BUSINESS LAW 207

Edited by Professor Chris Carr

California Polytechnic State University - San Luis Obispo

Orfalea College of Business

CAL POLY
ORFALEA
COLLEGE OF
BUSINESS
San Luis Obispo

University Readers™
San Diego, CA

First published in the United States of America in 2013 by University Readers, Inc.

Printed in the United States of America

ISBN: 978-1935551-99-7

University Readers™
800.200.3908 | www.universityreaders.com

Contents

Course Reader Materials for the First Exam
Chapter Two: Introduction to Law
Chapter Three: The Anatomy of a Civil Case; Judges, Courts & Their Jurisdiction; and Alternative Dispute Resolution (ADR)

1. Lessons Learned in Business School 1
   By Robert Prentice, Professor of Business Laws at the McCombs School of Business at the University of Texas at Austin

2. Surveying – Mastering Management 3
   By Constance Bagley, Professor of Business Law, Yale University

3. Chapter Two – Introduction to Law 7
   Study Outline

4. Chapter 3 – The Anatomy of a Civil Case; Judges, Courts and Jurisdiction; and ADR 15
   Study Outline

5. Hardin Loses Andersen Case But Wins Fans Among Jurors 21
   The Wall Street Journal

6. Martindale-Hubbell Law Directory (excerpt) 23

7. Example of a Summons 33

8. Example of a Complaint 35

9. Example of an Answer 37

10. Request for Entry of Default 39

11. Articles Re: Default Judgments 41

12. Written Interrogatory Example 43

13. Request for Production of Documents Example 49

14. Some Advice Re: Emails and Facebook 53

15. Document Shredding Shows Importance of Having a Policy on What is Preserved 55
The Wall Street Journal

16. When the Jury Box Runs Low, Deputies Hit the Wal-Mart 57
New York Times

17. Duty? Maybe It's Really Self Help 59
Newsweek

18. Jury Service is Your Business 61
By Mike Vallante, Pacific Coast Business Times

19. Jumping to be Jurors 63

20. Power of 12 65
American Bar Association Journal

21. Juror Prospect Says Nicole 'Deserved It' 71
Associated Press

22. Jury Selection in the Simpson Murder Trial 73

23. Building the Jury: Occupations Count in Job Bias Trials 75
By M. Frances Ryan, The National Law Journal

24. Lawyers Find Jury Pools Polluted by Antibusiness Biases 81
The Wall Street Journal

25. Jury Instructions Are Key in Andersen Trial 85
The Wall Street Journal

26. Prosecutors Seek Unusual Directive 87
The Wall Street Journal

27. Andersen Jurors Begin Deliberating the Company's Fate 89
The Wall Street Journal

28. Andersen Verdict Could Hinge on Critical Ruling From Judge 91
The Wall Street Journal

29. Jury Cuts Off an Andersen Appeals Route 95
The Wall Street Journal

30. Foreman Was Last to Be Persuaded 97
The Wall Street Journal

31. Pair of Jurors Caught Some Z'S During Arthur Andersen Trial 99
The Wall Street Journal

32. When Jurors Decide to Write Books 101
The National Law Journal

33. Selecting a Fair and Impartial Jury—A Piece of Cake?? 103

34. Lender Liable for $6.6 Million 105
The National Law Journal

35. $19M Award in Bank Battle 107
The National Law Journal

36. Chapter 3 — The Anatomy of a Civil Case; Judges, Courts and Jurisdiction; and ADR 109
Study Outline (continued)

37. How to Judge a Judge? 113
SLO New Times

38. Judicial Qualifications: A Sampling of Views 115

39. You Be the Judge: Local Elections Are Just Around the Corner 117
SLO New Times

40. Judicial Salaries: Making Less Than New Lawyers 121
The National Law Journal

41. Elderly Judges Handle 20% of U.S. Caseload 123
The Wall Street Journal

42. California Courts and Judges 125
By Deborah Bogen

43. Practice Problem Re: Jurisdiction and the Applicability of Long-Arm Statutes 135

44. Rules and Regs: Who Sets the Rules? 137
By Rob Gavin

45. Roberts Court Unites on Business 139
By Nick Timiraos

46. The Last Word: The 2008 Bench Press 143
By Anna Quindlen, Newsweek

47. U.S. Supreme Court: Law Clerks 145

48. Chapter 3 — The Anatomy of a Civil Case; Judges, Courts and Jurisdiction; and ADR 147
Study Outline (continued)

49. Alternative Dispute Resolution 149

50. ADR Finds True Believers 151
By David Hechler, The National Law Journal

51. Private Justice: Millions Are Losing Their Legal Rights 155
By Reynold Holding, San Francisco Chronicle

52. Private Justice: Can Public Count on Fair Arbitration? 165
By Reynold Holding, San Francisco Chronicle

53. Judges' Action Cast Shadow on Court's Integtrity 171
By Reynold Holding, San Francisco Chronicle

Course Reader Materials for the Second Exam
Chapter Six: Intentional Torts; Negligence; and Strict Liability
Chapter Twenty: Agency Law

54. Torts and Business 179
Study Outline

55. England v. S & M Foods, Inc. 187

56. "He's Back" 189

57. Flight Attendants Say They Lack Training for New Role in Security 191
The Wall Street Journal

58. Defamation in Cyberspace 193

59. Employee References 195

60. Islamic Charity Sues Media Companies for Defamation 197
By Michael Orey, The Wall Street Journal

61. WWF, Parents' Group Settle Libel Case 199
The National Law Journal

62. Lewis v. Equitable Life Assurance Society 201

63. Maybee v. Jacobs Motor Co. 205

64. Promises, Promises 207

65. En-Ruse? Workers Say They Had to Pose as Busy Traders to Impress Visiting Analysts 209

66. Photos of Women Who Get Abortions Go Up on Internet 211
By Yochi J. Dreazen, The Wall Street Journal

67. Big Brother Knows You're Speeding 215
The Wall Street Journal

68. Disaster Raises New Legal Issues In the Workplace 219
By Michael Orey, The Wall Street Journal

69. Ivy Imbroglio: Princeton Says It Spied on Yale 221
The Wall Street Journal

70. Colonel Stores, Inc. v. Fishel 223

71. False Imprisonment 225

72. The (Not-So) Friendly Skies 227

73. Abductions Cost Mo. Pastor $26.1M 229
National Law Review

74. Intentional Infliction of Emotional Distress 231

75. E-Mail Crusade Against Intel: Is It Trespass? 233
The Wall Street Journal

76. The Tort of Negligence 237
Study Outline

77. Kelly v. Gwinnell 241

78. Ann M. v. Pacific Plaza Shopping Center 243

79. Wal-Mart Not Liable in Shootings 247
The National Law Journal

80. Bahamian Resort Battles Allegations in Shark Attack 249
By Mark Fineman, The Los Angeles Times

81. Breach of Duty 251

82. Jury Says Home Depot Must Pay Customer Hurt By Falling Merchandise $1.5 Million 253
The Wall Street Journal

83. K-Mart to Pay $3 Million for Selling Gun to Suicidal Teen 255
The National Law Journal

84. Forseeable Type of Harm 257

85. Is a Singer Liable When Someone Acts Upon His Lyrics? 259

86. Griffith v. Valley of Sun Recovery, Inc. 261

87. No Penalty 263

88. The Billy Idiot-Delta Poo Poo Incident 265

89. The Tort of Strict Liability 267
Study Outline

90. Fla. Jury Awards Wounded Teller $26.9 Million 273
The National Law Journal

91. Tire Trial Ends with $29 Million Verdict 275
The National Law Journal

92. Agency Relationships In Business 277
Study Outline

93. Kuwait Air 287

94. Stieger v. Chevy Chase Savings Bank 289

95. Hausam v. Schnabl 291

96. Edgewater Motels, Inc. v. Gatzke 293

97. Firm Sued for Fatal Crash when Lawyer was Phoning 295
The National Law Journal

98. Landlord May Be Sued for Manager's Sex Harrassment 297

99. Estate Wins $46 Million for Killing 299

100. Pizza Delivery Assault: Boss Liable for Rape by Driver 301
The National Law Journal

101. Children Injured on Paper Routes Often Go Uninsured 303
The Wall Street Journal

102. Appendix A: Common Law Factors Used to Determine Employee Status 307
Internal Revenue Service

103. The Stella Steinbeck vs. McDonald's, and the Michael vs. RRL Incident 309

Course Reader Materials for the Third Exam
Introduction to Contracts & Contract Law; Agreement (Offer & Acceptance); Consideration; Defenses to the Enforcement of a Contract

104. Introduction to Contracts and Contract Law 315
Study Outline

105. Hair-razing Experience Is No Grounds for Lawsuit 319
By H. Dennis Beaver

106. A Deal Is a Deal, Even If It's Not in Writing 321
The National Law Journal

107. Practice Problems 323

108. Agreement Outline, Part 1A 325
Study Outline

109. Do Bob and Katrina Have an Enforceable Contract? 331

110. Fidelity's Johnson, a Billionaire, Wins Case Over Sum Of $160,000 333

111. Contract Issues In Cyberspace 335

112. Lyon v. Adgraphics 337

113. Agreement Outline, Part 1B 339
Study Outline (continued)

114. Time of Acceptance—The Mailbox Rule I & II 343

115. Consideration 345
Study Outline

116. The Shrinking Pledge 349
The Wall Street Journal

117. Promissory Estoppel 353

118. Contract Defenses Outline 355
Study Outline

119. Writing Requirements 367
Study Outline

120. Auto Auctions May End Up Costing You Plenty 371
By H. Dennis Beaver

121. Stambovsky v. Ackley 373

122. Church's New Trial 375
By Margaret Cronin Fisk

123. Mutual Mistake 379

124. $27.97 Air Fare to Paris, China? United: 'Oops' 381

125. Unilateral Mistake 383

126. BlueLight Nixes Accidental MP3 Discount 385
By Greg Sandoval, CNET News

127. High Court to Rule on Dispute Over Car Advertising 387
By Davan Maharaj, The Los Angeles Times

128. Calif.'s Top Court Bags Lawyer's Suit Over Jag 391

129. Duress – An Example 393

130. Undue Influence – An Example 395

131. Entering Into a Contract with a Minor Is Inadvisable 397

132. Minors – A Practice Problem 399

133. A Louisiana Lawsuit Challenges Rates, Fees at GE-Owned Bank 401
The Wall Street Journal

134. Contract Defenses – Examples 407

135. Test Your Knowledge of Home Contracts 409

136. Specializing in Sex Trade Law 411
By Bob Van Voris, The National Law Journal

137. He's No Sperm Donor. He's a Father 413
The National Law Journal

138. Contract Returns to Haunt 415

139. Artists Seek to Ease Recording-Pact Law 417
The Wall Street Journal

140. Not-So-Safe Deposit Boxes 419

141. More Contracts Practice Problems & Related Materials 423

Course Reader Materials for the Fourth Exam
Business Entities and Organizations; Sole Proprietorships, Ordinary Partnerships, Limited Partnerships (LPs), Limited Liability Partnerships (LLPs), Limited Liability Companies (LLCs), and Corporations

142. Introduction To Business Entities—Forms Of Business 439
Study Outline

143. Small Business, Big Decisions 447
The Wall Street Journal

144. Besieged Church Tries to Protect Vast Real Estate 451
The Wall Street Journal

145. Example of Fictitious Business Name Statement Form 457

146. Partners Forever? Within Andersen, Personal Liability May Bring Ruin 459
The Wall Street Journal

147. Andersen Partners Are Enron Targets 463
The Wall Street Journal

148. LLCs Offer Entrepreneurs Tax Breaks 465

149. Ordinary Partnerships 467
Study Outline

150. Example of a Written Partnership Agreement 481

151. Liender Liable for $6.6 Million 489
The National Law Journal

152. Limited Partnerships: LPs, LLPs and LLCs 491
Study Outline

153. Corporations 497
Study Outline

154. Sample/Example Articles of Incorporation 507

155. Sample/Example of a Set of Bylaws 511

156. Examples of Piercing the Corporate Veil 513

157. "DOs and DON'Ts" Re: Piercing the Corporate Veil 515

158. TRW Rebuffs Northrop, Offers Own Plan 517
The Wall Street Journal

159. Enron Board's Actions Raise Liability Questions 521
The Wall Street Journal

160. After Enron, Companies Confront Dearth of Willing Board Members 525
The Wall Street Journal

161. A Smart Investment 527
Best's Review Property/Casualty Insurance Edition

162. Andersen Ex-Party Pleads Guilty, In a Significant Blow to the Firm 529
The Wall Street Journal

163. Arthur Andersen Breaks Off Talks to Settle Criminal Case 531
The Wall Street Journal

164. Corporations Aren't Criminals 535
The Wall Street Journal

165. Business Entity Comparison Tables 537

Course Reader Materials for the First Exam

Chapter Two

Introduction to Law

Chapter Three

The Anatomy of a Civil Case;

Judges, Courts & Their Jurisdiction; and

Alternative Dispute Resolution (ADR)

1 Lessons Learned in Business School[1]

New York Times

By Robert Prentice — Professor of Business Laws at the McCombs School of Business at the University of Texas at Austin

Austin, Tex. — When Joseph Wharton established the nation's first business school at the University of Pennsylvania in 1881, he made business law one of five basic business school disciplines. More than a century later, the study of business law has given way to the study of business ethics.

But business students do not need to study business ethics so much as they need to study business law. The scandals at Enron, WorldCom and ImClone did not occur because executives were not conversant with the difference between teleological and deontological approaches to resolving ethical questions. It goes without saying that these scandals involved serious ethical lapses. But they also involved serious violations of business laws. They occurred, at least in part, because their participants had an insufficient knowledge of, appreciation for and, yes, fear of the law. Business schools have played a role in this disaster.

Because today businesses face far more complicated rules and regulations than they did a century ago, the need for managers to have a realistic appreciation of the legal environment in which they operate is more important than ever. Some business schools still have strong business law programs, but most have spent much of the last three decades reducing, marginalizing and often eliminating their business law faculty as other disciplines grew in stature and popularity. Consequently, in many business schools most students get their only look at the legal environment in which they will operate from faculty who view the law as an impediment.

Finance professors have told me that insider trading rules and financial disclosure requirements simply undermine the efficiency of the markets. Accounting professors have explained to me that rules limiting the ability of accounting firms to provide internal auditing services to a client (and thereby prepare the same books that they later purport to audit independently) are pointless, because accountants would never risk their reputation by acting improperly. (Many accounting professors still believe this, but they are quieter in the aftermath of Enron.) No wonder many business professors impart to their students an impression that the law exists simply to be manipulated or evaded.

At several leading business schools, many of the faculty that teach business law no longer even have law degrees; economists and political scientists offer policy courses that focus on lobbying. Indeed, much finance and economics research and teaching is built on the silly (though occasionally useful) assumption that man is a rational maximizer of his own utilities—and that these utilities can be measured financially. Not only is this unrealistic but, as the law professor Charles Pouncy has noted, it

1 Note from Professor Carr: This is an excellent introductory article for this course.

also encourages the view that any business strategy or activity that does not maximize monetary reward is suspect. This is the message that business schools tend to send—and companies like Enron tend to follow.

With the help of well-intentioned donors, several business schools have established business ethics centers. Unfortunately, research shows that it is very difficult to teach ethical values to undergraduates, harder still to teach them to M.B.A. students and all but impossible to get through to those enrolled in executive M.B.A. courses. If they didn't get a sense of right and wrong from their families or their faith, it's unlikely a business school professor can instill one.

Ethics courses can help those who are truly well-intentioned find their way through ethical dilemmas where the law gives no clear answer. But even these people will founder when they go to work for companies that value results over honesty; at such firms, acting ethically is always difficult.

There has never been a more crucial time to emphasize law in a business curriculum. Too many people forget that capitalism was saved from its own excesses by the securities laws passed in the 1930's. Recent scholarship shows that countries with strong judicial systems administering rigorous financial laws enable companies to raise money more quickly and facilitate more efficient stock markets. Legitimate companies want laws that require accurate financial disclosure and rules that punish fraudulent firms.

Centers for the study of business ethics are necessary to represent the ideals to which we aspire. But most business students will always view business ethics as hortatory rather than mandatory, as extra credit rather than required.

Instead, business law professors should explain to students that legal requirements are not optional. Such requirements enable our free-enterprise system to function—and disobedience carries a personal as well as a societal cost.

My colleagues and I must tell this story more forcefully than we have in the past. But to do so we need a more prominent forum in the business schools of America.

2 Surveying – Mastering Management[1]

The Financial Times

By Constance Bagley, Professor of Business Law, Yale University

LAW HAS RARELY been so important to managers, yet so in flux. Courts and legislatures are struggling to keep up with advances in technology, especially the transformation of the internet from a vehicle for communication among scientists and academics to an engine of global commerce. According to Forrester Research, internet retail sales were $20bn in 2000 and are expected to climb to $130bn by 2004. The Christian Science Monitor has reported that commerce between businesses conducted over the internet is even larger; $176bn in 1999 and estimated to increase to $1,300bn by 2003.

A company's most important assets are now often its intangible intellectual property. The market capitalisation of Microsoft is based not on its bricks and mortar but on its ability to use copyright law to prevent others from duplicating its software. Amazon.com's strategy of creating a strong brand and a loyal customer base depends on using trademark law to prevent others from using its name and on laws protecting trade secrets to prevent former employees from using or selling its customer lists. Patents, once primarily a concern of pharmaceutical, chemical and manufacturing companies, now protect computer software and even business processes, such as Netcentive's use of frequent flyer miles as rewards for consumers buying telephone services or borrowing money.

The recording industry and other entertainment companies are aggressively defending their right under copyright law to prevent unauthorised distribution of music and video on the internet. For example, MP3.com, a US company, had created a database containing hundreds of thousands of copyrighted songs, which users of its internet service could access. In September, Judge Jed Rakoff, sitting in a district court in New York, ordered MP3.com to pay royalties to the owners of the copyrighted music. Rakoff said some companies on the internet had "a misconception that, because their technology is somewhat novel, they are somehow immune from the ordinary application of laws of the United States, including copyright law." On the contrary, Rakoff declared, "the law's domain knows no such limits." As of mid-November, MP3.com had paid more than $150m to settle copyright claims by the five major record labels.

Napster, which makes it possible for millions of users to play and record music that other users have copied onto their computer hard drives, is defending copyright infringement lawsuits by the Recording Industry Association of America, major recording studios and artists (including such otherwise anti-establishment artists as Metallica). Napster claims that its service is not liable for music its users might have pirated because the service has substantial non-infringing uses, such as legally distributing the work

---

1 **Note from Professor Carr: This is also an excellent introductory article for this course.**

of new and unknown artists who are not represented by traditional record companies [...]

The European Union is wrestling with the proper forum for lawsuits by consumers against people selling goods and services on the internet. Should consumers be able to sue in their home country, or be required to sue in the country where the seller has its principal place of business?

Courts in the US have held that the mere presence of a website accessible in a particular state does not confer personal jurisdiction over the site owner, but are divided over just what activity is enough to give a state's residents the right to haul an out-of-state seller into local courts.

Both the US and EU have adopted laws on electronic commerce. A US law that went into effect in October gives electronic signatures the same validity as written signatures. This will enable consumers to obtain insurance and loans online. Companies continue to search for cheap yet reliable ways to authenticate digital signatures.

The US Securities and Exchange Commission (SEC) was one of the first agencies to embrace the internet and its use in selling securities and distributing information to investors. The technology enables companies to hold shareholder meetings online and to give individuals access to the analyst conference calls that routinely follow a company's announcement of quarterly earnings.

In September 2000, in an effort to give individuals, especially day traders (who quickly move in and out of stocks), access to the same information available to analysts and institutional investors, the SEC adopted regulations that prohibit companies from selectively disclosing private information to analysts and favoured investors but not to the public. Executives fear the new rules will subject them to liability if they have one-on-one conversations with analysts and warn this will reduce the quality of information available to the market.

The global reach of the internet makes it increasingly difficult for countries to regulate information flows across their national borders. For example, France sued Yahoo!, the web search engine and portal, for giving French citizens access to auctions of Nazi paraphernalia clearly prohibited by French law. After court-appointed experts concluded it was feasible to block access to the offending sites for 90 per cent of French surfers, the French court ordered Yahoo! to implement a filtering system proposed by the experts within 90 days of its November 20 ruling, or face fines of $100,000 in French Francs for each day it exceeded the deadline.

Germany has been unable to keep Germans from accessing neo-Nazi sites. Unlike pamphlets or books, which can be intercepted by customs at the border, websites are difficult to block. Similarly, efforts by the US Congress to protect children from pornography on the internet have been derailed because of the technological difficulty of keeping pornography from children without infringing adults' freedom of speech.

Managers and law

Given these uncertainties, what are managers to do? The first thing is to get into the game, even if the rules are not clear. For example, even if a manager is not convinced that obtaining a patent will give a company a competitive advantage, it is critical to have a bargaining chip if charged with infringing someone else's patent. It is increasingly common for a company to respond to a charge of patent infringement by denying the infringement and asserting infringement of its own patents. The resolution often involves an agreement whereby each company gives the other the right to use the patented technology.

Second, managers need to understand how the law can minimise risk and create value. Well-drafted representations and warranties in an acquisition agreement can flush out hidden problems and expressly allocate risk to one party. For example, the buyer of a factory could require the seller to disclose all environmental liabilities and to indemnify the buyer for all hazardous waste clean-up costs, even if they result from conditions not known to the seller.

Process patents

Amazon and Priceline.com are defending their business process patents for one-click shopping and computerised buyer-driven auctions, respectively. A US federal appeals court surprised many in 1998 when it embraced the patentability of business processes, and courts and legislatures are wrestling with the appropriate scope of these patents.

Critics claim the US Patent and Trademark Office has been too ready to grant patents for processes that are not novel and worthy of protection. For example, some argue that Priceline received a patent for a process that is basically a computerised version of the Dutch auctions that have been used to sell tulips since the 16th century. In addition, the completion of the Human Genome Project and the prospect of patents for human genes raise serious public policy questions about what information should belong to every member of the human race and what should be proprietary.

One area that has become more settled is the application of trademark law to internet domain names. Because a domain names is given to whomever registers it first, holders of registered trademarks had to deal with so-called "cybersquatters," who would register names (such as McDonalds.com and Panavision.com) then offer to sell them to the trademark holders.

A flagrant example was one company's use of "candyland.com" as the domain name for a child pornography site when Hasbro held a registered trademark for "Candy Land," which it had used for decades as the name of a children's board game. The US Congress responded by passing laws barring the use of marks that would tarnish or dilute a famous trademark (such as Candy Land) and prohibiting would-be cybersquatters from registering domain names in bad faith. Disputes are increasingly being resolved not by the courts but through arbitration by the World Intellectual Property Organisation.

Companies are aggressively going after former employees suspected of stealing trade secrets. General Motors recovered $100m from Volkswagen plus a promise to buy $5bn of GM parts after a former executive took pricing information with him when he was hired by Volkswagen.

Pepsico went further when it sued a former marketing executive who had developed marketing strategies for All Sport and powdered teas. When the executive left Pepsico he went to Quaker Oats to work on the marketing of Gatorade and Snapple drinks.

There was no evidence that the executive had taken any written materials with him, or had disclosed any trade secrets to his new employer. Nevertheless, an appeals court barred him from working for Quaker Oats for six months, after concluding that, given his assignment to work on directly competitive products, it was inevitable that he would use or disclose Pepsico trade secrets. A number of other courts in the US have embraced this doctrine of inevitable disclosure.

In the US Justice Department's suit against Microsoft, the parties sharply disagree about the proper role of competition law and judicial intervention when the technology is constantly changing and network effects and high switching costs cause consumers to gravitate to one standard for maximum interoperability.

The convergence of communications, media and computers makes it increasingly difficult for regulators to define the relevant market and to assess the anti-competitive effects of mergers involving major industry players [...]

Employers should require employees with access to confidential information to sign written nondisclosure agreements, in which the employee agrees not to use or give out trade secrets. Assignments of inventions can ensure that any copyright able work or invention conceived of by an employee belongs to the employer.

In some jurisdictions, employers can require staff to sign covenants not to compete. To be enforceable, they must be reasonable as to duration, geographic scope and range of prohibited activities. Some jurisdictions, such as the state of California and India, refuse to enforce any employee covenants not to compete (except in connection with the sale of a business) on grounds that they unduly restrict individuals' ability to ply their trade. Others, such as France, enforce them only if the former employer agrees to pay the same salary offered by the prospective employer. Yet even a pro-employee jurisdiction like California will enforce a non-disclosure agreement and assignment of inventions.

Because employers face the possibility of suits by former employees for wrongful termination, discrimination or sexual harassment, many companies require employees to agree to arbitrate all employment disputes. To be enforceable, these agreements must provide a fair way for resolving disputes. For example, in August, the California Supreme Court struck down a clause that limited the employee's available damages, did not require the employer to arbitrate and required the employee to bear a portion of the costs of arbitration.

Savvy managers understand that legal risks must be factored into business decisions in the same way as other risks, such as currency risks. Often, the manager will need an attorney to explain the options, but unless the attorney advises that an action is illegal, the manager, not the attorney, should decide whether the risk can be reduced and whether the benefits of the deal outweigh that risk.

Finally, managers should realise that legal disputes are inevitable. Indeed, if one is never challenged, it may mean that opportunities to create value are being lost due to an overly conservative legal strategy. Instead of delegating such disputes to attorneys, successful managers realise that every legal dispute is a business problem requiring a business solution. Too often, managers treat the law as a black box and leave it up to the lawyers, rather than taking responsibility for disputes.

3 Chapter Two – Introduction to Law

Study Outline

***Note that this chapter and material covers primarily definitions/definitional concepts. I won't spend much, if any, time on this material in class as it's material and concepts that are self-explanatory and that you should be able to master on your own.

*****Make _sure_ that you do the sample practice problems posted on Blackboard as it will help you master this material, test you to see if you "really" know and understand it, etc. You can expect similar problems to be on the exam. ☺**

I. Business Law – Why Is It Important/Why Is This Class Important For You To Take?

  A. Law and legal issues confront you at every turn
  B. Management deals with the law and legal issues practically every day
  C. Thus, you have to understand it, its importance, how it affects you, its nature, functions, and how judges interpret it
  D. <u>See also the Robert Prentice NY Times op-ed piece at page 1–2 and Constance Bagley Financial Times article at pages 3–6 of this textbook!! Relatedly, and as examples to help this "come to life" for you, also see/refer/think back to the: (1) wine/appellation/vitucultural example ("using the law to gain/maintain competitive advantage"); and the (2) consulting firm-MBA student contract example ("bargaining in the shadow of the law") that we went over the very first day of class!</u>

II. Types of Law
(I.e., – When we say "types of law" what are some of the options in the universe of possibilities? See the below.)

  A. State and federal constitutions
    1. Functions:
      a) They establish the structure of the government and allocate power among its various branches and subdivisions
        (1) E.g. – through its separation of powers, the U.S. Constitution establishes that: (1) Congress has the power to legislate and make law; (2) the President has the power to execute and enforce the law; and (3) the Federal Judiciary interprets the law
      b) They also prevent units of government from taking certain actions or passing certain laws, especially those laws that restrict individual rights

(1) E.g. – statutes passed by Congress which prevent flag burning are an unconstitutional violation of free speech

B. Federal & State Statutes – law that is created by Congress or a state legislature; they are contained in statute books (sometimes called code books)

1. Note: many state statutes/codes were originally drafted as Uniform Acts (which are model statutes that states can look to and adopt)
   a) E.g., – the Uniform Commercial Code (UCC), the Uniform Partnership Act (UPA), the Revised Uniform Limited Partnership Act (RULPA), etc. We will get to and study all of these Uniform Acts later in the course.
   b) Note that these Uniform Acts do not become "law" until they are passed/enacted by the legislature. Also, state by state variations in these Uniform Acts are common

C. Common Law (also called judge-made law or case law; it is called "judge-made law" because it involves judges/courts stepping in and making law that governs and regulates us/business activity in areas where there has been an absence of legislative or administrative action)

1. In cases where common law is applied, courts look at ***precedent*** and decide whether to apply the doctrine of ***stare decisis*** (which states that the present case should be decided the same way as past cases presenting the same facts and legal issues) or ***distinguish*** the case ***(this is called case law reasoning)***

2. Much of our tort, contract, property, agency law, etc. that govern business and business transactions comes from the common law!!

3. See also the material on the next several pages on the "Common Law" – this material does an excellent job of explaining, from a different angle, what the common law is all about, how it works, why it is important, etc.
   a) **Note: the common law controls/prevails <u>only</u> if there is no other type of law that applies to the case. E.g., if there is a conflict between a statute on the books and a common law court decision, the statute must prevail & the court must follow that statute**
      (1) Rationale: the legislature (which presumably is an expression of the will of the majority of the people in our democratic system!) has stepped in and expressly spoken on the issue and its rule must therefore be followed!

***

The Common Law

Overview: "Common law" refers to the system of jurisprudence that originated in England and was later applied in the United States, which is based on *judicial precedent*, rather than legislative enactments. It is to be contrasted with civil law, the descendent of Roman law prevalent in some other Western countries. Originally based on the unwritten laws and ancient customs of English merchants, the common law is generally derived from principles rather than rules; it does not consist of absolute, fixed, and inflexible rules, but rather on broad and comprehensive principles based on justice, reason, and common sense. It is of judicial origin and promulgation. These judicial principles have been determined by the social needs of the community, and have changed with changes in such needs. These judicial principles are also susceptible of adaptation to new conditions, interests, relations and usages, as the progress of society may require.

The common law is sometimes called "judge-made law," as contrasted with law made by legislatures, and because the common law changes, decision by decision, in litigated cases. In this sense, common law refers to law with both continuity and the capacity for change; a continuous growth of precedent in similar cases, with High Court decisions often controlling. With changed facts, judicial precedent is distinguished, yielding new law, usually a little at a time.

Some History on the Origin and Development of the Common Law: The Norman conquest of England in 1066 under William the Conqueror laid the groundwork for the development of the common law. To extend royal authority over this dominion, William's successors created permanent courts (called "King's Courts" or *curia regis*), staffed by judges appointed by the king, to administer the law of the realm. From the twelfth century onward, the English monarchs also dispatched "traveling justices" to rule in the king's name in the country courts. By the thirteenth century, the kings had succeeded in establishing a "common" set of legal procedures and legal standards throughout England.

But what legal procedures were the royal judges to follow in deciding cases, and what legal principles were they to employ? The judges could not rely upon parliamentary enactments for guidance—Parliament's emergence as a legislative body was still several centuries in the future. Nor could the judges rely much on royal edicts, for these did not extend to many of the legal problems confronting the judges. Rather, as William Blackstone observed in his famous treatise on the common law, the judges looked to a body of "unwritten law," the common law, for guidance. In speaking of the common law as "unwritten," Blackstone did not mean that it was transmitted by word of mouth. Rather, he was emphasizing that the doctrines of the common law, unlike legislative enactments, "are not set down in any written statute or ordinance, but depend merely upon immemorial usage." Judges served as the "depositories of the law," and their written decisions served as "the principal and most authoritative evidence that can be given of the existence of such a custom as shall form a part of the common law." Thus, the common law originated in written judicial decisions, which enunciated authoritative legal principles, presumably drawn from the customs and practices of the society, in the course of resolving disputes between litigants.

As these written judicial decisions accumulated, they comprised a body of law that judges could draw upon to resolve the cases coming before them. Recurrence to *precedent*—that is, to the judges' own earlier decisions or to those of their predecessors or colleagues—facilitated judicial decision-making by giving judges standards that they could rely upon in deciding the cases before them. Initially, "there was merely a tendency to establish a procedure, and perhaps adopt a few substantive principles which, taken together, constituted the custom of the court" and provided a standard for judicial decisions. Over time, however, as the practice of publishing written reports of judicial decisions developed, judges could easily consult the rulings of other courts. Over time, too, the authority of these precedents increased. This is reflected in the judges' acceptance of the *doctrine of stare decisis* (to stand by precedents and not to disturb settled points).

The doctrine of *stare decisis* is the policy of courts in common law countries to abide by, or adhere to, previously decided cases. In general, once a court has decided a matter, it will decide subsequent cases containing substantially similar facts and issues consistent with its earlier decisions. Previous cases become binding precedent for future cases. When a matter comes before a court, therefore, it looks to past cases to determine present issues. In a common law system, where the body of law develops case-by-case, the doctrine of *stare decisis* is **critical** for the development of a consistent and reliable body of law. For example, think of what would happen to business activity in the United States and our economy if the doctrine of *stare decisis* did not exist to require contracts to be honored and enforced!

Despite the proliferation of legislation and administrative regulations over the last two centuries, judge-made law continues to govern very important areas of life in common-law countries.

The Common Law in the United States: During the seventeenth century, most colonists emigrated to North America from England, and the brought the English legal system with them. When the United States declared its independence from England, the new states retained their common-law legal systems. Thus, like their English counterparts, American judges have had to enunciate legal standards in the absence of legislation in order to resolve disputes between litigants. This in turn has guaranteed American judges a major role in lawmaking.

U.S. courts have nevertheless modified the body of common law that they received from England in several important respects. In the decades following independence, American judges expunged aspects of the common law that reflected the aristocratic character of English society and were therefore inappropriate for the more democratic society being created in the United States. During the nineteenth century, they also adapted common-law doctrines that originated in an agrarian society in order to encourage economic development and accommodate industrialization.

***

Practice: The following quote by The Honorable Judge Learned Hand nearly 80 years ago does an excellent job of capturing the essence of the common law (this is also an essay question that I once gave – after reading the above material, you should be able to answer it/have something meaningful and relevant to say in response to the question):

"The Common Law stands as a monument slowly raised, like a coral reef, from the minute accretions of past individuals, of whom each built upon the relics which his predecessors left, and in his turn left a foundation upon which his successors might work."

Learned Hand, *Judge Cardozo's The Nature of the Judicial Process*, 35 Harvard Law Review, p. 479 (1922). Please discuss Justice Hand's quote from nearly 80 years ago with reference to how, exactly, the common law grows "like a coral reef."

Further, discuss whether the common law and a common law legal system (and its framework) is an asset or deterrent to the global and technology based trade and commerce of the future.

***

D. Administrative regulations and decisions ("Administrative Law")
   1. State and federal legislatures have the power to and often create administrative agencies to handle problems because they lack the time and/or expertise to do so. These agencies in turn get their power to make law by a *delegation* of power from the legislature
   2. Two types of law are created by administrative agencies:
      a) Administrative regulations – enacted by the agency itself, not the legislature
         (1) E.g., – Internal Revenue Service (IRS) regulations, the Securities & Exchange Commission (SEC) regulations, and Environmental Protection Agency (EPA) regulations
      b) Agency decisions – some agencies have internal court structures and procedures. The resulting decisions are another kind of law

E. Treaties
   1. Made by the President with foreign governments. Requires two-thirds Senate approval
      a) E.g., – the Panama Canal treaty, NAFTA, etc.

F. Ordinances
      a) Made by school districts, municipalities, etc.
      b) E.g., – zoning ordinances, building ordinances, etc.

G. Executive orders
   1. Made by Presidents or Governors
      a) Gives Presidents/Governors the power to issue and make laws. This power results from legislative delegation and is implied from the Constitution.
      b) E.g., – the President sending troops overseas

III. Priority of Laws

A. The Federal Supremacy Clause – a clause in the U.S. Constitution that states that "federal law is the supreme law of the land." This means that state legislatures and courts cannot pass or interpret their (state) laws differently to provide fewer/less rights to an individual or business than does a conflicting federal law, ruling by the U.S. Supreme Court and/or provision in the U.S. Constitution. **If/when there is such a conflict, the Supremacy Clause provides that the federal law must prevail.**

1. But note that individual states may provide *more* (but as noted above cannot provide *less*) protection for citizens than is provided by the U.S. Constitution, the U.S. Supreme Court and/or the U.S. Congress
   a) For example and as a hypothetical ... if the U.S. Supreme Court ruled that the government can only hold/incarcerate a person charged with a crime for 120 days before a trial must be held (i.e., holding anyone longer than that without a trial was unconstitutional), a state legislature, if it chose to do so, could come in a pass a law that set that time period at 90 days. I.e., any accused in that state would be getting *more* rights given to him/her than the U.S. Supreme Court granted him/her under the U.S. Constitution!

IV. Classifications of Law (addresses the issue of how should/can we categorize law? ... note that there are different ways – see below)

A. Public and Private Law
1. Public – concerns the powers of the government and the relations between government and private parties
   a) E.g., – constitutional law (when can the government search your home without a warrant?); administrative law (what can the SEC require a company to disclose to investors on its financial statements?)
2. Private – establishes a framework of legal rules the enable private parties to set the rights and duties they owe each other
   a) E.g., – the rules of contract (when do private parties have to honor contracts they enter into with one another?); the rules of property (how close can your neighbor build his house to your house?)

B. Criminal and Civil Law
1. Criminal – government prosecutes someone for the commission of a crime; criminal law regulates behavior so threatening that society outlaws it altogether
   a) Penalty – prison and/or a fine
   b) E.g., – "Law and Order"; The People v. O.J.
2. Civil – one party sues another party; *note that the government can be a party to such lawsuits*; civil law regulates rights and duties between persons (individuals and/or businesses) in our society
   a) Penalty/Remedy – money damages and/or equitable relief such as an injunction
   b) E.g., – Smith v. Jones
3. ALWAYS REMEMBER ..... a whole different set of rules applies to both civil and criminal law. E.g., the burden of proof, etc.!! In a civil case, the burden of proof is "beyond a preponderance of the evidence" and in a criminal case it is "beyond a reasonable doubt"

C. Substantive and Procedural Law
1. Substantive – substantive rights of the people are affected
2. Procedural – controls the behavior of government bodies (usually the police and courts) as they establish and enforce the rules of substantive law

3. Example – a statute charging O.J. with a crime = substantive law. All of the stuff that happened at trial re: the conduct the of the trial (e.g., the right to a speedy trial, the sequestering of the jury, evidence battles, etc.) = procedural law

D. Note: A law can be classified more than one of the above!! (e.g., our three strikes law = a criminal, substantive *and* public law)

V. Jurisprudence and Jurisprudential Schools (Legal Schools of Thought)

The schools of thoughts addresses the issue of "what is law" and/or "what should law be try to accomplish"? And the reason that this is important is because one client, attorney and/or judge may be a disciple or believer in one school and another client, attorney and/or judge may be a disciple/believer in another school, and hence, that is one reason we have disagreement and a fair amount of litigation in our society and legal system!

A. *Natural Law*

1. Defines law as (says that law should be) all commands of a recognized political authority which are not unjust (i.e., it recognizes a higher law). "Unjust law is not law." Its practical tendency is that the unjust laws of a political authority should not be enforced or obeyed.
   a) Advantage: protects the "little guy," the underdog, the oppressed, etc.
   b) Disadvantage: a bit pie in the sky; what would life/society be like if everyone believed unjust laws need not be obeyed?; disagreements re: morality (e.g., the perception of morality and what it "moral" may be very different in Iowa vs. Los Angeles)
2. Examples of Natural Law Thinkers—Nelson Mandella, Martin Luther King, Jr., Ghandi, etc.

B. *Legal Positivism (called command or ruling class law/theory in your textbook)*

1. Defines law as (says that law should be) the command of a recognized political authority. "Law is law, just or not." Its practical tendency is that the law of a recognized political authority should be enforced and obeyed, regardless of whether it is fair or just!
   a) Advantage: promotes stability and predictability.
   b) Disadvantage: what if it is enacted by a corrupt authority such as a Stalin or a Hitler, etc.?
2. Examples of Legal Positivism Thinkers—Robert Bork (the United States Supreme Court nominee several years ago); and probably most judges!!

C. *Legal Realism*

1. Defines law as (says that the law should be) what public decision-makers (e.g., judges) actually do. Their behavior is what counts, not the rules in the books. In other words, law is what public decision-makers say it is! Its practical tendency is that "law in action" is more important than "law in the books."
   a) Advantage: More "real world" and practical than the other two schools
   b) Disadvantage: Even in this school there is disagreement regarding the relationship between law and morality and the duty to obey the law

***** Again, I encourage you to do the practice problems that I have posted on Blackboard dealing with Chapter 2. You may "think" that you know/understand the above material, and, you may. But you may also not. Doing these practice problems—many of which involve application—is a great way (the only way, really) to see if you really do know and understand this material.—Prof. Carr**

4 Chapter 3 – The Anatomy of a Civil Case; Judges, Courts and Jurisdiction; and ADR

Study Outline

*****Note that in this textbook at pages 21–107 I have inserted a number of newspaper articles, supplementary materials, sample documents, etc. that relate to this material. These materials are required reading, and, also fair game for the exam.**

*****Make *sure* that you do the sample practice problems posted on my web site as it will help you master this material, test you to see if you "really" know and understand it, etc. You can expect similar problems to be on the exam. ☺**

The Anatomy of a Civil Case

I. The Anatomy of a Civil Case (see also class lecture, power point frames, and Chapter 3 of the textbook chapter posted on Blackboard for additional details); our system, for better or worse, like or not, is an *adversarial legal system* – *i.e., it often involves and is based on conflict and "butting heads"*

A. The Selection of Legal Counsel – refer to class discussion, power point frames, videos shown in class, and, pages 21–31 in this textbook

B. The Pleadings

1. Service of the ***Summons*** & ***Complaint*** – refer to class discussion, power point frames, and materials/example in this textbook at pages 33–36.

a) The complaint – The purpose of the complain is that it is a document that: (1) describes the factual basis for the plaintiff's suit; (2) explains why the court has jurisdiction over the case; (3) outlines the legal theory on which the plaintiff relies; and (4) indicates the damages or other relief that the plaintiff seeks. I.e., the complaint notifies the defendant what the plaintiff claims he/she did wrong and what remedy the plaintiff seeks. The filing of a complaint **also** serves the purpose of formally commencing the case in the court system!

(1) For an example of a summons and complaint, see this textbook at pages 33–36.

b) Once the plaintiff has filed his/her summons and complaint with the court, the defendant must then be "*served*" with a copy of those documents

2. The filing of the ***Answer*** – once, if and after the defendant has been "served" (see above), the defendant must file his/her answer with the court within 30 days in state court (in federal court it is 20 days) from the date on which the plaintiff's complaint and summons was served on him/her
   a) For an example of an answer, see the this textbook at pages 37–38.
   b) In answering the plaintiff's complaint, the defendant may admit or deny some of the allegations in the complaint
      (1) E.g., – a skydiving instructor may admit that a student died during a jump, but deny that the student died due to the company's negligence
   c) If this is not done (i.e., the defendant fails to file an answer on time), the plaintiff can have a ***default judgment*** entered against the defendant which cuts off the defendant's right to file an answer and it effectively ends the case (i.e., defendant loses because he/she did not timely pursue a defense!!)
      (1) In this textbook at pages 39–42 I have inserted several documents that relate to the issue of default judgments (e.g., a Request for Entry of Default; an article about a default judgment taken against the British *au pair* who was also prosecuted for murder; and an article about a default judgment taken against the ex-chairman for Christies' auction house)
3. The ***counter-claim/cross-complaint***
   a) Filed by the defendant with and when he/she files the answer
      (1) E.g. – the defendant may have a claim back against the plaintiff (counter-claim), or, a claim against a third party (cross-complaint) that the plaintiff did not sue/name as a defendant in the complaint

C. Preliminary Motions to Dismiss the Case – designed to weed out and dismiss frivolous lawsuits, untimely lawsuits, defective lawsuits, etc., short of and before a full-blown trial
   1. ***Motion to dismiss*** – may be made on various grounds (e.g., improper service of the complaint, lack of jurisdiction, etc.)
   2. The ***demurrer*** – basically this motion says "so what?" … even if the facts alleged in the plaintiff's complaint are true and correct, the laws that are on the books still do not allow the plaintiff to recover anything against the defendant so the complaint should be dismissed!

D. ***Discovery*** – involves the pretrial exchange of all relevant information (e.g., documents, identities of witnesses, etc.) between parties in a lawsuit; always remember that the scope of discovery is broad (refer to class discussion and power point frame on this issue)
   1. Rationale/Purpose Behind Discovery: helps avoid surprise/ambushes at trial; helps to predict the outcome of a trial; helps pin the parties and witnesses down so they can't change their story at trial and if they do then that discovery can be used to impeach/discredit them; the full disclosure of all relevant information may encourage the two sides to settle, etc.
   2. Tools of Discovery

a) ***Depositions*** – oral questions/answers under oath and under trial like condition transcribed by a court reporter (also refer to class lecture and videos; see also article at page 51 of this textbook)
b) ***Interrogatories*** – written questions submitted to the other side to answer and they must be answered and signed under oath (see example in this textbook at pages 43–48)
c) ***Request for production of documents*** ("Document Request") (see example and related articles in this textbook at pages 49–50 and 53–56)
d) ***Request for physical and/or mental examination*** – often used where the plaintiff claims some physical/mental/emotional injury

E. Later Pre-Trial Motions filed by the Plaintiff or Defendant to try and win the case early and before/without the necessity of a full-blown and expensive trial
1. ***Summary Judgment Motion*** – is a "trial by paper"/trial by affidavit. I.e., think of it as a mini-trial only it takes place with a motion, supporting papers, affidavits, etc. versus live witnesses like a real/normal trial would entail
a) Also, it is granted where the moving party has established that "no genuine issue of material fact" exists in the case

F. ***Pretrial conference/hearing*** – takes place right before the trial where the attorneys for the parties meet with the court/judge to discuss and address administrative issues (e.g., what facts can and will the parties stipulate/agree to so as to save time at trial; what witnesses will be presented, how many, etc.)
1. As part of this conference/hearing, there will also often be settlement discussions/pressures imposed by the court on the parties in the form of a ***mandatory settlement conference***

G. The Trial (note that there are two types of trials – ***court trials*** (the judge is the trier of fact) and ***jury trials*** (the jury is the trier of fact)
1. The Stages of a Trial (refer also to class discussion, videos and power point frames)
a) Chose/decide whether to have a court trial or jury trial
b) Jury selection (only, of course, in a jury trial)
(1) ***Voir Dire (jury selection takes place).*** (The phrase *voir dire* is a French phrase which means "to speak the truth.")
(i) ***For cause*** – where a prospective juror is excused by the court automatically (e.g., the prospective juror is the brother of the plaintiff)
(b) Rationale: obviously you don't want someone on the jury that can't be fair and impartial, might have a health problem that would prevent them from paying attention to the trial and evidence presented, etc.
(2) ***Peremptory challenges*** – where the attorneys can excuse a prospective juror for any reason at all (except, e.g., based on race)
(i) Rationale: keep the dispute fair; gives each side a chance to excuse potential jurors who flat out would not give a fair hearing to a party
(ii) In California, in a civil case, each attorney/each side gets six (6) peremptory challenges

c) Opening statement of the plaintiff's attorney (in civil cases) or the prosecutor (in criminal cases)
d) Opening statement by the defendant's attorney
e) Presentation of the plaintiff's/prosecution's case
    (1) Motion for directed verdict – often made by the defendant at this point in the trial (see below for more details on this motion)
f) Presentation of the defendant's case
g) Rebuttal witnesses
h) Closing argument for the plaintiff/prosecution
i) Closing argument for the defendant
j) Rebuttal closing argument for the plaintiff/prosecution
k) The judge the reads ***jury instructions*** to the jury (if a jury trial)
l) Deliberation by the judge (if a court trial) or the jury (if a jury trial)
m) Announcement of the verdict

Note: I have a number of very good articles in this textbook at pages 57–107 that are designed to highlight the above material and many of the steps listed at a – m above to make it come to life. Make <u>sure</u> you read that material. Again, this material is fair game for the exam.

H. Trial and Post Trial Motions (after the verdict is rendered) (these motions are designed/intended to cure/fix/address faulty, defective, or "crazy" things that might have happened during the trial – i.e., think of these motions as "safety valves" in the process to fix/cure trial anomalies):
   1. ***Motion for directed verdict*** – usually make right after the plaintiff presents his/her case in chief (i.e., the defendant stands up and asks the judge to dismiss the case and not let it go to the jury on the ground that the plaintiff failed to prove his/her case)
   2. ***Motion for judgment notwithstanding*** **the verdict ("*motion for JNOV*")** – where the defendant asks the judge to set aside all or a part of the jury's verdict on the ground that it (the jury's verdict) was in no way supported by the evidence and/or the law
   3. ***Motion for a new trial*** – either party can make, but is usually made by the "loser." If granted, new trial is granted on all or limited issues

I. Appeal
   1. Options available to an appellate court: affirm in whole or in part, reverse in whole or in part, remand back to the trial court, etc.
   2. Note that the role of an appellate court is NOT to re-litigate the case. Rather, it is to ensure that the law (not facts) was correctly interpreted and applied at lower trial court level. Appellate courts normally only examine the record of the case on appeal and determine whether an error of law (not fact) was committed at the trial court level (only trial courts conduct trials, take witness testimony, enter documents/exhibits into evidence, and make determinations of both fact and law).

J. Enforcing the Judgment/Collection – if the plaintiff is lucky enough to win, then he/she *still* has to collect on that judgment that the court/jury awarded in his/her favor!! This is often the most difficult and frustrating part of the case for a plaintiff!!
   1. The tools for enforcing a judgment are (assuming a defendant **has** assets **and** you can locate them!):
      a) ***Writ of execution*** – allows sheriff to seize and sell the defendant's property
      b) ***Garnishment*** – allows sheriff to seize property, $$ or employment wages in the hands of a third party and then give it to the plaintiff

*** **Again, folks … I encourage you to do the practice problems that I have posted on Blackboard dealing with Chapter 3. You may "think" that you know/understand the above material, and, you may. But you may also not. Doing these practice problems—many of which involve application—is a great way (the only way, really) to see if you really do know and understand this material.—Prof. Carr**

5 Hardin Loses Andersen Case But Wins Fans Among Jurors[1]

The Wall Street Journal

HOUSTON—EVEN WHEN RUSTY Hardin loses cases, he still can win over jurors.

The lead lawyer for Arthur Andersen LLP received some high praise from the 12-member jury that convicted his client Saturday of obstructing justice.

"He kept focused," said juror Jack Gallo, a 58-year-old airline general manager. "You never know what is going to come out of his mouth." He added: "We all respected him; we all loved him."

Despite the decision, Mr. Hardin pushed the case to the limit—the verdict came on the 10th day of deliberations—and won a moral victory of sorts. He blunted the impact of David Duncan, the government's star witness. He didn't lose points with the jury by openly battling a judge who frequently ruled in favor of the Justice Department. And he made a tight race out of a case that was supposed to be easy for his opponent.

Rusty Hardin

Going into the trial, "it was assumed that the government had a slam dunk," Mr. Hardin said Saturday in the hallway outside the courtroom.

From donning light-colored suits that defy courtroom convention to getting jurors to call him by his first name to playing songs in court, Mr. Hardin long has connected with jury panels. "It is very important that juries like the lawyer," says Dick DeGuerin, a Houston criminal-defense lawyer. "And juries just like Rusty."

In the six-week Andersen trial, Mr. Hardin—who still looks a bit boyish at 60 years old—used a mix of humor, hometown charm and an ability to make complex items more understandable in presenting his case for reasonable doubt.

Though the Andersen case promises to catapult him more firmly onto the national stage, Mr. Hardin is a household name in Texas legal circles. His legend blossomed during his 15 years as a prosecutor in Houston, where he helped put 14 people on death row. Former colleagues say the ex-Army intelligence officer and Vietnam veteran never lost a major felony case. "He is the best trial lawyer I have ever seen come through this office—and I've been

1 **Note from Professor Carr: Even though he technically "lost" he was still a real hit and really connected with the jury. I.e., this article can and should teach you how important the selection of legal counsel can be in our—a common law—legal system. Further, it shows how much power/sway legal counsel can have in shaping/making public policy that impacts business!!**

This article relates nicely to our class discussion of selection of legal counsel. I would also submit to you that Andersen would not have had a chance in this case had it not been for the high quality of Mr. Hardin's advocacy and trial skills.

here 32 years," says Bert Graham, the first assistant district attorney in Harris County and a friend of Mr. Hardin's.

In the past decade, Mr. Hardin successfully has defended clients ranging from sports stars Wade Boggs and Warren Moon to the son of the late oil tycoon J. Howard Marshall, whose pinup widow Anna Nicole Smith sued for his fortune. (Mr. Hardin in the past has represented Dow Jones & Co., publisher of *The Wall Street Journal.*)

It is Mr. Hardin's ability to work with jurors that impresses fellow lawyers the most. At the start of one of Mr. Hardin's more-celebrated cases as a prosecutor, the 1987 case in which Cynthia Campbell Ray was on trial for murdering her wealthy parents, Mr. Hardin raised eyebrows on both sides of the aisle while questioning prospective jurors. He spoke with one prospective juror for about an hour. Later that day, during questioning by the defense attorney, the man spat out, "Well, as Rusty said a while ago..." The defense attorney, flabbergasted, said: "What do you mean, 'Rusty said'? You mean Mr. Hardin?"

"If you get them to use your first name," says Lyn McClellan, a Houston assistant district attorney who worked on the case,"you know you have made a connection."

To be sure, he has critics. Even some supporters question his conduct defending Andersen, which was accused of destroying documents with the intent of impeding a Securities and Exchange Commission probe. During the trial, Mr. Hardin openly fumed at U.S. District Judge Melinda Harmon, accusing her of bias. She frequently sided with the government on motions and objections.

She, in turn, charged that Mr. Hardin's team was being "underhanded." Mr. Hardin responded that he deeply resented her "impugning" his integrity.

"That is not the way a professional lawyer is supposed to respond," says Johnny Holmes, the former Harris County district attorney and one of Mr. Hardin's greatest influences. During the trial, the judge said the record would reflect her fairness.

Meanwhile, the Andersen jury didn't seem offended. "We thought he was an excellent defense attorney," said Mr. Gallo, the juror.

Mr. Hardin began working as a prosecutor in Houston shortly after graduating from Southern Methodist University's law school. Known for sometimes-brutal cross-examinations, he knows when befriending a witness can prove more useful. In the Andersen case, he effectively turned the government's chief witness, Mr. Duncan, the firm's lead auditor on Enron Corp., into an Andersen witness. By making Mr. Duncan comfortable, he elicited testimony showing Mr. Duncan questioned for many months whether he had committed a crime.

In the end, the Andersen jury didn't find that Mr. Duncan was a "corrupt persuader" who intended to impede an official inquiry. Instead, the panel pointed the finger at his colleague Nancy Temple.

6 Martindale-Hubbell® Law Directory[1]

(excerpt) Volume 3; California S – Z

CALIFORNIA–SAN FRANCISCO[1]

BROBECK, PHLEGER & HARRISON LLP[2]
A Partnership including a Professional Corporation
SPEAR STREET TOWER
ONE MARKET
SAN FRANCISCO, CALIFORNIA 94105
Telephone: 415–442–0900
Facsimile: 415–442–1010
Email: info@brobeck.com
URL: http://www.brobeck.com

Los Angeles California Office: 550 South Hope Street. Telephone: 213–489–4060. Facsimile: 213–745–3345.

Palo Alto, California Office: Two Embarcadero Place, 2200 Geng Road. Telephone: 650–424–0160. Facsimile: 650–496–2885.

San Diego California Office: 12390 El Camino Real. Telephone: 858–720–2500. Fax: 858–720–2555.

Irvine. California Office: 38 Technology Drive. Telephone: 949–790–6300. Facsimile: 949–790–6301.

Austin, Texas Office: 4801 Plaza on the Lake. Telephone: 512–330–4000 Facsimile: 512–330–4001

Broomfield, Colorado Office: 370 Inter lockcn Boulevard, Suite 500. Telephone: 303–410–2000. Facsimile: 303–410–2199.

New, N.Y. Office: 1633 Broadway, 47th Floor. Telephone: 217–581–1600. Facsimile: 212–586–7878.

Washington; D.C. Office: 1333 H Street, N.W., Suite 800. Telephone: 262–220–6000. Facsimile: 202–220–5200.

Dallas: Texas Office: 300 Crescent Court, Suite 1400. Telephone: 972–715–2700. Fax: 972–715–2704.

*Reston Virginia Office: 2*100 Reston Parkway; Suite 203. Telephone: 703–621–3000. Fax: 703–621–3001.

Associated International Offices:

London, England Office: Brobeck Hale and Dorr International, Hasilwood House, 60 Bishopsgate, London EC2N 4AJ. Telephone: + 44 171 638 6688. Facsimile: 44 171 638 5888.

Oxford England Office: Brobeck Hale and Dorr, Park Gate. 25 Milton Park, 31. Abingdon; OX 14 4RY. Telephone: +44 1235 82 30 00. Fax: +44 1235 82 30. 30.

Munich Germany Office: Brobeck Hale and Dorr, Maximilianstrasse 31. D-80539. Telephone: +49 89 24 213–0. Fax: +49 89 24 213–213.

1 **Note from Professor Carr: This is one of the better legal directories out there that lists attorneys, their bios, legal pedigrees, etc. This firm bio and directory actually goes on and on for many, many pages, but to save time, copy costs, etc., I have only included several pages of the firm bio. I think/suspect that it's enough to give you a good picture and feel for this firm, how it's structured, the quality of its attorneys, its type of practice, what it's all about, etc. You can also access this directory on-line at the Lexis-Nexis database on the Cal Poly Kennedy Library web page.**

2 **Note from Professor Carr: This was a large San Francisco Law Firm (and a well-respected one)**

General Practice, including Business and Technology, Business Litigation, Securities Litigation, Patent and Trademark Litigation; Technology Litigation. Environmental Litigation, Product Liability Litigation, Insurance Coverage Litigation on behalf of Policyholders, Intellectual. Property (including Patent and Trademark Prosecution, Copyright Trade Secrets and Licensing), Labor Law, Financial Services and Insolvency (including Bankruptcy and Loan Workout), Real Estate, and Tax, Executive Compensation, Employee Benefits and Estate Planning.[3]

CHAIRMAN

RICHARD S. ODOM, born Galveston, Texas, 1944; admitted to bar, 1970, California; 1991, U.S. Supreme Court. *Education:* Stanford University (B.S., 1966; J.D., 1969). Editor, 1967–1968; Managing Editor, 1968–1969, Stanford Law Review. Author: "Alternatives to the Present Check Collection System," Volume 20, Stanford Law Review. [Legal Officer, U.S. Army, 1970–1971]. ***PRACTICE AREAS:*** Complex Commercial Litigation; Products Liability. ***Email:*** rodom@ brobeck.com

MANAGING PARTNER

RICHARD L. PARKER, born Santa Monica, California, 1950; admitted to bar, 1978, California. *Education:* California State University, Los Angeles (B.A., 1973); University of California School of Law, Davis (J.D., 1977); New York University (LL.M. in Taxation,–1978). Professor, Taxation and Business Planning, University of Baltimore School of Law, 1988–1992. Member. State Bar of California, Tax Section; American Bar Association, Tax Section. ***PRACTICE AREAS:*** Taxation and Business Planning. ***Email:*** rparker@brobeck.com

PARTNERS

ROCHELLE D. ALPERT, born 1950; admitted to bar, 1975, California. *Education:* University of Michigan (B.A., 1972); University of Michigan Law School (J.D., 1975). Order of the Coif. ***PRACTICE AREAS:*** Trademark; Copyright; Intellectual Property; False Advertising; Unfair Competition. ***Email:*** ralpert@brobeck.com

JAMES P. BAKER, Born Washington DC 1952 admitted to bar, 1980, California; 1981, District of Columbia; U.S. Supreme Court; U.S.. District Court, Northern, Eastern and Central Districts of California; U.S. Court of Appeals, Ninth and Seventh Circuits. *Education:* University of Paris, Sorbonne: University of Santa Clara (B.A. 1975; J.D., 1980); Georgetown University Law Center (LL.M., 1982) Author "Microsoft's Miscalculations," Los Angeles Daily Journal, June 8, 1999; "Design and Funding of Particular and Special Severance Arrangements," Chapter Four, Employment Severance Answer Book, 1998; "Equal Pay For Equal Work? The Law of Domestic Partner Benefits," ABA The Labor Lawyer, Summer 1998; "Double Down: Dual Health Coverage Will Not Vitiate a Qualified Beneficiary's COBRA Rights," article in special issue of Employment Law, 8/7/98; "Make Your Company's Domestic-Partner Benefits Foolproof," article in Workforce Magazine, 2/98; "Retired Care. Still Cuttable," article in Legal Times, 2/16/98. Recognized by the National Law Journal as one of the forty best ERISA employee benefit attorneys in the United States. Early Neutral Evaluator, ERISA, U.S. District Court for the Eastern District of California. ***LANGUAGES:*** French. ***PRACTICE AREAS:*** ERISA Litigation; Employee Benefits Litigation; Class Actions. ***Email:*** jpbaker@brobeck.com

GRADY M. BOLDING, born Shreveport, Louisiana 1951; admitted to bar, 1977, California. *Education:* Harvard University (B.A. 1973; J.D., 1977). (Also at Palo Alto, California Office). ***PRACTICE AREAS:*** Corporate Tax Law; Partnership Tax Law; Estate Planning Law. ***Email:*** gbolding@brobeck.com

---

3 Note from Professor Carr: Type of law this firm practices.

DONALD J. BOUEY, born San Francisco, California, 1952, admitted to bar 1978, California. *Education:* Harvard University (BA, 1975); University of California, Hastings College of the Law (J.D., 1978). ***PRACTICE AREAS:*** Health Care; Corporate; Administrative. ***Email:*** dbouey@brobeck.com

MARK H. BOXER, born Milwaukee, Wisconsin,–1953; admitted to bar, 1988, California: *Education:* Drake University (B.S., 1975); University of Wisconsin (M.B.A., 1976); University of San Francisco (J.D., 1968); New York University (LL.M., 1989), ***PRACTICE AREAS:*** Employee Benefits Law. ***Email:*** mboxer@brobeck.com

MARGO N. BRADISH, admitted to bar, 1993, California *Education:* Brown University (A. B., magna cum laude, 1990); University of California, Boalt Hall School of Law (J.D., 1993). Phi Beta Kappa. Author. "Building on the Past: A Road Map to Compliance With Historic Preservation laws," California Real Property Journal, Spring 1997. ***PRACTICE AREAS:*** Land Use Law; Entitlements; California Environmental Quality Act; National Environmental Policy Act. ***Email:*** mbradish@brobeck.com

SARA B. BRODY, born Boston, Massachusetts, 1960; admitted to bar, 1987, California; 1990, District of Columbia. *Education:* University of California at Berkeley (B.A. 1982); Smith College; Emory University School of Law (J.D., 1987). ***PRACTICE AREAS:*** Securities; Securities Litigation; Securities Fraud Class Actions; Shareholder Derivative Actions Regulatory; Investigations; Insurance Coverage. ***Email:*** sbrody@brobeck.com

DAVID J. BROWN, born Oakland. California, 1943; admitted to bar, 1973, California, U.S. District Court, Northern and Central Districts of California and U.S. Court of Appeals, 9th Circuit; 1974, U.S. District Court, Southern and Eastern Districts of California; 1978, U.S. Supreme Court; 1988, US. District Court, Southern District of Illinois; 1989, U.S. Court of Appeals, 7th Circuit. *Education:* University of California, Berkeley (B.S., 1966); University of the Pacific, McGeorge School of Law (J.D., 1973). (Also at Los Angeles, California Office). ***PRACTICE AREAS:*** Financial Services Litigation; Health Care Services .Litigation; Class Actions; Securities Litigation; RICO; Commercial and Home Real Estate Loan Litigation; Civil Litigation; Complex Bankruptcy. ***Email:*** djbrown@brobeck.com

DONALD W. BROWN, born Cleveland, Ohio, 1953; admitted to bar, 1978, California. *Education:* Ohio University. (A.B., 1975); Yale Law School (J.D., 1978). ***PRACTICE AREAS:*** Insurance Coverage, Litigation; Bad Faith and Consumer Fraud Litigation. ***Email:*** dwbrown@brobeck.com

JAMES E. BURNS, JR., born Berkeley, California, 1946; admitted to bar, 1972, California. *Education:* St. Mary's College (B.A., 1968); University of Chicago (J.D., 1972). ***PRACTICE AREAS:*** Securities Law; Litigation; Complex Commercial Litigation; Corporate and Securities; Transactions. ***Email:*** *jburns@brobeck.com*

SHANE M. BYRNE, born Dublin, Ireland, 1963; admitted to bar, 1990, New York; 1996, California: *Education:* University College Dublin, Dublin, Ireland (B.C.L., 1984); Incorporated Law Society of Ireland, Dublin, Ireland (1987). *Member:* American Bar Association (Member, Science and Technology Section). ***PRACTICE AREAS:*** Business Law; Internet Law; Securities; Corporate Law. ***Email:*** sbyrne@brobeck.com

ROY E. CRAWFORD, III, born Topeka, Kansas; 1938: admitted to bar, 1964, California and U.S Court of Military Appeals. *Education:* University of Pennsylvania (B.S., 1960) Stanford University (LL.B., 1963). Editor, Stanford Law Review, 1962–1963; Author "Taxation of Multi-State Banking Activities in California," ABA National Institute on Multi-State Banking, 1984; "Currency Exchange Problems in California's Worldwide Unitary Taxation," International Bureau of Fiscal Documentation, 1986; "Sale and Uses Taxes," and "Franchise and Corporate Income

Taxes," California Taxes, California Continuing Education of the Bar, 1988; "California Unitary Taxation and Water's Edge Election," International Bureau of Fiscal Documentation, 1989; "The Distinction Between Business and Nonbusiness Income," The State and Local Tax Portfolio Series, 1989. Chairman, State and Local Tax Committee, Taxation Section, American Bar Association, 1979–1981. ***PRACTICE AREAS:*** State Taxation; Local Taxation. ***Email:*** rcrawford@brobeck.com

GEORGE A. CUMMING, JR., born Washington, D.C., 1942; admitted to bar, 1967, California; 1974, U.S. Supreme Court. *Education:* College of San Mateo (A.A., 1962); San Francisco State College (A.B., 1963); University of California, Boalt Hall School of Law (J.D., 1967). Order of the Coif. Note and Comment Editor, California Law Review, 1966–1967. Fellow, American College of Trial Lawyers. ***PRACTICE AREAS:*** Antitrust Law; Commercial Litigation; Appellate Practice. ***Email:*** gcumming@brobeck.corn

SUSAN R. DIAMOND, born Vancouver, British Columbia, Canada, 1957; admitted to bar, 1983, California. *Education:* Stanford University (B.S., 1979); Massachusetts Institute of Technology (M.C.P., 1983); Harvard University (J.D., 1983). Phi Beta Kappa; Lamda Alpha. Arthur: "Upping the Ante .in the Approval Process," Urban Land, Sept. 1993; "A Transportation System Management Ordinance," Land Use Law and Zoning Digest, April, 1985; "The San Francisco Office-Housing Program," 7 Harvard Environmental Law Review 449, 1983., Visiting Lecturer, University of California at Berkeley Graduate Business School, 1985–1989. *Member:* American Planning Association. ***PRACTICE AREAS:*** Land Use Environmental Law. ***Email:*** sdiamond@brobeck. com

BRENDAN G. DOLAN, born Dungarvan County Waterford, Ireland, 1959; admitted to bar 1986, California: *Education:* University of California at Berkeley (A.B.,1981); University, of San Francisco, (J.D., 1986), Member, McAuliffe Honor Society. Managing Editor, University of San Francisco Law Review, 1985–1986. *Member:* Bar. Association of .San Francisco. ***PRACTICE AREAS:*** Litigation; Labor Law; Employment Law. ***Email:*** bdolan@brobeck.com

REBECCA D. EISEN, born Pensacola, Florida, 1949; admitted to bar, 1980, California: *Education:* University of California at Berkeley (B.A., 1971); San Francisco State University (M.A., 1973); University of San Francisco (J.D., 1980). Member, McAuliffe Honor Society. ***PRACTICE AREAS:*** Employment Litigation and Counseling. ***Email:*** reisen@brobeck.com

SUSAN P. VOMUND, born Houston, Texas, 1963; admitted to bar; 1995, California. *Education:* Texas A *&* M University (B.E.D., 1986); Golden Gate University (I.D., 1994). National Dean's List. Notary Public, California; 1992. Litigation Section, State Bar of California, 1995—. ***PRACTICE AREAS:*** Business and Technology; Securities. ***Email:*** svomund@brobeck.com

JUDITH A. WHITEHOUSE, born Rochester, New York, 1947; admitted to bar, 1998, California; 1999, U.S. District Court, Northern, Eastern, Central and Southern Districts of California. *Education:* Syracuse University (B.A., 1969); Golden Gate University (J.D., 1998). *Member:* Bar Association of San Francisco; American Bar Association; San Francisco Bank Attorneys Association. ***PRACTICE AREAS:*** Banking and Financial Services; Mergers and Acquisitions. ***Email:*** jwhitehouse@brobeck.com

ASSOCIATES

MICHAEL D. ADAMS, born Wilmington, Delaware, 1971; admitted to bar, 1996, California and U.S. District Court, Northern District of California. *Education:* University of California at Santa Cruz (B.A., with honors, 1993); Stanford University (J.D., 1996). ***PRACTICE AREAS:*** Commercial Litigation; Internet Law; E-Commerce; Construction Defect Litigation; Products Liability. ***Email:*** madams@brobeck.com

RONIT MICHELLE ALCHECK, born Redwood City, California, 1974; admitted to bar, 1998, California. *Education:* Georgetown University (B.S., 1995); University of California School of Law, Los Angeles (J.D., 1998). ***LANGUAGES:*** Hebrew. ***PRACTICE AREAS:*** Intellectual Property Counseling and Litigation. ***Email:*** ralcheck@brobeck.com

JAMES W. ANDREW, JR., born May 9 1969: admitted to bar, 1999, California *Education:* University of California, Berkeley (B.A.); Stanford University (J.D.). [Lieut., U.S. Navy, 1991–1996]. ***LANGUAGES:*** Spanish. ***PRACTICE AREAS:*** Land Use Law: ***Email:*** jandrew@brobeck.com

PAUL A. ANDRONICO, born Oakland, California, 1967; admitted to bar, 1995, California. *Education:* University of California at Santa Barbara (B.A., 1989); University of San Diego School of Law (J.D., 1995). Order of the Coif. Member, 1993–1995 and Executive Editor, 1994–1995, San Diego Law Review. *Member:* American Bar Association. ***PRACT1CE AREAS:*** Real Estate. ***Email:*** pandronico@brobeck.com

JOSEMARIA (JOE) ANGULO, born Los Angeles, California, 1970; admitted to bar, 1997, California. *Education:* University of California, Berkeley (B.A., 1993); Harvard University (J.D., 1997). *Member:* Bar Association of San Francisco; American Bar Association; State Bank of California. ***LANGUAGES:*** Spanish. ***PRACTICE AREAS:*** Corporate; Emerging Growth Companies ***Email:*** jangulo@brobeck.com

BARBARA ANTONUCCI, born New York, N.Y. 1974; admitted to bar, 2000, California *Education*: Columbia University (B.A., 1996); University of California; Boalt Hall School of Law (J.D., 2000): ***LANGUAGES:*** Italian and Spanish ***PRACTICE AREAS:*** Labor and Employment Law ***Email:*** bantonucci@brobeck.com

CHRISTOPHER J. BANKS, born 1973; *Education*: University of Nebraska at Lincoln (B.A., Internationals Affairs, 1994); George Washington University (M.A, International Affairs, 1997); Georgetown University (J.D., 2000). ***Email:*** *cbanks@brobeck.com*

MATTHEW S. BARTUS, born West Hartford, Connecticut, 1970, admitted to bar, 1999, New York; 2000, California. *Education:* Syracuse University (B.A., 1992); New York University (J.D., cum laude, 1998). *Member:* New York State and American Bar Associations. ***PRACTICE AREAS:*** Mergers and Acquisitions; Securities; Venture Capital; General Corporate ***Email:*** mbartus@brobeck.com

WILLIAM W. HUCKINS, born Kankakee, Illinois, 1958; admitted to bar 1994, Hawaii; 1998, Colorado; 1999, California. *Education:* University of Colorado at Boulder (B.S., cum laude, 1981); University of Utah (J.D., 1994). William H. Leary Scholar. Recipient, American Jurisprudence Awards: Contracts; Legal Writing and Research; Bankruptcy. ***PRACTICE AREAS:*** Litigation; Bankruptcy. ***Email***: whuckins@brobeck.com

MICHELLE P. HUDSON, born 1972; admitted to bar, 1999, California. *Education:* University of California at Santa Barbara (B. A., 1995); University of California, Boalt Hall School of Law (J.D., 1999). *Member:* California Law Review. ***Email:*** mhudson@brobeck.com

TAZAMISHA HESHIMA IMARA, born Hayward, California, 1972; admitted to bar, 1999, California. *Education:* Harvard College (A.B., 1993); John F Kennedy School of Government (Masters of Public Policy, 1995); University of California, Boalt Hall School of Law (J.D., 1998). ***PRACTICE AREAS:*** Labor and Employment. ***Email;*** timara@brobeck.com

CATHERINE A. JACKSON, born Anaheim, California, 1972; admitted to bar, 1997, California. *Education:* University of California at Los Angeles (B.A., cum laude, 1993); Georgetown University (J.D., 1997). ***PRACTICE AREAS:*** Business Litigation; Civil Litigation. ***Email:*** cjackson@brobeck.com

ROBERTO J. KAMPFNER, born Mexico City, Mexico; 1970; admitted to bar, 1995, California.

Education: University of Michigan (B.A., with distinction, 1991); Stanford University (J.D., 1995). Golden Key. *Member:* Bar Association of San Francisco; American Bar Association. ***LANGUAGES:*** Spanish. ***PRACTICE AREAS:*** Bankruptcy; Creditors' Rights; Commercial Law; Secured Finance. ***Email:*** rkampfner@brobeck.com

STEVEN S. KAUFHOLD, born Riverside, California; 1966; admitted to bar, 1991, California and U.S. District Court, Northern District of California. *Education:* University of California at Los Angeles (B.A., 1988); University of California, Hastings College of the Law (J.D., 1991). Phi Beta Kappa. Law Clerk to the Honorable Samuel Conti, U.S. District Judge, Northern District of California, 1993–1994. *Member:* Bar Association of San Francisco (Member, Board of Directors, 1998—); State Bar of California; The Barristers Club of San Francisco. (Member, Board of Directors, 1998–; President, 1999–); Consumer Attorneys of California; San Francisco Trial Lawyers Association. ***PRACTICE AREAS:*** Securities Litigation; ***Email:*** skaufhold@brobeck.com

CATHERINE DUDEN KEVANE, admitted to bar, 2001, California. *Education:* Barnard College (B.A., 1994); Boalt Hall School of Law University of California (J.D., 2001). ***LANGUAGES:*** French. ***PRACTICE AREAS:*** Securities Litigation. ***Email:*** ckevane@brobeck.com

LESLEY ELIZABETH KOTHE, born San Francisco, California, 1975; admitted to bar, 2000, California. *Education:* Duke University (B.A., 1996); University of California School of Law; Los Angeles (J.D., 2000): ***PRACTICE AREAS:*** Business Litigation. ***Email:*** lkothe@brobeck.com

MIHO M. KUBOTA, born Tokyo Japan, 1970; admitted to bar, 1999 California. *Education:* Wesleyan University (B.A., 1993); Boston University (J.D., cum laude, 1999). ***LANGUAGES:*** Japanese: ***PRACTICE AREAS:*** Corporate Low. ***Email:*** mkubota@brobeck.com

ELISA S. LEE, born Wyandotte, Michigan, 1969; admitted to bar, 1998, California. *Education:* University of Michigan (B.A., English Literature, 1991; J.D., 1998). ***PRACTICE AREAS:*** Business Law; Technology Law. ***Email:*** elee@brobeck.com

FELIX LEE, born Provo, Utah, 1972; (admission pending). *Education:* Stanford University (B.A., 1994); Harvard Law School (J.D., 1997). ***PRACTICE AREAS:*** Securities Litigation. ***Email:*** flee@brobeck.com

ELIZABETH H. LEFEVER, born Harrisburg, Pennsylvania; admitted to bar, 1995, New York; 1999; California *Education:* Middlebury College (B.A., 1989); Tulane Law School (J.D., 1994). ***LANGUAGES:*** Russian and French ***PRACTICE AREAS:*** Corporate Law; Securities. ***Email:*** elefever@brobeck.com

SAVITA N. LEPORE, born Washington, D.C., 1968; admitted to bar, 1995, Georgia; 1999, *Education:* Amherst College (A.B., cum laude, 1989); Emory University (J.D., 1995). ***PRACTICE AREAS:*** Intellectual Property; Trademarks, Copyrights, Domain Names, Advertising, E-Commerce and Licensing ***Email:*** slepore@brobeck.com

KRISTA JOY MARTINELLI, born San Francisco, California, 1973; admitted to bar, 1998, California. *Education:* Cornell University (B.S., with honors in Human Development and Family Studies, 1995); University of California, Hastings College of the Law (J.D., 1998). Phi Alpha Delta; Queen's Bench, San Francisco, 1998. Recipient, American Jurisprudence Awards: Moot Court, Criminal Law. Law Clerk: San Mateo County District Attorney's Office, Consumer and Environmental Unit, 1996; Alameda County Public Defender's Office. 1997 Author Public Law Research Institute (PLRI) Reports 1998 University of California Hastings College of the Law, "The Role of The California Attorney General in Enforcing Civil Rights Statutes" (Spring 1998). (Also at Palo Alto, California Office). ***LANGUAGES:*** Spanish **REPORTED CASES:** Preferred MSO of America-Austin LLC v. Quadramed Corp., 85 F. Supp. 2d 974 (CDCA :

1999). ***PRACTICE AREAS:*** Securities Litigation. ***Email:*** kmartinelli@brobeck.com

JULIE M. McEVILLY, born Torrance, California, 1972; (admission pending). *Education:* University of California at Santa Barbara (B.A., 1994); Loyola Law School (J.D., 1998). ***Email:*** jmcevilly@brobeck.com

NIKKI S. McKENNEDY, born Warwick, Rhode Island, 1971; admitted to bar, 1996, California. *Education:* Pepperdine University (B.A., summa cum laude, 1993; J.D., magna cum laude, 1996). Member Bar Association of San Francisco; Defense Research Institute; Queen's Bench. ***PRACTICE AREAS:*** Products Liability; Commercial Litigation. ***Email:*** nmckennedy@brobeck.com

ERIC MECKLEY, born Altoona, Pennsylvania, December, 1998; admitted to bar, 1993, California; 1995, U.S. Court of Appeals; Ninth Circuit *Education:* Pennsylvania State University (B.A., with honors, 1990); University of California, Boalt Hall School of Law (J.D., 1993). Phi Beta Kappa. *Member:* San Francisco County and American Bar Associations; Barrister's Association. ***PRACTICE AREAS:*** Labor and Employment Litigation. ***Email:*** emeckley@brobeck.com

PETER P. MERINGOLO, born Mineola, New York, 1969; admitted to bar, 1998, California. *Education:* University of Notre Dame (B.A., 1991); University of California, Hastings College of the Law (J.D., 1998) Senior Executive Editor, Hastings Law Journal, 1997–1998. ***PRACTICE AREAS:*** Complex Business Litigation. ***Email:*** pmeringolo@brobeck.com

LAUREN M. MICHALS, born Plainfield, New Jersey, 1959, admitted to bar, 1996, California. *Education:* University of Michigan (A.B.,1980); University of California at Santa Barbara (M.A., 1985); Stanford University; University of Chicago (J.D., 1996). *Member:* American Bar Association ***PRACTICE AREAS:*** Products Liability; Toxic Torts; Environmental Law. ***Email:*** lmichals@brobeck.com

JACQUELINE R. MIJUSKOVIC, admitted to bar, 1997, California. *Education:* University of California at Los Angeles (B.A., 1992); University of San Francisco (M.B.A., 1997; J.D., 1997). ***Email:*** jmijuskovic@brobeck.com

PETER G. MUGO, born Kenya, 1971; admitted to bar, 1997, Kenya; 2000, New York (Not admitted in California). *Education:* University of Nairobi, Nairobi, Kenya (LL.B., with honors, 1995); Kenya School of Law (Diploma in Law, 1996); Boston University (LL.M., with honors, 1998). Member: New York State and American Bar Associations, Law Society of Kenya ***LANGUAGES:*** Swahili and Kikuyu ***PRACTICE AREAS:*** Business Law; Technology Law. ***Email:*** pmugo@brobeck.com

SUE J. NAM, born Seoul, Korea, 1969; admitted to bar, 1995, New York; 1996, U.S, District Court, Northern District of California and U.S. Court of Appeals, Ninth Circuit, 2001, U.S. District Court, Central District of California. *Education:* Northwestern University (B.A., with distinction, 1991); Yale Law School (J.D., 1994). Clerkship with U.S. Court of Appeals, Second Circuit, 1994–1995. ***LANGUAGES:*** Korean and French. ***PRACTICE AREAS:*** Intellectual Property. ***Email:*** snam@brobeck.com

CALIFORNIA–SAN LUIS OBISPO

FARMER & READY
A LAW CORPORATION
Established in 1976
1254 MARSH STREET
P.O. BOX 1443
SAN LUIS OBISPO, CALIFORNIA *93406*
Telephone: 805-541-162
Fax: 805-541-0769
Email: info@farmerandready.com

General Civil and Trial Practice. Bankruptcy, Insolvency, Real Property, Commercial and Collection Law.[4]

DAVID Y. FARMER, born Minneapolis, Minnesota, April 16, 1945; admitted to bar, 1971, California, U.S. District Court, Northern District of California and U.S. Court of Appeals, Ninth Circuit; 1975, U.S. District Court, Central District of California; 1977, U.S. District Court, Eastern District of California;. 1979, U.S. District Court, Southern District of California. *Education:* Occidental College (B.A., 1967); Hastings College of the Law; University of California (J.D., 1970). Adjunct Faculty, California Polytechnic State University, San Luis Obispo, 1971–. Panel Trustee, Bankruptcy Court, Central District of California, 1979–. *Member:* San Luis Obispo County and American Bar Associations; State Bar of California; National Association of Bankruptcy Trustees; American Bankruptcy Institute (Member, Committee on Consumer Bankruptcy); (Certified Specialist, Personal and Small Business Bankruptcy Law, State Bar of California Board of Legal Specialization). ***PRACTICE AREAS:*** Bankruptcy; Commercial Law; General Civil and Trial Practice, ***Email:*** dyfarmer@farmerandready.com.

PAUL F. READY, born San Luis Obispo, California, October 7, 1956, admitted to bar, 1982, California; 1983, U.S. District Court, Central and Southern Districts of California; 1985, US. District Court, Eastern and Northern Districts of California; 1989, U.S. Court of Appeals, Ninth Circuit. *Education:* California Polytechnic State University (B.S, 1979); McGeorge School of Law University of the Pacific (J.D., 1982). Phi Delta Phi. Member, Adjunct Faculty, California Polytechnic State University, San Luis Obispo, 1983–; General Counsel, California Polytechnic University Alumni, 1994–1998. Planning Commissioner, 1995–2001 and Chairman, 1999–2001, City of San Luis Obispo. *Member:* San Luis Obispo County and American Bar Associations; State Bar of California ***PRACTICE AREAS:*** Real Property; Bankruptcy; Commercial and Collection Law; General Civil and Trial Practice ***Email:*** pfready@farmerandready.com.

REPRESENTATIVE CLIENTS: Chicago Title Co.; Mid-State Bank & Trust; The Real Estate Group of San Luis Obispo; Attorney Service of San Luis Obispo; First American Title Co.; Apio Inc.; Pacific West Produce-Mid Coast Land Co.; All Quaglino, Inc.; C. Dunn Homes; First Bank of San Luis Obispo.

REFERENCE : Mid State Bank & Trust, San Luis Obispo.

4 **Note from Professor Carr: Again, the type of law this firm practices.**

FITZPATRICK & BARBIERI
A PROFESSIONAL LAW CORPORATION
Established in 1980
1326 CHORRO STREET
SAN LUIS OBISPO, CALIFORNIA
93401–4006
Telephone: 805-541-6400
Fax: 805-541-3702
Email: FANDBLAW@CHARTER.NET
URL: http://www.lawyers.com/fizpatrick&barbierilaw

General Civil and Trial Practice, Subrogation Law, Personal Injury, Estate and Gift Taxation, Estate Planning, Business, Corporation, Probate, Real Estate Law and Construction Litigation, Private and Public Works.

DAVID C. FITZPATRICK, born San Luis Obispo, California, August 29, 1949; admitted to bar, 1975, California and U.S. of District Court, Estate District of California. *Education:* California State Polytechnic University (B.S., 1972); McGeorge School of Law, University of the Pacific (J.D., 1975). Phi Delta Phi. Member, Traynor Honor Society. *Member:* San Luis Obispo County Bar Association; State Bar of California. [With California Army National Guard 1971–1976]. ***PRACTICE AREAS:*** Business Law: Corporate Law; Probate Law; Estate Planning; Estate and Gift Taxation; Real Estate Law. ***Email:*** dfitz@thegrid.com.

EVANS J. BARBIERI, born Jefferson City, Missouri, July 30, 1947; admitted to bar, 1977, California and U.S. District Court, Eastern District of California. *Education:* University of the Pacific (B.A., 1971); McGeorge School of Law, University of the Pacific (J.D., 1977). Phi Alpha Delta. Member, Traynor Honor Society. *Member:* San Luis Obispo County Bar Association; State Bar of California; The Association of Trial Lawyers of America. Member, San Luis Obispo County Builders Exchange. Certified as a Civil Trial Advocate by The National Board of Trial Advocacy. (Also Of Counsel, Schweitzer, Dorrance & Bird, Ventura). ***PRACTICE AREAS:*** General Civil Trial Practice; Construction Litigation.

REPRESENTATIVE CLIENTS: City of San Luis Obispo; Industrial Indemnity/Fremont Compensation; Mervyn's California; Reiss Consulting, Inc.; Central Coast Fabricators, Inc.; Bergantz Interior Systems, Inc.; Waltech, Inc.; Nick E. Pokrajac Construction, Inc.; Evans Plastering, Inc.; Bunnell Construction, Inc.; Antone Sylvester Tug Service, Inc.; York Mountain Winery; Talley Vineyards; Pool Company; San Luis Mechanical; Sansone Company; Advance Adapters, Inc.

REFERENCES: First Union Securities; First Bank of San Luis Obispo; Bank of America.[5]

5 Note from Professor Carr: These are two small (but normal/typical) San Luis Obispo law firms. Note the differences between these firms and the San Francisco firm (the Brobeck firm listed in the preceding pages) with respect to the size of the firms (as in number of bodies they can throw at a case), the breadth of practice, the legal pedigrees of the attorneys, etc. I am not saying that one type of firm is better than the other—I am only saying that they are different, have different structures, different types of practices, etc., and hence, different strengths and weaknesses.

7 Example of a Summons

***Note from Professor Carr: This is a document that is attached to and served on a defendant with the complaint (see next page).

SUMMONS
(CITACION JUDICIAL)

FOR COURT USE ONLY
(SOLO PARA USO DE LA CORTE)

NOTICE TO DEFENDANT: ***(Aviso a Acusado)***

YOU ARE BEING SUED BY PLAINTIFF:
(A Ud. le está demandando)

*For state court; for federal court it is <u>20</u> days

You have 30 CALENDAR DAYS after this summons is served on you to file a typewritten response at this court.

A letter or phone call will not protect you; your typewritten response must be in proper legal form if you want the court to hear your case.

If you do not file your response on time, you may lose the case, and your wages, money and property may be taken without further warning from the court.

There are other legal requirements. You may want to call an attorney right away. If you do not know an attorney, you may call an attorney referral service or a legal aid office (listed in the phone book).

Después de que le entreguen esta citación judicial usted tiene un plazo de 30 DIAS CALENDARIOS para presentar una respuesta escrita a máquina en esta corte.

Una carta o una llamada telefónica no le ofrecerá protección; su respuesta escrita a máquina tiene que cumplir con las formalidades legales apropiadas si usted quiere que la corte escuche su caso.

Si usted no presenta su respuesta a tiempo, puede perder el caso, y le pueden quitar su salario, su dinero y otras cosasde su propiedad sin aviso adicional por parte de la corte.

Existen otros requisitos legales. Puede que usted quiera llamar a un abogado inmediatamente. Si no conoce a un abogado, puede llamar a un servicio de referencia de abogados o a una oficina de ayuda legal (vea el directorio telefónico).

The name and address of the court is: *(El nombre y dirección de la corte es)*

CASE NUMBER: *(Número del Caso)*

The name, address, and telephone number of plaintiff's attorney, or plaintiff without an attorney, is:
(El nombre, la dirección y el número de teléfono del abogado del demandante, o del demandante que no tiene abogado, es)

DATE: *(Fecha)* Clerk, by *(Actuario)* ______________________, Deputy *(Delegado)*

(SEAL)

NOTICE TO THE PERSON SERVED: You are served

1. ☐ as an individual defendant.
2. ☐ as the person sued under the fictitious name of *(specify)*:
3. ☐ on behalf of *(specify)*:

under: ☐ CCP 416.10 (corporation) ☐ CCP 416.60 (minor)
☐ CCP 416.20 (defunct corporation) ☐ CCP 416.70 (conservatee)
☐ CCP 416.40 (association or partnership) ☐ CCP 416.90 (individual)
☐ other:

4. ☐ by personal delivery on *(date)*:

(See reverse for Proof of Service)
SUMMONS

8 Example of a Complaint

Law Office
Big Shot Attorney
8934 Rathburn Avenue
Malibu, California 94456

MUNICIPAL COURT OF CALIFORNIA, COUNTY OF LOS ANGELES
LOS ANGELES JUDICIAL DISTRICT

COLLEGE SETTLEMENT CORPORATION,)) Plaintiff,)) vs.))) ACADEMIC BETTERMENT) CORPORATION, and DOES ONE through) TEN, inclusive)) Defendant))	PLAINTIFF'S COMPLAINT

> ***Note from Professor Carr: The original would be filed with the court clerk; and a copy would need to be served on the defendant.
>
> This document is attached to and served with the "Summons" (see previous page).

Plaintiff alleges:

I

Plaintiff is and at all times herein mentioned was, a corporation organized and existing pursuant to the laws of the State of California.

II

Defendant ACADEMIC BETTERMENT CORPORATION (hereinafter referred to as "ABC") is, and at all time herein mentioned was, a corporation organized and existing pursuant to the laws of the State of California, with its principal place of business in the County of Lost Angles, State of California.

III

The true names or capacities, whether individual, corporate, associate or otherwise of defendants sued herein as DOES ONE through TEN, inclusive, are unknown to plaintiff as this time and are therefore sued by such fictitious names. Plaintiff is informed and believes, and thereon alleges, that each of defendants designated herein as a DOE is legally responsible in some manner for the events and happenings herein referred to and caused injury and damages actually and proximately thereby to plaintiff as herein alleged. When such true names and capacities become known, plaintiff will amend this complaint to show these true names and capacities.

IV

At all times herein mentioned, defendants DOES ONE through TEN, inclusive, were the agents and employees of defendant ABC and each of their DOE codefendants referred to in this paragraph, and were acting within the course and scope of said agency and employment, and with the permission and consent of their said codefendants, and with the knowledge and under the supervision of said codefendants.

V

Within the last four years, defendants ABC and DOES ONE through TEN, inclusive, became indebted to plaintiff upon an open book account n the sum of $12,000.00, for balance due and owing on goods purchased from plaintiff at said defendants' special instance and request.

VI

Said amount has come due, plaintiff had demanded same, said amount from said defendants, and said defendants refused and have continued to refuse to pay said sum, or any part thereof.

WHEREFORE, PLAINTIFF PRAYS FOR JUDGMENT AGAINST DEFENDANTS ABC AND DOES ONE THROUGH TEN, AND EACH OF THEM AS FOLOWS:

1. General damages in the sum of $12,000.00

2. Interest at the rate of 7 percent per annum from March 16, 2009 forward

3. Cost of suit and reasonable attorney's fees incurred herein, and

4. For such other and further relief as the court deems just and proper.

By__________________________

Big Shot Attorney
Attorney for Plaintiff ABC

9 Example of an Answer

Academic Betterment Corporation
Bob Macquire
15888 Nordman Street
Westwood, California 98445

MUNICIPAL COURT OF CALIFORNIA, COUNTY OF LOS ANGELES
LOS ANGELES JUDICIAL DISTRICT

COLLEGE SETTLEMENT CORPORATION, Plaintiff, vs. ACADEMIC BETTERMENT CORPORATION, and DOES ONE through TEN, inclusive Defendants	ANSWER OF DEFENDANT ACADEMIC BETTERMENT CORPORATION

Comes now the defendant, ACADEMIC BETTERMENT CORPORATION, a corporation for itself and itself alone, and in the answer to plaintiff's complaint, admits, denies and alleges as follows:

Admits paragraph II thereof and denies each and every other allegation therein contained specifically paragraphs I, III, IV, V and VI thereof.

WHEREFORE, this defendant prays:

1. That plaintiff be granted no relief in this action, and

2. For defendant's costs in this action, together with such other and further relief as the court may deem just and proper.

ACADEMIC BETTERMENT CORPORTION,
a Corporation

By ______________________________
Bob Macquire, President

***Note from Professor Carr: The defendant files this document in response to being served with a copy of the plaintiff's complaint. If he/she fails to do so in a timely manner, the plaintiff can take/enter a default judgement against the defendant.

*Also, when filing an answer, the defendant may also choose to file a counterclaim against the plaintiff or even a cross-complaint against an outside third party that the plaintiff failed to name in his/her complaint.

10 Request for Entry of Default

ATTORNEY OR PARTY WITHOUT ATTORNEY (Name and Address): TELEPHONE NO.: FOR COURT USE ONLY

Chris A. Carr

San Luis Obispo, CA 93405

ATTORNEY FOR (NAME): Plaintiff Supercom, Inc.

Insert name of court, name of judicial district, and branch court, if any:

LOS ANGELES SUPERIOR COURT

NORWALK BRANCH (SOUTHEAST DISTRICT)

PLAINTIFF: SUPERCOM, INC.

DEFENDANT: ANWAR SALEH, ANWAR ELECTRONICS, JAMAL SALEH

ORIGINAL FILED

DEC 20 1995

SOUTHEAST DISTRICT

REQUEST FOR ☒ ENTRY OF DEFAULT ☒ CLERK'S JUDGMENT
(Application) ☐ COURT JUDGMENT

CASE NUMBER: YC 019311

***Note from Professor Carr: This is the form to fill out and file with the court to enter a default judgment against you if you do not file a timely answer to the complaint!!

1. TO THE CLERK: On the complaint or cross-complaint filed
   a. On (date): May 12, 1995
   b. By (name): Plaintiff, Supercom, Inc.
   c. ☐ Enter default of defendant (names):

   d. ☐ I request a court judgment under CCP 585(b), (c), 989, etc. (Testimony required. Apply to the clerk for a hearing date, unless the court will enter a judgment on an affidavit under CCP 585(d).)
   e. ☒ Enter clerk's judgment (as to Defendant ANWAR SALEH, an individual)
      (1) ☐ For restitution of the premises only and issue a writ of execution on the judgment. CCP 1174(c) does not apply. (CCP 1169) ☐ Include in the judgment all tenants, subtenants, named claimants, and other occupants of the premises. The Prejudgment Claim of Right to Possession was served in compliance with CCP 415.46.
      (2) ☒ Under CCP 585(a). (Complete the declaration under CCP 585.5 on the reverse (item 3).)
      (3) ☒ For default previously entered on (date): October 25, 1995

2. Judgment to be entered

	Amount	Credits Acknowledged	Balance
a. Demand of complaint	$ 522,375.00	$ 0	$ 522,375.00
b. Statement of damages (CCP 425.11) (superior court only)*			
(1) Special	$ 0	$ 0	$ 0.00
(2) General	$ 0	$ 0	$ 0.00
c. Interest	$ 0	$ 0	$ 0.00
d. Costs (see reverse)	$ 1,833.85	$ 0	$ 1,833.85
e. Attorney fees (see Civil Code § 1717.5)	$ 7,113.75	$ 0	$ 7,113.75
f. TOTALS	$ 531,322.60	$ 0.00	$ 531,322.60

g. Daily damages were demanded in complaint at the rate of: $ per day beginning (date):

Date: December 18, 1995

Chris A. Carr, Esq.
(TYPE OR PRINT NAME)

> Chris Carr
(SIGNATURE OF PLAINTIFF OR ATTORNEY FOR PLAINTIFF)

* Personal injury or wrongful death actions only.

FOR COURT USE ONLY
(1) [ ] Default entered as requested on (date):
(2) [ ] Default NOT entered as requested (state reason): default previously entered 10/25/95
By:

(Continued on reverse)

REQUEST FOR ENTRY OF DEFAULT
(Application to Enter Default)

COPY

11 Articles Re: Default Judgments

JUDGMENT SOUGHT AGAINST CHRISTIE'S EX-CHAIRMAN

The Wall Street Journal

LAWYERS FOR CLASS-ACTION plaintiffs who are suing Sotheby's Holdings Inc., Christie's International PLC and several of the auction houses' former executives have asked a federal judge to enter a default judgment against former Christie's chairman Sir Anthony Tennant for his failure to respond to their lawsuits.

According to a filing in U.S. District, Court in Manhattan, Sir Anthony was served with the complaint on July 5 in London. He had 20 days to respond to the lawsuit,[1] which alleges that he helped mastermind and carry out an alleged scheme in which Sotheby's and Christie's colluded to fix prices. Sir Anthony was chairman of Christie's from 1993 to 1996.

Individuals with knowledge of the government's continuing investigation into alleged price fixing said Sir Anthony hasn't spoken with prosecutors who are probing his involvement in an alleged conspiracy. These people said that Christopher Davidge, former chief executive officer of Christie's, has told prosecutors that he contacted Sotheby's then-president, Diana D. Brooks, in 1994 at the direction of Sir Anthony. Individual who have spoken with lawyers for Sir Anthony said he vigorously denies any links to the alleged price-fixing conspiracy.

It isn't clear whether Sir Anthony ever intends to respond to the lawsuits or to speak with U.S. prosecutors who are investigating him. Sir Anthony serves as a senior adviser to U.S investment-banking firm Morgan Stanley Dean Witter & Co. In London, his assistant said he was vacationing this week and unavailable for comment. His London lawyer, Richard J. J. Taylor, was also vacationing and unavailable for comment. Individuals with knowledge of the continuing probe said Sir Anthony has retained U.S. counsel though, no one has ever entered a court appearance on his behalf.

A default judgment means, in effect, that a defendant can be found liable for the actions alleged by plaintiffs without trial, and that damages can later be assessed. The defendant who allows such a judgment to stand unopposed gives up his legal rights. Even if such a judgment were entered, however, Sir Anthony could still fight it.

According to an affidavit submitted by the London-based private detective who was retained by U.S. plaintiffs' lawyers, Sir Anthony was served with the complaint as he was about to get into his Saab outside his Morgan Stanley offices. Sir Anthony shouted "Go away" and threw the papers onto the street, according to Mark Castle, the detective. "When I returned to the scene some two minutes later, the documents had been removed,"

1 **Note from Professor Carr: In federal court it is 20 days and in state court it is 30 days.**

Mr. Castle said. "I assumed that Sir Anthony had taken the documents with him." Sir Anthony was given until July 25 to respond to the complaint. When he hadn't done so by last week, plaintiffs lawyers sought the default judgment.

If U.S. District Judge Lewis Kaplan, who is presiding over the class-action lawsuits, finds Sir Anthony in default, lawyers said Sir Anthony could then oppose it, perhaps arguing that he wasn't properly served in London. Also, because he is a British citizen, a United Kingdom court would be required to enforce any default judgment against him. And were a U.S. court later to assess damages, a British court would decide whether to enforce potential claims on assets outside the U.S.'s jurisdiction.

JUDGE TO DECIDE AU PAIR DAMAGES

SLO Telegram–Tribune

BOSTON (AP)—The parents of the baby who died in the care of British au pair Louise Woodward asked a judge Monday to force her to pay several million dollars in compensation.

Sunil and Deborah Eappen sued Woodward for the wrongful death of 8-month-old Matthew. Since she did not respond to the lawsuit, the Eappens won by default.[2] Now it's up to a judge to decide how much to award the couple.

In court papers, the Eappens asked for damages to cover the loss of their son's companionship and what he might have earned in his lifetime. She did not file an answer to the plaintiff's complaint, so her default was taken.

---

2 Note from Professor Carr: She did not file an answer to the plaintiff's complaint, so her default was taken.

12 Written Interrogatory Example

<table>
<tr><td colspan="2">ATTORNEY OR PARTY WITHOUT ATTORNEY (Name and Address):

ATTORNEY FOR (Name)</td><td>TELEPHONE NO.:</td></tr>
<tr><td colspan="3">NAME OF COURT AND JUDICIAL DISTRICT AND BRANCH COURT, IF ANY:</td></tr>
<tr><td colspan="3">SHORT TITLE OF CASE:</td></tr>
<tr><td colspan="2">FORM INTERROGATORIES — ECONOMIC LITIGATION
Asking Party:

Answering Party:
Set No.:</td><td>CASE NUMBER:</td></tr>
</table>

Sec. 1. Instructions to All Parties

(a) These are general instructions. *For time limitations, requirements for service on other parties, and other details, see Code of Civil Procedure section 2030 and the cases construing it.*

(b) These interrogatories do not change existing law relating to interrogatories nor do they affect an answering party's right to assert any privilege or objection.

Sec. 2. Instructions to the Asking Party

(a) These interrogatories are designed for optional use in proceedings under the provisions for Economic Litigation in Municipal and Justice Courts, Code of Civil Procedure sections 90 through 100. However, these interrogatories also may be used in superior courts.

(b) There are restrictions on discovery for most civil actions in municipal and justice courts. These restrictions limit the number of interrogatories that may be asked. For details, read Code of Civil Procedure section 94.

(c) Some of these interrogatories are similar to questions in the Case Questionnaire and may be omitted if the information sought has already been provided in a completed Case Questionnaire

(d) Check the box next to each interrogatory that you want the answering party to answer. Use care in choosing those interrogatories that are applicable to the case and within the restrictions discussed above.

(e) The interrogatories in section 116.0, Defendant's Contentions—Personal Injury, should not be used until defendant has had a reasonable opportunity to conduct an investigation or discovery of plaintiff's injuries and damages.

(f) Additional interrogatories may be attached, subject to the restrictions discussed above.

Sec. 3. Instructions to the Answering Party

(a) Subject to the restrictions discussed above, an answer or other appropriate response must be given to each interrogatory checked by the asking party.

(b) As a general rule, within 30 days after you are served with these interrogatories, you must serve your responses on the asking party[1] and serve copies of your responses on all other parties who have appeared. See Code of Civil of Civil Procedure section 2030 for details.

(c) Each answer must be as complete and straight-forward as the information reasonably available to you permits. If an interrogatory cannot be answered completely, answer it to the extent possible.

(d) If you do not have enough personal knowledge to fully answer an interrogatory, say so, but make a reasonable and good faith effort to get the information by asking other persons or organizations, unless the information is equally available to the asking party.

(e) Whenever an interrogatory may be answered by referring to a document, the document may be attached as an exhibit to the response and referred to in the response If the document has more than one page, refer to the page and section where the answer to the interrogatory can be found.

(f) Whenever an address and telephone number for the same person are requested in more than one interrogatory, you are required to furnish them in answering only the first interrogatory asking for that information.

(g) Your answers to these interrogatories must be verified, dated, and signed. You may wish to use the following form *at the end of your answers:*

"I declare under penalty of perjury under the laws of the State of California that the foregoing answers are true and correct.[2]

__________ ____________________________"

(DATE) (SIGNATURE)

Sec. 4. Definitions

Words in **BOLDFACE CAPITALS** in these interrogatories are defined as follows:

(a) **INCIDENT** includes the circumstances and events surrounding the alleged accident, injury, or other occurrence or breach of contract giving rise to this action or proceeding.

(b) **YOU OR ANYONE ACTING ON YOUR BEHALF** includes you, your agents, your employees, your insurance companies, their agents, their employees, your attorneys, your accountants, your investigators, and anyone else acting on your behalf.

(c) **PERSON** includes a natural person, firm, association, organization, partnership, business, trust, corporation, or public entity.

(d) **DOCUMENT** means a writing, as defined in Evidence Code section 250, and includes the original or a copy of handwriting, typewriting, printing, photostating, photographing, and every other means of recording upon any tangible thing and form of communicating or representation, including letters, words, pictures sounds or symbols, or combinations of them.

(e) **HEALTH CARE PROVIDER** includes any **PERSON** referred to in Code of Civil Procedure section 667.7(e)(3).

(f) **ADDRESS** means the street address, including the city, state, and zip code.

1 Note from Professor Carr: You have 30 days to answer.

2 Note from Professor Carr: Better make sure that your answers are accurate <u>and</u> truthful!

101.0 Identity of Persons Answering These Interrogatories

☐ 1011 State the name, **ADDRESS**, telephone number, and relationship to you of each **PERSON** who prepared or assisted in the preparation of the responses to these interrogatories. (Do not identify anyone who simply typed or reproduced the responses.)

102.0 General Background Information — Individual

☐ 102.1 State your name, any other names by which you have been known, and your **ADDRESS**.

☐ 102.2 State the date and place of your birth.

☐ 102.3 State, as of the time of the **INCIDENT**, your driver's license number, the state of issuance, the expiration date, and any restrictions.

☐ 102.4 State each residence **ADDRESS** for the last five years and the dates you lived at each **ADDRESS**.

☐ 102.5 State the name, **ADDRESS**, and telephone number of each employer you have had over the past five years and the dates you worked for each.

☐ 102.6 Describe your work for each employer you have had over the past five years.

☐ 102.7 State the name and **ADDRESS** of each academic or vocational school you have attended, beginning with high school, and the dates you attended each.

☐ 102.8 If you have ever been convicted of a felony, state, for each, the offense, the date and place of conviction, and the court and case number.

☐ 102.9 State the names, **ADDRESS**, and telephone number of any **PERSON** for whom you were acting as an agent or employee at the time of the **INCIDENT**.

☐ 102.10 Describe any physical, emotional, or mental disability or condition that you had that may have contributed to the occurrence of the **INCIDENT**.

☐ 102.11 Describe the nature and quantity of any alcoholic beverage, marijuana, or other drug or medication of any kind that you used within 24 hours before the **INCIDENT**.

103.0 General Background Information — Business Entity

☐ 103.1 State your current business name and **ADDRESS**, type of business entity, and your title.

104.0 Insurance

☐ 104.1 State the name and **ADDRESS** of each insurance company and the policy number and policy limits of each policy that may cover you, in whole or in part, for the damages related to the **INCIDENT**.

105.0 *[Reserved]*

106.0 Physical, Mental, or Emotional Injuries

☐ 106.1 Describe each injury or illness related to the **INCIDENT.**

☐ 106.2 Describe your present complaints about each injury or illness related to the **INCIDENT**.

☐ 106.3 State the name, **ADDRESS**, and telephone number of each **HEALTH CARE PROVIDER** who treated or examined you for each injury or illness related to the **INCIDENT** and the dates of treatment or examination.

☐ 106.4 State the type of treatment or examination given to you by each **HEALTH CARE PROVIDER** for each injury or illness related to the **INCIDENT**.

☐ 106.5 State the charges made by each **HEALTH CARE PROVIDER** for each injury or illness related to the **INCIDENT**.

☐ 106.6 State the nature and cost of each health care service related to the **INCIDENT** not previously listed (for example, medication, ambulance, nursing, prosthetics).

☐ 106.7 State the nature and cost of the health care services you anticipate in the future as a result of the **INCIDENT**.

☐ 106.8 State the name and **ADDRESS** of each **HEALTH CARE PROVIDER** who has advised you that you may need future health care services as a result of the **INCIDENT**.

107.0 Property Damage

☐ 107.1 Itemize your property damage and, for each item, state the amount or attach an itemized bill or estimate.

108.0 Loss of Income or Earning Capacity

☐ 108.1 State the name and **ADDRESS** of each employer or other source of the earnings or income you have lost as a result of the **INCIDENT**.

☐ 108.2 Show how you compute the earnings or income you have lost, from each employer or other source, as a result of the **INCIDENT**.

☐ 108.3 State the name and **ADDRESS** of each employer or other source of the earnings or income you expect to lose in the future as a result of the **INCIDENT**.

☐ 108.4 Show how you compute the earnings or income you expect to lose in the future, from each employer or other source, as the result of the **INCIDENT**.

109.0 Other Damages

☐ 109.1 Describe each other item of damage or cost that you attribute to the **INCIDENT**, stating the dates of occurrence and the amount.

110.0 Medical History

☐ 110.1 Describe and give the date of each complaint or injury, whether occurring *before or after* **INCIDENT**, that involved the same part of your body claimed to have been injured in the **INCIDENT**.

☐ 110.2 State the name, **ADDRESS**, and telephone number of each **HEALTH CARE PROVIDER** who examined or treated you for each injury or complaint, whether occurring *before or after* the **INCIDENT** that involved the same part of your body claimed to have been injured in the **INCIDENT** and the dates of examination or treatment.

111.0 Other Claims and Previous Claims

☐ 111.1 Identify each personal injury claim that **YOU OR ANYONE ACTING ON YOUR BEHALF** have made within the past ten years and the dates.

☐ 111.2 State the case name, court, and case number of each personal injury action or claim filed by **YOU OR ANYONE ACTING ON YOUR BEHALF** within the past ten years.

112.0 Investigation — General

☐ 1112.1 State the name, **ADDRESS**, and telephone number of each individual who has knowledge of facts relating to the **INCIDENT**, and specify his or her area of knowledge.

☐ 112.2 State the name, **ADDRESS**, and telephone number of each individual who gave a written or recorded statement relating to the **INCIDENT** and the date of the statement.

☐ 112.3 State the name, **ADDRESS**, and telephone number of each **PERSON** who has the original or a copy of a written or recorded statement relating to the **INCIDENT**.

☐ 112.4 Identify each document or photograph that describes or depicts any place, object, or individual concerning the **INCIDENT** or plaintiff's injuries, or attach a copy. (If you do not attach a copy, state the name, **ADDRESS**, and telephone number of each **PERSON** who had the original document or photograph or a copy.)

☐ 112.5 Identify each other item of physical evidence that shows how the **INCIDENT** occurred or the nature or extent of plaintiff's injuries, and state the location of each item, and the name, **ADDRESS**, and telephone number of each **PERSON** who has it.

113.0 *[Reserved]*

114.0 Statutory or Regulatory Violations

☐ 114.1 If you contend that any **PERSON** involved in the **INCIDENT** violated any statute, ordinance, or regulation and that the violation was a cause of the **INCIDENT,** identify each **PERSON** and the statute, ordinance, or regulation.

115.0 Claims and Defenses

☐ 115.1 State in detail the facts upon which you base your claims that the PERSON asking this interrogatory is responsible for your damages.

☐ 115.2 State in detail the facts upon which you base your contention that you are not responsible, in whole or in part, for plaintiff's damages.

☐ 115.3 State the name, **ADDRESS**, and the telephone number of each **PERSON**, other than the **PERSON** asking this interrogatory, who is responsible, in whole or in part, for damages claimed in this action.

116.0 Defendant's Contentions — Personal Injury

[See Instruction 2(e)]

☐ 116.1 If you contend that any **PERSON**, other than you or plaintiff, contributed to the occurrence of the **INCIDENT** or the injuries or damages claimed by plaintiff, state the name, **ADDRESS**, and telephone number of each individual who has knowledge of the facts upon which you base your contention.

☐ 116.2 If you contend that plaintiff was not injured in the **INCIDENT**, state the name, **ADDRESS**, and telephone number of each individual who has knowledge of the facts upon which you base your contention.

☐ 116.3 If you contend that the injuries or the extent of the injuries claimed by plaintiff were not caused by the **INCIDENT**, state the name, **ADDRESS**, and telephone number of each individual who has knowledge of the facts upon which you base your contention.

☐ 116.4 If you contend that any of the services furnished by any **HEALTH CARE PROVIDER** were not related to the **INCIDENT**, state the name, **ADDRESS**, and telephone number of each individual who has knowledge of the facts upon which you base your contention.

☐ 116.5 If you contend that any of the costs of services furnished by any **HEALTH CARE PROVIDER** were unreasonable, identify each service that you dispute, the cost, and the **HEALTH CARE PROVIDER.**

☐ 116.6 If you contend that any part of the loss of earnings or income claimed by plaintiff was unreasonable, identify each part of the loss that you dispute and each source of the income or earnings.

☐ 116.7 If you contend that any of the property damage claimed by plaintiff was not caused by the **INCIDENT**, identify each item of property damage that you dispute.

☐ 116.8 If you contend that any of the costs of repairing the property damage claimed by plaintiff were unreasonable, identify each cost item that you dispute.

☐ 116.9 If you contend that, within the last ten years, plaintiff made a claim for personal injuries that are related to the injuries claimed in the **INCIDENT**, identify each related injury and the date.

☐ 116.10 If you contend that, within the past ten years, plaintiff made a claim for personal injuries that are related to the injuries claimed in the **INCIDENT**, state the name, court, and case number of each action filed.

117.0 ***[Reserved]***

120.0 How the Incident Occurred — Motor Vehicle

☐ 120.1 State how the **INCIDENT** occurred.

☐ 120.2 For each vehicle involved in the **INCIDENT**, state the year, make, model, and license number.

☐ 120.3 For each vehicle involved in the **INCIDENT**, state the name, **ADDRESS**, and telephone number of the driver.

☐ 120.4 For each vehicle involved in the **INCIDENT,** state the name, **ADDRESS**, and telephone number of each occupant other than the driver.

☐ 120.5 For each vehicle involved in the **INCIDENT,** state the name, **ADDRESS**, and telephone number of each registered owner.

☐ 120.6 For each vehicle involved in the **INCIDENT,** state the name, **ADDRESS**, and telephone number of each lessee.

☐ 120.7 For each vehicle involved in the **INCIDENT,** state the name, **ADDRESS**, and telephone number of each owner other than the registered owner or lien holder.

☐ 120.8 For each vehicle involved in the **INCIDENT,** state the name of each owner who gave permission or consent to the driver to operate the vehicle.

150.0 Contract

☐ 150.1 Identify all **DOCUMENTS** that are part of the agreement and for each state the name, **ADDRESS,** and telephone number of the **PERSON** who has each **DOCUMENT**.

☐ 150.2 State each part of the agreement not in writing, the name, **ADDRESS**, and telephone number of each **PERSON** agreeing to that provision, and the date that part of the agreement was made.

☐ 150.3 Identify all **DOCUMENTS** that evidence each part of the agreement not in writing, and for each state the name, **ADDRESS**, and telephone number of the **PERSON** who has each **DOCUMENT.**

☐ 150.4 Identify all **DOCUMENTS** that are part of each modification to the agreement, and for each state the name **ADDRESS**, and telephone number of the **PERSON** who has each **DOCUMENT**.

☐ 150.5 State each modification not in writing, the date and the name, **ADDRESS**, and telephone number of the **PERSON** agreeing to the modification, and the date the modification was made.

☐ 150.6 Identify all **DOCUMENTS** that evidence each modification of the agreement not in writing and for each state the name, **ADDRESS**, and telephone number of the **PERSON** who has each **DOCUMENT.**

☐ 150.7 Describe and give the date of every act or omission that you claim is a breach of the agreement.

☐ 150.8 Identify each agreement excused and state why performance was excused.

☐ 150.9 Identify each agreement terminated by mutual agreement and state why it was terminated, including dates.

☐ 150.10 Identify each unenforceable agreement and state the facts upon which your answer is based.

☐ 150.11 Identify each ambiguous agreement and state the facts upon which your answer is based.

13 Request for Production of Documents Example

YOUNG & YOUNGER
10 Higuera Street
San Luis Obispo, CA 93401
(805) 555-1212

Attorneys for Plaintiff MID CITY HOSPITAL

SUPERIOR COURT OF THE STATE OF CALIFORNIA

FOR THE COUNTY OF SAN LUIS OBISPO

MID CITY HOSPITAL Plaintiff, v. BOB'S JANITORIAL SERVICE; and DOES 1 through 100, Defendants.	CASE NO. CV 000XYZ REQUEST FOR INSPECTION OF DOCUMENTS AND OTHER TANGIBLE THINGS [C.C.P. 2031] Set No. One Assigned Judge: Hon. Roger Picquet

PROPOUNDING PARTY: Plaintiff, MID CITY HOSPITAL

RESPONDING PARTY: Defendant, BOB'S JANITORIAL SERVICE

SET NO.: ONE (1)

Plaintiff, MID CITY HOSPITAL, through its attorneys, hereby requests, pursuant to the provisions of the Code of Civil Procedure section 2031, production of the following documents or other tangible things for inspection and copying. The inspection and copying will not permanently alter or destroy the item involved.

Production of these items is scheduled for the law offices of Young and Younger, located at 10 Higuera Street, San Luis Obispo, California, thirty (30) days after service of the demand. Personal

REQUEST FOR INSPECTION OF DOCUMENTS, SET ONE

attendance by defendant or its representatives is not required, provided that prior to the production of documents defendant, or its representatives, delivers by mail or other suitable means the items designated herein. Failure of responding party to comply with the provisions of Code of Civil Procedure section 2031 shall be responded to by this party with a motion pursuant to Code of Civil Procedure sections 2031(k) and 2023.

Plaintiff hereby offers to reimburse defendant for reasonable expenses incurred in copying the items designated herein. Where the demand requests photographs, propounding party, requests that color laser photocopies of photographs be sent, rather than black and white photocopies of such photographs.

In accordance with the foregoing, plaintiff designates the following items and categories of items for production:

REQUEST FOR PRODUCTION

1. Any and all documents, writings, or other written memorandum reflecting any services you performed for the plaintiff.

2. Any and all writings, documents, or other written memorandum regarding any payment you received for any work you performed for the plaintiff.

3 True and correct copies of any and all files you maintained regarding the plaintiff.

4 True and correct copies of all correspondence between you and the plaintiff.

Dated: ______________ YOUNG & YOUNGER

____

***Note from Professor Carr: See also related article on the next page!!

DEPOSITIONS REQUIRE A SKILL SET LEADERS DON'T USE ON THE JOB

The Wall Street Journal
By George Anders

MOST OF THE time, hard-charging managers like to take command of a meeting going badly. They redefine the agenda around what they believe are the key issues. They argue their case so passionately that skeptics rally to their side. And if necessary, they overpower stubborn opponents with logic, humor or steely-eyed toughness.

Such techniques help leaders rocket up the organization. Go-getters use them to win customers' orders and get budgets approved. But all those techniques lose their magic if a company is being sued and a star manager is summoned by the opposing side's lawyers to give pretrial evidence in the form of an oral deposition. Suddenly strong-willed managers can end up feeling like cowering idiots. They spend hours under oath, unable to duck even the most impertinent question. If they try to argue, joke or bluster their way out of an awkward spot, every word of their answers will be picked apart for inconsistencies or signs of arrogance that might hurt their company's ability to defend itself.

Tim Foley

Like it or not, the deposition is becoming a major rite of passage for ambitious managers. It's a lot less fun than getting stock options or seeing one's promotions announced in press releases. But as executives gain prominence, it's increasingly likely that they will be the person chosen to explain their company's conduct in the face of suits alleging anything from patent infringement to product liability.

TO SURVIVE being deposed, attorneys and executives say, it helps to keep four things in mind. Make answers brief and tightly focused, avoiding the temptation to expand beyond what was asked. Prepare diligently beforehand. At the deposition, stay calm and truthful. And understand your side's legal strategy well enough that you don't undermine your value as a witness for the company if the case goes to trial.

In Dallas, attorney C. Vernon Hartline Jr., a partner in the firm of Hartline, Dacus, Barger, Dreyer & Kern, says his first priority in advising executives is to get them to understand that this isn't another business meeting to be attacked and conquered.

"Nothing you can say or do will make the case go away," Mr. Hartline explains. "The other side is just looking for a sound bite that will make you appear deceitful, insensitive or stupid." The more talkative a witness is, the greater the chance of blundering into trouble.

To drive home that point, California attorney Lon Allan years ago told clients: "If you can get through this whole thing without saying more than 150 words, I'll buy you lunch. If you say more, then you have to buy for both of us."

Lately Mr. Allan has served as a director of several small high-tech companies. When he is deposed, "I really have to bite my tongue," he says. "We all have this psychological need to explain things. But this is not a social setting. The more information that anyone volunteers, the more questions they will get asked."

Minor habits of speech matter, too. Attorney Barbara Moses, a partner in the New York firm of Morvillo, Abramowitz, Grand, Iason & Silverberg, says she cringes when executives use phrases such as "To be candid," and "I hate to admit it, but … ." Such language suggests other remarks aren't candid, she observes.

In some situations, Ms. Moses insists on a mock deposition ahead of time, then has executives watch the videotape. "That usually gets their attention," she says. "If they realize they are coming across badly, maybe they will spend more time preparing."

DURING HER own depositions, executive recruiter Valerie Frederickson says she avoids witty turns of phrase that could come back to bite her. She also gets up for a break—which is allowed in most jurisdictions—if she feels her temper is rising. "One deposition came right after I had knee surgery," Ms. Frederickson recalls. "Anytime the deposition got awkward, all of a sudden my knee hurt too much to continue."

If lawsuits go to trial, then corporate executives may be asked to tell their side of the story under friendly questioning from their own attorneys. But more than 90% of corporate litigation is dismissed or settled before trial. And in a deposition, it's the opposing side's lawyers that are running the show.

So corporate legal strategists constantly debate whether it's wiser to encourage cautious, tight-lipped depositions or to let executives take a higher profile with an eye to preserving their credibility as defense witnesses if the case later goes to trial. "You can't remember something at trial if you spent your whole deposition insisting that you didn't know anything about it," says Mr. Allan, the California director. In the late 1990s, Microsoft Chairman Bill Gates adopted an extremely cautious stance when being deposed in federal antitrust litigation. When that case went to trial, a videotape of his long pauses and terse answers was widely seen as detrimental to Microsoft's defense.

"I tell clients that if you come across as stupid in a deposition, you've been neutralized," says Boris Feldman. a corporate-defense specialist at the Palo Alto, Calif., law firm of Wilson Sonsini Goodrich & Rosati. "Be careful. Don't be flip. But show that you tried to do a good job."

14 Some Advice Re: Emails and Facebook

SOME ADVICE RE: EMAILS

> *"My wife once told me that you should never put anything in an e-mail that you don't want to be shown to 12 strangers on a big movie screen."*
>
> —a really smart husband
> (whose wife is a really smart attorney)

Once you graduate, you are to be cautioned about the e-mails you write and send at work or in connection with your job. Lawyers are increasingly searching company e-mails during discovery (which I discuss in class). What are they looking for? Roger Matus, in his blog Death by Email, reproduces a top 10 list that will likely raise red flags for e-discovery sleuths and in turn find that document in email form that will hang you/your firm at trial:

1. "I could get into trouble for telling you this, but..."
2. "Delete this email immediately."
3. "I really shouldn't put this in writing."
4. "Don't tell So-and-So." Or, "Don't send this to So-and-So."
5. "She/He/They will never find out."
6. "We're going to do this differently than normal."
7. "I don't think I am supposed to know this, but..."
8. "I don't want to discuss this in e-mail. Please give me a call."
9. "Don't ask. You don't want to know."
10. "Is this actually legal?"

As Matus wisely advises, if you find yourself typing one of these phrases, perhaps you should delete the entire email.

SOME ADVICE RE: FACEBOOK

Employers, particularly in this economy, are interested in hiring only the most qualified and desirable individuals and they naturally want to use every tool at their disposal to weed out potential bad hires. More and more employers are turning to the Internet, and specifically to "social networking" websites such as MySpace and Facebook, to conduct research on job applicants. The information that can be learned about applicants through social networking websites is potentially very interesting to employers. For example, information may be available about: the accuracy of resume data; the applicant's communication skills (or lack thereof); evidence of criminal behavior or drug/alcohol use; and the applicant's general professionalism and judgment (or lack thereof). The potential availability of this information with just a few keystrokes makes the temptation great for the employer to engage in such research methods.

Indeed, a recent survey of hiring managers conducted by an Internet job search website revealed that more then 10% of the responders had used social networking websites to conduct applicant research (that number is sure to increase in the future), and more than 60% of that group had decided not to hire applicants based upon information discovered in the social networking websites. A recent survey by the National Association of Colleges and Employers, revealed that over 80% of the responding college students had profiles on social networking websites, and yet nearly half of those did not expect or were unsure about potential employers contacting them through such profiles.

While most social networking websites have privacy statements that limit the use of information contain in member profiles for the private use of its members, did you know that what many employers now do is obtain your consent to conduct an Internet search on you? That is, before extending you an offer of employment or even after making you an offer of employment they make any such offer contingent upon the results of a background check and Internet search?

15 Document Shredding Shows Importance of Having a Policy on What is Preserved[1]

The Wall Street Journal

THE REVELATIONS BY Arthur Andersen LLP last week that it had destroyed documents relating to its work for Enron Corp. highlight a critical question for companies; just what must you keep, and for how long?

Clearly businesses can't keep everything: space limitations and storage costs make that prohibitive. What's key, say lawyers who advise businesses on such matters is to have a defined policy on what is preserved and what gets purged.

"Not having a policy is an invitation to creating problems," says George Terwilliger III, a white-collar defense attorney at White & Case in Washington, D.C. "Without a policy, you're open to an allegation that there was some nefarious purpose for destruction of documents."

If a corrupt motive for the destruction is proved during a government investigation, it can lead to obstruction-of-justice charges. In civil suits, courts can order sanctions, ranging from a default judgment to instructions that jurors can infer that the destroyed material contained damaging information.

When the destruction occurs is key. To be a federal offense, it must happen while a judicial proceeding or congressional or regulatory investigation is pending. A number of state laws, however, are stricter, making it a crime to destroy or conceal evidence if a proceeding is imminent or likely.

Lawyers generally advise clients to stop routine document destruction once any proceeding begins. Last week, Andersen said it suspended its records-management policy after the Enron revelations, but didn't say what its policy had been.

Lawyers say no single document policy suits all companies. The right approach varies with the needs of the business, as well as the regulatory and litigation environment it operates in. For example regulators require insurance companies and banks to hang on to certain kinds of information for specific time periods. And sfederal law governing employee-benefit plans requires retention of records for six years.

It is precisely because situations vary so greatly that the American Institute of Certified Public Accountants doesn't set document-retention standards for its accounting-firm members, says Chuck Landes, an AICPA official. It is, he says, a "management issue" that an accounting firm must resolve "in consultation with legal counsel and others."

1 **Note from Professor Carr: This article is relevant and important. For example, if I used the discovery tool called a "Request for Production of Documents" (see pages 49–50 of this textbook for an example), and flushed out the fact that you had relevant/responsive documents but had engaged in this type of activity (shredding), you can hopefully see why and how it will come back to haunt you in a BIG, BIG WAY!!**

Even when such policies are in place, it's not uncommon for courts to grapple with allegations that documents or electronic data have been improperly destroyed. For example, in a malpractice suit now pending against accounting firm, Grant Thornton LLP in Circuit Court for Baltimore City, Carnegie International Corp. alleged that J.W. Michael Starr, a Grant partner, internationally deleted e-mails and notes relating to Carnegie from his computer. Carnegie, a small Internet and telecommunications concern, asked for entry of a default judgment.

In October, Judge Kaye Allison refused to resort to that extreme sanction but ruled that Mr. Starr "had knowledge that a lawsuit against Grant was imminent when he deleted his computer files" and was "in violation" of court rules.

Tom Rafter, Grant's general counsel, wouldn't comment on the judge's order. But he says the case involved "a routine deletion of e-mails" and that the e-mails were ultimately obtained from the recipients and turned over to Carnegie. "There was no intent here to destroy any documents that were relevant," he says, adding that Grant has "a very, very firm policy against any kind of destruction of evidence."

In 1997, Federal District Judge Alfred Wolin slapped Prudential Insurance Co. of America with a $1 million fine and other sanctions after concluding it had engaged in widespread document destruction during litigation over its sales practices. At the time, Prudential blamed the destruction on managers who didn't follow company directives but agreed to pay the fine.

Deborah Rhode, a legal-ethics expert at Stanford University law school, says the prospect of sanctions often isn't enough to deter destruction. "There are a lot of lawyers who think that, whatever penalties would attach to the destruction of documents, it would be less severe than if the documents themselves surfaces," she says. That, she says, produces "a great incentive to remove smoking-gun documents."

But Mr. Terwilliger, a former deputy attorney general, says that impulse often backfires, "More criminal cases are born of attempts to cover up through document destruction ... during an administrative proceeding or investigation than any other single cause,," he says.

Judah Best, another Washington attorney, points out that in this age of electronic document creation and duplication, "it's impossible to destroy all copies of documents. They inevitably show up."

16 When the Jury Box Runs Low, Deputies Hit the Wal-Mart[1]

New York Times

[Article re: juries and the common law legal system]

SHELBY, N.C.—MICHAEL KANZ was pushing a grocery cart toward the checkout lane at the Wal-Mart Supercenter here when a woman wearing a gun walked up and told him to follow her orders—or face the consequences.

It wasn't a mugging, but a jury summons to report to court within an hour. And it's a perfectly legal way some judges have in recent years been getting jurors at the last minute.

The jury summons by mail doesn't always get the job done anymore. Because of out-of-date records obtained from voter registrations and agencies that issue drivers licenses, some summonses go to wrong addresses, or are just ignored.

To avoid declaring a mistrial for lack of jurors, courts across the nation, especially rural ones, have periodically authorized sheriff's deputies to fetch a kind of fill-in known as a talis juror. The term comes from a Latin phrase meaning bystander. In southwestern Colorado, deputies have been sent out twice in the past year, once in La Plata County and once in neighboring Archuleta County.

"The jury wheels we're using have such outdated records that a huge percentage of summonses are returned undeliverable,," says Judge David Dickinson in Archuleta, who sent deputies to a grocery store in March to round up jurors.

Those getting pinched couldn't be more shocked. "This, doesn't happen,," Mr. Kanz, a 34-year-old Baptist missionary, recalls thinking two years ago when the deputy told him to go to the Cleveland County Courthouse. The deputy took down information from his driver's license and told him that if he failed to show up, he could be held in contempt of court, which might mean going to jail, Mr. Kanz says. The court has resorted to lining up jurors this way four or five times in the eight years the current sheriff has been in office.

On the way out of the store, Mr. Kanz and his wife, Cathy, say they told entering (shoppers, "Don't come in! You'll get a subpoena!" Customers fled. But many of those inside the store got nailed. Fifty-five passers-by got pressed into service that day, many from Wal-Mart, including an assistant manager.

Originally, bystander jurors were plucked from the courtroom, as they were for the trial of a British soldier involved in the Boston Massacre. In Shelby, retired men used to loiter outside the

1 **Note from Professor Carr: I have to admit that I was fairly depressed after reading this article. I mean … c'mon … whatever happened to the idea of public service and isn't jury duty a way to fulfill our respective obligation to our society and communities? And, how can the system work if folks want so badly to get out of jury duty??**

But not all hope should be lost … See the articles on the next few pages and maybe after reading them you will see jury duty in a new light.

white-columned courthouse hoping to earn a little extra money—currently $12 a day—by filling jury holes.

But lately, with few people doing that sort of volunteering, judges are ordering sheriffs to go out and get jurors, often from malls, supermarkets and, of course, the local Wal-Mart. "I believe that when we schedule court, we need to hold court," says Superior Court Judge Don Bridges, who ordered the juror roundup here in Shelby.

Sgt. Gwen Carothers, 48, says that when the sheriff assigned her to round up jurors at Wal-Mart, she thought he was joking. "But then I looked at him and he was real serious."

Among the people nabbed at the Wal-Mart that day was assistant manager Robert Wilson. The store manager, Johnny Wise, suspects Mr. Wilson was singled out because he was returning from lunch and looked like a customer.

Dragooned jurors are often irked at having to fill in for people who failed to report when summoned.

Bob Cheney was one of the unlucky ones. A 60-year-old part-time surveyor, Mr. Cheney, on a day off last year, went to buy a carton of milk at the City Market in Durango, Colo. Inside the door, he encountered three deputies, one of whom asked whether there was any reason he couldn't serve on a jury that afternoon. Mr. Cheney was caught off guard. "I tried to think of [an excuse] and I couldn't, so I had to go," he says.

He asked how long the trial would last, but the deputy said he could say nothing else—and wrote Mr. Cheney a summons.

As he proceeded to buy his milk, Mr. Cheney says, he was a little annoyed. "Maybe it's old age, but I don't like anything that interferes with my routine," he says.

Two years after jurors were recruited from outside the Houston Kroger, Randy Ponce arrived for his very first day of work as manager and asked employees how much business came from the courthouse across the street. One replied, "Actually, sometimes they take your customers away," he recalls.

In Shelby, "the Wal-Mart people kind of frowned on it," says Cleveland County Sheriff Dan Crawford, "they wished we would spread it out." At Wal-Mart headquarters in Bentonville, Ark., the company says it does hear about customer roundups but doesn't see reason to protest. "We try to be a part of the community," says a spokesman.

Sheriff Crawford has set a new guideline for his deputies for the next juror roundup: In the future, they are forbidden to go to businesses.

Must bystanders confronted by juror-seeking deputies acquiesce? Tom Munsterman, founder of the Center for Jury Studies in Arlington, Va., says they must. "A summons can be enforced," he says. Can deputies "grab them at the moment and drag them kicking and screaming?" he wonders aloud. "I guess they can."

A more-polite approach might not work. In Jensen Beach, Fla., Sgt. Laura Murphy went to the Treasure Coast Square mall three years ago to solicit jurors from among the early-morning mall-walkers. She didn't issue commands, thinking that would constitute harassment. But her good-cop tactics backfired: No one volunteered.

17 Duty? Maybe It's Really Self Help[1]

If Being a Juror Is So Bad, Why Do So Many of the People Who Serve Feel So Good afterward?

Newsweek

[Article re: juries and the common law legal system]

THIS COURTROOM HAS a disconcerting decorative duality, like a person dressed only from the waist down. The lower half of the cavernous room has glowing wood wainscoting, and the well is set off by a surround of ornamental spindles. But above, the walls are flat and characterless, as though the money ran out, or the interest. Above the bench is the ubiquitous legend in mustardy gilt: IN GOD WE TRUST. The font is slightly off in several of the letters, as though they wore out from sheer exhaustion and had to be imperfectly replaced.

With apologies to true believers, this is undoubtedly a place in which trust is put squarely in human beings, the fidgety, polyglot, slightly ill-humored who are waiting to see if they will be chosen to serve on a jury. Each has been given a pamphlet explaining why jury service is good for the nation. Few seem to be convinced that it is good for the soul.

"Americans should be thrilled to serve on juries, since even a cursory study of our national personality would suggest that we have become the most judgmental people on earth. The popular TV shows have this as their bedrock; one wrong answer to some meaningless trivia question and you become the "Weakest Link" in the minds of millions. On Court TV online, viewers can weigh in on whether a woman charged with killing her husband in Las Vegas should be sentenced to life in prison, whether they know the facts of the case or simply don't like the way she wears her hair. The average American with a television, a computer or a newspaper becomes casually expert in conviction or acquittal in the court of public opinion with only a modicum of information: he's a bad guy, she was provoked, the cops acted properly. Darryl Strawberry, Robert Downey Jr., Bob Kerrey: stop a dozen people on the street, and they will not hesitate to pass judgment with perfect certainty.

Real judgment is quite different from and substantially more demanding than this instant-messaging variety, which may be one of the many reasons, along with the disruption of their daily routines, that people try to avoid jury duty. In Dallas County last year, according to The Dallas Morning News, less than 20 percent of those summoned showed up. New York City's numbers were once even worse, but its courts do better now, with attendance sometimes topping 50 percent, because of widespread changes in the system: eliminating jury-service exemptions for doctors and lawyers, adding welfare rolls to the voter-registration and licensed-driver lists as sources for summonses, increasing the pay to $40 a day. For those who actually show up, there may be hours of

1 Note from Professor Carr: Perhaps a different/ more positive way of looking at jury duty?? ☺

waiting, then the often tedious voir dire, the questioning to discern bias, point of view, fitness. If they are chosen, there are the days,

perhaps weeks, of trial testimony, the need to pay attention, to listen carefully to the judge's instructions and to consider seriously the standard of reasonable doubt The slam-bang judgments of modern life are like "Jeopardy!" questions; jury service is a blue-book exam, a term paper.

Yet while people complain in advance that they won't get paid at work, that they need to care for their children, that they have doctor's appointments and vacation plans, at the end many people who serve on juries feel enlarged, even ennobled by what they have done. At a time when so many rituals and civic experiences have lost that sense of moment, when wedding vows have become increasingly fungible and voting has been devalued by the dangling chads of Florida and the big money of campaign finance, service on a jury remains perhaps the only public service that for all its shortcomings, its inconveniences, its impracticalities, still has the power to elevate an ordinary citizen. In his typical offhanded profundity, G. K. Chesterton once wrote of society. "When it wishes anything done which is really serious, it collects twelve of the ordinary men standing round. The same thing was done, if I remember right, by the Founder of Christianity."

No romantic illusions about the process: it is flawed. Stephen Adler, in his book "The Jury," did a marvelous job of documenting through case histories how badly it can go wrong, how poorly it sometimes functions. In Virginia last year a task force recommended several common-sense ways to make the process better, including letting jurors take notes, letting them ask questions and forcing judges and lawyers to write jury instructions so that they are comprehensible to those who are not members of the bar. In_his book Adler suggests that those instructions be given at the beginning of a trial instead of at the end, so that "juries can learn the rules before they play the game."

But perhaps there is also no better way to sell jury duty to those called to its service. In voir dire in that courtroom in New York, when a juror invoked human nature to explain an understandable bias, one of the attorneys replied, "Throw human nature out the window." But that's not exactly right. Serving well on a jury requires the highest level of human nature, the part that is thoughtful, intelligent, empathetic and fair. In this self-help age, if someone offered a short course that would teach you to better find, use and value those qualities in yourself, thousands would plunk down good money to enter that particular lecture hall, confident that what they would learn would make them better parents, partners, workers, people.

"What if that lecture hall is really a courtroom? What if we found a way in our everyday lives to listen to all the facts, to refuse to judge by appearance or charm alone, to seek to understand the rules and to apply them fairly? What if it turned out, in avoiding jury service, that we were avoiding one of our best chances at becoming, not only better citizens, but better human beings? That old standby of democracy de Tocqueville said it so eloquently that it bears repeating: "By obliging men to turn their attention to other affairs than their own, it rubs off that private selfishness which is the rust of society."

18 Jury Service is Your Business[1]

Opinion

By Mike Vallante, *Pacific Coast Business Times*

[Article re: juries and the common law legal system]

THOMAS JEFFERSON ONCE said, "The jury is the only anchor ever yet imagined by man by which a government can be held to the principles of its constitution," and added that "the jury is the ultimate safe guard of our civil rights."

With such an endorsement from one of our founding fathers, one would assume that citizens would be climbing over each other to serve on a jury when called.

The truth is quite the opposite, of course, and here in California—businesses, unfortunately—are a big part of the problem. That's to their own detriment too, as California's businesses have the most to lose when jury proofs don't include those of "our peers" who understand business issues.

Currently, California's jury response rate is less than 20 percent. With that kind of support for one of the very tenets of our democracy, it's impossible to expect that every jury will include at least one person who understands important business issues, such as contracts, product liability, insurance or employment.

As a result, we see outrageous lawsuits and astronomical awards that threaten jobs and can put the very survival of a small business in jeopardy. That's why a recent study by the U.S. Chamber of Commerce ranked California 45th in terms of the fairness of its juries, and an even more deplorable 48th in terms of juries' predictability.

Do Californians avoid serving because they don't believe in the jury system? Do they have an inherent disregard for the courts and the rule of law? No. The No. 1 reason Californians fail to serve when called or seek excusal is their jobs. They don't think they can afford to take the time off.

Employers need to make a dedicated effort to encourage their employees to serve when called, thereby ensuring that the jury pool represents a much broader cross-section of society. This in turn can lead to greater benefit in terms of fairness and balance in jury verdicts.

Some small businesses are worried they cannot afford to let employees take time off to serve. However, 33 out of California's 38 courts have adopted the "One Day, One Trial" policy, allowing citizens who are not seated on a jury to return to work the next day, guaranteed. According to research from the California Judicial Council, "One Day, One Trial" system returns the majority of employees to work the next day after reporting for service.

1 **Note from Professor Carr: Can you see why we so desperately need good, smart patient and open-minded jurors to serve, especially in business and commercial cases? And why/how the "system" can't work real well if that is not happening?? ☺**

California's entrepreneurs are among the greatest critics of the state's civil justice system. If we are to stop the spiral and ensure the courts provide justice for all, employers must take responsibility to make sure jury service is a viable option for all.

19 Jumping to be Jurors

[Article re: juries and the common law legal system]

COURT OFFICIALS AROUND the country are reporting one big change because of the Sept. 11 terrorist attacks: more interest in jury duty.

Tom Munsterman, director of jury studies at the National Center for State Courts, based in Williamsburg, Va., says court administrators and judges nationwide have reported that there is a reversal in a decade-long decline in public participation in jury service.

Munsterman says that jury service, only months ago seen as a burden by most citizens, has suddenly become a trendy way of showing patriotism, like waving an American flag or giving blood.

In a speech to the Council of Appellate Lawyers of New York, the state's chief judge, Judith Kaye, described a visit she made to a Manhattan courthouse after the Sept. 11 attacks.

"When I gave a group of jurors the happy news that they could go because they would not be needed, they were plainly disappointed," Kaye says. "Many even declined offers to be excused."

Munsterman and court officials around the country say they have also witnessed fewer people trying to get out of jury duty.

And it goes beyond that. Judges, Munsterman says, are reporting to him that juries appear more attentive during trials and are taking longer in deliberations.

EVALUATING THE JURY

"[T]rial by jury is more than an instrument of justice and more than one wheel of the constitution: it is the lamp that shows that freedom lives." (Lord Justice Devlin, English judge)

"Although jurors are extraordinarily right in their conclusion, it is usually based upon common sense 'instincts' about right and wrong, and not on sophisticated evaluations of complicated testimony ... Because Judges, sometimes, consciously reject this laymen's approach of who is right or wrong and restrict themselves to the precise legal weights, they come out wrong more often than the juries." (Louis Nizer, defense attorney)

"The jury ... represents an impressive way of building discretion, equity, and flexibility into a legal system. Not the least of its advantages is that the jury, relieved of the burdens of creating precedent, can bend the law without breaking it." (Harry Kalven and Hans Zeisel, legal scholars)

"Jurymen seldom convict a person they like, or acquit one that they dislike. The main work of a trial lawyer is to make a jury like his client, or, at least to feel sympathy for him; facts regarding the crime are relatively unimportant." (Clarence Darrow, famous defense attorney)

"The jury contributes most powerfully to form the judgment, and to increase the natural intelligence of a people; and this is, in my opinion, its greatest advantage. It may be regarded as a gratuitous public school ever open, in which every juror learns to exercise his rights ... I think that the practical intelligence and political good sense of the Americans are mainly attributable to the long use which they have made of the jury in civil causes." (Alexis de Tocqueville, French commentator on America)

Sources: Erwin Griswold, "1962–1963 Harvard Law School Dean's Report," pp. 5–6, quoted in Harry Kalven, Jr., and Hans Zeisel. *The American Jury* (Boston: Little Brown, 1966), p. 5; Patrick Devlin, *Trial by Jury* (London: Stevens, 1956) p. 164; *Skidmore* v. *Baltimore & Ohio Railroad,* 167 F.2d 54 (2d Cir. 1948); Louis Nizer, *My Life in Court* (New York: Jove, 1978), p. 359; Jerome Frank, *Courts on Trial; Myth and Reality in American Justice* (Princeton, NJ: Princeton University Press, 1949), p. 132; Kalven and Zeisel, *The American Jury,* p. 498; Clarence Darrow, quoted in Valerie P. Hans and Neil Vidmar. *Judging the Jury* (New York: Plenum Press, 1986), p. 131; Alexis de Tocqueville, *Democracy in America,* Richard D. Heffner (Ed.) (New York: New American Library, 1956). p. 128.

20

Power of 12[1]

Jurors increasingly are sending loud messages of censure with megabuck verdicts. But critics charge that a jury is the least qualified body to decide public policy.

American Bar Association Journal

[Article re: juries and the common law legal system]

DIANE LEININGER IS no maverick or activist. At 50, she works as an interior designer, while her husband is a salesman for a pharmaceutical company. They live in the quiet Florida coastal town of Delray Beach.

But on Jan. 4, 2000, Leininger and five other Palm Beach County citizens decided that they had seen enough and were determined to send a message they hoped would dramatically change how health care is administered in this country.

For more than a month, Leininger was a juror in a case in which the parents of 9-year-old Caitlyn Chipps, who suffered from cerebral palsy, sued their insurance carrier, Humana Health Care, for repeatedly denying payment for their daughter's treatments.

"We were stunned by the testimony," Leininger says. "The company sent bonus checks to claims reviewers who saved the company money by denying the most medical claims for patients. And the company made its claims process so egregious and difficult just to increase their chances that families would eventually give up seeking reimbursement for treatments rather than continuing to fight to get their money."

The most disturbing revelation, according to Leininger, was that this practice wasn't unique to Humana but rather a course of conduct for many major health maintenance organizations.

"That's when we decided we had to send a message that would get not onlv Humana's attention but the attention of every HMO out there," she says.

Their verdict: $79.6 million, the largest damage award ever handed down in an individual case in Palm Beach County.

A spokeswoman for Humana called the verdict "erroneous and excessive." The company is appealing the judgment.

Legal analysts say the Humana jury reflects a growing trend among jurors to use their power to demand social changes that reach far beyond the specific case in which they are involved.

During the past two decades the clout of the American jury and the authority it wields have grown to historic levels, according to judges, lawyers and law professors.

Like no time before, the 12 people seated in the jury box regularly demonstrate an increasing willingness—even a clamoring—to force basic American institutions, such as government, business and even

1 **Note from Professor Carr: This article should give you a pretty darn good feel for how important and powerful juries are in our common law legal system!!**

private social organizations, to change the way they operate.

Trial lawyers and state attorneys general, recognizing the new pro-active attitude, are capitalizing on the trend by asking juries to use individual cases to make monumental decisions that impact entire industries or even establish de facto public policy, legal experts say.

A Really Hard Line

Consider these recent examples:

• Last year, a jury in Miami issued a $144 billion punitive damage verdict against the major tobacco companies. The jurors said their verdict was designed to force the cigarette makers to change how they do business or go bankrupt.

• Jurors in Canton, Texas, handed down a $23.3 million judgment in August 1999 against pharmaceutical maker American Home Products for withholding evidence about the dangers of the diet drug Fenphen. Following the decision, jurors said they wanted pharmaceutical companies to change their policies regarding disclosure of health risks to the public. The verdict led to a national, multibillion dollar settlement.

• A New York jury in 1999 told 15 U.S. gun makers to pay the families of seven crime victims $560,000. The panel found that the companies intentionally marketed their products in a way that they should have known would promote illegal gun distribution. While the verdict is on appeal, it fueled dozens of similar lawsuits still pending. It also convinced manufacturer Smith & Wesson to reach a settlement in its cases by agreeing to historic changes in the way it does business.

• In 1998, a Dallas jury awarded the family of a young child $62 million after the family's medical insurer, an HMO, refused to pay for needed medical care. Members of the jury said the award was designed to tell HMOs they must stop putting profits ahead of medical care.

• Similarly, in January 2000, a West Palm Beach, Fla., jury ordered Humana Inc. to pay $80 million in punitive damages to the family of a 9-year-old girl with cerebral palsy after the HMO denied doctor-recommended treatments for her. Lawyers in the litigation viewed the verdict as an indicator that the public is unhappy with the status of managed care and health insurance.

"Our founding fathers would be stunned and dismayed to learn of the issues that today's juries are deciding," says Frank Newton, dean of the Texas Tech University School of Law.

"Are guns unsafe? Are HMOs putting profits ahead of health? Are police using racial profiling in drug stops? Are our schools and churches doing enough to protect our children? Are our nursing homes properly treating our grandparents?"

Newton and other legal experts say that each of these cases involved major public policy questions that Congress and state legislatures failed to address. Frustrated by the lack of action, activists have taken their causes to court seeking relief from what they hope will be sympathetic juries.

And legal analysts say the 12 people in the jury box are frequently identifying with the activists and issuing verdicts that they believe will lead to change.

"I think we are witnessing the emergence of an activist jury pool," says University of Georgia law professor Ron Carlson. "People are frustrated by the inaction of the other branches of government and realize that, as jurors, they hold incredible powers of change and they are ready and willing to wield them.

"Juries have always held immense power in our system of self-government but only in recent years have jurors learned to use it," says Carlson.

A 16-month study by *The Dallas Morning News* and the *Southern Methodist University Law Review* identified more than 700 cases since 1990 in which jurors stated publicly that they intended their verdicts to have impact beyond their individual cases.

Between 1970 and 1990, the study found fewer than 100 such cases. In the 70 years prior, researchers identified only 17 cases in which jurors indicated they wanted their verdicts to have some kind of broader influence.

In addition, a survey of nearly 1,000 trial judges in Texas and federal judges nationwide by the *Morning News* and the *SMU Law Review* found that nearly half have had cases in which jurors used their verdict to send a message about a broader issue.

"Today's jurors come to court angry and full of biases, and they are exacting revenge," says Victor Schwartz, a nationally recognized litigation expert and general counsel of the American Tort Reform Association. "I don t like it and don't think that it's healthy, but there's no question it's happening."

DePaul University law professor Stephen Landsman, an expert on the role of the jury in American culture, agrees that deciding social and public policy through jury verdicts is a lousy way of governing.

"Juries are so unpredictable and cumbersome," he says. "Yet, when no one else has the courage to address the truly controversial issues and problems of our time, juries over and over have shown a willingness and ability to roll up their sleeves, study the facts and come to conclusions."

No Rational Basis

Even so, leaders of corporate America say that we are asking too much of jurors to decide issues that even scientists disagree on.

"We are now asking ignorant juries to make decisions on which scientists make the most sense," says William Lytton, general counsel and senior vice president at International Paper. "Does smoking cause cancer? Do silicone implants cause disease? Do electric power lines emit radiation and cause cancer?

"Juries are the least informed, the least represented and the least qualified body to determine public policy," he says.[2] "For 12 people to put Philip Morris out of business, what is next? Will 12 people decide fatty foods are inappropriate and put McDonalds out of business? That is a very undemocratic and potentially dangerous result."

Harvard law professor E. Kip Viscusi, who specializes in economics, argues that those jurors who punish companies via punitive damage awards actually have little or no positive impart.

In a recent study funded by Exxon, Viscusi found no safety or environmental differences between states that allow punitive damages and states that don't.

"Thus, there is no deterrence benefit that justifies the chaos and economic disruption inflicted by punitive damages," he wrote.

However, the *Morning News* and the *SMU Law Review* study identified more than 250 cases in which jury verdicts led to some change.

Those changes ranged from corporations recalling potentially dangerous products and manufacturers modifying how they dispose of waste, to businesses reforming how they treat their employees and police departments rewriting rules on car chases and excessive force.

"Don't tell me that juries don't make a difference, because the evidence contradicts that," says Stephen Daniels, a research fellow for the American Bar Foundation. "The anecdotal evidence is pretty overwhelming."

Daniels and other analysts point to the Dalkon Shield, the Ford Pinto, asbestos, Fen-phen and other products that companies have removed from the marketplace or fixed following jury verdicts.

True, trial lawyers have long asked juries to use their verdicts to send messages. But legal historians say that prior to the 1980s, those pleas mostly fell on deaf ears.

"There have been scattered jury verdicts throughout history where jurors were outraged and sent some political message," says Bill Nelson, an expert on the history of the American jury system and a law professor at New York University. "But

2 **Note from Professor Carr: Do you agree?**

those traditionally have been few and far between," he says. "Until now."

Nullification in Order

Most of the early examples of jurors demonstrating their independence came in so-called jury nullification in criminal cases involving William Penn in England or John Peter Zenger in New York. In those matters, jurors simply refused to find people guilty if they didn't like the law or felt law enforcement was overreaching.

But the practice is even more widespread today. For example, jurors in Atlanta in the mid-1990s started acquitting sports bookmaking defendants on a regular basis, even though such cases were usually slam dunks. In post-trial interviews, jurors said they saw no moral difference between sports betting and playing the Georgia lottery.

In Dallas, jurors started digging in their heels in 1999 in cases involving lewd dancing. The revolt began, according to lawyers, in a case in which there was little doubt that the women had danced closer to patrons than allowed by law.

The jury in one case publicly criticized police for wasting taxpayers' money investigating and prosecuting what amounted to victimless crimes. The jurors' statements made news and soon other juries in similar cases were refusing to convict.

"Now, when a dancer decides to fight these cases to a jury, they almost always win," says Houston lawyer Mike Maness. "It's absolutely a case of jurors telling police this is not appropriate public policy."

Tom Charron, director of the National District Attorneys Advocacy Center, says jury nullification isn't always bad. He says there are thousands of outdated laws still on the books that could and might still be prosecuted were it not for the willingness of jurors to refuse to convict.

"Today's jurors are not used to being told what to do." Charron says. "They take their personal beliefs into the jury room and they are more willing to act on those beliefs.

The first significant example of jurors sending a message in a civil case surfaced in 1962. Texan John Henry Faulk, a famous radio and television personality, sued when he was blacklisted after being identified by Aware Inc., a political action group, as being sympathetic to communism.

A New York jury ordered Aware to pay Faulk $3.5 million, which at the time was the largest damage award in history. The jury's verdict effectively put Aware out of business and ended institutional blacklisting by those who claimed to be experts on communism.

Legal analysts say the real trend toward juror activism in political, cultural and social issues had its birth in Jackson, Miss., in 1982. That's when East Texas trial lawyer Scottie Baldwin sued an asbestos maker for a client's lung disease. There had been scores of previous suits against the makers of asbestos, but most jurors had awarded only small damages to plaintiffs or found in favor of the defendants.

But this time, jurors reacted angrily to evidence of intentional misconduct by the corporate defendants Johns-Mansville and Raybestos-Manhattan. The panel awarded $1 million in punitive damages to James Jackson of Pascagoula.

The verdict spawned thousands more lawsuits and prompted Chief Justice William H. Rehnquist to ask Congress to take action. When that didn't happen, jury verdicts continued to pour in and billion-dollar companies were forced out of business.

Then came tobacco. As with asbestos, juries declined to punish cigarette makers for decades. The tide turned in August 1996 when a jury in Jacksonville, Fla., heard the case of Grady Carter, who developed lung cancer after 44 years of smoking Lucky Strike cigarettes.

The jury, after hearing evidence that the industry had conspired for decades to lie about the dangers of smoking, found the cigarettes were "unreasonably dangerous and defective" and ordered Brown & Williamson Tobacco Co. to pay $750,000. The company paid that judgment to Carter in March

2001 after the Florida Supreme Court upheld the jury's decision.

While tobacco giants Philip Morris and R.J. Reynolds weren't defendants in that suit, officials at both companies say the jury's decision resonated throughout their corporate offices.

"It was definitely a wake-up call," says Philip Morris vice president Steve Parrish.

After winning every jury trial for four decades, suddenly the gates opened.

"If you have a defective product, and you know it's defective and kills people but you keep selling it because people are addicted to it and it makes you billions of dollars, then that is just pathetic," says Michael Criscola. Criscola is a pizza parlor operator and the foreman of a San Francisco jury that slapped Philip Morris and R.J. Reynolds tobacco companies with a $20 million judgment in March.

"I found it shocking that these companies behaved in such a disgraceful manner and that the government has allowed them to get away with it," he says.

In the Miami case that resulted in the $144 billion verdict, lawyers for the industry told jurors in closing arguments that the tobacco companies got the message from other jury verdicts over the past four years.

The lawyers told the jury that because of those earlier verdicts, they had reformed how they do business and that they don't need to be punished any more.

"It's a startling admission from a powerful industry that jury verdicts do have an impact and can induce substantial changes," says University of Wisconsin law professor Marc Galanter. He says it was the fear of juries that sparked the tobacco industry to settle lawsuits brought by 41 state attorneys general for $246 billion.

Similarly, lawyers for gun manufacturer Smith & Wesson say it was a jury verdict last year that led it to agree to historic changes in how it does business.

The case involved the families of seven shooting victims who sued 25 gun makers for negligence in marketing their products in a manner that fueled illegal gun trading.

The Brooklyn jury deliberated for nearly a week, debating internally how their verdict would be viewed by the public.

On Feb. 11, 1999, the jurors returned a judgment of $560,000 against 15 of 25 gun manufacturers—the first such verdict in the nation. The verdict is on appeal.

"We really debated whether it was our job to send some message," says a Brooklyn man who served on the jury. "In the end, we decided, if not us, who? Nobody else was saying this is wrong and we believed it was wrong."

Spurred by the jury's decision, some 24 cities subsequently sued the gun makers making the same allegations. Some of those suits are expected to be presented to juries in the next year.

Even though Smith & Wesson was one of the 10 companies found not liable by the jury, lawyers for the gun maker say the jury's verdict emphasized just how vulnerable the industry is.

They privately admit that the Brooklyn jury was a major contributing factor in the company's decision to settle its lawsuits with a handful of cities.

Following the Brooklyn verdict, a few jurors explained their unhappiness to the lawyers for the gun makers.

"We told them our verdict expressed our opinion that the industry is not being as responsible as it should be," says one juror, who asked not to be identified.

Indeed, judges say that jurors are increasingly sending written messages with their monetary awards that seek to encourage some kind of reform.

That's exactly what happened on July 24, 1997, in a fourth floor Dallas courtroom. Jurors heard several weeks of testimony that leaders of the Dallas Catholic Diocese knew for years that one of its priests was sexually abusing young parishioners but did nothing about it.

In the deliberation room, the jurors decided they needed to send two messages—just to make sure their voice was heard clearly.

The first statement came in the form of a $119.6 million judgment against the church. But then the jurors issued a letter they read in open court in front of the bishop and the news media.

The note said that the church needed to make "significant changes to [its] policies in regard to child abuse."

"Just in case the diocese didn't understand exactly what message we were sending through the $119 million verdict, we decided to make it extra clear to them," says presiding juror Susan Koons, a 55-year-old housewife who delivered the message from her seat in the jury box.

Never Again

"We wanted to say to the religious community—but especially to the Catholic Diocese—that this must stop and never be allowed to happen again," says Koons.

"The message we intended to send was not just meant for the Dallas Catholic Diocese but for churches everywhere—that they are not properly supervising their priests and pastors," Koons says.

Lawyers in the case agree that the jury's verdict led to substantial reforms within the church. The verdict also led prosecutors to file criminal charges against the priest. The civil case settled a few months after the judgment.

"Changes have been made," says Randal Mathis, a Dallas lawyer who defended the diocese. "There is absolutely no doubt that the diocese received the jury's message very, very clearly."

As for Koons, she hopes the verdict caused other churches and private groups that deal with kids on a regular basis to re-examine their policies regarding child abuse.

"Every day, I look in the newspaper for two things: I look in the obituaries to see if one of those poor kids has killed himself, and I scour the paper to see if any other churches are having similar problems.

"I pray that pastors and priests and rabbis remember our verdict and work hard to make sure this never happens again," she says.

***

VIEWS FROM THE BENCH

In February 2000 *The Dallas Morning News* and the *Southern Methodist University Law Review* surveyed 594 U.S. District judges regarding their opinion of the jury system. These are some of the results of that survey:

Have you had a jury that clearly used its verdict to send a broader political or social message?

Yes	40.4%
No	59.4%

Which most closely categorizes the proper role of a jury?

Fact finders	23.8%
Truth-Seekers	46.1%
Conscience of the Community	15.5 %
Arbiters of Justice	11.6%

Have you presided over a clear case of jury nullification?

Yes	34.8%
No	63.5%

Have you had a case in which jurors delivered either a written letter or asked to make a statement when they delivered their verdict?

Yes	31.8%
No	67.9%

21 Juror Prospect Says Nicole 'Deserved It'[1]

Associated Press

[Article re: juries and the common law legal system]

SANTA MONICA (AP) – The jury candidate wasn't too impressed with Nicole Brown Simpson. But murder?

"She was a flirt. She deserved it," the man wrote on his questionnaire in the wrongful death trial against O. J. Simpson.[1]

Pressed by an attorney Tuesday on what "it" was, the candidate, an Asian man in his 30s, gave a variety of responses, settling on the suggestion Ms. Simpson deserved some sort of response from her former husband when she had sex with another man.

"If anybody comes home and sees his wife doing what she was doing, he would be angry and she would be yelled at," the juror prospect told plaintiff lawyer Daniel Petrocelli.

And as for Ms. Simpson's oft-broadcast 911 call for police help, the juror candidate said: "I don't think she was in great distress."

The prospect, who was dismissed by the judge, was one of the rare candidates to criticize one of the victims in the June 12, 1994, murders of Ms. Simpson and her friend Ronald Goldman.

When such criticism does come, it is directed at Ms. Simpson, with comments about her alleged wild lifestyle and propensity to push Simpson's emotional buttons. One prospect said he felt that former police detective Mark Fuhrman may even have been having an affair with Ms. Simpson.

1 **Note from Professor Carr: It would appear that getting a fair, unbiased and "open-minded" juror is not as easy as one might think!!**

22 Jury Selection in the Simpson Murder Trial[1]

FROM THE OUTSET, the prosecution and defense in O.J. Simpson's murder trial both knew that jury selection could be crucial to the outcome. The defense team retained Jo-Ellen Dimitrius, a crack jury consultant with a record of success with Los Angeles juries. Donald Vinson, president of Decision Quest, one of the nation's top jury consultants, offered his services for free to the prosecution.

Dimitrius and Vinson both polled residents of Los Angeles to determine their attitudes on the Simpson case, as well as on various issues that might arise at trial. In addition to polling, the defense conducted focus groups, whose discussions helped the attorneys devise the questionnaire to be submitted to prospective jurors during voir dire. The prosecution, meanwhile, staged "mock trials"—presentations of opening arguments before demographically diverse groups, with the groups' subsequent deliberations observed through a one-way glass.

With this information, Dimitrius and Vinson each constructed profiles of the ideal defense juror, and their profiles largely coincided: a blue-collar, middle-aged, African American woman who had some personal or familial experience with law enforcement. Simpson's attorneys heeded Dimitrius's advice and sought to select jurors who fit this profile. However, prosecutor Marcia Clark rejected Vinson's advice, confident that the spousal-abuse issue in the case and her experience in establishing rapport with African American women jurors would be decisive. The prosecution thus failed to employ its full allotment of twenty peremptory challenges, and the jury that finally acquitted Simpson included eight African American women, one African American man, two white women, and one Hispanic man.

Sources: Jeffrey Toobin, The Run of His Life: The People vs. O.J. Simpson (New York: Random House, 1996); Johnnie L. Cochran, Journey to Justice (New York: Ballantine Books, 1996); and Marcia Clark, Without a Doubt (New York: Penguin, 1997).

---

1 **Note from Professor Carr: What you may have not known or appreciated about the O.J. trial that the mainstream (i.e., non-legal) press never really picked up on and/or had a clue about.**

23 Building the Jury: Occupations Count in Job Bias Trials[1]

Jurors' Work Histories Are Often the Crucial Factor in Determining How They Will Evaluate Cases

By M. Frances Ryan, *The National Law Journal*

[Article re: jury selection and the common law legal system]

IN JOB DISCRIMINATION TRIALS, the juror's occupation and work history can be the single most important factor that determines how the juror perceives the evidence and evaluates the case. In the booming economy of the past 10 years, it has been hard for plaintiffs' lawyers to put together a jury stacked with disgruntled, out-of-work citizens looking for a chance to sock it to big business.

Now that the job market is becoming less friendly and the panel of potential jurors is less likely to be composed of busy, satisfied workers, the process of picking a winning jury becomes that much harder for defense counsel. More than ever, building the winning jury depends on understanding each potential juror's unique notion of justice in the workplace. There is no better gauge than examining each juror's personal work history and experiences.

In some ways, finding the right employment discrimination jury is similar to jury selection for other types of litigation. Each potential juror brings a wealth of strongly held beliefs formed by a lifetime of experiences. These beliefs and experiences are the prism through which the jury will interpret every piece of evidence and every argument. Picking a winning jury depends on understanding how each venire member will react to a particular case.

Unlike trials over personal injuries or business disputes, every discrimination case gives the jury the chance to second-guess managers' decisions about how to treat employees in the workplace. This is true regardless of the type of discrimination claimed. The plaintiff may be a 61-year-old man complaining that his layoff was based on his age, or a 25-year-old woman alleging that she was subjected to sex harassment in the workplace and that her company failed to put a stop to it.

In each case, the key issue at trial is how the defendant's management made its decisions, and whether the decisions were based on impermissible factors, such as sex, race, age or disability status. Another important issue in most discrimination trials is what the plaintiff has done to help himself. Did he bring about his own discharge through poor work performance or misconduct? Has he made rea-

1 **Note from Professor Carr: I put this article in the book to show how/why and some of the difficulties attorneys might encounter in selecting a jury in a job bias trial. Obviously, the process and considerations would be quite different in selecting a jury in say ... a real estate fraud case!!**

sonable efforts to mitigate his damages by looking for work elsewhere and holding down a job?

Ideal Jurors for Each Side

The plaintiff's theme in most discrimination trials is the same. The plaintiff is a good, hardworking, loyal employee who deserved to be hired/promoted/not fired/not subjected to harassment. The defendant's managers are bigots, sexists, ageists and liars who have proffered a false explanation for why they harmed the plaintiff. The plaintiff would obviously prefer to have jurors who are willing to substitute their judgment for a manager's, decide the manager is lying and at the same time accept the plaintiff as an innocent victim. The ideal juror will approach the defendant's explanations for its decisions with skepticism, and even hostility. Yet this juror will not question the plaintiff's testimony about her emotional injuries and loss of wages due to the defendant's conduct.

The defense wants jurors who will believe and accept management's nondiscriminatory explanation for the decisions that the plaintiff complains about without question. The defendant's theme is usually that the plaintiff brought about his own bad situation through ineptitude or misconduct or just plain bad choices. Defense jurors approach the case with the mindset that everyone is responsible for his or her own problems. If the plaintiff got fired, she probably deserved it. If a disabled plaintiff could not do his job anymore and complains that his company should have accommodated him with a different job, the defense juror says, tough luck—but not the company's fault.

How do winning lawyers screen out the nightmare jurors and try to pick their ideal jury? Given the limited amount of information most courts provide to counsel and the limited voir dire most courts permit, most lawyers fall back on occupation, geography and obvious characteristics that the potential jurors may share with the plaintiff or key defense witnesses. Geographic factors are similar for most types of litigation—plaintiffs prefer more liberal, urban jurors, while defendants count on the typical conservatism of the rural citizen.

Jurors' personal similarities with key witnesses or parties are also used by virtually all trial lawyers. In a discrimination trial, if a key defense witness—the alleged harasser or the manager who refuse to promote the plaintiff—is a 35-year-old male engineer, the plaintiff's counsel is likely to consider striking people like that from the panel.

Finally, one of the key things to find out on voir dire is whether any potential juror has himself filed charges of discrimination against an employer, or been accused of discrimination or unlawful harassment by a co-worker.

A Business Owner Often Makes a Pro-Defense Juror

How does the juror's occupation fit into the mix? Seasoned defense counsel report that in most types of discrimination trials, the final deciding factor for most strikes is the panel member's job. In many cases, the juror's job and work history are the best predictor of where the juror will fall on the scale between unquestioning deference to the defense manager's right to make workplace decisions, and outright animosity toward big business and its managers. Defense counsel is looking for managers first, and people who work (or have worked) very hard for a living, preferably in a non-union environment. Plaintiff's counsel is looking for jurors who have been ill-treated by the system and resent big business and management in particular, such as laid-off workers. Plaintiffs also favor the unemployed and professionals, nurses and teachers, who will not defer to the defendant's managers' judgment but will make their own decisions as to what should have been done for the plaintiff.

Business Owners, Managers

A juror who owns her own business is ideal from the defense perspective. She knows that in her world, which is the real world, decisions to hire and fire and promote are based on merit because she cannot afford to do otherwise. In her world, good employees are hard to find, and no rational business owner fires a good worker because of discrimination. She views the specter of being hauled into court to face a multimillion-dollar lawsuit based on one of her workplace decisions with horror.

Savvy plaintiffs' counsel use voir dire to find out if any member of the panel has ever owned a business, or has a close relative who has owned a business. These jurors can be a plaintiff's worst nightmare, because they can be people of any age, race or sex. This juror may even be someone plaintiff's counsel was counting on to lead the charge for a big verdict perhaps because of that person's current occupation or his resemblance to the plaintiff in age, sex or race.

One experienced plaintiff's counsel found out the hard way. He relates that in one trial of a Family and Medical Leave Act case, he thought he had a pretty good jury. It included a female nurse, whom he expected to be sympathetic to the cause of his client, a woman of approximately the same age and race as the nurse. After the jury returned a defense verdict, the plaintiff's counsel interviewed some of the jurors. He found out that the nurse was the daughter of small business owners and that she was one of the strongest advocates for the defense in the jury room.

For reasons that should be obvious, it is highly advantageous to the defense to have one or more managers on the jury. Managers are used to making decisions, including tough personnel decisions, and do not like the idea of having their own decision second-guessed by a jury somewhere. They are likely to be sympathetic with the defendant's key witnesses. And managers are more likely to be influential on other jurors' decision-making.

Absent some striking reason such as a manager who has himself filed a charge of discrimination against his employer, plaintiff's counsel typically wants to strike any and all managers on the panel.

The Unemployed

Some of the hardest jurors to predict are those who write on the questionnaire, "Occupation none." This juror may be retired, temporarily unemployed for personal reasons, laid off or fired and unable to find work, unable to work for medical reasons, a full-time homemaker or even independently wealthy. Unless the court allows individual voir dire on the potential juror's work history and reasons for not being employed, counsel is in the dark.

Absent compelling reasons to the contrary, many trial lawyers who represent defendants will strike the unemployed from the panel because it is simply too risky to keep them. If the juror has never been employed, she may not be responsive to the defense's argument that the plaintiff failed to meet her employer's expectations. If the juror was fired or had some other bad experience with management, he is likely to sympathize with the plaintiff. How can defense counsel predict now this juror will respond to counsel's arguments?

On the other hand, there is little down side for the plainttiff keeping the unemployed citizen the panel, so long as his residence location does not highlight him as a well-off individual who is likely a former manager or executive. The unemployed juror is less likely to be angry about being called for jury duty and to blame the plaintiff for the inconvenience than a juror who has been called away from the type of work in which jury duty means no earnings for every day of trial.

Union Members, Civil Servants

The juror who works either under a collective bargaining agreement or under the regulatory protection afforded to most civil servants brings unique issues to the table. His or her value to the defense or the plaintiff depends in large part on the specific issues in the particular case at hand. Plaintiffs' counsel who automatically assume that a union member will help the plaintiff's cause can be burned. Likewise, defense counsel can find a winning case torpedoed by a juror with the mindset of a represented worker or a civil servant.

While the unionized worker is typically sympathetic with other workers and strongly advocates the worker's rights over management prerogatives, he will likely view the evidence through the prism of his life experiences in a union shop. He may assume that the work rules that he takes as a given apply to every worker regardless of whether they are under a collective bargaining agreement. Most significantly, defense counsel can gain a huge advantage from having a strong union or civil servant seniority advocate on the jury if the defense can point to how the decision the plaintiff calls into question in the case benefited a worker with more seniority.

In a recent race discrimination trial, the plaintiff thought she had a home run. She was a manager of many years and she had been demoted by a white male manager who had a record of being disciplined for a racist, sexist comment. Knowing that there were several active and retired union workers on the jury, the defense called to the stand the sole manager in the plaintiff's department who had been retained in management when the plaintiff and two others were demoted in the reduction in force. As it turned out, this sole remaining manager had far more years with the company than the three who were downgraded. Never in a million years were union jurors going to be convinced that the plaintiff was demoted because of her race. The jury returned a defense verdict.

In a recent disability discrimination trial, one plaintiffs' attorney reports, the presence of a union member hurt the plaintiff's cause. The plaintiff claimed that after she had been out of work on an approved leave of absence because of a disability, the company failed to let her return to work because it continued to regard her as disabled and simply did not want disabled workers coming back. The defense argued that an ambiguous series of letters back and forth between the plaintiff and her supervisor showed that the company would have let the plaintiff come back to work, but she simply failed to come back. The plaintiff, who was a manager, argued that the letters were not clear and that she never received a clear indication from the company that she was permitted to return to work or which store she would be assigned to manage.

The jury ruled for the defense. One juror, a lifelong unionized worker, told the plaintiff's counsel that he voted for the defense because he thought the plaintiff should have simply showed up at work and started working. In his personal experience, that is what employees at his company do because of the terms of their collective bargaining agreement. He completely disregarded the plaintiff's testimony that she was waiting for clear orders as to when and where to report to work. Thus, plaintiffs' counsel must beware the union worker or civil servant on the jury who assumes that the plaintiff has the same rights as he does and that the plaintiffs workplace is governed by the same rules as the juror's.

In the right case, a worker with a union mindset can seriously hurt the defense on damages. In the union setting, a worker who wins an arbitration for wrongful dismissal typically expects to receive full back pay for the period spent out of work. Most union members would find it perfectly reasonable for any plaintiff to sit at home and wait to be recalled after layoff, or wait to be reinstated after a wrongful dismissal, without going out into the workplace and finding alternative employment. Thus, the common defense theme that the plaintiff failed to mitigate damages by seeking and holding work before trial will not go over well with this type of juror.

Professionals: Unpredictable

Professionals, too can be a mixed bag as jurors. Doctors, lawyers, teachers, accountants, nurses and the like bring their own issues to any case. The doctor or lawyer who is also a small business owner or who is responsible for managing others is typically good for the defense and bad for the plaintiff. But in a sex or race harassment case, or any other case in which defense counsel is trying to minimize the harshness of what may seem to the white-collar professional to be extremely ugly conduct, the defendant will typically look to avoid professionals on the jury.

In most cases, plaintiffs' counsel likes to find teachers and nurses on the panel. Teachers tend to be much more willing to substitute their own judgment for the judgment of a defense manager, much to the detriment of the defendant's case. Nurses are likely to be more empathetic than the average person with the injuries the plaintiff has suffered, and more judgmental and willing to punish the defendant for causing the injuries. In addition, nurses, as a profession, make a habit of believing the statements of their patients concerning the source of their injuries. Defense counsel will be trying hard to portray the plaintiff as someone who is misrepresenting his or her injuries and their cause. Thus, most management-side trial lawyers will avoid nurses on their juries.

It might seem like an obvious proposition that the plaintiff would prefer to have members of the plaintiff's own occupation on the jury, and the defense would prefer to avoid it. Certainly, one of the plaintiff's counsel's primary goals is to pick jurors who will identify with the plaintiff. In the right kind of case, however, this tactic can backfire. If the evidence in the case is going to show that the plaintiff behaved unprofessionally, or has poor, professional skills, the defense is better off with members of that occupation on the jury.

In any occupation, there are certain unpardonable sins that are better understood by the members of that profession. For example, the salesman who was laid off because of poor sales performance is going to have a hard time convincing the sales representative on the jury that sales numbers should be disregarded. Likewise, the secretary who was laid off for economic reasons will find little sympathy with the secretaries on the jury when they see her resume and correspondence are messy and full of typographical errors.

In sum, occupation often provides a window into the juror's mindset, assumptions and expectations about workplace behavior. When the jury is going to be asked to impose workplace justice, the lawyer who is guided by the juror's own lifetime of work experiences is going to be the better predictor of winning juries.

24 Lawyers Find Jury Pools Polluted by Antibusiness Biases

Continuing News of Alleged Fraud at Big Companies Takes Its Toll; Investment Losses Prompt Anger

The Wall Street Journal

[Article re: juries]

IN COURTROOMS AROUND THE country, companies are facing the specter of guilt by association.

With a daily drumbeat of news about **Enron** Corp., **WorldCom** Inc. and other scandals, corporate defendants are facing jury pools far more cynical about business ethics that just a year ago. Jurors who have seen the value of their stock portfolios plunge may be particularly primed to punish corporate wrongdoing and excess.

"You have an environment in which the average juror is fed up and they feel like there is a need for some significant justice to be done," says Allan Diamond, a Houston attorney who represents plaintiffs and defendants in commercial and financial litigation.

Nervous defense lawyers are going to unusual lengths to spot jurors who may be looking for payback. During jury selection in Los Angeles for a trial involving a rollover death against **Ford Motor** Co. last month, defense lawyers asked 50 prospective jurors their reaction to this statement: "Corporate executives will lie to increase their profits." More than half agreed.

"I don't really any proof of that," said Rosemary Watson, a postal clerk, when defense lawyers questioned her further. "It's just an image in my mind that I've gotten—news articles, things I've heard on the news, and some of the things that have been happening." The case was settled out of court under a secrecy provision.

"Right now is a very dangerous time," says Ford's lawyer in the case, Warren Platt of Phoenix, Ariz. "You start out with some substantial number of people in the jury pool who are going to give less credence to testimony of corporate executives just because they're corporate executives."

In a trial last month in Tulsa, Okla., involving allegations that an office-equipment distributor defrauded two former employees in connection with a stock-purchase agreement, plaintiffs' lawyer David Bryant told jurors that President Bush and Congress were attempting to address the problems in corporate integrity but said jurors needed to send a message, too. The jury awarded $2.23 million in compensatory damages and $500,000 in punitive damages, the maximum allowed under state law. Juror Fay Shackle, an elementary-school teacher, says awareness of corporate scandals "had a mild effect as background knowledge" in consideration of the punitive award.

Attorneys and jury consultants say the fallout is evident in everything from employment suits to intellectual-property disputes. "Ordinary people's trust has been dramatically shaken," says Christine Spagnoli, a lawyer for the plaintiffs in the Ford case. "It may be the equivalent of what Watergate did to people's trust in government."

Distrust of corporations has always been a worry for defense lawyers. The big difference now, says Mr. Platt, is how widespread and deep-seated the distrust has become. In recent mock trials conducted for clients preparing to face real juries, Chicago jury consultant Theresa Zagnoli found the percentage of prospective jurors who believe that executives lie to increase profits more than doubled to 67% from 30% a year ago.

The changed atmosphere is shaping trial tactics. In San Francisco Superior Court, plaintiffs' lawyer John Friedemann of Santa Rosa, Calif., was preparing a raft of arguments, including breach of contract, to recover damages m a complex suit between two banks. His client, Far East National Bank, a U.S. unit of Taiwan's **Bank Sino-Pac**, alleged that United Commercial Bank in San Francisco knowingly provided false information about a $3 million loan that Far East took over.

But with incessant news reports of corporate deceit, "we dumped the other theories before trial and sold the case as a fraud case through and through," says Mr. Friedemann. In arguing for punitive damages, he told jurors this was their chance to send a message that corporate fraud wasn't acceptable.

William Hebert, an attorney for UCB, says an already negative environment grew worse as the seven-week trial progressed. Jurors were allowed to read newspapers; near the trial's end, federal prosecutors in New York charged members of the Rigas family, founders of **Adelphia Communications** Corp., with looting hundreds of millions of dollars from the cable-TV company. "While the jurors were deliberating, those guys at Adelphia got dragged out in handcuffs," Mr. Hebert says.

On July 25, the jury awarded Far East $9 million, including $6 million in punitive damages. The plaintiff had asked for $3 million in compensatory damages and $21 million in punitives.

Juror Don Bannister, a 67-year-old, self-employed graphic designer, says he and the others focused only on the evidence to find UCB liable. But in considering punitive damages, he says he and four others argued for an award of as much as $20 million because they "were afraid this case would go unnoticed with what was going on in the outside world." They were overruled by other jurors. UCB, a unit of **UCBH Holdings** Inc. in San Francisco, is considering an appeal, Mr. Hebert says.

DecisionQuest, a Los Angeles jury consulting firm, has conducted more than 200 mock trials across the country over the past six months and found consistent anti-business bias, says Arthur Patterson, a director of jury research, In one mock case involving a contract dispute, a juror said misconduct by corporate managers "is a disease that infects all big companies."

In another mock trial involving an insurance company's obligation to cover damage from pollution, jurors discussed the possibility that documents had been shredded even though there was no allegation that they had.

While most civil cases are settled, some say the current environment is adding even more incentive to avoid trial. Houston attorney Stephen Susman says he recently represented a former executive of a large company who alleged that the company cheated him out of $8 million in stock options. Mr. Susman says he settled the case, possibly for "a lot less than I would have gotten a year ago because I'm worried about what a jury is going to think about an executive who gets $8 million in stock options.

At the same time, says Mr. Susman, who represents both plaintiffs and defendants, he suspects the executive's employer was worried that jurors would think that this is "one more example of how corporations deal dishonesty with everyone."[1]

SHAKEN CONFIDENCE

In a survey, 1,000 people addressed statements designed to gauge their attitudes about corporations.

Sample statement:

"A representative of a company will say whatever it takes to keep the company out of trouble."

Agree	50%
Strongly Agree	22%
Neither	17%
Disagree	11%
Disagree Strongly	0%

Source: Vinson & Dimitrius, jury consulting firm in Los Angeles.

---

1 Note from Professor Carr: Can you see how the bad-boy behavior of a few corporate executives ends up hurting all of you/us as business people?

Also, does this make you wonder just a bit about those folks who blame the legal system and "run-a-way juries" for their legal woes when the real blame/finger may need to be pointed right back at themselves??

25 Jury Instructions Are Key in Andersen Trial

For All Testimony So Far, Firm's Fate Could Hinge on Definition of "Corrupt"

The Wall Street Journal

[Article re: juries and jury instructions]

HOUSTON—THE BATTLE BETWEEN prosecutors and **Arthur Andersen LLP**, already pitched, is likely to intensify as the accounting firm's criminal trial ends.

Yesterday, a court filing by the prosecution, which is being led by Justice Department attorneys Samuel Buell and Andrew Weissmann, shed the first light on a long-running fight over the instructions that jurors should receive before they begin deliberations on whether to find the accounting firm guilty of obstructing justice.

For all the hours of testimony so far this month, Andersen's fate could hinge most on how U.S. District Judge Melinda Harmon decides to craft the instructions she gives to the jury after closing arguments—and whether the jury chooses to follow them. Heated arguments over the precise wording of jury instructions aren't unusual, of course. But the wording will be especially crucial in this trial, which could end as early as next week.

That is because of the unusual circumstances of the case. A key former Andersen auditor, David B. Duncan, already has pleaded guilty to an obstruction charge for illegally destroying **Enron** Corp.-related documents in the weeks before the firm received a Securities and Exchange Commission subpoena last fall. Prosecutors say they believe Mr. Duncan's plea is all the government needs to win a conviction against Andersen.

Juries are responsible for resolving questions of fact, not questions of law. Likewise, the circumstances under which an entire partnership can be held criminally culpable for a single member's actions is a legal issue for which Judge Harmon is responsible. So far, just about every major procedural and evidentiary ruling by Judge Harmon has gone the government's way and most trial observers expect her pro-government streak will extend to her jury instructions.

Samuel Buell

That would be bad news for Andersen, since her instructions to jurors on the issue of partnership culpability and other matters likely will play a pivotal role in shaping the jury's verdict. Still, it is entirely possible that jurors could choose the route of "jury nullification" and disregard some or all of her instructions in order to reach a "not guilty" verdict for Andersen, if they conclude that is the only way to reach a just outcome for Andersen. A hearing on the two sides' jury-instruction proposals could come as early as this week.

Attorneys for Andersen and the government have been arguing in court motions for nearly a month about how Judge Harmon should phrase her instructions, as well as the proposed instructions' legal underpinnings. However, prior filings by both sides on the subject had been filed under seal—and remain so—because they had been submitted to the court before jurors had been selected for the highly publicized case. Yesterday's filing by the prosecution marked the first public disclosure of the two sides' arguments on the matter so far.

For example, the witness-tampering statute under which Andersen is charged holds that it is a crime to "corruptly persuade" another person to destroy materials "with intent to impair the object's integrity or availability for use in an official proceeding."

Prosecutors have asked Judge Harmon to instruct the jury that acting "corruptly" simply means acting "with an improper purpose." Yesterday's filing quoted a previous Andersen memorandum asking Judge Harmon to instruct jurors that a person acts corruptly: "only if he or she (1) uses an improper method, such as bribery or other unlawful means, to induce that person to act; or (2) persuades the other person to do something they would not have had a lawful right to do had they been acting on their own."

On the partnership liability issue, jurors must find that Mr. Duncan was acting within the scope of his employment when he destroyed Enron related documents in order to hold Andersen criminally liable for his actions. Prosecutors have asked Judge Harmon to instruct jurors that it isn't necessary for the government to prove that an Andersen agent's sole or even primary motive for destroying documents was to benefit the partnership. Andersen, according to yesterday's filing, has asked Judge Harmon to instruct jurors that the government must prove that an Andersen agent's "primary" motive was to benefit the partnership in order to prove that the agent was acting within the scope of his or her employment.

Another point of contention is the definition of an "official proceeding." Andersen attorneys maintain the firm was legally allowed to destroy Enron-related documents until it received formal notice of the SEC's inquiry binto the firm's Enron audits on Nov. 8, when the firm received an SEC subpoena. The government contends it was illegal for Andersen to destroy Enron-related documents once the firm had reason to believe it would become a subject of the SEC's Enron inquiry.

The SEC didn't upgrade its informal Enron inquiry to formal invenstigation status until Oct. 30. Andersen has asked for an instruction that an informal SEC inquiry is not an "official procedding." According to yesterday's filing. Prosecutors have asked Judge Harmon to reject that request on grounds that government-agency proceedings aren't limited "to only those acts committed after a formal stage is reached."[1]

1 **Note from Professor Carr: See how key jury instructions can be in a case?!!**

26

Prosecutors Seek Unusual Directive

Anderson Judge Is Asked to Permit as Evidence Workers' Refusal to Testify

The Wall Street Journal

[Article re: juries and jury instructions]

HOUSTON—IN AN UNUSUAL move, prosecutors asked the judge overseeing Arthur Andersen LLP's document-shredding trial to let the jury consider three Andersen employees' refusal to testify as evidence that the firm obstructed justice.

The requested jury instruction, which U.S. District Judge Melinda Harmon took under advisement, drew vociferous opposition from Andersen lawyers, and raised what legal specialists said were novel questions about the scope of the Fifth Amendment.

Juries typically aren't permitted to draw any negative inferences from a person's invocation of the right against self-incrimination, considered a bedrock constitutional principle. To do otherwise, the thinking goes, would thwart the purpose of the amendment, which is that the government has to prove a person's guilt without his or her assistance. Such inferences are permitted in civil cases, where witnesses are unavailable for reasons other than having taken the Fifth.

The government's request underscores the importance of Judge Harmon's jury instructions in the case. In which the government alleges that Andersen obstructed justice by destroying tons of documents related to its audits of Enron Corp. Jury instructions are made by the judge after lawyers complete closing arguments and before the jurors deliberations on a verdict begin Essentially guidelines on the state of the law and elements of the crime that the government must establish, the framing of the instructions by Judge Harmon could provide an early clue to which side winSs the trial.

Yesterday's request came as the government begins wrapping up its case against Andersen; prosecutors said they intend to rest as soon as today. Among those who have declined to testify, citing their Fifth Amendment rights, is Nancy Temple, an Andersen lawyer, who sent an Oct. 12 e-mail to the firm's Houston offices, which the government has said was a signal to Andersen employees to start shredding tons of Enron documents.

Andrew Wiessmann

In addition, Tom Bauer, a senior Andersen partner on the Enron account, and Kate Agnew, an Enron auditor, who worked for him, have also asserted their right against self-incrimination. Mr. Bauer participated in meetings on Oct. 23 at Andersen's Houston office where the firm's document-retention policies in regard to Enron were discussed.

"The witnesses' refusal to testify ... is part of the government's case," prosecutor Andrew Weissmann told Judge Harmon. "These are really admissions that bind the partnership."

He said the government should be entitled to such an instruction because Andersen lawyers have attempted to make an issue of the government's failure to identify responsible individuals. Early on in the case, Andersen lead trial lawyer Rusty Hardin borrowed from a children's book, wondering out loud in court. "Where's Waldo?"

Mr. Weissmann said the jury should get the message: "Don't blame us if we couldn't produce Nancy Temple."

Mr. Hardin countered that Andersen employees chose not to testify because of government threats of prosecution and other pressures. He said if the judge approved the government's instruction, he should have the right to call attorneys for the employees, and ask questions about the government's interviewing tactics.

"They created a straw man, and now they want permission to knock it down," Mr. Hardin said.

What is clear is that the government's request is extraordinary, former prosecutors and criminal-law specialists say. Henry Hockeimer, a Philadelphia criminal defense lawyer and former federal prosecutor, said there was a major irony in the government's position: Prosecutors want to impute to Andersen the acts of employees for purposes of convicting the firm, but don't want to impute to the company the decision by the same people to invoke constitutional rights.

The government seems to want it both ways," Mr. Hockeimer said. "To allow invocation of the Fifth to create an adverse inference in a criminal case against a party just isn't done."

David Crump, a criminal-law professor at the University of Houston, said the precise issue—of whether an adverse inference can be permitted against a business entity from an employee's taking the Fifth Amendment—hasn't been definitively resolved by the U.S. Supreme Court. But he said he viewed the government's bid as an aggressive one in what is turning out to be a closer case than some observers previously thought.

"It just shows that the government is aware that proving intent beyond a reasonable doubt in an ambiguous situation is not an easy thing to do," Mr. Crump said.

Separately, Judge Harmon issued an unusual apology to the media after holding a bench conference out of public earshot after the jury had been dismissed for lunch. "Nothing happened at the bench conference that I was trying to keep from the press," the judge said. It turns out that prosecutors had expressed frustrations about Mr. Hardin's courtroom demeanor.

"We're a little tired of Mr. Hardin's speeches," prosecutor Samuel Buell said while leaving the court after the morning session, declining further comment.

27 Andersen Jurors Begin Deliberating the Company's Fate

The Wall Street Journal

[Article re: juries and jury instructions]

Houston

AFTER 21 DAYS of testimony and eight hours of summations, the Arthur Andersen LLP criminal case hinges on how jurors will fill an empty blank on a one-sentence verdict form: guilty or not guilty.

Yesterday evening, the 12 jurors in the obstruction-of-justice case ended their first day deliberating the fate of the 89-year-old accounting firm. They will resume this morning. During the deliberations, they had asked for yellow markers, copies of jury instructions and the entire transcript of the government's main witness.

Jurors began the day by picking as their foreman a middle-age college professor, one of the jury's five black members, who had been notable throughout the trial for his keen interest from his perch on the far-right seat of the jury box's front row. The balding, bespectacled man focused intensely on the proceedings and appeared particularly absorbed by prosecutor Samuel Buell's closing summation Wednesday.

The nine-man, three-woman jury later sent three notes to U.S. District Judge Melinda Harmon. The first asked for the highlighters and jury instructions. The second asked to see a large timeline of the case that Andersen attorney Rusty Hardin used during his summation, and for copies of a notebook binder containing dozens of exhibits presented by Mr. Buell.[1]

Judge Harmon declined to give jurors the items because they were "demonstrative" of the lawyers' cases. But she did agree to offer to list the exhibits in the government's binder, if the jurors wanted them, which they said they did.

In perhaps the most telling request, the jurors asked for the entire testimony of David B. Duncan, Andersen's lead partner on the Enron Corp. engagement team.

Judge Harmon ruled she would read excerpts only, upon request. "We will be here three weeks if we give them David Duncan's testimony," she said.

The request indicates jurors are trying to determine whether Mr. Duncan's testimony "is sufficient to by itself prove that Arthur Anderson is guilty" as prosecutors contend, said Gerald Treece, dean of South Texas College of Law, in Houston. "Both sides argued that Duncan's testimony helped them."

Still, Mr. Treece said, it is too early to tell what the requests signaled about jurors' leanings, other than that they are carefully reviewing the evidence. The fact that they were still studying the jury charge and evidence so late in the day could indicate that there is a disagreement among jurors, Mr. Treece said. If deliberations are not resolved by the end of

1 **Note from Professor Carr: Illustrates how these jurors were confused and/or needed/wanted additional clarification on certain important issues in the case.**

today, that likely would mean that the jurors "are starting to polarize," posing the risk of a hung jury, he said.

Both an acquittal and a conviction require a unanimous vote.[2]

During trial proceedings some jurors stood out for their cold stares and quirky behavior. During Mr. Buell's closing statement Wednesday, for instance, juror "No. 3" was the lone panelist who refused to open his exhibit notebook when Mr. Buell asked them to turn to particular pages showing the evidence he was describing. No. 9 occasionally drew whispered chuckles from the gallery when he would periodically nod off during witness testimony as trial entered its third week.[3]

While tensions have flared between the lawyers and Judge Harmon, they also have sizzled inside the jury box, as some members began getting on each other's nerves at the end of the month-long ordeal. One juror fretted in a letter to the judge Friday that another was "mad" and had remarked that "if one person gets mad at the rest of us, he can keep us here forever when deliberations are going on." Apparently, the juror was upset because one of the alternate jurors "is always late getting to the transit center in the morning, and we have to wait on her."

Others tried helping their fellow jurors endure the long days through random acts of kindness. Juror No. 15 who, as an alternate, was dismissed Wednesday night when deliberations began, occasionally was spotted massaging the shoulders of Juror No. 7, who sat in front of her. To date, Judge Harmon has declined to divulge jurors' identities.

---

2 **Note from Professor Carr: In a criminal case (a civil case is different).**

3 **Note from Professor Carr: Illustrates some of the quirky "human" factors, issues and characteristics that we (trial attorneys) have to consider, address, prepare for and overcome at a trial. Note, for example, Juror No. 3's behavior. Why do you think he was being so darn stubborn and uncooperative, and what, if anything, could/should a good prosecutor do to get that juror to "check back in" to the trial and proceeding??!!**

28 Andersen Verdict Could Hinge on Critical Ruling from Judge

The Wall Street Journal

[Article re: juries and jury instructions]

HOUSTON—A FEDERAL JUDGE'S response to an intricate legal question from the deadlocked jury in the Arthur Andersen LLP trial could make or break the government's obstruction-of-justice case against the beleaguered accounting firm.

Adding to the drama and tension at the trial, the jurors asked the judge to clarify a crucial point: Do they all need to agree on the identity of a single Andersen partner or employee who acted corruptly, or is it OK if various jurors think it was a different one of several Andersen employees?

If the judge says the lower standard is enough—for which there is some legal precedent—it would be easier for the jurors to break their deadlock over a verdict and find Andersen guilty, while a ruling by the judge that the higher standard is required would favor the defense.

The issue is important to the trial's outcome because U.S. District Judge Melinda Harmon in her jury instructions last week after testimony ended, said that to support a conviction the jury must conclude that at least one Andersen "agent" had tried to thwart a government investigation last fall by "corruptly" persuading another person to destroy work for Enron Corp.

However, Judge Harmon's instructions do not clearly state whether all the jurors, to support a conviction, must reach a unanimous conclusion about the identities of any individual "corrupt persuaders" at the firm. Judge Harmon, who was left to interpret her own wording, still had not ruled as of late yesterday afternoon.

Specifically, the jury asked in a note sent to judge Harmon, "If each of us believes that one Andersen agent acted knowingly and with corrupt intent, is it for all of us to believe it was the same agent? Can one believe it was Agent A, another believe it was Agent B, and another believe it was Agent C?"

At the trial, the government presented several Andersen employees as "corrupt persuaders," including the prosecution's star witness, former Andersen partner David B. Duncan, Enron's chief auditor, who has pleaded guilty to obstruction of justice. Others singled out in this role were Andersen in-house lawyer Nancy Temple and partner Michael Odom, the Houston office's practice director, among others. Ms. Temple took the Fifth Amendment at the trial, but previously had denied wrongdoing. Mr. Odom wasn't called to testify at the trial, and hasn't spoken publicly about his role.

In their arguments to the judge yesterday, the prosecution argued for the looser standard while defense attorneys insisted on the stricter one.

"As long as they agree on the bottom line, it isn't necessary for them to agree on the same actor," prosecutor Andrew Weissmann argued. But Andersen attorney Denis McInerney countered that Judge Harmon would be "deviating from what the law is" if she accepted that argument, and that she would be "changing your original charge."

"The bottom line is you cannot convict an entity without specific intent," Mr. McInerney said, adding that "each element must be satisfied by one person" upon whose identity all jurors agree.

Legal precedent favors the prosecution's position, according to Lawrence Barcella, a Washington defense attorney and former federal prosecutor not involved in the case. He said a majority of federal jurisdictions have ruled that jurors don't have to agree on one individual as the "corrupt persuader" under corporate liability laws. "You just have to find that somebody acted corruptly," he added.

But in a small number of cases judges have instructed jurors that they have to agree on "at least one of the same people. This is the minority position," he noted.

Walter Loughlin, a former law professor who co-authors a series of books on jury instructions that is widely used by federal judges, says he feels it is likely that Judge Harmon will instruct the jurors that they needn't all agree that a specific individual obstructed justice.

He said the law of corporate liability for the acts of individuals is unusually broad. "It seems to me that the state of mind necessary for a valid conviction on the obstruction charge can be aggregated, and that Nancy Temple was the corrupt persuader or that David Duncan was the corrupt persuader," said Mr. Loughlin, a former federal prosecutor, who is currently a corporate criminal defense lawyer in the New York office of Latham & Watkins.

Raging Debate

The jurors' uncertainty on the matter was the clearest sign yet to emerge of the debate now raging among jurors, who fold Judge Harmon late Wednesday that they were deadlocked in the case. Judge Harmon instructed the jury to redouble its efforts to reach a verdict, and the jurors sent the not on the corrupt-persuader issue within an hour of returning to the jury room from their hotel early yesterday. Two other notes followed, in which the jury asked to be read reams of additional testimony in the case, threatening to extend deliberations for days.

The "corrupt persuader" question exposed an ambiguity in Judge Harmon's 15-page jury instructions. The judge wrote that "in order to establish that Andersen is guilty" the government must prove that "each element of the offense ... Was committed by one or more agents of Andersen acting within the scope of their employment with the firm." This didn't address, however, whether all jurors had to agree on who the agent was.

Mr. Weissmann argued that Judge Harmon should tell jurors they don't need to agree on the same corrupt persuader to find the firm guilty. "The case law is abundantly clear," Mr. Weissmann said. He likened the situation to a crime scene at which six guns are found, but only one suspect. It wouldn't matter, he said, which gun was used in the crime, only that the suspect had committed it.

All that matters, Mr. Weissmann said, is that each juror "has found one" corrupt persuader. "Different jurors may be persuaded by different pieces of evidence as long as they agree on the bottom line," he said.

Andersen's lawyers argued that jurors must agree unanimously on the identity of at least one corrupt persuader to support a conviction against the entire firm, and that the requirement of specific intent cannot be aggregated—with different jurors disagreeing on that person's identity. The defense argues specific intent is an element of the crime, not just a means and method and that specific intent must be ascribed to at least one agent of Andersen, and done so unanimously.

Mr. McInerney, the Andersen lawyer, called the jury question "absolutely the most critical element in this case." He said that even if the government couldn't prove that a single Andersen partner or employee had committed a crime, under the government's proposed answer, "they would say 'that's OK,' the institution can still be convicted." Mr. McInerney told the judge that the "the bottom line is you cannot convict an entity without specific intent," adding that "each element must be satisfied by one person."

After hearing the arguments, Judge Harmon said she would review the case law cited by both sides and issue a ruling. There appeared to be no single case precedent cited by either side that is directly on point.

Mr. Barcella, the former prosecutor, said that if the judge applies the looser standard in answering the jury's question, it could be one of many issues that the defense could base its appeal on if there is a guilty verdict.

Taken together, yesterday's notes suggest that at least some jurors are taking a scalpel to Ms. Harmon's jury instructions, embarking on a painstaking person-by-person analysis to determine whether the actions of any one person at Andersen last fall would support a conviction against the entire firm.

29 Jury Cuts Off an Andersen Appeals Route

Linking an Employee to Criminal Act Makes Moot the Judge's Risky Procedural Ruling

The Wall Street Journal

[Article re: juries, jury instructions and jury deliberations]

HOUSTON—NOT ONLY DID the jury in **Arthur Andersen** LLP's criminal trial convict the firm of obstruction of justice. It also made a moot point out of one of the accounting firm's strongest potential grounds for appeal.

By unanimously agreeing, in a special jury verdict form, on the identity ofat least one person at Andersen whose actions brought criminal liability upon the accounting firm, jurors unwittingly headed off an unprecedented controversy whose emergence during the final days of jury deliberations provided the most dramatic moments of the firm trial.

It started Thursday with what lawyers in the case will long remember as Jury Note No. 9 And it posed an intricate legal question that the judge said has never been specifically addressed in a case of this kind: If the 12 jurors agree someone at Andersen corruptly intended to impede a government investigation—but they can't all agree on who that person is—can the jury still convict the firm?

Without any explanation of her reasoning, U.S. District Judge Melinda Harmon said "yes" Friday, substantially lowering the bar prosecutors needed to clear to win a conviction. She was quick to acknowledge there was a high risk some higher court would think she got the answer wrong. She even went so far as to ask if anyone in the audience or the press was aware of any judicial opinion anywhere that was directly on point. No one responded.

"I'm kind of in a position of a case of first impression, which is terrifying for a district judge," Judge Harmon said Friday. And especially so for Judge Harmon, whose own record before the U.S. Fifth Circuit Court of Appeals is hardly spotless, a frequent point of her own self-deprecation throughout the six-week trial.

In 1997, for example, an appeals court reversed a bank-fraud case she handled, upsetting the conviction of the former chairman of Texas National Bank-Westheimer. The appeals court said Judge Harmon erred when she allowed a federal bank examiner to express his opinions about the chairman's dealings with the bank and compounded the error when she refused to allow the chairman's lawyers to present expert testimony.

Widely viewed as the most pro-government federal district judge in the Southern District of Texas, she sided only rarely with the Andersen defense team on hundreds of evidentiary and procedural rulings. At one point, Andersen's lead attorney Rusty Hardin openly accused her of bias, a contention she has denied.

Even before the jury had returned from its deliberation room Saturday morning, a dejected Mr. Hardin was bemoaning how the ruling meant it was game finished for Andersen. Sure enough, at 10:25 a.m. local time, when Judge Harmon read aloud the jury's verdict, it was finished—but not for the reason Andersen anticipated.

In a special verdict form filled after the jury's guilty verdict was announced, the jurors all agreed on at least one Anderson employee who had acted corruptly by persuading another person to perform an act aimed at impeding the Securities and Exchange Commission's investigation into Enron Corp. last fall. Later four jurors confirmed, the "corrupt persuader" they all agreed upon was Anderson attorney Nancy Temple. As it turned out, according to jurors who spoke with reporters Saturday, they had made up their minds on Ms. Temple before they received Judge Harmon's answer. "If we had to be convicted," Mr. Hardin said, "I would have loved to have that issue."

Andersen attorneys said they believe they will still have plenty of grounds for appeal on Judge Harmon's evidentiary rulings and the manner in which she crafted her jury instructions. Among their beefs: Judge Harmon instructed jurors that, to support a conviction, they had to find a "corrupt persuader" had acted with specific intent to "impede" an official proceeding. Mr. Hardin said he feels that set the bar too low, and common-law precedent required her to use a stronger word like "undermine" or "subvert."

Andersen lawyers likely will argue on appeal that Judge Harmon shouldn't have allowed prosecutors to introduce evidence of Andersen's audit failures at Waste Management Inc. and Sunbeam Corp.; contending they prejudiced the jury, despite federal rules permitting the introduction of "prior bad acts" as evidence of a defendant's motive.

Andersen attorneys also got shot down several times when they objected to prosecutors' questions to witnesses about notes taken by Ms. Temple and others at Andersen who invoked their Fifth Amendment rights against self-incrimination. During one exchange last month, Mr. Hardin accused Judge Harmon of creating "totally reversible error" by doing so, and then by also refusing to allow Andersen to question those same witnesses about how they interpreted the statements of those unavailable witnesses.

"We couldn't present evidence of what Nancy Temple said to others, and the government in turn was able to demonize her," Mr. Hardin said. "We were powerless to do anything."

Still, winning an appeal is a long shot, statistically speaking. A report last year by the Justice Department's Bureau of Justice Statistics found criminal convictions in the federal courts were overwhelmingly upheld on appeal. Of 10,593 criminal appeals resolved in 1999, the latest year studied, lower-court rulings were affirmed, at least in part, in 85% of the cases.

And while district-court judges' rulings on novel legal questions do get closely scrutinized on appeal, appellate judges tend to cut them lots of slack on determining what factual information is admitted into evidence, said Henry Hockeimer, a former federal prosecutor and a Philadelphia corporate-defense lawyer. "Appellate courts typically defer to trial courts on evidentiary issues," Mr. Hockeimer said. "I would be less optimistic on that."

30 Foreman Was Last to Be Persuaded

The Wall Street Journal

[Article re: juries and jury deliberations]

HOUSTON—LOCKED FOR 72 hours in deliberations, it came down to just one juror holding back from convicting Arthur Andersen LLP of a felony.

Ironically for the group—huddled for their 10th day around a large conference table on the ninth floor of a downtown courthouse here—straying from the pack was the person the other jurors had elected as their foreman: Oscar H. Criner, a 62-year-old college professor.

But persuade Mr. Criner, they did. By 9:15 a.m. Saturday morning the jury had reached a unanimous verdict to convict the once-venerable accounting firm of obstructing justice, bringing the six-week trial to a close.

In one more of a string of unusual twists in the case, Andersen wasn't found guilty of such obstruction by shredding thousands of documentsrelated to its botched audit of Enron Corp., the highly publicized basis for the case. Instead, it was found guilty for editing a document—a document that was later turned over by Andersen to prosecutors.

Explaining the jury's decision, Mr. Criner said, "We had to ensure that someone corruptly persuaded someone else to do something that would result in the impairment of a fact-finding capability of an official proceeding." In the end, he added, "that almost had nothing to do with shredding documents."

U.S. District Judge Melinda Harmon turned over the case to the jury of nine men and three women on the evening of June 5. Among the first items of business: the foreman vote. A computer-science professor at Texas Southern University and a thoughtful speaker, Mr. Criner was chosen for his educational background.

The jury quickly laid out ground rules: Be honest. Talk one at a time. No name-calling. They then constructed a timeline of events from August through Nov. 9, the day the secretary of Andersen's lead auditor on the Enron account sent an e-mail calling for "no more shredding." The timeline took up one wall of the jury room.

At the outset, the jury was split on Andersen's guilt. Much of the first week was spent poring over the judge's dozen pages of highly complex instructions. "They were not easy reading," said Mr. Criner.

But by Wednesday, with about three people still not convinced, debate turned heated. "Some people were exasperated," said Mr. Criner. "Some people were tired of me shooting holes in arguments."

After nearly two weeks away from their families, nerves started to fray. "People were getting antsy that it was time to go home," said juror Jack Gallo, a 58-year-old airline general manager.

One juror missed his son's surgery, and another his forty-first wedding anniversary. A third discovered she might be pregnant. But the group tried to stay focused, and joined hands each morning and prayed.

Having reached an impasse, that afternoon they told the judge they were deadlocked. Her response was direct. They should redouble their efforts. "We needed our butts kicked," said Mr. Gallo. "That woke a lot of people up, and that's when we went into second gear."

The jurors returned to pore over the instructions, a foot-high stack of evidence, as well as their own notes—in some cases 140 pages or more. It was then that the final pieces began to fall into place. Compiling a list of five potential corrupt persuaders on a flip board, the jurors began eliminating them one by one.

Among them: Michael Odom, head of the Houston office's audit practice who had delivered a videotaped lecture on the firm's document-retention policy in early October. Jurors replayed the tape over and over, but ultimately dismissed his document-destruction comments as training instruction rather than an order to shred.

Eventually, the list was whittled down to two: the government's star witness David Duncan, Andersen's lead auditor on Enron who had pleaded guilty to obstructing justice just before the trial began, and Andersen Chicago-based lawyer Nancy Temple.

But some jurors doubted Mr. Duncan's testimony. "I felt very strongly that you couldn't trust David Duncan's testimony," said Mr. Criner. "He had already made an agreement with the prosecution."

By late Thursday, Mr. Criner was a lone challenger. "If you have 12 jurors in a room and one disagrees, you'd better look at what the other 11 think," said Mr. Gallo of the group's efforts to persuade him. "It took a couple of days, but we had to get him comfortable with that decision."

The group hit another wall: Were they all required to agree on the same corrupt persuader?" They put the question to the judge. She ultimately responded no, but by then the answer was moot.

Searching to match patterns in the instructions against the testimony, something had finally "clicked" for the mathematics professor Friday. What emerged was Ms. Temple's efforts to remove language from a memo that showed Andersen had disagreed with its lucrative client Enron over the wording of an earnings news release. At issue was the description of Enron's earnings as "nonrecurring," which Andersen thought was misleading but which its client used anyway.

"Arthur Andersen set about to alter documents to keep that away from the SEC," concluded Mr. Criner. The other jury members, too, were convinced, and unanimously agreed that Ms. Temple was a corrupt persuader.

The diverse group—which also included a Baptist minister, artist, jeweler and security guard—weren't swayed by the complexities of the accounting industry. During the trial one juror had asked what the Securities and Exchange Commission was—the regulatory body for the industry.

But by the end, they too, had adopted industry jargon: "There was a lack of auditor independence," stated David Schwab, an executive pastry chef, in the press conference after the trial.

Recognizing the magnitude of the task she had charged them with, Judge Harmon told the jury, as she dismissed them, that she had "never had a jury that have been so diligent in their decision."

Adding one final instruction, she told jurors to be sure to take their notes, to keep as a souvenir or discard as they wish. They could even "shred them," she added.

31 Pair of Jurors Caught Some Z'S During Arthur Andersen Trial[1]

The Wall Street Journal

[Article re: juries, jury conduct and jury deliberations, and even post-trial juror conduct]

HERE'S A PERK when serving on a jury in a long trial involving accountants: You can always catch up on your sleep.

That is apparently what two jurors did during testimony in the obstruction-of-justice case against Arthur Andersen LLP, Enron Corp's former auditor. Those same jurors voted to convict the accounting firm on June 15, paving the way for Andersen to eventually go out of business.

The jurors' frequent naps so worried their fellow jurors that at one point in the six-week trial, they tried to send a note to U.S. District Judge Melinda Harmon who presided over the case. But the judge never received the note, juror Jack Gallo said in an interview. The story of the dozing jurors was earlier reported in Texas Lawyer, a legal publication.

The two jurors, who weren't identified, clearly missed some crucial information from the trial, according to other jurors. This became obvious during the jury's 10 days of deliberations. One juror apparently believed that David Duncan, the Andersen auditor who oversaw the Enron account, was the one on trial. Mr. Duncan had already pleaded guilty to obstruction of justice and was the government's star witness.

Another of the jurors—perhaps believing the Securities and Exchange Commission has further reach than it really does—asked during deliberations whether NASA, the federal space agency, was involved in the case.

The revelation of the sleeping jurors comes as Andersen considers appealing the jurors' rationale in rendering the verdict. The defense team lost its most obvious appeal route when jurors revealed that they had all agreed that Andersen lawyer Nancy Temple was the "corrupt persuader" needed for a conviction. But Andersen lawyers are questioning the fact that the guilty verdict wasn't based on Andersen's document shredding but on an e-mail sent by Ms. Temple to Mr. Duncan in which she asked him to delete some words from a memo he had written showing that Andersen had disagreed with an Enron accounting decision. The defense lawyers argue that acting as a lawyer, Ms. Temple had a right to give legal advice to the firm.

Meanwhile, Mr. Gallo said another juror took one of the sleeping members aside during deliberation and filled him in on what he missed. That didn't help the man make up his mind: He switched his vote throughout the deliberations and at one point late in the process was one of only two jurors voting not guilty. "When it got down to the nitty-gritty, he voted with the rest of us," Mr. Gallo said in the interview. "We knew he would."

1 **Note from Professor Carr: Another obstacle that trial lawyers, unfortunately, have to plan for and try to overcome on behalf of their clients!!**

Mr. Gallo wrote a note to Judge Harmon about midway through the trial expressing concern about their dozing colleagues. But the jurors were informed by a federal marshal that the judge knew about the issue, so the note was never sent. "I was told the judge was well aware of it, so end of story, I forgot about it," Mr. Gallo said.

Andersen lawyer Rusty Hardin, who has said he will appeal the case, said he should have been informed of the note. Had that happened, Mr. Hardin told Texas Lawyer, "we would have asked for an inquiry of the jurors and would have raised the issue about whether these people were qualified to sit." Mr. Hardin didn't return a call seeking comment Friday.

32 When Jurors Decide to Write Books

Anderson Trial Raises Questions About the Impact on Deliberations

The National Law Journal

[Article re: juries, jury conduct and jury deliberations, and even post-trial juror conduct]

SHORTLY AFTER A Houston jury delivered its guilty verdict in the Arthur Andersen trial, the jurors began to talk to the press about their obstruction-of-justice finding.

Jury foreman Oscar Criner, a professor of computer science at Texas Southern University, revealed his intention to write a book about the Andersen/Enron scandal. Other jurors griped to the press that his note-taking during deliberations slowed the process down.

Though there is no evidence of it, his fellow jurors' allegations raise questions about whether Criner's book ambitions influenced the deliberations or verdict because of his hopes for a successful and lucrative book deal. While legal experts are uncomfortable with jurors' intent to profit from their experience, few believe there is much of a legal avenue to prevent jurors from profiting after the trial.

Criner said that the subject of financial scandals has interested him since the early 1960s and that while the idea of a book was one that had occurred to him early on in the process, it wasn't foremost in his mind during the trial. He asserted that his note-taking was not done in anticipation of a book, but to manage a lot of material in a complicated trial.

Criner is not the first juror to cash in on the experience. Jurors in the Bernard Goetz, O.J. Simpson and the Menendez brothers cases have spurred an interest in whether "jurors' journalism" is corrupting the legal process.

Currently, in the Georgia murder trial involving the Dekalb County sheriff accused of murdering his political rival, the state's star witness, jailer Patrick Cuffy, testified that he had been approached about a book deal that was dependent on a conviction.

As much as they don't like the smell of such involvement, legal experts know of no cases where publication ambitions, particularly of a juror, who ultimately helps decide the case, have changed a verdict. At least two states—New York and New Jersey—have laws that specifically prohibit jurors from negotiating book or movie deals before a verdict has been reached.

Tom Munsterman, the director of the center for jury studies at the National Center for State Courts in Washington, D.C., noted that the juror's right to publish is guaranteed under the First Amendment: Munsterman and others note that it would be difficult for a defense lawyer to prove there was prejudicial influence by the juror. Any such effort would likely result at best in ruling of "harmless error."

The center, which came out with a book about managing notorious cases, recommends that potential jurors be questioned in voir dire about any personal intentions they may have. Criner said no one ever asked.[1]

1 Note from Professor Carr: Do you think this fellow should be allowed to do this? If not, then how would you get around/defeat any First Amendment claim (free speech) he might raise?

33 Selecting a Fair and Impartial Jury—A Piece of Cake??

The following hypothetical attempts to raise what is often referred to in the legal profession as a "lender liability" issue. That is where a lender (e.g., a bank) steps out of its traditional role of simply lending money and letting the recipient of the loan run his/her business and the project, and instead becomes too involved in micromanaging the project (out of fear, of course, that the project will fail and it will never get repaid). Further, in the process of "micromanaging" the project the bank somehow screws things up/somehow harms the recipient of the loan.

To give you another example/different angle of how lenders can get into trouble in this regard, see the articles at page 105–107 of this text (right after this hypothetical). Once you read those two short articles, the below should make more sense.

Hypothetical

Bill owns a winery near Santa Maria. Bill's grandfather started the winery, it was passed on to Bill's father, and then to Bill. Bill is 46 years old, white, married, and has two children (a son who attends Cal Poly and a daughter who attends Stanford). Bill and his wife (a 44 year old Asian woman) are Jewish and very active in the Libertarian Party. When Bill was a teenager, he dropped out of high school so he could get an early start on learning how to make wine and run a winery.

Roughly seven years ago, a severe drought occurred (which resulted in decreased grape production) and Bill's winery began to lose money. During the last few years he also had some marital problems and he was not able to focus on making his winery as efficient as he probably should have. He also made some unwise business decisions for his winery (e.g., expanding too much and too fast).

As a result of his financial difficulties, Bill realized that he needed a large loan to cover operating expenses. Bill drove to San Luis Obispo and met with Stan, the vice-president of Stage-Coach Bank. Stan is 58 years old, white, Catholic, a Democrat, and the father of four wonderful and very talented children. Stan grew up in New York City and has an MBA from NYU. For years Stan has been active in the San Luis Obispo community and he is well liked and respected, although his reputation was recently tarnished when he left his wife ... for another man.

Stan reviewed Bill's financial records and statements and approved Bill's loan. As security for the loan, the Bank took a first deed of trust on Bill's winery. While Stan strongly suspected that Bill would not be able to turn things around and repay the loan, he nevertheless made the loan to Bill (in part because he considered Bill a friend).

Each year Bill's financial condition continued to worsen. Each year he had to return to the Bank and ask Stan for another loan, which the Bank approved. However, Stan and the rest of the officers at the Bank eventually decided that they simply could not loan any more money to Bill. Because Bill could not obtain any operating funds for his business, he closed his winery and the Bank foreclosed.

The Bank is in relatively good shape because although it will have to hire someone to manage the winery until it can be resold, all forecasts show that in another year (two at most), the value of wineries on the Central Coast will skyrocket. When that occurs, the Bank will be able to resell the winery at a large profit (probably to some rich lawyer from Los Angeles who wants to come to this area to retire and make wine).

Bill recently had to take a job as a janitor at the Santa Maria High School in order to make ends meet. Bill's son and daughter were also forced to take a leave of absence from college to work and raise money for school. Fortunately, Bill's marriage is stronger than ever.

Bill filed a "lender liability" lawsuit against the Bank. His basic theory of liability is that the Bank lured him in; kept loaning him money at exorbitant interest rates (which it knew he could never repay); and did so knowing that he would default on the loan payments, it could foreclose, and then eventually resell the winery at a nice profit.

The Bank's defense is simple: It was legitimately trying to help Bill out; it did everything it could do to help Bill succeed; it never made Bill any promises; the reason Bill failed was because he was a bad businessman; and Bill is just trying to blame someone else by suing a "deep pocket."

Tomorrow the trial starts and the parties will pick a jury. The trial will be held in the San Luis Obispo County Superior Court and is expected to last 4 to 6 weeks. The major witnesses at trial will be Bill, his wife, and Stan.

What type of person does Bill want on the jury? What type of person does the Bank want on the jury? From what demographic pool in San Luis Obispo County should/can Bill and the Bank go to in trying to select their ideal jury member?

Some demographic classifications to consider:

Gender
Race
Age
Occupation
Place/city/area of residence
Political patty
Religion
Education
Other?

34 Lender Liable for $6.6 Million[1]

The National Law Journal

NEWARK, N.J.—A CONSTRUCTION lender that exercises authority over management of a job site can be held liable for defects in a building, a New Jersey court has found.

Superior Court judge John Himmelberger, in Atlantic City, on Nov. 2 let stand a $6.6 million punitive damages verdict against the Bank of America, which financed a condominium complex rife with defects.

Lawyers in consolidated cases—*Gardner v. Bank of America,* No. ATL-L-184-99, and *Ocean Club Condominium Association v. Bank of America,* No. ATL-L-256-99—said it may be the first time in New Jersey a bank has been held liable for building defects absent a loan default by the developer.

Paul Sandars, a partner at Lum, Danzis, Drasco, Positan & Kleinberg in Roseland, N.J., the lawyer for Ocean Club Condominium Association of Atlantic City, argued that flaws in the complex, such as crumbling balconies, could be pinned to Bank of America's heavy handed supervision of the project.

Plaintiff Albert Gardner, half of a partnership that developed the two-building, 32-story project, wanted a contractor experienced in high-rise construction on oceanfront sites, which present special problems of soil condition, wind and salt air. But Bank of America insisted on a NewYork contractor, with which it had a business relationship.

On Sept. 17, after a three-month trial on liability, the jury found that Bank of America, had deviated from accepted standards of banking practice and had improperly exercised effective control over the construction. Himmelberger, who planned to have all damages tried separately, was about to excuse the jurors when Gardner's lawyer, Arthur Shanker, of counsel to the Law Offices of Richard Weiner of Montvale, N.J., said that *Herman v. Sunshine Chemical Specialties,* 133 N.J. 329 (1993), requires the jury that found liability to decide punitive damages. The judge agreed, despite protests from bank lawyer Paul Giordano of Philadelphia's Monteverde, McAlee & Hurd.

The jury returned its $6.6 million punitive damages verdict on Sept. 25.

1 **Note from Professor Carr: This article is an example of a classic "lender liability" case and shows how banks can get themselves in hot water.**

35 $19M Award in Bank Battle[1]

The National Law Journal

A LITIGATION MARATHON THAT began in 1988 yielded a $19 million verdict for a Louisiana man who alleged a bank officer engineered his financial ruin.

"This is about the most complicated case I've ever had," said Joseph R. Ward Jr. of New Orleans' Ward Nelson, who recently won the judgment for plaintiff Stanley Palowsky.

During the 1980s, Palowsky was a construction contractor and land speculator who had a keen interest in landing a seat on the board of directors of Ouachita National Bank, Ward said. As part of his campaign to win a director's seat, Palowsky brought clients to the bank's loan department, Ward said.

One of those clients, a doctor, defaulted on a $4 million loan. In 1986, a top bank officer allegedly extorted from Palowsky an agreement to purchase land the doctor had used as collateral by threatening to make public a trumped-up report by a private investigator that made several damaging allegations against Palowsky, Ward alleged.

Palowsky agreed to purchase and develop the land, in return for various commitments from the bank, all of which the bank reneged on, said Sedric E. Banks, a solo practitioner in Monroe, La., who handled discovery and motions on Palowsky's behalf. In 1992, a civil jury awarded Palowsky $1.7 million in a breach-of-contract suit against the bank after finding that he had been extorted into purchasing the land, Banks said.

The latest trial dealt with two consolidated cases, *Ouachita National Bank v. Stanley R. Palowsky Jr.*, No. 88-2879, and *Bank One v. Gulf States Land and Development Inc.*, No. 97-0544 (4th Judicial Dist. Ct., Ouachita Parish, La).

The earlier suit dealt with bank efforts to foreclose liens on property held by Palowsky, while the later suit stemmed from the bank alleging that Palowsky had wrongfully seized $1.7 million in bank assets to collect on the 1992 judgment.

Although both suits were brought by the bank, Judge Carl Sharp ruled that Palowsky's defense was grounded so firmly in allegations of wrongdoing by the bank that he would be regarded as the plaintiff, Banks said.

A key piece of evidence unveiled during the trial, Banks said, was the existence of a March 29, 1988, "criminal referral form" that detailed evidence the bank had accumulated about potential criminal wrongdoing by a top bank officer. Federal law requires banks to investigate and report such wrongdoing.

The form was eventually discovered in the bank vault, Banks said.

1 **Note from Professor Carr: This article is an example of a classic "lender liability" case and shows how banks can get themselves in hot water.**

36 Chapter 3—The Anatomy of a Civil Case; Judges, Courts and Jurisdiction; and ADR (continued)

Study Outline

*****Note that in this textbook at pages 113–146 I have inserted a number of newspaper articles, supplementary materials, sample documents, etc. that relate to this material. These materials are required reading, and, also fair game for the exam.**

*****Also, make *<u>sure</u>* that you do the sample practice problems posted on my web site as it will help you master this material, test you to see if you "really" know and understand it, etc. You can expect similar problems to be on the exam. ☺**

Judges, Courts and Their Jurisdiction

I note at the outset that the ability of any court system to function well and do justice depends on judges—and we need good, experienced and intelligent ones (especially in the business arena). Thus, before you read the below, go to the articles that I have inserted at pages 113–133 of this textbook. These articles address such important issues as ...

What are the attributes of a good judge? What makes for a good judge for **<u>business</u>** cases? What are some of the issues the legal profession is struggling with to keep our best and brightest legal minds on the bench (e.g., pay)?

You will also see that I inserted the biographies of several state court judges and one federal judge. What are their legal pedigrees? Are they impressive? Unimpressive? What are attorneys practicing before them saying about them? Relatedly, is there any difference between the legal pedigree of a state court judge vs. a federal court judge? If so, what are some of those differences?

I. Types of **<u>State</u>** Courts and Their Jurisdiction

   A. Jurisdiction

      1. What is it/what do we mean by it?

   a) It is a court's power to hear a case and issue a decision that is binding on the parties
2. The situation is that the plaintiff cannot sue the defendant in any state court he chooses. The plaintiff **must** sue in a court that has jurisdiction over the case. In other words, the court must have:
   a) Subject matter jurisdiction over the case (i.e., the power to hear the case), and, ***either of the following:***
      (1) *In personam (also known as "personal jurisdiction") over the parties in the case;* ***or***
      (2) What is called *in rem* jurisdiction over the *property* that is at the center of the case/dispute.

So ... now let's look at each of the above in greater detail ...

Subject matter jurisdiction—the court's power to decide the type of case at issue (this was already addressed above/earlier; it's also discussed below)

E.g., – a criminal court cannot hear a civil matter; $2,000,000.00 breach of contract claim cannot proceed in small claims court; a family law court would not/could not hear a probate matter, etc.

In personam (or personal) jurisdiction—is usually based on residence, location or activities of a defendant within the state (see the *Maritiz, Inc.* case and the *Cybersell* case in Chapter 3 of your textbook that is posted on Blackboard for an example of cases applying the *personal jurisdiction* concept/doctrine)

Question: But what do you do about/how does a court get/obtain personal jurisdiction over an out-of-state defendant??

That is where these things called "long-arm statutes" come into play. Such statutes often give courts *in personam (or personal)* jurisdiction over out-of-state defendants. In order for a long arm statute to apply, the out-of-state defendant must have certain "minimum contracts" with that state. E.g. -- he/she must have done business in the state, contracted to supply goods or services within state, committed a tort with state, etc.

See/refer to the example of a long arm statute that I gave in class/in your power point frames. See also the related articles at pages 135–138 of this textbook.

In rem jurisdiction—unlike *in personam* jurisdiction, this jurisdiction is based on the presence of ***property*** within the state (e.g., real estate, the probate estate of a deceased person). It allows the court to determine rights in that property even if the defendants are/reside outside of the state where the court hearing the case is located

For practice applying the jurisdiction concepts/rules noted above, see the practice problems that I have posted on Blackboard. You can expect to see similar problems on the exam

B. **State Courts of Limited Jurisdiction**

1. E.g., – ***Small Claims Courts*** (the subject matter jurisdiction to hear cases where the amount in controversy is $7,500 or less for a plaintiff individual or $5,000 or less for a plaintiff corporation) and ***Municipal Courts*** (have the subject matter jurisdiction to hear cases where the amount in controversy is $25,000 or less)
   a) Features of these courts: more informal, usually no transcript of the proceeding, faster, cheaper, parties in small claims court can argue their own cases (in fact, parties who are individuals (versus, say, a corporation, are not even allowed to have their/attorney appear and argue for them at the initial small claims hearing), etc.

C. **State Trial Courts of General Jurisdiction**

1. E.g., – ***Superior Courts*** (have the subject matter jurisdiction to hear cases involving any amount in controversy, but as a practical matter it is usually greater than $25,000)
   a) Features of these courts: not governed by limits on civil and criminal penalties that above-referenced courts are; keep detailed records of proceedings; slower, more expensive, more formal etc.

D. **State Courts of Appeal**

1. Features: decide legal questions of law and generally accept the lower trial court's findings of fact
   a) *****Note: San Luis Obispo sits/resides in the Second District Court of Appeal (which is actually located/hears cases in Ventura)**

Again, for practice applying the concepts/rules re: state courts and state court jurisdiction noted above, see the practice problems that I have posted on Blackboard. You can expect to see similar problems on the exam

II. Types of <u>**Federal**</u> Courts and Their Jurisdiction

A. **Federal District Courts (U.S. district court)** – in the federal system, the lawsuit begins here

1. Every state has at least one federal district court in it. California has four federal district courts (Northern, Southern, Central and Eastern)
   a) **Note: San Luis Obispo sits/resides in the Central District, (which is actually located/hears cases in Los Angeles)**

2. Federal District Court jurisdiction: the two (2) different bases for federal court jurisdiction are <u>(either one will suffice)</u>:
   a) **Diversity jurisdiction**—suit between citizens of different states ***<u>and</u>*** the amount in controversy exceeds $75,000
      (1) Corporation = is considered to be a citizen both where incorporated (e.g., Delaware) ***and*** the state where it has its principal place of business (e.g., such a company might have its principal place of business located in California). Thus, this has the effect of limiting the scope and reach of diversity jurisdiction.

b) **Federal question jurisdiction**—the case **"arises under"** federal law – e.g., the U.S. Constitution, a federal law/statute or a treaty of the United States (note: there is no amount in controversy requirement here)
   (1) E.g., – lawsuits which claim that a person's civil rights have been violated; violation of an EPA statute; violation of an IRS rule/regulation, etc.

B. **"Specialized" Federal Courts**
   1. Some cases are so unique and specialized that the federal government and the Constitution have designed "specialized courts" to hear them and the case <u>must</u> be filed only in that court
      a) E.g., – Claims Court (e.g., involves claims being made against the United States), International Trade Court, Tax Court, Bankruptcy Court, Patent and Copyright Disputes, etc.

C. **Federal Courts of Appeal**
   1. Hear appeals from federal district courts and state supreme courts
      a) **Here in California, we are located in the Ninth Circuit Court of Appeal (which is actually located/hears cases in San Francisco)**

Again, for practice applying the concepts/rules re: federal courts and federal court jurisdiction noted above, see the practice problems that I have posted on Blackboard. You can expect to see similar problems on the exam

D. **The United States Supreme Court**
   1. Most appeals to the U.S. Supreme Court come from federal courts of appeal and state supreme courts
   2. Case must fall within the court's ***certiorari*** jurisdiction in order to be heard. I.e., ***it is discretionary***. This means that you petition the Court to hear your case by filing what is called a ***writ of certiorari*** (from the Latin, "made more certain") and the Court can either grant your writ (and hear the case) or deny it.
      a) Only a very small percentage of cases are heard/writs are granted. At least 4 of the 9 justices of the Supreme Court must vote to hear the case/grant the writ (this is called the ***"rule of four"***). If at least 4 out of 9 do not vote to hear the case, then the writ of certiorari is denied and the lower court decision stands
   3. Also see/refer to class lecture for additional details. Be sure to also read the articles and materials that I placed in this textbook on the Supreme Court at pages 139–146. I inserted this material to help you better understand how the Supreme Court works. This material is fair game for the exam!

37 How to Judge a Judge?[1]

Always Remember that Justice Is More Important than the Law

SLO New Times

Editor's note: The following essay first appeared in New Times, and was later published by the 'Wall Street Journal,' the Texas Criminal Defense Lawyers Association, 'For the Defense,' 'Dayton Bar Briefs,' and other publications. With the race for SLO County Superior Court judge being decided on Tuesday we believe publishing it again may help readers more thoughtfully choose a candidate.

CHOOSING A JUDICIAL candidate can be confounding. How does one go about choosing a good judge? This is an important question. One that isn't asked often enough. After all, some of us—or someone we know and care about—may someday stand before a judge. That's the day we'd like to have a good one.

I have met many judges since admission to practice law, but no judge was as bad as Judge Morton of the Riverside Superior Court. Not that judge Morton was all bad. Eventually, he did everyone a favor. He died. The entire bar showed up at his funeral to make sure he was in that box.

On the opposite end of the scale, I never met a judge as good as judge Erman, one of the first justices of the peace I appeared before as a young lawyer in the California border town of Calexico.

Judge Erman, a retired mule trader, was somewhat short in his knowledge of the law. He was not very efficient and was slow in reaching his decisions. But he had a profound sense of justice and deep conviction for its need.

In addition, he had courage enough and wit enough to always bend the law in favor of justice. He had learned that to get any work out of a mule, you must you treat him with respect, not beat him to a pulp. Thus every criminal defendant in his court was always treated with at least as much respect as he would give a mule, which was considerable. Every municipal court judge I have known since ranks somewhere beneath him.

I will admit that most of the judges I've met or argued a case before have been reasonably intelligent and that only a few have been dullards. Some have even been smart enough to realize that intelligence was not the most important part of their jobs. Judges, after all, are inadequate to begin with, in need of on-the-job training. In the meantime we lawyers must try explaining their mistakes to our clients.

But enough of this. Let us remember that to be a good judge one must have 1) enough intellectual capability to reach a rational decision based on law and evidence, 2) enough wisdom to determine if this decision is also just, and 3) enough courage to reject

1 **Note from Professor Carr: Folks—In your view, what makes for a good judge? Who should we be appointing to the bench?? What types of people??**

or modify that decision to meet the requirements of justice.

I think that the main problem most people have is a failure to make the distinction between law and justice. The distinction should not be lost, or seen as quibbling over semantics.

Law, after all, is merely a bunch of rules written by the legislature; justice is based on the relationship between people and is certainly not just a bunch of rules. Anyone who cannot make this distinction should not be sitting on the bench.

Weimar Germany had many fine judges who were devoted to the enforcement of the law. When Hitler took over they continued to enforce the law without observing that it had become unjust. The horrors of the Nazi state became legal and enforced by those same fine German judges. Justice requires that no law can require you to commit an unjust act. The Germans who claimed this defense got hung.

I would say that all judges are at least intelligent enough for the job; after all, super-intelligence is too rare to be a requirement for any public office, and should not be expected in this one, either. It is character that makes a good judge.

The cynic's definition of a judge as "a lawyer who knew the governor" has enough truth in it to bear consideration. Today some are also assisted by campaign contributors, minorities, women or members of some other special interest group—and all of these characteristics are equally irrelevant to the question of justice.

Often the questions asked about a court relate only to its outward appearance, not its essential purpose, and this adds up to nothing more than efficiency, which is definitely not justice. What is being asked is how long the handle on the pump is without any thought as to the depth of the well or the amount of the water within.

One judge I've often appeared before is one of the most efficient judges I have ever seen. He carefully reads the defendant's rights, advises about counsel, and goes through the entire process so rapidly that no one untrained in law can possibly understand what he is saying. He is a hard-nose who takes pride in heavy sentences.

He honestly thinks equal sentences are fair sentences, but forgets that $100 means nothing to a man of wealth, whereas it can mean starvation to a poor working man. He sentences to jail, but accepts money in lieu of serving, so he is merely the collecting agency for the city, state and county. He is not unlike most judges today. He sells justice for a price.

Then there is the tendency to follow the popular will, a direction many judges are drawn to in their attempts to ensure their own re-election. These judges listen to the organized victims groups and do their bidding, while forgetting that it was the mob that influenced Pilate to condemn Jesus.

It may make a greater impression on today's judges if I remind them that shortly after the crucifixion, Pilate was recalled to Rome and considered unacceptable to continue as public official. Remember, too, that it was the mob that ordered the death of Socrates long before Christ, only to mourn at what it had done.

The popular will, then is to be avoided at all costs. There is no more dangerous group than a club of victims. Such practitioners of organized revenge—Mothers Against Drunk Drivers comes immediately to mind—can pervert justice even more than perjury. It always takes courage for a judge to speak up for justice instead of revenge. For it always takes courage to uphold justice against the law.

Some judges might even lose their jobs for being just. But that matters nothing at all, because it is a risk that comes with the position. For if judges are no more courageous than those they judge, they should be in the prisoner's dock instead of the bench.

38 Judicial Qualifications: A Sampling of Views

"All persons selected as judges should be of good moral character, emotionally stable and mature, physically able to discharge the duties of office, patient, courteous, and capable of deliberation and decisiveness when required to act on their own reasoned judgment." (American Bar Association)

"Judges ought to be more learned than witty, more reverend than plausible, and more advised than confident." (Francis Bacon, English philosopher)

"The trial judge ought to be neutral, detached, kindly, benign, reasonably learned in the law, firm but fair, wise, knowledgeable about human behavior, and in lesser respects as well, somewhat superhuman." (Judge Marvin Frankel)

"The more relevant things about an appointee are his breadth of vision, his imagination, his capacity for disinterested judgment, his power to discover and to suppress his prejudices." (Justice Felix Frankfurter)

"It is as important to a judge called upon to pass on a question of constitutional law, to have at least a bowing acquaintance with Acton and Maitland, with Thucydides, Gibbon, and Carlyle, with Homer, Dante, Shakespeare and Milton, with Machiavelli, Montaigne and Rabelais, with Plato, Bacon, Hume and Kant, as with the books which have been specifically written on the subject." (Judge Learned Hand)

"In the long run, there is no guarantee of justice except the personality of the judge." (Justice Benjamin Cardozo)

Sources: American Bar Association, *Standards Relating to Court Organization* (1990 ed.), Section 1.21; Francis Bacon, "Of Judicature," in Michael J. Hawkins (Ed.), *Bacon's Essays* (London: J. M. Dent & Sons. 1972), p. 162; Marvin Frankel, "The Adversary Judge: The Experience of a Trial Judge," in Mark W. Cannon and David M. O'Brien (Eds.), *Views from the Bench* (Chatham, NJ: Chatham House, 1985), p. 47; Felix Frankfurter and Learned Hand quoted in David O'Brien, *Judicial Roulette* (New York: Priority Press. 1988), p. 5; and Benjamin Cardozo, *The Nature of the Judicial Process* (New Haven, CT: Yale University Press, 1921), p. 149.

39 You Be the Judge[1]

Local Elections Are Just Around the Corner

SLO New Times

VOTING FOR JUDGE is the only way that citizens ensure themselves of a fair trial, yet most voters are reluctant to pick a candidate for judge. Most voters choose judges the way high school students race through the last five minutes of the SAT exam: filling in the blanks quickly and randomly, or not at all.

Yet the alternative—having judges assigned as political appointees—has so much more potential for corruption, that voting for judge is a downright patriotic act.

"To make a good judge, a person must have experience both in law and in life," says Don Ernst, president of the San luis Obispo County Bar Association. "It takes someone well-educated with a great knowledge of law to understand how businesses and people work. But the best judges are also wonderful human beings."

Public defender James Macguire, who has defended notorious criminals such as Rex Allan Krebs, says he looks for "a judge who is open minded and willing to listen, truly someone who doesn't pre-judge." Macguire also favors a judge who has studied the issues "so we are all up to speed and on the same page."

Seven candidates are competing for SLO Country Superior Court Judge : Terrence O'Farrel, Charles L. Carson, John A. Trice, Betty R. Sanders, Jacqueline Frederick, Walter Millar and Dale Gustin.

The most experienced candidate is Terrence O'Farrell, who has practiced both civil and criminal law for 27 years, and participated in 150 jury trials. He has tried eight murder cases, four as a prosecutor and four as a defense attorney. O'Farrell was defense counsel in the Dennis David Webb murder case (Trice, one of his opponents for judge, was prosecutor).

O'Farrell's priorities include expanding drug court to include juvenile offenders; shortening waiting time in the courts; and encouraging alternative dispute resolution.

Charles L. Carson is a civil trial lawyer, eager for new challenges. "The next judge should be a trial attorney— they work with judges on a daily basis," said Carson. "A trial lawyer is a mirror image of what a judge does; there is no better training."

1 **Note from Professor Carr: This article is from the New Times and pertains to a recent SLO County election for judge. As you read it, think to yourself "which of these candidates have the best/most BUSINESS AND COMMERCIAL LAW EXPERIENCE?" I think that you will see that many of them (but not all) do not have such experience. This in turn impacts you as a business person. I.e., public defenders and district attorneys may be wonderful/perfect judges for criminal cases, but not necessarily for business cases. Also, ask yourself ... which of these folks are likely to be elected by the voters? If you guessed the prosecutors/district attorneys, you guessed right! But again, does that help you/is that a good thing for business cases?**

Carson's priorities are to improve public access to affordable legal service; provide the public with more education to reduce substance abuse; and maintain community service with a strong law and order program.

According to Carson, the next judge should also be a civil lawyer. Conveniently, that would eliminate Deputy District Attorney John A. Trice from the race. Trice is famous for going after the most egregious criminals in SLO County, such as Krebs and Webb, and asking for and winning death penalty convictions. He is also known for winning a second degree murder conviction of the drunken driver who killed four-year-old Andrea Harris. (There have been live drunken driving murder prosecutions in the history of SLO County and Trice has tried two of those cases.)

Trice is also a Lieutenant Colonel in the Air Force reserve. As a military Judge Advocate General, he handled environmental, personal injury and labor law cases.

His priorities follow a law and order line: increasing security in the courthouse; saving the county money by employing a multi-departmental approach to probation cases; and modifying public defender programs to guarantee that only the needy receive free legal services.

Betty R. Sanders says that unfortunately lack of money is the greatest threat to a citizen's right to a fair trial. Her priority is "making the legal system fair and accessible to all by encouraging the use of alternative dispute resolution."

Sanders went to law school at night while working as a registered nurse, and then worked in a general law practice for 22 years.

She has handled every type of case, except criminal. Recently, she has specialized in elder law.[2]

Elder law has a gentle sound to it, but that can be deceptive as Sanders discovered at the hands of an infuriated plaintiff who found himself at the losing end of a contested will defended by Sanders. To get back at Sanders, the plaintiff secreted libelous fliers into circulated copies of the Feb. 21 issue of *New Times.*

Just as she confronts tough cases, Sanders also deals head-on with the gender issue. "It's no secret that SLO County is behind the curve when it comes to gender on the bench."

Only one other woman is running for judge. Jacqueline Frederick claims in her ballot statement that she is the "most experienced trial lawyer in the race," although she has no criminal prosecution or defense experience, and her civil practice has been limited to product liability malpractice, negligence, real estate, land use and environmental law. She has handled only 40 cases[3] in her career—although in the legal arena, where cases can go on for years, numbers may be misleading. When asked how she can claim to be the most experienced of the candidates, she points to the "complexity of the cases" she's handled.

"I have a passion for law and a passion for helping people, "Frederick says, describing her law career as one that has focused on victims. "In my 18 years of practicing law, I've observed an increased cynicism in people toward the legal system." Frederick vows to change that.

Frederick, who sits on the Nipomo Advisory Council, is known for her efforts in creating "Olde Town Nipomo." In her community work, she believes that she is forthright in hearing others' concerns, and letting them know the basis for her decisions.

Frederick listed her priorities as, "access of the courts to the public, insuring that truth and justice are paramount the courtroom; and making sure the law is administered with integrity."

Walter Millar spent a decade as a San Diego City police officer. He was "seduced by the law," as a result of night school classes he attended in order to

2 Note from Professor Carr: A pretty obscure area of the law, wouldn't you say?

3 Note from Professor Carr: After 40 cases, is she/can she be "old and wise" enough to be a good judge?

make himself a better officer. "I found it intriguing," he says. Most of his law career focused on product liability cases involving multiple deaths.

He says that he would bring to the bench an understanding of people, and an ability to be fair and impartial. His priorities are to be effective and efficient, and to respect the public service of citizens serving jury duty. He is a member of the San Luis Coastal Unified School District Board, a position he would have to relinquish should he win the race for judge.

The only candidate who is certified to serve in the juvenile court is Dale Gustin, a former blue-collar worker. He has practiced law since 1979, handling a variety of both criminal and civil cases.

He says he had to miss one candidate forum because he went to Long Beach to rescue a minority family that had been "kicked out of their home by the [Long Beach] district attorney due to an illegal foreclosure." Like Carson, Gustin would like to start a series of lectures and seminars to educate the public about the courts. "We have the best [legal] system in the world," he says, "but I don't think that average people think so."

At a recent debate hosted by the SLO County Bar Association, a questioner from the audience asked each candidate to choose one word—just one —that captures an essential quality of a good judge.

Sanders objected to being boxed in by such a question, but complied by answering: patience. Down the line, they responded. Gustin: compassion; O'Farrell: fair and impartial; Carson: experience; Trice: common sense; Frederick: understanding and working cooperatively with all people of all races and economic groups.

No one said succinct.

40 Judicial Salaries: Making Less Than New Lawyers[1]

The National Law Journal

IN FEBRUARY 2000, AS starting salaries of associates at major law firms rocketed to as much as $160,000, Judge Michael Luttig of the U.S. Court of Appeals for the 4th Circuit wrote a tongue-in-cheek letter to a friend at a prominent D.C. law firm, seeking a job there as a first-year lawyer.

Judge Luttig touted his experience as a former assistant attorney general for justices Antonin Scalia and Warren Burger. And, for good measure, he included "opinions that [he had] authored over the past nine years" as writing samples. The firm's rejection letter—likewise tongue-in-cheek–found Judge Luttig overqualified. The firm added that, while it had adopted a "casual Friday" policy, "black robes do not qualify as appropriate attire."

But underneath the humor lay a serious point. A recent study by the Federal Bar and the American Bar Associations demonstrates that federal judges are underpaid, by any reasonable measure. They are underpaid historically, based on what they used to earn; comparatively, based on what other lawyers make; and equitably, based on the value and importance of their work. And they are underpaid functionally, based on the compelling need to attract a diversity of talented lawyers to the bench.

Most judges took substantial pay cuts to join the bench, and had every right to expect—at a minimum—that the reduced salary they accepted would not diminish over time. But those expectations have been dashed. With only three modest cost-of-living adjustments since 1993, inflation has ravaged judicial salaries.

Judges have suffered a 13.4% decline in purchasing power during that period alone. Moreover, since 1969 court of appeals and district court judges have experienced a 24.6% loss in purchasing power, while Supreme Court justices have lost 38.3%.

In short, the salaries of federal judges are effectively much lower today than 30 years ago. And judges fear—not unreasonably—that their salaries will continue to decline.

Even as judicial salaries have dropped in real terms, lawyers earnings in the private sector have surged. As Chief justice William H. Rehnquist pointed out in his recent Year-End Report, "Many judicial law clerks, who work for federal judges for one or two years immediately after graduating from law school, leave their clerkships to work for top firms in big cities and immediately make as much as the judges for whom they clerked." And the judges' peers—senior partners in top law firms—often make at least three times a judge's salary.

1 **Note from Professor Carr: This article does a nice job of highlighting how desperately we/the business community need good judges, but, how hard it is to get/keep them on the bench due to salary issues.**

Opportunity costs

The concern here is not that federal judges are impoverished. And, of course there are other, nonmonetary rewards for public service—prestige, authority, professional satisfaction. But we cannot ignore what economists term "opportunity costs." As Nobel economist Paul Samuelson puts it, "opportunity cost is the value of the good or service foregone." For example, the out-of-pocket cost of a year at the University of Maryland is perhaps $13,000. But the opportunity cost of that year would include the additional $15,000–$20,000 that the student could have earned by working a full-time job instead.

Similarly, in analyzing judicial compensation, we should consider not only what judges are paid, but also the opportunities they forego—what they could earn in the private sector. In that light, those black robes cost a great deal indeed. Judges forego potentially hundreds of thousands of dollars a year for the rewards of public service.

Moreover, what we pay people reflects—or should reflect—the social value of what they do, their contribution to the public good. We expect our federal judges to decide the most difficult questions in our society: the right to die or to have an abortion, the role of religion, the scope of federal regulation, even the outcome of our elections. We expect judges to deal with mergers, globalization, emerging technologies and intellectual property disputes. We expect them to shoulder crushing caseloads. And we expect them to do so for life. Judges' compensation is out of kilter with these expectations.

We could lament the implicit social judgment that the skills of a first-year lawyer are worth more than those of our most distinguished jurists. But the more urgent matter is the practical consequence of these economic facts of life. We can ask people to sacrifice for public service, but only to a degree. The laws of economics are relentless. They teach that such a chasm in earnings between the public and private sectors inevitably will divert the best and the brightest from the bench.

Already we are witnessing an exodus from the bench—more than 50 judges left in the last decade alone, compared to only five in the 1960s. And according to the new FBA/ABA report, officials responsible for recruiting candidates for judgeships confirm that salaries are "the single most important factor discouraging potential candidates from seeking appointment."

Quality of the bench will suffer

To be sure, some gifted lawyers still will choose the bench as a career, despite the pay. Some will do so because they do not need the money. Others will simply make the sacrifice for public service. But all in all, the quality and the diversity of the federal bench will suffer. Our courts will be deprived of knowledge and experience that should inform the application of the law. And, in the end, society will pay a price.

No one suggests that federal judges should earn what senior partners at top law firms make. But judges deserve fair compensation. Congress' recent increase in the president's salary—doubling it to $400,000 a year—opens the door. Congress and the administration have a unique opportunity to arrest the downward spiral of pay erosion, and to enact comprehensive, long overdue salary reforms.

At a minimum, Congress should pass the Federal Judicial Fairness Act of 2001 (introduced by Congresswoman Judy Biggert, R-Ill.), which would give judges a "catch-up" pay raise of 9.6% (to restore the cost-of-living adjustment denied over the past eight years) and guarantee them annual cost-of-living adjustments in the future.

We can afford no less.

41 Elderly Judges Handle 20% of U.S. Caseload

The Wall Street Journal

HIS PIERCING BLUE eyes are rimmed with a bit of red. He wears headphones in court to amplify the sound, and he doesn't call lawyers late at night anymore.

But Milton Pollack, a federal judge who turned 95 last month, is still putting in 50-hour weeks, seeking out complicated securities cases and relishing his role in settling some of the biggest fraud cases in Wall Street history.

As for anyone who thinks he might be a little old for such an intellectually rigorous job, he says: "They don't know what they're talking about."

Judge Pollock, who sits in Manhattan, is one of a growing number of older federal judges who are keeping the judicial system afloat by continuing to work in "senior status" instead of retiring at age 65. Nearly 40% of the nation's more than 1,200 working federal judges are on senior status. Court officials say they are crucial to the justice system, as Congress has held up judicial nomination and caseloads have grown faster than the number of judgeships. These senior judges handle nearly 20% of the federal judiciary's work.

Critics question whether these judges can stay fresh. "It's a dinosaur graveyard," says Larry Klayman, chairman of Judicial Watch, a conservative group. He says older judges should be required to take competency tests or face a mandatory retirement age.

Marilyn Huff, chief district judge in San Diego, says competency tests for senior judges are unnecessary, because chief judges monitor senior judges' performance. "I don't know what we'd do without our senior judges," she says.

In Manhattan, they've never been more needed. Judge Pollack was in Houston when the World Trade Center collapsed and couldn't get back until Sept.18. But ever since, he's been in the thick of efforts to get the federal courthouse up and running. "This is salvage work to keep this leaky ship afloat," Judge Pollack says.

The courthouse, a 10-minute walk from the Trade Center site, still has only limited phone service. Security is extremely tight: The building is the site of numerous terrorist trials over the past decade, including one earlier this year in which four associates of Osama bin Laden were convicted in connection with the 1998 bombings of U.S. embassies in Africa.

Senior judges often handle reduced caseloads, but they still receive full pay. They say they are in essence donating their services because they receive full salaries for life, even if they decide to retire. Senior judges who maintain one-quarter of the average workload of active judges in their district are eligible for in [...]

Max Rosenn, a 91-year-old appellate judge in Philadelphia, still works nights and weekends. In Wichita, Kan., U.S. District Judge Wesley Brown, 94, eats lunch at his desk and handles three quarters of a full caseload. "I feel like I was appointed for life or good behavior, whichever I lose first." He says.

"It's gratifying to have something to look forward to every day."

Judge Pollack echoes the thought. "Having a daily occupation keeps me alive, and I have no plans to leave," he says, although he has stopped golfing and admits he can't read as much at a stretch as he used to.

Still, last summer, Judge Pollack jumped into the debate over a new type of securities suit: class action brought by investor against brokerage firms and analysts that hype stocks that later tank and who failed to disclose alleged conflicts of interest.

Judge Pollack sharply dismissed shareholder suits against Morgan Stanley and analyst Mary Meeker only three weeks after they were filed, writing that they contained "a collection of market gossip" that was hopelessly redundant, argumentative ... and to say the least in grossly bad taste." He gave plaintiffs' lawyer Fred Isquith 30 days to refile his case. Mr. Isquith says he was stunned: The defense hadn't even filed a motion to dismiss the suit. "I've never seen anything like it," Mr. Isquith says. "It came out of the blue." [...]

The son of Russian immigrants, Judge Pollack joined the bar just before the 1929 stock-market crash and was soon representing shareholders as trial counsel in lawsuits against brokerage firms and banks. By the late 1930s he was immersed in litigation stemming from investigations by the newly created Securities and Exchange Commission.

In the years since his appointment to the federal bench in 1967, and especially since he assumed senior status in 1983, Judge Pollack has played a leading role in some of Wall Street's biggest courtroom dramas. Pushing the lawyers with a barrage of late-night phone calls and faxes, he was largely responsible for the $1.3 billion global settlement of civil litigation against former junk-bond king Michael Milken and other former Drexel Burnham Lambert employees in 1992, as well as the deal a year earlier that allowed Drexel to emerge from bankruptcy proceedings.

At Drexel's request, Judge Pollack took over the bankruptcy case and, one afternoon, ordered the lawyers to go back to the jury room and come out with an agreement to divide up Drexel's assets. They emerged the same day with a signed yellow piece of paper that hangs framed in Judge Pollack's office. "That was a career achievement," says Michael Mukasey, Manhattan's chief federal district judge, adding that the case could have dragged on for years.

Judge Pollack still volunteers to hear cases, even if they don't involve high-profile defendants. A few months ago, he asked Judge Mukasey if he could take over a stock-fraud case that the chief judge was too busy to try. "In essence, he said, 'Give it to me and it will go away.'"[1]

1 Note from Professor Carr: Wouldn't one think that we would WANT to keep our older/wiser judges on the bench—especially if they are working hard like these judges are doing? Now, the counter-argument is that older judges can't keep up with the new developments of the day (e.g., technology issues)—but do you buy that? Aren't they bright enough people to get up to speed and handle such issues??

42 California Courts and Judges

By Deborah Bogen

[STATE COURT JUDGES][1]

BURKE, Earle Jeffrey
JUDGE, SUPERIOR COURT, San Luis Obispo County

Appointment/Election: Appointed by Governor Wilson May 27, 1997 (oath same day). Presiding Judge, 2000.

Other Judicial Office: Assistant Presiding Judge, 1999; Presiding Judge, Appellate Division, 1997–99.

Past Employment: Attorney, Burke, Smith, Helenias & Hayes, San Luis Obispo, Calif., 1968–97.

Memberships/Awards: Calif. Judges Assn., 1997—; American Board of Trial Advocates, 1980—; Court Executive Committee, 1999— (Chair, 2000); Civil Team Leader, 1999–2000; Team Leader, Civil Direct Calendar Program Design; Mediation Program Design; and Strategic Planning Committee. Former member: Association of Trial Lawyers of America; Calif. Trial Lawyers Assn.; Calif. Bar Assn.; American Bar Assn.

Teaching/Lectures/Panelist: Faculty, B.E. Witkin Judicial College, 1999—; C.J.S.P., Summer 1999, Winter 1999, Jan. 2000, Aug. 2000.

Publications: "Mediation Basics," CJER Aug. 2000.

Education: J.D. (1965) Stanford School of Law; B.A. (1962) Claremont McKenna College.

Born: Aug. 19, 1940; Atlanta, Georgia; Married. Two children.

Admission: Admitted to Calif. Bar Jan. 5, 1965: U.S. District Court. Southern and Northern Districts of Calif. Jan. 5. 1965: U.S. Court of Claims.

Office Address: County Government Center
Room 355 San Luis Obispo,
CA 93408

Office Phone: (805) 781-6421;
FAX. (805) 781-1071

PICQUET, Roger Thomas
JUDGE, SUPERIOR COURT, San Luis Obispo County

Appointment/Election: Succeeded to court upon unanimous written consent of judges in county [pursuant to Prop. 220] to convert Municipal Courts to Superior Courts, effective July 1, 1998.

Other Judicial Office: Judge, Municipal Court, San Luis Obispo County, appointed [succeeding Judge Michael L. Duffy, elevated] by Governor

1 **Note from Professor Carr: As of Fall 2008 these were two of our local SLO County Judges. Maybe you will see one of them in action if/when you went to our local courthouse to see the action.**

Wilson Oct.. 28, 1993 (oath Dec. 4, 1993), and elected June 7, 1994 (unopposed) to a 6-year term commencing Jan. 2, 1995.

Past Employment: Private law practice (with emphasis on municipal, land use, environmental and public agency law), San Luis Obispo, 1989–93 (sole practitioner, 1993; and partner, Lyon & Picquet, 1989–93). City Attorney: Paso Robles (1989–93) and Grover Beach (1989–93); City Attorney, San Luis Obispo, 1983–89. Served as Deputy and Assistant City Attorney, Modesto, Calif., 1978–83.

Memberships/Awards: Member: Calif. Judges Assn., 1993– Former member: San Luis Obispo County Bar Assn., 1983–93 (Vice President, 1993; Secretary, 1992; Chair. Legislative Committee, 1987); City of San Luis Obispo County Park and Recreation Commission. 1991–93; and Board of Directors, San Luis Obispo Children's Museum, 1990–93. Chair, Central Coast Public Counsel Association, 1985–91. Chair, City of San Luis Obispo Campaign Regulations Committee, 1989.

Military Experience: Served from Ensign to Commander, U.S. Navy (1969–74; Western & Southern Pacific) and U.S. Naval Reserve (1974–92). Recipient Naval Achievement Medal and Vietnam Service Medal. Surface Warfare Officer qualified.

Education: J.D. (1977), Hastings College of the Law, San Francisco, Calif.; B.A. (1969, History), Univ. of Calif., Berkeley. Attended Univ. of Missouri, Columbia, Sept. 1965 to June 1966; Graduate (1965), Cupertino High School, Cupertino, Calif.

Born: Sept. 18, 1947; St. Louis, Missouri; Married, Sharon Dvorak (Dental Hygienist). Three children.

Interests: Enjoys playing squash and basketball, skydiving, reading, and vexillology.

Admission: Admitted to Calif. Bar and to U.S. Dist. Court. Northern Dist. of Calif., Dec. 21, 1977; to U.S. Supreme Court Jan. 19, 1981; to U.S. Dist. Court Eastern Dist. of Calif., Nov. 23. 1981; to U.S. Dist. Court Central Dist. of Calif., March 16. 1988; and to U.S. Court of Military Appeals. April 4, 1989.

Political Affiliation/Religion: Catholic

Office Address: County Government Center
1050 Monterey Street
San Luis Obispo, CA
93408-2510

Office Phone: (805)781-5936

[ORANGE COUNTY SUPERIOR COURT JUDGE; STATE COURT]

HUNT, Derek W.[2]

JUDGE, SUPERIOR COURT, Orange County

Appointment/Election: Appointed [succceding Judge James Smith, retired] by Governor Wilson (oath Aug. 4, 1997).

Past Employment: Private law practice: Partner: Troy & Gould, Professional Corp., Los Angeles, Calif., 1981–97; Stradling, Yocca. Carlson & Rauth, Newport Beach, Calif., 1980; Troy, Majin & Pottinger, Professional Corp., Los Angeles, Calif., 1977–80; Associate. Mitchell, Silberberg & Knupp, L.A., 1972–77.

Memberships/Awards: Member. Assn. of Business Trial Lawyers, Los Angeles, Calif., 1973–1997; Complex Litigation Inn of Court, Los Angeles, 1992-97.

Education: J.D. (1972). Cornell Univ. Law School. Ithaca, N.Y. (Law Review); BA. (1965). Cornell Univ., Ithaca. N.Y.

Military: U.S. Army, 1967–69; Initial rank: 2nd Lieutenant. Final rank: 1st Lieutenant.

Born: June 15, 1943 in Washington, D.C.; Married. Two children.

Admission: Admitted to the State Bar of Calif., Dec. 1972; U.S. Court of Appeal, Ninth Circuit Dec. 1972; U.S. District Court, Central District of Calif., Dec. 1972; U.S. District Court, Northern

2 Note from Professor Carr: Note the attorney comments about this judge on the next page.

District of Calif., 1992; and U.S. District Court, Southern District of Calif., 1993.

Political Affiliation/Religion: Republican; Roman Catholic

Office Address: Department 9
700 Civic Center Drive West
P.O. Box 1994
Santa Ana, CA 92702-1994

Office Phone: (714) 834-3755

Ex Parte Hours: 1:30–4:30 p.m., Mon. through Fri.

ATTORNEYS' COMMENTS

Temperament/Demeanor

The comments collected about this judge's demeanor were not overly complimentary. Most people were put off by him. "He's been around for a couple of years now and I haven't heard a kind word about him yet." "I personally didn't enjoy my experience with him." "He can be mean and condescending to counsel." "He's an interesting guy. He's opinionated." When asked if Judge Hunt has ever lost his temper in the courtroom, one litigator replied. "Yes, but not in the sense that he'll raise his voice. He'll just get very abrupt." "He is a bit abrasive, but I can't say that it's always uncalled for. He'll let you know when he doesn't like something."

When asked if this judge's court would be a suitable place for a new attorney, answers were decidedly negative. "He's no picnic." "No way! Not unless you want to pay for therapy afterward." "No. It would be a disaster."

Intelligence /Knowledge

Most people opined that Judge Hunt is intelligent, but does not seem to have a real-world air about him. "He's smart." "He is a philosophy major [sic]." "Yes, he's intelligent. I'm sure he is." "He remembers everything. He'll let you know if you told him something different ten months ago." "I don't think he's unintelligent. The fact that he thinks he's more intelligent than he is, it clouds his thinking." "1 don't believe he was a trial lawyer, because he didn't have an understanding of what it's like to be an everyday trial lawyer dealing with scheduling, experts, problems with discovery. He seemed to be close-minded early in his judgeship. I remember when we were all sitting in there, and people were coming up to me and saying. 'Who is this guy?'"

Opinions about his accomplishment with legal scholarship were not glowing, but some interviewees credited him with being willing to look things up and to make tough decisions. "He made a very, very tough ruling. My client's accountant had essentially confessed that the plaintiff's view of the case was right and that they should be given money. I moved to exclude that on the grounds that it was opinion and prejudicial, and he granted it." "He reads everything and he'll learn it. Others don't know it, don't read it, don't care." "Some of the rulings he made were unfounded. I don't think he understood the issues. It was a complicated medical malpractice and you have to learn that." "I think his practice was too narrow before he took the bench, and now he's handling civil stuff and he really doesn't know the law that well. I heard he was antitrust and securities." "Malpractice he doesn't know."

On Motions

Attorneys were generally satisfied with the way Judge Hunt moves through his calendar, and most credited him with being eager to greet the day. "He's efficient. He seems to be prepared." "Reads the papers and understands them." "He said that he reads every word presented to him." "Oh, for sure." "Yes. That's his strong point. He's exceptional among the judges in terms of reading the papers and remembering the issues and facts. I was amazed. Our case was pretty complex, with all kinds of motions in limine and what not, and he would go through law and motion and decide a half dozen cases on obscure issues and get back to us and remember the arguments and the law and the facts on our motion. Tremendous memory."

He is known to be punctual and to expect the same from others. "He won't yell at you in front of the jury, but he will in front of other attorneys."

During the hearing itself, he is said to have a somewhat limited tolerance for oral argument, and a limited willingness to be persuaded. "No more or less than anyone else." "He will let counsel go for a while, and then he'll politely cut them off." "He'd listen too long initially, but he's changed now." "He tends to cut people off, in a way that is consistent with someone who is intelligent but only half as intelligent as he thinks he is. He's arrogant." "He will find issues that nobody briefs and nobody ever thought about which drives the lawyers up a wall because they haven't had a chance to address it or think about it or brief it." "He has something on the bench that looks like a big windwing. It looks like a folding desk of some sort and he'll raise it like a drawbridge and sometimes you can't see him during oral argument." "He can be persuaded, but it's not likely." "He's much like the others. It's rare that you can change his mind. He'll play devil's advocate. It would seem like you're having an open discussion with him, but he was just exploring different ideas and he had already made up his mind. If he had heard something he hadn't thought about,though, he might change his mind."

On Trial

Interviewees expressed mixed reactions when asked if they would readily keep this judge for trial, with the majority saying they would. "The problem is that you have to look at the alternatives, and there is the potential for someone worse. So, would I bump him? Probably not but he's not my first choice." "No, but there are worse." "1 wanted him for trial but the case settled." "I'm still waiting for the first kind word about him." "Only if I had to." "I would keep him for trial." "I did. I lost. I'd do it again." "I tried a case in front of him recently and he let's you try the case. He's pretty good on evidence, although ninety percent of the rulings go the way you would expect. But once in a while an oddball ruling comes along, a clinker, and leaves everyone scratching their heads." "He was a real disappointment because he was billed as a litigator and all of us trial lawyers were hoping we'd finally get litigator, but ..."

Continuances

Only complaints were registered on Judge Hunt's flexibility with respect to continuing proceedings. "He doesn't have a good grasp of running a civil calendar." "He's obsessed with sticking to the Fast Track and he shows little tolerance for schedule changes. He doesn't seem to get it that there are certain situations that do vary from the 'try it within a year' model. He's not sympathetic."

Settlement

The majority of respondents didn't have a favorable impression of this judge's facility of settlement negotiations. "He doesn't make much of an effort. I get the impression that he thinks everybody is a big boy and if we could have settled it we would have. In my case, it was true." "We took everything outside. We knew he wouldn't put the time into them. I wouldn't be too comfortable about talking confidentially to him because it wouldn't settle and then you'd have him for trial and he might look at you differently." "He's good at settlement. He facilitated a settlement for me."

Proclivities

There was general agreement that this jurist is considered to favor the defense. "He's pretty conservative." "Fundamentally conservative." "He has a defense leaning. I wouldn't call it a bias." "I get the impression he's very, very conservative, consistent with a defense corporate interest." "I think he's very conservative on the one hand, but on the other hand, he even told me on my case that he would grant an MSJ."

Summary

There was one warning: "Don't be late. When the plaintiffs attorney was late for the third time. Hunt said that if the guy didn't show up in fifteen minutes, he was going to dismiss the case. He'll put it on the record that you showed up late."

Some attorneys had general advice: "Speak up. He's deaf in one of his ears." "Have good posture. Be polite." "He is a freak about Alexander the Great.

If you want to impress him, mention Bicephalous (the horse)." "I believe he's prior military." "He likes to wear bowties." And every interviewee, without exception, warned: "Do not put your hands in your pockets, ever." When asked about the staff, most said, "They're all very nice."

[MARIN COUNTY SUPERIOR COURT JUDGE; STATE COURT]

TAYLOR, Lynn O'Malley[3]
JUDGE, SUPERIOR COURT, Marin County

Appointment/Election: Elected [succeeding Judge Henry J. Broderick. retired] Nov. 6, 1990 for term commencing Jan. 7, 1991, and reelected in 1996 for term commencing Jan. 1997.

Other Judicial Office: Judge, Municipal Court, Marin County Municipal Court [formerly Marin County, and before that Central] Judicial District. Marin County, Jan. 3, 1983 (effective date) to Jan. 7. 1991, elected [defeating Judge Robert A. Smallman] Nov. 2, 1982, and reelected in 1988. Presiding Judge, 1990 and 1986.

Past Employment: Private law practice (general civil practice), San Rafael, Calif., 1973–83 (sole practitioner; also in association with Law Offices of Norbert C. Babin, 1981–83: and with Law Offices of James M. Kennedy, 1974–81); Teacher: Grace Cathedral School for Boys, San Francisco, 1966–70; Richmond Unified School District, Richmond, Calif., Jan. Sept. 1966; and All Saint's Day School, Phoenix, Arizona, 1964–66.

Memberships/Awards: Member: Calif. Judges Assn., 1983 (Chair, Judicial Elections Committee, 1988 and 1987; member, Annual Meeting Seminar Committee, 1985; Civil Subcommittee); Judicial Council Task Force on Jury Instructions; The Mediation Society, 1999; Law and Economics Institute for State Judges, 1999; Terra Linda Rotary Club, 1987—; American Assn. of University Women, Marin County, 1978—; Board of Directors, Marin Property Owners (1978–94; President, 1980); Board of Directors, Marin Forum (1987–92; President, 1990–91), all in San Rafael: Board of Directors, Marin Council, Boy Scouts of America, 1983— (Vice President, Exploring, 1987–88); Marin Symphony Board of Directors, 1996—; Timothy Murphy School Board of Directors, 1996, 1997; Board of Directors, Marin Ballet, 1998, 1999. Former member, Marin County Criminal Justice Advisory Committee; National Assn. of Women Judges; Wednesday Morning Dialogue, 1982–87; National Woman's Political Caucus (honorary member); Calif. Women Lawyers; North Bay Women Lawyers; Selection Committee Marin Education Foundation, 1983–86; Marin County Bar Assn., 1972–82 (Secretary, 1982; Treasurer, 1981; Board of Directors, 1976–78; Delegate to State Bar Convention, 1981, 1979, 1976); and Marinwood Assn., Marinwood, Calif. (President and Secretary, 1977).

Teaching/Lectures/Panelist: Participant, CEB programs: "Developing Your Basic Trial Skills," 1991 and 1989; and Introduction to Municipal Court Practice, 1984. Faculty: Calif. Judicial College (CJER), Berkeley, 1987, 1988, 1995, and 1996; (CJER) Mediation Ethics, 2000; Hastings College of the Law Trial Advocacy Program, 1985—; Stanford Univ. Advocacy Skills Workshop, 1994—; U.S.F. Advocacy Skills Workshop, 1996—. Instructor: Dominican College (paralegal and business departments), San Rafael, 1977–81 (Business Law; Family Law; Evidence); and San Francisco City College, San Francisco, Calif., 1978–79 (Real Estate Law).

Education: Harvard Mediation Workshop, 1999; Harvard Advanced Mediation Worshop, 2000; J.D. (June 1972), San Francisco Law School, San Francisco, Calif.; B.A. (Aug. 1964, cum laude), Univ. of Arizona, Tucson (Phi Lamda Theta, honorary educational society); Attended Colorado College, Colorado Springs, Colorado, 1961–63;

---

3 Note from Professor Carr: Again, note the comment about this judge after her bio.

Graduate: Central High School (1961) and Madison School No. 1 (1957), both in Phoenix, Arizona.

Born: Nov. 6, 1943; Los Angeles, Calif.; Married. Three children.

Interests: Enjoys photography, water skiing, snow skiing, ballet and gardening.

Admission: Admitted to Calif. Bar, to U.S. Court of Appeals, Ninth Circuit, and to U.S. Dist. Court, Northern Dist. of Calif., Dec. 13, 1972.

Political Affiliation/Religion: Democrat; Episcopalian (Vestry member, Church of Nativity, 1979–81).

Office Address: Marin County Hall of Justice
Dept. 3
3501 Civic Center Drive
San Rafael, CA 94903.

Office Phone: (415) 499-6086

ATTORNEYS' COMMENTS

Temperament/ Demeanor

Judge Taylor is considered to be very personable and compassionate. "She is the most compassionate judge on the bench." "She is the sweetest, most lovely person." "She makes you feel welcome in her courtroom." "She is very social and civil to everyone." She exudes a "regular people type of comfortability." "She is very fair with propers." However, a few attorneys had contrary opinions. "She always stands which gives her a weird supercilious manner." "I don't like her."

Intelligence/Knowledge

Although she is well liked by most of the interviewed attorneys, her intelligence did not garner her high praise. "She is not very smart." "She is not an outstanding scholar." "She is not savvy on the law." "She is very insecure about what she does not know—which is a lot."

On Motions

Most attorneys believe that Judge Taylor's research attorneys read the majority of the motions presented and recommend the rulings. As a consequence, this judge rarely strays from her tentative rulings and many attorneys do not like going to her courtroom. "Oral argument is useless." "She does not change her mind on tentative rulings." "She had not read the papers."

A few attorneys commented that this judge's rulings appear well reasoned and timely. "She is very careful in her rulings." Most others opined, though, that her greatest fault is her unpredictability and indecisiveness on determinative issues. "She deliberately held off ruling on a summary judgment motion pending a settlement conference." "Cases have been known to settle with motions still pending before her."

On Trial

Many interviewees reported that they automatically challenge this judge for trial due to her unpredictability and tenuous grasp of the law. "She is not a good assignment for a court trial or for a complex case." "She sometimes make incorrect evidentiary rulings." "She does not understand the business records exception to the hearsay rule." Others did not agree and submitted that they think she is a good assignment for trial. "She is a good, practical judge."

It was reported by several respondents that she type notes in her computer during trial and has been known to stand throughout the proceedings due to a back problem.

Continuances

Judge Taylor is known to be a stickler for Fast Track rules and procedures. "She takes Fast Track seriously and will send the case to trial within one year of filing the Complaint." "She is chained to the Trial Delay Reduction Act and will mechanically set cases for trial without regard to the issues in the case." One attorney reported that Judge Taylor scheduled a trial date even though the defendant had not yet answered the Complaint.

Settlement

Judge Taylor is known to take an active role in settlement. Some attorneys complained, though, that her conduct was inappropriate and even judicially improper in their settlement conferences. "She screams and yells." "She threatened to hold me in contempt if my client did not reduce his settlement demand." Others reported finding her involvement to be helpful. "She made insightful comments that were right on the issue." "She is a terrific settlement judge."

Proclivities

It was mentioned that before assuming the bench, Judge Taylor practiced in Marin County as a defense attorney. Despite this background, most of the interviewed attorneys consider her to be plaintiff oriented.

One interviewee also reported encountering a possible phobia about bugs and rodents, noting that she has ruled vociferously against landlords in any case involving bugs and rats. It was also mentioned that she seems very concerned about her health and was once seen spraying a chair recently occupied by an attorney who was ill.

Summary

Opinions regarding this jurist varied from one extreme to the other. Although personally well liked, many consider her to be unpredictable in her rulings. Others said they believe that her reputation has suffered from ill-founded rumors. Be mindful of the Fast Track calendar.

[FEDERAL JUDGES]

NELSON, Dorothy Wright[4]

Senior Judge, United States Court Of Appeals, Ninth Circuit

Appointment/ Election: Assumed Senior Judge status Jan.1, 1995.

Other Judicial Office: Circuit Judge, same court. Nominated to Ninth Circuit by President Carter Sept. 28, 1979, confirmed by U.S. Senate Dec. 19, 1979, commission issued, and oath Feb. 1, 1980.

Past Employment: Private law practice, Los Angeles. Calif., 1954–80 (sole practitioner). Dean (1969–80), Interim Dean (1967–69), Professor (1967), Associate Professor (1961–67), Assistant Professor (1958–61), and Instructor (1957–58), Univ. of Southern Calif. Law Center, Los Angeles, (taught Judicial Administration, Wills, Trusts, and Legal Process).

Memberships/Awards: Member: American Law Institute; American Judicature Society (Vice President 1977–79; Board of Directors, 1972— (Chair, 1979–81): Executive Committee, 1976—; Research Advisory Committee, 1974—; and Editorial Advisory Board, Judicature, 1974—); American Bar Assn. (Chair, Committee on Education in Judicial Administration, 1972; member, Committee on Resolutions, 1973, and sections on Judicial Administration and Family Law); Board of Directors, ANISA, 1972—: Assn. of American Law Schools (Committee on Education in Judicial Administration, 1973–80 (Chair, 1976–80); and Nominating and Program Committees, 1972); The Supreme Court Historical Society, 1976—;. National Assn. of Public Administration, 1976—; Board of Directors, Council on Legal Education for Professional Responsibility Inc. (subsidiary of Ford Foundation), 1971—; Board of Directors, Constitutional Rights Foundation, 1971—; World Assn. of Lawyers, World Peace Through Law Center; Los Angeles County Bar Assn. (Chair, Subcommittee on Community Mediation, 1976–79; member, Committee on Economical Litigation, 1975–80; and Nominating Committee, 1979); Los Angeles Women Lawyers' Assn.; Los Angeles World Affairs Council; Legion Lex (USC support group); Town Hall; USC Alumni Assn.; and UCLA Law Alumni Assn. Board of Visitors, University of Chicago Law School, 1987–90, 1996—; Board of Advisors, Institute for the Study of Women and Men, 1987—; National Assn of Women Judges, 1987— (member, International Outreach Committee, 1998—); Chairman, Board of Directors, Western Justice Center Foundation,

4 **Note from Professor Carr: One of our FEDERAL court judges—see any difference between her qualifications/experience/legal pedigree in comparison to the state court judges you just read about?** ☺

Inc., 1987—; Advisory Committee, National Judicial Education Program to Promote Equality for Men and Women, 1988—; Advisory Board, World Law Institute, 1997—; Advisory Board, Tahirih Justice Institute to Assist Women Refugees; Chair, 9th Cir. Standing Committee on ADR, 1998—. Fellow: American Bar Foundation; and Hazen Foundation, 1977—. Lustman Fellow, Yale Univ., 1977—. Master of the Bench, Legion Lex American Inn of Court.

Former member: Calif. Judicial Council's Select Committee to Expedite the Calif. Supreme Court Workload (1987–88) and Advisory Committee for the Study of Unpublished Appellate Opinions (1976); President's Commission on Pension Policy, 1979; Committee of the Judicial Conference of the United States to Consider Standards for Admission to Practice in the Federal Courts, 1976–79; Judicial Process Task Force, Calif. Council on Criminal Justice; Advisory Board, National Study on Plea Bargaining in the United States, 1975–76; Governing Board, Calif. CEB, 1970–74; and Advisory Board, National Center for State Courts, 1971–73. Executive Director, Calif. State Bar's Conference on Trial and Appellate Reform, 1972. Director, Conference of Calif. Judges [now Calif. Judges Assn.] Judicial Seminar, 1964; Board of Directors, Federal Reserve Bank, San Francisco, Calif., 1977–80; Board of Directors, Farmers Ins. Group, 1974–80; Board of Directors, Southern Calif. Edison Co., 1977–80; Advisory Council, Junior League of Los Angeles, 1976–79; Board of Visitors, U.S. Air Force Academy, 1976–78; Board of Directors, Calif. Council for the Humanities in Public Policy, 1975; Advisory Board, Elizabeth Fry Center, 1973; City of Los Angeles Employee Relations Board, 1974–79; Los Angeles Mayor Tom Bradley's Ad Hoc Committee on City Finances, Subcommittee on City Expenditures, 1978 and 1975–76; Los Angeles Public Commission on County Government, 1974–75; and Mayor's Labor Management Advisory Committee, 1972. Co-Chair, Mayor Tom Bradley's Blue Ribbon Commission on Selection of Commissioners for City of Los Angeles, 1972. National Vice President, Order of the Coif, 1974–76. Delegate, International Women's Conference, Mexico City, Mexico, 1975; Beijing (1995); Selection Committee, Rockefeller Public Service Award, Princeton University, 1976–80; Board of Dispute Resolution Center, Pasadena, 1982–85; Board of Directors, *LJK*, County Bar Foundation, 1982–87; Co-Chair, U.N. Day Calif., 1982, appointed by Governor of the State of Calif.; Judicial Council, 9th Cir., 1985–87; Federal Judicial Center's Committee on Appellate Educational Programs, 1989–91. Recipient: "Justice Award" (1985), from American Judicature Society; Public Service Award for Education (1978) from CORO Foundation; "Pax Orbis ex Jure Medallion" (1975) from World Peace Through Law Center; "Torah [Humanitarian] Award" (1973) from Univ. of Judaism; "Ernestine J. Stahlhut Award" (1972) from Women Lawyers Assn. of Los Angeles; "International Award (1970) from AWARE; and "Professional Achievement Award" (1969) from Univ. of Calif., Los Angeles. Named "Woman of the Year" (1968) by Los Angeles Times; and "Law Alummus of the Year" (1967) by Univ. of Calif., Los Angeles; Hollzer Memorial Award for Commitment to Social Justice and Human Rights, Jewish Federation Council of Los Angeles, 1988; UCLA Medal of Honor, 1993; 1994 Distinguished Jurist, Indiana University of Law-Indianapolis; 1996 Emil Gumpert Judicial ADR Recognition Award from the Los Angeles County Bar Assn; 1997 YWCA Pasadena Julia Morgan Award—"Trail Blazing Architect for Racial Justice"; 1999 Samuel E. Gates Litigation Award from American College of Trial Lawyers.

Teaching/Lectures/request: Instructor, International Institute of Human Rights, "Human Rights and the Judiciary," Strasbourg, France, 1989; Co-Chair, Sino American Conference on Mediation and Arbitration (Beijing, 1992); Co-Chair, Seminar on Transition to a Global Society—Transition to a Just Society (Switzerland, 1992); Co-Chair,

International Colloquium on Alternative Dispute Resolution (Islamabad, Pakistan, 1990); Participant World Congress on Law and Medicine (New Delhi, India, 1985); Board of Directors, Pacific Oaks College, Children's School and Research Center (1996–98).

Publications: Author: *Judicial Administration and the Administration of Justice* (West Publishing Co., 1975); "High Court Orders Bakke Admission, Minority Enrollment Now up to Schools," The Los Angeles Dairy Journal (Sept. 11, 1978, 90th Anniversary Issue); "Carter's Merit Plan: A Good First Step." 61 Judicature 105 (1977); "Admission to the Federal Bar—The Work of the Devitt Committee," ABTL Journal (1977); "The Role of the Trial Judge in Clinical Legal Education," 13 The Judges' Journal 20 (1974); "Adam's Lib," 26 Okla L Rev 375 (1973); "Expediting Voir Dire: An Empirical Study" (with Judge William H. Levit), 44 USC L Rev 961 (1971); "Judicial Reform: The Holbrook Report Revisited," 38 LABB 383 (1963); "Variation on a Theme-Selection and Tenure of Judges," 36 USC L Rev 4 (1962); "Should Los Angeles County Adopt a Single Trial Court Plan?" 33 USC L Rev 17 (1960); and "Prc Trial—An Effective Weapon of Advocacy," 3 UCLA L Rev 381 (1957). Author of book reviews appearing in 44 USC L Rev 1140 (1971) and 34 USC L Rev 380 (1961) and of following papers: "Abolish the Blight of Plea Bargaining," Christian Science Monitor (Feb. 12. 1979); "Maintaining an Independent Judiciary" (delivered at annual meeting of Judicial Attorneys of Calif. at State Bar Convention, Sept. 1978). 54 State BJ 78 (1979); "Current Developments in Judicial Administration" (presented at Plenary Session of Assn. of American Law Schools, Dec. 1977). 80 Federal Rules Decisions 147(1978); "The Criteria Applied by the American Bar Association Standing Committee" (ABA Conference on Selection of Federal Judges. March 12 13, 1976): "Conference on Trial and Appellate Court Reform" (Editor of materials, State Bar of Calif., 1972); and "Myths in Education" White House Conference on Children and Youth, with Dwight Allen, 1970). Senior Research Associate for Survey of Metropolitan Courts—Los Angeles Area by James G. Holbrook (USC, 1956); Chapter in *Women Lawyers, Perspectives on Success,* Harcourt, Brace, Janovich, 1984; *Federal Ninth Circuit Civil Appellate Practice,* The Rutter Group, with Christopher Goeltz and Meredith Watts, 1995; *The Role of the Law Schools in Post Degree Education,* 5 Tel Aviv University Studies in Law 31; *Alternative Dispute Resolution—*A *Supermarket for Law Reform,* 14 New Mexico L. Rev. 467; *The American Court System: Problems of Today, Prospects of Tomorrow,* Court Management Journal 26 (1982); *The Future of Alternative Dispute Resolution: A Prospective Look From Three Viewpoints—Jurist, Educator and Practitioner,* 14 Pepperdine L. Rev. 769 (1986).

Education: LL.D. (Honoris Causa), University of Santa Clara (1990): LL.D. (Honoris Causa), University of San Diego (1997); LL.M. (1956), Univ. of Southern Calif. Law Center, Los Angeles, Calif.; J.D. (1953), Univ. of Calif., Los Angeles (Westwood), School of Law (Order of the Coif); B.A. (1950), Univ. of Calif., Los Angeles (Westwood), (Phi Beta Kappa: and Phi Kappa Phi); Graduate: Los Angeles High School (1946). Mt. Vernon Junior High School (1943), and Wilton Place Grammar School (1940), all in Los Angeles, Calif.

Born: Sept. 30, 1928; San Pedro, Calif. Married. Two children.

Interests: Enjoys swimming, tennis, gardening, camping, sailing, and fishing.

Admission: Admitted to Calif. Bar and to U.S. Dist. Court, Southern Dist. [now Central and Southern Districts] of Calif., Jan. 14, 1954.

Political Affiliation/Religion: Political Independent Member. Baha'i Faith (Vice Chairperson, National Spiritual [...]

43 Practice Problem Re: Jurisdiction and the Applicability of Long-Arm Statutes

PROBLEM:

Roller World, Inc., a family-owned corporation organized under Missouri law, operated a single roller skating rink in a small Missouri town. All of the corporation's business activities were confined to the state of Missouri, although sometimes persons from other states were customers at the rink. On one occasion, a twelve-year old girl, who lived in Idaho and was passing through Missouri while on vacation with her parents, was skating at the Roller World rink. She sustained serious injures as the result of a fall. Her parents, claiming that the fall and all the ensuing injuries were caused by Roller World's negligence in maintaining the rink, filed a lawsuit against Roller World in an Idaho court. Assume, for purposes of this question, that Idaho has a long-arm statue similar to the one discussed herein/in class/the relevant chapter posted on Blackboard.

Further, assume that Roller World's president occasionally travels through Idaho while on his way to visit his grandparents in Washington state. On the basis of these facts, may the Idaho court assert jurisdiction over Roller World? Why or why not?

ANSWER:

The Idaho court **cannot** constitutionally assert jurisdiction over Roller World, Inc. Roller World did not conduct any activities in Idaho. It did not have any particular connection with that state. Absent from the facts are the "minimum contact" with the state of Idaho required in order for the assertion of jurisdiction under a long-arm statute to be constitutional. Although isolated incidents may sometimes be enough to create the necessary minimum contact, the only connection with Idaho mentioned in the facts is that Roller World's president had occasionally traveled through Idaho on *personal matters*. That fact alone is not enough, under a constitutional long-arm statute, to give the corporation minimum contact with the state of Idaho. The fact that the plaintiffs are from Idaho does not automatically give an Idaho court the power to render a judgment against a foreign-defendant corporation (here, one from Missouri).

The plaintiff's suit against Roller World should be filed in an appropriate Missouri sate court, or, if the plaintiffs so choose, in a federal district court in Missouri (assuming that the amount in controversy in the case exceeds $75,000).

44 Rules and Regs: Who Sets the Rules?[1]

By Rob Gavin

THE CALIFORNIA SUPREME Court is expected later this year to hear a case that some observers say could make the Golden State the legal jurisdiction for cyberspace.

The high court will decide whether an Internet posting, made in another state but seen in California, can subject a person or business making the posting to California law. In August, the California Appeals Court held that it could, indeed, writing in its opinion that "the reach of the Internet is also the reach of the extension of the poster's presence."

Civil libertarians and technology-industry groups say if the Appeals Court is upheld, almost anyone, anywhere could be hauled into a California court for making an Internet posting alleged to be harmful to the state's residents or industries. "We believe that would result in a flood of litigation in California," says Jason Mahler, vice president and general counsel of the Computer and Communications Industry Association, a Washington, D.C., trade group likely to file a brief arguing for the Appeals Court decision to be overturned. "You post something on the Internet, [Californians] complain about it, and you might be beholden to courts across the country."

The case before the California Supreme Court involves a Texas man, Matthew Pavlovich, who, as a Purdue University student in Indiana three years ago, worked on a Web site on which were posted computer codes to break the DVD encryption that prevents movies from being illegally copied. In 1999, the DVD Copy Control Association, a movie and technology industry group based in Morgan Hills, Calif, that licenses the encryption software, sued 521 defendants including Mr. Pavlovich. In Santa Clara County Superior Court in San Jose to stop the posting of the decryption codes, arguing that they had violated the state's trade-secrets law. Mr. Pavlovich responded that California courts couldn't assert jurisdiction since he had not set foot in the state, made personal contacts, entered into agreements or specifically targeted any person or business in California. He also denied posting the decryption software.

The DVD Copy Control Association, however, argued that California courts have jurisdiction because Mr. Pavlovich knew, or should have known, that software that permits the illegal copying of DVDs would harm the motion picture industry that is centered California. Both the trial and appeals courts agreed.

Robert Sugarman, a New York lawyer representing the copy-control group, dismissed concerns that these rulings could extend California law to any

1 **Note from Professor Carr: This article relates nicely to our class discussion of doing business on the Internet and in the era of e-commerce and these things called "long-arm statutes."**

Again, you should be able to note and see (after reading this article) that one of the downsides of the Internet, Web, e-commerce, etc., is that it may cause you to become ensnared in litigation in a far away locale that you never imagined possible (in part due to these things called long-arm statutes!!).

place with an Internet connection as "doomsday rhetoric." The lower courts merely upheld established principles that allow states to protect their citizens from illegal acts aimed at them beyond their borders.

The California Supreme Court isn't expected to rule for several months.

45 Roberts Court Unites on Business

The Wall Street Journal Online

By Nick Timiraos

THE FIRST FULL term of the Roberts Court ended this past week with rulings that pushed the law in a direction favored by business.

Several key cases on affirmative action, abortion and free speech underscored how President Bush's nominees, Chief Justice John Roberts and Justice Samuel Alito, have solidified a five-vote conservative majority. The growing number of 5-4 decisions also illustrates the challenges facing the Chief Justice in his push for greater unanimity, which he hopes will allow the court's decisions to carry greater weight.

Business cases often showed greater consensus among the justices. While the court heard fewer cases than in past years, it considered a greater share of business cases. The U.S. Chamber of Commerce claimed victory in 13 of the cases it supported before the court, losing in just two.

Here's a closer look at some of the decisions:

Antitrust law: A series of rulings have shielded businesses from antitrust charges. In a split decision on Thursday, the court abandoned a 96-year-old law that prohibited manufacturers from setting minimum prices, allowing them to force retailers to sell goods at minimum prices as long as they promote competition.

In an 8-1 decision, the court made it harder for shareholders to file securities-fraud lawsuits against companies. That followed a 7-1 decision that dismissed an investor lawsuit that alleged an "epic Wall Street conspiracy" by firms to drive up the price of initial public offerings during the 1990s tech boom.

The court also made it easier for companies to win a speedy dismissal of certain antitrust claims by raising the standard required to prove that companies were colluding to raise prices. And it ruled unanimously in protecting the right of companies to bid up supply prices, overturning a $79 million award against timber giant **Weyerhaeuser** Co. brought by a smaller rival.

Punitive damages: The court set new limits on punitive damages when it voided an $80 million verdict against cigarette maker Philip Morris, ruling that juries couldn't use a single victim's lawsuit to punish a defendant for harm caused to hundreds of individuals. It also set aside a $55 million jury award against **Ford Motor** Co.

Employers won a 5-4 decision that said that businesses couldn't be sued for years-old pay discrimination by requiring employees to file a discrimination lawsuit no more than 180 days after their pay was set. Critics say the decision hampers employees' ability to pursue pay-discrimination suits because they often don't discover for years that other colleagues are being paid more for the same work.

The court also protected the insurance industry from millions in damages when ruling that insurers **Safeco** Corp. and Geico Corp. didn't have to notify customers that it had checked their credit reports.

Another ruling could make it harder for government whistle-blowers to win a share of damages in suits that claim that the government was defrauded. The court sided with **Boeing** Co. in ruling that whistle-blowers must have direct knowledge, not mere suspicion, of fraud.

Environment: One big defeat for business came in a split decision where the court ruled that states and environmental groups can sue the Environmental Protection Agency over its refusal to regulate car emissions that produce greenhouse gases, pressuring the government to regulate greenhouse-gas emissions.

The court sided with the EPA in requiring the electric-power industry to upgrade technology to reduce pollution when making improvements that increase power generation. A third case sided with developers and the EPA in a dispute with environmentalists about protecting endangered species.

Social issues: One of the court's most divisive decisions came on Thursday when it invalidated two public-school systems' use of race in assigning students to schools. Earlier this year, another 5-4 decision upheld a nationwide ban passed in 2003 on partial-birth abortions.

Free speech: In two closely watched cases, the court restricted a key portion of a landmark 2002 federal campaign-finance law by allowing corporations and unions to sponsor issue advertisements in the final days before a federal election. It also tightened limits on student speech by allowing schools to prohibit expression that might be construed as advocating drug use.

* * *

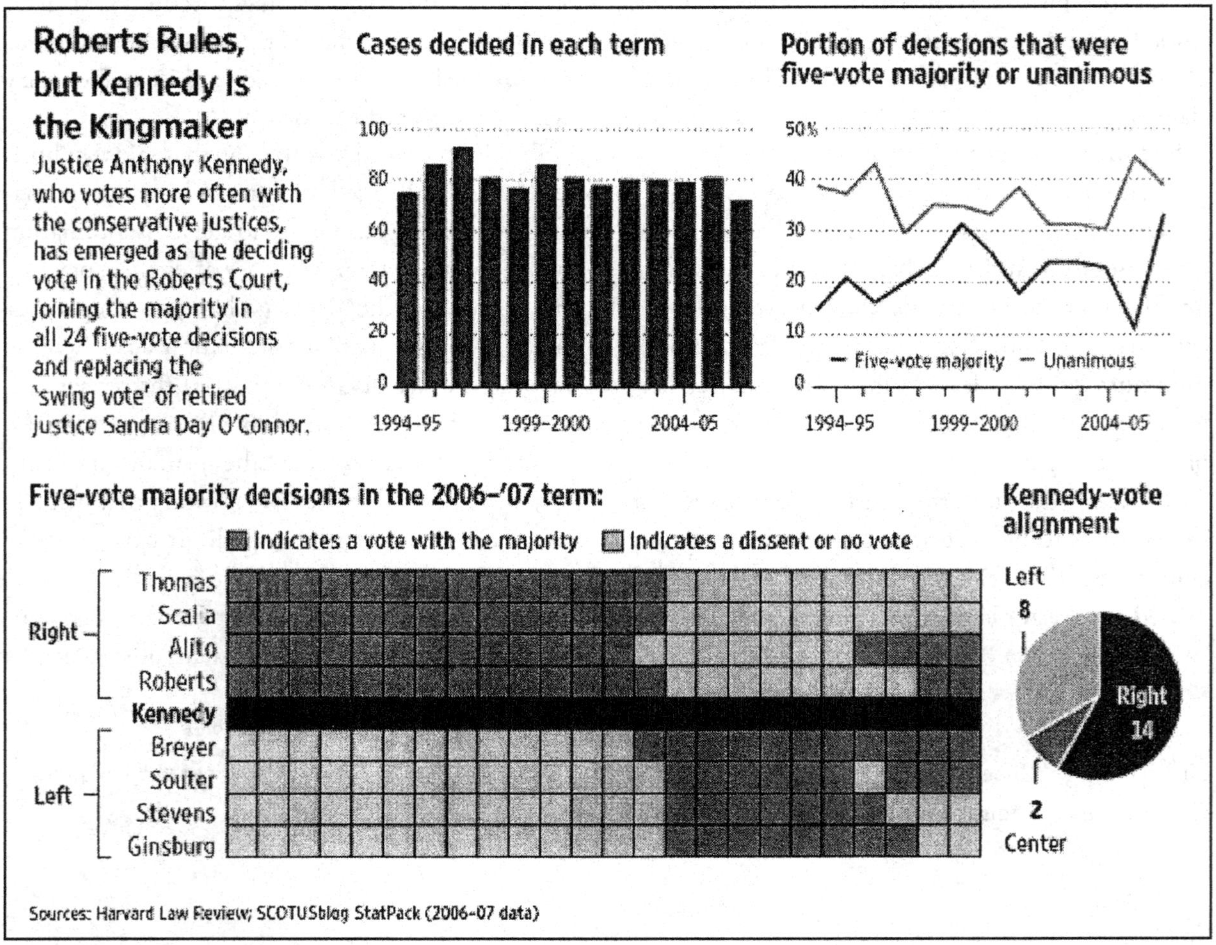

Facts

- The average age of the current court is 67. Chief Justice John Roberts, 52, is the youngest and Justice John Paul Stevens, 87, is the oldest. Oliver Wendell Holmes Jr. is the oldest to have served on the court and retired when he was 90.
- One sign of increased frustration among the court's liberal justices: Five times during the past term, justices read their dissents out loud, a tactic the court uses to convey great distress with the majority opinion.
- A May Gallup poll found that 51% of Americans approve of the job the Supreme Court is doing, with 36% disapproving. Last fall, the court's approval rating stood at 60%.
- In the last term, the Supreme Court heard 21 cases that had been decided by the Ninth Circuit Court of Appeals, more than any other court. It reversed or vacated 18, or 86%, of the court's decisions.
- One-third of all the cases were decided by a five-vote majority this year, the highest share in the last decade. Last year, only 13% of all cases were decided by a five-vote majority.

* * *

Corrections & Amplifications:

The Supreme Court ruled last week in favor of developers and the Environmental Protection Agency in a dispute with environmentalists about protecting endangered species. This article incorrectly reported that the court ruled in favor of developers against the EPA.

46 The Last Word: The 2008 Bench Press

By Anna Quindlen, *Newsweek*

JOHN ROBERTS COULD probably walk through any Home Depot in the nation unnoticed. Barack Obama or Hillary Clinton—chaos in the bathroom-vanity aisle. John McCain—autographs in power tools. But the chief justice of the U.S. Supreme Court could likely shop for a Phillips screwdriver and most people wouldn't look twice, even though he may be one of the most powerful people in America. Or at least one of nine.

Congress chips away at legislation, then sends some lowest-common-denominator version to the White House, to be signed or vetoed or later redesigned by the next president to take up temporary residence in Washington. But the work of the high court has had vast systemic influence over the lives of all Americans, an effect that lasts through generations. In the tripartite tussle, it's no contest: SCOTUS rules.

The display of the Ten Commandments in public buildings. The scope of eminent domain. The reading of rights to defendants. The ability of taxpayers to litigate against faith-based government-funded programs. School prayer. Medical marijuana. Campaign ads. And that's before you get to desegregation, abortion, affirmative action and capital punishment. If you try to register to vote in Indiana and are turned away because you don't have a government-issued photo ID, that's because the Supremes just ruled, 6-3, that that's OK.

So why are many Americans insensible to a body that has so much power over their lives? (Quick: can you name the nine? Yeah, that's what I thought.) Well, in our three-pronged system the justices are the only people we don't elect. But they are chosen by the person we do. So it makes sense that the presidential candidates be repeatedly asked specific and searching questions about what sort of justices they favor, especially since on Inauguration Day two thirds of the court will be 70 or older.

During the last general election, there were roughly four and a half hours of televised debate, and about five minutes of that were taken up with the Supreme Court. The usual code words and phrases applied. Strict constructionist = conservative; personal privacy = liberal. To listen to the questions, you would have thought the only issue before the court was abortion. This draws battle lines, but doesn't enlarge public understanding.

History tells us that virtually all presidents get blindsided by their court choices, that Richard Nixon thought Harry Blackmun would be a reliable conservative, not the guy who wrote *Roe v. Wade,* that Ike rued the expansionist Warren Court until the day he died. But, more important, history tells us that the decisions that made people angriest at the time are often the ones that seem most obviously just. *Brown v. Board of Education,* the landmark desegregation case, was excoriated. Limits on unreasonable searches, protection from self-incrimination—they were trashed until they became accepted as bedrock American principles. On every cop show a character shouts, "You can't come in here without a warrant!" and viewers nod as though it were Jeffersonian edict.

Today it's impossible to tell where prospective justices stand on some of these issues. The modern confirmation hearing has become kabuki theater, in which members of the Senate ask questions to which they already know they will not get answers. The nadir of this advise-and-consent travesty came when Clarence Thomas insisted he had never given any thought to whether *Roe,* the most contentious decision of the 20th century and the one which has been the litmus test for the far right for 35 years, had been correctly decided.

Republican presidents have made all but two of the appointments to the Supreme Court in the last 40 years. But the result has not yet been the ultra-conservative body dreamed of by the right wing, although there is no doubt that since Justice Sandra Day O'Connor was replaced by Samuel Alito, and Justice Roberts took over as chief, there has been a move in that direction. Men and women change in the job. Their view of the Constitution, a document whose interpretation is more art than science, often expands. Perhaps they can see the bigger picture from that neoclassical temple in Washington.

Maybe that's why we don't pay enough attention to the court: because it exemplifies the long view, and Americans are of the moment. So, too, are politicians. Their court appointments are too often an attempt to mollify supporters. But all people live with the results, whether the results are the expansion of rights and liberties or their diminution.

The next president will probably have the opportunity to appoint several justices, and therefore voters have the right to know precisely how the candidates will think about that monumental task. But no more pandering shorthand: cross-examination is in order. Which decisions in recent history have they admired, and why? If they favor strict constructionists, how can they support *Brown,* which was seen as judicial overreaching? Leaving the question of legal abortion aside, should Americans expect a constitutional right to privacy? Are there any circumstances under which execution is not cruel and unusual? The time for questions is not when the president is standing at the podium with a justice whose term may last for decades. It's when we're trying to decide who gets to stand at the podium and therefore who gets to sit on the court.

47 U.S. Supreme Court: Law Clerks[1]

IMAGINE BEING ONLY a couple years out of law school and yet drafting judicial opinions for the United States Supreme Court. Farfetched as this may sound, drafting opinions would likely be one of your responsibilities if you were one of the elite group of young lawyers chosen annually to clerk for the justices of the Supreme Court. This does not mean, of course, that the clerks determine how the Court decides—as Chief Justice William Rehnquist has emphasized, they are not "legal Rasputins," manipulating the justices to advance their own legal or policy goals. Yet working under the close supervision of the justice who selected them, these law clerks do play a crucial role in the operations of the Supreme Court.

The first justice to hire a law clerk was Justice Horace Gray, who had initiated the practice while a member of the Supreme Judicial Court of Massachusetts and brought his clerk with him when appointed to the Supreme Court in 1882. Gray's successor on the Court, Oliver Wendell Holmes, continued the practice, and gradually other justices followed their lead. Today, each justice chooses four clerks each year to assist her with her work. These clerks are truly a select group. Typically, they include the top graduates of major law schools—for a long time, Harvard and Yale dominated, but in recent years other law schools have contributed their share. Usually the clerks come to the Court with the experience of a year's clerkship for another judge, usually on a court of appeals. However, the justices are free to employ their own criteria in selecting their clerks, and some have been partial to clerks from their own region or law school. For example, Justice William O. Douglas, a native of Washington, characteristically chose Westerners as his clerks.

Because the clerks are to assist the justices, each justice determines the tasks his clerks will perform. Justice Gray, for example, asked his clerk's advice in picking out a ring when he became engaged at age 60, and Justice Hugo Black required his clerks to play tennis with him. However, almost all clerks share certain common tasks. The clerks assist their justice first of all in reviewing the petitions for certiorari, drafting memos that detail the issues and legal arguments in each case and recommend whether certiorari should be granted. Or if their justice belongs to the "cert pool," the clerks prepare memos on their assigned cases which are then circulated to all the justices participating in the pool. The limited data we have suggest that the justices usually go along with their clerk's recommendations, perhaps because those recommendations take into account the perspectives of the justice to whom they are addressed. Justice John Paul Stevens has underscored the importance of the clerk's work in screening petitions for review, noting, "I don't even look at the papers in over 80 percent of the cases that are filed."

Clerks also participate in preparing opinions, though the justices differ in the responsibilities they assign their clerks. All clerks conduct legal research for their justices. Some do little actual writing—one

1 **Note from Professor Carr: This is a nice article on law clerks and how they fit in and are utilized at the U.S. Supreme Court. Sounds like a pretty cool gig and job to me. Maybe this could be one of <u>you</u> some day?!**

of Justice Felix Frankfurter's clerks said that the justice wrote the opinion, and he wrote the footnotes. Most justices, however, allow their clerks to prepare rough drafts, along lines dictated by the justice. The justice will then revise the draft before circulating it to other members of the Court, and their comments will lead to further revisions. The opinion that is eventually published may bear little resemblance to the draft the clerk prepared. Finally, some clerks serve as "sounding boards" for their justices, providing them with opportunities to discuss the issues in the cases they are deciding. Justice Lewis Powell, for example, reputedly chose clerks whose views were more liberal than his own in order to ensure that he confronted the arguments against his own conservative proclivities. Although justices could conceivably be swayed by the arguments of their clerks, this probably does not happen often. For one thing, with their political experience the justices are used to working with a staff without being dominated by it. For another, the clerks themselves are transients—with rare exceptions. They serve for only a single year.

SUPREME COURT RULE 10: CONSIDERATIONS GOVERNING REVIEW ON CERTIORARI[2]

1. A review on writ of certiorari is not a matter of right, but of Judicial discretion, and will be granted only when there are special and important reasons therefore. The following while neither controlling nor fully measuring the Court's discretion, indicate the character of reasons that will be considered:

(a) When a federal court of appeals has rendered a decision in conflict with the decision of another federal court of appeals on the same matter …

(b) When a state court of last resort has decided a federal question in a way in conflict with the decision of another state court of last resort or of a federal court of appeals.

(c) When a state court of last resort or a federal court of appeals has decided an important question of federal law which has not, but should be, settled by this Court, or has decided a federal question in a way in conflict with applicable decisions of this Court.

2. The same general considerations outlined above will control in respect of petitions for writs of certiorari to review judgments of the Court of Claims, of the Court of Customs and Patent Appeals, and of any other court whose judgments are reviewable by law on writ of certiorari.

---

2 Note from Professor Carr: This is a Supreme Court rule which helps the Court decide which cases to take/hear/decide each year. Note that on top of this rule, one must also add the personalities, legal backgrounds, religious beliefs, social backgrounds, work experience, values, etc., etc.—obviously, such things/factors also influence what cases a justice may be interested in hearing and deciding! Don't forget to add the factors of political affiliation ideology and background as well!!

48 Chapter 3 — The Anatomy of a Civil Case; Judges, Courts and Jurisdiction; and ADR (continued)

Study Outline

ALTERNATIVE DISPUTE RESOLUTION (ADR)

IV. **Alternative Dispute Resolution ("ADR")** (See also class lecture, power point frames, video, and Chapter 3 of the textbook that is posted on Blackboard for additional details.)

A. Some of the purported pros of ADR -- greater flexibility, faster, cheaper, less formal, etc.

B. Some of the purported cons of ADR -- can result in "shoddy" justice; sometimes the so-called expert arbitrator or mediator is no "expert" at all and is instead incompetent, lazy, and or biased; usually no written record of the proceeding is made which thereby makes any meaningful appeal virtually impossible to file and/or win, etc.

V. Common forms of ADR

1. Arbitration (can be court-ordered or voluntary) (our focus will be here)
2. Mediation (our focus will also be here)
3. Settlement discussions and/or negotiations
4. Other – summary jury trials

*****Note that in this textbook at pages 149–176 I have inserted a number of articles, supplementary materials, sample documents, etc. that relate to this material. These materials are required reading, and, also fair game for the exam.**

*****Also, make *<u>sure</u>* that you do the sample practice problems posted on Blackboard as it will help you master this ADR material, test you to see if you "really" know and understand it, etc. You can expect similar problems to be on the exam. ☺**

49 Alternative Dispute Resolution

The Two Most Common Types of ADR Are *Arbitration* and *Mediation*

Arbitration

- Is the most similar to dispute resolution in court
- Like a court trial, it is an *adversarial* process with two or more parties competing with each other before a neutral decision maker called an "arbitrator"
- Like a judge, the arbitrator will hear evidence as judges do and will make a decision about who wins and who loses
- It is private
- It can take place anywhere
- Less formal than a court/jury trial (e.g., the rules of evidence are often relaxed)
- Can be binding or non-binding
  - If binding, the losing party can generally only appeal if the arbitrator showed bias, corruption, total incompetence, insanity, or, a significant error of law appears on the face of the arbitrator's written award/decision
- Sometimes the parties can pick their arbitrator
- Precedent may not be followed by the arbitrator in rendering his/her decision (thus, it can be unpredictable)

Mediation

- There is no decision maker, rather the neutral objective 3rd party, called the "mediator," acts as a facilitator
- The mediator's job is to try and get the warring sides to reach a settlement
- Is a *cooperative* rather than adversarial process
- Is informal
- It is private
- It can take place anywhere
- It can help the parties preserve their business relationship
- Parties are not obligated to accept or follow the mediator's recommendations/suggestions
  - I.e., the mediation itself is not binding on the parties. … It/the mediator tries to reach a settlement agreement/contract that is in turn/will be binding on the parties and enforceable

How Do You Get To ADR?

- In the majority of cases there is a provision in a contract that the parties entered into/signed that obligates/requires them to submit the dispute to some form of ADR (e.g., common in employment contracts, health care contracts, etc.—see your power point frames for an example of such a clause)
- After litigation commences, the parties may voluntarily agree to take their case out of the court system and go to some form of ADR

- Finally, the court may order the parties to go to some form of ADR

Purported Pros/Advantages of ADR

- See the articles at pages 151–154 of this textbook. This material is fair game for the exam

Drawbacks/Disadvantages of ADR

- Arbitrator or mediator may be bad/incompetent for the case/the parties at issue
- Fairness (one side can be at a significant disadvantage)
- Other—see also the articles at pages 155–176 of this textbook. This material is fair game for the exam

50 ADR Finds True Believers[1]

Companies Make the Leap—and Save Tens of Millions of Dollars.

By David Hechler, *The National Law Journal*

[ADR]

THE YEAR WAS 1992, and James W. Durham, general counsel of the Philadelphia Electric Co., was still grappling with a case he'd inherited three years earlier. It had all the elements of a litigation nightmare.

A nuclear power plant had been shut down by federal regulators after his company's control room operators had been found asleep on the job. The plaintiffs were three utilities with which his company had a continuing partnership, the claims totaled $300 million, attorney fees had been mounting for nearly four years and the last thing he needed was an expensive trial and more bad publicity.

Mr. Durham had been imploring the companies to try mediation and, 10 weeks before their trial date, they finally did. It took all of two days. The settlement totaled $131 million—with no trial, no appeals and no admission of liability. Mr. Durham still recalls the moment fondly: "When it was all said and done, the mediation cost less than the postage bill had been for the litigation."

To many people back then, alternative dispute resolution (ADR) was still something of a novelty. That was why Mr. Durham had trouble convincing the companies to give it a try. But by 1997, when David B. Lipsky and Ronald I. Seeber, two Cornell University professors surveyed the Fortune 1000, 87% of the companies responding had used mediation at least once during the previous three years and 80% had used arbitration.

Today, most of the organizations that collect ADR data report substantial increases in recent years. For example, of the cases filed between 1996 and 2000 with the American Arbitration Association, mediations and arbitrations combined almost tripled [see chart, Page A17]. In the wake of the U.S. Supreme Court's ruling in March 2001 that mandatory arbitration clauses in employment contracts are *legal (Circuit City Stores v. Adams,* No. 99-1379), many in the field, including the Cornell professors, expect the numbers to explode.

From their own widely cited research, Mr. Lipsky and Mr. Seeber conclude that roughly 10% of the Fortune 1000 dislike ADR and rarely use it. Another 80% are in what Mr. Lipsky calls an experimental mode: "There's a lot of benchmarking going on—companies looking at each other and trying to figure out what to do."

But he and Mr. Seeber were most intrigued by the remaining 10% that had institutionalized ADR

1 **Note from Professor Carr: This is definitely a "pro-ADR" article. As you read it, look for why that is the case and why or what are some of the purported pros/advantages of ADR.**

by implementing conflict management systems. This surprised the professors, who decided to zoom in from the wide-angle approach of their first study for close-ups.

The pair spent 18 months examining 19 companies from the *Fortune* 1000. In their study, which will be published later this year in a New York University labor law book, they will explain why companies made the leap.

Case study

One company they studied was Mr. Durham's. Philadelphia Electric is now part of Chicago-based Exelon Corp., and Mr. Durham retired in March 2001, but the system remains.

The legal department was different when he arrived in 1988. Nearly all legal work was done by outside firms that had little incentive to contain costs, Mr. Durham recalls. The in-house department consisted of six or seven lawyers who mostly assisted the hired hands. His mandate was to change that.

As president of the Oregon State Bar, Mr. Durham had created its first dispute resolution committee, and he was determined to introduce ADR to his new department. Even as he was hiring, he was grooming his staff, emphasizing from the first interviews his vision of lawyers as "problem solvers."

Within three years he had 25 lawyers handling their own cases. With 200 pending at any given time, Mr. Durham's goal was to "recalibrate the litigators to think about early evaluation" and, when appropriate, prompt settlement.

At Philadelphia Electric, a utility company, most cases were predictable: slip-and-falls, crashes into utility poles. As long as the claims were legitimate, he favored settling immediately: "It's important to be able to say, 'We screwed up.' Everybody makes mistakes. The important thing is how you resolve them after they're done."

Yet, Mr. Durham discovered, the vast majority of company disputes weren't even in his domain. Appliances damaged by power surges, for instance, passed through the claims department, which processed thousands each year. So Mr. Durham successfully lobbied to have them folded under his umbrella. To maintain public trust, Mr. Durham felt it was especially important to quickly resolve claims filed by customers.

The best way to do that, he reasoned, was to allow adjusters to settle on the spot, so he literally put checkbooks in their hands. The result: Adjusters processed more claims more quickly and the average settlement cost dropped. "So everybody won," he says.

Handling employment disputes

When it was appropriate, Mr. Durham didn't shy away from litigating. Each year, the company was hit with employee discrimination claims, most of which Mr. Durham deemed meritless. He "basically won them all" he says. Yet, he also recognized that these cases revealed a problem. Amicably resolving disputes with employees was as important as doing so with customers, and that wasn't likely to happen in court.

Mr. Durham believes this was a driving force behind the company's most ambitious ADR initiative of all: the development of a system to resolve employment disputes without having to go to court.Another factor was the need to change the relationship between workers and managers as the company braced for competition after deregulation. This was the human resources department's concern when it created a system in 1993.

Here's how it works: If a dispute involves a legally protected right, like the right not to be discriminated against, employees can opt for internal or external mediation or voluntary, binding arbitration, according to Ellen Wolf, director of employee dispute resolution. The company will even reimburse employees for up to $2,500 in legal fees.

When protected legal issues aren't involved, such as discipline for unauthorized absences, employees dissatisfied with a supervisor's decision may request a binding hearing before a peer review panel. Panels comprise three peers, a manager and a supervisor, none involved in the conflict and all volunteers with special training. Panels aren't authorized to change policies, procedures, performance ratings or salaries, Ms. Wolf says. They judge whether supervisors' decisions were consistent with existing policies. Sometimes the stakes couldn't be higher: They can reinstate a fired worker or restore back pay. But the system had problems.

Too adversarial

When Ms. Wolf was hired, in 1995, she found a system that was used but a process that was adversarial. Panelists themselves complained that many conflicts could have been resolved earlier by a simple conversation, Ms. Wolf recalls.

She assembled a team of a dozen employees from different levels and divisions, put together focus groups, and the result was a new option, part of a program called People*Solve. Before hearings, employees embroiled in disputes may now meet with trained peer coaches who prepare workers for conversations with their supervisors.

In 2000, 92% of the cases brought to the coaches were resolved, which meant 40% fewer panels than in 1999, according to Ms. Wolf. Employment lawsuits and cases brought by the U.S. Equal Employment Opportunity Commission were reduced 44% over the same period.

Another booster

Another company the Cornell professors studied was FMC Corp., a leading producer of chemicals and machinery. Like Mr. Durham, General Counsel Stephen F. Gates was already an ADR booster when he arrived. He had seen it succeed at Amoco, where he had worked for 23 years, the last five as GC. Early resolution of disputes had saved more than just time and money. Distraction was a hidden cost of litigation, which often took on a life of its own.

While he didn't find any real proponents at FMC, he found a sophisticated, 20-lawyer legal department that "was very receptive to ADR.

"The real knack in ADR is finding or inventing the right format for the particular dispute." Mr. Gates says. If two parties disagree about the correct reading of a contract. The best solution may be hiring a decision-maker . Where the issues are purely financial and the range of differences narrow, he's found negotiation will often suffice. For example, lawsuits on behalf of people injured or killed operating FMC construction cranes are most often resolved through settlement discussions.

On the other hand, Mr. Gates has enjoyed some of his greatest success with mediation—sometimes under unlikely circumstances. When he suggested mediating a case in which FMC was accused of selling defective Bradley fighting vehicles to the U.S. Army, the case had been litigated for 14 years. FMC had already lost in court. A judge had reduced the jury's $380 million verdict to $87 million, boosted to $110 million with interest and legal fees. Still, both sides were appealing, so Mr. Gates suggested mediation. In two days, they settled for $80 million.

Mr. Gates hasn't yet formalized a system at FMC, as he did at Amoco, because he's only been on the job a year. "It's on the agenda," he says. In the meantime, the tools and the mind-set are there, and he believes they are already practicing it.

What do the companies that have implemented conflict management systems have in common? That was one question the Cornell professors set out to answer. Many companies had a crisis, usually in the form of a large lawsuit, Mr. Lipsky says. Some had smaller suits that rolled in regularly.

Virtually all the companies had a James Durham or a Stephen Gates.

An ardent ADR advocate

"There's always someone who is an ardent advocate for ADR," Mr. Lipsky says. When the champion is a lower-level employee, he continues, the company may take an ad hoc approach. When a company adopts an integrated system, the champion is usually an executive.

Conversely, the pair also found common features among the skeptics. "A lot of CEOs are saying, 'What's the real business case?' " notes Mr. Seeber. Without an ADR champion or a litigation crisis, the issue may be off a company's radar screen, or it may have emerged all too visibly in a bad experience.

The professors speak of the need for institutionalization to ensure a system's survival. If a company's system is built by a champion on whom it depends, the system may collapse after the champion leaves. That is the test that determines whether the corporate culture has truly changed.

FMC will face the test this fall, when the company splits in two and Mr. Gates becomes a consultant to both but general counsel to neither. He has confidence that both companies will retain the same approach, he says.

Exelon is already in the post-Durham era. Mr. Durham believes ADR concepts are accepted by the people and built into the contracts. Besides, he says, he doesn't have time to worry. He's too busy pursuing the new role he's fashioned since he "retired."

"I'm on the other side of the table now," he declares. "I'm a mediator."

Number of arbitrations and mediations filed with the American Arbitration Association:

1996	72,200
1997	78,769
1998	95,143
1999	140,188
2000	198,491

ADR Websites

1. ADRWorld: www.adrworld.com
2. American Arbitration Association: www.adr.org
3. American Bar Association Section of Dispute Resolution: www.abanet.org/dispute
4. CPR Institute for Dispute Resolution: www.cpradr.org
5. JAMS (Judicial Arbitration and Mediation Services): www.jamsadr.com

51 Private Justice: Millions Are Losing Their Legal Rights[1]

Supreme Court Forces Disputes from Court to Arbitration—A System with No Laws

By Reynold Holding, *San Francisco Chronicle*

[ADR]

A PRIVATE BRAND OF civil justice, one without laws or juries or constitutional rights, has swept quietly across the nation's commercial landscape, shielding corporations from costly verdicts, compromising judges and stripping the public of its right to a day in court.

Tens of millions of Americans can no longer get medical treatment, a job, a home, a credit card or a host of goods and services without agreeing to resolve future disputes in confidential, unregulated proceedings riddled with conflicts of interest.

They cannot claim injury, fraud or discrimination without paying filing fees that may reach thousands of dollars. They cannot rely on legal guarantees of due process and fair treatment. They cannot appeal, except in rare circumstances.

And most of them don't even know it.

They have been forced into binding arbitration, a quasi-legal process that allows private individuals to pass final judgment on the disputes of the parties who hire them.

Voluntary arbitration has a long history in corporate commerce, organized labor and professional sports, where it has earned praise for efficiently resolving conflicts between adversaries of equal strength.

But over the past two decades, corporate America has imposed mandatory arbitration on the public as a condition of doing business with the blessing of the U.S. Supreme Court.

Legal experts, including advocates of voluntary arbitration and several members of the court itself, have accused the justices of ignoring the intent of Congress and distorting the Federal Arbitration Act so that business interests can avoid the costs and risks of lawsuits and judges can lighten their workloads.

"The Supreme Court rewrote that statute as a service to corporations that don't like jury trials," says Professor Paul Carrington of Duke University School of Law.

The result, critics say, is a second-class justice system in which obscure clauses buried deep in bank statements, phone bills and job applications deprive millions of people of their legal rights:

1 **Note from Professor Carr: This is the first of three articles that recently appeared in the San Francisco Chronicle. They are designed to show/illustrate for you that there is/may be a "dark-side" to ADR that many folks do not like to talk about or address.**

—Lost rights: In mandatory arbitration, high fees can discourage individuals from pursuing cases. The system lacks the procedural safeguards of court, and limited awards can make hiring a lawyer difficult. Arbitrators don't have to be lawyers and may not follow the law or justify their rulings. Their decisions are confidential and final.

—Conflicts of interest: Some arbitration firms have invested in the companies whose disputes, the firms' arbitrators hear, creating the appearance of conflicts that would never be tolerated in court. Studies show that arbitrators may favor large corporations and other frequent clients.

—Compromised judges: Soaring demand and potentially high pay have lured an increasing number of sitting judges into arbitration—particularly in California—and pressured some to act in ways that may impress arbitration firms but weaken public confidence in the courts.

"Mandatory arbitration allows corporations to undermine the whole system by which we hold them accountable," says Montana Supreme Court Justice Terry Trieweiler. "Every day it becomes more pervasive, and more oppressive."

Taking a case through mandatory arbitration can be financially and emotionally devastating.

While a vice president at Nations Bank Capital Markets, Renee Cecala says male bosses grabbed, cursed and pawed her. A stripper dressed as a pizza delivery boy disrobed as she stood on the trading floor. For Halloween, she received a small coffin containing a nude figure with a penis as long as its body.

In 1998, under securities-industry rules, her complaint was assigned to a panel of three arbitrators.

The panel's chairman was a retired music teacher. The second arbitrator had run a small stock-brokerage firm in Indiana and, Cecala says, "was immensely hard of hearing." The third, a small-town lawyer and diabetic, often slept during the proceedings as his insulin pump whistled in the background.

"I remember walking into the room, seeing these three and thinking, 'Oh, my God,'" says Cecala.

Transcripts show the panel losing control of the attorneys, misstating the law and making bizarre rulings. The hearings lasted 18 days over more than two years and cost Cecala almost $25,000 in arbitrator and hearing fees alone. Then the panel ruled against her.

Cecala says she fell into deep depression, unable to sleep for days at a time.

"In terms of the massiveness of the mess, it's hard to top her case," says Cecala's current attorney, Mitchell Aberman, who is asking a federal judge to overturn the arbitrators' ruling.

In response to mounting criticism, several arbitration firms have adopted fairness standards. But the protocols are sometimes ignored and, in any event, cannot be enforced in court.

Reforms that would protect the public have been proposed in Congress and state legislatures. On Sept. 26, Gov. Gray Davis signed a bill calling for rules requiring arbitrators to disclose conflicts of interest. A bill now before the U.S. House of Representatives would prohibit employers from imposing arbitration on most workers.

But the prospects for further reform are uncertain. The California Chamber of Commerce, the American Insurance Association and other business interests from Silicon Valley to Wall Street have consistently fought to defeat proposed limits.

"What you're talking about here," says Rep. Dennis Kucinich, D-Ohio, a sponsor of the House bill, "is a classic struggle between the basic rights of workers and the desire of corporations to have absolute control of the workplace."

On Wednesday, the U.S. Supreme Court will hear arguments in a case that could extend the reach of mandatory arbitration even further. The court will decide whether the federal Equal Employment Opportunity Commission can sue an employer on behalf of Scotty Baker, a fired short-order cook who unwittingly signed away his right to a jury trial.

The case may show how far the court is willing to go in limiting not only the rights of individuals but the authority of the agencies created to protect them.

"Employers see a green light posted on the front steps of the Supreme Court, emboldening them to make arguments that 20 years ago would have been deemed outrageous," says San Francisco attorney Michael Rubin, author of a brief supporting the EEOC's position. "This time, I hope the Supreme Court tells them that they have finally pushed too far."

FEDERAL ARBITRATION ACT[2]

For years, the nation's courts refused to enforce arbitration agreements, frustrating companies eager to conduct business without lawyers or courts.

Then, in 1923, Republican Rep. Ogden L. Mills of New York introduced a bill that would make arbitration contracts enforceable in federal court.

Critics of arbitration worried the legislation would undercut the rights of individuals. But the bill's authors and supporters said it would only apply to "merchants" in contract disputes.

The Federal Arbitration Act became law in 1925, and for decades the nation's courts honored the limits Congress intended to impose on the act.

But by the mid-1970s, the fear of an explosion in litigation gripped the federal judiciary. Business interests warned of skyrocketing lawsuits. Insurance company Crum & Forster ran a full page advertisement in Time magazine, condemning lawyers for filing more than 1 million product liability cases each year. Although the actual number never exceeded about 80,000, the point had been made.

In 1983, without explanation, the Supreme Court declared that the Federal Arbitration Act had created a "liberal federal policy favoring arbitration," meaning arbitration agreements should be upheld whenever possible.

The pronouncement marked a stark change in the high court's thinking, and the new policy soon drew criticism from its own members, including Justice Sandra Day O'Connor, who said the court "utterly fails to recognize the clear congressional intent underlying the Federal Arbitration Act."

But the court repeatedly invoked the new policy as it expanded mandatory arbitration throughout the nation's commercial life—even when civil rights were at stake.

The court had long maintained that arbitrators "may be wholly unqualified" to decide civil rights cases and similar legal matters, said Justice Hugo Black.

But in 1991, the justices ruled 7 to 2 that Robert Gilmer, a 62-year-old financial services manager replaced by his 28-year-old protege, must take his age discrimination case to arbitration.

The ruling cleared the way for companies in every industry to prohibit their employees from going to court with their grievances.

HIDDEN WAIVERS

In its rulings, the Supreme Court has treated arbitration clauses as ordinary contracts between consenting parties.

But for individuals, the clauses are much more. They are waivers of the constitutional right to a jury trial. And in all contexts other than arbitration clauses, federal courts have consistently ruled that such waivers must be "knowing, voluntary and intentional," says Jean Sternlight, a law professor at the University of Missouri.

Yet thousands of medical patients, credit cardholders, homeowners and employees give up that right every day without even knowing they have done so.

Many mandatory arbitration clauses are tucker into shipping materials. Some lurk in the dense pages of bills and bank statements. Often the clauses appear in tiny type.

---

2 Note from Professor Carr: Some important history.

In 1992, the Bank of America started slipping mandatory arbitration clauses into bills sent to its credit card and account holders. Customers who continued to use their card or account, said the notices, would agree not to sue.

But a group of cardholders sued the bank, arguing that the so-called "bill sniffers" were unfair and deceptive. In 1998, the California Court of Appeal in San Francisco ruled in their favor, becoming one of the few courts in the nation to say that a business imposing arbitration on its customers "must clearly and unambiguously show" that they have agreed to waive their constitutional right to a jury trial.

For a while, the decision discouraged bill stuffing in the state. But in July, Berkeley resident Darcy Ting and other phone customers received "Dear AT&T Customer" letters. If they made one more long-distance call, the letters said, they would have to resolve all disputes of more than $5,000 in arbitration.

Ting was outraged. She led a class-action suit against AT&T in federal court in San Francisco.

"Why should I lose my rights?" asked Ting. "It is really unfair."

PROHIBITIVE FEES

Filing a case in California Superior Court typically costs from $90 to $185.

If the complaint involves discrimination, a state agency such as the California Department of Fair Employment and Housing or the federal Equal Employment Opportunity Commission might take the case for free. In certain employment disputes, the state Labor Commission might take the case, also for free.

But mandatory arbitration can require thousands of dollars to file a case. As a result, some people must pay fees they cannot afford or drop their legal complaints.

Lorraine Aho had to make that choice earlier this year in her wrongful firing case against Maxager Technology in San Rafael.

The American Arbitration Association ordered her to pay a $3,000 filing fee, plus any fees the arbitrator might charge. Her attorney, Mary Dryovage, says the fees could have topped $50,000.

"We told them to forget it," Dryovage says. "I wasn't going to let one of my clients get into a situation of having to declare bankruptcy to pursue her case."

Some arbitration firms charge less. Several courts, including the California Supreme Court, have ruled that employers must foot the bill in employment discrimination cases.

But American Arbitration Association, the nation's largest arbitration firm with more than 140,000 cases each year, charges up-front fees ranging from $500 for claims under $10,000 to more than $7,000 for claims above $1 million in commercial cases.

NO CLASS ACTIONS

Mandatory arbitration agreements often prohibit class actions, lawsuits that combine many claims so awards are large enough to cover legal fees and other costs. Class actions help people of modest means afford litigation and, although subject to abuse, enforce consumer protection and civil rights laws.

The National Arbitration Forum has assured potential clients that its rules will shield them from class actions and improve "the bottom line."

FleetBoston Financial Corp., Citigroup Inc. and MBNA Corp. recently barred credit card customers from joining any class actions against the companies, including suits already filed but not yet "certified" by courts.

NO JUDGES

Although many arbitrators are former judges, they are rarely required to follow the law. Some arbitrators are not even lawyers.

In 1997, Carl Posey's defamation and wrongful firing case against Paine Webber Inc. was assigned to a panel of three arbitrators in Nashville, Tenn. Two of the arbitrators weren't lawyers. The third, the panel's chairman, showed up wearing a white T-shirt and a khaki vest adorned with fishing lures.

"I remember asking the case administrator, 'Where did you get these guys—off a barstool?'" says Posey's attorney, Jeffrey Liddle.

After a full day of opening statements, the panel asked if the lawyers could go through the statements again. It soon became clear that the arbitrators would never grasp the case's nuances, says Liddle, so they agreed to quit.

A second panel was appointed. But when its chairman, a nonlawyer, leaped to his feet to stop Posey from getting documents he was legally entitled to, Liddle sensed more trouble. After a three-hour discussion, the second panel also quit.

Ultimately, the case was filed in federal court and settled.

"They just had a total misunderstanding of what we were about," says Posey, who had to pay the arbitrators $10,000 for the aborted hearings.

Paine Webber, now UBS PaineWebber, declined to comment.

LOST RIGHTS

Although supporters of arbitration praise the system's swift resolution of disputes, critics say speed and efficiency come at a price: the loss of rights guaranteed in court.

In 1999, San Francisco investment banker Nicholas Prassas sued Smith Barney Inc., claiming the bank fired him for not lying about campaign contributions that could have disqualified the firm from doing a bond deal with the state of Hawaii.

Smith Barney forced Prassas into arbitration, preventing, the allegations from being, aired in open court. During the case, his attorney says, the firm turned over few documents and gave superficial answers to his written questions. When the attorney tried to take deposition testimony from witnesses, the arbitrators stopped him.

Left with scant information to make his case, Prassas settled without a hearing.

"It was awful," says Prassas. "There seemed to be no rationale behind the arbitrators' decisions."

Smith Barney, now Salomon Smith Barney, declined to comment.

SMALL AWARDS

In many cases, arbitration agreements limit the size of awards.

In July, for example, AT&T's customer notice said disputes with the company would go to arbitration rather than to court and that the company would only pay for faulty phone service or direct damages to property—not for indirect, punitive or other damages normally allowed by law.

Award limits can make finding an attorney difficult. In December, the California Research Bureau, the Legislature's research wing, reported that almost a third of the medical patients who go to arbitration don't have attorneys.

Cliff Palefsky, a San Francisco attorney who has led the legal opposition to mandatory arbitration, says he has advised many women—particularly securities industry professionals—not to pursue a discrimination case in arbitration.

"The high costs, the amount they could win and the chances of winning all militate against pursuing it, because of the damage it could do to their careers," he says. "It breaks my heart to have to give someone with a good case that kind of advice."

NO EXPLANATION

Three years ago, after Sherri Warner lost her discrimination and wrongful firing suit in mandatory arbitration, a San Francisco arbitrator not only charged her nearly $16,000 for his time, he ordered her to pay her opponent's legal fees of more than $207,000.

The fee award would probably not have been allowed in court, and it forced Warner into bankruptcy.

But after her lawyer, Stephen Gorski, asked the arbitrator to explain his decision, the arbitrator refused when reminded no rules required him to do so.

Arbitrators rarely issue written opinions, making requests for review virtually impossible.

The National Association of Securities Dealers generally limits arbitration opinions to the names of the participants and their attorneys, the claims asserted and the outcome. In some cases, major clients of arbitration firms have prohibited arbitrators from even issuing opinions.

MCI telecommunications Corp., for example, agreed in 1994 with Endispute, which later merged with Judicial Arbitration and Mediation Service now JAMS, that awards, "shall not include any findings of fact or conclusions of law."

As a marketing company pointed out in its 1996 lawsuit against MCI, an arbitrator's finding that MCI had engaged in "willful misconduct" would have exposed the company to increased liability under federal regulations.

UNENFORCED ETHICS CODES

In recent years, mounting complaints about arbitration have prompted the nation's largest arbitration firms to adopt fairness standards.

Starting in 1995, for example, American Arbitration Association agreed to abide by "protocols" for running arbitrations in employment, consumer and health care cases. In health care, the association said it would accept only cases that people had voluntarily agreed to submit to arbitration after the dispute arose.

But the standards are not enforceable, and the association seems to ignore them.

In 1999, for example, Maureen Alexander filed a complaint against Blue Cross of California, claiming that a doctor removed her gown during a routine checkup and, for no apparent reason, poked her breasts and pelvic area with a pin, according to court papers.

Blue Cross forced her into arbitration, and American Arbitration took the case, even though Alexander said she didn't know she had signed an arbitration clause.

The arbitrator failed to apply the association's health care rules, including requirements for sharing documents and other information, and ruled against Alexander.

She sued Blue Cross to overturn the award, claiming the arbitrator was biased and ignored applicable laws, but she lost. She then sued the American Arbitration Association for breaching its own protocols, but a federal court dismissed her suit earlier this year.

Meanwhile, in a separate case last year, American Arbitration Senior Vice President Robert Meade submitted a sworn affidavit saying the organization 'does not require compliance with the (health care) protocol for cases we administer."

In other cases, the association has also failed to require its arbitrators to follow the consumer or employment protocols.

American Arbitration spokeswoman Kersten Norlin says the association enforces the protocols unless a case "doesn't fall under one of the defined categories. You may have an employment arbitration clause involving a health care company, for example. So it's not always black or white."

Palefsky says that's nonsense.

"The protocols," he says, "are all just a marketing ploy."

THE LAST BARRIERS

On Wednesday, attorneys for the Equal Employment Opportunity Commission will appear before the U.S. Supreme Court on behalf of 27-year-old Scotty Baker.

In November 1992, Baker's white Corolla flipped off a rain-slickened highway near his home in South Carolina. He walked away with a bump on his head, but a week later started to have periodic seizures.

In 1994, he filled out an application for a job cooking at the Waffle House in Columbia. He got the job, but turned it down. A few weeks later, he applied for a similar job at the Waffle House in West Columbia.

The manager hired him on the spot, without asking Baker to complete an application. When Baker mentioned his seizures, the manager just said, "Show up for work at 7 a.m.," Baker says.

About two weeks into the job, Baker suffered a seizure, and the manager fired him. The manager said, "It's bad for business to have you spazzing out in front of the customers," says Baker.

Eight months later, he consulted a lawyer about suing Waffle House for discriminating against a disabled employee. That was when he learned about the arbitration clause at the bottom of the application he had filled out for the Wattle House in Columbia.

In barely readable type, a four-line paragraph said any dispute involving the company would go to binding arbitration.

Baker says he never saw the arbitration clause. Besides, the clause was on the application he had completed at the first Waffle House, not at the Waffle House in West Columbia where he worked.

But arbitration was his only recourse. And he would have to pay half the costs, including the arbitrator's fees. Out of work and seeking reinstatement to a job that paid $5.50 an hour, Baker couldn't afford it.

In 1996, the Equal Employment Opportunities Commission sued Waffle House in the U.S. District Court in Columbia, S.C., claiming the company had violated the Americans with Disabilities Act by firing Baker for his seizure. Waffle House, as expected, moved to force the case into arbitration.

Waffle House and its attorneys declined to comment on the case.

When a federal judge ruled that Baker wasn't bound by any arbitration agreement, Waffle House appealed. In October 1999 the appeals court reversed the ruling deciding not only that Baker must go to arbitration, but that the "strong policy favoring arbitration" barred the EEOC from suing Waffle House for damages and, in effect, doing an end run around the agreement.

The court, though, also acknowledged the EEOC's congressionally mandated duty to protect the public's interests. The agency could, therefore, seek an order stopping Waffle House from illegally firing any disabled workers.

That is the issue now before the U.S. Supreme Court. Can a federal watchdog like the EEOC use every means provided by Congress, including suing for damages, to enforce the laws against employment discrimination and other civil rights violations?

"I can't imagine the court will stop the EEOC from enforcing the law," says Carrington, "but who knows? And if workers have to protect themselves from discrimination without the EEOC, to bargain for their own rights, then that means they don't have any rights."

SUPREME COURT RULINGS EXPANDING THE ROLE OF ARBITRATION

In a series of controversial rulings since 1983, the U.S. Supreme Court has encouraged companies to impose mandatory arbitration on the public. But critics say the rulings misinterpret the Federal Arbitration Act.

Federal Arbitration Act

For years courts allowed people to back out of bad arbitration agreements. In 1925, Congress passed a bill making arbitration agreements as enforceable as any other contract. During congressional debates, the bill's support assured critics that the new law would apply only to "merchants" who entered agreement voluntarily.

1983—New policy favoring arbitration

In the mid-1970s, fears of a litigation explosion prompted judges and companies to push arbitration as an alternative to laws. In 1983, without explanation, the high concluded that the Federal Arbitration created a "liberal federal policy favoring arbitration."

1984—Trumping state law

Citing that "federal policy," Chief Justice Warren Burger wrote for the court that arbitration clauses preempt state laws protecting the public's right to go to court dissent, Justice Sandra Day O'Connor said decision "utterly fails to recognize the congressional intent underlying the (Fed Arbitration Act)."

1985—Fair and competent

In a case enforcing an arbitration agreement an antitrust action, the high court called arbitration just as fair and competent as legal system. Justice John Paul Stevens disagreed, calling arbitration "despotic decision making."

1989—Ignoring consumer protections

Reversing an earlier ruling, Justice Anthony Kennedy wrote for the court that a securities firm could force a disgruntled customer into arbitration, even though arbitrators might not enforce the consumer protections of securities laws. Justice Stevens compared the decision to "an indefensible brand of judicial activism."

1991—Lost civil rights

The high court ruled that an employee must take age discrimination case to arbitration, breaking with its longstanding position that civil rights cases were too important and legally complex to handle in arbitration.

1995—Undermining state protections

The Supreme Court held that states could not limit mandatory arbitration with, for example, laws ensuring that consumers, employees and others understand the rights they are giving up by agreeing to arbitration.

2001—Covering employees

Earlier this year, the high court ruled for the first time that the Federal Arbitration Act applied to all employees, except transportation workers.

STARK DIFFERENCE BETWEEN COURT AND ARBITRATION

Advocates of arbitration say the process is swift, efficient and inexpensive. But critics say arbitration can mean high filing fees, unqualified arbitrators, lost legal rights, limited awards and no appeals.

FEES

Court: Filing a case in state Superior Court costs from $90 to $185, depending on the amount claimed.

Arbitration: Filing fees for arbitration can cost thousands of dollars, depending on the case and the arbitration firm. Fees for hearing rooms and the arbitrator's time can run tens of thousands of dollars more and discourage individuals from pursuing a case.

JUDGES

Court: Judges or other judicial officers hear cases.

Arbitration: Many arbitrators are former judges, but some are not even lawyers. Arbitrators are rarely required to follow the law and are regulated in only two states.

PICKING JUDGES

Court: Judges are usually assigned according to a rotation or by a presiding judge.

Arbitration: Parties select arbitrators, usually from a list compiled by an arbitration firm. Firms offer parties various methods of striking names from the list and reducing them to one. If the parties cannot agree, the firm may designate an arbitrator.

INDIVIDUAL RIGHTS

Court: The right to a fair process is protected by legal safeguards such as discovery, testimony and evidence rules.

Arbitration: Court rules do not apply, meaning the arbitrator—sometimes guided by an arbitration agreement or the rules of an arbitration firm—controls the process.

AWARDS

Court: Judges and juries decide how much an injured party should receive.

Arbitration: Awards are generally lower than in court, and arbitration agreements sometimes limit the type of damages an individual can recover..

APPEALS

Court: Judges' decisions are public record and subject to appeal.

Arbitration: Most decisions by arbitrators are confidential. They cannot be appealed and are subject to judicial review only in narrow circumstances.

CIVIL RIGHTS TAKE A BEATING

The stories of three people who discovered how hard it is to fight mandatory arbitration.

—No arbitration, no job

For three years, Donald Lagatree worked as a legal secretary at a Long Beach firm, receiving regular bonuses and pay raises. Then in June 1997, the firm asked him to agree "that any claims arising out of or relating to my employment ... shall be resolved by final and binding arbitration."

When Lagatree refused, the firm fired him.

Several months later, he took another secretarial position, this one at a Los Angeles law office. On his first day, he was handed a letter to "confirm" the deal, including his agreement to take all disputes to arbitration.

Again Lagatree refused to agree to arbitration, and, once again, he was fired.

He sued both firms for wrongful termination and lost in the state courts. The federal Equal Employment Opportunity Commission is pursuing the case before the U.S. Court of Appeals in San Francisco.

The right to go to court "just seemed too important to give away," said Lagatree.

—Even egregious decision stands

Rosalind Smith says her co-worker ogled her breasts, licked his lips and gyrated against her from behind. He complimented her "onion-shaped butt," bragged of his sexual prowess and repeatedly asked for a "one-night stand."

When Smith, a secretary at a Pennsylvania social services agency, finally complained to her supervisor, she was fired. In 1999, she filed a claim against the agency and her co-worker, charging them with sexual harassment and retaliation.

At the formal hearing, her co-worker admitted asking her for a one-night stand and making vulgar comments about her body. But the arbitrator ruled against Smith.

So she went to federal court, seeking to overturn the arbitrator's decision.

The judge acknowledged that her case met all the requirements for proving sexual harassment.

And when she argued that the arbitrator was simply wrong about the law, the judge agreed.

But courts are prohibited from overturning even the most egregious decision by an arbitrator, unless it makes virtually no sense at all.

In declining to reverse the ruling in Smith's case, the judge wrote that he could not "conscientiously conclude that the arbitrator's ... decision exceeded all bounds of rationality."

—"Plaintiffs have themselves to blame'

Three years ago, when Gabriel Martinez lost his job with Scott Specialty Gases Inc. in Fremont, he and his wife sued the company in Alameda County Superior Court, claiming the firm had fired him illegally and ruined their lives. The company responded that Martinez was bound by the arbitration agreement he had signed when he had signed when he started work.

Although Martinez insisted that he had repudiated the agreement when it was presented to him, the court ordered him to arbitration.

Martinez appealed, and late last year the state Court of Appeal in San Francisco ruled against him and his wife.

Then the court informed Martinez that by pursuing his case in court, he had waived his right to take the case to arbitration. Martinez was left with no recourse against his former employer, either in court or in arbitration.

"While perhaps genuinely regretting this now, ... " the court wrote, "plaintiffs have themselves to blame for their predicament."

THE FINE PRINT

Waffle House's policy requiring parties to settle disputes through arbitration—and give up their right to a jury trial—appears in small, barely readable type at the bottom of its employment application form. An excerpt:

"The parties agree that any dispute or claim concerning Applicant's employment with Waffle House, Inc. ... or the terms, conditions or benefits of such employment, including whether such dispute or claim is arbitrable, will be settled by binding arbitration."

52 Private Justice: Can Public Count on Fair Arbitration?[1]

Financial Ties to Corporations Are Conflict of Interest, Critics Say

By Reynold Holding, *San Francisco Chronicle*

[ADR]

THE NOTICE THAT arrived in Darcy Ting's mailbox early last July was troubling enough.

AT&T, her long-distance phone company, was cutting off her right to sue. If Ting made one more long-distance call from her Berkeley home, the notice said, she would have to resolve claims of more than $5,000 against the company through the American Arbitration Association.

What the notice didn't disclose was that the association had invested $100,000 in AT&T bonds the previous November.

"How can I possibly count on their being fair?" asks Ting, who has sued AT&T on behalf of California customers who received the notice.

In fact, the American Arbitration Association, the nation's largest arbitration firm, owns millions of dollars' worth of stocks and bonds in major corporations whose legal disputes its arbitrators have heard. Some of the corporations also buy "memberships" in the association, and their executives sit on the association's board of directors.

The association denies that any of these financial relationships affect its ability to provide fair and neutral arbitrators.

But critics say the arbitration industry is riddled with conflicts of interest that would never be tolerated in court.

"Virtually any lawyer who has had to use arbitration doubts the integrity of the system in a way we never doubted the integrity of the public courts," says Arne Werchick, a lawyer, arbitrator and former president of the California Trial Lawyers Association.

Over the past two decades, the U.S. Supreme Court has allowed corporate America to impose mandatory arbitration on the public so that companies can avoid lawsuits and judges can lighten their workloads. But the pressure to generate income and attract new clients has driven some arbitrators and their firms to engage in practices that cast doubt on the fundamental fairness of the process:

—Financial investments. The American Arbitration Association and other arbitration firms own millions of dollars in stocks and bonds in some of the companies whose disputes the firms' arbitrators hear.

1 **Note from Professor Carr: This is the second of three articles that recently appeared in the San Francisco Chronicle. They are designed to show/illustrate for you that there is/may be a "dark-side" to ADR that many folks do not like to talk about or address.**

—Undisclosed contracts. Large arbitration firms sell administrative and consulting services to many clients they provide arbitrators to, contracts that aren't revealed to people forced into arbitration.

—Soliciting clients. Many arbitration firms court corporate clients by stressing the small awards and cursory procedures, sometimes asking ostensibly neutral arbitrators to help salesmen solicit new business.

—Repeat players. Researchers have found that some arbitrators may succumb to the pressure of ruling for the clients who use their services repeatedly.

—Captive operators. Some arbitration firms have such a close relationship with their clients that arbitrators may rule in the companies' favor to keep the business.

Last year, the American Arbitration Association's own arbitrators and mediators sharply criticized the firm for filing a legal brief that supported electronics company Circuit City's position before the U.S. Supreme Court. Circuit City wanted to enforce an arbitration clause against an employee, and American Arbitration didn't disclose that the clause named it to handle the dispute.

The association insists the brief merely explained how arbitration worked. But in a Sept. 15, 2000, letter to the association, American Arbitration mediator Elaine Leitner wrote that the brief "is not only unseemly, but [...]

Even arbitration's strongest supporters insist that an industry based on neutrality cannot tolerate the appearance of a conflict of interest.

"The only thing that keeps arbitrators in business is their integrity," says Arnold Zack, former president of the National Academy of Arbitrators.

FINANCIAL INVESTMENTS

AT&T is not the only corporate client in which American Arbitration has held a financial interest.

The association also has owned shares of Bank of America, Aetna, Cigna Corp., General Electric and other corporations whose disputes its arbitrators have heard.

Several corporate officers of General Electric, Sprint and other companies that use the association's arbitrators have been directors of American Arbitration. And last year the association received more than $2.1 million in membership fees from Aetna, GE Industrial Systems and other corporations, institutions and individuals.

Kersten Norlin, spokeswoman for American Arbitration, said an outside investment firm manages all the nonprofit association's investments and the association's actual knowledge of the investments "is extremely limited." And whatever the affiliations of its directors or members, she explained, arbitrators are largely independent from the organization and usually selected from panels by the parties themselves.

"Our neutrals decide the outcome of cases. AAA doesn't," Norlin said.

But critics stress that the association has substantial control over the cases it resolves: American Arbitration Association sets the arbitration rules, selects and trains the panels and chooses arbitrators when parties cannot.

"Do you honestly believe," says Alabama plaintiffs' attorney Charles Robinson Jr., "that a consumer has a fair chance when the company on the other side of the table pays yearly fees to AAA?"

UNDISCLOSED CONTRACTS

Two years ago, several long-distance phone customers complained that MCI WorldCom Inc. had concealed a mandatory arbitration clause in documents filed with the Federal Communications Commission. The clause required customers to file all complaints with Irvine-based JAMS, formerly Judicial Arbitration and Mediation Service.

But JAMS, argued the customers, was financially beholden to MCI under side agreements that had never been made public.

One of the customers, a company owned by George Hopper of Lexington, Ky., said in legal papers supporting a complaint to the FCC that JAMS had earned more than $325,000 providing administrative and consulting services to MCI had received phone service from MCI, and, until 1999, owned primarily by investment firm Warburg, Pincus & Co.

As a result, Hopper argued, the arbitration rules were "unjust, unreasonable, unlawful and unenforceable."

JAMS President Steve Price says MCI never paid for JAMS' long-distance service, the investment firm "never attempted to influence JAMS" and "any claim that this program was biased is just not true."

In 1998, a federal appeals court upheld the contract with MCI.

Another major arbitration firm, National Arbitration Forum in Minnesota, cited the MCI decision in a paper presented to the American Bar Association last year.

"Irrespective of allegations of bias," the company said, "the fact remains that the arbitration administrator—and its employees—cannot affect the outcome of an arbitration hearing any more than courthouse employees can affect the outcome of litigation."

But critics point to the overwhelming success of First USA N.A., one of the forum's biggest clients.

The bank has filed more than 50,000 collection cases with the forum and paid it several million dollars in fees, according to deposition testimony. And since 1998, First USA has won 99.6 percent of the cases, according to figures produced in a class-action lawsuit.

The forum's managing director, Edward Anderson, rejects the figures, saying the bank might have done as well in federal court.

"The forum is neutral, the arbitrators are neutral and the system has all sorts of protections against any claimant getting a leg up," Anderson says.

But on Sept. 30, 1999, a federal judge in Florida refused to enforce a mandatory arbitration agreement against a First USA credit cardholder because the card company had "failed to demonstrate ... that the National Arbitration Forum is a neutral, inexpensive and efficient forum."

On June 1, the U.S. Court of Appeals reversed the decision, saying First USA was not required to demonstrate the forum's neutrality.

SOLICITING CLIENTS

Formed in 1996, the American Arbitration Association had little competition for decades. But in the late 1980s and early 1990s, the Supreme Court dramatically expanded the role of mandatory arbitration, and the demand for arbitrators soared.

JAMS, National Arbitration Forum and other competitors commanded an increasing share of the market, and the association was forced to fight for business.

American Arbitration arbitrators began to accompany the firm's salesmen on calls to potential client—helping to solicit business from companies whose disputes the association hoped to resolve say former association employees.

In a Jan. 14, 2000, memo, Regional Vice President Paul Van Loon in San Francisco asked arbitrators for introductions to corporations and to "indicate ... if you would like to make the call with us.

Van Loon declined to comment, but association spokeswoman Norlin says he was referring to phone calls rather than personal calls, which, she says, arbitrators are barred from attending.

Although American Arbitration stresses that it does not tell potential clients they will prevail over employees, consumers and other individuals more often in arbitration than in the courts, that is the message the companies receive.

On the sales calls, often with arbitrators, "we would educate people on how arbitration was a less expensive, faster and confidential process," says one former salesman.

On a videotape played for workers at Red On a videotape played for workers at Red Lobster restaurants, American Arbitration arbitrator Bruce Chapin advised that a workplace dispute "is not a matter that would be best tried in front of a jury."

And the association's brochures have stressed "more rational outcomes than (in) the jury system."

REPEAT PLAYERS

Even reputable arbitrators are vulnerable to what has come to be known as the "repeat player" problem.

The problem arises because parties that frequently use arbitrators tend to have an advantage over individuals who go to arbitration once or twice. A repeat player who chooses an arbitrator and wins is more likely to select the same arbitrator in future cases. The prospect of more business gives the arbitrator a financial incentive to rule in the repeat player's favor.

In a 1997 study, Lisa Bingham, director of Indiana Conflict Resolution Institute, found that employees won just 16 percent of their cases against repeat players, defined as employers in arbitration at least twice a year. But the employees won 71 percent of their cases against nonrepeat players. Even when employees beat repeat players, the employees generally won no damages, the study found.

Last year, Bingham presented a revised study that accounted for new industry standards designed to make arbitrations fairer. Employees still won only 29 percent of the cases against repeat players compared with 51 percent against nonrepeat players.

Michael Young, co-chair of JAMS' Committee on Professional Standards and Public Policy, said in a recent article that "the risks of the repeat player advantage are real and can be disturbing," although he noted many arbitrators "take seriously their ethical obligations to be impartial."

By trying to reduce arbitration costs, the courts may have aggravated the repeat player problem.

In 1997, the U.S. Court of Appeals in Washington said an employee can't be forced into arbitration and then charged fees he wouldn't have incurred in court. The California Supreme Court reached a similar conclusion last year.

But making one party pay the fees skews the system, says Zack, who argues that parties should split the bill.

"I would like to think that if I did these cases, I would do what I think is fair regardless of where the chips fall," he says. "But I do have a gnawing feeling that if I hadn't had any cases for a while, and I saw the possibility of a lot of cases coming in from an employer, it might influence my decision."

CAPTIVE OPERATORS

Outside the major arbitration firms, thousands of arbitrators ranging from individual lawers to company-controlled panels operate beyond scrutiny or industry guidelines.

And in some cases, the close relationship between these independent operators and their clients has cast doubt on the fairness of their proceedings.

"It's the unregulated, cowboy arbitrators," says Bingham, "and the private panels that employers set up below the radar that you really have to worry about."

In March, a federal judge in Indiana ruled that a chain of restaurants called Ryan's Family Steak Houses could not enforce an arbitration agreement imposed on two waitresses who accused their manager of sexual assault.

The agreement required employees to resolve disputes before Employment Dispute Services Inc., a private company the restaurant paid to provide arbitration whenever the need arose. Employees made no comparable payment which the court found disturbing.

Employment Dispute Services "clearly has an incentive to maintain its contractual relationship with Ryan's," said the court. And since Employment Dispute Services also made the rules and picked the arbitrators, the court ruled there was "a strong potential for bias," and threw out the agreement.

It is rare, though, for a court to consider the fairness of an arbitration process before an award is issued. It is even rarer for a court to overturn an award—even when the process is fraudulent.

In a lawsuit filed four years ago, for example, three Los Angeles landlords say they agreed to a commercial tenant's demand for an arbitration clause that named the Southern California Arbitration Association to resolve any disputes.

Unknown to the landlords, said the complaint, the tenant's officers were business associates of the arbitration firm's principals.

Within a few months, the tenant fabricated complaints that the association then resolved in their favor, costing the landlords hundreds of thousands of dollars in bogus awards, the complaint said.

Other victims of the association had failed to overturn similar awards because judges are essentially powerless to disturb arbitration decisions. But last year, a Los Angeles Superior Court judge slapped the now-defunct association and related businesses with a $5.1 million fraud and racketeering judgment.

Legal experts acknowledge that arbitration scams may be common—but are very difficult to detect.

The lack of oversight in this (arbitration) business creates a giant loophole," said Gregg Martin, an attorney for the landlords. "It's not going to take a rocket scientist to figure out how to do this again and again."

NEW ETHICAL CODES

The financial pressure to get new business also can influence whether an arbitrator discloses information that might keep him off a lucrative case.

The U.S. Supreme Court acknowledged the problem as early as 1968. In a case involving an arbitrator who had failed to disclose $12,000 in income from one of the parties, Justice Hugo Black stressed that judge or jury foreman in that position would have been lacked off the case.

"We should, if anything, be even more scrupulous to safeguard the impartiality of arbitrators than judges," Black wrote for the court, "since the former have completely free rein to decide the law as well as the facts and are not subject to appellate review."

In 1994, several instances of egregious conflicts of interest persuaded the California Legislature to require that arbitrators, like judges, disclose certain potential conflicts.

But judges and arbitrators face different financial considerations.

"In court, if a judge recuses himself, nothing happens," explains William Cahill, a mediate and arbitrator and former San Francisco Superior Court judge. "But if you recuse yourself in the arbitration world, it's more complicated, because you might have to refund money. Some people don't easily do that."

In June 2000, a commission sponsored by Georgetown University Law Center and the CPR Institute for Dispute Resolution drafted code of ethics for arbitrators and arbitration firms.

The code calls on the firms to disclose "any interests or relationships" that "might reasonably create the appearance" of bias.

In a comment to that provision, the code's drafters say "it is essential to hold (the firms) ... to the highest standards of quality and competence."

William Slate, president of American Arbitration Association, is a member of the commission. But the firm has declined to say whether it will ever comply with the code.

53 Judges' Action Cast Shadow on Court's Integrity[1]

Lure of High-Paying Jobs as Arbitrators May Compromise Impartiality

By Reynold Holding, *San Francisco Chronicle*

[ADR]

TO KRISTY SHUBIN, IT just didn't seem fair.

Her boss had greeted the news of her pregnancy by demoting her, Shubin claimed, so she sued him for sex discrimination.

But a clause in her employment contract said she couldn't sue. She could only take her complaint to mandatory arbitration, a private process of resolving disputes without judges, juries or the rule of law. The same clause, though, allowed her boss to sue her in certain circumstances, a double-standard that Shubin cited in persuading a trial court to strike down the clause as "unconscionable."

But Shubin's employer appealed, and on Nov. 14, Justice Daniel Hanlon and two colleagues at the state Court of Appeal in San Francisco ruled the clause, with slight modifications, should stand.

The ruling outraged Shubin. What she didn't know was that while her case was pending, Hanlon had accepted a job with JAMS, formerly Judicial Arbitration and Mediation Service—the very firm that Shubin's contract had named to hear her dispute. In fact, the day before Hanlon and his colleagues issued their decision, JAMS advertised in the San Francisco Daily Journal, a legal newspaper, that it had hired Hanlon.

"There was a clear conflict of interest," says Professor Erwin Chemerinsky, a constitutional law and ethics expert at the University of Southern California Law School. "The judge had something to gain financially by enforcing clauses that might send cases to JAMS."

Hanlon declined to comment. But JAMS President Steve Price said, "it's inconceivable to suggest that a preeminent jurist who has served on the bench for more than 20 years with an impeccable reputation for nonbias ... would compromise his record in any way."

Price added that JAMS wouldn't have heard Shubin's case because the arbitration clause failed the firm's fairness standards.

For more than a decade corporate America has forced the public into mandatory arbitration—with the blessing of the Supreme Court.

While the system has enabled companies to avoid the costs and risks of jury trials, the nation's judges have benefited, too: Mandatory arbitration not only eases their workload, it offers them

1 Note from Professor Carr: This is the third of three articles that recently appeared in the San Francisco Chronicle. They are designed to show/illustrate for you that there is/may be a "dark-side" to ADR that many folks do not like to talk about or address.

potentially lucrative jobs as arbitrators after they leave the bench.

Nowhere have judges flocked to arbitration firms faster than in California, where private judging blossomed more than 20 years ago.

But today the business is "one of the single biggest problems facing the California judiciary," says Justice Anthony Kline of the state Court of Appeal in San Francisco.

Critics believe the allure of mandatory arbitration has caused sitting judges to act in ways that may compromise the integrity of the judicial system:

—Impressing arbitration firms. Some judges have tried to make themselves more attractive to arbitration firms by requesting specific assignments and pushing for swift settlements in complex disputes. One Los Angeles arbitration consultant gives judges a list of 10 ways to impress a potential employer.

—Financial conflict. By upholding disputed arbitration clauses shortly before joining arbitration firms, judges may have created at least the appearance of financial conflicts of interest.

—Clearing caseloads. Judges eager to clear their dockets of difficult and time-consuming discrimination lawsuits have forced such cases into arbitration, where important civil rights issues are resolved by arbitrators who are rarely required to know or follow the law.

—Client conflicts. Former judges working as arbitrators who return to court on temporary assignments have been accused of conflicts of interest by hearing cases involving clients of their current employers.

—Blocked decisions. In some cases, the state Supreme Court has blocked anti-arbitration decisions from being cited as legal precedent after being asked to do so by corporations, arbitrators and former judges.

Bills that would reform the arbitration industry are working their way through Congress and the state Legislature. But many businesses view mandatory arbitration as a shield against the risks and costs of lawsuits, and their financial and political clout may block efforts to restrain a system that even some judges believe is out of control.

"One might call mandatory arbitration the do-it-yourself approach to law reform," says Professor Jean Sternlight at the University of Missouri law school. "The company need not convince any legislature to pass revised laws, or persuade any judicial body to change court rules, but merely choose to eliminate pesky lawsuits on its own."

PRESSING ARBITRATION FIRMS

In recent years, the demand for private judges has soared.

Today the American Arbitration Association, JAMS and several other arbitration providers compete to hire the biggest names on the bench.

Although arbitrators need not be judges, or even lawyers, most are. And former judges are preferred because "lawyers don't trust each other," says Lucie Barren, head of Action Dispute Resolution Services in Los Angeles.

The attractions for judges are obvious. A Superior Court judge earns $133,055 a year, while top arbitrators can make $10,000 or more a day, in addition to retirement pay.

Judges who want to become arbitrators often beg off the criminal bench, where the number of cases is rising, and request assignments in civil court, where caseloads are down, so they can hone their settlement skills.

Barron, who advises judges wanting to become arbitrators, says it's a smart move.

"I have about 10 things that I work over with them while they are still on the bench," she explains. "I tell them to settle cases, develop an expertise, get on panels, do a lot of speaking, develop synopses of their cases, that sort of thing.

[...] arbitration and mediation because his salary as a Los Angeles Superior Court judge wasn't enough to support two kids in college. He prepared by getting assigned to the Court's family law calendar, he says, "knowing it would be useful" in attracting business.

Chernow says the lure of private judging makes sitting judges "more polite and respectful. Otherwise, they're not going to get any business."

But other judges find the practice troubling.

"Understandably," says Justice Kline, "lawyers are increasingly worried about the objectivity of judges who seek assignments they think will enhance their chances of landing a job as a private arbitrator."

FINANCIAL CONFLICTS

No one has accused judges of issuing favorable rulings to impress arbitration firms.

But critics say judges undermine the judiciary's credibility by joining the firms shortly after issuing opinions that uphold controversial arbitration clauses, particularly when those opinions are reversed on appeal.

"There's the appearance that the decisions are based on self-interest," says Professor Chemerinsky, "and that's very troubling."

On March 13, 1997, for example, U.S. District Judge Eugene Lynch ruled that securities broker Tonyja Duffield must go to arbitration with the sexual discrimination and harassment claim she had filed against her employer.

Duffield argued that she had not agreed to arbitration "knowingly" which the U.S. Court of Appeals had determined was a requirement for enforcing such agreements against employees. Lynch ruled against her anyway.

Less than four months later, JAMS announced that Lynch was joining its panel of arbitrators.

Ten months after he joined JAMS, the U.S. Court of Appeals in San Francisco overturned his ruling in the Duffield case.

Lynch declined to comment.

While stressing Lynch's "impeccable reputation," JAMS President Price explained that "at the end of the day, it doesn't matter to us how they (judges) rule in any individual case."

In a September 1999 decision, state Court of Appeal Justice William Masterson and two colleagues ruled that a law firm could fire legal secretary Donald Lagatree for refusing to sign a mandatory arbitration agreement more than three years after he was hired.

After discussing his options with Barron, Masterson retired to become a private judge in June 2000—five months before a federal judge barred Lagatree's former law firm from imposing arbitration on its employees. The law firm has appealed the decision. Last August, Masterson joined JAMS.

He says there may be sitting judges, who tailor their behavior to impress arbitration firms, but "I just don't see that happening."

Chemerinsky and others acknowledge that any appearance of conflict depends on how soon a judge becomes an arbitrator after upholding an arbitration clause.

In 1999, for example, Justice Christopher Cottle and two colleagues on the state Court of Appeal in San Jose ruled that San Diego's Technology Integration Group could force administrative assistant Amanda Lee to arbitrate her [...] and sexual discrimination suit—even though Lee didn't know she had waived her constitutional right to a jury trial.

The ruling reversed a trial court's decision and conflicted with the federal appeals court's ruling in the Duffield case.

The state Supreme Court agreed to review Lee's case, but then dismissed the appeal after the parties settled.

Earlier this year, Cottle retired from the bench and announced that he was discussing a job with JAMS. He has since decided to practice arbitration independently.

But Cottle says any conflict created by becoming an arbitrator after upholding an arbitration clause "was so remote that it never even came up as an issue in my mind."

Blocked decisions

In some cases, corporations, arbitration firms and former judges have lobbied against lower court rulings hostile to arbitration, and the state Supreme Court has "depublished" the decisions, in effect striking them from the books. Of about 850 published state Court of Appeal decisions last year, 22 were depublished.

In 1994, for example, the state Court of Appeal in San Francisco struck down an arbitration clause that a mortgage company had duped elderly borrowers into signing. The mortgage company had printed the clause in small, dense type, effectively preventing the borrowers from realizing that they were waiving their right to a jury trial, the court said.

The decision troubled the American Arbitration Association, its client, Bank of America, and others. The association and state Attorney General Dan Lungren asked the high court to depublish the ruling so that it could not be cited as legal precedent.

A Bank of America spokesman said Lungren was asked to get involved by the bank, which had contributed to his re-election campaign and was facing a class-action lawsuit accusing it of sneaking mandatory arbitration into agreements with card and account holders. A Lungren spokesman said the attorney general acted on the issue's merits.

On July 28, 1994, the state Supreme Court voted 6 to 1 to grant the request.

Two years later, Justice Armand Arabian joined American Arbitration and Chief Justice Malcolm Lucas joined JAMS. Both voted to depublish the decision.

The following year, the state high court depublished another controversial decision involving private judges.

When Edgar Rushing sued his employer, Lancaster Radiology Medical Group, for race discrimination, Los Angeles Superior Court Judge Victor Chavez ordered procedural matters resolved before a private judge—at the parties' expense. Rushing said he couldn't afford the process, but the judge ignored his objections.

Rushing's share of the bill totaled more than $18,000, and when Chavez ordered Rushing's lawyer to pay it, she refused.

The case went before the state Court of Appeal, and in 1996 Justice Miriam Vogel struck down Chavez's order, saying it would "slam the courthouse doors in the face of the poor."

Once again, the decision prompted calls for depublication, including a letter from former high-court Justice David Eagleson and five other retired California jurists working as private judges.

On February 5, 1997, the Supreme Court acquiesced to the request of its former colleagues and struck Vogel's ruling from the books.

It was a lamentable act of censorship," says Professor Stephen Barnett of Boalt Hall School of Law at the University of California at Berkeley. "It was made even worse in this case by the unfortunate fact that the future economic interests of the justices arguably were affected well."

CLIENT CONFLICTS

Conflicts can also arise when former judges working as arbitrators return temporarily to the bench.

In July 1999, for example, Escondido (San Diego County) restaurant owner Ruben Estrada sued Crusader Insurance Co. for denying his insurance claim. The case was assigned to a retired judge, Kenneth Ziebarth, who was filling a temporary vacancy on the San Diego Superior Court.

When Estrada's attorney, Jack Winters, discovered Ziebarth also worked at JAMS, he demanded that the judge step aside. Many insurance companies—including Crusader—use JAMS, and Crusader could "easily reward Judge Ziebarth for his handling of this case" by subsequently hiring the judge or one of his JAMS colleagues, argued Winters.

But Ziebarth refused to step down. Estrada appealed to the state Court of Appeal in San Diego, and last year the court ordered Ziebarth to explain why he should remain on the case. Instead, the judge stepped down.

"I didn't believe then, and I still don't believe there was as conflict," says Ziebarth. "I was in a no-win situation. If I ruled for the plaintiff, the defense would have thought I was bending over backward not to be biased. If I had favored the defendant, it would have solidified the plaintiffs belief."

Clearing caseloads

For decades, the U.S. Supreme Court insisted that civil rights cases be heard in federal court because arbitration's abbreviated procedures and minimal legal protections would give the cases short shrift.

But in 1991, the high court changed its mind—and federal judges took full advantage.

A study by the U.S. Court of Appeals in New York four years ago found that federal judges consider discrimination cases too difficult and time-consuming. So with the high court's blessing, the judges have forced such cases into mandatory arbitration at an increasing rate—and, say some legal experts, at a troubling cost.

"What the (Supreme) Court has not yet recognized," warns Professor David Schwartz of the University of Wisconsin Law School, "is that it has allowed corporations to avoid not only the courts, but the regulatory impact of the law."

Even some judges are critical

Montana Supreme Court Justice Terry Trieweiler says rulings upholding mandatory arbitration illustrate "an all too frequent preoccupation on the part of federal judges with their own caseloads and a total lack of consideration for the rights of individuals."

Mandatory arbitration, he says, "subverts our system of justice as we have come to know it."

PROSPECTS FOR REFORM

In February, California Sen. Sheila Kuehl, D-Santa Monica, introduced a bill that would allow employees bound by mandatory arbitration to file employment disputes with the state's Department of Fair Employment and Housing.

In June, Reps. Dennis Kucinich, D-Ohio, Barney Frank, D-Mass., and other members of Congress introduced a bill that would overturn the recent Circuit City decision, in which the U.S. Supreme Court granted employers in almost every industry the power to impose arbitration on employees.

"Circuit City made it mandatory," says Kucinich, "that we address arbitration's destructive undermining of a wide range of civil rights protections."

But both bills are likely to face intense resistance from business interests, and politicians from Sacramento to Washington, D.C., are keenly aware of that opposition, as Kuehl recently discovered when she ran into Gov. Gray Davis at a party.

"He started shaking his head," says Kuehl, "and said, 'That employment arbitration bill, I really don't want to see it on my desk.'"

Davis declined to comment.

Kuehl has postponed any action on the bill until next year.

REFORMS PROPOSED FOR FAIRER SYSTEM

Proposals to reform mandatory arbitration essentially fall into two categories: Make it fairer or make it voluntary. Each raises difficult issues.

Several courts have required fairer procedures. The state Supreme Court, for example, ruled last year that arbitration imposed on employees must provide a neutral arbitrator, enough discovery to make a case, a written decision and limits on costs. Companies and arbitration firms also have adopted rules to protect individuals' rights.

Professor Samuel Estreicher at New York University law school says there has been "a lot of progress" toward making arbitration fair, and additional protections would "just jack up costs" in most cases.

But critics say the changes don't go far enough. And reforms such as granting employees rights to appeal or to obtain more information from an employer could make arbitration just as slow and expensive as court.

In any event, says Cliff Palefsky, a San Francisco attorney who leads the legal opposition to mandatory arbitration, "to work, a justice system must be perceived as fair. And mandatory arbitration will never be perceived as fair so long as someone is forced into it by a stronger party that sets the rules."

Palefsky and others advocate making arbitration voluntary. "If people really are better off in arbitration," he says, "they'll choose it."

And to arbitration advocates who say a voluntary system would produce too few cases to make arbitration practical, Palefsky says, "So what? Increasing the arbitration caseload is not the objective here."

Estreicher, though, says the objective is a better system of resolving disputes, and companies could not afford to create such a system unless enough consumers and employees committed to using it.

He also stresses that mandatory arbitration is as "voluntary" as any other contract term. "It's one of an array of things that an employer or company offers that you may or may not find acceptable," Estreicher says. "But you can't disfavor arbitration by saying you need special standards to apply."

Note from Professor Carr: After reading the pro-ADR article that I gave you ("ADR Finds True Believers") and the three "dark side of ADR" articles I gave you (the S.F. Chronicle articles), which one/side do you find more compelling/credible/convincing, and why? If I were able to give you an essay question on the exam, this would be a very good question to ask you to see if you read the articles, understood them, and "knew your stuff." Note that these articles are fair game for questions on the exam!!

Course Reader Materials for the Second Exam

Chapter Six

Intentional Torts; Negligence; and Strict Liability

Chapter Twenty

Agency Law

54 Torts and Business

Study Outline

*****Note that in this textbook at pages 187–235 I have inserted a number of newspaper articles, supplementary materials, misc. documents, etc. that relate to this material. These materials are required reading, and, are also fair game for the exam.**

*****Make *<u>sure</u>* that you also do the sample practice problems posted on Blackboard as it will help you master this material, test you to see if you "really" know and understand it, etc. You can expect similar problems to be on the exam.**

I. Nature and Function of Tort law

A. Torts are private (civil) wrongs against persons or their property. The primary aim of tort law is to compensate injured persons for such harms. Injured persons can sue for actual (compensatory) damages, and possibly punitive damages (where applicable)

II. Intentional Torts

A. **Battery** – occurs where the defendant *intentionally* does an act that results in a *harmful* **<u>or</u>** *offensive* touching (i.e., contact) of another without his/her consent

1. Harmful -- means that it produces any bodily injury
2. Offensive -- means that it is calculated to offend a person of ordinary sensitivity's reasonable sense of personal dignity and is unwarranted by the social usages prevalent at the time and place at which the contact is made
3. Intentional -- means that the defendant either desired to bring about the consequences of his act, acted recklessly, ***<u>or</u>***, believed that harmful or offensive consequences were *substantially certain* to follow from what he did
   a) See the ***England*** case in this textbook at page 187 for a good example of the "substantial certainty" rule/doctrine
4. Note: Direct contact between the plaintiff and the defendant is not necessary (e.g., a rock or baseball throw suffices).
5. Note: Making contact with anything connected with the plaintiff's body is sufficient (e.g., the defendant hits the plaintiff's purse, sunglasses (see O.J. article in this textbook at page 189), dog while the plaintiff is holding the dog's leash, hat, etc.)

6. Note: Doctrine of ***transferred intent*** applies – where you intend to injure one person or do throw something this is substantially certain to injure another person, but you miss and actually injure another (e.g., if I throw a rock at Bill, and miss and hit Paul, then I have committed a battery on Paul even though he is not the person I wanted/intended to hit!)
7. Note: The plaintiff need not be aware of the contact in order for a battery to occur (e.g., if you are asleep and somebody touches you with a knife, legally, that is a battery). Now, of course, whether and how much money a jury may award you for contact being made while you are unaware/asleep, etc., is an altogether different question.
8. Defenses:
   a) Consent to the contact-- must be free and voluntary; note that consent can be shown by words, acts, and in some cases even by silence and/or inaction!
   b) Self-Defense -- but force used must be reasonably necessary under the circumstances and not excessive
   c) Defense of others -- is a defense so long as reasonable under the circumstances
   d) Defense of property – is a defense so long as reasonable under the circumstances; but note that one can never use deadly force solely to protect or defend only property

See the cases and supporting articles in this textbook at pages 187–192 (and the practice problems posted on Blackboard) for practice and some good examples of some of the above concepts and rules re: battery.

B. **Assault** – any intentional *attempt or offer* to cause harmful or offensive contact with another is an assault, if it causes a ***well-grounded (i.e., reasonable) fear or apprehension*** of ***imminent harmful*** or ***offensive*** contact
   1. Threats of future harm/contact no are generally not sufficient (e.g., "I am going to beat you up next week") because not considered imminent, and, the law expects you to take the high road and avoid such confrontations (e.g., not show up next week and fight).
   2. Also, whether contact actually occurs between the plaintiff and the defendant is irrelevant (i.e., no contact is necessary for there to be an assault – an assault occurs when the plaintiff reasonably "fears" or "apprehends" harmful or offensive imminent contact)
   3. Threatening words alone are also generally not enough to constitute a civil assault (e.g., to say to someone, "I am going to pound your head in" is generally alone not enough; now, if you said that while holding a hammer in your hand and you were two inches from the other person's face, then that would probably be enough to be an assault!)
   4. Fear and apprehension are also not the same thing (either one will suffice).
   5. The plaintiff must also be ***aware*** of the threat (e.g., if you stand over someone's bed and waive a knife over them while they are asleep, legally, no assault has occurred)
   6. Defenses -- same as battery (see above)

Again, see the England case and supporting articles in this textbook at pages 187–192 (and the practice problems posted on Blackboard for practice and some good examples of some of the above concepts and rules re: assault.

C. **Defamation** -- tort designed to protect a person's ***reputation***. In order to prevail on a claim for defamation, the plaintiff must prove beyond a preponderance of the evidence that the defendant: (1) "published"; (2) a false <u>and</u> defamatory statement; (3) about another person

1. Libel – written defamation (includes television and radio). Because more "permanent" in nature than oral defamation, deemed to be more serious and is actionable without any proof of "special damage" to the plaintiff (i.e., evidence of the actual loss of anything of monetary value)
2. Slander – oral defamation. Generally, requires proof of special damage (meaning the plaintiff has to prove that he/she was actually somehow injured), but not when ***slander per se*** is involved in which the defamatory and harmful nature of the statement is *presumed*. In other words, these situations (slander per se) are deemed to be so bad/harmful that we/the court will PRESUME that the plaintiff was injured and he/she does NOT need to therefore prove that he/she was somehow damaged or injured in such situations/cases by the alleged defamatory statement at issue. But ... if it is NOT a slander per se case or situation, and only an "everyday/normal" oral defamation case, THEN, the plaintiff must ALSO prove some type of damage or injury in order to recover/prevail against the defendant.
   a) Examples of slander per se (where it will be presumed that the plaintiff was injured or damaged):
      (1) Where someone makes a false statement about another re: the commission of a crime of moral turpitude (e.g., rape, embezzlement); having a loathsome disease (e.g., AIDS); being professionally incompetent or guilty of professional misconduct; ***or*** guilty of serious sexual misconduct
3. *Defamatory* -- means it harms the reputation of another by injuring the community perception of him or by deterring others from associating or dealing with him.
4. *Publication* -- only need be from one person to another. Widespread communication is ***not*** necessary, and, making the statement to ***only*** the plaintiff does not normally count
   a) But see the ***Lewis*** case in this textbook at pages 201–203 which carves out an exception to the normal rule that "making the statement to only the plaintiff is not enough" (this case is an example of the common law in action and how it carves out/creates a new rule of law in the defamation area in order to do justice and equity for the plaintiff at issue
      (1) This case illustrates the "*self-publication doctrine*"— self-publication occurs where the defamed person in some way is compelled to communicate the defendant's statement to a third person, and it is reasonably foreseeable to the defendant that the defamed person would be so compelled. This case should teach you to be careful about what you say/don't say as a future employer to departing employees!
5. Miscellaneous rules regarding Defamation
   a) Groups -- individual member of a group of people that has been defamed cannot recover unless the group is so small that statement can reasonably be understood to refer to specific member; or, statement is such that it is reasonable to conclude that a particular group member is being referred to
   b) Opinions -- not actionable because not a statement of fact (obviously the line between a statement of fact vs. opinion is gray and murky)

6. ***Defenses*** available to a plaintiff in a defamation case (meaning that even if the plaintiff proves his/her case in chief, if the defendant can show that one or more of the below apply, then the defendant is NOT liable to the plaintiff)
   a) *Truth is an absolute defense* (but this can often be hard to prove)
   b) Absolute privileges -- statements by participants in judicial proceedings, legislators or witnesses in legislative proceedings, executive officials in the course of their duties, and between spouses in private (these are called absolute privileges because even if they are "abused' by the person who holds them -- e.g., they outright lie and defame a person in such a proceeding -- they still work and are valid!)
      (1) Rationale behind absolute privileges – in order for such proceedings, situations, relationships, etc. to be effective, open, etc., then as a policy matter we need people to feel completely free to say any and all things
   c) Conditional privileges -- Examples are intra-corporate communications (e.g., sending out an email that states to employees of the firm, "Bill (or someone) is believed to have stolen company property, and if anyone knows anything, please email back with the details"); a former employer answering questions about a former employee (but this can be/get risky so watch out for this one and if you answer such questions, do it carefully! – ***see, e.g., the article in this textbook at page 195 titled, "Employee References"***); fair comment (media reports of defamatory matter in reports of proceedings of official action, or originating from public meetings), etc.

      Basically, each of these examples is an example of making a statement to protect the interest of another/others

      (1) ***But if abused or exceeded (e.g., the person making the statement is lying, he/she knows it, and just wants to "get" the person they are defaming), <u>conditional privileges are lost</u>. An example of a conditional privilege being abused or lost would be a former employer providing defamatory information that is NOT related to job performance (such as lifestyle information)***

Again, see the defamation articles and cases at pages 193–203 of this textbook (and the practice problems posted on Blackboard) for practice and examples of some of the above concepts re: defamation.

D. **Fraud** – to recover for fraud in a civil case, a plaintiff must prove ALL of the following elements by a preponderance of the evidence:
   1. A false statement of fact (not opinion);
   2. Knowingly made by the defendant;
      a) "Knowingly" means the defendant knew that it was not true, did not believe it to be true, ***or,*** to recklessly disregard the truth of the statement. Negligently making the statement is not enough!! (We will study fraud more when we get to and study contracts)
   3. Made with the intent to induce the plaintiff to <u>rely</u> on the statement, which, in fact causes the plaintiff to rely;
   4. The plaintiff's reliance on the statement was reasonable and justifiable; <u>and</u>

5. The plaintiff was also somehow injured/damaged

Note that a fraud can occur not just through an affirmative misstatement (e.g., I sell you a car and lie by telling you that the car has 40,000 miles on it (and the odometer has that number on it), and, the car really has over 130,000 miles on it); a fraud can ALSO occur through non-disclosure (e.g., not disclosing a material fact that to the other party that you should disclose) – one example would be the ***Stambovsky*** case (that haunted house case) at pages 373–374 in this textbook.

Again, see the cases and supporting articles in this textbook at pages 205–210 (and the practice problems posted on Blackboard) for practice and some good examples of some of the above concepts and rules.

E. **Invasion of Privacy** (there are four different types/torts of invasion of privacy)
   1. *Intrusion of Solitude* -- intentional intrusion on the solitude or seclusion of another where the intrusion is highly offensive to a reasonable person and violates someone's reasonable expectation of privacy (e.g., open mail, tap phone or bank account, search home or body, harassing phone calls, etc.)
      a) Defenses – the intrusion was not highly offensive/the expectation of privacy was not reasonable; note that this cause of action is not available to dead persons or corporations because it is a personal right that is involved
   2. *Publicity Concerning Private Facts* -- publicity of such facts that are highly offensive to a reasonable person (e.g., a person's failure to pay debts, his illness, details re: sex life, etc.)
      a) Here, unlike defamation, the publicity must be widespread
      b) Defenses – the fact disclosed is a matter of public record or legitimate public interest; truth of the publicized fact is not a defense here; this cause of action is not available to dead persons or corporations because personal rights are involved; public officials and figures have no right of privacy concerning information that is reasonably related to their public lives
   3. *False Light* -- publicity that places a person in a false light in the public's eye can be an invasion of privacy if that false light is highly offensive to a reasonable person (e.g., signing a person's name to a telegram, attributing an inferior or scholarly work to the plaintiff, etc.)
      a) Here/for this tort, the publicity must be widespread
      b) Defenses -- truth is a defense here; this cause of action is not available to dead persons or corporations because it is a personal right; and defendants here enjoy the same constitutional protections as defamation defendants (e.g., free speech)
   4. *Appropriation of Name or Likeliness* -- using a well-known or famous person's name, likeness, picture, etc., in an advertisement or for other commercial purposes without their consent
      a) E.g., using Tiger Woods' picture in an advertisement without his permission

For some great examples of how a privacy legal issue can come up in today's e-commerce world, see the articles and materials as pages 211–222 in this textbook. Also, refer/remember back to the "**Not as Private as You Think**" 60 Minutes video that (time permitting) I may show you in class.

And again, see the cases and supporting articles in this textbook at pages 211–222 (and the practice problems posted on my Blackboard) for practice and some good examples of some of the above concepts and rules.

F. **False Imprisonment** – the intentional ***confinement of another*** for an appreciable length of time (a few minutes is enough) ***without his consent***
   1. Defenses -- consent, plaintiff's lack of knowledge or awareness of the confinement (e.g., someone is asleep and you lock the door on them while they are asleep)
   2. Store owners and shoplifters
      a) Traditional rule -- the store is liable if the plaintiff is later found to be innocent of shoplifting
      b) The more modern and applicable rule – the store is not liable if it had a reasonable belief the plaintiff shoplifted, acted reasonably and only detained the plaintiff for a reasonable period of time. [Note from Professor Carr: This is a more flexible rule; but shopkeepers are only protected if they act REASONABLY in these various facets. **This is often called or referred to as the "shopkeepers privilege"]**
         (1) Rationale: to accommodate and balance the interests of store owners and the public

Again, see the cases and supporting articles in this textbook at pages 223–230 (and the practice problems posted on Blackboard) for practice and some good examples of some of the above concepts and rules re: false imprisonment.

G. **Intentional Infliction of Emotional Distress** -- e.g., prank telephone calls, co-worker stalking another co-worker, a credit collection agency making harassing telephone calls to a debtor every morning between 1:00 a.m. and 5:00 a.m., etc.
   1. Elements:
      a) Defendant's conduct must be "so outrageous in character, and so extreme in degree as to go beyond all possible bounds of decency, and to be regarded as atrocious and utterly intolerable in a civilized community"
      b) The plaintiff's emotional distress must also be severe in order for him/her to recover
         (1) Note: is proof of bodily harm or injury (e.g., a physical injury such as an ulcer; break out in hives, etc.) required here in order for the plaintiff to recover/to prove that the plaintiff suffered "severe emotional distress"? (Possibly -- it depends on the state; some states require it and others do not)
         (2) Note: remember that the "intent" to cause intentional infliction of emotional distress works the same way as it does for assault and/or battery. … The intent can be the intent to actually cause the plaintiff to suffer extreme emotional distress OR if it is "substantially certain" to cause such distress to the plaints (remember the **English** case herein – flying hamburger case!) —Professor Carr

Again, see the cases and supporting articles in this textbook at pages 227–232 (and the practice problems posted on Blackboard) for practice and some good examples of some of the above concepts and rules re: intentional infliction of emotional distress.

H. **Trespass** -- is an offense against the right to ***possession*** of ***property*** (note that "property" can be real property (i.e., real estate) or personal property (e.g., a company's computer system)

1. Elements:
   a) The intentional and unlawful entry onto/into property in the possession of another (e.g., hiking on someone's property without their consent; having a party that sends loud sound waves across a neighbor's property; hacking into another's website or computer system)
   b) Unlawfully remaining on/in another's property, after lawful entry (e.g., after your lease expires you don't leave the rental unit)
   c) Unlawfully causing something to enter onto/into property possessed by another (e.g., throwing a beer can on your neighbor's property), ***OR***
   d) Failure to remove something from property which you have a duty to remove (e.g., your neighbor says you can park your car at his house for one month and you fail to come pick it up after the one month expires and just leave it there)
2. In most jurisdictions, no actual harm or damage to the property is required for there to have been a trespass
3. Defenses: trespass was warranted/reasonable/justified (e.g., entering the property to assist someone in danger), showing that the purported owner did not actually have the right to possess the property, etc.
   a) Note that mistake is generally NOT a defense here (e.g., you were on a hike and did not realize that you were on somebody else's property). Thus, watch where you are going!!

Again, see the cases and supporting articles in this textbook at pages 233–235 (and the practice problems posted on Blackboard) for practice and some good examples of some of the above concepts and rules re: trespass. See also the two examples of trespass below.

Two other examples of the tort of trespass:

1. At 11:30 one night, Jeff Berg, the Chairman of ICM in Hollywood, received an emergency phone call from a company assistant. Unexpectedly returning to the office, the assistant had come upon several employees hauling boxes of files out to station wagons and cars. The culprits were four top employees leaving to start their own creative management firm. "This was an act of trespass," Mr. Berg said. "We have been advised by counsel that this conduct is actionable." Mr. Berg added that the material taken involved documents about clients and the firm's business matters. ICM represents stars such as Mel Gibson, Julia Roberts, Michelle Pfeiffer and Jodie Foster. Under pressure from Mr. Berg, the employees returned all the files by dawn.

2. Marisa owns all of the apartment buildings on Elm Street, except one. Many of the apartments are rented to students. She hired Rajiv to manage the units and tells him that, under the terms of the leases, she has the right to ask guests to leave if a party becomes too rowdy. But she forgets to tell Rajiv that she does not own one of the buildings, which happens to house a college sorority.

One night, when the sorority is having a rambunctious party, Rajiv hustles over and starts ejecting the noisy guests. The sorority is furious and sues Rajiv for trespass. If the sorority wins its suit against Rajiv, Marisa would have to pay the judgment, plus Rajiv's attorney's fees, because she had told him to quell noisy parties, and event though he did not realize he was trespassing.

*****Again, folks, I encourage you to do the practice problems on intentional torts that I have posted on Blackboard. You may feel that you know/understand the above material, and, you may. But you also may not. So, be safe and do these practice problems. Many of them involve the application of the above concepts and that is a great way to learn (the only way, really) to see if you really do know and understand this material. – Prof. Carr**

55 England v. S & M Foods, Inc.[1]

511 So.2d 1313 (La. Ct. App. 1987)

[Assault and battery]

BETTY ENGLAND WORKED at a Dairy Queen restaurant owned by S & M Foods in Tallulah, Louisiana. One day while she was at work, her manager, Larry Garley, became upset when several incorrectly prepared hamburgers were returned by a customer. Garley allegedly expressed his dissatisfaction by using profane language and throwing a hamburger that hit England on the leg. England filed a battery suit against Garley and S & M and won a $1,000 judgment. Garley and S & M appealed.

Jones, Judge

Defendants contend no battery was committed because Garley did not intend to inflict bodily harm upon England. They argue Garley was disgusted about the returned hamburgers and threw one toward the trash can and it inadvertently splattered on her and Alcie Rash, another employee. They contend that England's embarrassment was caused as much by her overreaction to the situation as by Garley's conduct.

England said that Garley used profane language when he told her to prepare the hamburgers correctly. She said Garley, while looking straight at her, then threw the hamburger which hit her on the leg. She testified that she argued with Garley about the matter and that several patrons observed the incident which caused her to cry and become emotionally upset.

Rash said that she did not see Garley throw the hamburger, but observed it hit the floor and splatter mayonnaise and mustard on her and England.

A battery is any intentional and unpermitted contact with the plaintiff's person or anything attached to it. In the area of intentional torts, intent means the defendant either desired to bring about the physical results of his act or believed they were substantially certain to follow from what he did. Mental distress and humiliation in connection with a battery are compensable items of damage.

The totality of the evidence provided a substantial basis for the trial judge to conclude Garley must have been substantially certain the hamburger would hit England or splatter on her when he threw it toward her. His contact with her was, therefore intentional and unpermitted and constituted a battery.

Judgment for England affirmed.

1 **Note from Professor Carr: This case is an excellent example of a battery and the unique way that it can come up in a business context. Also, if Betty saw the hamburger coming at her and she felt a well-founded (i.e., reasonable) "fear" or "apprehension," of "imminent contact" then the defendant has <u>also</u> committed an assault!! Now whether and to what extent a jury would award damages for such a tort is another issue/ question!!**

56 "He's Back"

[Assault and battery]

AP/WIDE WORLD PHOTOS

HE'S BACK *O.J. Simpson, right, gestures as he talks with his attorney Yale Galanter, left, in Miami circuit court on Oct. 10 for the second day of jury selection for his trial. Simpson faces two to 16 years in state prison if convicted of auto burglary and battery charges based on an angry road encounter last Dec. 4 during which he allegedly snatched the sunglasses off a motorist's face.*[1]

1 Note from Professor Carr: Illustrates how O.J. may have committed the tort of battery by making "contact" with something "attached" to the plaintiff (here, the plaintiff's sunglasses). Also, if the motorist also saw O.J.'s grab/reach coming <u>and</u> felt reasonable "fear" or "apprehension" of "imminent contact" there may also be an assault!!

57 Flight Attendants Say They Lack Training for New Role in Security

The Wall Street Journal

[Assault and battery]

WITH MOST PILOTS soon to be locked with cross bars behind cockpit doors, suddenly vulnerable flight attendants are asking themselves, their unions and companies, "What do we do now?"

They know if there is trouble in the cabin, they must rely on their wits to keep would-be terrorists from making their way into the cockpit. Yet they have no new training or weapons for being sky cops and they fear the heightened airport security is too superficial to keep other suicidal hijackers from getting on planes.

"I'd really like to have some protection for myself—stun guns or mace or something—because we've been told the cockpit will not be coming out to help us," says Cindi Fisk, a 16-year Delta Air Lines attendant. "That was always our ace in the hole."

Most airlines are quickly deploying stopgap security measures and the government plans to trail a phalanx of sky marshals. Pilots continue to give guidance in preflight briefings. But for the first time, flight attendants are largely on their own as they assume the unwelcome job of being the first line of defense against mayhem. "We're asking them to do something that wasn't in their job description," says one executive at a major airline.

Airlines say they understand their attendants' concerns and are working, hard to keep them safe. Carriers are communicating new marching orders to their cabin crews through briefings, circulars in mailboxes, on e-mails and by posting bulletins on secure Web sites. The companies won't say precisely what they are telling them or what the new procedures are.

It is known that some steps include parking catering carts in front of the cockpit door, prohibiting coach-class passengers from using the first-class lavatories, taking cockpit keys away from attendants and encouraging them to enlist the aid of passengers if a problem arises. Airline ground personnel are searching all the planes every day before they fly, and some are putting "tamper-detection tape" on food carts that attendants now inspect.

Fundamentally, "the hijacking training we had dealt with a different threat," says Dixie Daniels, a 29-year veteran of Trans World Airlines, now owned by American Airlines. "They wanted to go to Cuba, to get their buddies out of prison, to get money. Not a suicide mission. We need to get up to speed on the new terror tactics."

As if the nation's 100,000 flight attendants didn't have enough to worry about. In the four separate hijackings on Sept. 11, they lost 25 colleagues, and some attendants are too depressed or fearful to return to work. Bill Lehman, an America West Airlines attendant and union official, says one of his colleagues was stepping out the door to head for the airport when her eight-year-old daughter grabbed her leg and said "Mommy, please don't die." She didn't fly that day or for several weeks, and sought counseling for herself and her child, he says.

Others are balking after they've eyeballed the passengers or studied the flight manifest. Last week, a United Airlines cabin crew raised alarms about the name of a passenger on a flight to Washington from Orlando, Fla. The FBI cleared the passenger, but the attendants refused to fly.

So the flight was canceled.

Making matters worse, the airlines, hit by a devastating drop in traffic, are laying off thousands of workers, including nearly 17,000 flight attendants, so far, who have been terminated, put on furlough or taken voluntary unpaid leave. Among the lowest paid of all airline workers, with base salaries ranging from $12,000 to $50,000 a year, the mostly female attendants don't have much savings to fall back on.

Their unions are trying to help. Organized labor is pushing for a bill to extend unemployment benefits to laid off airline workers. The Air Line Pilots Association is pressing for pilots to be allowed to carry firearms. And the Association of Flight Attendants is lobbying for new training in self-defense and permission for members to carry pepper spray, mace or stun guns.

The AFA worries, though, that not enough is being done on the ground to keep planes safe once they take off. Regulators and the industry are making no moves to require widespread screening or luggage that goes into airplane cargo holds, nor are they adopting a system to match baggage with passengers on domestic flights. Moreover, "law enforcement officers with guns are standing around the [airport] screening points," says Jeff Zack, an AFA spokesman, "but the same underpaid, poorly trained people are doing the screening."

"Security is a joke," says Mary Baker, a 29-year United flight attendant. "People are getting stuff through. I talked to a passenger yesterday who said, 'I forgot this razor blade in the bottom of my purse.'"

For now, pilots largely are setting the tone. United's Ms. Baker said the captain of her first flight after Sept. 11 told her to "use whatever means necessary to prevent someone from getting into the cockpit." She retorted, "How about some training here." The pilot told her to use a blanket to subdue a hijacker. Ms. Baker says she has thought of hitting an attacker with a fire extinguisher but wonders, "what is my professional liability if I kill an innocent person, or hurt somebody."

To avoid being sitting ducks, flight attendants are taking their own precautionary measures. America West's Mr. Lehman says he now locks his crew bags onboard, something he never did before. He monitors the boarding process more closely and makes eye contact with each person.

Delta's Ms. Fisk has thought of how she would deal with a threat. "Most women know where you can give a swift kick to a guy," she says, "I just hope I have on my concourse shoes with the heels and [not] my in flights with the little padded soles."

One attendant who didn't want to be named says she and her colleagues are covertly racially profiling the passengers. On her first trip after the attacks last month, she says, she encountered three young, quiet passengers who appeared to be Middle Eastern. She reckons they probably were "intimidated" by the negative attention they were getting. Nevertheless, she says she approached "a couple of big, burly guys" sitting nearby and told them, "If any of them makes a false move, you tackle 'em." The men replied, "With pleasure."[1]

1 Note from Professor Carr: Possible assault and battery?? (We may discuss in class.)

58 Defamation in Cyberspace

[Defamation]

Defamation—an untrue statement by one party about another to a third party.

Defamation In Cyberspace

The elements of defamation remain the same in cyberspace. You must show that someone said or wrote something false that portrayed you in a bad light and that the statement, written or oral, was published, or heard, or read by others. That the defamation occurs in a chat room does not change the application of tort law. However, the pervasive nature of the Internet could make the damages for defamation greater because so many obtain the information so quickly and damage can be done so rapidly. FOR EXAMPLE, Mark S. Jakob, a securities trader who had lost $100,000 in August 2000 with poor trades in Emulex, Inc. stock options, decided to correct his declining earnings trend by posting a false press release on the Internet that Emulex's earnings were overstated and that its CEO would resign. The news release was distributed to various Web sites. The overall loss in the value of Emulex stock was $2.5 billion before trading was stopped and the false nature of the press release revealed. Mr. Jakob had made $240,000.[1] It is the tort of defamation that would permit the investors to recover their losses. Mr. Jakob had defamed the company, and the damages were extensive and quite easy to establish because the stock's decline was directly attributable to trades made immediately following the posting of the false information by the fake press release.[2]

Even though the methods for publication have changed and make damages more extensive, the tort of defamation remains the legal tool those harmed are able to use in seeking recovery.

One of the interesting issues that arises in cases of defamation via the Internet is whether the companies providing the servers must reveal the identity of customers who have posted defamatory information. FOR EXAMPLE, on one message board an employee posted false information about his employer and its CEO. The employer requested Yahoo! to reveal the identity of "Aquacool_2000," the screen name of the person who had posted the false and defamatory statements. Yahoo! did reveal the identity of Aquacool; and Aquacool has filed a multi-million-dollar invasion of privacy suit against Yahoo.[3] The suit is pending even as the Justice Department seeks to prosecute the young man for wire fraud. Although revealing information about Internet users to private companies raises questions about the invasion of privacy, server companies must reveal such information under warrants from law enforcement agencies. The issue of revealing the identity of those who have posted defamatory information remain in litigation, but the ultimate answer

---

1 Alex Berenson, "Man Charged in Stock Fraud Based on Fake News," New York Times, 1 September 2000, Cl, C2.

2 Note from Professor Carr: A good example of how defamation can come up!!

3 Matt Richtel, "Yahoo Says It Is Discussing Internet Privacy with the F.T.C.," New York Times, 31 March 2000, Bl.

to the question of whether the identity of users can be revealed to third parties will be determined by the very staid law on invasion of privacy and the notion of expectation of privacy.

59 Employee References[1]

Employment Law: Knowing When Not to Recommend

[Defamation]

ALL PERSONNEL MANAGERS, supervisors, and other individuals called on for job references, take note: You can be liable for failing to disclose adverse information, if the failure presents a substantial, foreseeable risk of physical injury to someone.

Recently, a junior high school student alleged that she was molested by a vice principal at her school. She sued, among others, the individuals who wrote letters of recommendation for the vice principal (and the school districts for which they worked), for negligent misrepresentation and fraud in failing to disclose earlier charges against him of sexual improprieties. The California Supreme Court found, in *Randi W. v Muroc Joint Unified School District* (1997) 14 C4th 1066, that the; defendants who wrote letters of recommendation should have been able to foresee that the plaintiff's school district would rely on their favorable letters in hiring the vice principal, and that, after being hired, he might molest or injure a student. The court stated that the defendants could have avoided liability by writing a full disclosure letter revealing all relevant facts or writing a "no comment" letter that merely verified basic employment data. Instead the court said, the letters constituted misleading half-truths.

Most employers will not find themselves in the situation of recommending employees for jobs where prior conduct is relevant to future physical injury to third parties. Still, an employer should consider the job the applicant is seeking. For example, if a former delivery driver had been cited by an employer for reckless driving, a cautious employer would provide a "no comment" letter.

The truth of any facts disclosed may not prevent the former employee from suing the former employer for interference with prospective employment. Employers may have a defense, however, in the qualified privilege for job performance references contained in section 47 of the Civil Code.

1 **Note from Professor Carr: This article does a nice job of highlighting how an employer can get caught in the "no-man's land" that can exist between defamation and negligence. I.e., do you recommend or not recommend??**

60 Islamic Charity Sues Media Companies for Defamation

By Michael Orey, *The Wall Street Journal*

[Defamation]

THE GLOBAL RELIEF Foundation, which describes itself as one of the largest U.S.-based Islamic charitable organizations, filed a defamation suit last week against a half-dozen media organizations.

In reports during the past two months, the New York Times, Associated Press, ABC's "Good Morning America" and other news outlets falsely linked GRF with fund raising for terrorist groups, the charity alleges in a complaint filed in federal district court in Chicago.

The result, according to the organization, has been a significant drop in donations. Prior to mid-September, the foundation says in its complaint, it was receiving "upwards of 50 donations a day by mail." After the news reports, that number dropped to three or four a day.

"That was the real motivation" for the suit, says Asim Ghafoor, a spokesman for the organization. Global Relief reported annual contributions of about $5 million for both 1999 and 2000.

Named as defendants are New York Times Co. and its Globe Newspaper unit, the Associated Press, Walt Disney Co.'s ABC, Hearst Corp. and the Daily News of New York.

The suit comes at a time when some are expressing concern that the government has been too sweeping and indiscriminate in investigating individuals and institutions for possible ties to terrorism. But Global Relief's suit is aimed squarely at the news media. In its complaint, the organization states it believes that "no government source exists for any of the claims made each of the defendants." Roger Simm Global Keller's lead lawyer in the case, says he hopes the very filing of [...] they need to be more careful.

"This group does a whole lot of things ... to make sure it's not being illicitly used for terrorist organizations," says Matthew Simmons, another of Global Relief's attorneys. "We need to clear our client's name." But media-law experts not involved in the lawsuit said Global Relief likely faces an uphill fight.

Bruce Johnson, a media defense attorney in Seattle, said courts generally treat organizations that solicit public funds as "public figures." That means Global Relief probably faces the higher burden of showing that news organizations acted intentionally or recklessly in publishing a false report. Matthew Simmons said he hopes the court will determine that Global Relief is a "private figure," which would require it to show only negligence. But he said the case doesn't depend on that.

One risk for organizations pursuing such suits, Mr. Johnson notes. Is that they may be required to provide defendants with names of their donors and information about where funds were distributed. "We are prepared for that possibility," Roger Simmons says, adding that Global Relief has nothing to hide.

According to the suit, ABC's "Good Morning America" reported on Sept. 24 that the U.S. had named GRF as an organization that was "getting funds to bin Laden." A reference to Osama bin Laden. Later that day ABC posted a retraction on its Web sites stating "this is not the case." But, GRF says in its complaint, ABC never broadcast the retraction, so most people who saw the original report were unaware it was made. A spokesman for ABC said Friday that the network hadn't yet seen the suit and couldn't comment. On Oct. 1, the New York Times reported that "administration officials are recommending" that Global Relief be included on a new list of charities that would have their assets frozen because of suspected terrorist links. It also described Global Relief's home city of Bridgeview, III. as "a hub of militant Islamic activity." The statements, implications and innuendo" in the Times article are defamatory. Global Relief says in its complaint. As of Friday the government hadn't requested or subpoenaed any of GRF's records or taken any steps to freeze Global Relief assets Mr. Simmons said.

"We believe the case is without merit," said a spokeswoman for the *New York Times*, which also publishes the Boston Globe, another defendant in the suit.

David Tomlin, assistant to the president of AP, said the wire service believes its report was "accurate and responsible." The other defendants couldn't be reached.

61 WWF, Parents' Group Settle Libel Case

The National Law Journal

[Defamation]

WORLD WRESTLING FEDERATION Entertainment has settled a suit against a group claiming that televised wrestling causes violence in children.

In a recently announced defamation settlement involving media Research Center, a nonprofit conservative corporation, the Parents Television Council and various other defendants, the pro wrestling organization will receive $ 3.5 million.

Beginning in 1999, the Parents Television Council and its parent organization the Media Research Center, began to target the wrestling show *Smackdown* for what they believed was inappropriate content for broadcast television.

The organizations, both run by L. Brent Bozell III, sought out sponsors and advertisers, to convince them of the in appropriate content of the television program.

According to the plaintiff's complaint, a representative from the Parents Television Council called *Smackdown*, "one of the most violent, sexually graphic, racist, sexist and foul mouthed programs to air on prime time television" at a meeting in 2000.

The settlement included damages stemming from a fund-raising video of the parents' group claiming that the murders of four children by minors were caused by the murderers' learning moves from *Smackdown*.

The video's focus was the murder of Tiffany Eunick, 6 who was killed by Lionel Tate, 12, in Florida in 1999.

On the video, Tate's lawyer, Jim Lewis, claimed that the murder was caused by moves that Tate learned by watching the show.

However, the murder was committed before *Smackdown* went on the air. Bozell wrote and apology to the wrestling group admitting that the deaths bore no relation to *Smackdown*.

The Media Research Center is a conservative organization whose mission, according to its Web site, is to "bring balance and responsibility to the news media." The Parents Television Council ranks television programs and its mission is "restore television to its roots."

According to Wrestling Federation lawyer Jerry McDevitt of Pittsburgh's Kirkpatrick & Lockhart, the parent groups made repeated public declarations, including Bozell's statements at the Conservative Leadership Conference and on CNN's *Crossfire* that kids are killing other kids because of such programs as *Smackdown*.

62 Lewis v. Equitable Life Assurance Society[1]

389 N.W. 2d 876 (Minn. Sup. Ct. 1988)

[Defamation]

Carole Lewis, Mary Smith, Michelle Rafferty, and Suzanne Loizeaux were employed as dental claim approvers in the St. Paul, Minnesota, office of the Equitable Life Assurance Society of the United States. In October 1980, they were sent to assist in Equitable's Pittsburgh office. None of the women had ever traveled on company business before, and they departed for Pittsburgh without being given copies of Equitable's travel expense policies or being told that expense reports would have to be filed. Instead, they were verbally given information on Equitable's daily meal and maid tip allowances and told to keep receipts for hotel bills and airfare. In addition, each was given a $1,400 travel allowance which, having no instruction to the contrary, they spent in full.

When they returned to St. Paul, each of the women received a personal letter from management commending her on her on job performance in Pittsburgh. Each was also told for the first time that she would have to submit expense reports detailing he daily expenses in Pittsburgh. This they did, but a dispute subsequently arose over the amount of allowable expenses because Equitable's written guidelines differed from the instructions they had received prior to departure. After first changing their reports with respect to maid tips, they were asked to change their reports again, the net effect of which would have been to obligate each employee to return approximately $200 to Equitable. They refused to do this, arguing that the expenses shown on their reports were honestly incurred, a claim that Equitable never disputed. Subsequently, the women were fired for "gross insubordination."

In seeking new jobs, each woman was asked by prospective employers why she had left Equitable, and each said she had been terminated, When asked in interviews to explain their terminations, each stated that she had been terminated for gross insubordination and attempted to explain the situation. Only one of the women found a new job by being forthright with a prospective employer about her termination from Equitable. The others had various difficulties finding new jobs. They filed a defamation suit against Equitable, and when a jury ruled in their favor, Equitable appealed.

Amdahl, Chief Justice

In order for a statement to be considered defamatory, it must be communicated to someone other than the plaintiff, it must be false, and it must tend

1 **Note from Professor Carr: This is a good and interesting example of the "self-publication" doctrine that can come up in a defamation case. This case should teach you to watch what you say as a future employer.**

to harm the plaintiff's reputation. Generally, there is no publication where a defendant communicates a statement directly to a plaintiff, who then communicates it to a third person. Plaintiffs themselves informed prospective employers that they had been terminated for gross insubordination. They did so because prospective employers inquired why they had left their previous employment. The question raised is whether a defendant can ever be held liable for defamation when the statement in question was published to a third person only by the plaintiff.

We have not previously been presented with the question of defamation by means of "self publication." Courts that have considered the question, however, have recognized a narrow exception to the general rule that communication of a defamatory statement to a third person by the person defamed is not actionable. These courts have recognized that if a defamed person was in some way compelled to communicate the defamatory statement to a third person, and if it was foreseeable to the defendant that the defamed person would be so compelled, then the defendant could be held liable for the defamation.

Several courts have specifically recognized this exception for compelled self-publication in the context of employment discharges. The trend of modern authority persuades us that Minnesota law should recognize the doctrine. Compelled self-publication does no more than hold the originator of the defamatory statement liable for damages caused by the statement where the originator knows, or should know, of circumstances whereby the defamed person has no reasonable means of avoiding publication of the statement or avoiding the resulting damages. In such circumstances, the damages are fairly viewed as the direct result of the originator's actions.

The St. Paul office manager admitted that it was foreseeable that plaintiffs would be asked by prospective employers to identify the reason that they were discharged. Their only choice would be to tell them "gross insubordination" or to lie. Fabrication, however, is an unacceptable alternative.

Finding that there was a publication, we next turn to the issue of truth. True statements, however disparaging, are not actionable. The company contends the relevant statement to consider when analyzing the defense of truth is the one that plaintiffs made to their prospective employers, that is, that they had been fired for gross insubordination. Plaintiffs counter that it is the truth or falsity of the underlying statement—that they engaged in gross insubordination—that is relevant.

Requiring that truth as a defense go to the underlying implication of the statement, at least where the statement involves more that a simple allegation, appears to be the better view. Here, the company's charges against plaintiffs went beyond accusations and were conclusory statements that plaintiffs had engaged in gross insubordination. The record amply supports the jury verdict that the charge of gross insubordination was false.

Even though an untrue defamatory statement has been published, the originator of the statement will not be held liable if the statement is published under circumstances that make it conditionally privileged and if privilege is not abused. The doctrine of privileged communication rests upon public policy considerations. The existence of a privilege results from the court's determination that statements made in particular contexts or on certain occasions should be encouraged despite the risk that the statements might be defamatory.

In the context of employment recommendations, the law generally recognizes a qualified privilege between former and prospective employers as long as the statements are made in good faith and for a legitimate purpose. Plaintiffs argue that a self-publication case does not properly fit within the qualified privilege doctrine, but the logic of imposing liability upon a former employer in a self-publication case appears to compel recognition of a qualified privilege. A former employer in a compelled self-publication case may be held liable as if it had actually published the defamatory statement directly to prospective employers. Where an employer would be entitled to a privilege if it had actually published the statement, it makes little sense to deny the privilege where the identical communication is made to identical third parties with the only difference being the mode of publication. Finally, recognition of a qualified privilege seems to be the only effective means of addressing the concern that every time an employer states the reason for discharging an employee it will subject itself to potential liability for defamation. It is in the public interest that information regarding an employee's discharge be readily available to the discharged employee and to prospective employers, and we are concerned that, unless a significant privilege is recognized by the courts, employers will decline to inform employees of reasons for discharges.

This conclusion does not necessarily determine that the company's statements were privileged. A qualified privilege is abused and therefore lost if the plaintiff demonstrates that the defendant acted with actual malice. The jury found that the company's statements were "actuated with actual malice."

Judgment for the plaintiffs affirmed.

63 Maybee v. Jacobs Motor Co.

519 N.W.2d 341 (S.D. Sup. Ct. 1994)

[Fraud]

Deceit (or fraud) is the formal name for the tort claim that is available to victims of knowing misrepresentations. Liability for deceit usually requires a false statement of material important fact, knowingly or recklessly made by the defendant, with the intent to induce reliance by the plaintiff, actual and justifiable reliance by the plaintiff, and harm to the plaintiff due to his reliance, Because most deceit actions arise in a contractual setting, and because a tort action for deceit is only one of the remedies available to a victim of fraud, a fuller discussion of this tonic is deferred until Chapter 13.

Can a defendant be liable in deceit for the *nondisclosure* of facts material to the transaction? The following Maybee case presents the *Restatement (Second)* rule on this subject.

JOHNIE MAYBEE PURCHASED a 1984 Chevrolet van from Jacobs Motor Company for $8,700. No one at Jacobs told her that the van's original engine had been replaced with a rebuilt engine using a 1966 engine block. According to Maybee, the salesman with whom she dealt "just said that it was an '84 van that was in good condition and that they had used it around the business." In addition, no Jacobs employee mentioned that the van had dieseling and oil leakage problems. Although Maybee had the opportunity to ask questions and to have the van inspected by a mechanic, she declined.

About one month after the purchase, Maybee's husband took the van to a garage because it had been leaking oil. The mechanic discovered the 1966 block and also determined that the engine was in poor shape. In addition, an expert witness for Maybee later testified that, due to its high compression ratio, the engine required high octane aviation fuel for its proper operation. Eventually, Maybee claimed, she parked the van in her yard because it "didn't work."

Maybee sued Jacobs for fraud and deceit. The jury found Jacobs liable, awarding Maybee $14,700 in compensatory damages and $75,000 in punitive damages. Because the $14,400 in compensatory damages was more than 10 times the $1,450 cost of replacing the engine, the trial court ordered a new trial on the damages question. Maybee appealed this order, and Jacobs appealed the jury's determination that it was liable for fraud and deceit.

Henderson, Justice

Deceit requires proof that the misrepresentation was material to the formation of the contract and that other party relied on the misrepresentation to her detriment. Such misrepresentations include true statements which the maker knows or believes to be materially misleading because of the failure to state additional or qualifying matter. [According to] *Restatement (Second) of Torts* section 551(2)(e):

> One party to a business transaction is under a duty to exercise reasonable care to disclose to the others before the transaction is consummated...
>
> (e) *facts basic to the transaction*, if he knows that the other is about to enter into it under a mistake as to them, and that the other, because of the relationship between them, the customs of the trade or other objective circumstances, would reasonably expect a disclosure of those facts.

When a person purchases a 1984 vehicle, is the presence, within that vehicle, of an engine built for a 1966 model, which requires a fuel typically not used by vehicles on the road today, a fact basic to the transaction? The jury so found and this court finds that the evidence can support such a finding.

Nevertheless, a new trial on the issue of damages is warranted due to our decision on the second issue. During closing argument, *Maybee's counsel stated that $1,500 would compensate his client.* Somehow, the jury calculated compensatory damages at $14,750 and additionally awarded $75,000 in punitive damages. The jury verdict indicates passion and prejudice as well as inconsistencies with the instructions and law. A trial solely on Maybee's damages would require essentially the same evidence as a trial on both the substantive merits of the fraud claim and damages. A new trial on damages is warranted.

Trial court decision reversed; case returned to the trial court for a new trial on damages.[1]

---

1 Note from Professor Carr: The jury made a MISTAKE re: the amount of damages that the plaintiff should have been awarded. BUT, the fact that a fraud occurred/was proven was pretty obvious! The new trial was only on the issue of the amount of damages to be awarded.

64 Promises, Promises[1]

Internet Companies Stand Accused of Fraudulent Inducement

[Fraud]

THINGS HAPPEN QUICKLY in the dot-com world. But usually not this fast. Consider: In February a 33-year-old marketing director, lured away from her Old Economy job by the promise of stock options, was fired by the dot-com start-up she signed up with—before her first day on the job.

The company's executives explained that their venture capital funding came up short. The woman, who was unable to return to her former job, responded with a lawsuit.

Her lawyer is Mark Rudy, a San Francisco-based attorney with Rudy, Exelrod, Zieff & True—a firm that since the first of the year has handled more than ten cases involving employees who felt they had either been lied to or misled by their New Economy employers. Fraudulent inducement is the most obvious cause of action here. But in other cases claims are also being made under California Labor Code section 970, which provides relief for those who relocate to take new jobs and under promissory estoppel, which obligates employers to live up to their promises. Some also claim negligent misrepresentation of facts.

It's a predictable phenomenon, given how aggressively dot-com companies are hyping themselves. "You always hype your company because you want to attract the best people," Rudy allows. "But companies have to be very careful about letting employees make representations that are simply untrue because they want to entice people to work for them."

Fraudulent inducement is clearly the claim du jour, agrees Fred Alvarez, who is head of the employment group at Palo Alto's Wilson Sonsini Goodrich & Rosati, which primarily serves a high-tech clientele. In fact, in the termination complaints he's seen lately, anywhere from one-half to two-thirds have invoked fraudulent inducement as a cause of action, with most of the alleged misrepresentations involving either the company's finances, product development, or merger prospects. Recruiting is so intense in the high-tech industry, Alvarez notes, that the line between exaggeration and outright fraud often becomes highly blurred, if not overtly crossed.

At McGuinn Hillsman & Palefsky in San Francisco, plaintiffs attorney Cliff Palefsky observes that many start-up hiring managers will try to obscure how far away a product is from release by hiding behind a veil of secrecy. "They'll say to a job candidate, "We can't talk about it now because you're not onboard," explains Palafsky. Other times, they'll claim to be in beta testing or even that they're ready to ship, when in reality they're nowhere near that stage.

As egregious as a company's misrepresentations might be, both plaintiffs and defense attorneys agree that fraudulent inducement claims can be very difficult to prove. One way that companies protect themselves is by including in their employment

1 **Note from Professor Carr: This article is another good example of the tort of fraud and how it can come up in the business setting.**

agreements a "superseding clause" that effectively preempts whatever else might have been offered or said during the recruiting process.

Another thing that companies will do, on the advice of counsel, is to make their financial records available to potential hires with the expectation that most recruits won't bother to look very hard. That way, if a dispute comes up, the company can just say, "Look, you had access to all the records and all the financials. So why are you claiming you didn't know?"

How might such defenses be surmounted? One Achilles' heel is e-mail, which can show a very different side, to how a company portrays itself. There are other ways, too, that a company can trip up. Rudy, for one, thinks he has a particularly strong case with the marketing director who was fired before her first day on the job. "The company was foolish enough to put in writing that they were funded at a certain level when in fact they were funded at only 70 percent of that amount," say Rudy. At this writing, Rudy believes that a settlement is imminent. Meanwhile, his client has since found a new job. But this time, it's *not* with a dot-com.

65 En-Ruse? Workers Say They Had to Pose as Busy Traders to Impress Visiting Analysts[1]

[Fraud]

IT'S NOT ONLY **Enron** Corp's financial accounts that were phony.

Some current and former employees of Enron's retail-energy unit say the company asked them to pose as busy electricity and natural-gas sales representatives one day in 1998 so the unit could impress Wall Street analysts visiting its Houston headquarters.

Enron rushed 75 employees of Enron Energy Services—including secretaries and actual sales representatives—to an empty trading floor and told them to act as if they were trying to sell energy contracts to businesses over the phone, the current and former employees say.

"When we went down to the sixth floor, I remember we had to take the stairs so the analysts wouldn't see us," said Kim Garcia, who at the time was an administrative assistant for Enron Energy Services and was laid off in December.

"We brought some of our personal stuff, like pictures, to make it look like the area was lived in," Ms. Garcia said in an interview. "There were a bunch of trading desks on the sixth floor, but the desks were totally empty. Some of the computers didn't even work, so we worked off of our laptops. When the analysts arrived, we had to make believe we were on the phone buying and selling electricity and natural gas. The whole thing took like 10 minutes."

Penny Marksberry—who also worked as an Enron Energy Services administrative assistant in 1998 and was laid off in December—and two employees who still work at the unit also say they were told to act as if they were trying to sell contracts.

"They actually brought in computers and phones and they told us to act like we were typing or talking on the phone when the analysts were walking through," Ms. Marksberry said. "They told us it was very important for us to make a good impression and if the analysts saw that the operation was disorganized, they wouldn't give the company a good rating."

Peggy Mahoney, Enron Energy Services' spokeswoman, confirms some employees were told to move to the sixth floor for a visit by 150 analysts from Wall Street firms who were in town for a convention. But she said it was just a handful of employees who participated, not 75, and Enron didn't ask anyone to pose as traders or sales reps.

"We weren't trying to mislead anyone," Ms. Mahoney said. "There were some employees who were moved down there. They were told to just sit there. I don't know why. Analysts were brought in, and we showed them our operation. We were just showing them how we structured deals and contracts."

Enron filed for bankruptcy-law protection in December after questions were raised about a

1 **Note from Professor Carr: Another good and classic example of the tort of fraud and how it can come up in a business setting.**

number of off-balance-sheet partnerships run by Enron executives. Controversial accounting related to the partnerships was the major factor contributing to Enron's collapse. A report by a three-member special Enron board committee and its staff said the company "improperly" implemented various transactions "to conceal from the market very large losses" resulting from some of its business operations.

In the 1998 trading-floor incident, analysts were led around by Ken Lay, then Enron's chairman and chief executive, and the EES floor appeared busy with actual work, said an analyst who recalled the visit to Enron headquarters.

"The big push then was EES and retail electricity in California," the analyst said. "The trading floor looked fully staffed. There was a presentation in a little auditorium right where EES was operating. It looked like people were very busy. We didn't interact with any of the employees on the floor."

Enron Energy Services was set up in late 1997 to sell energy and advisory services to large consumers that had been freed or were expected to be freed from their local utilities by newly hatched deregulation. The unit was still small in 1998.

Enron executives, including Mr. Lay, escorted the analysts through the floor and returned later to tell the employees that they had done a good job, said Ms. Garcia, the administrative assistant.

"I think a bunch of us asked him why did we just do this, and he said the analysts needed to see a bunch of warm bodies working so Enron could get a good I credit rating," Ms. Garcia said. "He said the trading part of Enron was the company's bread and butter."

66 Photos of Women Who Get Abortions Go Up on Internet[1]

Activist-Photographers Prowl Clinics, Feed Web Masters Like Georgia's Mr. Horsley

By Yochi J. Dreazen, *The Wall Street Journal*

[Privacy]

'A Bull's-Eye on Their Backs'

DENVER—AS SOON AS he saw the blue minivan turning into the parking lot of Planned Parenthood's small abortion clinic here, Kenneth Scott grabbed his digital camera, clambered up his rickety metal ladder and started snapping pictures.

"You'll have nightmares about this day the rest of your life," he bellowed, photographing the blond woman gingerly leaving the minivan. Then he turned his camera to her escort. "Your sin won't be hidden or forgotten," he screamed.

Mr. Scott is doing his best to make sure of that. Within hours of his Photo expedition early this month, he was home downloading the pictures onto his computer so he could e-mail them to Neal Horsley, fellow activist in Carrollton, Ga. Mr. Horsley runs a Web site devoted to deterring "homicidal mothers" from seeking abortions by posting photos of women seen entering abortion clinics. New pictures he gets are often on the Web within days.

The site, Abortioncams.com which Mr. Horsley claims gets almost two million hits a month, marks a tactical shift by the antiabortion movement. Increasingly, protesters are targeting women who seek abortion not just doctors who perform them. The weapon of choice: the camera.

"Shame enough women into realizing that eternal damnation awaits them if they murder their baby and the abortionists won't have any work to do," says Mr. Scott, whose aging brown van bears a small handwritten sign reading "Smile! You're on Christiangallery.com!" (It's another Horsley Web site.)

"Mr. Scott and his wife, Jo, are part of a loose-knit network of several dozen activists from 24 states who send photos to Mr. Horsley's and a handful of other Web sites. In Portland, Ore., an affable man named Paul deParrie takes photos of women entering clinics for Mr. Horsley as well as for his own antiabortion site, Portlandporcupine.com. Mr. Horsley hopes to have contributing photographers in every state by the end of the year. He also says he hopes to start adding the women's names and addresses. Some postings already show license plate numbers.

The tactic poses difficult legal questions that courts are just beginning to tackle. Last year, an

1 Note from Professor Carr: This article is an excellent example of how the tort of invasion of privacy can come up (Intrusion of Solitude; and Publicity Concerning Private Facts).

Illinois woman whose photo and medical records were posted online sued the activists who took the photo and the man who ran the Web site, a friend of Mr. Horsley's. Her pending damage suit says the posting violated her privacy and subjected her to humiliation and potential harm.

A "right to privacy" doesn't appear in the Constitution or the Bill of Rights, but for the past 37 years, courts have increasingly held that Americans have a right to keep many details of their lives secret. Among issues the courts could someday have to weigh with regard to this tactic is whether women going in for abortion lose any of this protection because they're in a public place—or, to the contrary, whether entering a clinic for medical procedure affords additional privacy protection. Courts may have to consider whether the Web sites implicitly threaten violence against the women. And they'll certainly have to weigh the claim of the activists that they are journalists whose work is protected by the First Amendment right to free speech.

"This is a new area for the law and there's no easy answer based on past cases that makes this a slam dunk in either direction," says Jonathan Zittrain, co-director of Harvard Law School's Berkman Center for Internet & Society.

In Denver, a Planned Parenthood clinic set in low-slung gray building in a poor residential area is the site of a strange game of cat and mouse. When protesters first began carrying still and video cameras here last summer, clinic employees strung tall gray curtains alongside the parking lot to block the view from the sidewalk. The protesters brought in ladders. Then Planned Parenthood's volunteer escorts began carrying huge umbrellas to try to shield the women's faces.

Stan Roebuck, Planned Parenthood's security director for the Colorado region, says the presence of the cameras "ratchets up the tension for women who are already under extreme stress." To Kate Michelman, president of the National Abortion and Reproductive Rights Action League, "This is like drawing a bull's-eye on the backs of these women and inviting those who are irrationally zealous to take action." The activists say they're doing nothing to incite or threaten violence.

One California mother of two says she was shocked when she was told by a friend that her photo was on Mr. Horsley's site. "Getting an abortion was the most difficult and personal decision I've ever had to make," says the woman, requesting anonymity because she doesn't want friends and family to know she had one. "I couldn't believe that some stranger had the nerve to share it with the world."

Fighting Back

One woman is fighting back in court. She suffered a cervical tear while a patient at the Hope Clinic in Granite City, Ill., and needed to be rushed to a hospital. As clinic staffers wheeled her toward a waiting minivan, one of a group of antiabortion protesters outside, Daniel Michael of nearby Highland, Ill., saw what was happening and snapped a picture of her. Within days, her picture as well as her medical records—obtained through an unknown source—were on a Web site called Missionaries to the Unborn. It didn't name her but included her age, the name of her tiny hometown, the fact that she was married and the age and sex of her only child.

Identified as "Jane Doe" in court papers, the woman alleges the photo and records revealed her identity, violating her privacy and opening her to potential public humiliation and physical violence. She said in a deposition in state court in Edwardsville, Ill., that she feared an extremist could try to track her down and harm her. She declined to comment for this article.

The defendants include Mr. Michael, his wife, Angela, and Stephen Wetzel, who runs the Web site. The suit also names the hospital, recently renamed Gateway Medical Center, for failing to make sure her records stayed confidential. Mr. Michael and Mr. Wetzel say the records came to them anonymously.

The woman is seeking more than $400,000, mostly in punitive damages. State court judge George Moran issued a temporary restraining order last summer ordering removal of her photo and medical records from Missionaries to the Unborn and another Web site. The case is pending.

Mr. Wetzel says the woman has no reason to fear for her safety. "Nobody's going to go after a girl for getting an abortion," he says. "They're as much a victim as the babies are." Mr. Michael says the medical records shouldn't have been put online. He says the woman has a right to privacy but adds that it wasn't violated because the photos were blurry and the records were redacted to exclude her name and address. "This wasn't meant to harm her—it was just to let the world know what happens at that clinic," he says. The hospital didn't return a call seeking comment.

One tough legal question likely to arise as these tactics continue is whether posting women's photos on a site such as Mr. Horsley's—which likens abortion to murder and speaks of divine punishment for patients and their doctors—amounts to a threat against their safety. A person making such a claim could have a high bar to clear. Courts nave generally found that plaintiffs alleging threats to their safety must show the defendant directly threatened to do violence against them.

In a 1982 Supreme Court case, NAACP v. Claiborne Hardware, black activists working to enforce a civil-rights boycott against several white-owned businesses in Mississippi stood outside and wrote down the names of blacks who continued to shop there. The names were read aloud at a nub-lie meeting and published in a newspaper, leading to several assaults and arsons. Later, an organizer was quoted as saying that if he caught anyone "going in any of them racist stores, we're gonna break your damn neck." The high court said the statement was constitutionally protected because there was no evidence the organizer had authorized a specific act of violence or threatened to commit one himself.

Mr. Zittrain and other legal experts say that current privacy laws don't appear protect a person from being photographed while in a public place but that women could potentially sue the photographers or the sites for intentional infliction of emotional stress or illegal intimidation.

A Suit in Oregon

The women could benefit from a recent appellate-court decision that touched on another Web site Mr. Horsley runs, Nuremberg Files, which carries abortion providers names, addresses and photos and crosses out their names when they've been killed. It was cited in a lawsuit against others—a group called the American Coalition Life Activists—as evidence of intimidation.

Planned Parenthood, several doctors and a clinic in Portland, Ore., filed the suit in federal court in Portland. It alleged the Coalition had in cited violence and broken a 1994 federal law that allows doctors and clinic workers to sue anti-abortion protesters they believe have tried to intimidate them into no longer doing the procedure.

In 1999, a jury awarded the plaintiffs nearly $107 million, virtually all punitive damages. Two years later a three-judge panel of the U.S. Court of Appeals for the 9th Circuit in San Francisco overturned the verdict, saying that though the site and some of the group's posters used inflammatory language and imagery, they didn't contain any explicit threats of physical harm to an individual.

But this month the full 9th Circuit reversed that decision and said that the activists had "made statements to intimidate the physicians reasonably foreseeing that physicians would interpret the statements as a serious expression of intent to harm them." The court said the doctors had begun wearing bulletproof vests as a direct result of the posters arid Web site, and concluded the protesters' activities "amounted to a true threat and not protected speech." The activists promise to appeal, and many observers expect the Supreme Court to take the case because of me thorny questions of free speech and abortion access it raises.

Mr. Scott, the picture-taking end of the Scott-Horsley operation, says he had a personal experience with abortion 23 ago, when he got a girlfriend pregnant and paid for her to have an abortion. Later he married, and he says that after his second marriage fell apart he became a born-again Christian. Now he spends much of his free time protesting at abortion clinics across the country. He met his third wife, Jo, at an antiabortion protest near the 1996 Republican convention in San Diego.

The two, devout Grace Christians, play the part of bad cop and good cop; Mr. Scott screams at the women about hell and damnation, while Mrs. Scott quietly approaches cars pulling into the clinic to offer women ultrasound tests, financial help or advice about adoption.

One afternoon earlier this month in Denver, Mr. Scott yelled at a woman in a green jacket hurriedly walking toward the clinic doors with a tall man in a red T-shirt. "Don't kill your baby," he said. "You'll always wonder if it was a boy or a girl."

His words had the desired effect: The man turned to swear at Mr. Scott and raised his middle finger, while the woman pivoted to see what the commotion was. Mr. Scott, wearing a placard around his neck reading "Life begins at conception and ends at Planned Parenthood," quickly took several photos.

By the end of the day, he had snapped more than 90 pictures in all, the scenes ranging from the confrontational to the prosaic. In one photo, a woman in a green jacket was running toward the facility while her male companion, a tall man with a pony tail and goatee, raised his fist at the camera. In another, two women stepped out of a parked car. The women's faces were all clearly visible.

At home in a suburb of Boulder, Colo., Ms. Scott hooked the camera to a desktop computer in her basement and transferred the photos to an online picture-sharing service called Ofoto. Minutes later, they were on their way to Mr. Horsley in Georgia. There, in a home office cluttered with tripods, guitars, an overflowing bookcase and photos of his college-age children, Mr. Horsley soon began downloading the photos into a computer.

Getting them online takes time. The first step is choosing, sometimes from as many as 500 pictures sent him in a week, he says. Mr. Horsley says he is a journalist trying to tell a story, and wants to avoid using pictures with poses or expressions too similar to others he has posted on the site. He also resizes the photos and edits their color and lighting, though he says the Scotts' photos rarely need much retouching. "They're pros," he says.

"From my point of view," Mr. Horsley says, "this is a news report that has the ability to send a message. I want images that capture the look on a woman's face as she goes to a place where babies are being killed."

After picking the photos, the final step is to make duplicate versions of each photo, including a miniature that will appear on a Web page full of other shots from each state and a full-size image that viewers can access by clicking on the small one. The whole process takes about 15 minutes per picture.

Maintaining the site costs about $10,000 a year. Mr. Horsley pays for much of it through his day job as a computer and Internet consultant. He also gets donations from other antiabortion activists. He tries to update the site every day, and says he's always looking for new photographers. "Get out there to your local butchertorium with your zoom lenses and get those cameras rolling," he writes on his Web site. "Point and click."

67 Big Brother Knows You're Speeding[1]

Rental-Car Companies Install Devices that Can Monitor a Customer's Whereabouts

The Wall Street Journal

[Privacy]

YOU'RE ON A road trip to California in a rental car and opt for a quick detour to Las Vegas. As the neon sparkle comes into view, a voice suddenly blares from the speaker phone. The car's antitheft tracking system has detected deviation from the travel plans you indicated on your rental from, and a customer service representative is inquiring if everything is all right.

It is, in that the car is safe. But to those concerned about individual privacy, the idea that a driver's every twist and turn is being remotely monitored sounds like Orwell's worst nightmare. Yet it is becoming possible at a growing number of rental-car agencies.

Trucking companies have used such monitoring for years to keep tabs on their drivers, but now the technology has become cheap enough, and powerful enough, to be practical for car-rental companies. For as little as $20 to $30 per vehicle per month, mobile-fleet operators can outfit their inventory with "telematics"—a combination of a global positioning satellite system, such as that used in the map devices that can help drivers navigate, and a wireless phone. Unlike a GPS system alone, telematics can transmit an automobile's location and status—if stopped, for example, or how fast it's "going—with or without the driver knowing.

"When your single biggest investment is your moving capital, it makes sense to keep track of it as best you can," says Don Simmonds, chief executive of AirIQ Inc. of Toronto, one of a handful of fleet-tracking companies specializing in the rental-car industry. "

With the AirIQ system, a hidden black box connects vehicles, via the cellphone network, to an online data warehouse. Information about each car, determined by the GPS system, is routed to a password-protected Internet site where the client can view a vehicle's location, speed and direction. Fleet owners benefit from quicker recovery of stolen trucks or cars and real-time inventory tracking. Using the technology can even lower insurance premiums. The system stores the information indefinitely, says Miguel Gonsalves, AirIQ's vice president of commercial transport.

AirIQ already has established contracts with licensees of Ford Motor Co.'s Hertz Corp., Budget Group Inc.'s Budget Rent A Car Corp., Cendant Corp.'s Avis Group Holdings, Dollar Thrifty Automotive Group Inc.'s Dollar Rent A Car Systems Inc. and Thrifty Car Rental, ANC Rental Corp.'s National Car Rental, Rent-A-Wreck of America Inc., U-Save Auto Rental of America Inc. and some independent rental operators.

---

1 **Note from Professor Carr: This article is an excellent example of the tort of privacy (in particular, intrusion of solitude).**

Most rental-car companies say they use telematics only if cars are stolen, not to police rental-contract rules such as prohibitions on taking cars into Mexico, on back-country roads or past predetermined boundaries. Both Budget and Hertz keep the devices in passive mode on their high-end rentals such as Jaguars, activating the system only if a car is reported missing.

David Sobel an attorney with the Electronic Privacy Information Center in Washington D.C., says just the fact that companies could be storing tracking information is worrisome, potentially giving police, lawyers and suspicious spouses information never collected before. He cites Linda Tripp's recording of a telephone call with former White House intern Monica Lewinsky as an example. It was "information that didn't need to be created, but once it was created it was there for the taking," Mr. Sobel says.

One car-rental company that does actively use the telematics data is Acme Rent-a-Car of New Haven Conn, which has charged the credit cards of renters who speed $150 for each violation according to the Connecticut Department of Consumer Protection. Acme has its AirIQ system programmed to report a car's location every time the car exceeds 80 miles per hour for at least two minutes, according to Paul Konzlowski, owner of the rental agency.

Most rental concerns say they track only those cars that are stolen, but privacy advocates are alarmed.

Last month, the department filed a complaint against Acme, saying the company failed to inform customers how AirIQ's technology was being used and violated the state's unfair trade practices law by charging customers without any damage to the vehicle being sustained. Former customer James Turner is suing the car-rental company in small-claims court for monitoring his driving and then fining him $450 for speeding. "They tracked me across seven states," he says. "My privacy was invaded."

Mr. Kozlowski says a bold-print sign visible upon entering the rental office and a notice at the top of all rental contracts inform customers that cars are equipped with GPS tracking equipment.

Acme's attorney, Max F. Brunswick, says the company believes it has a right to track how fast people are driving its property as long as customers are informed that their driving will be monitored. And tracking speeders makes good business sense, he adds. The cost of having AirIQ installed is far offset by reduced insurance premiums and reduced fleet loss.

Yet other car-rental companies have publicly criticized Acme's speeding fines. The move was "a bad decision," says Kimberly Mulcahy, a spokeswoman for Budget, that "doesn't make any sense" from the perspective of trying to attract and maintain customers.

RentalTrack.com, an Irvine, Calif., fleet-tracking company, is targeting another market: parents who want to keep tabs on their teens. It offers a consumer version of its tracking system through its parent company, Aircept.com LLC. Aircept's tracking box costs $595 to install plus a $5 to $35 monthly fee that varies with the amount of tracking an individual wants.

Aircept's device also has a $49 add-on that creates a special tracking boundary. When the driver moves outside the programmed boundary, the system's user—a parent, spouse, boss or whoever—is notified by e-mail, fax or however he or she chooses, the same way rental car companies are notified of a car's location or direction, for example.

No rental-car company has ever asked for this tracking feature, says Stephen Cyros, vice president of sales for RentalTrack.com. It is, however, very popular with parents, he says.

AirIQ's Mr. Simmonds defends the tracking technology as simply the latest advancement in need of guidelines. All tools have the potential to be abused, and telematics technology is no different, he says.

"One can butter toast with a knife or you can kill someone with a knife," he says. "We should be aware of the potential abuses and develop protections—not throw it all out."

68 Disaster Raises New Legal Issues In the Workplace

By Michael Orey, *The Wall Street Journal*

[Privacy]

CAN A COMPANY fire employees who refuse to get on an airplane? Is it legal for a business to remove pictures of employees of Middle Eastern background form a marketing brochure?

America's war with terrorists is provoking a host of questions in the workplace, and employment attorneys say they are being peppered with inquires form businesses seeking guidance on how to respond.

Many of the questions raise classic issues of privacy, discrimination or compliance with labor laws. Others, however, are leading attorneys into uncharted terrain. "I think lawyers don't have a clue about how to advise their clients on some of these things," says Robert D. Lipman, an attorney in Jericho, N.Y. "A lot of these problems don't have a legal remedy because nobody contemplated something like this."

New problems can elicit conflicting opinions. For example, an executive who was killed while attending a meeting at the World Trade Center on Sept. 11 had stock options that were due to vest on Oct 1. No death certificate had been issued by that date. Should the options vest?

No, says Michael Lotito, a partner in the San Francisco office of Jackson Lewis, an employment law firm that got such an inquiry from a client it declines to name. Since the executive had ceased working for the company on Sept. 11, Lipman, whose four-lawyer firm represents both management and employees, isn't so sure, since the executive hadn't officially been declared dead as of the vesting date.

Far from ground zero, employers are coping with workers unnerved by the terrorist attacks. Mr. Lotito says one California client had employees who were resisting flying, even after the company arranged for them to travel on private jets. A group of workers at another company didn't want to return to work on the 52nd and 53rd floors of a New York office building.

Can these employees be fired?

Mr. Lotito and other employment attorneys emphasize that the initial response of most companies has been to cut back on travel or allow telecommuting for anxious workers. At some point, though, Mr. Lotito notes, "the company has a right to pursue its business," and if getting on an airplane—or working on a high floor—is necessary to job, and an employee refuses to do it, he or she can be fired.

There are, however, some caveats. A little known provision of the National Labor Relation Act protects "concerted activity of even non union employees. Thus, if anthrax fears lead two or more employees to object to mail-handling procedures, they can't be fired or disciplined for agitation for better protection. Also, if a worker claims he or she can't perform certain functions because of posttraumatic stress disorder or another diagnosed condition, an employer may have to make accommodations under the Americans with Disabilities Act.

Companies could also be at legal risk if they aren't complying with guidelines issued by authorities for dealing with current threats. Terri M. Solomon, an attorney at Littler Mendelson in New York, says she was contacted by a client who told her that a mailroom worker's insistence on wearing gloves to deliver company mail was creating fear among other employees. "To which I said, 'Too bad,'" says Ms. Solomon, who notes that a number of federal agencies have suggested precisely that precaution.

While employers may ask employees about past convictions, many states forbid inquiry into arrests.

Efforts by companies to improve security since Sept. 11 have spurred numerous legal questions. Tom Finkbiner, chief executive of Quality Distribution Inc. in Tampa, Fla., which operates the largest chemical tank-truck fleet in the country, says some chemical makers have asked Quality to provide them with names, addresses and other background information on its 3,350 drivers. After consulting with in-house counsel, Mr. Finkbiner concluded that "a lot of the things they're requesting are invasions of privacy." Quality is providing names and photo IDs but not employment histories and home addresses.

Managers of office buildings trying to prepare evacuation plans have asked tenants to supply lists of employees with disabilities that might hinder their escape in an emergency, raising privacy concerns.[1] But in a recent bulletin, the Equal Employment Opportunity Commissions said employers may ask employees if they will need assistance, as long as answering is voluntary. The EEOC also said companies can provide this information to building security officers and others responsible under any emergency evacuation plan.

There are few limits on companies conducting security checks of employee's bags or work areas, attorneys say, provided the company clearly informs its workers of the inspection policy.[1] In presentations for employers, Ms. Solomon's firm advises them to maintain broad rights to conduct searches, suggesting, for example, that they "expressly reserve the right to enter all lockers, desks, and vehicles at any time."

Newfound security concerns have sent many employers rushing to perform background checks on workers. Here too, there are certain legal requirements to navigate. The Fair Credit Reporting Act, for example, requires job applicants and employees to consent to checks of their credit history and, in certain circumstances, to employers obtaining drug test reports, driving records and interviews with friends or associates. And while companies are free to inquire about past convictions, many states forbid inquiry into arrests, notes Ms. Solomon.[1]

Because background checks can be expensive, the question was raised at a Nov. 12 meeting of human resource officials in Pittsburgh whether it would it possible to conduct them just for foreign nationals. That, says John Hill, a Jackson Lewis attorney who attended the meeting, would be a bad idea. To avoid potential discrimination claims, he says, "if you do it for one person, do it for everybody."

David Ross, an attorney for Seyfarth Shaw in New York, says his firm gave similar advice to the company that inquired about removing pictures of workers of Middle Eastern background from its marketing materials. Although it's not illegal, he says, "we cautioned them that that could come back to haunt them in others contexts" such as discrimination lawsuits because it shows separate treatment of people based on their heritage.

---

1 Note from Professor Carr: Potential tort for invasion of privacy??

69 Ivy Imbroglio: Princeton Says It Spied on Yale[1]

The Wall Street Journal

[Invasion of privacy, fraud, and tresspass]

IN A FEAT OF Ivy League counter-espionage, Yale University caught Princeton University accessing confidential Internet records to see whether its rival had admitted or rejected students that had applied to both schools.

Princeton admitted the intrusion and said it had suspended, with pay, associate dean and director of admissions Stephen LeMenager, pending an investigation of the incident. Mr. LeMenager couldn't be reached for comment.

"We deeply regret that information provided by students in good faith to the university was used inappropriately by at least one official in our admissions office," Princeton spokeswoman Marilyn Marks said.

Yale, whose campus is in New Haven, Conn., reported the incident to the FBI and state authorities yesterday and also notified the 11 students that Princeton was checking on. Princeton was able to use the publicly available Yale.edu Web site to get the confidential admissions data because it had the student's passwords—the names, Social Security numbers and dates of birth they had provided on their Princeton applications.

Yale said it traced 18 attempts to log in to the site to computers at Princeton, including several in Princeton's admissions office. Yale spokesman Tom Conroy said that the records available on the page included the admissions decision and, if the student was accepted, a brief extracurricular and academic profile. The records also indicated whether the candidate had applied for financial aid, although no details of the award were provided.

Ms. Marks, the Princeton spokeswoman, said that Princeton plans to contact the students whose records were accessed. She said she didn't know whether those students were accepted, or intend to attend either Yale or Princeton.

The break-in, reported on the Web site of the Yale Daily News student newspaper, comes as elite universities are vying ever more strenuously for top students. In this environment, knowing whether a rival has accepted an sought after student can be valuable strategic information and useful in shaping a competitive financial aid offer.

Yale and Princeton in particular have been intensely competitive in recent years, lobbing financial-aid changes back and forth in a contest in which Princeton is widely considered to be more aggressive, even as it has become more generous. Princeton has also been a leader among schools that use early decision programs to lock in commitments

1 **Note from Professor Carr: An excellent and interesting article that highlights several torts—invasion of privacy, fraud, and trespass. The irony is ... one would think that well educated, smart, prestigious, well-trained schools and university employees such as this would know better than to engage in this type of activity. ☺**

from the best students months ahead of the regular admissions deadlines.

Princeton's computer actions bring up a host of legal concerns in an uncharted field, said Lee Gesmer, a Boston attorney who practices privacy law. "Only a brilliant law professor could think up a question this hard," he said.

Mr. Gesmer said that Princeton could be in trouble on three fronts: civil trespass, for accessing computer network it was clearly not supposed to use; fraud, for its employees' misrepresentation of their identities; and invasion of the privacy rights of the students whose records were peeked at.

"Half the time these guys consider themselves colleagues and half the time they are directors of marketing of competitors," said John Katzman, who founded the Princeton Review test-preparation company. "If I could just log into a Web site and understand which families I was winning or losing, which schools I was winning or losing, I would do it. It is just good sport. Of course, it's totally wrong."

Until 1991 the Ivy League schools and other private colleges in the Northeast met around a conference table each April to fix financial-aid packages for students who were admitted to more than one school. That year, after the Justice Department sued the schools, accusing them of rampant antitrust violations, the universities agreed to stop the practice.

That set the stage for a series of thrusts and counterthrusts as schools focused on wooing the legions of middle-class applicants who couldn't afford their $35,000-a-year pricetags. In 1998, Princeton radically change the playing field by making several changes that lowered parental contributions in aid awards; Yale and others followed suit. Then, last year, Princeton announced it would fund with grants all the money students had previously taken out as loans. Yale responded in September with a $7.5 million increase in its aid budget.

Yale officials say the current contretemps began when they heard "verbally" that Princeton had used the site. To nail down the rumors, the school enlisted Alexander Clark, a Yale sophomore who created the Web site. Mr. Clark reviewed electronic access logs for the site and discovered that several computers bearing a unique identifier, called an IP address, belonging to Princeton and located in New Jersey, had accessed the site within hours—and sometimes minutes—of other computers logging in under the same name from other parts of the country.

Yale then contacted the students involved and asked if they had used computers near Princeton to check their accounts. No one said yes, and Mr. Clark traced the IP addresses of the Princeton computers to the admissions office. The other log-ins, he concluded, were legitimate checks by the students.

Lauren Weinstein, the founder of the Privacy Forum, an electronic-rights group, said Princeton's actions were clearly wrong but Yale's site should not have relied on Social Security numbers and birth dates, which can sometimes be retrieved from public records, to secure the data.

"It's not enough to have a weak Web site and depend on the good ethical behavior of others not to penetrate it," he said. "Similarly, it is not adequate to say that just because you found the weak Web site you should go ahead and penetrate it."

By comparison, Harvard University, in Cambridge, Mass., chose to notify applicants of decisions this year by e-mail rather than a Web site because it was concerned about security.

70 Colonel Stores, Inc. v. Fishel[1]

288 S.E.2d 21 (1981) Court of Appeals of Georgia

[False imprisonment]

Facts

HANK FISHEL WAS stopped by an armed guard while he was shopping at the Big Star Supermarket in Savannah, Georgia. The store is owned by Colonial Stores, Inc. (Colonial Stores). The security guard accused Fishel of stealing a bottle of aspirin that Fishel had in the top pocket of his sweater. The guard detained Fishel and called the store manager. Fishel informed the store manager and the guard that he had purchased the aspirin at a drugstore prior to coming into the Big Star Supermarket and that he was looking at the aspirin in Colonial's store to compare prices. Fishel suggested that if the manager would count the aspirins in the bottle he would find that Fishel had already taken two of the aspirin. Fishel also suggested that if they would go to the drugstore where Fishel had purchased the aspirin, they would find the empty aspirin box in the trash receptacle in front of the drugstore. The manager and the guard ignored both requests. The manager and the security guard took Fishel to the stockroom, where they searched him and then handcuffed him to a large metal container. The store manager called the police. When the police arrived, the manager filed a criminal complaint against Fishel. The store had a policy of prosecuting almost everyone the guard apprehended for shoplifting. At the criminal hearing, the charge against Fishel was dismissed because the guard failed to appear as a witness. Fishel brought this action against Colonial Stores to recover damages. The jury returned a verdict in favor of Fishel and awarded him $400 actual damages and $175,000 punitive damages. Colonial Stores appealed.

Issue

Is Colonial Stores, Inc., liable for the intentional tort of false imprisonment?

Opinion. Pope, Judge.

A determination by the jury that the store manager failed to act reasonably in investigating the shoplifting incident prior to initiating the prosecution against Mr. Fishel would allow a finding of liability against Colonial Stores. Evidence presented indicated that the store manager was aware of a reliable source of information that was readily available by telephoning or by sending someone to the nearby drugstore in an attempt to verify Mr. Fishel's story. Also, the store manager had the ability to look in his own store for the box that Mr. Fishel supposedly "ditched" but he failed to do this before

1 **Note from Professor Carr: This is a good example of the tort of false imprisonment and how it can come up in a business context. See also next page for related and supplemental reading.**

Mr. Fishel was placed in police custody and charged with a crime.

The jury was justified in its determination that the Colonial Stores's manager acted unreasonably by allowing Mr. Fishel to remain handcuffed and immobilized in the back room of the store and by initiating prosecution of the shoplifting charge for which he was never convicted.

Colonial Stores finally claimed that $175,000 as punitive damages was excessive. A jury may award additional damages in tort where there are aggravating circumstances either in the act or in the intention. Mr. Fishel was arrested, handcuffed and held in the back room of a grocery store, accused of a crime he was never shown to have committed. The store manager's conscious indifference and refusal to attempt to ascertain the truth as to whether or not the aspirin had been purchased elsewhere, or to further substantiate the case against Mr. Fishel, justified the award by the jury.

Holding.

The appellate court found no error in the trial court's finding that the defendant, Colonial Stores, Inc., committed the intentional tort of false imprisonment.

CASE QUESTIONS

Critical Legal Thinking. Should a store owner be able to stop and search a patron suspected of shoplifting? Is the present law adequate to protect the interests of both parties?

Ethics. Did Colonial Stores act ethically in prosecuting Hank Fishel in this case?

Business Implication. Are merchant protection statutes easy for businesses to follow? Was the award of $175,000 punitive damages warranted in this case?

71 False Imprisonment[1]

[False imprisonment]

FALSE IMPRISONMENT IS **the intentional restraint of another person without reasonable cause and without consent.** Suppose a bank teller becomes seriously ill and wants to go to doctor but the bank will not permit her to leave until she makes final tally of her accounts. Company official physically bar her from leaving the bank against her wishes. That is false imprisonment. The restraint was unreasonable because her accounts could have been verified later.

False imprisonment cases most commonly arise in retail stores, which sometimes detain employees or customers for suspected theft. Most states now have statutes governing the detention of suspected shoplifters. **Generally, a store may detain a customer or worker for alleged shoplifting provided there is a reasonable basis for the suspicion and the detention is done reasonably.** To detain a customer in the manager's office for 20 minutes and question him about where he got an item is lawful. To chain that customer to a display counter for three hours and humiliate him in front of other customers is unreasonable, and false imprisonment.

Assume that you are a junior vice president of a chain of 15 retail clothing stores, all located in your state. The president has asked you to outline a sensible plan, to be given to all employees, for dealing with suspected shoplifters. Here are some ideas to consider:

- There are competing social values. Shoplifting is very costly to our society, causing businesses to lose anywhere from $5 billion to $25 billion annually. On the other hand, no one wants to shop in a "police state" environment.
- What is a "reasonable" suspicion of shoplifting? What if a clerk sees a customer hurry out wearing a sweater identical to those on display? Must the clerk have seen the customer pick up the sweater? Put it on?
- What is "reasonable" detention? Can you tackle someone running through the parking lot? Can you shoot him?
- How private should the detention be? If you make your accusation publicly, in the store, you will deter many others from committing theft. But if you are wrong, what tort have you committed?
- How much questioning do you want to do, and how much would you prefer to leave to police?

Some people in our society are biased against others, based on race or gender, while others are entirely free of such biases. How do you take that into account?

Some states have passed new statutes called "civil fine" statutes, which allow stores to demand, in writing, a fine from the shoplifter of up to three times the value of the goods taken. Often the shoplifter pays up immediately to avoid criminal prosecution. Should you spend time lobbying the state legislature to pass such a statute?

---

1 Note from Professor Carr: Supplemental/related reading re: the tort of false imprisonment.

There are no perfect answers to these questions, but a manager clearly needs to consider them and to craft and approach that meets the legal standard: Reasonable suspicion of shoplifting and reasonable detention.

72 The (Not-So) Friendly Skies[1]

A Slew of Suits Follows Northwest's Treatment of Passengers During Jan. 2 Blizzard

[False imprisonment]
[Intentional infliction of emotional distress]

WHILE A BLIZZARD kept her plane stranded for more than six hours on the tarmac at Detroit's Metro Airport in early January, Northwest passenger Marti Sousanis sat and cried quietly in her seat.

Flight attendants told Sousanis that despite chronic back "pain" she couldn't stand up, and if she did, she could be arrested.

"It was a Kafka-esque nightmare," the San Francisco woman says, the exasperation still evident in her voice more than five months after her ordeal.

Sousanis was one of the thousands of passengers left stranded in Detroit on Jan. 2 when a nasty winter blizzard kept 27 Northwest flights frozen on the runway. Some passengers, whose pain and frustration was well-chronicled by *The Wall Street Journal, 20/20* and *Dateline NBC,* were stuck in their planes for as long as 11 hours.

Three class actions claiming false imprisonment and negligence are in the works against Northwest. The largest, which potentially could have as many as 8,000 claimants, is set to be certified in a Michigan courtroom on June 18.

Sousanis is a part of the class action headed by Charfoos, but she is also bringing an individual suit against Northwest for the way she was treated by the supervising flight attendant on her flight from Detroit to San Francisco.

Sousanis' attorneys say the motivation of the suit is not money. Rudolph Reyes Jr. of Hanson, Bridgett, Marcus, Vlahos & Rudy says the main objective of her suit is to bring attention to the fact that airline passengers have no rights aboard an aircraft and to address the deterioration of flight crew service.

"Marti's claim is distinguished because she was specifically mistreated," said Reyes, whose co-counsel on the case is Andrew Giacomini, also of Hanson, Bridgett.

Sousanis' suit seeks compensatory and punitive damages for intentional infliction of emotional distress, breach of contract, and breach of the implied covenant of good faith and fair dealing. The Northwest supervising flight attendant will be named in the suit, which at its core stems from the fact that Sousanis suffers from chronic back pain.

Sousanis says that while the plane was stranded on the runway for more than six hours the captain left the "Fasten seatbelt sign" on almost the entire time. Twice, when Sousanis stood up to stretch her back she was told to sit down. Worried her back might go into spasms, Sousanis asked to speak to the supervising flight attendant.

1 **Note from Professor Carr: A good article that highlights the torts of false imprisonment and intentional infliction of emotional distress.**

"The flight attendants were extremely rude from the get-go," she says. "Instead of being sympathetic and compassionate, they were hostile, which aggravates a situation."

Sousanis says she was told that if she stood up again she would be interfering with the operation of the aircraft. She says the head flight attendant threw an informational warning sheet into her lap and told her, "When you get to San Francisco the authorities will be there to pick you up."

For the remainder of the time the flight was stuck on the ground, Sousanis sat in her seat, crying.

The lawsuits underscore a wider rebellion among airline passengers over what they say is shoddy treatment on the part of the nation's air carriers.

According to the Department of Transportation, the number of passenger complaints against airlines increased 26 percent from 1997 to 1998. Through March of this year, passenger complaints jumped to 2,840, increase of nearly 69 percent from the 1,682 complaints filed during the same period in 1998.

But the lightning rod of the movement clearly is what happened aboard those Northwest flights in Detroit in January. Lawrence Charfoos of Detroit's Charfoos & Christensen, who is heading up the largest class action, is seeking $80 million from Northwest, or about $10,000 per passenger. "The conduct of Northwest was outrageous," he said.

Northwest sees things a little differently "We don't think they're warranted." Northwest representative John Austin said of the class actions, and while he conceded that the passengers were "horribly inconvenienced and horribly treated," Northwest believes an "effusive apology" and the offer of free Northwest airline tickets is enough "We don't believe it rises to the level of a legal action."

Congress has already reacted to the passenger ordeals in Detroit by drafting the Passenger Bill of Rights. Introduced by Rep. Bud Shuster, chairman of the Committee on Transportation and Infrastructure, the Passenger bill of Rights would require airlines to compensate Passengers any time they are kept waiting on the runway for more than two hours and to explain the reasons for delay, cancellation or diversion of any flight.[2]

2 Note from Professor Carr: Shows how if you do not have your act together as a business, then Congress may step in and regulate you. To learn more about this issue, take BUS 404!!

73 Abductions Cost Mo. Pastor $26.1M[1]

Defendant's Pro Se Performance Slams Jews and Quotes the Bible

National Law Review

[False imprisonment]
[Intentional infliction of emotional distress]

A MISSOURI JURY HAS returned a $26.1 million award against a preacher and two of his children for the false imprisonment and emotional distress suffered by eight of his grandchildren when he allegedly kidnapped them and indoctrinated them with anti-Semitic beliefs.

The lawsuit was brought by two of the now-adult grandchildren and their fathers. It was resolved on May 4. *Leppert v. Winrod,* No. CV301-402CC (Laclede Co., Mo., Cir. Ct.).

The fathers, North Dakota farmers Tim and Joel Leppert, had married two daughters of the Rev. Gordon Winrod. After acrimonious divorces in the early 1990s, the Lepperts were granted sole custody of the 11 children the two couples had borne.

In 1994, shortly after the custody battles ended, eight of the 11 children were abducted from the Lepperts' farm. When the two eldest children, Nathan and Erika, were dispatched back to North Dakota to kidnap the three remaining children, they instead alerted law-enforcement officials. The notice culminated in a 100-officer raid on the Winrod compound outside Gainesville, Mo. Four of the Winrods, including the Lepperts' ex-wives, are serving prison terms related to the kidnappings.

Father and son

Winrod is a former Lutheran minister and the son of the regionally well-known "Jayhawk Nazi," the Rev. Gerald B. Winrod, a Kansas preacher tried several times for sedition in the 1940s. The younger Winrod is serving a 30-year sentence in Missouri for the abductions. Known for the rabidity of its rhetoric, his publication, *The Winrod Letter,* is quoted on the Anti-Defamation League's Web site as blasting everyone from Bill Clinton to members of the "jewdiciary" for crimes including child molestation and cannibalism.

The Winrods initially refused to participate in the proceedings, leading to a declaratory judgment. At trial, which went forward on damages, the younger Winrod and two of his children, Steven and Carol, defended themselves against the Lepperts' claims, including false imprisonment and intentional infliction of emotional distress. The pro se performance included Bible quotations and references to Jewish conspiracies.

---

1 Note from Professor Carr: Another good article that highlights to torts of false imprisonment and intentional infliction of emotional distress

After four hours of deliberation,[2] the jury returned the award, some of which the Lepperts' attorney, David B. Pointer, hopes to recover from a prejudgment attachment on the Winrods' Our Savior's Church.

"This was the strangest fact situation I ever hope to come into contact with," Pointer said. The Winrods were unavailable for comment.

2 Note from Professor Carr: The jury came back quickly. 4 hours is not a long time for a jury to deliberate!!

74 Intentional Infliction of Emotional Distress

[Several nice examples of this tort and how it can come in a business context]

FROM THE TRENCHES

LETA FAY FORD won a suit against cosmetics manufacturer Revlon, Inc. for intentional infliction of emotional distress after company officials failed to stop ongoing harassment by her supervisor Karl Braun.

The harassment began in April 1980 after Braun invited her to dinner, supposedly to discuss business. However, at the end of the evening, when Ford tried to leave, Braun told her to stay because he planned to spend the night with her. When she rejected his advances, he told her, "You will regret this." This was only the first of several incidents in which Braun harassed Ford, including one a month later at a company picnic at which Braun held Ford in a choke hold, fondled her, and made lewd comments to her.

Although Ford had not reported the first incident to Revlon management, after the company picnic incident she initiated a series of meetings with several members of Revlon management to report her complaints. She told them that she was afraid of Braun, that she wanted help, and that the strain of dealing with Braun and his advances was making her sick.

The harassment continued throughout 1980 with Braun threatening to destroy Ford and promising her that as long as she worked for him she was never going to go anywhere. When no action had been taken by Revlon Management by December 1980, Ford contacted a manager to whom she had complained earlier. The manager told Ford that the situation was too hot to handle, and that Ford should put the matter in the back of her mind and try to forget about it. During the time of the harassment, Ford developed high blood pressure, a nervous tic in her left eye, chest pains, rapid breathing, and other symptoms of emotional distress.

In February 1981, Ford requested a job transfer and met with a personnel representative to try to resolve her grievance. Not until three months later did the personnel representative submit a report on Ford's complaint to a Revlon vice president. The report confirmed Ford's charge of sexual assault and recommended that Braun be censured. In May 1981, a full year and a month after Braun's initial act of harassment, Braun was issued a letter of censure from Revlon.

In October 1981, Ford attempted suicide. Later that month Revlon fired Braun. In April 1982, Ford sued both Braun and Revlon for assault and battery, and for intentional infliction of emotional distress.

The Arizona Supreme Court upheld a jury verdict against Revlon, holding that Revlon's conduct in ignoring Ford's situation for months was outrageous and extreme, and thus fulfilled the requirements for intentional infliction of emotional distress.

Source: Ford Revlon Inc., 734 P. 2d 580 (Ariz. 1987).

$1 MILLION FOR CREMATION OF WRONG BODY[1]

A FUNERAL HOME THAT cremated the wrong person should pay close to $1 million for the mix-up, a jury has decided.

Car crash victim Matthew Miller, 20, was sent to the Akins Funeral Home to be buried.

Instead, the Russellville, Ala., home cremated him after confusing him with another victim of the same accident.

A jury awarded $950,000 to Miller's relatives, finding the funeral home negligent and wanton in handling a human body. *Miller v. Kilgore-Green Funeral Home,* No. CV 2000-261 (Walker Co., Ala., Dist. Ct.).

Plaintiff's attorney Garvey Ivey Jr. of Jasper, Ala.'s Ivey & Ragsdale said the trial emphasized the family's "strong religious and personal beliefs" against cremation and the fact that the funeral home allegedly "showed no remorse." Defense attorney Larry Bradford of Birmingham's Bradford & Donahue did not return calls.

Alabama 'outrage'

The auto accident happened in February 2000 as Miller was driving on Alabama Highway 5 with two friends, Johnny Russell and Louise David. His car was struck by an 18-wheeler. All three were killed. According to the complaint, Miller's brother came to the accident scene and "while under extreme emotional distress, allegedly identified the Russell body as being the Miller body."

Russell's family wanted him to be cremated, and Miller's family opted for burial for Matthew. But when an Akins Funeral Home representative came to the coroner's office to pick up Miller's body for burial, they took Russell instead.

According to Ivey, the Miller family went to the funeral home that afternoon to view Matthew's body, but Akins allegedly refused to let them in until they advanced certain sums of money."

"In the meantime the other body was cremated," Ivey said.

When the Millers arrived at Tharptown Friendship Holiness Church for Matthew's funeral, the body they saw in the casket was not Matthew Miller's. It was Russell's.

Only later did Miller's family learn that their son had been cremated.

"If they would have let the mother and spouse look at the body, the cremation would never have happened," Ivey said "It's irreversible."

At trial, grief counselor Dr. Judy Davidson of Berea, Ky., explained the funeral process and the closure it provides to the victim's family.

In addition to the negligence charge they jury returned one count of "outrage," an Alabama version of intentional infliction of emotional distress that Ivey said is reserved for an extreme act, like mishandling a body.

75 E-Mail Crusade Against Intel: Is It Trespass?

The Wall Street Journal

[Trespass]

WHEN KEN HAMIDI was fired from Intel Corp. in 1995 after a long workers' compensation battle, he didn't go quietly.

Mr. Hamidi, 55 years old, spent the next two years criticizing the company in e-mails sent to thousands of co-workers. Convinced he was a victim of age discrimination, Mr. Hamidi even publicized his campaign by dressing as a cowboy and going on horseback to distribute printed versions of his messages to employees entering Intel's Folsom, Calif. facility, where he once worked.

Now, the California Supreme Court will determine whether the former employee's e-mail is a form of electronic trespassing, as Intel claims, or an expression of free speech.

The case, one of the most closely watched in cyber law, is gaining wider attention and could be heard before the month is out. Although Intel already has won three court rounds, the state Supreme Court decided earlier this year to review the case partly because of the doggedness of Mr. Hamidi's young Harvard-trained lawyer, and partly because a cadre of "cyber rights" advocates have come to Mr. Hamidi's defense.

Battle lines hardened this past week with the filing of friend-of the-court briefs on both sides of the case by groups as diverse as the American Civil Liberties Union, the Electronic Frontier Foundation and the U.S. Chamber of commerce.

It all started with a painful back injury that Mr. Hamidi, an Intel engineer, suffered on work time in 1990. Mr. Hamidi contends that the company didn't want to pay for workers' compensation costs related to the injury; Intel says Mr. Hamidi was fired for incompetence. Convinced that Intel's real motive was to be rid of an older, more costly employee, Mr. Hamidi launched his campaign, including his Internet missives.

At issue is whether an unwanted, unsolicited e-mail can be actionable as a form of trespass. After Intel repeatedly asked Mr. Hamidi to stop sending his e-mails and he refused, the company sued him in 1998. Charging him with "trespass to chattels"—a 17th century tort that prohibits meddling with and damaging another person's property for personal gain. Chattels is an old English word for "property," and the trespass-to-chattels tort has rarely been used in hundreds of years. Intel couldn't use the more common "trespass to land" complaint because Mr. Hamidi didn't actually step on Intel property.

Mr. Hamidi's supporters argue that in charging him with "trespass to chattels" Intel is, in effect, trying to erect borders across the Internet. A ruling for Intel could set a precedent allowing anyone to sue anybody else for trespass at the mere presence of an electronic signal, they argue. For example, Yahoo inc. could be sued by a company that doesn't want its Web site controlled by yahoo's search engine. Or, eBay Inc. could sue a smaller online auctioneer for simply linking to its Web site.

Intel's reaction to Mr. Hamidi's e-mailings highlights a growing problem at many companies, especially; those in the technology field. Criticisms from disaffected shareholders and angry, laid-off employees often appear on a company's own electronic chat boards, Web-sites and through e-mails.

"The Internet gave a megaphone to a lot of people who before weren't able to speak," says Cindy Cohn, legal director of the Electronic Frontier Foundation, which filed a brief on Mr. Hamidi's behalf. "A lot of big companies are uncomfortable with this more intrusive freedom of expression and they are trying to shut it down."

"We are trying to make the public aware that the soul of the Internet is at stake here," says William McSwain, a lawyer at Dechert LLP in Philadelphia, the firm representing Mr. Hamidi on a pro bono basis. Being represented by Dechert also makes Mr. Hamidi's case highly unusual: Deehert has earned a reputation for representing powerful companies, not individuals waging crusades.

Mr. Hamidi first came to the attention of Mr. McSwain, 33, when he was studying law. A former infantry officer in the U.S. Marines Corps, Mr. McSwain's 1999 Harvard law-review article in support of Mr. Hamidi caught the eye of the ACLU, the EFF and other groups.

Soon after graduating and landing a job as an associate at Dechert, Mr. McSwain managed to persuade the firm to let him represent Mr. Hamidi at no charge.

"Dechert cares about this case because we care, and! our clients care, about the "long-run development of the Internet," Mr. McSwain says. "The Internet is not going to achieve its commercial potential if "everybody who has an e-mail inbox, or who operates a Web site, can erect a virtual 'no trespassing' sign around that inbox or that Web site," he adds. "This could turn millions of Americans into criminals overnight, simply for looking at Web pages or sending unsolicited e-mails."

Intel spokesman Chuck Mulloy says the company never complains when Mr. Hamidi and his supporters stage protests outside its buildings, which the group has done a number of times. Mr. Hamidi may speak against Intel as often as he likes, Intel says, just not on the company's computer screens. "E-mail is where we draw the line," Mr. Mulloy says.

No one disputes that Mr. Hamidi is more than a minor irritant to the tech titan. Along with allegations of discrimination, his e-mails also often contained warnings of layoffs at Intel and calls to current Intel employees to be wary of management.

His messages haven't gone unheard: His organization, FACEIntel, has hundreds of members, mostly other former Intel workers with grievances. And his e-mails often reveal detailed information about Intel that suggests someone inside is tipping him off.

In a message he sent shortly after the inauguration of the FACEIntel Web site he wrote: "Annual review time is very close, unfortunately many of you will be put on CAP [Intel's program to improve employee performance] or will be terminated; Regardless of were [sic] you are contact us we can help. We all together can influence Intel to once again become the employee oriented company that it used to be!!!"

Perhaps most maddening about Mr. Hamidi's crusade is that while he is brash and indignant, he also is reasoned—and he obeys the law. His stunt on horseback was in response to a court order to stop his e-mail campaign, an order he followed immediately.

Mr. Hamidi's supporters say his e-mails can't be considered trespass because they didn't damage any of Intel's physical computer equipment.

For its part, Intel says its wins so far represent a victory for any business seeking to control its workplace. Plus Intel says, the e-mails harm employee morale, they threaten worker productivity and cost Intel money in the form of the time its technicians spent attempting to block the messages—a task they never achieved because Mr. Hamidi used a variety of tactics to outwit the screening programs of Intel's servers.

Mr. Hamidi, who now works for the state government but doesn't want to disclose which department, says he simply wants to warn Intel employees about company policies that he sees are disguised forms of age and disability discrimination. "I am the only person who cannot communicate with the very people I need to communicate with," he says. "This is about free speech and nothing else."[1]

---

1 Note from Professor Carr: Normally we think about a trespass only occurring on/over real property (land) but as this article nicely illustrates, the Internet and e-commerce have given rise to a new way that the tort of trespass may occur.

Also note that this is an excellent example of how the common law works—an old tort that has been around for centuries (trespass), with its broad and flexible elements, is being asked/used to address business conduct brought about by new technologies and societal change.

How would you rule in this case, and why?

76 The Tort of Negligence

Study Outline

III. The Tort of Negligence

A. When we say that a defendant acted "negligently," we mean that the defendant *failed to exercise reasonable care* and act as a "reasonably prudent person" would have acted under the circumstances, and the plaintiff was injured as a result. The question often becomes .... how extensive is this duty/how far does it go? (To answer this question, see below discussion regarding duty.)

B. Elements of Negligence: duty, breach of duty, causation, damages/injury, and no defenses apply

1. **Duty** – again, it's the duty to exercise "reasonable care"/act as a "reasonable person" would act under the circumstances (this is an objective test, not a subjective one)

    a) *How far/high does this duty go/how extensive is this duty? It depends on:*
        (1) The level of danger posed to the consumer/plaintiff/public
        (2) The reasonable forseeability of that injury occurring
        (3) The burden on the defendant in meeting/complying with that duty

    Obviously this is a flexible, sliding scale/balancing test that will vary with each case and situation.

    In effect, we ask ... how would a reasonable person have behaved/acted in this situation?

    But note: if a person/defendant has a mental or physical defect (e.g., mentally retarded, blind, etc.), then the "reasonable person" takes on those qualities as well. I.e., such a defendant is NOT penalized or held to the "ordinary" or "normal" reasonable person standard. See the practice problems that I have posted on Blackboard for some good examples of this distinction

See the cases and supporting articles in this textbook at pages 241–250 and 253–256 (and the practice problems posted on Blackboard) for practice and some good examples of how the "duty" component/aspect of negligence works

2. **Breach** – this duty must have been breached by the defendant

a) A person is guilty of a breach of duty if he exposes another to an ***unreasonable, foreseeable*** risk of harm (i.e., the defendant fails to act or behave the way a "reasonable person" would have behaved or acted under similar circumstances). Again, as with the duty element of negligence, in deciding the reasonableness of the risk, courts often balance the social utility of a person's conduct and ease of avoiding or minimizing the risk against the likelihood that harm will result and the probable seriousness of the harm

Again, see the cases and supporting articles in this textbook at pages 251–256 (and the practice problems posted on Blackboard) for practice and some good examples of how the "breach" component/aspect of negligence works

3. **Causation** – the breach of this duty of care must have caused damage/injury to the plaintiff (remember - both actual <u>AND</u> proximate causation must be satisfied)

   a) ***Actual causation*** – The breach of duty must have been the ***actual cause*** of the plaintiff's injury. Here, courts apply a "***but/for***" test

      (1) Ask …… but-for (or were it not for) J.T. slugging Chris without provocation while they were at Farmer's Market, would Chris' $3,000 gold necklace have been stolen by a thief as he lay on the ground unconscious?

         (a) With respect to the gold necklace being stolen and that part of Chris' injury/damage, the answer is NO! -- thus, the "but-for" test is satisfied, and actual causation is therefore satisfied. If the answer is "yes", then the but-for test fails/is not satisfied and the defendant wins because the plaintiff cannot prove a required element in his/her negligence claim

   b) ***Proximate causation*** – In addition to being the actual cause of the plaintiff's injury the breach of duty must have *<u>also</u>* have been the *proximate (or legal) cause* of the plaintiff's injury (here, the idea is to place a legal limit on defendant's liability. Thus, although the defendant's conduct may have been the actual cause of the plaintiff's injury, he is only liable if his conduct was *<u>also</u>* the proximate cause of that injury). **The test for what constitutes "proximate cause" is one of *<u>foreseeability</u>***

      (1) Ask …….. was it <u>reasonably</u> foreseeable that a thief would steal Chris' $3,000 gold necklace after J.T. struck Chris and knocked him out?

         (a) Probably not (in my view) and thus the defendant would win as this element has not been satisfied (as SLO is a relatively safe place, it was daylight out, lots of people/witnesses around, SLO in general has very few thieves -- but these are obviously debatable points). On the other hand, if Chris was lying unconscious in the street in a ghetto at night in New York after being struck by J.T., then such harm/injury would probably be "reasonably foreseeable" and the plaintiff would have successfully established this element of his/her negligence claim

      (2) **What about a superseding cause or "intervening force" (i.e., an outside, independent force)??** -- if the superseding cause or intervening force that injures the plaintiff is

a reasonably foreseeable one, either because it frequently occurs in the ordinary course of human events *or* because the defendant's negligence substantially increases the risk of its occurrence, it will not relieve the defendant from liability. But if the intervening force is unforeseeable, most courts will absolve the defendant from liability and treat the force as a *superseding cause* of the plaintiff's injury

(a) In the above example, an example of a superceding cause or "intervening force" (i.e., an outside independent force) would be an airplane flying over SLO during Farmer's Market and crashes right on top of Chris and kills him. Most folks/members on a jury would probably say that this is an ***unforeseeable*** superceding cause of Chris' death; and, therefore, the causal chain is broken (and J.T. its not liable for Chris' death)

(b) See also the practice problems posted on Blackboard as they will help you better see and be able to recognize what is/what is not a superceding/intervening cause and practice applying this rule/test

See the cases and supporting articles in this textbook at pages 257–260 (and the practice problems posted on my Blackboard) for practice and some good examples of how the "causation" component/aspect of negligence works

4. **Damage/Injury**

a) The plaintiff must have suffered damage or injury as a result of the defendant's negligent act

b) The damage or injury can be economic (e.g., lost profits) or non-economic (i.e., personal injury, pain and suffering, etc.)

c) Ordinarily the plaintiff has physical injuries so this is not an issue. But what about purely emotional injuries??

(1) Most courts have dispensed with the "physical impact/contact or injury" requirement and allow for the recovery of purely emotional injuries. However, some of these courts still require, as a precondition of recovery, proof that some physical injury or symptom resulted from plaintiff's emotional distress. Obviously juries are more skeptical of pure emotional injury cases than ones in which/where the plaintiff can show some actual physical injury to his/her body

5. **Defenses** – Finally, in order for the plaintiff to recover, none of the below defenses can apply

a) **Contributory negligence** -- plaintiff fails to exercise reasonable care for his own safety. This is a total bar to any recovery by the plaintiff!! This doctrine and defense means that if the defendant was 99% negligent and the plaintiff was only 1% negligence, the plaintiff loses and recovers nothing!!

b) **Comparative negligence (also called comparative fault)**-- looks at the relative fault of parties and assesses liability accordingly. This doctrine and defense was developed and adopted by courts in most states to help mitigate the harshness and potential unfairness to plaintiffs of the contributory negligence doctrine and defense discussed above.

Different states have different types of comparative negligence systems. For example ...

(1) ***Pure*** comparative negligence jurisdiction: plaintiff recovers a portion of his damages, even if he was more at fault (percentage wise) than the defendant (e.g., if the plaintiff was 60% negligent and the defendant was 40% negligent, then if the plaintiff's total damage was $10,000, the plaintiff recovers $4,000 against the defendant). California is this type of a jurisdiction. (See the practice problems posted on Blackboard for more practice applying the pure comparative negligence rules.)

(2) ***Mixed*** comparative fault jurisdiction: plaintiff recovers a portion of his damages, but only so long as his percentage of fault is less than the defendant's percentage of fault (e.g., the plaintiff can only recover if his negligence was 49% or less. E.g., if the plaintiff was 49% at fault, and the defendant was 51%, and the plaintiff's total damage are $10,000, then the plaintiff only recovers $5,100 against the defendant; but if the plaintiff was 51% at fault, he/she would recover $0!). (See the practice problems posted on Blackboard for more practice applying the mixed comparative negligence rules.)

c) **Assumption of risk**--plaintiff who ***voluntarily*** exposes himself to a ***known and specific danger or risk*** (note that this is different than a *general* danger or risk) created by defendant's negligence cannot recover.

(1) Note that the plaintiff's assumption of a risk can be express (e.g., via an exculpatory clause or a waiver of liability in a contract that he/she signed) or implied (e.g., by conduct)

(a) See the articles at pages 263–264 in this textbook for a good example of the assumption of risk doctrine/defense

Again, see the cases and supporting articles in this textbook at pages 263–266 (and the practice problems posted on Blackboard) for practice and some good examples of how the "defenses" component/aspect of negligence works

And ... for a good example of a case that ties all of the various elements of negligence together (including defenses), see the *Griffith* case in this textbook at pages 261–262. For another good example that ties together the duty, breach and causation aspect of negligence (but not defenses), see also the "Grand Theft Auto" video that I may show you in class, time permitting.

*****Finally, folks, I again encourage you to do the practice problems on negligence that I have posted on Blackboard. You may feel that you know/understand the above material, and, you may. But you also may not. So, be safe and do these practice problems. Many of them involve the application of the above concepts and that is a great way to learn (the only way, really) to see if you really do know and understand this material. – Prof. Carr**

77 Kelly v. Gwinnell[1]

96 N.J. 538, 479 A.2d 1219, Supreme Court of New Jersey, 1984

[Negligence — Duty. This case is a good example of the DUTY element of negligence, when a duty is owed and what that duty is.]

Facts: Marie Kelly was seriously hurt in a head-on collision with a car driven by Donald Gwinnell. Kelly alleges that just before the accident, Gwinnell had spent an hour or two at the house of his friend, Zak, drinking. Zak accompanied Gwinnell to his car and saw him drive off. Twenty-five minutes later he telephoned the Gwinnell house to make sure Gwinnell had reached it safely, only to learn of the accident. After the accident, a blood test indicated that Gwinnell's blood alcohol concentration was 0.286. An expert testified that Gwinnell must have consumed the equivalent of 13 drinks, must have been severely intoxicated, and must have shown signs of it while at Zak's home. Kelly sued Gwinnell. She also sued Zak for serving alcohol to Gwinnell; this case deals with the suit against Zak.

Issue: Does a social host, who causes a guest to become drunk, have a duty to the victim of an automobile accident caused by the guest?

Chief Justice Wilentz: Under the facts here defendant provided his guest with liquor, knowing that thereafter the guest would have to drive in order to get home. [One] could reasonably conclude that the Zaks must have known that their provision of liquor was causing Gwinnell to become drunk, yet they continued to serve him even after he was visibly intoxicated. By the time he left, Gwinnell was in fact severely intoxicated. A reasonable person in Zak's position could foresee quite clearly that this continued provision of alcohol to Gwinnell was making it more and more likely that Gwinnell would not be able to operate his car carefully. Zak could foresee that unless he stopped providing drinks to Gwinnell, Gwinnell was likely to injure someone as a result of the negligent operation of his car. In a society where thousands of deaths are caused each year by drunken drivers where the damage caused by such deaths is regarded increasingly as intolerable [and] where liquor licensees are prohibited from serving intoxicated adults, the imposition of such a duty by the judiciary seems both fair and fully in accord with the State's policy.[1]

We therefore hold that a host who serves liquor to an adult social guest, knowing both that the guest is intoxicated and will thereafter be operating a motor vehicle, is liable for injuries inflicted on a third party as result of the negligent operation of a motor vehicle by the adult guest. We impose this duty on the host to the third party because we believe that the policy consideration served by its imposition far outweigh those asserted in opposition. While we recognize the

1 **Note from Professor Carr: The court is saying that the level of danger posed to the plaintiff is high AND the foreseeability of that injury occurring is also high!! Thus, the duty owed is ...**

concern that our ruling will interfere with accepted standards of social behavior; will intrude on and somewhat diminish the enjoyment, relaxation, and camaraderie that accompany social gatherings at which alcohol is served; and that such gatherings and social relationships are not simply tangential benefits of a civilized society but are regarded by many as important, we believe that the added assurance of just compensation to the victims of drunken driving as well as the added deterrent effect of the rule on such driving outweigh the importance of those other values.

[The court admits that in some cases social hosts could incur so much liability that they lose their house.] In any event, it is not clear that the loss of a home by spouses who, by definition, have negligently caused the injury, is disproportionate to the loss of life of one who is totally innocent of any wrongdoing.

Most courts that have considered the problem have disagreed with the New jersey Supreme Court. For example, across the Hudson River in New York, the state's highest court refused to go along with *Kelly.* The court said that at common law, it was only the drunk driver who was liable, not a social host who poured the alcohol. If the legal duty were to be extended to social hosts, that must be done by the state legislature not by the courts.

The high courts of Iowa and California, like New Jersey, held that social hosts were liable. Yet in both of those states, angry legislators decided that the court had gone too far. They voted to repeal the social host liability and return to the old common law rule, leaving only the driver himself liable. Ask yourself the following questions on this conflict:

The New Jersey Supreme Court has taken the lead on this issue of soc host liability. Is it right to do that? Is the court engaging in "social engineering"? There are indications society is fed up with drunk drivers. Who should make the decision about social host liability, a court or a legislature? Over which one do the citizens have greater control?

Many states now have differing kinds of dram acts, making liquor stores, bars, and restaurants liable for serving drinks to intoxicated customers who later cause harm. Why might a state choose to make liquor stores and bars liable while not holding social hosts liable?

78 Ann M. v. Pacific Plaza Shopping Center[1]

6 Cal. 4th 666, 863 P.2d 207, 1993 Cal. Lexis 6127
Supreme Court of California 1994

[Negligence — Duty]

LAW SHOWS US trends in social issues. Regrettably, a major concern of tort law today is how to respond to injury caused by criminals. If a criminal assaults and robs a pedestrian in a shopping mall, that act is a crime and may be prosecuted by the state. But prosecution leaves the victim uncompensated. The assault is also an intentional tort (discussed in Chapter 5 at page 114) and the victim could file a civil lawsuit against the criminal. But most violent criminals have no assets; all too often, a plaintiff could win such a lawsuit without recovering any money. Given this economic frustration, and the flexibility of the common law, it is inevitable that victims of crime look elsewhere for compensation.

As crimes now occur in the workplace, in shopping malls, and parking lots, plaintiffs increasingly seek compensation from the owners of these facilities. Here we look at a landowner's liability for crime; later we consider an employer's liability.

Facts: Ann M. worked at the Original 60 Minute Photo Company in the Pacific Plaza Shopping Center, a strip mall in San Diego. About 25 commercial tenants occupy the center. She was the only employee on duty one day when a man walked in "just like a customer," pulled a knife, went behind the counter and raped Ann M. He robbed the store and fled. He was never apprehended.

Ann M. sued Pacific Plaza, claiming that it was negligent in failing to provide security patrols in the common areas of the shopping center. Under the terms of the lease, Pacific Plaza had exclusive control of these areas, and the right to police them if it chose. It was not obligated to provide patrols, and it did not do so.

Issue: Is Pacific Plaza liable for negligence in failing to provide security patrols?[2]

Judge Panelli: While the record includes some evidence of criminal activity on the shopping center's premises prior to Ann M.'s rape—bank robberies, purse snatchings, and a man pulling down women's pants—there is no evidence that Pacific Plaza had knowledge of these alleged criminal acts. In fact,

1 **Note from Professor Carr: Another good/interesting case dealing with the DUTY element of negligence**

2 **Note from Professor Carr: I.e., Did the defendant have a duty to provide security controls?? (See the next page for the answer!)**

Pacific Plaza offers uncontroverted evidence that it is the standard practice of [Pacific Plaza] to note or record instances of violent crime, and that [their] records contain no reference to violent criminal acts in the shopping center prior to Ann M.'s rape.

Ann M. presented evidence that the employees and tenants were concerned about their safety prior to her rape. These concerns centered around the presence of persons described as transients, who loitered in the common areas. One of the employees of the photo store called the police on two different occasions prior to the incident involved herein to complain that she felt threatened by persons loitering outside her employer's store. The photo store ultimately granted this employee permission to bring her dog to work for protection. This employee worked a late night shift, while Ann M. worked during the day. During periodic meetings of the merchants' association, an organization to which all tenants belonged, the tenants voiced complaints about a lack of security in the shopping center and the presence of transients.

It is now well established that California law requires landowners to maintain land in their possession and control in a reasonably safe condition. In the case of a landlord, this general duty of maintenance, which is owed to tenants and patrons, has been held to include the duty to take reasonable steps to secure common areas against foreseeable criminal acts of third parties that are likely to occur in the absence of such precautionary measures. In this state, duties are no longer imposed on an occupier of land solely on the basis of rigid classifications of trespasser, licensee, and invitee.

We turn to the heart of the case: whether Pacific Plaza had reasonable cause to anticipate that criminal conduct such as rape would occur in the shopping center premises unless it provided security patrols in the common areas. For, as frequently recognized, a duty to take affirmative action to control the wrongful acts of a third party will be imposed only where such conduct can be reasonably anticipated. In this, as in other areas of tort law, foreseeability is a crucial factor in determining the existence of duty.

Unfortunately, random, violent crime is endemic in today's society. It is difficult, if not impossible, to envision any locale open to the public where the occurrence of violent crime seems improbable. The scope of [a landlord's] duty is determined in part by balancing the foreseeability of the harm against the burden of the duty to be imposed. [I]n cases where the burden of preventing future harm is great, a high degree of foreseeability may be required. On the other hand, in cases where there are strong policy reasons for preventing the harm, or the harm can be prevented by simple means, a lesser degree of foreseeability may be required.

While there may be circumstances where the hiring of security guards will be required to satisfy a landowner's duty of care, such action will rarely, if ever, be found to be a "minimal burden." The monetary cost of security guards is not insignificant. Moreover, the obligation to provide patrols adequate to deter criminal conduct is not well defined. No one really knows why people commit crime, hence no one really knows what is "adequate" deterrence in any given situation. Finally, the social costs of imposing a duty on landowners to hire private police forces are also not insignificant. For these reasons, we conclude that a high degree of foreseeability is required in order to find that the scope of a landlord's duty of care includes the hiring of security guards. We further conclude that the requisite degree of foreseeability rarely, if ever, can be proven in the absence of prior similar incidents of violent crime on the landowner's premises. To hold otherwise would be to impose an unfair burden upon landlords and, in effect, would force landlords to become the insurers of public safety, contrary to well-established policy in this state.

Turning to the facts of the case before us, we conclude that violent criminal assaults were not sufficiently forseeable to impose a duty upon Pacific Plaza to provide security guards in the common area. We, therefore, conclude that Pacific Plaza was entitled to summary judgment on the ground that it owed no duty to Ann M. to provide security guards in the common areas.[3]

3 **ANSWER: The court says "no" to the question of whether a duty is owed (because of the reasons discussed above).**

79 Wal-Mart Not Liable in Shootings[1]

The National Law Journal

[Negligence — Duty]

A TEXAS JURY HAS rejected the contention of two victims of a shooting rampage 10 years ago that Wal-Mart was liable for selling a semi-automatic handgun to the shooter—a mentally unstable attorney.

The plaintiffs unsuccessfully contended that store personnel should have been trained to ask provoking questions that might have revealed the customer's dangerous paranoia.[2] Plaintiff's counsel Art Brender of the Fort Worth, Texas, Law Offices of Art Brender, said the verdict underscored the difficulty of picking a jury on the highly polarized gun issue. "We did some focus groups on this and there are really only two positions on guns," he said. "There are the people who don't think they ought to be sold at all, and those people frankly are more honest about their feelings, and people who feel that sellers shouldn't be held responsible for the guy who pulled the trigger. Despite nearly a full day of voir dire, we ended up with a jury that had decided before they ever sat down that unless there was overwhelming evidence they were not going to hold the seller responsible."

Defense counsel Ramona Martinez of Dallas' Cowles & Thompson said the jury simply rejected the plaintiff's theory that gun sellers have a duty to "screen potential purchasers for dangerous mental illnesses. "They [the plaintiffs] were looking for an application of the law that just wasn't, there." she said.[3]

The suit was brought by the family of Chris Marshall, an assistant district attorney in Tarrant County, Texas, who died in the shooting spree, and by retired Judge Clyde Ashworth, who was wounded. The killer, Gregory D. Lott, was convicted of killing two people and wounding three others in a rampage on July 1, 1992, at the Court of Appeal in the Tarrant County Courthouse.

Lott, a lawyer who practiced law sporadically for seven years before surrendering his law license in 1988, has since been executed. Brender described Lott as a "manifestly irrational" person who came to view the Tarrant County court system as his enemy following a bruising divorce and custody battle between Lott and his former wife, Margaret Best. A court-ordered family study by a psychologist concluded that Lott had a paranoid disorder and a violent temper.

On May 2,1992, Lott, apparently bent on revenge against the Tarrant Country courts, purchased a 9-millimeter Glock semi-automatic handgun

1 Note from Professor Carr: Another article dealing with/highlighting the DUTY aspect/element of negligence

2 Note from Professor Carr: The plaintiff was arguing that the store had a "duty" to ask such questions.

3 Note from Professor Carr: But ... as you can see, the jury disagreed with the plaintiff's argument/position.

from a Wal-Mart store, then known as Hypermart, in Arlington, Texas. Brender argued that store personnel should have been trained to ask "screening questions" that might have provoked a suspicious reaction from persons suffering paranoid disorders. "If you ask what is the purpose for purchasing the weapon you don't expect Lott to answer, 'I am going to shoot people at the court of appeal' but you will get a reaction out of the ordinary," he said.

Martinez said gun sellers have no legal obligation to determine the mental health of gun purchasers beyond a standard of what is reasonable. Lott, she said, gave no outward appearance of having mental problems.

"He didn't appear aggressive or angry," she said. "He was a graduate of law school. He was a smart man. This mass murder was a plotted event: I don't doubt that even if he is a crazy man and very angry, he could mask that for the 20 minutes it takes to buy a firearm."

Brender said screening questions, like those used by airlines, will elicit revealing responses from dangerously mentally ill people. *Marshall v. Wal-Mart Super Centers Inc.,* No. 236-154399-94, (Tarrant Co., Texas, Dist, Ct.).

80 Bahamian Resort Battles Allegations in Shark Attack[1]

By Mark Fineman, *The Los Angeles Times*

[Negligence — Duty]

Caribbean: Wife of mauled guest contends **lifeguards** did nothing to help, an accusation that company officials and witnesses deny.

BODY:

When Hong Kong real-estate powerhouse Hutchison Whampoa Ltd. was planning the $400-million resort that opened in December on Grand Bahama Island, senior management knew that it was entering a competitive market filled with potential pitfalls.

But General Manager Eric Waldburger conceded Wednesday that no one foresaw the tale of the Wall Street banker and the shark, nor the major damage-control operation Our Lucaya Beach & Golf Resort had to mount this week after its guest was attacked offshore.

"In 105 years in the Bahamas as a whole," Waldburger said, "there have only been 39 such incidents, and only three of them in Grand Bahama."

Long Island resident Krishna Thompson, 36, was in an intensive-care unit Wednesday at a Miami hospital after losing most of his left leg while celebrating his 10th wedding anniversary at the resort. His wife, Ave Maria Thompson, insists that lifeguards at the Caribbean's second-largest resort did nothing when a shark attacked him Saturday in 4 feet of water about 18 feet offshore—an accusation that the resort and witnesses deny.

The attack and its aftermath illustrate the risks of doing business in the tourism-dependent Caribbean.

In a region of extraordinary beauty that is plagued by its share of disasters both natural and human-made—from hurricanes to rising drug trafficking and crime—resort owners have had to defend their white-sand beaches and luxury suites during the past year amid reports of tourist slayings, the mystery of a missing travel writer and even a massacre in a Roman Catholic cathedral.

It was against that backdrop that Ave Maria Thompson, a New York City prosecutor, appeared Tuesday before reporters at Miami's Jackson Memorial Hospital, where her husband remained in serious but stable condition after doctors amputated his leg above the knee.

"He was screaming for help and nobody came. Nobody came," she said, weeping as she reported her husband's first words after the ordeal.

"When you scream for help and you're a lifeguard, you're supposed to get in there," she said.

1 **Note from Professor Carr: A final article that addresses the "DUTY" element/aspect of negligence. After reading the article, ask yourself "did the lifeguards have an affirmative duty to jump in earlier than they did to try and rescue this fellow?" Why or why not? I.e., apply the factors listed in this textbook on page 237. Further, what facts would be important to you in conducting such an analysis/evaluation??**

"One of the first things he said to me when they removed the ventilator was that he was screaming and they wouldn't come. He had to swim to them."[2]

Krishna Thompson's efforts—beating the shark with his fists, then grabbing his almost-severed leg as he swam toward shore, where his last act before passing out was scrawling the couple's room number in the sand—drew largely local news coverage in Florida when he was airlifted here Saturday. After all, 16 of the 31 shark attacks recorded worldwide this year by the International Shark Attack File, which is run by the Florida Museum of Natural History in Gainesville, took place off the state's shores.

But Ave Maria Thompson's emotional news conference Tuesday drew national attention.

On Wednesday, resort manager Waldburger and a Bahamas-based doctor who was jogging by when Krishna Thompson came ashore found themselves giving a battery of interviews swearing to quite a different version of events.

Lavishing praise on Our Lucaya's lifeguards, Waldburger said they saved Thompson's life.

"They did not hesitate to jump in" the moment they spotted Thompson's head above the surface near the fin of the shark, Waldburger said. The guards swam out to Thompson, formed a human chain and brought him hand to hand to shore, where they used a lifeguard's belt to apply a tourniquet to the leg and wrapped the wound in towels, he said.[3]

"The fact that they jumped in there in total disregard of their own lives is remarkable," Waldburger said. "They saved a man's life."

Dr. Nicholas Namias, the surgeon who amputated Thompson's leg in Miami, said it was a miracle that he didn't die from blood loss after the shark tore most of the flesh, nerves and muscle from his calf.

Rolando Corral, the Grand Bahama surgeon who was jogging by at the time of the attack, said during TV interviews Wednesday that the lifeguards' performance was exemplary.

The resort's manager and its publicists declined comment Wednesday on what may have motivated Ave Maria Thompson's account; she confirmed that she was in her room at the time of the attack and attributed all details to her wounded husband.

"We have done what we are supposed to do," said Waldburger, when asked whether the resort or its owners have offered any compensation to the Thompsons. "We have fulfilled our obligation."

Ave Maria Thompson did use her news conference to profusely thank the resort staff and managers who accompanied her and prayed for her husband at hospitals in the Bahamas and Miami.

She told reporters that before doctors removed her husband's ventilator she asked him if there was anything he wanted or needed. He wrote her a note that said, simply, "a leg."

2 Note from Professor Carr: The plaintiff is arguing that hotel/lifeguard had a duty to swim to him.

3 Note from Professor Carr: The hotel will argue that the duty it owed was exactly was it did/satisfied. I.e., that it fulfilled its duty to rescue him in the time and manner in which it did and it did not have a duty to do anything faster/differently.

81 Breach of Duty[1]

[Negligence — Breach]

THE SECOND ELEMENT of plaintiff's negligence case is *breach of duty*. The plaintiff must show that the defendant had a duty to him and breached that duty by not being sufficiently careful. But how careful is "careful"? Courts apply the *reasonable person* standard: a defendant breaches his duty of due care by failing to behave the way a reasonable person would under similar circumstances. Reasonable "person" means someone of the defendant's occupation. If the defendant is a taxi driver, he must drive and treat passengers as a reasonable taxi driver would. If the defendant is a heart surgeon, she must perform bypass surgery with the care of a trained specialist in that field.

Two medical cases from Texas will indicate how one court applies the reasonable person standard. In *Gooden v. Tips*[2] the plaintiff, Gooden, was struck by an automobile driven by Dr. Tips' patient, who was under the influence of prescription Quaaludes at the time of the accident. Gooden claimed that the doctor breached his duty of due care by failing to warn his patient not to drive while taking the drug. The court held Dr. Tips liable for breaching his duty.

In *Casarez v. NME Hospitals, Inc.*,[3] Dr. Vasquez admitted a patient to a hospital who was terminally ill with acquired immune deficiency syndrome (AIDS). In his admission instruction he stated that the patient was HIV positive; he also told the nurses of the patient's condition. Dr. Vasquez did not, however, instruct anyone on the procedures to use with the patient. Casarez, a certified nursing assistant, was caring for the patient when he involuntarily spewed blood on Casarez's mouth, eyes, and arm. The patient died the next day. Casarez tested HIV positive.

Casarez sued Dr. Vasquez (among others), claiming that he was negligent in failing to warn him of the dangers and instruct him how to handle an AIDS patient. Casarez was indeed obligated to take precautions with an AIDS patient, but he did everything reasonably required by being sure that the staff knew of the patient's illness. He had no obligation to instruct staff in special procedures for such a patient because all hospital staff were already trained. Casarez and all others knew precisely what precaution to take, and Vasquez was not liable.

CRIME AND TORT REVISITED: NEGLIGENT HIRING AND RETENTION

From July 1992 to July 1993, more than 2 million people in the United States were physically attacked in the workplace, according to a Northwestern National Life Insurance Company study. In 1992, there were 2,000 violent incidents on the job at the U.S. Postal Service alone, 138 homicides in

1 **Note from Professor Carr: Materials re: the BREACH aspect/element of negligence.**

2 51 S.W.2d 364 (Tex. Ct. App. 1983).

3 883 S.W.2d 360, 1994 Tex. App. LEXIS 2091 (Tex. Ct. App. 1994).

the workplace in New York City, and 1,004 such homicides nationwide. This makes homicide the leading cause of death in New York's workplaces and the second leading cause of workplace death, nationwide.[4]

A corporation can be liable for negligence if it hires someone known to have a history of violence. In *Gaines v Monsanto*, for example, a mailroom clerk with a previous rape and robbery conviction followed a secretary home after work and fatally assaulted her. Even though the murder took place off the company premises, the court held that the defendant would be liable if it knew or should have known of the mail clerk's criminal history. In other cases, companies have been found liable for failing to check an applicant's driving record, to contact personal references, and to search criminal records.

An employer who does an adequate background check before hiring must still pay attention to his employee's behavior. Courts have found companies negligent for retaining an employee. Consider *Yunker v. Honeywell, Inc.* Honeywell employed Randy Landin from 1977 to 1979, when he was imprisoned for the strangulation death of Nancy Miller, a Honeywell co-worker. When Landin was released from prison, Honeywell rehired him as a custodian in its General Offices facility in South Minneapolis. Because of workplace confrontations Landin was twice transferred to different facilities. Later he began to harass and threaten fellow employee Kathleen Nesser at work and at her home. At the end of June 1988, Landin's behavior prompted Nesser to seek help from her supervisor and to request a transfer out of the St. Louis Park facility.

On July 1, Nesser found a death threat scratched on her locker door. Landin did not come to work on or after July 1, and Honeywell accepted his formal resignation on July 11. On July 19, approximately six hours after her Honeywell shift ended, Landin killed Nesser in her driveway with a close-range shotgun blast. Landin was convicted of first degree murder and sentenced to life imprisonment.

The heirs and next-of-kin of Kathleen Nesser sued Honeywell. The Minnesota Court of Appeals held that Honeywell had not been negligent in hiring Landin, but that a jury could properly find that Honeywell had breached its duty to Nesser by *retaining* Landin after these incidents.

What can an employer do to diminish the likelihood of workplace violence? Many things.

Make workplace safety a priority. Many employers still do not believe that violence can occur in their company. Sadly, they are mistaken.

Seek the assistance of security experts and mental health personnel in planning a company-wide safety program.

Evaluate the workplace for unsafe physical features. Install adequate lighting in parking lots and common areas, hire security guards if necessary, and use closed-circuit television and identification cards. Ensure that the company uses thorough pre-hire screening, contacts all former employers, checks all references, and conducts criminal checks.

Respond quickly to dangerous behavior. In many cases of workplace violence, the perpetrator had demonstrated repeated bizarre, threatening, or obsessive behavior on the job, but his supervisors had not taken it seriously.

Offer counseling where appropriate and fire employees when necessary.

---

4 **Mathew Purdy, "Workplace Murders Provoke Lawsuits and Better Security,"** *New York Times,* **Feb. 14, 1994, p. Al.**

82 Jury Says Home Depot Must Pay Customer Hurt By Falling Merchandise $1.5 Million[1]

The Wall Street Journal

[Negligence — Duty and Breach]

AMID RISING CONCERNS over safety at so-called big-box stores, a Louisiana state-court jury ruled that Home Depot Inc. was negligent and must pay $1.5 million to a customer injured by falling merchandise. The Atlanta home-improvement retailer said it will likely appeal the verdict.

Home Depot and other retailers such as Wal-Mart Stores Inc. have been under increasing pressure from plaintiffs and consumer advocates to improve safety in their cavernous warehouse stores. In recent years, there have been several cases of customers killed or seriously injured by bulky merchandise falling from store shelves high above.

Don Patrick Avery sued Home Depot in October 1998 for negligence in the 19th Judicial State Court in the Parish of East Baton Rouge. The case stemmed from a February 1998 incident at a Home Depot in Baton Rouge. The suit alleged that a 70-pound bag of sand fell from a rack and landed on Mr. Avery. The suit said Mr. Avery suffered injuries to his back, hand and mouth. Mr. Avery and his Baton Rouge attorney couldn't be reached for comment.

Three people have died from falling merchandise at Home Deport stores since 1999, according to the company. Amid those deaths and increasing litigation over falling merchandise, Home Depot earlier this year named its first-ever safety officer and hired 130 safety managers to monitor store compliance with new safety measures. The retailer is rolling out a program nationwide this year that essentially bans the use of forklifts and other stocking activities during regular shopping hours. At Home Depot, some customers have been injured by forklift operators inadvertently knocking merchandise off shelves onto shoppers.

Earlier this year, Home Depot also mandated that top-self merchandise be secured to a pallet and wrapped in plastic to keep items from falling. Consumer advocates have pushed for additional safety measures, such as restraining bars on store shelves or a requirement that customers wear a hard hat in the store. But retailers have opposed those measures as unnecessary.

---

1 **Note from Professor Carr: This article does a nice job illustrating/highlighting how Home Depot owed its customers the DUTY, to keep/maintain a safe store premises and how it BREACHED (failed) to satisfy that duty (i.e., it failed to act as a reasonably prudent person/store owner under the circumstances—a "reasonable store owner" would not have had an unsafe store premises like this!).**

83 K-Mart to Pay $3 Million for Selling Gun to Suicidal Teen[1]

The National Law Journal

[Negligence — Duty and Breach]

At a Glance
CASE TYPE: Wrongful death
CASE: Eslinger v. Kmart Corp. No. 2:97CV0981
COURT: U.S. District Court for the District of Utah
VERDICT: $3 million

ON MAY 22, 1996 Ryan Eslinger, 19, went to the Kimball Junction, Utah, Kmart to buy a shotgun. Before making the purchase "he had been adjudicated as a mental defective," said plaintiffs' attorney James McKenna. Nevertheless, when filling out the Bureau of Alcohol, Tobacco and Firearms (ATF) weapons form, Eslinger answered "no" to the question regarding mental illness.

Although Eslinger didn't have a driver's license for identification, a Kmart clerk, 17-year-old Jared Ryan, accepted Eslinger's passport, even though it did not include his current address.

The next day, Eslinger brought the gun back. It was in pieces and he wanted Kmart to reassemble it. "Maybe he took it apart because he didn't want to kill himself," McKenna said. "The store security manager took a look at [Eslinger], pulled the ATF form and saw that it didn't have proof of current, address." He called Kmart's legal department, but they never called back, alleged McKenna.
Although the security manager was against giving Eslinger the gun back, he was overruled by the store manager. Eslinger walked out with it and, several hours later, shot himself to death.

Ellinger's parents sued Kmart, charging violations of gun-control laws requiring proof of residence. They also alleged negligent training and supervision of store personnel.[2] At trial, McKenna played a training video on gun sales. It warned that "the most important sale is the one you don't make" and cautioned against selling to anyone "who looked even a little funny."

At the time of the sale, Eslinger allegedly fit that description. On a heavy dose of the psychotic Clozaril, which causes an overproduction of saliva, "he was literally drooling," said McKenna. Also, he had self-inflicted scars and burn marks on his neck and arms, McKenna added.

1 **Note from Professor Carr: Here, the plaintiff successfully argued/convinced the jury that the Kmart employees had a DUTY to check for proper I.D., ask this young man the right questions, which would have brought to light what a messed up person he was, etc., and then in turn NOT sell him this gun. Further, the plaintiff successfully argued/convinced the jury that the defendants breached this duty by selling him the gun (i.e., the defendants failed to act as a "reasonable person" would have acted under the circumstances)**

2 **Note from Professor Carr: They are arguing the theory of negligence.**

Kmart contended that it complied with the laws on gun sales, that Eslinger appeared clean-cut and normal and that the sale was not a proximate cause of his death. On Sept. 12, a Salt Lake City jury awarded the Eslingers $1.5 million, then added $1.5 million in punitives the next day. Kmart's attorney declined to comment.

84 Forseeable Type of Harm[1]

[Negligence — Causation]

FOR THE DEFENDANT to be liable, the *type of harm* must have been reasonably foreseeable. In the case above, Dom could easily foresee that bad brakes would cause an automobile accident. He need not have foreseen exactly what happened. He did not know there would be a cyclist nearby. What he could foresee was this *general type* of harm involving defective brakes. Because the accident that occurred was of the type he could foresee, he is liable.

By contrast, assume the collision of car and bicycle produces a loud crash. Two blocks away, a pet pig, asleep on the window ledge of a twelfth-story apartment, is startled by the noise, awakens with a start, and plunges to the sidewalk, killing a veterinarian who was making a house call. If the vet's family sues Dom, should it win? Dom's negligence was the factual cause: it led to the collision, which startled the pig, which flattened the vet. Most courts would rule though that Dom is not liable. The type of harm is too bizarre. Dom could not reasonably foresee such an extra ordinary chain of events, and it would be unfair to make him pay for it.

Another way of stating that Dom is not liable to the vet's family is by calling the falling pig a *superseding cause*. When one of the "dominoes" in the row is entirely unforeseeable, courts will call that event a superseding cause and the defendant is off the hook. Negligence cases often revolve around whether the chain of events leading from the defendant's conduct to the injury was broken by a superseding cause.

In Kowkabany v The Home Depot Inc., Mr. and Ms. Remseyer bought four eight-foot landscape timbers at a Home Depot store. Mr. Remseyer and a Home Depot employee loaded the timbers into his car, placing them in the back seat protruding about three feet out the front passenger window. After 20 minutes of driving, Remseyer approached Eva Kowkabany and another girl, both on bicycles. A car was coming from the other direction. Remseyer thought he could pass the girls safely, but the approaching car "squeezed him" and the timber struck Eva Kowkabany, severely injuring her. Kowkabany sued the Home Depot.

The Home Depot defended by saying that Remseyer's negligent driving caused the accident. Remseyer had indeed been negligent. Was his negligence a "superseding cause?" No, held the court.

A [superseding] cause should only be found where the circumstances are highly unusual, extraordinary, bizarre or, stated differently, seem beyond the scope of any fair assessment of a danger created by the defendant's negligence. Applying the "highly unusual, extraordinary, bizarre" circumstances standard to the facts of this case, a jury could very reasonably find that Remseyer's poor judgment in driving his automobile, which resulted in the timber striking Ms. Kowkabany, was not so unusual or bizarre that it could not have reasonably been foreseen.

WEATHER or not is the question that Dr. Mark D. Shulman asks himself whenever a famous case comes to trial. As a forensic meteorologist, he is

---

1 Note from Professor Carr: Material re: the CAUSATION element/aspect of negligence

less concerned with who done it than with how the weather might have affected critical pieces of evidence or testimony. Was it sunny, cloudy, raining, dry, hot or cold? Was the moon shining or the wind blowing, and if so, in which direction? If a storm was involved, was it a freak occurrence or one that people should have been prepared for?

In one case, the insurance company for a New Jersey warehouse near New York Harbor had refused to pay for extensive flood damage to stored equipment after a thunderstorm. The insurer asserted that the warehouse should have anticipated the risk of flooding and taken measures to protect the equipment. But Dr. Shulman examined data from the National Climatic Data Center and research reports from the National Weather Service and concluded that the storm had been of extraordinary intensity, producing winds of hurricane force and record-high tides in the harbor.

"Even if the National Weather Service had issued early warnings of severe weather," he concluded "the warehouse could not have anticipated a storm of this magnitude and would not have been able to protect the equipment that got damaged as a result.

When a sign blew down in a western New jersey shopping center one January and injured a woman, was it negligence (did the owner fail to secure and maintain the sign properly?), or was it, in insurance lingo, an "act of God," the result of a wind so unusually intense and unpredictable that the owner could not have anticipated it? If negligence was determined, the owner would have been held personally liable for the woman's injuries, but if the accident was deemed an act of God, the insurance company for the shopping center would pay.

By checking the hourly data recorded at the nearest National Weather Station at Philadelphia International Airport, Dr. Shulman determined that based on changes in temperature, wind speed and wind direction, a strong cold front passed through the area at the time of the accident. A further analysis of many years of data that the National Oceanic and Atmospheric Administration, collected about climatological conditions for January at the airport revealed that "a wind of this intensity was a rare occurrence, "Dr. Shulman said. "So the intense wind that knocked down the sign fell within the category of an act of God."

85 Is a Singer Liable When Someone Acts Upon His Lyrics?[1]

[Negligence — Causation]

CONTEMPORARY PERSPECTIVE

MANY PEOPLE, PARTICULARLY youths, are influenced by singers, musicians, sports figures, movie stars, and other celebrities. Some listeners, readers, or watchers will be moved to love; others to tears; some to creativity, spirituality, or fear. But what happens when a person is so moved by a song, a movie, or a book that he commits a crime or engages in other dangerous conduct? Is the songwriter, singer, author, scriptwriter, or movie company liable for this conduct? This question was posed to the *court in McCollum v. CBS, Inc., and Osbourne.*

John "Ozzie" Osbourne is a well-known singer of rock and roll music and has become a cult figure. The words and music of his songs demonstrate a preoccupation with unusual, antisocial, and even bizarre attitudes and beliefs, often emphasizing such things as satanic worship, the mocking of religious beliefs, death, and suicide. CBS Records (CBS) produced and distributed Osbourne's albums.

On Friday night, October 26, 1984, John Daniel McCollum (John) listened over and over again to certain music recorded by Osbourne. He was a 19-year-old youth who had a problem with alcohol abuse as well as serious emotional problems. John was in his bedroom using headphones to listen to the final side of Osbourne's two-record album, *Speak to the Devil,* when he placed a .22 caliber handgun next to his right temple and took his own life.

One of the songs that John had been listening to was called "Suicide Solution." Three of the verse of the song stated:

Wine is fine but whiskey's quicker
Suicide is slow with liquor
Take a bottle drown your sorrows
Then it floods away tomorrows
Made your bed, rest your head
But you lie there and moan
Suicide is the only way out
Don't you know what it's really about
Ah know people
You really know where it's at
You got it
Why try, why try
Get the gun and try it
Shoot, shoot, shoot

John's relative, Jack McCollum, and John's estate sued Ozzie Osbourne and CBS for negligence, alleging that the lyrics of Osbourne's music incited John to commit suicide. When the trial court dismissed the action, the plaintiffs appealed. The appellate court held that although Osbournes's lyrics might

1 **Note from Professor Carr: A good example re: the CAUSATION aspect/element of negligence**

have been an actual cause of John's suicide, they were not the proximate cause of the suicide.[2] The court stated, "John's tragic self-destruction, while listening to Osbourne's music, was not a reasonably foreseeable risk or consequence of defendant's remote artistic activities."

The court further stated, "It is simply not acceptable to a free and democratic society to impose a duty upon performing artists to limit and restrict their creativity in order to avoid the dissemination of ideas in artistic speech that may adversely affect emotionally troubled individuals. Such a burden would quickly have the effect of reducing and limiting artistic expression to only the broadest standard of taste and acceptance and the lowest level of offense, provocation, and controversy." [*McCollum v. CBS, Inc., and Osbourne,* 202 Cal. App. 3d 989, 249 Cal. Rptr. 187 (Cal. App. 1988)]

---

2 Note from Professor Carr: I.e., both elements of causation were not satisfied; thus, the defendant wins!!

86 Griffith v. Valley of Sun Recovery, Inc.[1]

126 Ariz. 613 P.2d 1283 Arizona Court of Appeals

Facts: Don Gorney was a "repo man." A repossession person is someone authorized to find and take cars whose owners are behind on payments. A repossessor is allowed to drive away in such a car, provided he can do it peacefully. Gorney worked for Valley of Sun Recovery. He sought a car being used by Linda Marsalek and Bob Williams. Gorney knew that there had been other, failed efforts to repossess the Marsalek car, including a violent confrontation involving attack dogs. He thought he could do better.

Gorney went to the car at 4:00 in the morning. He unscrewed the bulb in an overhead street lamp. He unlocked the car, setting off its alarm, and quickly hid. The alarm aroused the neighborhood. Williams and a neighbor, Griffith, investigated and concluded it was an attempted theft. They called the police. Gorney watched all of this from his hiding place. When everyone had gone, Gorney entered the car, again setting off the alarm and arousing the neighborhood. Williams and Griffith again emerged, as did another neighbor, dressed in his underwear and carrying a shotgun. They all believed they had caught a thief. Williams shouted for the gun and the neighbor passed it to him, but it went off accidentally and severely injured Griffith. Griffith sued Valley of Sun. The trial court granted summary judgment for Valley of Sun, and Griffith appealed.

- Did Valley of Sun have a *duty* to Griffith?
- If so, did the company *breach* its duty?
- If so, was the breach the *factual cause*[2] of the injury?
- If so, was *this type of injury foreseeable?*[3]

Argument for Griffith: Your Honors, Mr. Griffith should be allowed to make his case to a jury, and let it decide whether Valley of Sun's repossession led to his injury. Mr. Griffith has demonstrated every element, of negligence. First, Valley of Sun had a duty to everyone in the area when they attempted to repossess a car. They could easily have foreseen injury.[4] Car repossessions always involve antagonism between car owner and the repo company.

Obviously Gorney breached his duty.[5] He was caught up in some fantasy, your honors, dreaming that he was Harrison Ford in an adventure film. That is great in the movies but extremely dangerous in the real world. He knew from previous repossession attempts that trouble was certain. Everything he did showed that he anticipated the worst. But

1 **Note from Professor Carr: This is a case that does an excellent job of highlighting and tying together <u>all</u> of the elements of negligence (duty, breach, causation and damages).**

2 **Note from Professor Carr: Actual causation**

3 **Note from Professor Carr: Proximate causation**

4 **Note from Professor Carr: Duty**

5 **Note from Professor Carr: Breach of the duty**

rather than taking steps to minimize the danger, he exacerbated it. He unscrewed a light bulb, guaranteeing poor visibility and confusion. He set off the car alarm *twice,* making the whole neighborhood jittery. He saw police arrive, and angry, frightened neighbors appear. He hid and watched, and relished the whole thing—and caused [...]

Factual causation is indisputable.[6] Had it not been for preposterous game playing, no neighbors would have been outside, no guns present—and no accidental shooting. And this type is easily foreseeable.[7] Gorney expected violence, he played cops and robbers, he did everything he could to increase the chance of violence—and he got it. We should have a chance your honors, to take our case to a jury.

Argument for Valley of Sun Recovery: Your honors, this is a case that should never have been a case, and the trial court correctly granted summary judgment. There are three good reasons to end this case today: no duty, no breach, no causation.[8]

It is preposterous to suggest that Valley of Sun has a legal duty to an entire neighborhood. Car owners behind on their payments live in all parts of all communities. Is a repossession company to become an insurer of the entire city? Your honors, we are in a lawful, and important business. People may not like the idea of car repossession, but they would like it even less if there were no such companies. These companies deal with delinquent owners, people who feel like driving new cars without paying.

Yes there is some danger involved, because delinquent owners are irresponsible and sometimes dangerous. Should we therefore allow them to keep their cars? Of course not. We must act, and that is what Valley of Sun does.

They do it safely, your honors. Even if there had been a duty, there was no breach. Mr. Gorney attempted to repossess when it was least likely anyone would see him. Opposing counsel calls this "playing cops and robbers," but opposing counsel has never repossessed a car. What should Mr. Gorney have done, asked for permission to take the car? *That* is a recipe for violence. If the owner were reasonable, there would be no repossession in the first place. Repo men do everything possible to minimize danger.

There is also no causation here your honor. Factual causation? Valley of Sun did not create this situation. The car owner did. He bought the car and failed to pay for it. That is the factual cause of this chain of events. Even if there were factual causation, Valley of Sun is not liable because there is a superseding cause: the negligent use of a firearm by one of Mr. Griffith's neighbor's. Mr. Griffith's counsel refers to Mr. Gorney as a vigilante, when in fact the only vigilante here was the foolish neighbor, thinking he should take the law into his own hands. No jury should hear this case, your honors, because there is no case.

---

6 **Note from Professor Carr: Actual causation**

7 **Note from Professor Carr: Proximate causation**

8 **Note from Professor Carr: There was no duty owed, no breach, and the required causation element was not satisfied. Read on as to why ...**

87 No Penalty[1]

[Negligence — The Assumption of Risk Defense]

Teams and leagues are usually shielded from liability when spectators are injured during action, but that doesn't mean Brittanie Cecil's family won't be compensated.

ADDRESSING THE MEDIA before his team's first home game since Brittanie Cecil's death, Columbus Blue Jackets coach Dave King said, "We have to do as much as we can to help the family through this." It was an admirable sentiment, but it was based on social responsibility, not legal obligation. Under the common law doctrine of "assumption of the risk," sports teams and leagues are generally shielded from liability when fans are injured in foreseeable ways during play.

The thinking: There are certain risks that are so inherent in an activity that they cannot be eliminated. In the case of sports spectators, that can include getting hit by a foul ball, a hockey puck or a car part. "The law isn't favorable to fans," says Harvard Law School professor Paul Weiler, an expert in both torts and sports law. "It essentially says, Look, you know what you're getting yourself into. If you don't like the risks, don't come."

Some fans struck by objects have overcome this presumption, but the circumstances have been extraordinary. For instance, a Los Angeles Kings fan won a $3 million settlement from the team, the San Jose Sharks and Joe Murphy in September 2000 after the fan was hit in the head by a puck that Murphy rifled into the stands after an L.A. goal. Though it was reasonably foreseeable that the fan might be hit with a puck during the action, that wasn't the case once play had stopped. In Brittanie's case, however, no such peculiarity was apparent.

Another possible legal gambit: Fans can't assume risks they don't understand. In one of the few Ohio cases that could provide favorable precedent to the Cecil family, a Cleveland man who was attending his first hockey game, in 1948, was hit by a flying puck. He successfully circumvented the "assumption of risk" defense by maintaining that he didn't know that sitting in an unscreened area was dangerous. Still, the attorney retained by Brittanie's family last week

Legal doctrines be damned, it's a rare jury that would favor a sports franchise over the family of a deceased 13-year-old cheerleader would have a hard time maintaining that Brittanie, an avid hockey fan, was unaware of the risks.

On the spot Aside from sending condolences to the Cecil family, as of Monday, NHL commissioner Gary Bettman had not spoken publicly of the tragedy.

Spectators injured during play have also won cases on the grounds that the teams' facilities were inadequate or unsafe. In 1999 a Florida Marlins fan sitting near the bullpen was severely injured by a wild pitch that flew over the screening and was awarded $2.5 million when a jury ruled that the

1 **Note from Professor Carr: An excellent article that highlights the Assumption of Risk doctrine/defense**

team should have known the netting was too low. The plexiglass in Columbus's Nationwide Arena, however, conformed to accepted NHL standards. Given that Brittanie was the first fan in league history to be killed by a puck, it would be difficult to contend that the standards were negligent.

What of the language on the back of the tickets that warns fans of flying pucks and usually claims to discharge the team of responsibility? While no reasonable court would regard that as a binding contract, it's a further indication that the risks have been made apparent and foreseeable to fans.

Yet just because the Blue Jackets likely don't have to compensate the Cecils doesn't mean they won't. Were the Blue Jackets to tell the Cecils that, in so many words, "they're outta luck," the public relations consequences could be disastrous. If the case went to trial, legal doctrines be damned, it's the rare jury or elected judge that would favor a deep-pocketed sports franchise over the family of a deceased 13-year-old cheerleader.

E. Michael Kelly, a Chicago attorney, successfully defended the White Sox in a recent $1 million suit brought by a fan hit in the eye by a foul ball. If he were counseling the Blue Jackets, Kelly would advise the team to proffer to the family $1 million, minimum, for waiving their right to sue. "Maybe it would be different if it had been a loudmouth with 15 beers in him," he says. "But this? This is a tragedy beyond belief with the most sympathetic plaintiffs imaginable."

88 The Billy Idiot-Delta Poo Poo Incident[1]

Billy Idiot, a twenty-year old student attending Cal Poly University and majoring in computer science, pledged the local chapter of Delta Poo Poo, a national fraternity with local chapters on thirty-five campuses. The local chapter to which Billy pledged is an unincorporated association.

During the course of his initiation ceremony, Billy and other pledges attended a "hell night," during which they underwent a series of hazing activities mandatory for all pledges. The activities, which began at approximately 8:00 p.m., required the pledges to strip down to their underwear, sing songs, be sprayed with beer and soda, to attend a coed party clad a such, and to drink massive amounts of alcohol.

The active fraternity brothers goaded the pledges to drink excessively and ridiculed them when they drank only small amounts. Following the directions of the fraternity brothers, the pledges "chugalugged" 40 ounce pitchers of beer and drank from a quart bottle of whisky. Billy became so drunk that he vomited and, after another initiation activity, passed out at approximately 11:00 p.m. One of the pledges and two fraternity brothers carried him to bed where they thought he would "sleep it off." They checked on him just after midnight, noticed his face was pale and discolored, and were unable to wake him. Afraid that they would be charged with criminal conduct and unsure whether they should call emergency medical help, they decided to leave Billy in the bedroom.

The next morning, a fraternity brother discovered Billy in the bedroom and called the local emergency rescue service. Billy was transported to a local hospital where he received medical care. Unfortunately, Billy suffered permanent neurological damage to his arms and hand as a result of a near fatal blood-alcohol content.

Alleging that the fraternity members unduly pressured him to consume excessive quantities of alcohol, Billy commenced a personal injury (i.e., negligence) action against the members of the Cal Poly chapter of Delta Poo Poo, the local Delta Poo Poo chapter, the national Delta Poo Poo organization, and Cal Poly.

During discovery, Billy provided two expert reports.

In the first report, a physician from the University of California, San Francisco medical school qualified as an expert in the field of emergency medicine, opined that the proximate cause of Billy's permanent injuries was the failure of the members of the fraternity to promptly obtain emergency medical assistance.

In the second report, an expert clinical psychologist from Stanford University opined that the pledge's desire to join the fraternity, the prestige of being a member of the fraternity, and

1 **Time permitting we will go over this case/hypothetical in class**

the psychological and social dynamics involved in hazing activities diminished the pledge's ability to refrain from excessive drinking.

Questions:

1. What must Billy establish in order to succeed in his personal injury action against the local chapter of Delta Poo Poo?

2. May the named defendants escape liability for Billy's injuries because Billy voluntarily participated in the hazing activities? I.e., do any negligence defenses apply?

3. What might colleges and universities, national fraternity organizations, local fraternity chapters, and members of fraternities do to reduce or eliminate their liability for injuries suffered by pledges during initiation ceremonies?

89 The Tort of Strict Liability

Study Outline

IV. **The Tort of Strict Liability**

For some activities, defendants are held strictly liable for injuries that such activities cause. This is the case regardless of the fact that the defendant did everything possible to prevent the harm and/or he did not intend to cause the harm.

Strict liability theory states that if you did it/engaged in the act, and, if strict liability theory applies (and none of the defenses apply), then if the plaintiff was damaged or injured you have to pay for that damage – period and end of story.

What can justify making people liable irrespective of their level of fault? The standard argument is the risk-spreading argument -- because they face the greater recoveries that strict liability makes possible, defendants will self-insure or purchase insurance. This costs money, but most defendants will be in a position to pass on the greater costs in the form of higher prices. Thus, the economic risk associated with the defendant's activity is (partially) spread about through society.

Strict liability applies to the following activities/situations:

A. Abnormally Dangerous (or Ultrahazardous) Activities

1. Activities that necessarily involve a risk of harm to others that cannot be eliminated by the exercise of reasonable care (e.g., blasting, crop dusting, stunt flying, fireworks shows, etc.)

B. Statutory strict liability

1. Workers' compensation (e.g., if you get hurt on the job, and, if workers' compensation applies, you get paid out of the workers' compensation fund for your injuries regardless of whether your employer was/was not at fault)
2. Dram Shop statutes (e.g., they make a tavern owner or bartender civilly liable for injuries caused to or by patrons who are served too much alcohol and then get in a car, drive away and kill/injure someone)
3. Operators of aircraft for ground damage resulting from aviation accidents

C. Strict Products Liability (Strict Liability for the sale of Defective Products – Not Services) (**we will spend the bulk of our time in class on this one**)

1. Product Liability Law – What is it?
    a) The legal liability of the manufacturer or seller of a product which, because of a defect, causes injury to the purchaser, user, or bystander. In theory, liability extends to anyone in the business of selling the goods or in the chain of distribution.

2. The Evolution of Product Liability Law
    a) The 19th century
        (1) Product liability rules were very much in favor of sellers and manufacturers. It was an era of *caveat emptor* (let the buyer beware)
    b) The 20th century
        (1) A more protective climate emerged. Product liability law moved from a *caveat emptor* emphasis to a stance of *caveat venditor* (let the seller beware)

3. The current (perceived) crisis in product liability law

    a) Many sellers and manufacturers contend that it's becoming too difficult or prohibitively expensive to obtain liability insurance. This in turn may be passed onto the consumer and/or deter the development and marketing of new products. As a result, there has been a movement seeking to cut back what is perceived to be "pro-plaintiff" product liability law primarily through state and/or federal legislation (which, for example, cuts back on the amount of damages a plaintiff can recover in such lawsuits). This is often referred to as the "tort-reform movement." In some states this movement has gained traction and in others not. For the time being the environment of *caveat venditor* (let the seller beware) prevails.

4. **Strict Product Liability** – "The Rules/Elements"

    Note that a major benefit of this theory for the plaintiff is that it eliminates the need for the plaintiff to prove that the defendant owed and breached a duty (as is required by negligence – see the preceding negligence outline in this textbook)

    a) Requirements/elements of strict liability theory (i.e., this is what the plaintiff must prove beyond a preponderance of the evidence in order to recover against the defendant):

        (1) *The seller must be engaged in the business of selling the product that harmed the plaintiff (vs. an occasional seller)*; ***and***

            (a) Note that liability under this theory extends to anyone in the chain of distribution – manufacturers, wholesalers, distributors, and retailers. I.e., they are all considered "sellers" for purposes of strict products liability law. Thus, for example, a person injured by a product purchased from a retail store can sue, among others, any one (or more) of these potential defendants

(2) *The product must __also__ be in a "defective condition" when it left the hands of the manufacturer or seller, __**and**__ it must also be "unreasonably dangerous" because of that condition*

(a) The test of whether a product is in a "defective condition" is whether the product meets the reasonable expectations of the average consumer

(i) E.g., a consumer expects a stepladder not to break when stands on the bottom step and the ladder is being used

(b) An "unreasonably dangerous" product is one that is dangerous to an extent beyond the reasonable contemplation of the average consumer (some courts also balance the social utility of a product against its danger when analyzing whether a product is unreasonably dangerous)

(i) Note that a product may be "unreasonably dangerous" because of a manufacturing defect, a design defect, or inadequate warnings, labeling, or instructions

********Always remember ... product liability lawsuits can be brought under either strict liability theory and/or negligence theory!!**

b) __**Defenses**__ -- to a strict products liability lawsuit

(1) Assumption of risk

(a) But remember that the facts must show that the plaintiff ***voluntarily consented to a __specific__ and __known__ danger*** (note that this is different than a *general* danger) order for this defense to work for a defendant

(i) See the ***McDonald's*** case study/hypothetical in this textbook at pages 309–312 for an example of this defense. Did Stella assume a "specific and known" risk in that case? We will discuss this case study in class

(2) Obviousness of the Risk

(a) If the use of a product carries an obvious risk, the defendant will not be held liable for injuries that result from ignoring the risk

(i) E.g., a Volkswagen microbus was held not to be defective even though the shortened front end resulted in more serious injuries in a collision

(3) Product Misuse (i.e., the plaintiff is injured because he/she was misusing the product)

(a) General Rule: usually available to a defendant as a valid defense

(b) Exception: not available where the defendant knew of or had reason to foresee the particular misuse involved

(i) E.g., it is foreseeable that a child will misuse most toys, so the defendant has to plan for this!

(4) State-of-the-Art Defense

(a) This defense is based on a manufacture's compliance with the best available technology at the time (which may or may not be synonymous with the custom and practice of the industry). The state-of-the-art-defense shields a manufacturer from liability if no safer product design is generally recognized as being possible at the time

(i) For example, an Indiana statute provides: "It is a defense that the design, manufacture, inspection, packaging, warning, or labeling of the product was in conformity with the generally recognized state-of -the-art at the time the product was designed, manufactured, packaged, and labeled."

(ii) A Missouri statutes provides that, if the defendant can prove the that the dangerous nature of the product was not known and could not reasonably be discovered at the time the product was placed in the stream of commerce, then the defendant will not be held liable for the failure to warn

(5) Comparative Negligence (also called comparative fault)

(a) In product liability actions, the plaintiff's damages may be reduced by the degree to which the plaintiff's own negligence contributed the injury. I.e., the same rules and concepts apply here as discussed under negligence theory. (See the negligence study outline in preceding pages of this textbook at the "Defenses" section.)

(b) Note that *contributory negligence* is ***not*** a defense in a strict products liability action

For a good example of a product liability case that illustrates strict liability (and negligence theory), see the ***McDonald's*** case study/practice hypothetical in this textbook at pages 309–312. We may discuss this case study in class

Be sure to see the other cases and supporting articles in this textbook at pages 273–276 for practice and some good examples of how strict liability works and how it can come up in a business context

*****Again, folks, I encourage you to do the practice problems on strict liability that I have posted on Blackboard. You may feel that you know/understand the above material, and, you may. But you also may not. So, be safe and do these practice problems. Many of them involve the <u>application</u> of the above concepts and that is a great way to learn (the only way, really) to see if you really do know and understand this material. – Prof. Carr**

Miscellaneous – for now omit/don't worry about the other torts discussed in Chapter 6 of the textbook that is posted on Blackboard (i.e., they will not be on the exam; we may come back and discuss them later if we have time)

90 Fla. Jury Awards Wounded Teller $26.9 Million[1]

The National Law Journal

[Strict Liability]

A SMALL FLORIDA FIRM has won a $26.9 million judgment for a bank teller shot and paralyzed in a robbery by applying products liability law to Foreline Security Corp., the company that designed and installed the bank's security alarm system.

"This was one of the first, if not the first, case to use product liability theory against a security alarm company," asserted Bryan W. Crews of Crews & Bodiford of Orlando, Fla.

The plaintiff, Marishia Scott, 28, became a quadriplegic after being shot in the neck on March 20, 1999, during a robbery at the tiny Mt. Dora, Fla., branch of United Southern Bank. Her co-worker, Heather Young, was shot dead during the robbery. According to facts established at both the criminal trial of the robber Fred Anderson Jr., and during the civil litigation, Anderson had visited the bank manager the day before the robbery posing as a college student researching a paper on the banking industry. He saw that the VCR connected to the bank security cameras was sitting on a credenza in the manager's office.

During his criminal trial it was revealed that Anderson, a petty criminal well known to local police, had concluded he could successfully rob the bank by murdering the two tellers and removing the VCR.

During the robbery, a passerby summoned the police, who arrived within one minute.

Anderson, who is now on death row, was arrested carrying a pistol, a waste paper basket containing $70,000 and the VCR.

Crews and his partner, Raymond O. Bodiford, built their case around the theory that the alarm system was a defective product, despite complying with the minimum standards of the Federal Bank Protection Act. The two crucial defects were the placement of the VCR in an unsecured location and the failure to install panic buttons at the teller stations.

"We had a criminologist testify that Foreline made the bank a soft target by placing the VCR in an unsecured place," Bodiford said. "The fact the robber was arrested with the VCR under his arm made that a powerful argument."

Crews and Bodiford argued that the security system was defective based on implied warranty of fitness, implied warranty of merchantability and strict liability.

---

1 **Note from Professor Carr: An interesting and excellent article that highlights how the tort of strict product liability can come up.**

In addition, they contended Foreline both negligently and fraudulently misrepresented[2] that the system complied with standards set by Underwriters Laboratory. The jury found in favor of the plaintiff on each point but split liability evenly between the bank and the security firm. The bank, however, is shielded from litigation by Florida's worker's compensation law. A judge must decide how much of the award goes to Scott.

VCR location pivotal

Foreline was represented by Roland "Jerry" Sutcliffe of Orlando's Zimmerman, Sheffield, Kaiser & Sutcliffe. Sutcliffe said the pivotal factual issue was the placement of the VCR in the manager's office, which he said was done at the insistence of the bank.

"We designed the system to have the VCR in a secure closet, but they wanted it in the manager's office because it is he who changes the tapes and reviews the videos," Sutcliffe said. "There was nothing illegal about having it there. It didn't violate any standards to have it there."

Crews and Bodiford argued that under strict liability, Foreline remained liable for defects in the security system regardless of whether the system complied with minimum standards.

As for the argument that the bank management directed placement of the VCR, they noted the manufacturer of the VCR included with its instructions a warning that it should be located in a secure place.

"We plowed new legal ground but it ended up well," said Crews. "The jury checked all the product theories in our favor, as well as negligent misrepresentation and negligent failure to warn."

Sutcliffe said Foreline will appeal, though upon what grounds is still being studied. *Scott v. Foreline Security Corp.*, No. 00-129 (Lake Co., Fla, Cir. Ct.)

---

2 Note from Professor Carr: Note that the tort/ theories of both <u>negligence</u> and <u>fraud</u> were alleged by the plaintiff in its complaint and at trial.

91 Tire Trial Ends with $29 Million Verdict[1]

The National Law Journal

[Strict Liability]

A TEXAS JURY HAS awarded $29 million to the family of a man who died in a rollover accident involving a Bridgestone/Firestone tire.[1]

Jurors made the award in connection with a Chevrolet Blazer that veered off the road and flipped after the tread separated on its left rear tire. Sears Roebuck had previously repaired a puncture in the tire.

After a day-and-a-half of deliberations, the jury assigned 65% of the blame to manufacturer Bridgestone/Firestone and 35% to Sears, which sold the tire.

Jurors found that Sears and Bridgestone/Firestone were negligent and agreed that the Dueler APT had design and manufacturing defects. *Christine J. Tripp v. Sears Roebuck and Co.*, No. A00482-C (Orange Co., Texas, Dist. Ct.).

The family of the plaintiff had reached a confidential settlement with Bridgestone/Firestone about six months before the case went to trial.

Several litigation attorneys said the Texas verdict and award should not be viewed as a bellwether for other tire tread separation cases because the circumstances of the fatal accident were so unusual.

Federal officials have blamed rollover accidents involving Ford Explorers and Firestone tires for more than 200 deaths and more than 700 injuries. A recall two years ago led to the replacement of nearly 30 million of those tires. The Dueler APT was not part of that recall, and Sears no longer sells the tire.

Sears, the country's largest tire seller, has not yet decided whether it will appeal. A spokeswoman said the verdict will have no impact on other Sears tire cases.

"We just don't feel it's going to change how we handle any litigation we have now," said Jan Drummond. "That may change six months from now. It's a really new verdict." Sears' trial attorney, Louis A. Lehr of Arnstein & Lehr in Chicago, referred questions to Drummond.

Plaintiff's attorney Richard Mithoff of Houston said he sought to lay the lion's share of the blame on Sears, which sells $800 million worth of tires annually. He argued during the four-and-a-half day trial that though the tire had an underling defect, Sears bore more responsibility for its failure because

1 **Note from Professor Carr: Note how this article illustrates how the plaintiff alleged and proved two different tort theories of liability against the defendant—strict liability and negligence. But also remember and note, as we discussed in class, that these two theories require the plaintiff to prove different things/elements. Know what those elements are for the exam!!!**

the retailer had gathered data that detailed tire problems. That information should have led the retailer to replace—not just repair—the punctured tire, Mithoff said.

The Dueler APT was covered by a road hazard warranty when a nail punctured it 15,000 to 20,000 miles before the September 2000 accident that killed 35-year-old passenger Terry Tripp. The plaintiff's experts contended that the repair was done improperly—a claim defense experts rejected. Mithoff, a partner at Mithoff & Jacks, suggested that the jury assign Sears 70% and Bridgestone/Firestone 30% of the blame for Tripp's death. The panel assessed $17 million and punitive damages against Sears, but nothing will be awarded, Mithoff said, because the jury did not find that Sears had acted maliciously. Jurors said after the trial that they made the malice award "to send a message to Sears that they should do something about the Dueler APT, Mithoff said.

Because the tire manufacturer had settled before trial, Judge Pat Clark is expected to deduct either the amount of the settlement or 65% of the award from the $29 million.

Mithoff said the trial introduced "a dynamic of tension between Bridgestone/Firestone and Sears" as each blamed the other for the tire's failure. "I think it will add to that dynamic—or should add to that dynamic—in these cases," he said.

Tab Turner, a Little Rock, Ark., attorney, said the verdict won't have any bearing on three Dueler APT tread separation cases he's filed in three states. "I'm sure somebody's got a case like it," he said, "but that case will not have a whole lot of relevance on how people value something because the issues there are so unique." Turner, of Turner & Associates, said he'll focus on design defects.

Richard M. Zielinksi, who defends mass torts and products liability cases for Hill & Barlow in Boston, said: "I don't see this as a landmark, groundbreaking case that's going to change people strategies. It's just a data point."

92 Agency Relationships In Business

Study Outline

*****Note that in this textbook at pages 287–312 I have inserted a number of newspaper articles, supplementary materials, misc. documents, etc. that relate to this material. These materials are required reading, and, are also fair game for the exam.**

*****Make *sure* that you also do the sample practice problems posted on Blackboard as it will help you master this material, test you to see if you "really" know and understand it, etc. You can expect similar problems to be on the exam. Please note that I will NOT spend a lot of time on the agency material in class – it's some of the easier and more straightforward material we cover and you should be able to master it on your own – especially if you do the agency law practice problems posted on Blackboard along the way.**

I. Agency

A. Definition: A two party relationship in which one party (the agent) is authorized to act on behalf of and under the control of, the other party (the principal)

B. **Why do we have agency law/why is this material important for you to know?**

1. It is virtually impossible to run a modern business without hiring agents. Agency law helps stimulate commercial activity. For example, it does so by increasing the number of transactions that can be completed within a given period of time. And, since the principal often benefits from the agent's work and actions, he/she may have to accept the downside as well for those actions (e.g., liability!)

II. The Creation Of An Agency Relationship

A. How Is An Agency Relationship Created Between Two Parties?

1. **Agreement:**

a) An agency can be created by the agreement of two parties (written (although it is not required to be in writing) oral, and/or implied by their conduct) that one party (the agent) will act for the benefit of the other (the principal)

(1) For example, a person hired to manage a business such as a restaurant would have the *express authority* to manage the restaurant; he/she would also normally have the *implied authority* to make repairs to the restaurant

2. **Ratification:**
   a) Where, *after the fact*, the principal, either by act (conduct) or agreement, ratifies the conduct of an agent who acted outside the scope of his/her authority or the conduct of a person who is in fact not an agent
      (1) For example, where a person who is hired to stock shelves at night at a Rite-Aid store goes out (without permission) and buys an expensive computer system for use at the store. Such an employee probably does not have either the express of implied authority to do this. But when the bill for the computer system is then received by the store and its owner doesn't grumble and pays the bill, we would say that the store owner (the principal) had *ratified* the agent's act after the fact

3. **Estoppel:**
   a) When the principal (not the agent) does something that causes a third person to reasonably believe that a person is his or her agent, and the third person deals with the supposed agent on that basis, the principal is "estopped" from denying the existence of an agency relationship
      (1) For example, when a NAPA Auto Parts store gives a person a shirt and hat that says "NAPA" on it, a car to drive around during deliveries that has a "NAPA" sign on it, then the owner of that store (the principal) has done something (see above) to give third party members of the public (e.g., a creditor or supplier) the impression that the person at issue is, in fact, an employee. In such a situation, the owner of the store (the principal) will be "estopped" from arguing that the other person was not his/her agent
      (2) In reality, this is a form of "apparent authority" -- which is discussed in greater detail below

4. Miscellaneous:
   a) For a very good example illustrating when an agency relationship is/is not created, ***see the article in this textbook at page 287 about Kuwait Air***

III. Duties Owed By The Agent To The Principal

A. Regardless of whether or not an agency relationship is contractual in nature (i.e., created by an express written or oral contract), agency law establishes certain ***fiduciary duties*** that the agent owes the principal, and *vice-versa*

1. **Duty of Loyalty** -- this includes:
   a) Avoiding conflicts of interest with the principal, which includes:
      (1) Not dealing with himself (unless the principal knowingly and voluntarily consents after knowing all of the facts)

(2) Not competing with the principal regarding the agency business so long as he remains an agent

(3) Not acting on behalf of the other party to the transaction unless the principal knowingly consents

(4) Not using or disclosing any confidential and proprietary information acquired during or throughout the agency

(a) Note: after the termination of the agency relationship, in the absence of an agreement to the contrary, an agent may usually compete with principal. However, the duty not to use or disclose confidential and proprietary information learned while you were the principal's agent continues after the termination of the agency agreement/relationship and cannot be breached!! The former agent may, however, utilize ***general knowledge and skills*** acquired during the agency

2. **Duty to Obey the Principal's Instructions (Obedience)**

a) An agent has the duty to obey the principal's reasonable instructions for carrying out the agency business. An agent obviously has no duty to obey orders to behave illegally or unethically

3. **Duty to Perform Duties with Reasonable Diligence and Skill (Performance)**

a) Agents (and paid agents in particular) must possess and exercise the degree of care and skill that is a standard in the locality for the kind of work the agent performs. Agents (particularly paid agents) that represent that they possess a higher than customary level of skill may be held to a higher standard of performance (e.g. a CPA or an attorney).

4. **Duty to Notify the Principal (Notification)**

a) An agent must promptly communicate to the principal matters within his knowledge that are reasonably relevant to the agency business and that he knows or should know are of concern to the principal

5. **Duty to Account to the Principal (Accounting)**

a) An agent must give to the principal any money or property received in the course of the agency business (unless, of course, the principal and agent agree to the contrary)

(1) Note: This includes profits received, gifts, bribes, etc.

b) An agent must also account for his work

(1) An ***accounting*** includes such things as keeping accurate records and accounts of all transactions, disclosing them to the principal when he makes a reasonable demand for them, not commingling principal or agency property with his own property

(2) **Example**: A manager is sent by his company, at company expense, to a national high tech trade show and conference. Various exhibitors have donated door prizes to be awarded to attendees based on free tickets they have received upon registration. The manger wins by lottery drawing a valuable prize worth about $12,000. The certificate he receives is in his name so that the initial title resides in him. When he returns to

his office the corporate CEO informs him that the prize actually is company property and insists that he assign it or its value to his employer.

(a) Some questions that arise (i.e., this would be a good question for an essay question on an exam!): Does the employer have a valid claim? Does the intent of the prize donor matter? Is this similar to cases involving frequent flier miles issued initially to business employees?

IV. Duties Owed By The Principal To The Agent

A. The most important duties are the principal's obligations to compensate the agent, reimburse the agent for money spent in the principal's service, and to indemnify (or reimburse) the agent for losses suffered in conducting the principal's business:

1. **Duty to Compensate the Agent (Compensation)**
   a) Generally, the principal-agent contract/agreement controls the scope of this duty.
      (1) For example, if the contract/agreement provides that the agent is to do sales, only get paid if he/she makes a sale, he/she is responsible for all of their expenses, etc., then the agent is bound by that agreement.
      (2) But where there is no written or oral contract/agreement between the parties, or, where there is one but it does not address the specific issue at hand, then the relationship of the parties, the surrounding circumstances, industry custom, etc. determine whether and in what amount the agent is to be compensated.
         (a) For example where the contract is silent on the issue of compensation, or, it notes that compensation is due but its amount is not expressly stated, the amount due is the market price or the customary price for the agent's services, or, if neither is available, their "reasonable value," whichever is appropriate

2. **Duty to Reimburse the Agent (Reimbursement)**
   a) General rule: the principal has a duty to reimburse the agent for expenditures expressly or impliedly authorized by the principal while the agent was acting on the principal's behalf
   b) Exception: there is a written or oral contract/agreement between the parties to the contrary

3. **Duty to Indemnify the Agent (Indemnification – i.e., "Reimbursement)**
   a) Agency law implies a promise by the principal to indemnify (or reimburse) an agent for losses that result from the agent's *authorized activities*
      (1) However, with certain exceptions, the principal is usually ***not*** required to indemnify an agent for losses resulting from *unauthorized acts* (e.g., slugging a fellow employee)

4. **Duty to Provide Safe Working Conditions for the Agent**
5. **Duty to Cooperate and Assist the Agent in Performing His/her Duties**

V. Liability In Agency Relationships

A. Liability For Contracts -- when is the principal liable for a contract that an agent enterers into? Generally, it depends on whether one of the below are present (actual authority, apparent authority, and/or ratification)

1. **Authority** -- an agent can ***only*** legally bind his principal to a contract when he has the ***authority*** to do so

a) Types of Authority:

(1) ***Actual authority*** -- exists where the principal's consent to act is communicated to the agent by ***words, writing or conduct***

(a) Types of actual authority:

(i) *Express* – see above and the textbook chapter posted on Blackboard for the details

(ii) *Implied* – see above and the textbook chapter posted on Blackboard for the details (note that implied authority cannot contradict express instructions given by the principal – see some of the practice problems posted on Blackboard for an example of this)

(2) ***Apparent authority*** – this is different than actual authority. Apparent authority arises when the principal's behavior causes a ***third party*** to form a ***reasonable belief*** that the agent is authorized to act in a certain way. Apparent authority is communicated to the ***third party*** (versus the agent). Here, the principal is liable for the agent's actions even though the agent was *not* authorized to act/do what he or she did!

See the ***Steiger*** case and the ***Hausam*** case in this textbook at pages 289–292 for two very good examples applying the above two concepts. These cases are fair game for the exam. I would also *strongly* encourage you to do the agency law practice problems posted on Blackboard as they will help you better understand and be able to apply the concepts of actual express authority, actual implied authority and apparent authority

b) **Ratification** -- can also bind the principal for an agent's unauthorized act/unauthorized entering into of a contract

(1) Ratification is the affirmation by the principal of an agent's unauthorized act or promise *after the fact*. For the ratification to be effective, the principal must obviously be aware of all material facts

B. Liability for Torts:

1. Liability for an Agent's Torts – of course an agent is always liable/legally responsible for his or her own torts; but when is a *principal* liable/legally responsible for a tort committed by his/her agent that injures a plaintiff?

a) The Doctrine of *Respondeat Superior*

(1) Under this doctrine, the principal who is an ***employer*** is liable for torts committed by agents who are ***employees*** (versus independent contractors) ***and*** who commit the tort while acting ***within the "scope of their employment."*** This applies to an employee's negligent act, and depending on the facts, the situation and the job, even an intentional tort. This is a rule of ***imputed*** or ***vicarious liability*** (which means that the liability of the agent/employee is imputed to the employer/principal personally and the employer/principal is as liable for that tort as if he has committed it himself!)

(a) "Scope of employment" -- *what does it mean?*

(i) Some courts ask whether the employee was on a ***frolic*** of his own (for which the principal is NOT liable), or simply a ***detour on the job*** (for which the principal IS liable)

(ii) In doing this analysis, there are a number of factors that a court may consider:

(a) Was it the ***kind of conduct*** the employee was employed to perform?;

(i) To meet this test, the employee's conduct need only be of the same general nature as the work expressly authorized, or be incidental to its performance

(b) Did it occur substantially within the employee's authorized ***time period*** of work?;

(c) Did it occur substantially within the ***location*** authorized by the employer?; ***and***

(d) Was it motivated at least in part by the purpose of serving the employer?

To the extent that the answer to the above questions is "yes," then that points to the doctrine of respondeat superior being satisfied (i.e., the principal being legally responsible for the tort of the agent). If, on the other hand, the answers are "no," then that converse would be true.

b) Direct Liability

(1) This differs considerably from *respondeat superior*. Here, the principal himself is at fault, and there is no need to even impute the agent's liability to him. Also, no scope of employment issue exists here

(2) **Rule**: a principal is *directly liable* for an agent's tortious conduct if the principal directs that conduct and intends that it occur. In such cases, the agent's conduct can be intentional, reckless or negligent

(a) The typical direct liability case involves harm caused by the principal's own negligence (e.g., giving the agent improper or unclear instructions; failing to make and enforce appropriate regulations to govern the agent's conduct; negligently hiring an unsuitable agent; failing to discharge an unsuitable agent; furnishing an agent with improper tools, instruments, or materials; carelessly supervising an agent, etc.)

(3) Of course, a principal might be liable under ***both*** a *respondeat superior* and *direct liability* theory of liability!!

c) See the articles at pages 293–302 of this textbook for excellent examples of these concepts (respondeat superior and direct liability). These materials are fair game for the exam. Also be sure to do the agency law practice problems posted on my website dealing with respondeat superior and direct liability!!

VI. Employees vs. Independent Contractors

A. Normally, all employees who deal with third parties are deemed to be agents of the principal, and thus, all of the rules and exceptions discussed above would apply.

However, what about independent contractors? Well, those rules don't apply (but see exceptions below). That is, independent contractors are ***not*** usually deemed to be agents of his/her principal; and that is the very reason that many firm/companies structure the employment relationship this way ….. it helps avoid or minimize messy things like liability!! Independent contractors are also cheaper for a company to use than are employees (e.g., how many independent contractors do you know that have health benefits??)

For an ***excellent example*** of how a firm might structure an employment relationship to take advantage of these rules (and thereby gain/maintain competitive advantage over its competition), see the article at pages 303–306 of this textbook titled "Children Injured On Paper Route Often Go Uninsured"

B. But what is the legal difference between an employee and an independent contractor?

1. No sharp line delineates what is an "employee" vs. what is an "independent contractor"

a) Courts use a number of factors in analyzing this issue. See pages 361–362 in the textbook chapter posted on Blackboard (Chapter 20) for a discussion of these factors. See also the IRS handout in this textbook at page 307 for the factors the IRS looks at for federal income tax purposes. Obviously, many people/firms run afoul of these factors in their attempt to try to make it "look like" a person is an independent contractor when in reality that person is an employee!!

C. Liability for the Torts of Independent Contractors

1. General Rule: a principal is ***not*** liable for the torts of his independent contractors
   a) Rationale: the principal has no right to control the details of the work, so why should he/she be liable?
   b) Of course, the independent contractor remains liable for his/her own torts

2. Exception: a principal can be ***directly liable*** for tortious behavior connected with the retention of an independent contractor (e.g., negligently hiring an incompetent/unsuitable independent contractor)
3. Exception: a principal is liable for an independent contractor's failure to perform a ***non-delegable duty*** (e.g., a common carrier's duty to transport its passengers safely; a city's duty to keep its streets in repair; a railroad's duty to maintain safe crossings; a landlord's duty to make repairs and use care in doing so; etc.)
4. Exception: a principal is liable for an independent contractor's negligent failure to take the special precautions needed in order to conduct certain ***highly dangerous or inherently dangerous activities*** (e.g., excavations in publicly traveled areas; the clearing of land by fire; the construction of a dam; the demolition of a building; etc.)

VII. Miscellaneous:

A. Tort Suits Against Both the Principal and Agent

1. Both the principal and the agent are sometimes legally liable for an agent's torts (as to when, see above discussion on respondeat superior and direct liability). In such cases, the parties are ***jointly and severally liable***.

   a) This means, as a practical matter, that the third party (i.e., the plaintiff) may sue both such defendants in one/the same lawsuit and get a judgment against both of them (i.e., the principal and the agent). The plaintiff can then elect to collect the judgment/damage award against any one of the two defendants. It's the plaintiff's option/choice. This in turn means, as a practical matter, that since the employer/principal is the one with the money, he/she is going to have to pay the judgment for his/her agent's tort; he/she can then can seek to be indemnified (i.e., reimbursed) from the agent, but let's face it … how may agents/employees out there can afford/will be able to in fact reimburse the employer/principal?? Virtually none, of course!

   b) Note that once (and if) the third party (plaintiff) collects from either the principal or agent, no further recovery is permitted (i.e., the third party/plaintiff cannot recover twice)

***Again, folks, I encourage you to do the practice problems on agency law that I have posted on Blackboard. You may feel that you know/understand the above material, and, you may. But you also may not. So, be safe and do these practice problems. Many of them involve the application of the above concepts and that is a great way to learn (the only way, really) to see if you really do know and understand this material. – Prof. Carr

93 Kuwait Air[1]

[Agency Law — Kuwait Air]

PRINCIPALS ARE LIABLE for the acts of their agents because they exercise control over the agents. If principals direct their agents to commit an act, it seems fair to hold the principal liable when that act causes harm. In the following example, did Northwest Airlines exercise control over Kuwait Air?

The horse-drawn caisson wound slowly through Arlington National Cemetery and stopped in front of lot number 59, the section reserved for victims of terrorist acts. The flag-draped casket of William L. Stanford, one of the two Agency for International Development auditors killed by plane hijackers in Iran, was carried to the gravesite amid full military honors. Three volleys of rifle fire pierced the unusually warm December air as scores of family, friends and colleagues lowered their heads and wept. Stanford, 52, was killed as he was traveling to join his wife and 13-year-old daughter in Karachi, Pakistan, where he intended to spend the holidays.

The hijacked plane—with William Stanford aboard—was on a Kuwait Airways (KA) flight from Kuwait to Pakistan. Stanford had originally purchased a ticket on Northwest Airlines but had traded in his Northwest ticket for a seat on the KA flight. Stanford's widow sued Northwest on the theory that KA was Northwest's agent. The airlines had an agreement permitting passengers to exchange tickets from one to the other. In this case, however, the court found that no agency relationship existed because Northwest had no *control* over KA. Northwest did not tell KA how to fly its planes or how to handle terrorists; therefore it should not be liable when KA made fatal errors. An agent and principal must not only *consent* to an agency relationship, the principal must also have *control* over the agent.

1 Note From Professor Carr: This article nicely illustrates <u>when</u> an agency relationship between two parties is/is <u>not</u> created.

94 Stieger v. Chevy Chase Savings Bank[1]

666 A.2d 479 (D.C. App. 1995)

[Agency Law — Actual and Apparent Authority]

PAUL STIEGER GAVE his Chevy Chase Bank credit card to a Ms. Garrett during a business trip. He told her to use the card only for a car rental and for hotel lodging. After Stieger returned from the trip, he found that Garrett had made 15 unauthorized uses of his card. For 13 of these purchases, Garrett signed Stieger's name to the charge slip; for the other two, she signed her own name.

Stieger eventually obtained a $3,200 judgment against Garrett but was able to collect only $750 on that judgment. After Chevy Chase refused to cancel Garrett's unauthorized charges, Stieger sued for a declaration that he should not be liable for those charges. The trial court ruled in Chevy Chase's favor on all 15 charges, and an appellate court ruled in the bank's favor on the 13 charges Garrett signed in Stieger's name. Stieger appealed this ruling.

Pryor, Senior Judge The Truth-in-Lending Act was enacted to protect credit cardholders from unauthorized use by those able to obtain possession of a card from its original owner. The act limits liability for the cardholder to a maximum of $50 for charges made by third parties that are "unauthorized ." However, the act does not limit liability for third-party charges that are made with "actual implied or apparent authority." Since actual and implied authority are not alleged in this case, the issue is whether Garrett had apparent authority to use the card.

Apparent authority arises when a principal places an agent in a position which causes a third person to reasonably believe that the principal had consented to the exercise of authority the agent purports to hold. Where a credit cardholder voluntarily permits the use of his credit card by another person, the cardholder has authorized the use of that card and is thereby responsible for any charges as a result of that use, even if he requested that the other person not charge over a certain amount or make charges only for specified purposes. Nearly every jurisdiction that has addressed a factual situation where a cardholder voluntarily and knowingly allows another to use his card and that person subsequently misuses the card, has determined that the agent had apparent authority and therefore was not an unauthorized user.

Stieger argues that he had the right to expect Garrett to use the card only for the charges he authorized, and that he cannot be liable for [Garrett's]

1 **Notes from Professor Carr: This case nicely highlights the concepts of:**

1. Actual authority; and

2. Apparent authority

Here, the principal = Paul Stieger

Here, the agent = Ms. Garrett

Note that Stieger, via agency law, was held liable for 13 of the 15 charges that Garrett rang up (and it is because of the apparent authority doctrine!).

acting beyond the scope of her authority. Stieger also asserts that Garrett could not reasonably present herself as Paul Stieger, and that a merchant should be required to give greater scrutiny to the person using the card. [However,] Stieger placed Garrett, by voluntarily giving her the card, in such a position as to mislead third persons into believing that [she was] clothed with authority which in fact she [did] not possess. To a merchant, voluntary relinquishment combined with the matching of a signature is generally a reasonable indication of apparent authority to use the credit card. However, the same cannot be said of the two charges where Garrett signed her own name. It is an unreasonable extension of apparent authority for a merchant to accept charges, where the signatures do not match, without any additional factors to mislead the merchant into believing that the person presenting the card is the agent of the cardholder.

Lower court decision in Chevy Chase's favor on 13 of the 15 charges affirmed.

95 Hausam v. Schnabl[1]

887 P.2d 1076 (Idaho Ct. App. 1994)

[Agency Law—Actual and Apparent Authority]

JOHN SCHNABL[2] RAN RW Logging as a sole proprietorship. When John experienced health problems early in 1989, he placed his son Wade[3] in charge of the business. John told Wade that he had authority to hire and fire employees, to seek logging contracts, to assign jobs, and to pay himself whatever he wanted. However, John did not explicitly give Wade the authority to borrow money on the business's behalf.

Nonetheless, Wade borrowed $20,000 for RW in January 1990. He signed a promissory note obligating the business to pay the lender, Neal Hausam, $28,000 on or before July 31, 1990. After Hausam forwarded the money to RW early in 1990, Wade stopped managing the business and it ceased operations early in 1991. Never having been repaid, Hausam sued John and Wade on the loan obligation. After Hausam obtained default judgment against Wade, the court dismissed his claim against John. Among other things, the court held that Wade was not authorized to borrow money on RW's behalf. Hausam appealed.

Walters, Chief Judge Both express and implied authority are forms of actual authority. Express authority refers to that authority which the principal has explicitly granted the agent. Implied authority is necessary, usual, and proper to accomplish or perform express authority. Apparent authority is created when the principal voluntarily places an agent in such a position that a person of ordinary prudence, conversant with the business usages and the nature of a particular business, is justified in believing that the agent is acting pursuant to existing authority.

In the instant case, there clearly was express authority for Wade to operate his father's business. However, there was not express authority for Wade to borrow money. Therefore, Wade's authority to borrow money, if it existed, must have arisen from either implied or apparent authority.

Hausam asserts that included in the express authority to run a business is the implied authority to acquire the money necessary to operate that business. However, the trial court found that although John had placed Wade in charge of the day-to-day operations of the business, there was no evidence that the authority to borrow money was necessary to those functions. John's uncontradicted testimony was that the business did not need to borrow money at the time Wade obtained the loan from Hausam. John testified that even if the company had been in need of money, he would not have borrowed it from

1 **Note from Professor Carr: This case also nicely highlights the concepts of actual authority and apparent authority.**

2 **Note from Professor Carr: Here, the principal = the father (John)**

3 **Note from Professor Carr: Here, the agent = the son (Wade)**

a "stranger." There was no implied authority for Wade to borrow money on behalf of the business. The apparent authority of the agent is determined by the acts of the principal, not by the acts of the agent. The declarations of an agent, standing alone, are insufficient to prove the grant of power exercised by the agent and to bind the principal to third parties. To establish apparent authority, the principal must do something to lead the third party to believe that the agent has authority. In the instant case, John placed Wade in charge of the day-to-day operations of RW Logging. It cannot be said that such an action could lead Hausam to believe that Wade had authority to borrow money on behalf of RW. An agent with actual authority for one purpose does not thereby become an apparent agent for all other types of transactions.

Trial court judgment in John's favor affirmed on the question of John's contract liability on the loan.[4]

4 **Note from Professor Carr: The father (John) was held NOT liable for the debt Wade incurred because neither the actual or apparent authority doctrines applied/were satisfied!!**

96 Edgewater Motels, Inc. v. Gatzke[1]

277 N.W.2d 11 (Minn. Sup. Ct. 1979)

[Agency Law — The Doctrine of Respondeat Superior]

A J. Gatzke, a district manager for the Walgreen Company, spent several weeks in Duluth, Minnesota, supervising the opening of a new Walgreen restaurant there. He remained at the restaurant approximately 17 hours a day, and he was on call 24 hours a day to handle problems arising in other Walgreen restaurants in the district. While in Duluth, he lived at the Edgewater Motel at Walgreen's expense. After some heavy drinking late one night, Gatzke returned to his motel room and spent some time at a desk filling out an expense account required by his employer. Gatzke was a heavy smoker, and he testified that he probably smoked a cigarette while completing the expense account. Shortly after Gatzke went to bed, a fire broke out in his motel room. Gatzke escaped, but fire damage to the motel totaled over $330,000. An expert witness testified that the fire was caused by a burning cigarette or a match and that it started in or near a wastebasket located beside the desk at which Gatzke worked.

Edgewater sued Walgreen for Gatzke's negligence. The jury found for Edgewater, in the process concluding that Gatzke acted within the scope of his employment when he filled out the form and disposed of the cigarette. The trial court, however, granted Walgreen's motion for judgment notwithstanding the verdict. Edgewater appealed. The question for the appellate court was whether Gatzke's negligent conduct occurred within the scope of his employment.

Scott, Justice Gatzke's negligent smoking of a cigarette was a direct cause of the damages sustained by Edgewater. The question is whether the facts reasonably support the imposition of vicarious liability on Walgreen's for the conceded negligent act of its employee.

"For an employer to be held vicariously liable for an employee's negligent conduct, the employee's wrongful act must be committed within the scope of his employment. To support [such] a finding, it must be shown that his conduct was, to some degree, in furtherance of the interests of his employer. This principle is recognized by *Restatement (Second) of Agency* section 235, which states: "An act of a servant is not within the scope of employment if it is done with no intention to perform it as a part of or incident to a service on account of which he is employed." Other factors to be considered in the scope-of-employment determination are whether the conduct is of the kind that the employee is authorized to perform and whether the act occurs substantially within authorized time and space restrictions.

The question is whether an employee's smoking of a cigarette can constitute conduct within

1 **Note from Professor Carr: This case nicely highlights the respondeat superior doctrine.**

It was applied to hold the principal (here Walgreens) liable for the tort of its agent (here, Gatzke).

his scope of employment. The courts which have considered the question have not agreed on its resolution. A number of courts have ruled that the act of smoking, even when done simultaneously with work-related activity, is not within the employee's scope of employment because it is a matter personal to the employee which is not done in furtherance of the employer's interest. Other courts have reasoned that the smoking of a cigarette, if done while engaged in the business of the employer, is within an employee's scope of employment because it is a minor deviation from the employee's work-related activities, and thus merely incidental to employment. We agree with this analysis and hold that an employer can be vicariously liable for an employee's negligent smoking of a cigarette if he was otherwise acting in the scope of his employment at the time of the negligent act.

Thus, we must next determine whether Gatzke was otherwise in the scope of his employment at the time of his negligent act. Even assuming Gatzke was outside the scope of his employment while he was at the bar, Gatzke resumed his employment activities after he returned to his motel room and filled out his expense account. The expense account was completed so that Gatzke could be reimbursed by Walgreen's for his work-related expenses. In this sense, Gatzke is performing an act for his own personal benefit. However, the completion of the expense account also furthers the employer's business in that it provides detailed documentation of business expenses so that they are properly deductible for tax purposes. In this light, the filling out of the expense form can be viewed as serving a dual purpose: that of furthering Gatzke's personal interests and promoting his employer's business purposes. Accordingly, the completion of the expense account is an act done in furtherance of the employer's business purposes.

Additionally, the record indicates that Gatzke was an executive type of employee who had no set working hours. He considered himself a 24-hour-a-day man; his room at the Edgewater Motel was his "office away from home." It [is] therefore reasonable to determine that the filling out of his expense account was done within authorized time and space limits of his employment.

Judgment reversed in favor of Edgewater.

97 Firm[1] Sued for Fatal Crash when Lawyer[2] was Phoning[3]

The National Law Journal

[Agency Law — The Doctrine of Respondeat Superior]

WASHINGTON—A LAWYER ALLEGEDLY making business calls from her cell phone while driving, swerves off the road and strikes and kills a teenager. Should her firm be held liable?

That's a $30 million question in the case of Jane Wagner, a former Cooley Godward associate in Reston, Va.

Last month, the father of 15-year-old Naeun Yoon, who was killed last year by Ms. Wagner while walking along Route 7 in Great Falls, Va., filed a wrongful death suit against Ms. Wagner, her husband and Cooley Godward. The crux of Youngki Yoon's claim against the firm: Ms. Wagner made business calls around the time of the accident and Cooley billed for them.

Richard Hibey, head of Winston & Shawn's Washington, D.C., litigation practice group, believes that Cooley could find itself open to liability in *Yoon v. Wagner*, filed in Virginia's Loudoun County Circuit Court.

'I don't think it's a stretch'

"Basically, if she's making calls from her car phone or anywhere else in the course of practicing law for the firm ... and that conduct is the proximate cause of the injuries and caused in this case the death of that pedestrian, then I don't think it's a stretch to hold the law firm liable for that conduct," he said. "If they chose to bill that, then she's acting within the scope of her employment."

But some defense attorneys doubt that the case will get before a jury.

"I'm skeptical that they could establish causation," said Frank Winston Jr., a partner in the McLean, Va., office of D.C.'s Shaw Pittman. "I doubt if the firm directed her to make cell phone calls from her car while driving 50 miles per hour."

Ms. Wagner, an associate in Cooley's Reston office, was driving home when she hit something she claimed she thought was a deer. It was Ms. Yoon, who died that night.

According to the civil complaint, Ms. Wagner logged cell phone calls just before, after and around the time of the accident and continued to handle work assignments after she arrived home.

Represented by criminal defense attorney Rodney Leffler of Fairfax, Va.'s Leffler & Hyland, she pleaded guilty to failing to stop after an accident

---

1 **Principal/Employer**

2 **Agent/Employee**

3 **This article is another good example of the respondent superior doctrine being applied. If you own a company and have employees using cell phones while they are on the job (e.g., while driving), you had better train them to be darn careful or you may be responsible for their tort!**

and was sentenced to five years in jail, with all but a year suspended. Ms. Wagner lost her job and her law license.

The suit asks for $25 million in compensatory damages and $5 million in punitives.

Cooley Godward has not decided whether to retain outside counsel, said chief operating officer Mark Pitchford.

Though the girl's death was tragic, he said "we don't believe the facts or the law will support a judgment" against the firm.

Associate law Professor Susan Carle of American University's Washington College of Law sees the case as the simple application of older legal principles to new workplaces that are being "restructured by new technology."

"I think it's a pretty good theory;" she said. "It is an interesting extension of the employer liability theories … but it's not wild, it's not crazy."

Plaintiffs' attorney Diane Cooley of D.C.'s Coale, Cooley, Lietz, McInerny & Broadus said that phone records could reveal if Ms. Wagner was working on firm business. "I think causation is going to be relatively easy to prove," she said.

The plaintiff's bigger problem is foreseeability, Ms. Cooley said: "Did they know this was going on? Did they foster it?"

Ms. Wagner's leaving the scene also raises the question of what caused the student's death, the accident or the delay, attorneys said.

If Cooley Godward loses, the effect on employers could be significant.

With cell phone use commonplace, "people could be working for the employer when the employer's not really aware of it," said George Mason University School of Law Professor Lloyd Cohen, who specializes in law and economics.

98 Landlord May Be Sued for Manager's Sex Harrassment[1]

[Agency Law—The Doctrine of Respondeat Superior]

LINDA RENTS AN apartment in a building where James is the resident manager. Chris is the landlord. Linda noticed James staring at her while she was lying by the apartment swimming pool in her swimsuit, after which, she alleged, James "began making off-color, flirtatious and unwelcome remarks."

Shortly thereafter James went to Linda's apartment to repair a water leak in her shower. While in the apartment, James allegedly put his arm around Linda, told her she was an attractive woman, and made a remark about her breasts, referring to them as "headlights."

Linda pushed James away. He then allegedly "grabbed her breast, and after being pushed away again, grabbed her buttock as she walked away from him."

After consulting her attorney, Linda sued resident manager James and landlord Chris for sex discrimination in "operation of their apartment complex."

She alleged violations of state and federal housing discrimination laws.

Linda's lawsuit alleged landlord Chris should be liable for the unwanted advances of resident manager James under the legal theory of "respondeat superior" whereby an employer is "responsible for the employee's acts. James and Chris asked the court to dismiss the lawsuit.

Should Linda be allowed to proceed to prove her allegations that sexual harassment is a form of housing discrimination for which a landlord may be held liable for the actions of a resident manager?

The judge said yes.

Under the theory of respondeat superior, the judge emphasized, a landlord[2] may be held liable for the acts of an employee[3], such as the resident manager. Therefore, Linda's lawsuit may proceed to trial for proof of her allegations, the judge ruled. Based on the 1995 U.S. District Court decision in Beliveau vs. Caras, 873 Fed.Supp. 1393.

---

1 **Note from Professor Carr: Another good and interesting example of the doctrine of respondeat superior being applied to hold the principal (landlord) liable for the tort of its agent/employee (property manager)**

2 **Employer/Principal**

3 **Employee/Agent**

99 Estate Wins $46 Million for Killing[1]

[Agency Law—The Doctrines of Respondeat Superiora nd Direct Liability]

AT A GLANCE

CASE TYPE: Negligent hiring, wrongful death
CASE: Gurkin v. The Nurse Connection Inc., No. OCN-L-4017-95
COURT: OCEAN Co., N.J., Super. Ct.

IN APRIL 1993, SCOTT Baker was hired by The Nurse Connection Inc., a home health care company, as a nurse's aide. In July of that year, he was assigned to help Beatrice Baskin, 74, care for her husband, David, an Alzheimer's patient. While on duty, Baker "saw cash laying around and decided to come pack and rob them," said plaintiffs' lawyer Lane M. Ferdinand. After working briefly for another Nurse Connection client, Baker got himself reassigned to the Baskins.

This time, however, he showed up in a ski mask and surgical gloves and was accompanied by two accomplices. The trio stole about $60,000 from the Baskins and, after Beatrice Baskin tore the mask off Baker's face, he stabbed her 75 times. She bled to death and, in 1997 Baker was convicted of murder.

Her family sued The Nurse Connection for negligent hiring, charging that it failed to do a proper background check on Baker. After he disclosed a prior conviction for burglary, the firm made no attempt to find out any details about the case, which included a recommendation by the judge that Baker get help learning to deal with his anger.

The defendant ignored another red flag. A previous nursing home had fired him and, said Ferdinand, "They never bothered to find out why."

The defense countered that there was no violent behavior in Baker's past. "His conviction was for throwing a brick through a supermarket window," said defense attorney Richard Grossman. The plaintiffs focused on proving severe pain and suffering, noting that 27 of the stab wounds were inflicted while Baskin was conscious, as shown by autopsy photographs of defensive wounds on her arms and hands.

On Feb. 19, a New Jersey jury found Baker 60% and The Nurse Connection 40% liable, awarding $46 million to the estate of Baskin for her pain and suffering and $600,000 to the estate of her husband, who died 23 months later. The defense will move for JNOV and a new trial.

---

1 This article is a GREAT example of the direct liability doctrine in action. Here, the employer engaged in a negligent background check/ negligent hiring.

2 Question from Professor Carr:

Q: Would "respondeat superior" work here to hold the Nursing Connection, Inc., (the employer/ principal) liable for its agent's torts?

A: Probably not. This was an intentional tort (assault, battery, false imprisonment, etc.) committed by the agent/employee. Thus, it would be/fall "outside the course and scope of the employment relationship."

BUT ... DIRECT LIABILITY (i.e., negligent hiring), as noted in the article, would work to hold the employer/principal liable for this agent/employee torts!!

100 Pizza Delivery Assault: Boss Liable for Rape by Driver[1]

Jury Awards $175,000 for Prior Offender's Act

The National Law Journal

[Agency Law—The Doctrines of Respondeat Superior and Direct Liability]

THE OWNER OF a pizza restaurant in Omaha, Neb., was found liable by a jury for failing to do even a rudimentary background check on a newly hired delivery driver who raped a customer.

During the trial it was revealed that the driver, David Taitte, had a criminal history of sexual assault, including stalking a woman he'd met while working as a delivery driver for another pizza shop. Taitte was prosecuted for raping the plaintiff and sentenced to 25 years in prison, according to plaintiff attorney Steve Lefler of Omaha's Lefler & Mullen.

Lefler successfully argued that management of TK Pizza, a local franchise of Domino Pizza Inc., had not even completed a check of Taitte's driving record, as Domino Pizza franchises are required to do, before unknowingly sending the convicted sex offender to deliver pizzas to people's homes

Taitte claimed to have a clean driving record, but he had numerous violations that would have precluded his hire for insurance reasons, Lefler said. "If they had just checked his driving record they would have known he is a liar and an unsafe driver and they would not have hired him," he asserted. Lefler claimed that for $10 TK Pizza could have received a copy of Taitte's criminal record from the local police. That would have revealed a conviction for attempted first-degree sexual assault on a child and his arrest in March 1999 for stalking a woman he met while delivering for another pizza shop.

"There is a difference between hiring somebody to make pizzas and hiring somebody to deliver pizza," he said. "Who among us hasn't given a teenage babysitter or Grandma $20 and told them to order a pizza?"

Defense attorney Albert Engles of the Omaha firm of Engles, Ketcham, Olson & Keith, argued that Taitte alone, not TK Pizza, was responsible for the 1999 sexual assault. "The claim is my client was negligent in hiring this guy, which we deny, but even if my client was negligent the action supersedes any level of negligence," he said.

1 **Note from Professor Carr:**

Q: Would respondeat superior apply here to hold the employer/principal liable for this agent/employee's tort?

A: Probably not...because this tort (assault and battery, false imprisonment, etc.) was "outside the course and scope of the employment relationship."

Q: What about "DIRECT LIABILITY?"

A: Yes!! The jury here said the employer defendant was directly liable for failing to do a basic background check when it hired the agent!!

$1 million sought

The plaintiff asked for $1 million. The defense at one point offered $25,000, Lefler said. The jury awarded the plaintiff $175,000. He cited several factors that he believed complicated the task the jury faced in determining damages, beginning with the fundamental question of assigning liability.

"I was afraid that maybe the jury would not find liability, that David Taitte raped this woman, not TK Pizza, so why punish TK Pizza," he said. "We faced a very sympathetic defendant, a young man who literally built and operated two pizza shops... and he has already lost everything."

Lefler noted the plaintiff was unemployed at the time of the assault, so lost income was not a factor, and her medical bills totaled less than $5,000. Most complicated of all, he said, was determining her emotional and psychological suffering. The woman had already suffered six years of sexual abuse throughout her childhood and was raped previously as an adult. The defense used that history to argue that the emotional pain and suffering she suffered when assaulted by Taitte could not be completely distinguished from the emotional damage of the previous abuse, Lefler said.

"Yes, she has had a terrible life but she had managed to cope until this terrible incident that occurred in her home that she had made with her children," he said. "Basically, I asked the jury to determine what they thought was fair compensation for the sickening experience of being raped by that man."

Engles said TK Pizza has filed post-trial motions.

Domino Pizza Inc. was named in a separate suit but settled for an undisclosed sum. *Jane Doe v. TK Pizza,* No. 988 (Douglas Co., Neb., 1st. Ct).

101 Children Injured on Paper Routes Often Go Uninsured[1]

'Little Merchants' on Bikes Pay Own Medical Bills, Don't Get Death Benefits

The Wall Street Journal

[Agency Law — Independent Contractor-Employee Distinction]

Nelson Chong Gum was zipping across the street on a motorized scooter one Sunday in January, delivering the Honolulu Star-Bulletin, when a van hit him. The 14-year-old paperboy spent 12 days in the hospital. The injury left him with a disfigured leg and medical bills so far totalling more than $80,000. The Star-Bulletin, owned by privately held Black Press Ltd. of Canada, isn't legally obligated to pay those bills.

The paperboy long ago became an American icon, and generations of kids have gained important experience—not to mention income—delivering newspapers. "Why be a newspaper carrier?" asks an industry recruiting advertisement. "The lessons learned can carry over into a bright future." The ad goes on to name more than 100 famous former carriers, including billionaire Warren Buffett, astronaut John Glenn, and Olympic speed-skating gold medalist Chris Witty.

But largely unknown is what happens when a child gets hurt or killed delivering newspapers. In most cases, the newspaper is not responsible for paying medical bills or providing workers' compensation benefits. The industry has argued for decades that the children aren't employees, but are "little merchants," independent contractors who buy papers wholesale and sell them at retail prices. This independent status saves newspapers money on workers' compensation insurance and essentially absolves them of any responsibility for the welfare of their child deliverers—a position that dismays some legal and workplace experts.

A Special Exemption

That kids can work in the newspaper business at all is an unusual exception to federal law. The industry won an exemption to child-labor laws in 1949, and

1 **Note from Professor Carr: This article does an excellent job of highlighting some of the differences between an independent contractor and an employee, why businesses/employers try to structure relationships as ind. contractor relationships (e.g., to save money, limit potential liability for any tort committed by an ind. contractor, etc.), and, how and why courts sometimes may "call" them on this business strategy and reclassify such people as employees even though the business/employer is trying to call/label such people as "employees."**

On a related question, in your view, is this type of business strategy "ethical"? How would you handle this/what would you do if you owned such a newspaper/business??

delivering newspapers is one of only six kinds of employment legally available to children 13 years old and younger. They can also act, babysit, do certain kinds of farming, work for some family businesses or make Christmas wreaths at home. The list of jobs children 14 and older are permitted to hold grows less restrictive as they reach age 18.

In 1990, kids made up 68% of the home delivery force. With newspapers getting heavier, and morning delivery deadlines earlier, that number dropped to 35% in 2000, according to the Newspaper Association of America. Still, that means that roughly 140,000 youngsters are tossing newspapers on to front lawns and doorsteps, according to the latest industry figures.

The job has its hazards. Sixteen youths under age 18 were killed delivering newspapers or collecting fees from subscribers between 1992 and 2000, the most recent year for which figures are available, according to the U.S. Department of Labor's Bureau of Labor Statistics. No national data are compiled for how many kids are injured on their newspaper routes.

Last month a 12-year-old papergirl was sexually assaulted in Ogden, Utah, while delivering the privately held Standard-Examiner. In 1994, Andrea McNeil, also 12, got struck and killed while delivering the family-owned Daily Times Chronicle by bike in Reading, Mass. A year earlier Jeralee Underwood, 11, was abducted and murdered while collecting money from subscribers for the family-owned Idaho State Journal in Pocatello. That same year 14-year-old Mark Caljouw was hit and killed by a van while riding his bike to pick up a bundle of Patriot Ledger newspapers to deliver in Hanover, Mass.

Of the six job-related deaths of youths in Massachusetts between 1991 and 1999, half were newspaper carriers, according to Letitia Davis, director of the state's Occupational Health Surveillance Program. It was only while studying those deaths that Ms. Davis, an epidemiologist, learned that the young paper carriers were not covered by workers' compensation, child-labor laws or standards set, by the U.S. Occupational Safety & Health Administration. They were not even required to wear bike helmets, she says.

"It was surprising to us that the youngest and most vulnerable of our workers were the least protected," she says.

Marc Linder, a University of Iowa law professor who has studied the issue, says he can't "understand how anyone with legal training can accept that a 13-year-old boy is running a delivery service like UPS."

In other industries, state and federal regulators have been cracking down on employers of under-age workers. In March the Illinois Department of Labor refused to let kids under age 14 work as paid umpires at little league ball games. (Responding to irate parents, the state last month passed a law allowing 12- and 13-year-olds to work as umpires under certain conditions.) Last year, the U.S. Department of Labor fined Red Robin International of Englewood, Colo., for employing 14- and 15-year-olds at prohibited times or for too many hours at 26 of its burger restaurants. Two years ago, federal regulators fined the Waltham Public Library in Massachusetts for paying 14- and 15-year-olds to shelve books on school nights for more than three hours and past 7 p.m., two violations of child-labor laws.

Federal law doesn't limit the hours child newspaper deliverers can work and even allows them to work in the middle of the night. Some states have stricter guidelines.

Few States Require Coverage

Meanwhile only a handful of states, including New York, Wisconsin, Nevada, Kentucky and Maryland, require workers' compensation coverage for youth carriers. (Most adult carriers also work as independent contractors and are not covered by the insurance, although the latter four states require it.) Workers' compensation laws require employers' or their insurers, to pay medical bills and some lost wages to injured workers, as well as death benefits for employees who are killed on the job.

In other states, legislators have tried without success to force newspapers to provide workers' compensation to carriers. Publishers this year convinced Rhode Island lawmakers to drop a provision from a bill that would have required coverage for paper carriers at daily newspapers. It was the second time in recent years that newspapers successfully fought such a law in Rhode Island.

John Howell, owner of the biweekly Warwick Beacon, says that if he were required to carry such insurance, his 120 carriers—85% of whom are under age 18—would be out of a job, because he would be forced to mail the paper. Mr. Howell says he knows of no Beacon deliverer who has ever been hurt on the job.

State legislators in Nebraska tried in 1994, 1996 and 1997 to pass laws that would have required newspapers to provide workers' compensation benefits for paper carriers. But the Nebraska Press Association argued that such a law would dry up job opportunities for young people, and the bills never passed.

At least one paper voluntarily takes financial responsibility for injured child carriers. Under no statutory pressure to do so, the family-owned Columbus (Ohio) Dispatch for two decades has made its 1,100 youth carriers, about half of its total delivery force, employees instead of independent contractors, thus covering them with workers' compensation insurance. When 11-year-old Sean Allen was struck by a car and killed delivering the paper in 1997, the Dispatch paid his medical bills, as well as $6,200 in death benefits. Life insurance the paper buys for its carriers paid an additional $5,000. The boy's mother, Linda Allen, was so moved by the paper's support that she kept her son's route and now delivers it herself. "I keep doing it in Sean's memory," she says.

Over time, parents have challenged the newspaper industry's "little merchants" position in court, with mixed results. Twelve-year-old Jenny Larson was struck by a car while delivering the Fremont (Nebraska) Tribune in 1991. Reduced to a persistent vegetative state, she must be watched round the clock, fed through a tube in her stomach and have her diapers changed.

When her medical bills neared $1 million, her parents filed a workers' compensation claim.

The paper and its insurer said the girl, now 23, was not eligible for such coverage. Hometown Communications Inc., which then owned the Fremont Tribune, no longer exists. Rupert Phillips, a part owner of the company at the time, says he had a limited role in the case, but noted that "the vast majority of newspapers considered carriers independent contractors."

It took four years and four courts to resolve the issue. A Nebraska workers' compensation judge ruled that Jenny was the paper's employee and was eligible for workers' compensation benefits. "It is beyond sophistry and closer to outright dishonesty to characterize a 10-year-old party to a contract as a 'little merchant' and thus an independent contractor," the judge wrote. The newspaper appealed, and the Nebraska Supreme Court ultimately affirmed the lower court decision in 1995.

Difficulties in Court

But many courts have ruled against families. Ron Da Silva was delivering the News-Times in Danbury, Conn., in 1983 when someone in a passing car threw a snowball, hitting his right eye. Mr. Da Silva, 14 years old at the time, underwent seven operations and was left legally blind in that eye. Initially his medical bills were covered by accident insurance he had purchased from the News-Times for 50 cents a week. But that insurance was capped, leaving him with $35,000 in unpaid medical bills. His parents had no insurance at the time of his accident, so Mr. Da Silva filed a workers' compensation claim. The News-Times challenged the claim. Rob Sypek, its circulation director, said in an interview that the paper's carriers are all independent contractors who each run "their own little business." He says the paper didn't want to pay in Mr. Da Silva's case and thus set a precedent that its carriers were employees. "It wasn't just for the News-Times, it was to stand up for every newspaper," says Mr. Sypek.

Scott McCarthy, Mr. Da Silva's attorney, argued that the paper had a duty to cover its young workers. "The characterization of newsboys as independent contractors is an outdated legal fiction used by publishers to avoid responsibilities to minors and runs contrary to the public policy of this state," Mr. McCarthy said in a court brief.

But the News-Times prevailed at the Connecticut workers' compensation review board and the Appellate court of Connecticut. That court ruled in 1995 that as a paper-boy Mr. Da Silva was an independent contractor because, among other things, he kept all money and tips above the wholesale cost of the paper, was billed each week by the paper even if subscribers failed to pay him, and was free to deliver other papers as well.

At that point, about 13 years after the accident, medical-bill collectors tried to garnish Mr. Da Silva's wages as a textile-plant worker. In 1997, at the age of 28, he filed for personal bankruptcy protection.

The News-Times is owned by Dow Jones & Co., publisher of the Wall Street Journal, through its Ottaway Newspapers Inc. unit. A Dow Jones spokesman declined to comment further on the Da Silva case.

About 15% of the carriers for Dow Jones community newspapers are kids under 18 years old, and the company provides workers' compensation coverage for about half of them because the papers they work for operate in states that require the coverage, the company says. The other children are offered accident insurance, but is it not as comprehensive as workers' compensation coverage.

Dow Jones says it does not know if any youth carriers deliver the Journal. About 31% of the newspaper's home-delivery circulation is handled by adult employees, who are covered by workers' compensation. The Journal contracts the rest of its deliveries to independent distribution firms and other publishers, and also mails some papers.

In Hawaii, the family of Nelson Chong Gum, the 14-year-old hurt delivering the Honolulu Star-Bulletin, hasn't tried holding the newspaper responsible for his injury. Nelson's father, Ibang Chong Gum, says he didn't think he could get help from the paper. Don Kendall, the publisher and president of the Star-Bulletin, says that Nelson was employed by an independent distributor at the time of the accident. Phil Paragoso, the distributor, says that the boy's contract stipulated that his company was not liable for injuries suffered delivering papers.

The personal-injury insurance of the driver who hit Nelson covered $20,000 of his medical costs, but that left more than $67,000 in unpaid bills. Neither the boy's father, a security guard, nor his mother, a restaurant kitchen worker, has insurance. They have hired a lawyer to sue the driver of the van and the cleaning company she was working for at the time. The suit has not yet been filed, and the family's attorney says he has not ruled out filing a workers' compensation claim.

Meanwhile, Mr. Chong Gum, whose six other children also deliver the Honolulu Star-Bulletin, has applied for and received state assistance for uninsured kids. "To me, my children work for the newspaper company, even if they say they are independent," Mr. Chong gum Say, "Without the kids, their customers are not going to get the newspaper."

102 Appendix A: Common Law Factors Used to Determine Employee Status

Internal Revenue Service

[*Agency law—the distinction between an employee and independent contractor*]

INDEPENDENT CONTRACTORS[1]

For federal income tax purposes, a worker is considered to be an employee if the worker:

1. Must comply with employer's instructions regarding the work.
2. Receives training from or at the direction of the employer.
3. Provides services that are integrated into the business.
4. Provides services that must be rendered personally.
5. Hires, supervises, and pays assistants for the employer.
6. Has a continuing working relationship with the employer.
7. Must follow set hours of work.
8. Works full-time for a employer.
9. Must work on the employer's premises.
10. Must work in a sequence set by the employer.
11. Must submit regular reports to the employer.
12. Receives payments of regular amounts at set intervals.
13. Receives payments for business and/or travel expenses.
14. Relies on the employer to furnish tools and materials.
15. Lacks a major investment in facilities used to perform the service.
16. Cannot make a profit or suffer a loss from the service.
17. Works for one employer at a time.
18. Does not offer services to the general public.
19. Can be fired by the employer.
20. May quit work at any time without incurring liability.

Source: Rev. Rul. 87-41, 1987-1 C.B. 296.

103 The Stella Steinbeck vs. McDonald's, and the Michael vs. RRL Incident

[Time permitting we will go over the below hypothetical in class – Professor Carr]

Part One of the Story …

JIMMY SMITH IS 21 years old. He graduated from Paso Robles high school, and works for RRL. RRL is a firm that designs and manufactures plastic moldings for a variety of purposes. Its headquarters and plant are located in Paso Robles and it employs approximately 60 people. Jimmy has worked for RRL for the last two years. He works 25 hours a week, and his job is essentially the firm "handyman/errand-boy" -- whatever needs to be picked up, delivered, etc., Jimmy is the man for that job.

Jimmy's boss approached him and advised him that one of the plant's molding machines had broken down. The necessary parts to repair the machine could only be obtained at a shop in Santa Maria. Jimmy's boss instructed Jimmy to take the company truck (which had RRL's logo on both sides of it), drive *directly* to Santa Maria to pick up the parts and then return *directly* to Paso Robles. Jimmy, being a good soldier, hopped in the truck and headed south down Highway 101 toward Santa Maria.

As Jimmy drove to Santa Maria, he realized that he was out of his favorite chewing tobacco – Skoal – and he *really* needed a "pinch." He also felt the urge to go to the bathroom (a Number One). He decided to exit at the city of Nipomo, pop into a convenience store located just off the freeway, take care of business, and then hop back onto the freeway and continue his trip down to Santa Maria.

He went into the convenience store (he was also wearing a hat that had the "RRL" logo on it), bought his can of Skoal, decided to go ahead and use the bathroom while he was there to (again, a Number One), and he also decided to buy a lottery ticket for himself before he headed out the door.

Before he left Paso he had grabbed $5.00 from RRL's petty cash box to cover any miscellaneous expense that might come up on his trip -- RRL's employees routinely did this -- and he dipped into this $5.00 to buy his lottery ticket, but he planned to pay RRL back for this "little advance." Re: the can of Skoal he bought, he talked the manager into letting him pay for the Skoal with a personal check.

While Jimmy was in the convenience store he also saw that it was having a special sale on high end Pinot Noir wine at ¼ the normal price. Remembering that his boss had mentioned that he was on the lookout for such wine for RRL's upcoming company picnic, he decided to take the initiative and buy eight (8) cases of the wine for the company and that event. The problem was … Jimmy did not have the cash needed to pay for the wine, so he asked the convenience store manager (a buddy of his from high school who also knew that Jimmy worked for RRL) if he could take the wine "on credit", have the store send RRL the bill and RRL would in turn pay that bill within 15 days of receipt. The store manager agreed.

Part Two of the Story ….

Coffee, when it's poured at most places that serve coffee, is normally 150 to 160 degrees. Stella Steinbeck, an 81-year-old grandmother and former department store clerk, bought a 49-cent cup of coffee at the McDonald's located in Nipomo just off the freeway. After purchasing the cup of coffee at the drive-in window, she drove away and turned onto a main street. She came to a stoplight, stopped her car, and while waiting for the light to turn green, she opened the lid on her cup of coffee. She did this to add cream and sugar. She did not have it or place it between her legs. The cup disintegrated and the coffee spilled on her thighs and groin area, thereby causing second- and third-degree burns to her inner thighs, groin, buttocks, and labia.

Michael Jones just happened to be walking by this intersection at the time of this incident. After Stella spilled the coffee and was burned, and after hearing Stella scream, Michael rushed over to her car, opened the door, picked up Stella, placed her on her back in the back seat of the car, jumped back into the car on the driver's side, and proceeded to drive toward Santa Maria toward the nearest hospital.

Unfortunately, while leaving Nipomo for the hospital, and as Jimmy was pulling out of the convenience store, there was another terrible accident …

Jimmy was not watching where he was going as he pulled out of the convenience store parking lot and hit Stella's car broadside as it drove by. Michael was severely injured as a result of the collision (he broke both legs). Miraculously, even though she was in the back seat and not buckled in with her seatbelt, Stella suffered no injuries as a result of this automobile accident – her injuries were solely due to the coffee burns.

Stella requested McDonald's to cover her medical bills (just over $2,000), plus the lost wages of her daughter who stayed home to care for her. Stella offered to settle the case for $2,600 (she even sent receipts) and a promise by McDonald's to turn down the temperature of the coffee. McDonald's countered with a "take-it-or-leave-it offer" of $800 and promised to litigate the case "as far as necessary" should she decline. As a result, Stella filed a lawsuit against McDonald's in the San Luis Obispo County Superior Court.

McDonald's does not believe that it should be liable for Stella's burns. It contends that she contributed to her own injuries by holding the cup while in the car and not removing her clothing immediately after she spilled the coffee. It also contends that Stella's age may have caused her injuries to have been worse than they might have been in a younger individual, since older skin is thinner and more vulnerable to injury.

Michael has also sued Jimmy and his employer (RRL) for his injuries. RRL does not believe it should be responsible for the injury and damages that Jimmy caused Michael – rather, it feels that Jimmy is solely responsible for these injuries – after all, Jimmy was the one doing the driving and his boss had instructed him to go *directly* to and from Santa Maria.

These cases are scheduled to go to trial next week. Discovery in these cases has revealed the following:

STELLA VS. MCDONALD'S

Stella spent seven days in the hospital and required dozens of skin grafts (during this period she lost 20 pounds – to 83 pounds – almost 20% of her body weight). When she was burned, she was wearing a sweat suit and was sitting in the bucket seat of her car. She also spent three weeks recuperating at home. Stella has never before filed a lawsuit.

McDonald's, known for its careful control over its franchisees, requires that its coffee be prepared at hot temperatures in order to extract the flavor during brewing. McDonald's operations and training manual states that its coffee must be brewed at 195 to 205 degrees, and then held (i.e., poured) at 180 to 190 degrees for optimal taste. McDonald's marketing department believes that the hotter the temperature, the more its customers perceive that its coffee tastes good.

> The following statement was on Stella's coffee cup … "Caution – Contents Hot".

McDonald's received over 700 complaints of coffee burns during the ten (10) years preceding the Stella incident, ranging from mild to third-degree burns. In one of those cases, McDonald's quality assurance manager, Jim Zorn, testified at trial that in spite of these burn incidents, "he was aware of the risk and had no plans to turn down the heat."

During his deposition in this case, a McDonald's executive also testified that he believed that consumers were unaware of the risk posed by a liquid of the temperature at which their coffee was served, but that McDonald's was and had been aware of the danger for a number of years. He also admitted that McDonald's coffee is "not fit for consumption" as and when sold because it will cause severe burns if spilled <u>or</u> ingested. However, he also testified that McDonald's had decided not to warn customers about the possibility of severe burns nor did it have any plans to change any of its coffee policies or procedures saying that "people in America need to learn to take responsibility for their own actions and stop blaming others" and "there are more serious dangers in restaurants."

McDonald's (domestic, U.S.) sells over one billion cups of coffee each year, with daily coffee profit (domestic, U.S.) exceeding $1.3 million. One of McDonald's expert witnesses, Dr. Robert Kanaff, testified during his deposition that hot-coffee burns were "statistically insignificant" when compared to the billions of cups of coffee that McDonald's sells annually. Specifically, he testified that 700 complaints was about 1 in 24 million coffee cups which was "basically trivially different from zero."

Another McDonald's expert testified during his deposition that any coffee hotter than 130 degrees can produce third-degree burns, so it did not matter whether McDonald's coffee was hotter than that (i.e., hotter than 130 degrees). However, a doctor who testified on behalf of Stella stated during his deposition that lowering the serving temperature to about 160 degrees could make a significant difference -- because at 190 degrees it takes 3.5 seconds to cause third-degree burns to skin, muscle and fatty tissue, while it takes about 12 to 15 seconds to do so at 180 degrees, and about 20 seconds to do so at 160 degrees.

McDonald's coffee in the city in which this burn occurred (Nipomo) was served at 190 degrees – at least 20 degrees hotter than any other venue tested in the area and 25 degrees hotter than any machine available to consumers that produces coffee. This is a temperature that causes third degree, full thickness burns to skin, muscle and fatty tissue in 3.5 seconds.

MICHAEL VS. RRL & JIMMY

Jimmy makes $7.00 an hour and he is classified by RRL as an "independent contractor" – although in reality, depositions in the case revealed that RRL exercised a significant amount of control over the how, when and why (i.e., the details) of Jimmy's work.

Jimmy found out about and applied for his job with RRL after reading an ad that RRL has posted in the local paper for a "handyman/errand-boy." When Jimmy was hired he had been ticketed on two (2) previous occasions for reckless driving and at least four (4) times for speeding. RRL did not know about these violations as it had not done any type of background check on Jimmy when it hired him.

Jimmy's boss did not like the wine he purchased, and RRL refused to pay for it. The convenience store refused to take it back, and has filed a small claims action against RRL (and Jimmy) for the $$$$ due and owing on the wine.

Jimmy was also fired from his job at RRL. He felt that his firing was unfair as he was only trying to do his job and do it the best he could, and that RRL was trying to make him a scapegoat. Two weeks after he was fired, Jimmy, in an attempt to extract some revenge from his RRL, called up one of RRL's suppliers and ordered $3,000 worth of computers to be delivered to RRL's plant in Paso Robles. When the computers arrived, RRL refused to pay for them. As expected, this supplier wants its bill paid and is threatening litigation against RRL.

Oh, and that lottery ticket? It turned out to be a winner. It was the winning ticket for the $20 million lottery that week. RRL has taken the position that it owns those proceeds -- not Jimmy.

Product Liability Questions:

1. Does Stella have a case against McDonalds under strict product liability theory? (I.e., in light of the evidence above, can she prove each of the elements of this theory of liability?)
2. What defenses are available to McDonald's, if any?
3. How might ADR have been used to resolve the Stella vs. McDonald's dispute? Could it have done so?
4. Perhaps no case has so inflamed the American people against the civil legal system in recent years as this case. The case prompted House and Senate floor debates in Washington, and was cited regularly as emblematic of the every excess in the legal system that could be cured through tort reform. Stella's case presents some interesting facts, very few of which were widely publicized by the media, and all of which lead to the following questions.... was the case, as the media and politicians widely suggested, a frivolous one?
5. Relatedly, what is the role of the media in creating and sustaining public perceptions of the law and legal system? Are state and federal legislators, in their effort to maintain popularity and/or get re-elected complicit in creating this perception?

Agency Law Questions:

6. Is RRL legally responsible for the wine that Jimmy purchased?
7. Is RRL legally responsible for the $3,000 worth of computer equipment that Jimmy ordered after he was fired?
8. Who owns the $20 million lottery proceeds? RRL or Jimmy?
9. Is RRL legally responsible for injuries that Jimmy inflicted on Michael as a result of the car crash?

Course Reader Materials for the Third Exam

Introduction to Contracts & Contract Law;

Agreement (Offer & Acceptance);

Consideration;

Defenses to the Enforcement of a Contract

104 Introduction to Contracts and Contract Law

Study Outline

*****Note that in this textbook at pages 319–323 I have inserted several introductory newspaper articles, supplementary materials, misc. documents, etc. that relate to this material. These materials are required reading, and, are also fair game for the exam.**

*****Make *sure* that you also do the sample practice problems posted on Blackboard ("Introduction to Contracts and Contract Law Practice Problems") as it will help you master this material, test you to see if you "really" know and understand it, etc. You can expect similar problems to be on the exam. Please note that I will NOT spend a lot of time on the this "Introduction to Contracts and Contract Law" material in class – it's some of the easier and more straightforward material we cover and you should be able to master it on your own – especially if you do the practice problems posted on my website along the way.**

I. Introduction

A. Definition of a contract -- an agreement that can be enforced in court; formed by two or more parties who agree to perform or to refrain from performing some act now or in the future

B. Other definitions you need to quickly master:

1. Offeror -- the person who makes the offer
2. Offeree – the person receiving the offer
3. Breach – this means that one of the parties who was obligated to do/not do something under the contract failed to do that (i.e., we say they "breached" the contract and as a result may be liable to the non-breaching party for monetary damages)
4. Voidable – mean s that the contract can be cancelled (or rescinded by the damaged/injured party). For example, if you enter into a contract someone as a result of their fraud, you may be able to cancel the contract/get out of having to perform your obligations under the contract

II. The Nature of Contracts

A. Basically, in order for a promise to be treated as a contract you need several things: an ***offer***, ***acceptance***, valid ***consideration***, and ***no defenses*** to the formation or enforcement of the contract can apply. (But see also below discussion on promissory estoppel and quasi-contract that qualifies this statement.)

III. The Function and Social Utility of Contracts

A. Enables us to facilitate private business planning, know what to expect, and also know that we can call upon the law to ensure that such agreements will be honored (i.e., contracts and contract law promote predictability and stability in the marketplace)

IV. Basic Contract Concepts, Types, and Related Doctrines

A. Bilateral Contract -- involves a promise in return for a promise (e.g., "If you promise to put a new roof on my house, I promise to pay you $5,000." Once the roofer makes the requested promise to put a new roof on the house, a bilateral contract is created at that point)

B. Unilateral Contract -- involves a promise in return for some type of an act or performance (e.g., "I will pay you $500 if you run to the top of Mt. San Luis within 30 minutes." Here, an enforceable contract is *only* created once (and if) you make it to the top of Mt. San Luis within the allotted time). If you do not do so, then I am not obligated to pay you any money.

1. Note: The importance of the difference between bilateral and unilateral contracts will become more apparent later when we discuss offer, acceptance, consideration, etc. In particular, unilateral contracts present some interesting problems and issues

C. Express Contract -- parties expressly create a contract either by words (oral) or in writing

D. Implied Contract -- parties create a contract by their *conduct* (e.g., when you go to a doctor for treatment a contract is implicitly formed; when you take a drink from a bartender after ordering; when you go/walk through a grocery store checkout line, etc.). The key is to focus on the parties' ***conduct*** and the particular facts and circumstances at issue

1. For an example of this concept see the article titled "Hair-Razing Experience is No Ground for Lawsuit" at page 319 of this textbook (as well as the practice problems posted on Blackboard)

E. Promissory Estoppel -- situation where one person relies on a promise made by another, but because one or more of the required elements of a contract is missing, a contract has not been created

1. Rule: A promise which the promisor should ***reasonably expect*** to ***induce*** action or forbearance (i.e., reliance) on the part of the promisee/a third person and which does induce such action or forbearance is binding if injustice can be avoided only by enforcement of the promise
   a) The key here is ***reliance***--should the promisor foresee that the promisee is likely to rely on his promise?
   b) Also, in terms of damages, here, <u>a court will either enforce the promise, or, allow the plaintiff to recover his/her reliance losses/damages</u>

2. See the related articles and practice problems in this textbook at pages 321–323

F. Quasi-Contract—is not a contractual obligation created by the parties, but is instead is an obligation imposed by law in order to avoid the ***unjust enrichment*** of one party at the other party's expense. As a matter of law, the benefited party usually is required to pay **the reasonable value of the benefits or services** he received. Also, in order for this doctrine to apply, the benefited party must have ***knowingly accepted and retained*** the benefit

1. See the related articles and practice problems in this textbook at page 323

V. The Uniform Commercial Code (the "UCC")

A. Background:

1. Origin -- Created by the American Law Institute (the "ALI") and the National Conference of Commissioners on Uniform State Laws. All states have adopted some version of the UCC except Louisiana

2. Purpose -- to promote uniformity among the states where commercial transactions are involved; create a body of rules which would realistically and fairly solve common problems which occur in commercial transactions; and formulate rules which would promote fair dealing and higher moral and ethical standards in the market place. ***In short, to encourage and promote commerce through a stable and predictable body of law***

3. Scope of the UCC -- the UCC has nine articles. We will focus on only Article 2 of the UCC which involves the ***sale of goods***

   a) Nature of Article 2 – In many cases the UCC and its rules of contract are the same as the common law rule. However, in other cases it is different from the common law contract rule (and, for example, a court that applies the UCC is more likely to find that a valid contract was created than is a court that applies traditional common law contract rules)

   When the difference between the UCC and common law rule of contract is important I point that out in the study outline in this textbook. For the exam, make sure that you know which one/rule to apply and then be able to correctly apply it!! Note that a contract for a "good" is different than a contract to provide a service

(1) Examples of "goods" under the UCC would be a computer system (hardware and/or software), a bus, a bicycle, etc. – NOT something like the sale of an office building or real property (not considered a "good" under the UCC)

B. Application of the Article 2 of the UCC

1. Article 2 ***only*** applies to contracts involving the "sale of goods." Goods are essentially defined by section 2-105 as "tangible, movable, personal property." Goods do ***not*** include things such as real estate, stocks, bonds, etc. Also, Article 2 does ***not*** apply to ***service*** contracts

a) What about ***"hybrid transactions"?***

(1) Definition of a "hybrid transaction": a contract that has both a good and a service component to it. E.g., when a mechanic repairs your car, is he/she providing a good, a service, or both? The answer is both! Hence, it is called a hybrid transaction

(a) The ***"Predominant Factor Test"***

(i) Under contract law, if the good aspect/component of the transaction/contract "dominates", then the UCC and its rules apply. If, however, the service component dominates, then regular (i.e., non-UCC) common law contract rules apply

b) Don't know/can't recognize what a hybrid transaction is and/or how to apply the predominant factor test?? Well, then the thing to do is go to the practice problems I have placed in your Course Reader at the "Introduction to Contracts and Contract Law" section and do practice on those problems!

*****Again, folks, I encourage you to do the practice problems on "Introduction to Contracts and Contract Law" that I have posted on Blackboard. You may feel that you know/understand the above material, and, you may. But you also may not. So, be safe and do these practice problems. Many of them involve the application of the above concepts and that is a great way to learn (the only way, really) to see if you really do know and understand this material. – Prof. Carr**

105 Hair-razing Experience Is No Grounds for Lawsuit

You and The Law

By H. Dennis Beaver

[Implied Contract]

BEFORE TAKING A barber to Small Claims Court, I need some advice. You seem to have a good sense of humor and common sense, and a solution to this problem requires both."

So began a letter from a naval officer in Lemoore, Calif.

"My father-in-law is from the Philippines and is 80. He's in excellent physical condition. But his speech is a little impaired. This hasn't been too much of a problem. As his English has always consisted of a great deal of smiling, head nodding and saying *Yes*!"

"He lost his wife some years ago and still has eyes for pretty ladies and that's one of the reasons he purchased an expensive toupee. It cost over $1,500, but it's beautiful. Wearing it, he has long hair, so long that when he tosses his head back, the years melt away. It makes him look and feel young and I think it's one of the reasons he is so popular with women.

"His only real hair is what looks like a ring around his head at ear level, and it grows at an amazing rate. Every two weeks I take him to the barbershop for a trim, and that's why I am writing you.

"The owner of the shop knows that the only area to trim is that ring around his head. He is careful not to harm the toupee.

"Last week when I took him in the owner wasn't there and the shop was full. While waiting for his turn, I was paged and made a phone call from a pay phone inside the shop. Dad was called to the chair and he hopped in.

"Things then happened very quickly. I was still on the phone, but heard the barber mention a trim, and my father-in-law nodded his head affirmatively with a big smile."

According to my reader, the barber then said, "I've got to do something about this long hair of yours, it's getting in your eyes!" At this point the barber started trimming the toupee! It was only when the old man began to cry that he realized something was wrong.

"This ruined the toupee and terribly upset Dad. I believe the owner should be responsible for the damage. He had an obligation to tell his employees that my father-in-law's hair wasn't really his hair, if you follow me. But he blamed me for not warning the barber."

"If I go to court, what will be the outcome?"

Arguments to be Made

If this case actually made it to court, a judge would ask these questions.

1. Was a contract made?
2. Was it reasonable to expect the barber to know of the toupee?
3. Did my reader have an obligation of telling the barber about it?
4. Should the owner have warned his other employees about this particular customer?

Liability here would depend, in part upon a breach of what we refer to as an implied-in fact contract.[1] By sitting down in the chair after being called, it is clear to anyone looking on that the gentle man has consented to a haircut.

This question of consent is important especially after the suggestion to do "something about the long hair." Nodding and saying "yes, yes" conveys only one thing, and that's agreement.

My opinion is that the barber cannot be held responsible, on either contract principles or any theory of negligence. The son in law had a duty to watch out for what must be a very charming older man. He had a chance to act. But his phone call took greater priority.

A toupee can be replaced, and I hope my reader will do so promptly. This man of 80 has a lot of living to do!

---

1 Note from Professor Carr: This is an excellent example of an IMPLIED contract (i.e., one that can arise/is created by conduct and/or the behavior of the parties

106 A Deal Is a Deal, Even If It's Not in Writing[1]

Plaintiff's Business Wins Despite Lack of Contract

The National Law Journal

[The Doctrine of Promissory Estoppel]

THE LESSON TO BE learned from the business dispute involving my client is that you can overcome the preconceived notion that all business deals must be governed by written contract.

Due to circumstances beyond my client's control, it did not have a written agreement with the defendant. Yet on March 18, a jury in San Antonio awarded my client a $21.8 million verdict, including $15.5 million in punitive damages.

My client Corporacion Pipsa S.A. de C.V., a supplier of raw materials for car batteries in Monterrey, Mexico, sued Johnson Controls Inc. a Milwaukee-based battery maker, and two related companies. Pipsa, relying on promissory estoppels and fraud claims, alleged that the defendants had promised to be long-term buyers, with a minimum guarantee of a seven-year contract. In reliance of that promise, Pipsa spent $6.5 million to upgrade its facilities.

The defendants claimed that there were several failed attempts to negotiate a five-year extension to an earlier two-year agreement. But after the two-year contract had expired, Pipsa and Johnson continued doing business until the negotiations broke off on the five-year extension and Johnson took its business elsewhere.

The challenge in voir dire was the common perception most jurors have that a business deal must have written documentation.

We eliminated several jurors for cause who admitted that no amount of instructions from the judge would overcome that notion. We made repeated references in voir dire and throughout the trial that this was not a breach-of-contract case, and took every opportunity to drive home the concepts of promissory estoppels and fraud and how these differed from breach of contract.

The events and key documents were part of a time line presented on a giant poster board, as well as with Power Point. On the time line were correspondence between the parties and notes and minutes from meetings that confirmed Johnson's urging that Pipsa upgrade its facilities, Johnson's involvement in the upgrading and suggestions on purchases to improve the plant.

In turn, it was shown that Pipsa continually informed Johnson that it was making those costly changes in reliance on Johnson's promise of a long-term contract that would allow Pipsa to recoup its investment.

1 **Note from Professor Carr: The case discussed in this article is an excellent example of the promissory estoppel doctrine in action. Note how a key part/requirement of this doctrine is RELIANCE.**

Pretrial discovery had revealed internal memos and e-mails showing that as Pipsa was obtaining assurances and making investments, the defendants were conducting analysis and negotiating with Pipsa's competitors to have options on the sources of raw materials.

INTERNAL DOCUMENTS A KEY

The time line also emphasized that at the same time as assurances of a seven-year deal with Pipsa were being made, Johnson's internal documents spoke of its effort to explore options and to keep the process secret so as to not jeopardize Pipsa as its source. When Johnson executives were confronted with these documents on cross-examination, no adequate explanations were given.

The closing argument consisted of a Power Point presentation that brought the time line to life, showing documents, meetings, telephone calls and plant upgrade purchases and putting it into context.

No one document or event stood out as a "smoking gun," but the cumulative effect allowed the jury to conclude that fraud and promissory estoppels existed and that punitive damages were appropriate. The defendants are appealing.

107 Practice Problems

QUASI CONTRACT

DON EASTERWOOD LEASED over 5,000 acres of farmland in Jackson County, Texas from PIC realty for one year. The next year he obtained a second one-year lease. During each year, Easterwood farmed the land, harvested the crops, and prepared the land for the following year's planting. Towards the end of the second lease, after Easterwood had harvested his crop, he and PIC began discussing the terms of another lease. While they negotiated, Easterwood prepared the land for the following year, cutting, plowing, and disking the soil. But the negotiations for a new lease failed, and Easterwood moved off the land. He sued PIC Realty for the value of his work preparing the soil.

Did Easterwood have an express contract? Clearly not. The lease was their contract, it had expired, and they failed to create a new one. Did he have an implied contract? No. The parties were actively trying to create a new express contract, so their conduct would not create any kind of an implied agreement. If he had neither an express nor an implied contract to pay him for the value of the work he has done, how could he make any legal claim? By relying on the legal theory of a *quasi-contract*—even when there is no contract, a court may use quasi-contract to compensate a plaintiff who can show that:

- The plaintiff gave some benefit to the defendant,
- the plaintiff reasonably expected to be paid for the benefit and the defendant knew this, and
- the defendant would be unjustly enriched if he did not pay.

PROMISSORY ESTOPPEL

I OFFER TO SELL you my car for $3,000. I tell you I will keep the offer open for a week. You tell me that since I'm willing to keep the offer open for that period of time, you are going to go out and get a loan during the week to enable you to buy the car. You obtain the loan, at 9% interest, including paying a loan origination and processing fee, and return with the money to buy the car. As I see you approach, I say, "Oh, yeah, you're the one who was interested in buying the car. It's already sold to someone else!" If you sue me, the best legal theory to win the case would be:

(a) Breach of express contract
(b) Promissory estoppel[1]
(c) Quasi-contract

1 **Note from Professor Carr: There was reasonable reliance (going on out and getting the loan). Answer: B**

108 Agreement Outline, Part 1A

Study Outline

*****Note that in this textbook at pages 331–337 I have inserted several newspaper articles, supplementary materials, misc. documents, etc. that relate to this material. These materials are required reading, and, are also fair game for the exam.**

*****Make *<u>sure</u>* that you also do the sample practice problems posted on Blackboard ("Agreement (Offer & Acceptance) Practice Problems") as it will help you master this material, test you to see if you "really" know and understand it, etc. You can expect similar problems to be on the exam.**

I. What is an ***Offer***?

A. Definition: An offer is a promise or commitment to perform or refrain from performing some specified act in the future

B. The most important thing that courts usually look at to determine whether an offer has been made, as opposed to mere negotiations or invitations to deal, is some ***objective*** (<u>not</u> subjective) indication/evidence of a ***present intent to contract***. I.e., there must be, according to this objective test, a "meeting of the minds" between the two parties on the relevant and important terms of the contract. In analyzing this issue courts consider:

1. **Definitiveness or Certainty of the Terms** -- the more definitive and certain the terms, the more likely an offer

a) Note: preliminary negotiations, invitations to deal, expressions of opinion, statements of intention, etc., are not offers!

b) Note that "objective" means/looks at "what would a reasonable person conclude here?" whereas "subjective" means "what the defendant meant/intended." Those are two very different standards, and, as noted above, it's the former standard (objective) and not the latter (subjective) that courts look at and consider important in determining whether an offer was made and hence whether a contract was formed

c) Also, by "terms" we mean such things as price, quantity, identity of the subject matter of the contract, time of delivery, method and time of payment, any warranties, etc. etc.

d) For a good example of the above, see the articles in this textbook at pages 331–336; also see and do the practice problems I have posted on Blackboard

C. Communication to the Offeree

1. General Rule – the offeror must also communicate the offer to the offeree

a) Rationale: if the offeror did not communicate the offer to the offeree, this is good evidence that he lacked the present intent to contract which is necessary for an offer!

II. Special Offer Problem Areas

A. Advertisements

1. General Rule: Advertisements are generally NOT regarded as an offer (because they are not certain or definitive enough) and instead are viewed as only *invitations* from the merchant-seller to deal/bargain/negotiate to and with the consumer

a) Rationale for this general rule: it's because, for example, such important terms such as price, duration, subject matter, etc. are generally not discussed or made clear in the ad so how could it be an offer?

2. Exception: If the terms ***are*** certain or definitive enough (according to an objective -- reasonable person standard … see above), then an advertisement may, in fact, be an offer!

B. Rewards

1. General rule: a public offer for a reward is an offer, but it is a *unilateral offer* (meaning that in order to accept, the offeree must perform the requested act)

a) Also, in order to be entitled to the reward, most states require the offeree to have performed the act with knowledge of/because of the offer

C. Auctions

1. With reserve: The person making the bid is the offeror and the seller of the item is the offeree. Acceptance only occurs when the auctioneer (who is the seller's agent) brings the hammer down and says "sold." The auctioneer may withdraw the goods at any time before acceptance

2. Without reserve: The seller of the item is treated as the offeror and the bidders are the offerees. After the auctioneer (the seller's agent) calls for bids on the property, the auctioneer cannot withdraw the property (unless, of course, no bids are made). The item is sold to the highest bidder. A bidder can also retract his bid at anytime before the hammer comes down. A bidder's retraction does not revive a previous bid

D. Bids

1. Advertisements for bids are generally treated as invitations to deal (unless advertisement states the contrary, e.g., "the contract will be awarded to the lowest bidder"). Those who submit bids are treated as the offerors. Bidders can withdraw bid at any time before acceptance. Note that for government contracts special rules and statutes apply

III. Termination of Offers

In order for a contract to be formed, the offer must be accepted by an offeree **before** it expires/terminates (otherwise, there is nothing for the offeree to accept!). So ... how and when can an offer expire/terminate? (See the below)

A. By the **Terms of the Offer** itself -- the important point to remember here is that the offeror is the "*master of his offer*" and can therefore give it the length of life he wants, lay down the ground rules for how it needs to be accepted, etc.

I.e., an offer may terminate by the very terms of the offer itself when the conditions necessary to timely accept it are not satisfied!

1. For some very good examples of this concept, refer to class lecture (and example), **and**, do the practice problems on "Agreement (Offer and Acceptance)" posted on Blackboard

B. Revocation

1. General rule: offeror can revoke his/her offer at any time, even if he promises to hold it open for a certain period of time (but see below exceptions to this rule)

2. Exception: option contract supported by consideration

a) See Chapter 8 of the textbook chapter posted on Blackboard at page 164 for an example of an option contract; see also the practice problems posted on my website for an example of the option contract exception and how to apply it

3. Exception: UCC "Firm Offer" [UCC 2-205] -- a writing (could be any ol' piece of paper, even the back of a napkin!), signed by a merchant (a merchant is someone who specializes in selling the good(s) at issue), promising to buy or sell goods, **and** which promises to hold the offer open

for a certain period of time (or if no time is stated, for a reasonable time, but in no case can it exceed three months)

a) Again, see Chapter 8 of the textbook chapter posted on Blackboard at page 164 for an example of a UCC Firm Offer; see also the practice problems posted on my website for several examples of the UCC Firm Offer exception and how to apply it

4. Exception: Unilateral contract is involved and the offeree starts to perform the requested act

a) Once the offeree starts to perform (versus beginning preparations), the offeror must hold the offer open for a reasonable period of time. For example, if I tell you I will pay you $1,000 to run up to the top of Mt. San Luis under 30 minutes, and, you take off and start running up the hill, I have to hold that offer open and let you try to make it – I can't wait until you are halfway up the hill and yell "I changed my mind and herby revoke my offer"!!

5. Exception: Promissory Estoppel: in some cases, the offeree ***relies*** on the offer being kept open, and the offeree will suffer an injustice if the offeror is allowed to revoke, so the doctrine of promissory estoppel can operate to prevent the offeror from revoking his/her offer prior to acceptance (e.g., comes up often in construction contracts and in particular, the general contractor -- subcontractor relationship)

6. **Effectiveness of revocation (when is a revocation of an offer by the offeror effective??)**

a) General Rule: Upon receipt by the offeree

(1) See the ***Lyon*** case on page 337 of this textbook for an example

b) Exception: The offeree indirectly learns that the offeror has revoked the offer (e.g., a reliable third party informs the offeree the offer has been revoked)

C. Rejection by the offeree -- can be express, implied by conduct, making of a counteroffer, etc. The effect is to automatically terminate the offer. The offeree cannot later go back and try to "revive" it and then accept it. If he does so, he has made his own ***offer/counteroffer*** (whichever you want to call it)

For an example of this concept/rule, see the practice problems posted on Blackboard

1. **Effectiveness of rejection (when is a rejection of an offer by the offeree effective??)**

a) Rule: Upon receipt of the rejection by the offeror

D. Lapse of time -- if no time stated as to how long the offer will remain open, then the law deems it to remain open for a "reasonable" period of time

E. Death or insanity of either party--automatically terminates the offer without notice

   1. Rationale: a meeting of the minds is impossible when one of the parties has died or become insane

F. Destruction of the subject matter of the contract

   1. If, prior to the acceptance of the offer, the subject matter of the contract is destroyed without the knowledge or fault of either party (e.g., a tornado destroys the item), the offer is automatically terminated

G. Intervening illegality (e.g., grain embargo, arms embargo, technology embargo, etc.)

***Again, folks, I encourage you to do the practice problems on "Agreement (Offer and Acceptance)" that I have posted on Blackboard. You may feel that you know/understand the above material, and, you may. But you also may not. So, be safe and do these practice problems. Many of them involve the <u>application</u> of the above concepts and that is a great way to learn (the only way, really) to see if you really do know and understand this material. – Prof. Carr**

109 Do Bob and Katrina Have an Enforceable Contract?

[Offer and Acceptance—Meeting of the Minds]

The Scene. A glitzy café, New York. Evening. Bob, a famous director, and Katrina, a glamorous actress, sit at a table, near a wall of glass looking onto a New York sidewalk that is filled with life and motion. Bob sips a margarita while carefully eyeing Katrina. Katrina stares at her wine glass.

Bob (smiling confidently): *Body Work* is going to be huge—for the right actress. I know a film that's gonna gross a hundred million when I'm holding one. I'm holding one.

Katrina (suddenly perking up): It *is* quirky. It's fun. And she's very strong, very real.

Bob: She's you. That's why we're sitting here. We start shooting in seven months.

Katrina (edging away from the table): I have a few questions. That nude scene.

Bob: The one on the toboggan run?

Katrina: *That* one was O.K. But the one in the poultry factory—very explicit. I don't work nude.

Bob: It's not really nude. Think of all those feathers fluttering around.

Katrina: It's nude.

Bob: We'll work it out. This is a romantic comedy, not tawdry exploitation. Katrina, we're talking $2.5 million. A little accommodation, please. $600,000 up front, and the rest deferred, the usual percentages.

Katrina: Bob, my fee is $3 million. As you know. That hasn't changed.

Katrina picks up her drink, doesn't sip it, places it on the coaster, using both hands to center it perfectly. He waits, as she stares at it in silence.

Bob: We're shooting in Santa Fe, the weather will be perfect. You have a suite at the Excelsior plus a trailer on location.

Katrina: I should talk with my agent. I'd need something in writing about the nude scene, the fee, percentages—all the business stuff. I never sign without talking to her.

Bob shrugs and sits back.

Katrina (made anxious by the silence): I love the character, I really do.

Bob: You and several others love her. (That jolts her.) Agents can wait. I have to put this together fast. We can get you the details you want in writing. *Body Work* is going to be bigger than *Sleepless.*

> That one hooks her. She looks at Bob. He nods reassuringly. Bob sticks out his hand, smiling. Katrina hesitates, lets go of her drink, and SHAKES HANDS, looking unsure. Bob signals for the check.

Is there an enforceable contract between Bob and Katrina? In your view, are there enough terms and are they certain and definitive enough for a court to enforce them? What was the "offer"? What was the "acceptance"? Discuss and defend your position. (This would be an excellent question to give you as an essay question—seems to me that both sides/arguments can be made here.—Prof. Carr).

110 Fidelity's Johnson, a Billionaire, Wins Case Over Sum Of $160,000

WHAT'S A COUPLE hundred thousand dollars to a billionaire? Small change, but apparently worth a fight for Edward C. Johnson III, the chairman of Fidelity Investments.

Yesterday, Mr. Johnson, whose net worth is estimated at more than $4 billion, won a court case over $160,000 in fees sought by Richard W. Larson, a longtime friend who has worked for Mr. Johnson as a caretaker of his properties in Maine.[1]

Mr. Larson, 71 years old and a family friend for 30 years, oversaw construction of a $2 million woodworking shop and upstairs apartment at Mr. Johnson's summer estate on exclusive Mount Desert Island, off Maine's coast. The two men had long enjoyed playing tennis and socializing with one another's families. But last year, Mr. Larson filed suit in U.S. District Court in Bangor, Maine, saying Mr. Johnson, also 71, reneged on a promise to pay him.

In 1995, Mr. Johnson turned to Mr. Larson, then a retired plumbing and heating contractor who also worked five years in Fidelity's real-estate operations, to build a country home on Mount Desert Island. The original budget for the 4,000-square-foot house: about $1 million.

Mr. Johnson—well-known at Boston-based Fidelity for his attention to detail—asked for 535 changes, calling Mr. Larson three times a week, staying in touch even while on the road in the Far East and England, according to the suit. By the time the house was complete, costs ballooned to about $5 million. Mr. Johnson ended up paying Mr. Larson about $376,000 for his part in the project. Their friendship remained intact.

Afterward, Mr. Johnson let Mr. Larson live rent-free in one of his Mount Desert Island homes, named Prays Meadow, in exchange for Mr. Larson's oversight of the magnate's Maine property. But the pair soon would have their falling out.

In November 1999, Mr. Johnson again asked for Mr. Larson's help-this time to build the workshop, complete with a basement wine cellar, antique storage and an apartment with an Oriental motif and "a ceiling of Douglas fir and Alaskan yellow cedar." Mr. Larson asked Mr. Johnson to pay him $6,700 a month—his rate for the previous project, his suit says. Mr. Johnson answered by saying his old friend should "trust the Great Oracle," referring to himself, and would "take care of" Mr. Larson, according to the complaint.

But Mr. Johnson, who went to Bangor to testify in the case, said he never agreed to pay Mr. Larson but merely told him to take on the project in return for the rent-free use of the Prays Meadow. After repeatedly asking for payment and being turned down, Mr. Larson sued in March of last year.

Late yesterday, a jury sided with Mr. Johnson, saying he owed Mr. Larson nothing.

1 **Note from Professor Carr: Here, the jury apparently said/found that there was no "meeting of the minds" between the two parties re: the essential terms of the contract. Hence, there was no contract and that's why the plaintiff loses!!**

111 Contract Issues In Cyberspace

FORMATION OF CONTRACTS IN CYBERSPACE

CONTRACT FORMATION IN cyberspace is simply the result of a desire for speed and better communication in business. If you wanted to form a contract with a New York seller 20 years ago and you were in Los Angeles, you drafted a proposal and mailed it to the seller. The back-and-forth negotiations took time through the mail. Then overnight delivery service arrived to speed up your cross-country negotiations. Next came faxes and their instantaneous exchanges of terms and negotiations. Now that there was speed, however, businesses wanted to reduce the amount of paperwork involved in transactions. They also recognized the flaws in the paper system: Had the letter arrived? Did the fax get through? Was it legible? Paperless contracts were born with the availability of electronic digital interchange (EDI), and companies using EDI have had a set of contract formation guidelines they have followed for almost 20 years. EDI is simply the electronic exchange of business forms. Contracts are formed using purchase orders and invoices submitted via computer.

Even EDI, however, had its flaws in requiring the comparison of forms and numbers, and verification of the interchange. With the Internet, e-mail, and the ability to attach documents, cyberspace provided business with yet another method for forming contracts.

Despite this new way of doing business with the instantaneous response to new term proposals, basic contract issues exist in cyberspace contracts that are no different from the contract issues that existed when the law merchant first began its work in finding uniform ways of doing business. Contract issues that continue to dominate discussions in cyber law are: *When is a contract formed? What are the contract terms?*

The formation of contracts in cyberspace is governed by the same laws that apply when a contract is formed in a business office. Was there an offer and acceptance, and when did those two requirements come together? Some issues that arise in contract formation in the new economy are, for example, whether a contract is formed when someone downloads a program from the Internet. He or she may have paid for the program by credit card and simply downloaded it on the computer. Does the click of the mouse accepting the program mean that all the terms of the contract have been accepted? How does the seller of the program make sure that the buyer is aware of all the terms in the contract that governs the sale of the program? Can the click of the mouse constitute a signature for purposes of contracting?

Several new laws currently govern the formation of contracts. [...]

The Electronic Signatures in Global and National Commerce Act (called **E-sign**) is a federal law that recognizes digital signatures as authentic for purposes of contract formation. Even though E-sign recognizes the validity of electronic signatures, states are responsible for passing laws regulating the authenticity and security of signatures.

States have responded to the need for legislation on contract formation and authentication with the

Uniform Electronic Transactions Act (UETA) and the Uniform Computer Information Transaction Act (UCITA). UETA is a uniform law that has been adopted in 18 states; UCITA has been adopted in 2 states.

112 Lyon v. Adgraphics

40 A.2d 398 (Conn. Ct. App. 1988)

[When is the revocation of an offer effective?]

Edward Sherman engaged V. R. Brokers as listing agent for the sale of Adgraphics, his business. On December 5, 1985, William Lyon made a written offer to purchase the business for $75,000 and attached certain conditions to the offer. Later the same day, Sherman signed a written counteroffer offering to sell for $80,000 and rejecting two of the conditions contained in Lyon's offer. On December 7, at 11:35 A.M., Lyon signed the counteroffer before a notary public and then brought it to the office of V. R. Brokers around noon on that day. Before Lyon could hand the signed counteroffer to Robert Renault, the principal of V. R. Brokers, Renault told him that Sherman wanted to cancel his counteroffer. Lyon filed a breach of contract suit, and, when the trial court ruled in his favor, Sherman appealed.

Borden, Judge It is a basic principle of contract law that in order to form a binding contract there must be an offer and acceptance based on a mutual understanding of the parties. The counteroffer by Sherman created a power of acceptance in Lyon. That counteroffer, however, was revocable by Sherman at any time prior to acceptance by Lyon.

The trial court's conclusion that Lyon's acceptance of the counteroffer was effective when he signed it was contrary to our law. Revocations of an offer in order to be effectual must be received by the offeree before he has exercised his power of creating a contract by acceptance of the offer. Acceptance is operative, if transmitted by means which the offeror has authorized, as soon as its transmission begins and it is put out of the offeree's possession. Lyon's act of signing the written counteroffer failed to communicate the acceptance to Sherman or his agent and failed to put the acceptance out of Lyon's possession. It was therefore, ineffective to create a contract.

When Sherman, through his agent, informed Lyon that the counteroffer was withdrawn, Lyon's power to accept the counteroffer no longer existed. This was done before Lyon had properly accepted the counteroffer by transmitting the signed counteroffer to Renault. Accordingly, no enforceable contract between the parties was ever created.

Judgment reversed in favor of Sherman.

113 Agreement Outline, Part 1B

Study Outline (continued)

*****Note that in this textbook at pages 343–344 I have inserted several newspaper articles, supplementary materials, misc. documents, etc. that relate to this material. These materials are required reading, and, are also fair game for the exam.**

*****Make *sure* that you also do the sample practice problems posted on Blackboard ("Agreement (Offer & Acceptance) Practice Problems") as it will help you master this material, test you to see if you "really" know and understand it, etc. You can expect similar problems to be on the exam.**

I. What is an ***Acceptance***?

You just finished reading about and studying the offer component/element of a contract. But in order for there to be a legally enforceable contract, there must **also** be a timely and valid ***acceptance*** of that offer.

So. … let's look at the rules of acceptance—specifically, what is an acceptance, how does it occur, when is an acceptance effective, etc.? …

A. An acceptance is a voluntary act by the offeree that shows assent, or agreement, to the terms of an offer. It can take place by words and/or conduct. In analyzing this issue courts will look at whether there was an:

1. Intention to accept -- did the offeree (according the ***objective*** "reasonable person" test; not what the offeree subjectively meant/intended) indicate a ***present intent*** to accept?; *and*

2. Intent and acceptance of the offeror's terms

a) Common law "**mirror image rule**" – *states that the offeree's acceptance must exactly mirror the terms of the offer. If anything at all is changed or modified when the offeree attempts to accept the offer, then there is no acceptance, and the offeree's attempt to accept the offer was/is really a counteroffer/his own offer (whichever you want to call it)!*

(1) Example – if you offer to sell me your car for $500 and I say "I'll take it but I also want you to wash it before I pick it up" -- there is not yet a contract as my attempt to accept your offer did not "mirror" the terms of your offer – I tried to add an additional term.

Hence, there is not yet a contract and instead, my statement to you is really my own offer/counteroffer to you which you are free to accept/reject (and, further note that we have switched roles – I have gone from becoming the offeree to the offeror, and you have gone from being the offeror to the offeree!)

(a) This is a very important concept and rule for you to understand. You must know it and be able to apply it on the exam. So ... go practice! See and do the practice problems I have posted on Blackboard on this issue

(2) Note: an mere inquiry regarding the terms of the offer (e.g., "when you say $500 for your car do you mean that to also include it passing the state's smog test?" ... or ... a "grumbling acceptance" — e.g., "ggggrrrrrrrr .... I think your price of $500 is way to high and ridiculous but I guess I don't have a choice ... I'll take it") ... are probably not rejections of the offer and/or one's own offer/counteroffer

(a) Note that a mere inquiry is just that ... a request for clarification and hence, there is not yet an acceptance of any offer by the person asking for the clarification. But a "grumbling acceptance" is a little different – here, there IS an acceptance of the offer; there is not a rejection of the offer or a counter offer by the person making the "grumbling acceptance" (again, the offeree)

b) **The UCC and the "Battle of the Forms"** (vs. the Common Law "Mirror Image" Rule)

Folks, note that the UCC acceptance rule is quite different than the common law mirror image rule. For a discussion of the UCC acceptance rule, see your textbook chapter posted on Blackboard.

The reality is, this rule is quite complicated, and we do not have enough time to cover it in class. So, you are lucky ... I won't test you on the UCC acceptance rule.

However, for purposes of the exam, do know, be aware of and appreciate that there is a UCC acceptance rule, and that it is quite different than the common law acceptance-mirror image rule, as you might see a question that requires you to know that there are two sets of rules out there, that they are different, etc.

One thing is certain for the exam, though, you HAVE to know and be able to apply the common law mirror image rule (see above)

B. Communication of an Acceptance (i.e., ***when is an acceptance of an offer by the offeree effective?***)

1. Acceptance by *instantaneous* forms of communication (e.g., we are talking/doing the deal on the phone) -- here, there is generally no problem or issue because the parties are dealing face to face, by telephone, etc. In such situations the acceptance is instantaneous

2. Acceptance by *non-instantaneous* forms of communication (e.g., letter, fax, email, messenger, etc.)

    a) ***Mailbox Rule – states that the acceptance is effective and valid upon posting/dispatch by the offeree***

    (Note that the above rule holds even if the acceptance never arrives/gets to the offeror—e.g., the post office loses or mis-delivers a mailed acceptance)

    (1) Exception: Offer expressly says acceptance only effective upon ***receipt*** by the offeror (see earlier discussion on the offeree being the "master of his/her own offer")

    (2) Exception: If the acceptance was improperly addressed or the postage was incorrect, it is effective upon ***receipt*** by the original offeror

    For examples applying the mailbox rule, see the "Time of Acceptance – The Mailbox Rule I" and the "Time of Acceptance – The Mailbox Rule II" hypotheticals in this textbook at page 343–344; see also the practice problems posted on Blackboard – you can be sure that you will see some problems on the exam that require you to know this rule and be able to apply it

3. Stipulated means of communication

    a) If the offeror expressly conditioned acceptance upon the use of a certain medium (remember the earlier discussion on the offeror being the "master of his/her own offer"), and the offeree used another medium trying to accept, there is no acceptance upon dispatch because the attempted acceptance varies from the terms of the offer. Instead, that attempted acceptance becomes an offer/counteroffer itself which will be effective upon *receipt* by the *original* offeror!

C. Miscellaneous Rules Regarding Acceptance:

1. **Silence as an acceptance**

    a) General Rule – silence cannot/is not an acceptance

b) Exception: custom in the industry is otherwise; or, the past/prior relationship between the parties is/was otherwise

2. Who can accept an offer? Only the offeree (and/or his agent). If anyone else tries to accept, the attempted acceptance will be treated as an offer which the original offeror can accept or reject

3. Communication of an acceptance

   a) In order for an acceptance to be valid, it obviously needs to be communicated to the offeror

      (1) Special situation: depending upon the situation, sometimes notification or communication of the acceptance is necessary where a *unilateral contract* is involved

4. Manner of communication -- if the offeror states what needs to be done in order to accept, those conditions need to be followed or the attempt to accept fails. If the offer however, merely ***suggests*** a method or place of communication, or is ***silent*** on such matters, the offeree may accept within a ***reasonable time*** and by ***any reasonable manner*** of communication

5. Acceptance in unilateral contracts -- in order to accept, the offeree must perform the requested act

6. Acceptance in bilateral contracts -- in order to accept, the offeree must generally make the promise requested by the offer. This can be done expressly or implicitly

***Again, folks, I encourage you to do the practice problems on "Agreement (Offer and Acceptance)" that I have posted on Blackboard. You may feel that you know/understand the above material, and, you may. But you also may not. So, be safe and do these practice problems. Many of them involve the <u>application</u> of the above concepts and that is a great way to learn (the only way, really) to see if you really do know and understand this material. – Prof. Carr**

114 Time of Acceptance— The Mailbox Rule I & II

EXAMPLE I

When Masako faxes her offer to sell land to Eric, he mails his acceptance, the contract is binding the moment he puts the letter into the mail. In most cases, this mailbox rule is just a detail. But it becomes important when the offeror revokes her offer at about the same time the offeree accepts. Who wins? Suppose Masako's offer has one twist:

- On Monday morning, Masako faxes her offer to Eric.
- On Monday afternoon, Eric writes "I accept" on the fax.
- On Tuesday Morning, Eric mails his acceptance.
- On Tuesday afternoon, Masako faxes Eric a revocation of her offer.
- On Thursday morning, Eric's acceptance arrives at Masako's office.

Outcome? Eric has an enforceable contract. Masako's offer was effective when it reached Eric. His acceptance was effective on Tuesday morning, when he mailed it. Nothing that happens later, such as Masako's attempt to revoke, can "undo" the contract.

EXAMPLE II[1]

Attorneys for free-agent goalie Mike Vernon filed suit in federal court in Detroit, charging the Red Wings with breach of contract. The suit claims the Red Wings reneged on a two-year contract offer of $5.45 million made June 19, between games 1 and 2 of the Stanley Cup Finals.

According to [Vernon's lawyer] John R. Trentacosta, Vernon accepted the offer via fax June 30, a week after the Wings were swept by the New Jersey Devils. The Wings claim they withdrew the offer before Vernon accepted it. [Trentacosta and Larry Kelly, Vernon's agent] believed someone in the Wings organization soured on Vernon during the Finals and wanted to get out of the $5.45 million deal. "We really feel, more than anything, that Mike was mistreated," Trentacosta said.

The key points in Vernon's version of the case: On the morning of June 30 Kelly faxed the Wings an acceptance letter for the $5.45 million deal and confirmed the signing meeting for 3:15 P.M. that day. At the meeting, Wings senior vice-president Jimmy Devellano told Vernon that team owner Mike Hitch had withdrawn the offer. Kelly said it was already accepted and therefore binding. Devellano said that no fax was received, and further told Kelly that the fax number he used had been out

1 Note from Professor Carr: This is just another example of the Mailbox Rule & how it can come up.

of use for two years. Trentacosta's documentation shows that, not only is the fax number still in use, it also was the same number used to fax the original offer. Trentacosta has documentation from Sprint showing that the fax was received by the Wings on June 30.

[Red Wings legal representative Jay A. Bielfield, in a letter to Trentacosta, claimed that an earlier letter from agent Larry Kelly to the Red Wings amounted to a counteroffer.] The letter from Kelly to [the Red Wings] dated June 19 also stated "I would be grateful if you could clarify two points for me: (1) Do the playoff performance bonuses and individual bonuses apply to the 1994–95 season; and (2) Does your offer contain revisions equal to the bonuses we have discussed to date?"

"Larry [Kelly] certainly understands contract law and his letter was not a rejection of the June 19 offer," Trentacosta said.

Source: Chris McCosky, Vernon Suing Red Wings, Detroit News, August 9, 1995, p. 1B.

115 Consideration

Study Outline

*****Note that in this textbook at pages 349–353 I have inserted several newspaper articles, supplementary materials, misc. documents, etc. that relate to this material. These materials are required reading, and, are also fair game for the exam.**

*****Make *<u>sure</u>* that you also do the sample practice problems posted on Blackboard ("Consideration Practice Problems") as they will help you master this material, test you to see if you "really" know and understand it, etc. You can expect similar problems to be on the exam.**

I. The Idea of Consideration

A. It is "***legal*** value, ***bargained for*** and given in ***exchange*** for an act or a promise." The idea or concept involved is a "bargained for exchange" of something. It is the "glue that holds the bargain together"

1. See/do related practice problems posted on Blackboard; refer also to class lectures and examples

II. Legal Value

Here, the concept is the promisee doing or agreeing to do something he had no prior legal duty or obligation to do. His doing so or agreeing to do so has legal value. "Legal value" does ***not*** mean that the promise or act involved must have *monetary* or *economic* value

A. Adequacy of consideration – as long as the promisee's act/performance or promise satisfies the legal value test, courts will generally not ask or inquire whether what the promisor gave or promised to give was worth it (i.e., whether it was economically equivalent to what the promisee gave) (again, see/do the related practice problems posted on Blackboard)

1. Rationale/social policy behind this rule: freedom of contract includes the right to make bad bargains as well as good ones; courts have better things to do than second guess the parties and play the role of appraiser; the promotion of stability and predictability in commercial transactions by denying potential legal challenges made after the fact regarding the enforceability of a contract based upon in inequality of the exchange, etc.

   a) Qualification:

(1) Gross inadequacy of consideration *may* give rise to an independent basis for setting aside the contract based upon such grounds as fraud, duress, unconscionability, lack of capacity, it was a gift, etc.

2. Illusory promises: e.g., "I will wash your car if I feel like it" or "I will shingle your roof as soon as I can" is not valid consideration because the promisee is not really legally binding himself to do anything. Therefore, it fails the "legal value" test

   a) Again, for examples of this rule/concept, see the practice problems I have posted on Blackboard; refer also to class lecture and examples

3. Preexisting Duties (The Preexisting Legal Duty Rule)

   a) Common law rule: As a general rule, a promise to do what one is already legally obligated to do (i.e., what one has a preexisting public and/or private contractual duty to do) is not valid consideration (because no legal detriment or benefit has been received or incurred)

      (1) For examples of this rule/concept, see the practice problems I have posted on Blackboard; refer also to the class lecture and examples

   b) UCC contract modification rule (is different than the above common law preexisting legal duty rule)

      (1) Rule: Under the UCC (i.e., when it applies – again, it only applies to contracts involving the sale of goods) an agreement to modify a contract for the sale of goods (not services) does ***not*** need and new consideration in order to be binding

         (a) Again, for examples of the rule/concept, see the practice problems I have posted on Blackboard; refer also to class lecture and examples

III. Bargained for exchange – the essence of consideration is that it is given and accepted as the motive or inducement of the promise

A. Past Consideration

1. Rule: Agreeing to do something that has already taken place in the past is not valid consideration.

   a) Again, for examples of this rule/concept, see the practice problems I have posted on Blackboard; refer also to class lecture and examples

B. Moral Consideration:

1. Rule: Promises based on moral obligations are also generally held to lack adequate/valid legal consideration and are therefore unenforceable

a) E.g., where a parent promises to give a child money. Or, a grandmother's promise to provide for a grandchild in a will, or trust fund, or pay the grandchild's school loans. Such promises, made out of moral obligation or for moral reasons, are generally unenforceable

b) Again, for examples of this rule/concept, see the practice problems I have posted on Blackboard; refer also to class lecture and examples

C. Gifts:

1. Rule: Generally not enforceable because no bargaining took place and consideration therefore fails!

a) Also, think of the social policy that courts are seeking to implement by this rule. If they (courts) enforced every single promise of a gift made by people who had reneged that promise, they (courts) fear that they would be opening the floodgates of litigation and those cases would saturate the courts!

b) Again, for examples of this rule/concept, see the practice problems I have posted on Blackboard; refer also to class lecture and examples

IV. Substitutes for Consideration (or Exceptions to the Consideration Requirement)

What happens when the consideration element/component of a contract fails, there is therefore no contract, and, justice or equity demand/require that the promises the parties exchanged somehow be enforced? Well ... see the below substitutes for consideration – if they apply, all of their elements are satisfied, etc., then that means that a court/judge may come in and still enforce the promises/contract at issue to do justice/equity.

Thus, folks, on the exam, if you see a problem that is testing you on the consideration portion of a contract, you see/determine that the consideration element has failed, then stop, think and see if one of the below substitutes or "fallbacks" may apply to come in and save the contract/make it enforceable!! Nobody will be trying to "trick" you with a trick question; rather, the goal is to see/verify that you truly understand and have mastered the consideration material (including the substitutes for consideration) and can apply it.

A. The Doctrine of Promissory Estoppel – where the promisor should reasonably expect the promisee to rely on his promise, the promisee does in fact rely on that promise, and injustice results to the promisee as a result of relying on that promise, then a court may step in and enforce the promise

1. See "Promissory Estoppel Hypothetical – An Insurance Example" and the news article titled "The Shrinking Pledge" in this textbook at pages 349–353 for good examples of this concept; see also the practice problems I have posted on Blackboard; refer also to class lectures and examples

B. UCC Firm Offer – already discussed earlier/above under "offers"

1. Again, for examples of this rule/concept, see the practice problems I have posted on Blackboard; refer also to class lecture and examples

C. UCC Contract Modification Rule – discussed above

1. Again, for examples of this rule/concept, see the practice problems I have posted on Blackboard; refer also to class lecture and examples

***Again, folks, I encourage you to do the Practice Problems on "Consideration" that I have posted on Blackboard. You may feel that you know/understand the above material, and, you may. But you also may not. So, be safe and do these practice problems. Many of them involve the application of the above concepts and that is a great way to learn (the only way, really) to see if you really do know and understand this material. – Prof. Carr**

116 The Shrinking Pledge

The Wall Street Journal

[*Consideration and the Doctrine of Promissory Estoppels*]

Donors are quietly canceling or delaying pledges they made during the height of the boom. On why charities got caught up in the stock-market frenzy—and how they're paying for it now.

IT WAS SUPPOSED TO be the world's premier online university, launched with $100 million from software entrepreneur Michael Saylor. He envisioned an unparalleled mail-order diploma, with Bill Clinton teaching politics, Warren Buffett on investing and Steven Spielberg on film.

That was before his company's stock tanked.

In a reversal of fortune that's become all too common lately, Mr. Saylor watched his shares fall more than 90%. Ten months later? There is no foundation, no name, not even a mention on the corporate Web site. "Nothing has happened that's announceable," says a spokesman for Micro Strategy Inc., Mr. Saylor's company.

For the nation's nonprofits, it's shaping up to be a year of shrinking pledges and broken promises. From Harvard University to the Cheetah Conservation Fund, donors who made pledges at the height of the boom are now delaying or even canceling them. The New Schools Venture Fund, which promotes education projects, says about $1 million in promised gifts have been adjusted or postponed. Stanford recently saw one stock pledge, initially valued at $1 million, drop nearly 90%. And don't look for Texas-size grants from the Austin Entrepreneurs Foundation: Seven of the 60 companies that contributed stock to it have gone out of business.

While some of this is typical during an economic downturn, the problem threatens to be worse this time because so much charitable giving over the past decade has been based on stock. Indeed, to some degree charities got caught up in the same frenzy over IPOs, and dot-com riches that everyone else did. Not only did they aggressively pursue newly minted (and, now, former) millionaires, but non-profits across the country launched a variety of innovative efforts to encourage donations in stock.

"We hadn't realized what could happen," says Jack Wiant, of the Museum of Contemporary Art in Los Angeles, "and we need to deal with it." Mr. Wiant, the museum's chief financial officer, says it received a "substantial" gift of restricted stock last summer—but it lost more than half its value before SEC rules permitted the institution to sell. (Some shares owned by insiders must be held for a certain amount of time.) He adds that the museum is now revising some of its donation rules to ward off similar situations in the future.

What's the impact of all this? Some nonprofits have plenty of time and resources to make up for shortfalls. But others big and small are already feeling the hit, from the Community Foundation Servicing Boulder County, Colo., (it has shelved a planned back-office support center for local charities) to the University of Washington. It had been promised a $2 million donation from Internet executive Ravi Desai to fund new fellowships and a poets-in-residence program starting last fall. The contribution so far? $6,700.

DEAD POETS SOCIETY

"We're in negotiations," says David Wu, the university's acting vice president for development. Mr. Desai, in a statement, says he recently scheduled a conference call to finalize the agreement.

And, for now at least, there will be no 16,000-acre addition to the Cheetah Conservation Fund's sanctuary in Namibia. The reason: In November, a wealthy Canadian, who was heavily invested in U.S. stocks, called to say he was "unable to fulfill" his $500,000 pledge, says Vance Martin, president of the fund.

All this comes after a decade of windfalls for American philanthropies. One after another used the bull market as a chance to launch campaigns of unprecedented scope. It worked: Overall, the IRS recorded $109.2 billion in donations to charity on itemized returns in 1998—more than double the total from a decade earlier.

But what a difference a few months of economic jitters can make. The problem, says Charles Collier, Harvard's senior philanthropic adviser, is that some donors have large concentrations of wealth in a single security that has plunged in value. He cites a New York man who pledged $250,000 to Harvard, due in December: "Now it's on slow bleed. He's going to wait and see if he can make it by the fall."

While some donors have tried to prepare charities in advance for the bad news, the Austin Entrepreneurs Foundation didn't have a clue about failed pledges from several companies until reading about their demise in the newspaper. Follow-up phone calls weren't encouraging: "They said, 'Yeah, that's right we're gone, the stock's useless,'" says executive director Paula Fracasso.

In all, seven of the Austin foundation's corporate donors have gone under—including Garden.com, One Card, Baleo, All.Com and WebTaggers—leaving the charity holding worthless pre-IPO stock. And three others recently asked to postpone donations they promised last year, because they are devaluing the price of stock options they pledged. (In these cases, the foundation gets options, and then sells the stock as soon as it is legally possible.) The bottom line? The foundation, founded in 1999 to help local community groups, thought it would have given away $300,000 to $500,000 by now. Instead it has been able to give out only $150,000.

Some donors, of course, say they feel bad about bailing and are looking to make up the gap. "You can't give what you don't have," says Dave Kansas, editor of TheStreet.com, who has restructured several gifts he promised when his company's stock was riding high, including a five-year, $38,000 endowment to a college in Indiana. He made the first payment, he says, but not the second, promising to make it up this year. "A lot of people who got money too fast don't understand what it means to commit to giving it away," he says.

MAKING UP THE DIFFERENCE

William Nobrega, an Atlanta venture capitalist, pledged 30,000 shares of an Internet firm's pre-IPO stock to his local United Way. But because of market conditions, the company has delayed its offering, which delays cashing in the gift. "We'd all be naive to think the bubble wouldn't pop," says Mr. Nobrega, who promises to make up the difference, up to $500,000.

But not all donors can, or will, do that. At Stanford University, 1990 alumnus Michael Wolfe pledged stock, then valued at $1 million. Since then, the stock tanked—reducing the actual gift to just over $100,000. "It was a stock gift, not a cash gift, and that's it," says Mr. Wolfe, an executive at onetime highflier Kana Communications Inc. Mr.

Wolfe says he still intends to make future gifts to his alma mater.

New York-based fund-raising consultant Henry Goldstein says he's simply "lighting a candle and hoping for the best" on three "seven-figure" pledges to healthcare and educational institutions. They're overdue because the stock that was pledged has declined in value. "We aren't pushing them to give us the reduced-value stock, and we're not asking them to make it up in cash, he says. "We think they'll rebound."

These complications come on top of a slowdown in giving that began to hit some charities late last year. And charities will face new obstacles if the Bush Administration succeeds in rolling back estate taxes, which could reduce incentives for some large gifts (alternative measures to boost donations are also being considered).

The huge growth in so-called community foundations has also fueled the problems. The appeal of these groups, whose number has more than doubled in the last decade, is that they allow people to make donations in stock, and take the tax write-off immediately—deciding even years later where they want the money to go. Indeed, the percentage of charitable gifts on itemized returns that are "noncash" has more than doubled, to 27% of all U.S. contributions in 1998, compared with 13% a decade earlier. At Atlanta's United Way, about 30% of last year's major gifts were in stock, about, double the portion five years earlier.

THE PROBLEM WITH STOCK

Stock gifts can be the most vulnerable to an economic downturn, says Peter Dobkin Hall, a lecturer in public policy at Harvard. "With the new money, so much of the big giving is tax-driven. It's not driven by commitment, it's driven by self-interest." But cash gifts can be affected as well: Mr. Hall points to his own Episcopal Church in New Haven, Conn., where pledge fulfillment is down about 10% this year to $125,000.

Nonprofits have been known to fight back. In one case, Chicago's Museum of Contemporary Art sued a former chairman for failing to honor a $5 million pledge. The case was later settled when the chairman's widow, Camille Oliver- Hoffman, agreed to give the museum two paintings in lieu of the cash donation.

"There hasn't been much friction this time around. "He's fulfilled his commitment," says Julia Hartung, Stanford's director of class giving, of Mr. Wolfe's stock donation, now valued at nearly $900,000 less than when he made his pledge. As for the plunge in value: "Stanford has to stomach that."

If the economy continues to slow, taking the high road could get harder. Indeed, some charities have already begun to roll out new approaches to cope with the slowing market, from encouraging couples to put them on wedding registries to asking aging Baby Boomers to write them into their wills.

But some would-be philanthropists remain optimistic about fulfilling their past pledges. In a statement, Micro Strategy's Mr. Saylor says he is "more enthusiastic than ever" about his idea of an online university. But, noting the company's past "financial difficulties," a spokesman for Micro Strategy says there isn't, anything else to say about the plan for now.

THE SHRINKING PLEDGE

Note from Professor Carr: After reading this *Wall Street Journal* article, ask yourself the following questions (remember, doing this will be good practice for the exam!):

1. Are these promises/pledges of a gift enforceable contracts?
2. If not, does/would the doctrine of *promissory estoppel* come to the rescue of these charities?
3. If you headed up one of these charities, and a donor "backed out", how would you handle it? What would you do? Under what circumstances would you resort to the legal system to solve that disagreement?

117 Promissory Estoppel

An Insurance Example

A FIERCE FIRE SWEPT through Dana and Derek Andreason's house in Utah, seriously damaging it. The good news was that agents for Aetna Casualty promptly visited the Andreasons and helped them through the crisis. The agents reassured the couple that all of the damage was covered by their insurance, instructed them on which things to simply throw out and helped them choose materials for repairing other items. The bad news was that the agents were wrong: the Andreason's policy had expired six weeks before the fire. When Derek Andreason presented a bill for $41,957 worth of meticulously itemized work that he had done under the agents' supervision, Aetna refused to pay.

The Andreasons sued—but not for breach of contract. There *was* no contract, that was exactly the problem. The insurance contract had expired. So they sued Aetna under the legal theory of promissory estoppels: Even when there is no contract, a plaintiff may use promissory estoppel to enforce the defendant's promise if he can show that

- the defendant made a promise knowing that the plaintiff would likely rely on it,
- the plaintiff did rely on the promise, and
- the only way to avoid injustice is to enforce the promise.

A Utah Court of Appeals ruled in favor of the Andreasons (Andreason v. Aetna, 848, P.2d 171 (1993)).

118 Contract Defenses Outline

Study Outline

*****Note that in this textbook at pages 371–421 I have inserted several newspaper articles, supplementary materials, misc. documents, etc. that relate to this material. These materials are required reading, and, are also fair game for the exam.**

*****Make *sure* that you also do the sample practice problems posted on Blackboard ("Contract Defenses -- Practice Problems") as it will help you master this material, test you to see if you "really" know and understand it, etc. You can expect similar problems to be on the exam.**

I. Effect of the Defenses Discussed Below

A. Contracts induced by fraud, duress, mistake, undue influence, etc. are ***voidable*** at the option of the injured party. This means that the victim can rescind (or cancel) the contract. When this occurs, the contract is "unwound" and both parties return anything which he or she received from the other party

II. Fraudulent Misrepresentation (i.e., Fraud)

A. Elements (plaintiff must prove all five of the below elements):

1. An untrue assertion of a ***past or existing fact*** must have been made by the defendant;
   a) Assertion re: a future event – is not enough/is not fraud
   b) Active lie/concealment -- obviously constitutes fraud and is probably the most common type of fraud in the business world
      (1) But what about passive silence (e.g., nondisclosure; the failure to offer or volunteer information)? Is that a fraud?
         (a) Traditional view: not enough/was not fraud
         (b) Modern view: is enough/is fraud
   c) Problem area for this element: what about a statement of opinion (e.g., "puffing" or sales talk) vs. statements of fact? Is that a fraud?
      (1) General Rule: statements of opinion are usually <u>not</u> actionable because they are not a "statement of a past or existing fact"
      (2) Exceptions to the general rule:

(a) A relationship of trust and confidence exists between the parties
(b) The relying party is unusually susceptible/vulnerable
(c) The relying party reasonably believes that the person on whose opinion he is relying has superior skill or judgment

2. The fact asserted must have been ***material*** (vs. minor or insignificant);
3. The fraudulent assertion must also have been "knowingly" made by the defendant to the victim/other party/plaintiff <u>and</u> with the "intent to deceive"
   a) "Knowingly" -- means that the defendant knew that the statement he made was false, knew that he had no basis for making the statement, ***<u>or,</u>*** he made the statement without being confident that it was true
   b) Intent to deceive – is not the same thing as an innocent mistake; it pretty much means what it says/implies -- you "knowingly" (see above) intended to dupe somebody
4. The complaining party must have entered into the contract because of his ***reasonable and justifiable reliance*** on the assertion (or failure to disclose); ***<u>AND</u>***
   a) Problem area for this element: The relying party's failure to investigate the accuracy of the assertion
      (1) Traditional approach: the reliance of a person who did not attempt to discover readily discoverable facts was not justifiable
      (2) Modern approach: has decreased the complaining party's duty to investigate and has instead placed a greater degree of accountability on the person who makes the assertion of fact/failure to disclose
5. The relying/complaining party must have been ***injured or suffered damage***

For some good examples of the above and this defense, see this textbook at pages 371–377; also see/do the related practice problems dealing with fraud posted on my Blackboard; refer also to any class lecture and examples dealing with this defense

III. Mistake

A. Mistake: a belief about a past or existing fact (<u>not</u> a *future* fact/event) that is not in accord with the truth. A mistake is unlike a fraudulent misrepresentation in that the erroneous belief is not the result of the other party's untrue statement

B. Effect of mistake -- depends upon whether the mistake was ***mutual*** or ***unilateral***

1. **Mutual Mistake** -- occurs when *both* parties to a contract have erroneous assumptions about the *same* fact

   a) Elements:
      (1) The mistake related to the same basic assumption on which the contract was made (e.g., the identity, existence, quality, or quantity of the subject matter, as opposed to a mistake about a party's financial ability or market conditions);

(2) The mistake has a ***material*** effect on the agreed-on exchange (e.g., the situation is such that not only would it be unfair to require the complaining party to perform the contract, but the other party has received an unbargained-for advantage); ***AND***

(3) The party adversely affected by the mistake does not bear the risk of the mistake (e.g., buy something "as is" or contracts with a ***conscious awareness*** that he is ignorant or has limited information)

2. **Unilateral Mistake** -- only one of the parties makes a mistake about a basic assumption on which he made the contract

a) Elements:

(1) (The mistake made by the mistaken party must relate to a basic assumption on which the contract was made (e.g., quality, subject matter, quantity, etc.);

(2) The mistake must have had a material effect on the agreed upon exchange;

(3) The mistaken party must not have borne the risk of that mistake (e.g., bought the item "as is" or made his/her decision with a conscious awareness that he/she was ignorant or had limited information); ***and***

(4) The non-mistaken party caused *or* had reason to know of the mistake made by the mistaken party

For some good examples of the above and these defenses, see this textbook at pages 379–391; also see/do the related practice problems dealing with unilateral and mutual mistake posted on Blackboard; refer also to any class lecture and examples dealing with this defense

IV. Duress

A. Nature of duress -- it is the *wrongful coercion* such as physical compulsion, threats of physical, emotional or economic harm, etc.

1. Elements:

a) The contract was induced by an ***improper*** threat; ***AND***

(1) Basically, what constitutes "improper" is a judgment call. However, a threat to file a civil proceeding without a legal basis for doing so would clearly be improper. The threat to institute a criminal prosecution is always improper, even if the person making the threat has good reason for believing that the other person committed a crime

b) The victim had no ***reasonable*** alternative but to enter into or modify the contract

(1) Problem area: what about economic duress (e.g., threatening to breach a contract unless the other side agrees to modify its terms) … is that enough to set aside a contract based on the grounds of duress?

(a) Traditional approach: not enough/not duress

(b) Modern approach: can be enough/is duress if the facts and situation call for it/are egregious enough

For some good examples of the above and this defense, see this textbook at page 393; also see/do the related practice problems dealing with duress posted on my Blackboard; refer also to any class lecture and examples dealing with this defense

V. Undue Influence

A. Nature of undue influence -- it is unfair ***persuasion***, as opposed to coercion (which duress is based on). Comes up often in will contests in probate court

1. Elements:
   a) The relationship between the parties is either one of trust and confidence or one in which the person exercising the persuasion dominates the person being; ***AND***
      (1) Examples: parent-child, husband-wife, lawyer-client, a relationship in which on of the parties holds dominant psychological power over another that is not derived from a confidential relationship, such as a housekeeper caring for an elderly person. Look for a person who is in a position of particular vulnerability
   b) The persuasion is "unfair"
      (1) Here, courts will look at all of the surrounding facts and circumstances and make a judgment call

A common situation where undue influence comes up is kids who ignore their parents or grandparents for years and years, and then when the parent or grandparent dies the kids find out that in the will they were left nothing and most/all of the items in the estate were left to the "kindly neighbor" who came over and talked to the parent/grandparent, kept them company, looked after them, etc. I.e., the kids often try and argue that the neighbor who received everything under the will only got those things because *he/she used "undue influence" over the parent/grandparent.*

For some good examples of the above and this defense, see this textbook at page 395; also see/do the related practice problems dealing with undue influence posted on Blackboard; refer also to any class lecture and examples dealing with this defense

VI. Contractual Capacity – "capacity" means the ability to incur legal obligations and acquire legal rights

A. Effect of Lack of Capacity – makes the contract voidable a the option of the person who lacked it (capacity) … not the other party

B. Minor's Contracts

Note that for purposes of contract law, a "minor" is anyone under 18 (anyone 18 and over is not considered a "minor")

1. Minor's Right to Disaffirm

a) General Rule: a minor can disaffirm any contract he/she enters into

b) Exceptions to the general rule (and when the minor remains liable on the contract):

(1) Statutory exceptions -- contracts involving marriage, agreements to support their children, ***school loans (sorry folks!)***, life and medical insurance contracts, contracts for transportation by common carriers, sports contacts, contracts to employ a child actor, etc.

(2) Emancipated minor -- emancipation is the termination of a parent's right to control a child and receive services and wages from him. Emancipated minors are persons 18 years of age or under and married or they have received a declaration of emancipation from the court (i.e., a court order is required for a minor to become emancipated). In most jurisdictions, emancipated minors cannot disaffirm a contract

(3) Necessities -- a "necessity" is something that is essential for the minor's continued existence and general welfare that has not been provided by the minor's parents or guardian. Typical examples include food, clothing, shelter, medical care, tools of the minor's trade, and basic educational or vocational training. Beyond that, it will depend upon the facts and circumstances of each case (e.g., the minor's age, station in life, and personal circumstances)

(a) Under the necessity exception, the minor is liable not for the contract price of the necessity, but the ***reasonable value*** (i.e., this is quasi-contract and quasi contract value which we studied in an earlier class) of the item in question (note that the contract price and the quasi contract value/price may be the same or different!)

2. Time of disaffirmance (<u>when</u> can a minor cancel a contract that he/she entered into??)

a) Contract can be disaffirmed by the minor as soon as it is formed

b) Note: the minor's power to cancel the contract does not automatically end upon reaching the age of majority. In most jurisdictions, the minor can still disaffirm the contract within a ***reasonable time after reaching the age of majority***

3. Ratification -- after the minor reaches majority, he can ratify (or affirm) the contract. If he elects to do so, he is bound and cannot later change his mind and try to disaffirm the contract

a) Requirements for ratification -- there are no formal requirements. It can either be express (oral or written) or implied (e.g., by conduct, continued performance by the minor of his part of the contract, etc.)

4. Duty to return consideration upon disaffirmance

a) If neither party has performed or exchanged the agreed upon consideration, the parties' relationship will simply be canceled by the disaffirmance. But if something has been exchanged, both parties must return to the other any consideration that the other has given. If the minor is unable to return any consideration given to him by the adult, most states will still permit him to disaffirm the contract. Thus, adults beware!!

5. Must the disaffirming minor make restitution if he/she damaged or destroyed the subject matter of the contract (e.g., a car)?
   a) Situation: if the consideration given by the adult to the minor has been lost, damaged, destroyed or simply depreciated in value as a result of the minor's use, must the minor make restitution to the adult for the loss?
      (1) The majority of states say no!
      (2) A minority of states say yes

6. Effect of a minor's misrepresentation of age (what happens when a minor lies when entering into a contract – e.g., used a fake I.D.??)
   a) Traditional approach: A minor's misrepresentation of his age does *not* affect his right to disaffirm the contract and/or create any obligation to reimburse the adult for damages or pay for the benefits received
   b) Modern approach: today, in many states, a minor who misrepresents his age will be ***estopped*** (i.e., barred) from asserting his minor status as a defense to the enforcement of a contract

For some good examples of the above and this defense, see this textbook at pages 397–399; also see/do the related practice problems dealing with contracts with minors posted on Blackboard; refer also to any class lecture and examples relating to this defense

C. Contracts of Intoxicated Persons

1. Intoxication and Capacity
   a) Intoxication can be by alcohol and/or drugs
      (1) An example – how many business deals do you think get done on a golf course where the parties are having a fair bit to drink along the way??!
   b) Intoxication is a ground for lack of capacity only when it is so extreme that the person is unable to understand the nature of the business at hand; also, the non-intoxicated person must know or have reason to know of the other party's intoxicated state in order for this defense to work
   c) The rules governing the capacity of intoxicated person are very similar to those applied to mentally incapacitated persons (see below). However, in practice, courts have generally been less sympathetic to intoxicated persons than minors or mentally incapacitated persons and it is rare for a person to actually escape his contractual obligations on the ground of intoxication

For some good examples of the above and this defense, see/do the related practice problems dealing with contracts with intoxicated persons posted on Blackboard; refer also to any class lecture and examples dealing with this defense

D. Capacity of Mentally Impaired Persons

1. Test for mental incapacity
   a) Note at the outset that mental incapacity encompasses many things: mental illness, brain damage, retardation, senility, etc. Also note that a person can suffer from a mental illness or defect and still have the legal capacity to contract
   b) Test -- is a ***cognitive*** one. Under the test usually employed by most courts, courts will ask whether the person had "sufficient mental capacity to understand the nature and effect of the contract"
      (1) Criticism of this test -- it does not take into account the fact that a person suffering from a mental illness or defect may be unable to ***control*** his conduct
      (2) *Restatement of Contracts* test -- a person's contracts are voidable if he is unable to ***act*** in a reasonable manner in relation to the transaction ***and*** the other party has reason to know of his condition
         (a) This is an alternative test to the above – cognitive test that a minority of courts sometimes use
2. The right to disaffirm
   a) If contract is voidable, only the person who lacked capacity at the time the contract was made (i.e., the mentally incapacitated person) has the right to disaffirm the contract
   b) A person formerly incapacitated can ratify a contact if he regains his capacity. Thus if he regains his capacity and wants to disaffirm the contract, he must do so within a reasonable time, or he will be deemed to have ratified it
   c) As with disaffirming minors, a person disaffirming a contract on the basis of mental incapacity must return any consideration given by the other party that remains in his possession
   d) A mentally incapacitated person is also liable for the reasonable value of necessities in the same manner as are minors (see above)

For some good examples of the above and this defense, see/do the related practice problems dealing with contracts with incapacitated persons posted on Blackboard; refer also to any class lecture and examples relating to this defense

VII. Legality

A. For a contract to be valid and enforceable, it must also be formed for a legal purpose, not contrary to a statute, not violate public policy, etc.

1. Contracts Contrary to Statute:
   a) Usury/Usurious contracts -- means to charge excessive interest on a loan
      (1) Effect of a usurious loan -- some states allows the lender to recover only the principal and *legal rate* of interest (not the usurious rate charged), In California, for example, the legal rate of interest for many transactions is usually 10%; other states will allow the lender to *only* recover the principal as a penalty for trying to charge usurious interest (and not even the legal rate of interest!!)
         (a) Obviously, in many states, "lenders" such as credit card companies are exempt from the normal rules of usury that the rest of us have to live and

play by (and they often accomplish this through very aggressive lobbying campaigns before Congress and/or their state legislatures) – otherwise, how do you think it is that credit card companies can charge you such high interest rates on your credit card bill?!!

For some good examples of the above and this defense, see this textbook at pages 401–407; also see/do the related practice problems dealing with usurious contracts posted on Blackboard; refer also to any class lecture and examples dealing with this defense

b) Gambling Contracts (unless, of course, in states that have legalized the type of gambling at issue – e.g., Vegas – such contracts would be enforceable in that state)
   (1) Question: Virtually any and all contracts we enter into have some aspect of risk or "gamble" associated with them, right? But does that make them unenforceable "gambling contracts" according to this defense?
   (2) Answer -- No. The hallmark of a wager or a gambling contact for purposes of this defense and contract law is that neither party has any financial stake or interest in the uncertain event except for the stake that he/she has created by making the bet

For some good examples of the above and this defense, see this textbook at page 407; also see/do the related practice problems dealing with contracts with gambling contracts posted on my Blackboard; refer also to any class lecture and examples dealing with this defense

c) Contract Covered by Certain Licensing Statutes – this defense comes up for people such as doctors, attorneys, stockbrokers, accountants, real estate agents, engineers, architects, contractors, a hair stylist, masseuse, etc. who are required by statute to get some kind of a license or permit to practice their trade/profession and they fail to do so
   (1) Note the protection of public statutes vs. revenue raising statutes distinction
      (a) If the licensing statute in question is designed/intended to make certain people obtain a license in order to protect the public or the public's safety/welfare, the contract at issue will be illegal and unenforceable
         (i) The lesson to be learned here? If this applies to you, and, for example, you get into a dispute with a client over a bill, then you better make darn sure you have your license/permit and have complied with the relevant statute, or the client will be able to raise this defense against you as a bar to the enforcement of your claim/fees against the client!!
      (b) If the latter (i.e., the main purposes of the licensing statute is to raise revenue), the contract will probably still be enforceable
      (c) Example: If Spencer, a first-year law students, agrees to draft a will for Rowen for a fee of $500, Spencer could NOT enforce the agreement and collect the fee because he is not licensed to practice law (and the requirement to make people obtain a license to practice law is designed to protect the public). But suppose that Spencer IS a licensed and practicing attorney in his state but forgot to ay his annual renewal/registration fee to keep

his law license current. In that case, Spencer could probably enforce his agreement with Rowen as there is no compelling public interest or reason for inflicting such a hardship on Spencer (also, the renewal/registration fee requirement for Spencer would be to primarily raise revenue for the state bar).

(d) Note: Whether a licensing statute is a regulatory (public protection) statute or a revenue raising statute depends on the intent of the legislature, which, may/is sometimes clear and sometimes not.

For some good examples of the above and this defense, see this textbook at pages 407–410; also see/do the related practice problems dealing with contracts covered by licensing statutes posted on Blackboard; refer also to any class lecture and examples dealing with this defense

2. Contracts Contrary to Public Policy:

For two good and interesting introductory articles that highlight contracts that are contrary to public policy, see this textbook at pages 411–414

a) Agreements/Contracts to commit a crime/the purpose of which violates the law (i.e., Illegal Contracts)

(1) Where BOTH parties are aware that their contact is illegal, courts, for obvious public policy reasons, will not enforce the agreement, or, allow either party to recover/get back what they parted with

(2) What about ignorance of the law? Does that matter?

(a) If both of the parties to the contract are ignorant of the fact that their contract is illegal, courts will not permit them to enforce the agreement, but will allow them to recover/get back what they parted with

(b) If one party knows the contract is illegal and the other does not, then as long as the illegality is of a relatively minor character (e.g., does not involve an immoral act or pose a serious threat to the public), <u>and</u>, the innocent party pulls out of the contract before learning of the illegality, he/she can sometimes recover against the other party for any breach of that agreement

For some good examples of the above and this defense, see, e.g., the "Gambling Contracts" example in this textbook at page 407; also see/do the related practice problems dealing with illegal contracts posted on Blackboard; refer also to any class lecture and examples dealing with this defense

b) Contracts in Restraint of Trade or Competition (e.g., a contract or covenant not to compete)

(1) Such contracts are unenforceable unless they are "reasonable" in scope, time, geographic area, serve a legitimate business interest, etc.

For some good examples of the above and this defense, see this textbook at pages 415–418; also see/do the related practice problems dealing with contracts in restraint of trade posted on my Blackboard; refer also to any class lecture and examples dealing with this defense

c) Contracts the Contain Overbroad Exculpatory Clauses/Release From Liability Clauses/ Waiver from Liability Clauses
   (1) General Rule: such clauses are unenforceable if …
      (a) They attempt to exclude an intentional tort (e.g., assault, battery, fraud, etc.) **<u>or</u>** gross negligence;
      (i) (Note that gross negligence is worse and far different than the "ordinary" negligence we studied earlier in connection with Torts. Remember … "gross negligence" is different than "ordinary negligence". A good example of "gross negligence", which by its very name implies more egregious conduct/carelessness than ordinary negligence, would be a nightclub owner not having fire sprinklers and accessible fire exits in his club and then allowing a band to come in and use fire works during the band's performance. An example of "ordinary negligence" would be that same nightclub owner failing to repair a small crack in the floor of his or her club that a customer/patron in turn trips on or over and injures his or her ankle. Can you see/feel/sense the difference between the two??
      (b) The affected activity is an important public interest or an important public policy is involved (e.g., the business at issue involves a public utility, bank, common carrier, etc.);
      (c) The parties have greatly unequal bargaining power; <u>and/or</u>
      (d) The clause is not clearly written and/or visible

For some good examples of the above and this defense, see/do the related practice problems dealing with contracts with exculpatory clauses posted on Blackboard; refer also to any class lecture and examples dealing with this defense

d) Unconscionable Contracts/Clauses (sometimes also called/referred to as "Contracts of Adhesion")
   (1) Where the contract (or some of its terms) are so harsh, oppressive, unintelligible, contains inconspicuous print, etc., and/or one of the parties to the contract was legitimately victimized (e.g., he/she could not read, was not given the opportunity to read the contract or ask questions, was under severe duress in signing the contract, an emergency gave rise to the signing the contract, etc.), the questionable part of the contract or possibly even the entire contract may be declared by a court to be unconscionable and therefore, unenforceable

For some good examples of the above and this defense, see/do the related practice problems dealing with unconscionable contracts posted on Blackboard; refer also to any class lecture and examples dealing with this defense

***Again, folks, I encourage you to do the practice problems on "Contract Defenses" that I have posted on Blackboard. You may feel that you know/understand the above material, and, you may. But you also may not. So, be safe and do these practice problems. Many of them involve the <u>application</u> of the above concepts and that is a great way to learn (the only way, really) to see if you really do know and understand this material. – Prof. Carr**

119 Writing Requirements

Study Outline

The following is an excellent introductory example of why we have the Statute of Frauds and why you need to "get it in writing"... ☺

Twenty-seven years after the release of the 1969 hippie-biker film Easy Rider (which made famous the Steppenwolf song Born to Be Wild, played while a group of young hairs on motorcycles roared side by side cross country), the two lead actors, Dennis Hopper and Peter Fonda, were involved in a lawsuit over how the profits should be divided and who should get credit for creating this classic film. In keeping with the hippie themes of free love and drugs, the actors never wrote down the terms of their profit-sharing agreement. While Peter Fonda told the Wall Street Journal that he has an "extraordinarily accurate memory," the irony is that the lawsuit could have been avoided entirely if Hopper and Fonda had simply used common sense and written down on paper the agreed-upon split and credits.

Source: "Hey, Man, See you In Court: 'Easy Rider' Gets a New Epilogue," *Wall Street Journal*, Feb. 9, 1996 at A1.

I. The Statute of Frauds

A. Enacted in 1677. It states that certain contracts are so important that they *must* be in writing and signed by the party to be charged in order to be enforceable. If a contact falls within the Statute of Frauds ("SOF") and it is not in writing, it is unenforceable! This means that if the person you seek to enforce the contract against decides to honor the contract and perform under it, then "it's all good" and he/she can do so. But.... if they decide NOT to honor it, you are out of luck/there is nothing you can do – the contract cannot be enforced against that person (subject to the promissory estoppel exception doctrine – see below)

B. Contracts that fall within the Statute of Frauds (and therefore must be in writing and signed by the person charged in order to be enforceable; think of the Statute of Frauds as another possible defense to the enforcement of a contract):

1. Collateral contracts in which a person promises to perform the obligation of another person (i.e., a guaranty)
   a) A collateral contract is one in which one person (the guarantor) agrees to pay the debt or obligation that a second person (the principal debtor) owes to a third person (the obligee) if

the principal debtor fails to perform. In a collateral contact, the guarantor promises to pay ***only if*** the principal debtor fails to do so

(1) E.g., -- when a bank asks your parents to guaranty a loan you take out for a car or home, and that guaranty requires them to pay the bill if you don't ... well ... that normally has to be in writing to be enforceable against them!

2. Contracts that create or transfer an ownership interest in real property
   a) E.g. -- if I agree to sell you my house (which includes, of course, the dirt under it), then that contract must be in writing in order to be enforceable against me!

3. Contracts that by their terms cannot possibly be performed within one (1) year from the date of their formation
   a) Note: the mere fact that performance is unlikely to be completed within a year does not bring the contract within the SOF. If there is any possibility, however remote, that the contract can be performed within a year, the SOF does not apply and the contract need not be in writing. It is only if the contract ***cannot*** possibly be performed within a year does it fall within the SOF
   b) Computing the one year time period
      (1) Start counting from the day the contract comes into existence/is formed, not the date when performance under the contract begins

4. Contract for the ***sale of goods*** in the amount of $500 or more [UCC 2-201]
   a) E.g. – the sale of a box of baseball cards (which is a "good") valued at $510.00 must be in writing to be enforceable

5. Contract in Which Marriage is the Consideration
   a) Where one party's promise is given in exchange for marriage or the promise to marry on the part of the other party, the SOF applies and the promise must be in writing. The typical example of this type of an agreement is a *prenuptial agreement*

6. Promise of an Executor or an Administrator of an Estate to Personally Pay a Decedent's Debt
   a) If an executor or administrator promises to pay the decedent's debt out of the estates funds, the SOF does not apply and a writing is not required. However, if he promises to pay out of his own *personal* funds, it must be in writing or it is not enforceable

For some good examples of the above and these rules, see/do the related practice problems dealing with the Statute of Frauds posted on Blackboard; refer also to any class lecture and examples dealing with the Statute of Frauds

II. Meeting the Requirements of the Statute of Frauds

A. Nature of writing required (when we say "it has to be in writing" what does that mean??)

1. Memorandum
   a) The entire contract need not be in writing, but some type of "***memorandum***" of the parties' agreement is required. The memorandum must provide written evidence that a contract was made
      (1) A memorandum can be in virtually any form (e.g., on the back of a napkin can be enough, the back of an envelope, a yellow note pad, etc.)
   b) Contents of the memorandum (what does it have to say/address??)
      (1) Essential terms of the contract are required
      (2) Identity of the parties is required
      (3) Subject matter of the contract must be identified with reasonable certainty (especially true with respect to contracts involving real estate)
         (a) Contents of the memorandum under the UCC -- more flexible and a looser standard than the traditional approach. UCC 2-201 states that the writing must be sufficient to indicate that a contract for sale has been made between the parties, but a writing can be sufficient even if it omits or incorrectly states a term agreed on. However, the memorandum is not enforceable for more than the quantity of goods stated in the memorandum. Thus, a writing that does not indicate the ***quantity*** of goods to be sold would ***not*** satisfy the UCC's writing requirement
      (4) The memorandum must be signed by the ***party to be charged*** or his authorized agent

Again, for some good examples of the above and these rules, see this textbook at pages 431, and 435–436; also see/do the related practice problems dealing with the Statute of Frauds posted on Blackboard; refer also to any class lecture and examples dealing with the Statute of Frauds

III. Promissory Estoppel and the Statute of Frauds

A. Some states provide that when one of the parties would suffer serious losses because of his reliance on an oral contract, the other party is ***estopped*** from raising the SOF as a defense
   1. Policy: The SOF, which is designed to prevent injustice, should not be allowed to work an injustice
   2. However, the use of promissory estoppel as a means of circumventing the SOF is controversial. Some courts feel that the promissory estoppel doctrine/exception essentially "eats up" the rule of the SOF

IV. The Parol Evidence Rule

Do not worry about this material in your book for the exam. It's long and complicated materials, and, we simply do not have time to cover it.

*****Again, folks, I encourage you to do the practice problems on "Contract Defenses" that I have posted on Blackboard. You may feel that you know/understand the above material, and, you may. But you also may not. So, be safe and do these practice problems. Many of them involve the <u>application</u> of the above concepts and that is a great way to learn (the only way, really) to see if you really do know and understand this material. – Prof. Carr**

120 Auto Auctions May End Up Costing You Plenty[1]

By H. Dennis Beaver

[Fraud/Non-Disclosure]

HAVE YOU HEARD about the huge savings possible on a used car if you buy one from an auto auction? Well, it's true. You can save thousands of dollars. But you can also lose your shirt, which is what almost happened to Todd, a client of mine.

"I wanted to buy a used Lexus and a friend told me about a weekly car auction in Los Angeles. She bought a car there and saved a lot of money.

"So I drove down there in January of this year and looked at the cars before the auction began. I spotted what seemed to be a nice clean 1990 Lexus with only 51,000 miles.

"When they announced the car, things then moved very fast. It was like a cattle auction, no kidding," he said. "At most three minutes elapsed between the car being called and the deal closing.

"During this time the auctioneer said the vehicle was a recovered theft and was offered 'As Is.'

"Bidding was opened at $13,000, and then other bids pushed the price to $16,500. I offered $16,800 and got the car. Later I found out that there were what are known as 'jumpers' working there. These are people who literally jump up and shout out higher bids. But the average consumer doesn't know that and gets caught up in the whole thing," Todd explained.

"After registration fees and taxes—bringing the price up to a total of $18,000—I drove off in my car, a happy customer ... or so I thought."

And Todd was content with the deal, until he got home and found that the spare tire was missing along with the jack, not to mention the air filter. But for the price he paid, this was just a little annoyance. However, within a few months the Lexus needed a lot of work.

Attempting to "save money," Todd's first mistake was in not taking the car to a Lexus dealership, but to a shop that worked on foreign cars. "I wound up dropping almost $2,000 in repair costs and then decided that I just had to sell it," he told me.

In August he sold the car to Chuck for $20,000. When due for regular service, Chuck took it in to a Lexus dealer. That was when the full scope of what had actually happened to this vehicle became known.

"Within an hour of dropping the car off, the service manager was on the phone to me and said that he had some very disturbing news," Chuck said. "The odometer showed 64,000 miles, but according to the Lexus National Service Records, this car had 63,000 miles on it in November of 1994.

1 **Note from Professor Carr: This is a good example of how fraud can come of, how and why it is a defense to the enforcement of a contract (i.e., how it will allow an injured party to cancel, rescind/"unwind" such an agreement or contract).**

Recall that Todd purchased the vehicle at the auction in January of 1996 and at that time the odometer read 51,000.

"The service manager explained that it was obvious someone had tampered with the odometer because of the way it was sitting in the dash. The Lexus odometer is designed in such a way that it will just not fit back in correctly if it's been tampered with. This would be obvious to anyone in the business of selling used cars."

Chuck insisted upon a refund. Todd contacted the auto auction and they played the well-known game of, "We'll get back to you."

When I called the auto auction, the games stopped.

Their attorney first hid behind the words "As Is" on the contract, maintaining that the legally required mileage statement was "accurate to the best of our knowledge." But what about the little problem of the odometer sitting in the dash in a suspicious manner?

"After all," I pointed out, "your client is in the business of selling cars. It had a duty to at least visually examine this Lexus to see if the odometer appeared to have been tampered with. Had it done so, this entire mess would never have occurred. They could have still sold the car. But the words 'Unknown Mileage' would have appeared on the disclosure statement. So, how about a refund and we all go away?"

Within a week the auto auction agreed to buy the car from Chuck for precisely what he had paid for it.

And Todd's advice to anyone thinking of buying a car at auction? "It's not what I thought it would be. This had been a real eye-opener. I didn't have a clue and thought that I'd save a lot of money on a good car. I nearly wound up losing $20,000."

121 Stambovsky v. Ackley[1]

572 N.Y. S.2d 672 (N.Y. Sup. Ct. Div. 1991)

[Fraud]

NONDISCLOSURE CAN ALSO be the equivalent of an assertion of fact. Nondisclosure differs from concealment in that concealment involves the active hiding of a fact, while nondisclosure is the failure to volunteer information. Disclosure of a fact—even a fact that will harm the speaker's bargaining position—is required in a number of situations, such as when the person has already offered *some* information but further information is needed to give the other party an accurate picture, or when there is a relationship of trust and confidence between the parties. In recent years, courts and legislatures have tended to impose a duty to disclose when a party has access to information that is not readily available to the other party. This is consistent with modern contract law's emphasis on influencing ethical standards of conduct and achieving fair results. Transactions involving the sale of real estate are among the most common situations in which this duty to disclose arises. Most states now hold that a seller who knows about a latent (hidden) defect that materially affects the value of the property he is selling has the obligation to speak up about this defect. *Stambovsky v. Ackley*, which follows, involves an interesting application of the duty to disclose in the context of a sale of real estate.

Stambovsky v. Ackley *572 N.Y.S.2d 672 (N.Y. Sup. Ct. App. Div. 1991)*[2]

Jeffrey Stambovsky, a resident of New York City, contracted to purchase a house in the Village of Nyack, New York, from Helen Ackley. The house was widely reputed to be possessed by poltergeists, which Ackley and members of her family had reportedly seen. Ackley did not tell Stambovsky about the poltergeists before he bought the house. When Stambovsky learned of the house's reputation, however, he promptly commenced this action for rescission. The trial court dismissed his complaint, and Stambovsky appealed.

Rubin, Justice The unusual facts of this case clearly warrant a grant of equitable relief to the buyer who, as a resident of New York City, cannot be expected to have any familiarity with the folklore of the Village of Nyack. Not being a "local," Stambovsky could not readily learn that the home he had contracted to purchase is haunted. Whether the source of the spectral apparitions seen by Ackley are parapsychic or psychogenic, having reported their presence in both a national publication (*Reader's Digest*) and the local press (in 1977 and 1982, respectively), Ackley is estopped to deny their existence and, as a matter of law, the house is haunted. More to the point, however, no divination is required to conclude that it is Ackley's promotional efforts in publicizing her close encounters

1 **Note from Professor Carr: This is the Stambovsky (or haunted house) case. Another good example of how a fraud can come up.**

with these spirits which fostered the home's reputation in the community. In 1989, the house was included in a five-home walking tour of Nyack and described in a November 27th newspaper article as a "riverfront Victorian (with ghost)." The impact of the reputation thus created goes to the very essence of the bargain between the parties, greatly impairing both the value of the property and its potential for resale.

[The court discussed the fact that New York law does not recognize a remedy for damages incurred as a result of the seller's mere silence, applying instead the doctrine of caveat emptor. The court then proceeded to discuss the availability of rescission.]

From the perspective of a person in the position of the plaintiff, a very practical problem arises with respect to the discovery of a paranormal phenomenon: "Who you gonna call?" as the title song to the movie *Ghostbusters* asks. Applying the strict rule of *caveat emptor* to a contract involving a house possessed by poltergeists conjures up visions of a psychic or medium routinely accompanying the structural engineer and Terminix man on an inspection of every home subject to a contract of sale. The doctrine of *caveat emptor* requires that a buyer act prudently to assess the fitness and value of his purchase. It should be apparent, however, that the most meticulous inspection and the search would not reveal the presence of poltergeists at the premises or unearth the property's ghoulish reputation in the community. Therefore, there is no sound policy reason to deny Stambovsky relief for failing to discover a state of affairs which the most prudent purchaser would not be expected to even contemplate.

Where a condition which has been created by the seller materially impairs the value of the contract and is peculiarly within the knowledge of the seller or unlikely to be discovered by a prudent purchaser exercising due care, nondisclosure constitutes a basis for rescission as a matter of equity. Any other outcome places upon the buyer not merely the obligation to exercise care in his purchase but rather to be omniscient with respect to any fact which may affect the bargain. No practical purpose is served by imposing such a burden upon a purchaser. To the contrary, it encourages predatory business practice and offends the principle that equity will suffer no wrong to be without a remedy.

In the case at bar, Ackley deliberately fostered the public belief that her home was possessed. Having undertaken to inform the public at large to whom she has no legal relationship, about the supernatural occurrences on her property, she may be said to owe no less a duty to her contract vendee. Application of the remedy of rescission is entirely appropriate to relieve the unwitting purchaser from the consequences of a most unnatural bargain.

Judgment modified in favor of Stambovsky, reinstating his action seeking rescission (or cancellation) of the contract

122 Church's New Trial[1]

Attorneys Sue to Reopen Old Priest-Abuse Suits

By Margaret Cronin Fisk

[Fraud]

THE AMERICAN CATHOLIC Church may be vulnerable to a new wave of sexual abuse litigation—from plaintiffs who had previously settled their claims.
A lawsuit recently filed in Sacramento, Calif., accuses the diocese there of fraud, contending that the church fraudulently induced the plaintiffs to settle by falsely telling each of them that he was the sole victim of that particular priest.

Plaintiffs' attorneys in other previously settled cases are also considering reopening some of these lawsuits—complaining that the church failed to live up to agreements to remove the priests from the active ministry or eliminate the priests' contact with children.

Reviving settled lawsuits based on new information is "the logical outgrowth of what we're learning and it's a natural outgrowth of the fraud and deception by the Catholic church," says leading clergy-abuse plaintiffs' attorney Jeffrey Anderson of Minneapolis' Reinhardt & Anderson. "If church officials failed to disclose material information and this led to the settlement, the settlement may be void. If there's a fraud, why should the church benefit from it?"

But defense attorneys for the church warn that judges are unlikely to allow plaintiffs "to take a second bite of the apple," says Patrick Schiltz, interim dean of the University of St. Thomas Law School in Minneapolis, who represented the church in the past. "The massive publicity of the last few weeks, including some of the settlement numbers, has resulted in a lot of people seeking some way to reopen settlements. It's a form of buyer's remorse. But courts across the board are very reluctant to reopen settlement agreements."

A case of fraud?

At the heart of the Sacramento lawsuit is the theory that the church committed fraud and that "fraud vitiates a contract." Says plaintiffs' attorney Kathryn Kohlman Druliner of Sacramento's Law Offices of Kathryn Kohlman Druliner. "If you buy a car and find out that the seller lied to you, you can go back and void the contract." The same is true, she says,

1 **Note from Professor Carr: This article is yet another excellent example of how a fraud can come up. Here, the fraud is alleged to have been committed by the Church when it entered into these settlement agreements. Further, the parties who signed those agreements/contracts are/were the victims of the molestation. They are/will argue that these settlement agreements should be set aside (or rescinded) based on the fraud of the Church (i.e., that they—the victims—would not have signed and entered into these settlement agreements had it not been for the fraud perpetrated by the Church).**

of settlement agreements, if the plaintiff can prove he or she settled based on misinformation by the other side.

Her clients, Michael Beam and Paul Doe, contend they were sexually abused by Father Michael Walsh, that the Diocese of Sacramento knew Walsh was molesting parishioners but was allowed to continue working as a priest and that the diocese represented to each that there were no other victims. Neither Beam nor Doe was a child at the time of the incidents, though the claim does specifically allege Walsh had molested a girl who was under 18. *Beam v. The Roman Catholic Bishop of Sacramento*, No. 02-AS02480. (Sacramento Co. Calif., Super. Ct.) Beam was 18 when he came to Walsh for advice about which of two girlfriends he should continue to pursue. "Walsh drugged him and [Beam] woke up with his face next to Walsh's naked penis." Druliner says. "Walsh tried to talk the plaintiff into fondling his penis." Beam then jumped out of bed and fled Walsh's home. Beam had suppressed the incident for years. Druliner says. When he reported it to the church, "they first sent him to a psychiatrist who labeled him delusional." Subsequently, she contends, church representatives told Beam there had been no other victims, and paid him $25,000 to settle his claim.

Beam was not represented by counsel at that time, Druliner says.

The second incident cited in the new lawsuit occurred in 1985, several years before Beam had lodged his complaint. The plaintiff known as Paul Doe was considering becoming a priest and came to Walsh, who was then a chaplain at a Sacramento hospital. "Father Walsh invited Paul to his home," Druliner says. The first three or four times nothing untoward happened."

The final time, the complaint alleges, Doe came to Walsh's home and he "was drugged unconscious and forcibly sodomized by Walsh." Doe reported this allegation to the police, who investigated and turned it over to the district attorney's office. "The church pressured the prosecution to drop it," Druliner charges. In addition, she contends, the church did not supply any records about Walsh to the prosecutor's office. Doe was 19 at the time of the incident. Walsh was never charged, but Doe went to a lawyer and settled his case for $35,000.

The new lawsuit alleges, among other things, fraud and breach of fiduciary duty. The plaintiffs contend, according to the complaint, "that even though the Diocese knew of Fr. Walsh's sexual predilections, specifically that he was a predator, he was allowed to continue in the Diocese and continued to molest parishioners who were minors and boys under the age of 21 by drugging them."

The plaintiffs were advised by the church officials, the complaint adds, that the plaintiffs "and other parishioners need not worry about Fr. Walsh and that [church officials] would take care of it." But, Druliner says, no action was taken by the church and Walsh continued as an active priest. The church officials, the complaint maintains, "intended plaintiffs should rely on said representations as an inducement to be silent about Walsh, and not to commence litigation."

The statue of limitations does not apply to these plaintiffs because it was "a continuing fraud," Druliner says. "The statute runs from when you discover the lie." Whether this particular lawsuit will prevail, some plaintiffs' attorneys consider the theory that previous settlements with the church can be voided because of misrepresentation compelling. "It's a viable theory, if the agreement was induced based on fraudulent misrepresentation," says Roderick MacLeish of the Boston office of Greenberg Traurig. "It's fraud in the inducement." In addition to convincing plaintiffs to settle quickly for fear they might lose at trial, MacLeish says, plaintiffs might have settled for far less than their cases were worth because they were convinced they were the only victims. "If there were many other complaints, that would enhance the 'value' of the case."

"It's very important to know if it happened before," says plaintiffs' attorney Katherine K. Freberg of Irvine, Calif.'s Freberg & Associates. "It goes to the church's own knowledge and liability. If the church was not truthful, you've absolutely got a case for fraud."

"The church is very vulnerable" to charges of fraud in these settlements, says plaintiffs' attorney Stephen Rubino of Margate, N.J.'s Ross & Rubino. "There have been specific representations made to litigants and myself that it was a single event." Rubino is currently reconsidering some cases he settled in past years. If there is evidence that these representations were fraudulent we'd make an effort to reopen."

The charge of fraud could be used as well, Rubino says, in initiating or reviving cases that were never filed or were filed late, if misrepresentations "convinced the plaintiffs not to file the claim or caused them to file late."

No follow-through?

The church is also vulnerable to charges of fraud and breach of contract in cases that were settled if the church failed to fulfill promises to discipline priests, says MacLeish. MacLeish and his partner, Robert Sherman, represent plaintiffs accusing priests of sexual abuse and have won more than 150 settlements over the past decade.

"In all our cases, we didn't just take the money and run," says MacLeish. The settlement agreements included clauses binding the diocese to "commit to removing the priest from the active ministry and that the priest would have no more access to children." In several cases, he says, the church did not honor these commitments. In particular, MacLeish and attorney Robert Sherman, also of Greenberg Traurig, are considering reopening several lawsuits involving the Rev. Paul Shanley, who was arrested in California on May 2 on charges of raping three children. MacLeish and Sherman have recently sued the Boston archdiocese on behalf of a boy Shanley is alleged to have molested for several years, starting when the child was 6. In the mid-1990s, MacLeish and Sherman settled several lawsuits against the church involving previous incidents where Shanley sexually abused young boys.

There are, however, significant obstacles to reopening these cases. "If plaintiffs are seeking to set aside settlement agreements, they're facing an uphill battle," adds defense attorney Andrew Eisenzimmer of St. Paul, Minn.'s Meier, Kennedy & Quin, who has represented the church in numerous lawsuits. "Courts will not be sympathetic."

Most settlement agreements, Eisenzimmer says, will include language that precludes reopening the action. "Any of us in defense work use boilerplate language in these settlements, whether it's sexual abuse or an auto accident." These agreements include words to the effect that the settlement "is a compromise of a doubtful or disputed claim and not an admission of liability."

They also include waivers on relevant information withheld by ignorance or oversight. "If in discovery, the parties testified that there were no other victims, that may change the analysis," Eisenzimmer says. But these misrepresentations would have to be on the record.

Failure to provide information however, can be used as an element of proof of fraud, says Freberg, who recently won settlements of $5.2 million and $ 1.2 million in separate priest-abuse cases. If during discovery, she says, "you requested the employment files and didn't get them, then it's open season. You have them for fraud based on concealment."

123 Mutual Mistake

A MUTUAL MISTAKE OCCURS when both parties negotiate based on the same factual error.

Sherwood and Walker both thought Rose (a cow) was barren, both negotiated accordingly, and both were wrong. The Michigan Supreme Court gave judgment for Walker, the seller, permitting him to rescind (i.e., cancel) the contract because the parties were both wrong about the essence of what they were bargaining for.

If the parties contract based on an important factual error, the contract is voidable (i.e., can be cancelled) by the injured party.

Sherwood and Walker were both wrong about Rose's reproductive ability, and the error was basic enough to cause a tenfold difference in price. Walker, the party who would be injured by enforcing the contract, is entitled to rescind it.

Note that the error must *be factual.* Suppose Walker sold Rose thinking that the price of beef was going to drop, when in fact the price rose 60 percent in five months. He made a mistake, but it was simply a business prediction that proved wrong. Walker would have no right to rescind (cancel the contract).

124 $27.97 Air Fare to Paris, China? United: 'Oops'[1]

Eric Bescher almost flew to Paris for less than $30.

An elite level United 1 Airlines frequent flier from Los Angeles, Mr. Bescher visited United's Web site on Jan. 31 to search for low fare to Europe in March. The deal he found was a lot better than he'd bargained for—passage to France for less than the price of a bottle of good burgundy. A technical glitch at the site listed the round-trip fare from San Jose to Paris as just $27.98. "I snapped it up right away," he says.

Mr. Bescher wasn't alone in his good fortune. United Airlines says it inadvertently sold 143 tickets to destinations such as Hong Kong at *really* rock bottom prices via its Web site, ual.com, during a 55-minute period on the evening of Jan 31.

United says a computer bug "zeroed out" the fare on a number of international flights so that the amounts shown reflected only a portion of the taxes and miscellaneous fees. In fact, fares were in a free-for-all: One minute a round trip fare from San Francisco to Paris was $85.42; seconds later that same ticket sold for $24.98.

United spokesman Chris Brathwaite says the airline won't honor any tickets sold at those prices. "Anyone who thought they could fly from L.A. to Paris for $27 should have known better." Mr. Brathwaite says. He likens the situation to a bank error when the teller inadvertently hands the customer a $1,000 bill instead of $100. "It's clearly a mistake: everyone knows you don't fly first class to Paris for $29," he says, "You don't get something for nothing."

United is in the process of contacting customers to let them know what the "correct" fare is. As a consolation, United says it will waive any cancellation fees should passengers not wish to pay the difference.

Some travelers are fuming nonetheless. One United flier from Orange County, Calif., says United even sent an e-mail confirmation of his purchase of two tickets between San Jose and Paris for $85 each and now refuses to honor that price. As someone who spent more than $130,000 on United last year, the flier, who asked that his name not be used, says he believes the airline has a responsibility to honor the tickets because its own Web site was responsible for the error.

Moments after purchasing his ticket to Paris, Mr. Bescher also received an email confirmation of the $27.98 fare. But days later, United charged his credit card $573—what he assumes is the price he would have been quoted for the ticket had ual.com been working correctly.

Mr. Bescher immediately contacted United's customer service office about what he viewed as an unauthorized charge, and is still awaiting a re-

---

1 **Note from Professor Carr: This is another very good mistake example. But what type of mistake is it? A unilateral mistake? A mutual mistake? Both?**

If you were the CEO of United, how would you handle this "mess"?

Is it ethical, in your view, for people/customers to try to claim the $27.88 fare??

sponse. "If they don't come through with a goodwill gesture," he says, "I'm going to dispute it."

In the meantime, prices have returned to earth at ual.com. Two weeks after the glitch-driven fare sale, the lowest price for round-trip ticket for travel between San Jose and Paris next month is $510.

125 Unilateral Mistake

To rescind for unilateral mistake, a party must demonstrate that she entered the contract because of a basic factual error and that either (1) enforcing the contract would be unconscionable *or* (2) the non-mistaken party knew of the error.

Cosmo inherits his parents' house, along with 50 years of accumulated rubbish. He conducts a yard sale, and offers a dusty painting of a hummingbird for $25, "because it has a nice frame." Lucy recognizes the picture as the work of Martin Johnson Heade, a distinguished American artist. Knowing the picture to be worth at least half a million dollars, she buys it for $25, then promptly sells it for $800,000. When Cosmo sues for rescission he will win. Cosmo's basic factual error was his ignorance that a famous artist created the work. Lucy knew of Cosmo's error, since otherwise he would never sell the picture so cheap. Cosmo has proven both elements and gets his picture back. Notice that Cosmo could also argue that it would be unconscionable to let Lucy benefit so hugely at his expense. The uninjured party only needs to prove unconscionability *or* knowledge of the error, but typically the two go together: when one party knows of the other's basic factual error, it will usually be unconscionable to enforce the bargain.

By contrast, suppose that Cosmo does realize he has inherited a Martin Johnson Heade. He asks a dealer what it is worth, and the dealer tells him "about $600,000." Cosmo sells it to Vince for $550,000, and Vince promptly resells it for $850,000. Can Cosmo rescind? No. If he underestimates the value, that is his tough luck. He has made an error of judgment about the fine art market, but not a basic factual mistake about the nature of the object he inherited.

126 BlueLight Nixes Accidental MP3 Discount[1]

By Greg Sandoval, *CNET News*

BlueLight.com said it would not honor the thousands of orders it received for an MP3 player that was accidentally advertised at a price almost 90 percent below normal.

A "KEYING MISTAKE" ON Tuesday caused the online unit of Kmart to advertise the Nomad Jukebox for $26.89. Blue Light normally sells the Nomad for $299.99. News of the discount spread via an online message board and hordes of discount hunters swarmed the e-commerce site, according to spokesman Dave Karraker.

Blue Light corrected the glitch within minutes, but not before the company received the wave of orders, Karraker said, adding that some customers placed multiple orders. Blue Light e-mailed customers who ordered a Nomad notifying them that the company could not honor the $26.89 price.

Instead, Blue Light offered them the MP3 player for $274.99, which is the wholesale price that Blue Light pays. The company also offered the customers a coupon good for 20 percent off of their next purchases.

Much of the sentiment on message boards Thursday was that the company is alienating customers and should honor the sales.

Pricing glitches are nothing new to e-commerce sites. Most merchants, like BlueLight, refuse to honor the dramatically discounted prices that result from a pricing error.

"We want to be fair to our customers, but at the same time they have to be fair in what they expect from a company," Karraker said.

1 Note from Professor Carr: This is another good example of a possible unilateral mistake (Kmart could argue that one occurred here and that it should be excused from having to honor these contracts!)

127 High Court to Rule on Dispute Over Car Advertising[1]

By Davan Maharaj, *The Los Angeles Times*

[Unilateral mistake]

AND THERE IT was in a Lexus of Westminster ad. At $ 25,995, it seemed like a great deal. Donovan and his wife zipped over to the dealership to make sure it was not a junker. After test driving the vehicle, Donovan told the salesperson that he'd buy it—at the advertised price. No dickering.

The response he received—that the price was a misprint, an honest mistake—would set off a two-year court battle. As the case has evolved, the battle now pits the state's motor car dealers and newspaper executives against Donovan and some consumer activists.

The dispute has raised some basic legal questions that judges of the California Supreme Court have agreed to resolve: Does a car dealer have to sell a vehicle at its advertised price? And would the dealer still be obligated even if the advertised price was a misprint?

The stakes are high for consumers, car dealers and newspapers.

"If the Supreme Court says, 'Guess what, people, the dealer doesn't have to honor those prices,' then we'll be back in the era of bait-and-switch that California car dealers have been famous for," said Donovan, a 54-year-old Newport Beach attorney, in a recent interview.

Glen A. Smith, an attorney for Times Mirror, which publishes the Los Angeles Times and the Daily Pilot, the Newport Beach paper that printed the Lexus ad, says it appears that newspapers and Web sites that advertise cars or other items for sale could be held liable under a recent appellate court ruling that supports Donovan's position.

"A misplaced decimal point or a missing zero could have disastrous results." said Smith, an attorney with Baker & Hostedler in Los Angeles.

The case that began with a dispute over a number in a newspaper ad quickly turned into a battle of wills.

Donovan refused to pay the $37,016 price that Lexus of Westminster demanded for the 1995 Jaguar, and he bought a similar vehicle from another dealership—for $39,000. He filed a civil suit in Municipal Court in Newport Beach in 1997, demanding that the Lexus dealership pay him $13,000—the difference between the advertised price and the price he paid for the other vehicle.

At a trial lasting no more than two hours, Lexus of Westminster contended that the advertised price was a typographical error. Workers in the composing room of the newspaper pasted the $25,995 price tag under the 1995 Jaguar when that price was intended for a 1994 Jaguar. The dealership produced advertisements from other newspapers in which the 1995 car was advertised at the correct

1 **Note from Professor Carr: Another unilateral mistake example.**

price. Further, the dealership's attorney, James G. Lewis, contended that in any case, an advertisement was not a binding contract.

Judge Christopher W. Strople ruled for the dealership. The judge reasoned that the dealership was unaware of the misprint and that that therefore invalidated its "offer" to sell at the $25,995 price.

Municipal court cases—especially those with only $13,000 at stake—are seldom appealed. But Donovan, a lawyer who represents contractors in disputes with the federal government, intended to keep fighting. Strople also ruled that the advertisement resulted in a binding contract when Donovan offered to pay the advertised price for the vehicle.

But that contract became void, he said, because the newspaper had made "a good-faith unilateral mistake."

Donovan, a former Air Force investigator—he keeps sketches of fighter planes in his law offices—said he was angry that the attorney for the dealership had filed several motions to dismiss or delay the case.

"I know the games attorneys play, and they were playing games with me," Donovan said. "It became a principled fight. I thought how many times this happens to consumers who have no recourse because most lawyers won't take a case like this because there's not much money involved."

Donovan later found a passage in the state's vehicle code which he interpreted to mean that it is unlawful for a car dealer to "fail to sell a vehicle to any person at the advertised total price, exclusive of taxes" and fees.

A three-judge panel of the Orange County Superior Court agreed with Donovan's argument and reversed the lower court's decision. Donovan said he then called the dealership's lawyer and offered to settle the case for $15,000 but that the dealership instead took the matter to the 4th District Court of Appeal in Santa Ana.

In a decision for a unanimous three-judge panel. Justice William Rylaarsdam wrote that the dealership should have reviewed the advertisement before it was published.

"A dealer has a heavy responsibility to ensure that the advertisements are error-free," Rylaarsdam said.

The panel said that although "this is a close case," the vehicle code "tips the scale in favor of our construing the advertisement as an offer which could be, and was, accepted by an attempted tender of the purchase price."

The panel ordered that Donovan be paid damages.

Times Mirror, the California Newspaper Publishers Assn. and the California Motor Car Dealers Assn., all of which supported the Lexus dealership at the court of appeal have since convinced the state's high court to review Rylaarsdam's decision.

Lewis contends that a newspaper ad for a vehicle at a specified price "is not an offer subject to acceptance. It is an invitation to negotiate."

Furthermore, if the ruling remains on the books, Lewis says, advertisers would try to recoup their losses by suing the medium that made the mistake. "Do we want to create that many lawsuits?" he asks.

"People understand that advertisements regarding major purchases, such as of a house or car, are generally not contracts," said Peter Welch, an attorney with the car dealers' group.

Welch said the appeals court should not have based its decision on the vehicle code but rather on a well-settled principle that contracts can be rendered invalid when mistakes are made by third parties.

Smith, the attorney for Times Mirror, agrees.

"This new standard of care has been imposed without due regard for the practical realities of advertising given the volumes of these ads and short deadlines (sometimes instantaneous) that exist in old and new forms of communication," he wrote in a court filing.

Jim Ewert, legal counsel for the newspaper group, said that if the decision is upheld, dealers could try to hold newspapers responsible if they're forced to sell at advertised prices.

"It would be an unwarranted burden on the commercial speech of advertisers and newspapers," Ewert said.

For his part, Donovan said he has never believed that the ad was indeed a mistake, an attitude that is shared by others.

Rosemary Shahan, executive director of Consumers for Auto Reliability and Safety, a consumer watchdog group in Sacramento, said her group receives frequent reports about dealers using advertisements to lure customers into their showrooms, then refusing to sell at those prices.

Lewis, the attorney for the Lexus dealership, said his client does not participate in such practices and that the company is determined to vindicate its name.

"Everybody understands that mistakes happen and there's no reason why one party should be held liable for another party's mistake." he said.

128 Calif.'s Top Court Bags Lawyer's Suit Over Jag

[Mistake]

CONTRACTS

NEWPORT BEACH, CALIF., attorney Brian Donovan simply wanted to buy a Jaguar for his wife.

What he got was a four-year battle that finally ended last week with a ruling from the California Supreme Court.

Donovan had opened up the newspaper and found an ad for a sapphire blue XJ6 Vanden Plas priced at $25,995. He walked into Lexus of Westminster with a check in hand. But the dealer wanted $37,000 for the car and blamed the typographical error on the paper. Donovan—a government contract lawyer—insisted his refusal to sell the car was a breach of contract and sued.

The justices recently ruled that while Donovan was right about the ad constituting a contract between the dealer and consumers, the contract ultimately had to be rescinded because the error was due to oversight.

"No evidence presented at trial suggested that defendant knew of the mistake before plaintiff attempted to purchase the automobile, that defendant intended to mislead customers, or that it had adopted a practice of deliberate indifference regarding errors in advertisements," wrote Chief Justice Ronald George, leading the 4–2 majority in *Donovan v. RRL Corp.*, No. S082570. James Lewis, the Los Angeles attorney who represented the dealer, said the case resolves an issue that has come up before among car salesmen. "It gives dealers specific direction as to where they are if a mistake is made in an ad and it's not of their doing," he said.

In fact, much of the decision focuses on rescission theory and what's required to trigger it.

But in her dissent, Justice, Kathryn Mickle Werdegar called "the majority's grant of contractual rescission … relief that is both unsolicited and procedurally irregular." Werdegar pointed out that the argument of rescission was never even raised by either party.

Donovan took heart in Werdegar's dissent, saying the majority appeared to have "bent over backwards to find a way to not give me relief."

As for the car, he said he ended up buying a different model. He added, "I don't like Jaguars. Women like Jaguars. This was my wife's idea."

129 Duress – An Example

If one party makes an improper threat that causes the victim to enter into a contract, and the victim had no reasonable alternative, the contract is voidable (i.e., can be cancelled by the victim). The key issues are thus whether there was an improper threat and whether the victim had a reasonable alternative.

HYPOTHETICAL

On a Sunday morning, Bancroft Hall drove to pick up his daughter Sandra, who had slept at a friend's house. The Halls are black and the neighborhood was white. A suspicious neighbor called the police, who arrived, aggressively prevented the Halls from getting into their own car, and arrested the father. The officers took Hall to the police station for booking but eventually realized there might be some problems with the arrest, since neither of the Halls had violated any law or done anything wrong whatsoever. An officer told Hall that he could leave immediately if he signed a full release (stating that he had no claims of any kind against the police), but that if he refused to sign it he would be detained for a bail hearing. Hall signed the release, but later filed suit for false arrest, false imprisonment, battery, and civil rights violations. The police defended based on the release.

The court held that the release was voidable because Hall had signed it under duress. The threat to detain Hall for a bail hearing was clearly improper because he had committed no crime. He also had no reasonable alternative to signing. The Halls' suit went to trial, where the jury also awarded them compensatory and punitive damages, plus attorneys' fees, totaling over $525,000.

Source: Hall v. Ochs, 817F.2d 920 (1st Cir. 1987)

130 Undue Influence – An Example

SHE WAS SINGLE and pregnant. A shy young woman in a large city with no family nearby, she needed help and support. She went to the Methodist Mission Home of Texas where she found room and board, support ... and a lot of counseling. Her discussions with a minister and a private counselor stressed one point: that she should give up her baby for adoption. She signed the adoption papers, but days later decided she wanted the baby after all. Was there any ground to rescind? She claimed *undue influence*, in other words, that the Mission Home so dominated her thinking that she never truly consented.

Where one party has used undue influence, the contract is voidable (i.e., can be cancelled) at the option of the injured party. There are two elements to the plaintiff's case. To prove undue influence, the injured party must demonstrate

- a relationship between the two parties either of trust or domination, and
- improper persuasion by the stronger party.

In your view, are these two elements satisfied in this case? Discuss the argument for both sides.

131 Entering Into a Contract with a Minor Is Inadvisable

[Contracting with a minor]

"MY 15 YEARS OLD son Don bought a beeper and signed up for one year's worth of paging services, without my permission or knowledge. What is the law in this area? Can you help us cancel the contract?" That was Ann's question.

"Don had begged me to buy him a pager for months. I refused. But he's stubborn. So off to a pager store he went, paid $75 for a beeper and signed a yearlong contract."

"I discovered the beeper when it went off at about 2 a.m. a few days ago," Ann explained, adding, "I also got the truth from my son." The next day, both of us went to the store to speak with the manager.

"She admitted being aware that my son was a minor, but didn't care. She claimed to have checked with her lawyer who told her it was legal to sell to minors. No refund would be made."

This seemed like the time for a conference call, so I got the manager on the line, explained who I was and why I was calling, and asked if she could explain to me: (1) Why she sold the pager to a 15-year-old in the first place, and (2) Did she plan to cancel the deal and refund the money?

"I sell to anybody and I don't care how old they are," she told me. "My lawyer told me I could."

Now, I doubt any lawyer in his right mind would advise that it is legal for her to knowingly contract with a minor. I attempted to educate her.

"Ma'am, would you let me read to you from the California Family Code section 6710? It's the part about a minor being able to disaffirm a contract. That means cancel it, and I'm sure once you hear this language, you'll want to do the right thing," I said in my "Dr. Beaver, your neighborhood psychologist"-tone of voice.

Her answer? "I don't care what it says, it's my business and I'll sell to whoever I want to." Click. So much for business ethics.

An hour later, my secretary buzzed me with an urgent call. "It's some guy calling about a beeper." I grabbed the phone.

"Mr. Beaver, I am the owner of the beeper store," a humble-sounding voice began, "You were speaking to my wife. I must apologize. Of course, we should not be selling to minors. Have the customer return the pager and we will have a complete refund. I am very sorry for the trouble this has caused them."

Case solved, and not just in terms of getting a refund. We may prevent Don from being kicked out of school.

It is against the law in California to bring beepers onto school property. Clearly an effort to slow down the sale of drugs in schools, if a child is caught with a beeper, it can mean suspension and prosecution. Starting out life with a cloud over your name where drugs is concerned isn't a winning strategy.

A final note of caution on this issue of minors and contracts: If food, lodging, medical care or other "things necessary for support of the minor or the minor's family" have been furnished, they must be paid for. To disaffirm other contracts, the law requires that it be done *before reaching age 18 or within a reasonable time afterwards.*

132 Minors – A Practice Problem

FOR KEVIN GREEN (age 16), it was love at first sight. She was sleek, as quick as a cat, and a beautiful deep blue. He paid $4,600 cash for the used Camaro. The car soon blew a gasket and Kevin demanded his money back. But the Camaro came with no guarantee, and the dealer refused. Kevin repaired the car himself. Next, some unpleasantry on the highway left the car a worthless wreck. Kevin received the full value of the car from his insurance company. Then he sued the dealer, seeking a refund of his purchase price. The dealer pointed out that it was not responsible for the accident and that the car had no warranty of any kind. Yet the trial court awarded Kevin the full $4,600. How can this be? Should Kevin receive the full purchase price for a demolished car?

133 A Louisiana Lawsuit Challenges Rates, Fees at GE-Owned Bank[1]

The Wall Street Journal

[Usury]

NEW ORLEANS—JUST BEFORE Christmas 1995, Patricia Heaton bought three video recorders and other gifts from Campo Appliances, a local store. She paid $837.71 with a Campo credit card.

About two years and $476 in payments later, the amount she owed had risen to $1,041.53 because of late fees and interest running at an annual rate of 21.84%. That debt, a tiny speck in the vast U.S. credit card market, now is the subject of a high-stakes legal battle pitting Ms. Heaton against a unit of General Electric Co. that is one of biggest issuers of "private-label" credit cards for retailers.

On her side: two young New Orleans attorneys who have little experience in banking law but who have attracted the support of the Louisiana attorney general. On GE's side: four prominent law firms along with the company's in-house legal staff, a nationally known Harvard law professor, the Federal Deposit Insurance Corp. and a host of state banking regulators.

At stake is whether Monogram Credit Card Bank of Georgia, the GE-owned bank that issued the Campo card, can skirt consumer-protection laws in states such as Louisiana by basing its operations in Georgia, which has relatively permissive rules on interest rates.

A titan in the private-label market, Monogram is part of GE Card Services, and its primary business is issuing all of the GE unit's cards for major retailers such as Banana Republic, Exxon, Home Depot and scores more. Although GE won't say how many accounts Monogram has, the Nilson Report, an industry newsletter, estimates that GE Card Services has about 116 million U.S. private-label accounts. The bank charged Ms. Heaton rates perfectly legal by Georgia's standards but higher than those allowed under Louisiana law, which caps annual interest at 18% and monthly late fees at $15.

If the Heaton suit succeeds, Monogram and some other credit-card banks that now "export" high rates and fees from their home states, could face similar suits filed in the handful of other states that have consumer-protection caps, such as Colorado and Indiana, state banking regulators say. (Traditional banks that also issue credit cards wouldn't be affected.)

1 **Note from Professor Carr: This article is a nice example of how some firms/business entities use and try to get around usury law to their advantage.**

Also, note the section in the article that discusses the battle over venue—to locate these cases in state courts vs. federal courts. You can see that the defendants in this case want to venue the case in federal court because they are afraid that state court juries may be more sympathetic to consumer plaintiffs. Do you agree? Should such businesses/firms be allowed to make such strategy moves to their advantage??

"It would be a major, major explosion of litigation which would have liability in the billions of dollars," Burt Rublin, an outside lawyer for Monogram, argued in U.S. district court here in November 1999.

Skirmishing Intensifies

The Heaton case began in December 1997, when Monogram sued the shopper in small-claims court here over her debt to the bank. She counter-sued in state civil court in May 1998 with a suit that seeks class-action status on behalf of all card holders in Louisiana who have paid what she and her lawyers call excessive interest and fees to Monogram.

So far, the case has bounced from state court to U.S. district court and the Fifth U.S. Circuit Court of Appeals—all in an effort to determine which tribunal will sort out the merits. GE's deployment of massive legal firepower is understandable. If defeated, its bank could be forced to abide by individual state consumer law—a big bureaucratic burden for a company that issues cards nationwide.

Ms. Heaton demands that Monogram refund all of the late-fee and interest payments above the Louisiana limits that it has collected for up to 10 years from its customers here. Monogram has about 940,000 credit-card accounts in the state, although only 370,000 currently carry balances, according to GE Capital, the company's financial-services arm, which includes GE Card Services and the bank.

Bank Remains Confident

John Oliver, a GE Capital spokesman, says Monogram isn't troubled by the Heaton case. He explains that the November 1999 "explosion-of-litigation" statement by the Monogram lawyer was merely hypothetical. "Monogram Credit Card Bank of Georgia is very confident that its charges to credit-card customers in Louisiana have conformed with all legal requirements, and we are further confident that the courts will recognize that fact," the spokesman says. Even if Ms Heaton wins the procedural tussle, he adds, "There are still numerous other contract and Louisiana-statutory defenses, which would preclude any recovery."

Backing Monogram is the FDIC. Best known for its protection of consumer deposits, the agency in this case took several relatively unusual steps to help the bank. For instance, the FDIC signed a letter supporting the bank that had been drafted by an attorney hired by Monogram. The agency says it did this to protect its authority as a regulator.

But the federal trial judge who has presided over most of the lawsuit said at a hearing last December, "I'm very disturbed, I will say this, about the actions of the FDIC in this entire matter." Judge Carl Barbier added, "I thought the FDIC was there to protect the public, frankly, and consumers, and not to protect Monogram Bank and similar companies."

Mr. Oliver responds: "Because of our excellent track record on compliance issues, we have a good working relationship with the FDIC. But they have not shown any favoritism or special privileges to us." Douglas H. Jones, the FDIC's senior deputy general counsel, says the agency letter "merely confirmed" that the FDIC had independently concluded that Monogram's position was correct.

Origins of a Dispute

Ms. Heaton, a 42-year-old New Orleans native, works in a local government office that archives notarized documents. She and her husband, a local government official, have three children. She has never been involved on either side of a lawsuit before, Ms. Heaton says. She has a total of seven credit cards and hasn't run into any trouble with them in the past, she adds.

But she frequently missed the payment date on her Campo bills and in some months didn't pay at all. Her lawyers explain that she typically pays all of her bills in the middle of the month, rather than when they are due. As a result, she incurred a total of $297 in late fees on the Monogram card; her lawyers allege that each of the late fees was above Louisiana's cap.

Then, in mid-1997, Ms. Heaton says, she began receiving two monthly bills from Monogram with different amounts due. She says she contacted Monogram, but bank representatives failed to straighten out the confusion. So, she says, although she was financially able to pay the bills, she stopped doing so and threw the bills away,

GE Capital's Mr. Oliver says Monogram "has no record that supports this" account.

In December 1997, the bank filed its small-claims suit. It won a quick judgment and moved to garnish Ms. Heaton's wages.

Angry and feeling she had "been treated unfairly," Ms. Heaton found a lawyer, Todd R. Slack, a 32-year-old former computer scientist. He teamed up with Louis Plotkin, 34, who has an office near Bourbon Street and represents people filing occupational-health suits. Hoping the case would grow into a class action, the pair agreed to take as pay an as-yet undetermined percentage of any recovery.

The Heaton attorneys soon fastened on the issue of what kind of bank Monogram is. Traditional banks chartered by federal or state authorities have long been able to export to the rest of the country any rates and fees allowed by their home states. This arrangement is supposed to strengthen the banking system and assure wide availability or credit.

Unlike traditional banks that make a variety of loans and take deposits from customers, Monogram received a state charter from Georgia strictly as a credit-card bank. Still, it wanted the privilege enjoyed by more-traditional banks of exporting its rates and fees. To do that, it had to fit the technical definition of a "state bank," which according to federal law is an institution "engaged in the business of receiving deposits."

But in a further twist, the Georgia law under which Monogram was chartered in 1988 said at the time that credit-card banks could loan money only to card holders and take deposits only from corporate affiliates.

Ms. Heaton's attorneys reasoned that Monogram couldn't be "in the business of receiving deposits," if its activities were limited in this way. And, if Monogram didn't meet the definition of a "state bank," they concluded, it should have abided by Louisiana consumer-protection law.

The plaintiff's lawyers filed their suit in May 1998 in the district court for the Parish of Orleans, a drab linoleum-floored edifice that also houses the small-claims court. Within weeks, Monogram sought to move the case to federal court, which occupies a more-dignified building that is a 10-minute walk toward the Mississippi River. (Soon after that, Monogram dropped its small-claims case against Ms. Heaton.)

Ms. Heaton's lawyers say that Monogram's attempt to shift the venue was a standard corporate effort to avoid facing a state judge and jury, who might be more sympathetic to claim that a state consumer protection provision had been evaded.

Monogram's lawyers counter that federal court is the proper venue because the case involves the federal definition of a "state bank." On that point, Monogram has an important ally: The FDIC, which insures Monogram's deposits, had said for years that it met the federal definition.

Monogram submitted to the federal court a letter to that effect, apparently written by the FDIC and dated Sept. 25, 1998. In October, the first federal judge in the case ruled it should stay in federal court. Less than a week later, the case was reassigned to the newly appointed Judge Barbier, who let that decision stand.

But as Ms. Heaton's lawyers found out in late spring of 1999, during the pretrial fact-finding process known as discovery, there is more to the letter than met the eye.

Paper Trail

Monogram had hired a former FDIC general counsel, John Douglas, now a partner at the large Atlanta law firm of Alston & Bird, to draft the FDIC letter and submit it to the agency's Atlanta field office for approval, according to court filings by the plaintiff's side. When the FDIC received the draft letter, a staff attorney modified it lightly, put it on agency letterhead and signed it, according to these filings. Later, one of Monogram's trial lawyers added some minor revisions, after which the FDIC attorney signed the amended version. Neither the bank nor FDIC disputes this basic account.

In an interview, Mr. Douglas dismisses the whole topic of the letter as "silly stuff." GE Capital's Mr. Oliver adds, "It is customary in working with regulatory agencies such as the FDIC to prepare the initial draft [of such a letter] for their review."

But Mr. Jones, the FDIC's senior deputy general counsel, says the practice of agency officials signing draft letters provided by bank lawyers is "uncommon," though "not unique." In this case, he adds, the agency letter merely informed the court that the FDIC considered Monogram to be a "state bank."

Nonetheless, Ms. Heaton's lawyers asked Judge Barbier to reconsider the case, and he agreed.

At a hearing in November 1999, Monogram's lawyers were asked by Judge Barbier to explain why the FDIC provided the bank with deposit insurance in the first place. The only deposits Monogram had when the case began were about $670 million from other GE units—money intended to fund the bank's operations, and the only deposits permitted under its Georgia bank charter. Yet the GE-owned bank obtained FDIC insurance to safeguard GE's own money.

The FDIC's Mr. Jones says, "Legally, a deposit is a deposit, regardless of where money comes from."

But Ms. Heaton's lawyers argued in court that receiving GE funds didn't put Monogram "in the business" of taking deposits, as it had to be to meet the federal definition of a "state bank." Moreover, they added, the coverage provided by the insurance—0.39% of the amount deposited—was so negligible that its only purpose could have been to gain the FDIC's imprimatur on Monogram's being a "state bank" and therefore allowing it to export rates and fees.

"That's the sole reason for it, really" Judge Barbier said from the bench.

"Yes," acknowledged Mr. Rublin, the outside Monogram lawyer. But "there is nothing improper about that."

This time around, in late November 1999, Judge Barbier ruled that Monogram didn't meet the definition of a "state bank." He sent the case back to state court for a full trial.

Monogram appealed that decision to the Fifth Circuit, engaging Arthur Miller, a high-profile Harvard law professor to work on its brief. The FDIC filed a friend-of the-court brief, supporting Monogram, and the agency's general counsel's office issued a separate written opinion that confirmed Monogram's "state-bank" status. The FDIC says it acted to end the uncertainty created by the Heaton case.

But in a brief supporting Ms. Heaton, the Louisiana attorney general's office urged the court not to defer to the FDIC. Saying "the agency permitted Monogram to ghostwrite a letter," the state attorney general added that "the orchestration between Monogram and the FDIC, while Monogram was a defendant in private litigation, is disturbing." Last November, the appeals court dismissed Monogram's appeal, saying it lacked jurisdiction to intervene.

Within weeks, Monogram's lawyers were back before Judge Barbier, trying once more to keep the case in federal court. The FDIC took the uncommon step of seeking court permission to join the case as a full-fledged party alongside Monogram.

Judge Barbier didn't disguise his frustration. "God knows how much has been spent in attorneys' fees in this case," he told Gregory Taylor, an FDIC attorney, at a hearing in December. "If Monogram had just asserted its defenses in state court [rather than trying to shift to federal court], this case may be over with by now."

"The Judge added: "It seems to me it is just a terribly improper use of judicial resources, legal resources by the government, by the FDIC and by you."

"Your Honor, I guess the only thing I can say is that this is a very important issue for us," Mr. Taylor replied a little later.

In January, Judge Barbier ruled for Ms. Heaton again and sent the case back to state court. Three years after she first filed the suit, her lawyers are preparing for trial. A start date hasn't been set. The FDIC, meanwhile, is pressing its own appeal on the venue issue before the Fifth Circuit.

134 Contract Defenses – Examples

USURY

HENRY PAPER AND Anthony Pugliese were real estate developers. They bought prime property in West Palm Beach, Florida, worth $1.7 million, on which they intended to build an office building. Before they could begin construction, they needed $1 million. They had managed to raise $800,000 of it, but were unable to secure a loan for the last $200,000 at 15 percent interest. Gross knew the partners were desperate for the money, so when it came time to close the loan, he presented Paper and Pugliese with documents demanding not only the 15 percent rate of interest, but also 15 percent equity (ownership) in their partnership. The partners had no real choice, so they signed the documents, borrowing $200,000 for 18 months and agreeing to give Gross 15 percent equity in the partnership, as well as the interest rate he requested. But Paper and Pugliese never repaid the loan, and Gross sued. Although they had known exactly what they were agreeing to, the court held that they need not pay one cent to Gross.

How can that be? Because of usury laws!

GAMBLING

SOHEIL SADRI, A California resident, did some serious gambling at Caesar's Tahoe casino in Nevada. And lost. To keep gambling, he wrote checks to Caesar's, and then signed two memoranda pledging repay money advanced. After two days, with his losses over $22,000, he went home. Back in California, Sadri stopped payment on the checks and refused to pay the money he owed Caesar's. The casino sued. In defense, Sadri claimed that California law considers his payment agreements to be illegal and unenforceable. He was unquestionably correct about one thing: a contract that is illegal is void and unenforceable.

LICENSING STATUTES I

JEROME HOWARD WAS the agent for rap recording star Domino. Howard was delighted that his contract gave him a long-term relationship with an artist whose most recent album sold at "platinum" levels. But Domino was unhappy with the arrangement and walked away from it—legally. Howard was not licensed by the state of California to work as a music agent. His contract with Domino was void.

Why? Because of the law of licensing. The contract with Howard is void because this type of statute was probably designed/intended by the legislature primarily to protect the public rather than just to raise revenue.

LICENSING STATUTES II

YOU SUE YOUR next-door neighbor in small claims court, charging that he keeps a kangaroo in his backyard and that the beast has disrupted your family barbecues by leaping over the fence, demanding salad, and even punching your cousin in the ear. Your friend Foster, a graduate student from Melbourne, offers to help you prepare the case, and you agree to pay him 10 percent of anything you recover. Foster proves surprisingly adept at organizing documents and arguments. You win $1,200 and Foster demands $120.

Must you pay?

Again, the answer is determined by the law of *licensing.* Like the previous hypothetical, the answer is again probably "no"—the contract with Foster is void because this type of statute is designed/was passed primarily to protect the public rather than just to raise revenue (i.e., your friend Foster was engaging in the practice of law and by statute one has to have a license to do that (and he does not) and the purpose of that statute is to make it so not every Tom, Dick or Harry out there can open up a law practice and start giving people legal advice!).

135 Test Your Knowledge of Home Contracts[1]

[Licensing Statutes]

ARE YOU PLANNING to have work done to your roof, driveway or garage? How about some landscaping, painting or possibly adding a gazebo to your back yard?

Well if so, I would like to give you a little test. It's a test of your knowledge of law as it applies to home improvement contracts.

(1) The estimate for your new driveway is $5,500 and the contractor has requested a down payment of $1,500. Is this legal?

(2) True or False: Unlike buying a set of dishes or set of encyclopedias, there is no requirement of a three-day cooling-off notice when I'm having a new roof put on my house.

(3) A tree trimmer quoted a charge of $775 and the homeowner gave the go-ahead for the job that was done property. Afterwards, upon being asked to show a valid contractor's license, the tree trimmer admits that he is unlicensed. The homeowner refuses to pay and is sued in Small Claims Court. Who will win?

1 **Note from Professor Carr: This article does a nice job of highlighting how the lack of a necessary license (that is designed to protect the public vs. being a license (and licensing fee) designed primarily to raise revenue for the state/government) is a defense to the enforcement of a contract.**

Here are the answers: (1) No. (2) False. (3) The Homeowner.

How many did you get right? Before hiring a contractor, there is literally a massive amount of information that you need to know and it is important to be aware of your legal rights.

Let's begin with a few basics. If you are going to hire someone—or a company—to repair, remodel, alter, convert, modernize or add to residential property, this is called a Home Improvement. If the value of the improvement is $300 or more, a valid California Contractor's License is required for the license category in which the contractor is going to be working.

If the total cost of the project exceeds $500, by law the contract must be in writing.

Typical home improvements include: driveways, swimming pool, spas and hot tubs, patios, awnings, gazebos, storm windows, landscaping, fences, porches, garages, installation of a sprinkler system, installing a carpet, trimming trees, repairing a chimney, painting. In fact, just about anything you can imagine having done to your home will be a home improvement.

The written contract must show:

- The contractor's name, address and license number;
- Scheduled starting and completion dates;
- Description of the work to be done, including materials;

- Price agreed upon as well as any down payment (10 percent max in most cases);
- Notice regarding Mechanics Lien;
- Statement of Right to Cancel (three-day cooling-off period).

Using my first question as an example, if the price quoted for a new driveway is $5,500, at most a down payment of $550—10 percent—may be requested. If you are ever asked to make a down payment of more than 10 percent of the contract price, find another contractor. With swimming pools it's less: 2 percent or $200.

How about the three-day cooling-off period? This right to cancel a contract does apply to home-improvement contracts. You must be given the cancellation forms that will dearly state the last business day on which you may cancel. If not provided, California law gives you the right to cancel at any time, even after the work is done!

But by far the most dramatic and important rule of law consumers must know is this one:

Unlicensed contractors cannot enforce their contracts in court. This means that it you are ever sued by a contractor, he must prove that he had a valid license at the time of his contract with you or the case will be thrown out of court.

The Contractor's State License Board has a number of excellent pamphlets that clearly outline your rights. I recommend that anyone who is planning on hiring a contractor should order a free "Get Information to Build On" kit by calling the Contractor's State License Board at (800) 321-CSLB or (800) 321-2752.

136 Specializing in Sex Trade Law[1]

D.C. Lawyer Counsels Escort Services, Exotic Dancers and the Like.

By Bob Van Voris, *The National Law Journal*

[Contracts that violate public policy]

HOLLY FLOWERS' WEB SITE characterizes her practice as "a different kind of law firm." False advertising it is not.

Since setting up shop as a solo practitioner just last year, Flowers has built a Washington, D.C., practice out of representing clients many other lawyers shun: the rank-and-file workers of the sex industry.

Flowers, 29, provides legal advice to X-rated Web site operators, prostitutes, exotic dancers and escort services, among other outside-the-mainstream clients. She calls it "the sex-friendly firm with a social conscience."

Flowers, who also advocates for the rights of sex workers, says sex workers often have a hard time finding lawyers they can trust and feel comfortable working with. "I'm not threatening, and I'm not judgmental," said Flowers. There's a reason for that. While in college in Los Angeles, Flowers moonlighted in the adult entertainment industry, including working as an exotic dancer and nude model. She said her experience has made it easier for sex workers to trust her. "They know I'm not coming at this from a voyeuristic point of view," she said.

She worked for a labor union in Washington, D.C., before graduating from American University's Washington College of Law in 1998. She said she became interested in legal issues involved in the sex trade when she wrote a law review article on unionization in the adult entertainment industry.

As part of her research, she interviewed dancers at San Francisco's Lusty Lady peep show, where the workers voted to form a union in 1996—the first time adult entertainers had organized.

"This was done virtually without any attorneys involved [on the dancers' side]," said Flowers. "They were being shunned and turned away because of the stigma. That just struck me as so wrong."

In addition to sex workers, Flowers also gets clients with unusual lifestyles—people who might be reluctant to confide in a lawyer in wingtips and a Brooks Brothers suit.

Contract submissiveness

She once worked with a couple who were sufficiently serious about their dominant-submissive personal relationship that they wanted to spell out their obligations in an enforceable contract. The man, by night the submissive, owned the company where the woman worked during the day.

1 **Note from Professor Carr: What I like about this article is how it illustrates how this particular attorney, given the type of clients she has, has to think and structure contracts quite creatively so that they will be/remain enforceable and a court will not strike them down as void/violating public policy.**

Flowers knew that a contract of this kind would not likely be upheld in court, so she drafted an employment contract that incorporated aspects of the couple's personal interests.

Like any lawyer, her hours reflect those of her clients. Flowers said she is more likely to put in an 11 a.m.-to-1 a.m. day than one that runs 9-to-5. She also changed her name, leaving behind Holly Wilmet for the catchier Holly Flowers.

Sex workers have all of the same legal problems that other workers have, Flowers said, with a few more thrown in. For example, escorts and exotic dancers get into divorce fights like anyone else. But their work often becomes the center of disputes over child custody. She has drafted cease-and-desist letters for clients whose photographs are posted on Web sites without their consent.

Webmasters with pornographic sites consult Flowers to make sure they don't run afoul of obscenity laws, although she tells them there's no legal silver bullet. When Flowers does work for clients outside the sex industry, she focuses mainly on issues involving artistic freedom, employment law and civil rights.

She is a member of the Free Speech Coalition, an adult entertainment industry group, and has volunteered her time with a D.C. group that provides services to street prostitutes.

After graduating from law school, Flowers worked as an associate at Washington, D.C.'s Joseph D. Gebhardt & Assocs., where she practiced employment-discrimination law.

Flowers said she gets many of her clients through word of mouth and Internet contacts. It can be hard to get a solo practice off the ground, but she is confident hers will continue to grow. "I think it's coming along quite nicely, she said.

Her firm's Internet site is at www.flowerslawfirm.com.

137 He's No Sperm Donor. He's a Father[1]

Support in Sight for Girl Begot in the Usual Way.

The National Law Journal

[Contracts that violate public policy]

A BROWARD COUNTY, FLA., doctor who had signed away his paternal rights and responsibilities after agreeing to act as a "sperm donor" and impregnate his girlfriend through sexual intercourse may end up having to pay child support.

A three-judge panel of the 4th District Court of Appeal in West Palm Beach recently reaffirmed its Nov. 14 ruling that consenting adults who engage in sex for the sole purpose of having a baby cannot contract away that child's right to future financial support by either of the parents.

In the latest ruling, however, the court eliminated a provision from its November ruling that would have allowed Dr. Frederick Silverman to try to prove in state court that he should not be held financially accountable to his daughter. This paves the way for the mother to seek child support.

The new opinion does away with a specially concurring opinion by 4th DCA Judge Robert Gross that Silverman should be allowed to try and prove that because the child's mother took nearly 10 years to seek support, her claim should be barred by the doctrine of laches. That doctrine essentially says that such a delay could unfairly impair a defendant's ability to make a case.

Father's expectations

The Court of Appeal is saying "that it's clear from the contract that he expected her to come back and seek support," said Tracy Newmark, an appellate attorney with Fixel & La Rocco in Hollywood, Fla., who represented Tamara Budnick, the child's mother.

In 1989, Budnick asked her then boyfriend Silverman to impregnate her if she signed an eight-page preconception agreement essentially assuring Silver man that he would bear no responsibility for the child arid would be legally recognized as a "sperm donor."

Under Florida law, a sperm donor is bound to give away any rights as a parent. But the law applies only to assisted reproductive technology. Budnick got pregnant, in the words of the 4th DCA, in the "usual and customary" way and therefore, the court

1 **Note from Professor Carr: This article does a nice job of highlighting how courts will <u>not</u> allow certain rights and obligations to be contracted away. The rationale? Such attempts are against/violate public policy, and courts will simply not allow parties to do that by contract—even if they are adults, smart, intelligent people who do so voluntarily. And, of course, the courts will be on the lookout to try and protect the rights of children in these types of cases.**

held, Silverman should be viewed as more than a sperm donor.

Budnick's attorneys noted that the agreement included a provision that if Budnick did not comply with the deal, Silverman could assume "full and complete permanent custody and guardianship" of the child. They say this provision suggested that Silverman expected Budnick to try to gain child support at some time in the future.

Silverman's attorney, Andrew M. Leinoff of Miami, said he was still reviewing the opinion and had not decided what action he would take. *Budnick v. Silverman*, No. 4D00-4032.

138 Contract Returns to Haunt[1]

[Contracts that restrain competition]

LAST JUNE, SHORTLY after laser eye technician Debra Pilkerton went to work at the Annapolis, Md., office of the TLC Laser Eye Center, she signed employment papers that included a "non-competition agreement."

Under the agreement, if she left TLC, she could not work for a competing laser surgery facility within 50 miles for a year after her departure.

If you didn't sign it, Pilkerton said, "you didn't get the job."

Within months of joining the TLC staff, Pilkerton's relationship with her employer soured, and she was fired in October. With 23 years of experience as an optician, Pilkerton quickly found new work, first as a laser technician at the Baltimore Laser Eye Center, and then as manager of the office. She said she even got a raise.

Nonetheless, the non-competing agreement she had signed with TLC lurked like an explosive awaiting detonation. In late January, an attorney for TLC wrote to Pilkerton and her employer, saying that she was violating the agreement and insisted that Baltimore Laser Eye Center dismiss her.

A month later, when TLC renewed the demand and filed a complaint in Anne Arundel County Circuit Court, the Baltimore facility complied.

"They fired me," Pilkerton said.

Non-competition agreements have long been a fixture in the world of sales and marketing as companies have tried to keep strategies and customer lists as secret as military battle plans. Now more workers—and not just those at the top of the corporate ladder—are being required to sign such agreements before being hired.

The contracts are especially wide-spread in the technology sector, with some firms requiring that all workers sign the agreement no matter what their jobs.

"They have risen very dramatically in the last couple of years, said Steve A. Mandell, a Tysons Corner, Va., lawyer specializing in corporate law. "It is because companies are sensitive to the information germane to their well-being. The departure of this information will be lost, entirely to the benefit of the employee and his new company."

The American Society for Industrial Security, in a study last year, reported that Fortune 1,000 companies suffered losses of more than $45 billion in 1999 from theft of trade secrets.

With the excitement of a new job, few workers object to the non-competition agreements. But the documents can come back to haunt employees months or years later if they switch jobs, especially if they join a company that does work similar to that of the firm they left.

'Indentured servitude'

"It's the new indentured servitude," said Cliff Palefsky, a San Francisco employment lawyer. "It's entirely appropriate to protect trade secrets or

1 **Note from Professor Carr: This article does a nice job highlighting how certain contracts are not enforceable because they violate public policy (here, they unlawfully restrain trade/competition).**

customer lists. But the notion that a company that is not paying you or employing you can keep you from working someplace else is really outrageous in this economy."

R. Mark Halligan, a Chicago lawyer specializing in trade secrets, said: "Non-competes are very necessary when a company identifies what its competitive advantage is. Eighty percent of employees will abide by them because they signed them. The fact is they're abused. They're contracts of adhesion. There's no bargaining (over the terms) and that's an abuse."

Non-competition contracts typically prohibit workers from joining a direct competitor for a year, although some pacts limit job movement for up to three years. Most also include a geographic limitation, as Pilkerton's did.

Corporate lawyers defend the agreements, and even attorneys who have fought them on behalf of clients generally agree that they're legally enforceable if they're written to protect a corporation's demonstrated commercial interest and do not keep an individual from earning a living.

Banned in California

The exception to this is in California, which forbids such contracts in most cases, as an illegal restriction of an employee's right to move to a new job.

Pilkerton hired attorney T. Allen Mott of Baltimore to try to overturn her non-competition agreement with TLC. She said Baltimore Laser at first agreed to rehire her if the legal dispute could be resolved, but since has changed its mind.

Mott contended that TLC'snon competing pact is "fundamentally unfair."

"There's no legitimate proprietary enterprise to protect that would justify prohibiting her from working in her trained field," Mott said. "They're enforceable to protect proprietary and confidential information, not where you have a technician and it's a one-shot deal—you get your eyes done."

A TLC spokesman declined to discuss the case because it was in litigation.

In its court complaint, TLC said that Pilkerton was using "confidential and proprietary technological and business information of TLC ... and taking advantage of the technological training and experience, patient contact, and TLC policies and procedures."

Last March, TLC fired another laser technician, Robert Marinaccio, but didn't object when he went to work for Baltimore Laser's companion office, Washington Laser Eye Center at Tysons Corner.

Marinaccio said that when he was hired by TLC he objected to the non-competition clause and was told by TLC to add an addendum to the agreement that effectively negated it.

"They said they'd never gone after anyone," Marinaccio said.

139 Artists Seek to Ease Recording-Pact Law[1]

The Wall Street Journal

[Contracts that restrain competition]

LOS ANGELES—AS ARTISTS and music-industry executives gather here to fete themselves at the 44th annual Grammy Awards Wednesday, some will be buzzing about more than statuettes.

Major artists and their management companies have stepped up their efforts to win a growing industry conflict over recording contracts. At issue is a measure in the California Legislature over a law that some artists say ties them to record labels for unfairly long periods.

And how the issue plays out will be closely watched by some U.S. lawmakers to determine whether certain other music- industry issues are taken up at the federal level in the near future.

California is the only state that limits to seven years the time workers can be held to contracts for services. In 1987, however, that law was amended at the behest of record companies to allow certain exceptions for recording artists. Those exceptions can tie artists to their record companies for as long as it takes to release the number of albums specified by their contracts. In some cases, that could mean decades. In January, Democratic State Sen. Kevin Murray filed a measure that, if passed, would ensure that recording artists can't be bound by contracts for multiple albums that last longer than seven years.

Record companies strongly oppose the proposal, arguing that labels must be able to keep the small number of profitable acts on their rosters for as long as possible in order to offset losses incurred by the majority that fail. Hilary Rosen, president of the Recording Industry Association of America, the lobbying arm of the five major music companies, argues that, if passed, the Murray amendment wouldn't just force record companies to sign fewer artists, but would also create an incentive for them to take their business outside the state.

> *At issue is a California law that some artists say ties them to record labels for unfairly long periods.*

What happens in California over the year could largely determine how much time and money artists and record companies are willing to spend on contentious issues at the federal level, including

1 **Note from Professor Carr: This article highlights how even in spite of the rule that "contracts against public policy/that restrain competition" are not enforceable, there may still be, within that class or category of contracts, certain contracts that ARE or remain enforceable.**

Here, it is quite obvious that the record companies were able to push through the legislature these types of contracts and make them stand up/be enforceable.

Now, as to whether they are right or wrong, good or bad in doing that (or whether the artists are in the right or wrong), I leave up to you to decide.

industry accounting practices, copyright protection and royalty rates. In recent months, the Recording Artists Coalition, an artists' rights group with about 150 members, and the Recording Industry Association of America have stepped up spending to push their respective agendas in California where many record-company contracts are signed.

In the meantime, fund-raising efforts are under way on both sides to influence the escalating debate.

Artists and their business partners are holding fund-raisers, holding strategy sessions and enlisting the support of labor groups, including the AFL-CIO, to further their cause. Tomorrow, the Recording Artists Coalition plans to raise as much as $1 million at four fund-raising concerts featuring the Eagles, Billy Joel, Dwight Yoakam, No Doubt, and Beck, people familiar with the matter say.

Last week, a Beverly Hills entertainment company called the Firm, which manages a roster of artists including rock group Linkin Park and country singers the Dixie Chicks, raised more than $300,000 for the Democratic Congressional Campaign Committee at a reception billed "Winning Back the House and Winning Back Artists Rights." Joining the rock stars, entertainment lawyers and managers in attendance were House Democratic leader Richard Gephardt and Michigan Rep. John Conyers Jr., the senior Democrat on the Judiciary Committee, who aides say is drafting a federal bill intended to better protect artists rights. No record-company representatives were invited to the fund-raiser.

Ms. Rosen, of the Recording Industry Association of America, says the big record companies are more aggressively lobbying in Sacramento in light of the California bill but she declined to disclose the industry's spending on the issue.

Since early 2000, the Recording Artists Coalition, which includes big-selling artists such as Sheryl Crow and Billy Joel, says it has raised about $216,000 and recruited a trove of lawyers and managers to work pro bono on the group's behalf.

But more money is needed to go forward, says the Eagles' Don Henley, a cofounder of the coalition. Mr. Henley says he has met privately with artists such as U2 and Neil Diamond in hopes that they will join. But because artists by nature "aren't joiners," he says, building up the coalition hasn't been easy.

The group has had some success in the past. In 2000, it successfully lobbied Congress to change a so-called work-for-hire provision supported by the record companies, that restricted the right artists had to copyrights of their music after a 35-year waiting period expired. Mr. Henley says he hopes recent news of the accounting scandal at Enron Corp. will spur further interest. Indeed, some California lawmakers recently pledged to look into music-industry accounting practices.

140 Not-So-Safe Deposit Boxes[1]

Retrieving Charred Memories from World Trade Vault; A Searing Oven for Days

[Exculpatory Clauses]

WHEN WINNIE HOWE put the precious jewelry she received as wedding gifts into a safe deposit box, she thought twice about renting a box at the World Trade Center near her office.

"I should walk farther," she recalls thinking. "But I was pregnant at the time, so I said 'Oh forget it! What are the chances of it getting bombed again?'"

That was last August.

This week, she and her husband Eddie Wen, both 30 years old, went to retrieve what remains of their family treasures—mostly black ashes and twisted gold. Ms. Howe's mother in law had given her a jade pendant and a gold chain fashioned from all the gifts of gold given to her son as a newborn, a Chinese tradition. "I think the jade is ruined, although it still looks green," says Ms. Howe. "Jewelry, once it is ruined, it doesn't matter how ruined," she adds.

Paper burns at 451 degrees Fahrenheit; steel melts at 1,500 degrees. The 1,300 safe deposit boxes at the J.P. Morgan Chase & Co.'s Chase Bank branch of 5 World Trade Center literally cooked for days after the horrific events of Sept. 11th—although just how long and at what temperature is a matter of debate. What is clear is that no paper inside the boxes survived and some gold melted. Fire and debris from the nearby Twin Towers rained down on the building, leaving one side exposed like an open dollhouse. Then rubble burned uncontrollably around and below 5 World Trade, turning the bank vault on the second floor it into a searing oven.

Customers who rented the boxes, starting at $50 a year, have been facing a hard truth since then: the place where they stored their most precious possessions turned out to be vulnerable. And some are only now realizing that banks do not insure the contents of safe deposit boxes—that is the customers' responsibility. Chase, as required by state law, says in its box-rental agreement that contents "may not be fully protected against loss under insurance coverage maintained by the bank."

While the bank has been very clear that it has no liability, it has been telling customers that it will "work with" them on an individual basis. Customers must first document what was inside and provide appraisals for repair of damaged items or estimates of salvage value before presenting a claim to Chase.

---

1 **Note from Professor Carr: Here, we have a contract (these rental agreements for safety boxes). But ... they also have waivers of liability. In your view, should these waivers of liability (called exculpatory clauses) be upheld or struck down? Do they meet the test for upholding or striking them down that we discussed in class/is discussed in your study outline and other articles and materials in this textbook??**

"The fact that we have a box of stuff at all is better than we expected given the letters we got from Chase," says Mr. Wen.

Indeed, in September, Chase notified customers that it did not yet know the full status of the branch site and was "taking the necessary steps" to gain access. Then in early December, it warned that due to the weight of the debris and the extreme heat, "at this point, we have to consider the safety deposit boxes as unrecoverable due to this tragic disaster." That outraged some box holders who filed a lawsuit in Manhattan Supreme Court, seeking to force Chase to make more steps to recover their property.

Soon thereafter, Chase wrote to many customers that their boxes had been recovered and identified, and that while the overall condition was poor, they could make an appointment to inspect the contents. Chase said its about-face had "nothing to do with the lawsuit" and "everything to do with our commitment to our customers."

Scheduling just two appointments per hour, Chase has been letting customers visit the remains of the battered boxes, now housed in the basement of another Chase building a few blocks away from the Trade Center site. The misshapen blocks of metal drawers are warped and black—except for an eery pink neon paint that demolition workers sprayed on them before the building was demolished in December to help identify them later. Once opened with a genteel two-key system, most of the boxes can now be opened only with a hammer and crowbar.

So far, about 900 of the boxes have been recovered from the site, and some 200 people have come to retrieve their belongings. Many are shocked by what they find.

"I opened the box and saw all that black ash, like black tissue paper," says Sharon Ann Jordan, a trader at the New York Board of Trade, which was located in the Trade Center. Her papers had burned to cinders. A black Mabe pearl ring had disintegrated, leaving only the empty setting. Still, Ms. Jordan, 53 years old, says, "I didn't think of jewelry. I thought of the people I saw jumping from the World Trade Center. ... I was lucky to get out. I lost friends."

When asked in Chase's lobby what he had just seen in his box, Theodore McGraw Jr., a 47-year-old insurance broker, pulled a plastic bag out of his briefcase. He held it up and looked at it a moment and then turned and recited a litany of memories. The fused finger of black metal was once a gold penknife, given to his father by *his* mother at his confirmation. A gold pocketwatch from his grandfather and a mottled money clip, a gift to his father from his best man, were also bent and discolored. But Mr. McGraw found talking about them difficult. "Given the extent of loss, both personal and financial, to others, to dwell on my safe deposit box is not appropriate," he said.

Sheri Bethelmy, one of three plaintiffs in the lawsuit filed in Manhattan Supreme Court on Dec. 6, says her safe deposit box contained jewelry worth $40,000 to $50,000 and much more in sentimental value. When she opened it, she found powdery gray peas instead of her mother's pearls and a blackened platinum leaf-pin with little diamonds that her mother wore often. And most distressing: a disfigured ring that that was designed by her mother. "She loved it. She always wore it," says Ms. Bethelmy.

One of the biggest losses was of more than 40,000 photographic negatives of President John F. Kennedy and his family belonging to Jacques Lowe, the Kennedy's' personal photographer who died last May. The negatives, which were not insured, were estimated to be worth $2 million to $3 million.

David Wollmuth, a partner of Wollmuth Maher & Deutsch, the firm that filed the lawsuit, says part of the suit may be moot, since the bank has made many of the boxes available. But the plaintiffs are continuing to press the case, alleging that Chase breached its contract with box renters by failing to provide boxes able to withstand "damage/destruction from fire and debris." Chase declined to comment on the suit.

David McGuinn, founder of Safe Deposit Specialists, a consultant in Houston, says very few people read the fine print on their rental contract. He urges banks to give consumers a separate notice and post signs that insurance isn't provided. And he advises consumers to keep a detailed inventory list, including appraisals and receipts to prove ownership.

But no disclaimer could have helped Jim Tendean-Luce, who deposited his wife's gold jewelry, which he values at around $20,000 in the Chase branch a few years ago when he worked near the World Trade Center. He later changed jobs and his wife asked him to move the jewelry closer to his new office in midtown.

"She kept pushing me and pushing me and finally last August I told her that I'd done it, but I hadn't," says Mr. Tendean-Luce. He never confessed. But he says that last month in the middle of the night, his wife woke him up to say: "I know about the jewelry and it is all right."

141 More Contracts Practice Problems & Related Materials

The following are several practice problems (and related materials) that I pulled together for you.

The class before the exam, and time permitting, I will try to go over/cover as many of them as possible.

Irrespective of whether or not I am able to get to these problems during class, it seems to me that you can/should still "buddy" up with a study partner and go over these problems and this material with him/her as that would be very good practice for the exam. For example, if you can recognize the legal "issue" that the problem raises/presents, then that bodes well for you and most likely means that you understand that portion of the contracts material. We could also discuss one or more of these at the review session if you would like and we have time.

—Prof. Carr

INTELLECTUAL PROPERTY

A catch-all label for property that is recognized in works of the mind, without general acceptance of any definitive listing of what is covered by the expression. At a minimum, it includes copyright, patent, trademark, trade name, and service mark, as well as, generally, trade secrets.

LICENSE

A license is generally a right granted which gives the grantee permission to do something which he could not legally do absent such permission. With respect to intellectual property, a license is a variety of contract by which the owner of personal and/or intellectual property grants permission to another to make limited use of the intellectual property, subject to such terms and conditions as are imposed by the license. Generally, a license represents only a personal right, and gives a conditional privilege to a party, not the property itself, and therefore is generally not assignable.

SHRINK-WRAP LICENSE

A shrink-wrap license is a mass-market license which appears on certain products, most commonly computer software packages, which are sealed in transparent wrapping. The typical shrink-wrap license purports to obligate anyone who breaks the seal to comply with various contractual terms. Often, the terms are found only inside the box, and thus can't be reviewed until the seal has been broken. Typically, shrink-wrap licenses provide that the supposed purchase is really a perpetual lease subject to all of the use restrictions in the contract. Any lessee who doesn't like the terms, must return the software for a refund.

With the advent of the Internet, electronic shrink-wrap licenses, or "click here" contracts, have burst on to the scene. Although a user can read a "click here" contract before signing, the same use restrictions are likely to be included.

"E-LITIGATION: CLICKS AND CONTRACTS"

The National Law Journal

THINK BACK TO the first rule of contracts that you learned in law school: offer, acceptance, deal. This straightforward rule has applied in thousands of contexts.

Now, fast-forward to today. Electronic commerce is booming; One company alone racks up $1 billion per month in computer chip sales over the Internet; another, Amazon.com, sells $3.5 million worth of books daily without a single brick-and-mortar store. As more businesses move to the Internet, transactions increasingly are defined by data packets sent between computers rather than by sales slips and paper contracts. But the need for certainty—in choice of forum and law, liability and warranty, the basic terms for use of the product—is every bit as crucial in cyberspace.

But you can't sign a computer screen. Instead of a signature, e-commerce companies seek to bind consumers to electronic contracts with a simple "click" of a computer mouse.

Does the click of a mouse a contract make?

So does a click make a binding contract?

Absolutely, according to the first appellate court to address the issue squarely. See *Caspi v. The Microsoft Network,* 323 N.J. Super. 118, 732 A.2d 528 (1999). And a new proposed uniform state law—which may be coming soon to a legislature near you—agrees resoundingly. The Uniform Computer Information Transactions Act (UCITA), like the Caspi case, would provide that "an on-screen 'click' acceptance is binding" as long as the user had a sufficient opportunity to read the contract. The concept of a "click-wrap" license, an extension of the now established software "shrink-wrap" license, is on its way to widespread recognition.

The software industry has long relied on the concept of the shrink-wrap license to establish essential terms between software publishers and users. Think of it as a chance to set the rules of the game before the customer gets to play. By the simple act of removing the plastic cover of a shrink-wrapped software package, the end user has—in theory—agreed to the terms on which the software publisher is willing to sell the package to the consumer.

The need for this sort of contract in the software context is compelling. If a publisher can't define the proper uses of the product at the outset, an end user could make illegal copies or otherwise improperly exploit the product before agreeing to any licensing terms. Software publishers shipping thousands of packages of disks and CD-ROMs to consumers around the world simply cannot require signed license agreements. The shrink-wrap license became an expedient means of solving this problem.

In the 1980s, scholars and courts began debating whether shrink-wrap licenses should be enforced. Does a potentially unsophisticated user really agree to the fine print in a software license inside a box simply by ripping off the plastic and using the product? Is "acceptance by performance" really legal? The stakes were enormous, both because the copyright status of software—especially object code—had not solidified fully and because the worth assigned by the marketplace to these rights is extraordinary.

Shrink-wrap deals are enforceable, courts say

The consensus is yes—shrink-wrap licenses are enforceable. Shrink-wrap licenses join other contracts whose terms are discovered only after money is paid, including airline tickets, insurance policies and concert tickets. Although some early courts did strike down particular licenses as unconscionable contracts of adhesion, the U.S. Court of Appeals for the 7th Circuit enforced licenses in persuasive language in two cases that have become the standard. See *ProCD v. Zeidenberg,* 86 F.3d 1447 (7th Cir. 1996); *Hill v. Gateway 2000 Inc.,* 105 F.3d 1147 (7th Cir. 1997), cert. denied, 118 S. Ct. 47 (1997). There is nothing unconscionable about a shrink-wrap license, Judge Frank H. Easterbrook concluded in *Hill*, if one considers the alternative: If a salesperson were required to read the buyer the list of terms aloud before accepting a sale, "the droning voice would anesthetize rather than enlighten many potential buyers. Others would hang up in a rage over the waste of their time."

Enter the Internet. To permit effective electronic commerce—the buying and selling of goods ranging from software to underwear over worldwide networks—the still-new concept of the binding shrink-wrap license must be reinvented. Now the consumer isn't even charged with knowledge of terms when he or she unwraps a physical package. The buyer instead must mouse-click assent to the transaction.

Once again, a physical act of assent is essential. Although there is movement toward a standard for electronic signatures to supplant such tangible acts, the legal standards are quite fluid, and the technology is not yet widely available to consumers. Electronic commerce is booming now, and the technology for assent by mouse-click is ubiquitous. The click-wrap license has quickly become the norm in electronic commerce.

Retailers have bet millions on the enforceability of click-wrap licenses. The standard Internet transaction includes an opportunity to review screens of text on the Web site, followed by buttons labeled "I agree" or "I disagree." The prospective buyer must agree with the terms by clicking on the "I agree" button to proceed to the step of purchasing a product.

If this click of assent didn't create a contract, the certainty needed to support widespread electronic commerce would be impossible. Retailers could be sued anywhere that was home to a disgruntled customer and an amenable long-arm statute. The availability of contractual choice of law, so important to managing business risk, could be lost. And businesses' confidence in doing business on the Internet inevitably would be seriously impaired.

Fortunately for Internet sellers, the Appellate Division of the Superior Court of New Jersey resoundingly approved a "click" as assent to an electronic contract. The plaintiffs in *Caspi* were a potential class of Microsoft Network subscribers who claimed that their subscription fee had been raised impermissibly through a "negative option." New Jersey, one of 21 states whose attorneys general earlier had raised a similar allegation against America Online, would have been a sympathetic forum for such a claim.

But Microsoft Network understandably sought to move the litigation to its home county in Washington state, pursuant to a forum-selection clause in its standard member agreement. The plaintiffs vigorously opposed the change of venue on grounds that the member agreement was unenforceable against them.

The *Caspi* plaintiffs raised many claims that previously had been raised against shrink-wrap licenses. They argued that the contract should not be enforced because their acceptance of it was the result of a disparity in bargaining power; that enforcement of the contract would violate public policy; and that they never received adequate notice of the clause. The court rejected all of these arguments, finding that the plaintiffs had validly agreed to the contract.

A click is just as good as a signature

Most important the *Caspi* court found that the electronic contract agreed to by a click was just as binding as a written contract agreed to by a signature. "The scenario presented here is different because of the medium used, electronic versus printed," the court noted, "but, in any sense that matters, there is no significant distinction." Just as a party to a paper contract can read through the fine print before signing, the *Caspi* plaintiffs "were free to scroll through the various computer screens that presented the terms of their contracts before clicking their agreement." Accordingly, the court found, the contract could be enforced.

In fact, it is possible that a party to an electronic contract can spend more time reviewing that contract on a computer screen than a party to a paper contract might spend looking it over under the watchful eye of a salesman (and more than a consumer has with a shrink-wrap license, which binds the user to terms that are inside the package).

The *Caspi* court approved of the presentation of a contract in the standard Internet mode of screens of text followed by an "I agree" button. Because the plaintiffs had an opportunity to review the contract and had, in fact, clicked their agreement to it, the court held them bound and dismissed the case.

Caspi set the stage perfectly for the late July final vote of the National Conference of Commissioners on Uniform State Laws. The conference had been working for eight years in an often-controversial effort to craft an addition to the Uniform Commercial Code that would establish rules for commerce in information technology. It finally hammered out UCITA, and approved it on July 29.

To be sure, the act covers much more than click-wrap assent to electronic contracts, and its passage by states is not assured. (Some 24 state attorneys general objected to it in August on grounds other than click-wrap issues.) And it does not attempt to cover nonsoftware e-commerce transactions. But its resolution of electronic contracting issues is complementary to the broader Uniform Electronic Transactions Act.

Sec. 112 of UCITA establishes the test for "manifesting assent"—a term coined by the 1971 Restatement (Second) of Contracts—to an electronic contract. Sec. 112 also requires that the contracting party have a reasonable opportunity to review the contract. The proposed law defines "assent" broadly. It permits a contract to be formed when a contracting party intentionally engages in conduct "with reason to know that the other party or its electronic agent may infer from the conduct or statement that the person assents" to the term (§§ 112[a][1] and 112[a][2]).

This is relatively straightforward, but the always-vital reporters' notes elucidate the importance of the mouse click. The first illustration of this method of contracting involves an online service. In this illustration, the reporters note, a "party that indicates 'I agree' manifests assent to the license and adopts its terms."

Structuring enforceable e-contracts

Taking *Caspi* and UCITA into account involves essentially following the industry standard in integrating contractual terms into e-commerce sites.

The entire contract or term should be provided in a format that is reasonably accessible and legible. It need not be provided on one screen; the user can scroll. At its end, the consumer must have the opportunity to express an agreement with the contract itself.

And, of course, the system must be configured to retain electronic evidence of the consumer's assent. Those representing consumers seeking to challenge enforcement of click-wrap licenses should look for ways in which the challenged format did not provide an opportunity to review the contract or otherwise tilted the electronic playing field in favor of the Web site.

Enforcing click-wrap licenses is a sensible approach. Enforceable electronic contracts lead to reliable e-commerce and will contribute to increasing confidence in Internet business. In the end, both consumers and businesses will benefit.[1]

---

1 Note from Professor Carr: But see the next article for a different take on this issue (and result).

"CYBERSPEAK: TO MAKE LEGAL TERMS STICK, MAKE WEB USERS CLICK"[2]

WEB SITE OPERATORS who wish to bind site visitors to certain terms should probably do more than simply display those terms on the Web site. Rather, as a precondition to further action on the site, users should be required to click their assent to those critical terms that are sought to be enforceable.

This issue came home to roost in the recent case Sprecht v. Netscape Communication. In that case, the plaintiffs complained that as a result of usage of Smart Download software, Netscape and its parent company, America Online, wrongfully transmitted private information about users' file transfer activity in violation of the Electronic Communications Privacy Act and the Computer Fraud and Abuse Act. Netscape sought to compel arbitration of the case, arguing that binding arbitration was required by the relevant software licensing agreement. The plaintiffs responded that they were not bound to arbitrate the case because the manner in which the license agreement was presented did not lead to consent to arbitration or other terms in the agreement. A federal trial judge in New York agreed with the plaintiffs.

Internet users who wanted to obtain Smart Download from Netscape's Web site arrived at a page pertaining to the download of the software. There appeared a tinted button on this page labeled "Download." By clicking on this button, the user started the download. The only reference on this page to a license agreement appeared in the text only if the user scrolled down the page to the next screen. If a user did this, he would see an invitation to "please review and agree to the terms of the Netscape Smart Download license agreement before downloading and using the software." If a user clicked on this text, the user then would be taken to a page containing the license agreement, and by clicking through this agreement the user ultimately could find the language requiring arbitration of disputes.

Critical to the judge's decision that arbitration could not be required was the fact that Internet users were not required affirmatively to indicate their assent to the license agreement (and its arbitration terms), or even view the license agreement, before proceeding with the download of the software. This was different from a "click-wrap" license that requires the user to manifest assent by clicking on an icon; the product cannot be obtained unless the icon is clicked. The judge noted that the few other courts to have considered click-wrap contracts have upheld them as valid and enforceable.

Netscape tried to argue that there had been sufficient contractual assent simply by the unambiguous indication of assent; "the primary purpose of downloading is to obtain a product, not to assent to an agreement." In contrast, "clicking on an icon stating 'I assent' has no other meaning or purpose than to indicate such assent." Thus, Netscape's failure to require users of Smart Download to explicitly assent to the license agreement containing the arbitration requirement as a precondition to downloading its software was deemed "fatal" by the judge to Netscape's argument that a contract requiring arbitration had been formed.

The now obvious lesson is that if you want to make certain terms stick, require Internet users to affirmatively click their assent to critical terms before they can proceed further on the site.

---

2 Note from Professor Carr: The judge/court in this case said that under these facts/ circumstances, pointing, clicking and then downloading was <u>not</u> assent/an agreement by the person pointing and clicking to be bound by the terms of the web site/web page.

LEASE EXAMPLE: BARGAINING IN THE SHADOW OF THE LAW

Chris,

I am having some contracting trouble, which is kind of ironic because my new job is now contracting.

Nicole and I just moved in to an apartment in Huntington Beach, we were supposed to move into a one bedroom on June 9 for $1150. We signed a lease for a specific apartment for a specific price a couple of weeks before, a week or so prior to signing that lease we paid $100 to be on a waiting list that would then be applied towards our deposit. We also paid a $60 application fee. They did not give me a copy of the lease we signed that day, and said they would on the day we moved in. I didn't really question that since I figured they have problems with people losing junk like that on the move and didn't question it at the time. Well that apartment was no longer available because the tenant did not vacate and they were going to have to force him out.

In the meantime they were putting us in a studio for a month for another one bedroom across the hall for the same price available for us on July 9th. We moved in on a month-to-month lease, for the studio on June 9th and gave a cashier's check for $1,263. Well, that second apartment is no longer available. They keep trying to offer us other apartments that cost more and are less desirable. I believe that the original lease was a valid contract to take possession of a property on June 9th. That did not happen, and while it is beyond their control, isn't that a breach on their part? I believe it is, but then again, who am I?! Now they are saying since that date has come and gone thus making the contract null and void. Today I asked for a copy of my original lease since I never did receive it. The manager said she couldn't give me a copy of that lease unless she writes void on it. I said no, I just want a copy of my file which you have, and that I believe I have a right to see it. I explained that I want a copy of what I have signed my name to so I know my complete rights. She will not give me a copy until she speaks to her attorney.

My basic question is ... do I have a right to see my file, the original lease, and everything else? Do they have a right to void it, without my signature?

She is also saying that by not taking the original apartment I also "agreed" that the contract is void. I asked if we had an implied contract, she said no, then I said well that is why I want a copy of my lease to read what I have signed more closely.

Your thoughts?

xxxxxx

HYPOTHETICAL – 1

Kelly and Pat are siblings. Kelly, the elder of the two, wants to buy a house, and Pat's house is on the market. One night, as they leave the precinct meeting headed for the friendly neighborhood bar, Kelly says, "Pat, I'll take that house off your hands for $80,000."

"Surely you jest!" replies Pat: "I must net at least $90,000." After verbal negotiation, they compromise on $85,000. They both cross their hearts and hope to die that they mean it, and they write the terms of the agreement on a piece of paper to show Mom. Pat signs the paper.

a) Who, if anyone, was the offerer? Why?
b) Who, if anyone, was the offeree? Why?
c) Was there an agreement? If so, why? If not, why not?
d) Was a contract formed? If so, why? If not, why not?
e) If a contract was formed, was it bilateral or unilateral? Why?
f) If a contract was formed, was it oral or written? Why?
g) If a contract was formed, was it express or implied? Why?
h) If a contract was formed, was it an enforceable contract? Why? If not, why not?
i) What was the consideration, if any, of the offeree?
j) What was the consideration, if any, of the offerer?

HYPOTHETICAL – 2

Mary Smith owns a number of properties in the Central Coast area. One of these properties is a lot with an ocean view near Cambria.

One day Mary is approached by Bill, a retiree who recently moved to San Luis Obispo from Los Angeles. Bill heard about the lot that Mary owns near Cambria. He approaches her about selling the lot. To Bill's surprise, Mary says she is leaning toward selling the lot. Bill asks her to go ahead and write up an offer to sell and fax it over to him, and Mary says she will do so.

She faxes it (her offer) to him on Thursday morning. The selling price listed/stated in her offer is $160,000. The offer is silent as to how long it remains open and how it may be accepted.

Later that night, while she is having dinner with some friends at a posh restaurant in Morro Bay, Mary rummages through her purse and pulls out the offer again to take a quick look at it and refold it (it had unfolded in her purse and become crumpled). To her shock, she realized that she made a typo in the offer. The offer price should have read $190,00, not the $160,000 that she typed in. She has no idea how she missed this typo as she normally prides herself on being a "details person." Panicked, she calls you and asks what she should do.

MEMORANDUM

TO:	Plaintiff's Teams
FROM:	Managing Partner
RE:	*Baker v. Esprit*

Your law firm in San Luis Obispo has had referred to it by the New York Firm of Browbeat Flogg & Harass a litigation matter on behalf of its client, Richard Baker. The client wants a complaint filed in this matter next week, before Esprit can file a claim against him in a related matter. He wants to file first so as to control the choice of court and venue. Please prepare, for my review, by next Wednesday, a draft complaint in this matter. Because of the shortage of time, please utilize to the extent possible, the standard California Judicial Council forms for breach of contract and any related causes of action which you believe should be included in the same complaint.

The pertinent facts are as follows:

Our client, Richard Baker is a resident of Big Sur, in Monterey County, California. He is a former garment industry executive who formerly was president of one of the divisions of Esprit's apparel lines. He left the employ of the company in 2006 when the company was acquired by an off-shore vulture fund. There ensued certain litigation between Baker and Esprit concerning his separation from the company, his entitlement to executive severance pay, and issues of his reimbursement to the company of certain mortgage assistance and relocation loans.

After the filing of the litigation, but before it went to trial, Baker met with the then general counsel of Esprit, Kathleen Anderson, at the Inn at Morro Bay on or about July 12, 2008, to attempt to negotiate a settlement. They reached an agreement on all material terms. The next morning the general counsel returned to her office in San Francisco, where she prepared and forwarded a signed agreement to Baker, who was still at the Inn at Morro Bay. The agreement provided, *inter alia,* that Baker was to have the agreement reviewed by his own counsel, and to execute and return it by July 17; due to slow mail delivery, Baker did not receive the contract until the 17th. He immediately phoned Anderson to acknowledge receipt and said he was sending it to his attorney post haste, that it appeared to him to be consistent with the agreement they had reached in Morro Bay, and that to show his good faith, he was going to go ahead and send Anderson the sum of $20,000. Anderson told him not to worry about the date, just to get it done as soon as possible. Anderson received and Esprit deposited the $20,000 payment on July 20, 2008. In the meantime, Baker had the contract reviewed by an attorney, signed it, and placed it in the mail in Morro Bay to Anderson on July 27, 2008. Anderson had previously executed the draft she had sent on behalf of Esprit.

On July 28, 2008, Kathleen Anderson lost her life in a kayaking accident off of Coos Bay. Immediately thereafter the corporate secretary of Esprit on July 29, 2008, sent a facsimile to Baker, indicating that Esprit was withdrawing its offer to settle the pending litigation and was repudiating the settlement contract in its entirety. Esprit continued to refuse to honor its settlement agreement and continued to prosecute the litigation and a subsequent appeal in New York. Baker prevailed in the litigation, but incurred additional litigation expenses after July 12, 2008, of $200,000 and the loss of his severance which he had off-set against his loan obligations with in the amount of $270,000. The settlement agreement Anderson had signed on behalf of Esprit contained an attorney's fees clause.

LIMOSINE EXAMPLE BARGAINING IN THE SHADOW OF THE LAW

Dear Dr. Carr:

I'm in your business law class and have run into a real problem of my own.

I agreed to go to a prom with an old friend of mine and who is still in high school. About a week and a half ago she called a limo place to rent a limo for the prom. Well she did and arrangements were made. I called in a few days later to pay for the limo using one of my credit cards. Apparently she agreed to a price or at least thought she agreed to a price of $765.00, at $85.00 an hour and for 9 hours.

According to her the $765.00 was quoted to her by who I understand to be the owner. When I called in he told me he would be faxing me a sheet with the confirmation, which I would need to sign and fax back. The fax did not come till May 28. After reviewing the form I saw a portion that stated a $28.00 charge for gratuity. I called in and asked about this charge and he responded that the charge was for gratuity, tax, and any parking and bridge tolls that may be incurred. Also that the $28.00 was not part of the $85.00 an hour. In any case this bumped the total cost up to $979.20.

This is more than anyone in the party can afford to spend and we want to cancel but according to him it is too late to cancel, and he stated I would be billed even if we do not use the limo that night.

I was wondering if there is any claim we can make to get out of the contract. I looked back into what we learned so far and I don't know how the law relates to this situation. Also my date, the one who called in to make the reservation for the limo, recently turned 18.

If you could reply soon it would be much appreciated.

Thank you.

xxxxxx

PRACTICE PROBLEM 1

On November 11, 2008, Turner Broadcasting orally contracted to lease the Los Angeles Coliseum for a multi-sport millennium celebration December 31, 2009 in Los Angeles. However, Turner Broadcasting, early in 2009, after reviewing its disappointing 2008 financial results, and "recrunching" the numbers for its millennium celebration, realized that it had grossly miscalculated. In short, Turner Broadcasting realized that if it were to go ahead and honor its oral contract to rent/lease the coliseum, it would lose millions of dollars. The other contracting party, the City of Los Angeles, has a current employee named Tom Hanks, who is a senior manager with the City's Property Management Department. Hank's previous employer was Turner Broadcasting, for whom he did contract, lease and accounting work, but was fired because he had told an off-color joke about Mr. Turner's wife at a company retreat for executives. Hanks had been fired by Turner Broadcasting, and then hired by the City of Los Angeles, right before the lease was entered into. It is unclear at this point whether Hanks actually knew about Turner Broadcasting's miscalculation before the City of Los Angeles and Turner Broadcasting entered into the lease at issue.

For obvious reasons, Turner Broadcasting does not want to perform its obligations under the contract.

What defenses are available to Turner Broadcasting with regard to the formation and enforcement of the contract at issue?

PRACTICE PROBLEM 2

Jenny Jones is a 29 year old female. She is a bright, charismatic, attractive and funny investment banker who loves adventure.

Last year she left her job in New York City for a new job in San Francisco. She had six weeks to make the move before she started her new job. She boxed up all her belongings, shipped them to San Francisco using a moving company, and then decided get in her car and take a cross country trip from New York to San Francisco in order to see the country, decompress and engage on an adventure. And, an adventure she got ... that's for sure.

As she was driving west through Nevada, her car broke down on the freeway. She was approximately 10 miles from the nearest town. It was 10:00 p.m. at night when her car broke down. She took her cell phone, called ahead to the next town, was able to roust a tow truck operator out of bed; and he proceeded to drive out to hitch up her car and tow it into town.

When the tow truck operator (Ben) arrived, she profusely thanked him for coming and then asked him how much the tow was going to be. He stated that under such "emergency and short notice conditions" the price would be $750.00

Jenny's heart sank and inside she felt quite angry and taken advantage of. She was not averse to paying this fellow a fair wage for his time, help and work, but what she thought was "fair" was a very different figure than what Ben thought was "fair." Jenny said "okay" to Ben's quote of $750. Ben went ahead and hooked up her car and towed her into town.

Once they arrived in the town and Ben unhooked her car, Jenny had second thoughts about paying the $750. She felt that this guy—Ben—was taking advantage of her because of her desperate situation and because she was a female. She took out her wallet and gave Ben $300. She thought that was more than fair and stated that was all she would pay. Ben, of course, was not a happy fellow. Ben took the $300 but then later filed a small claims action in Nevada against Jenny to recover the remaining $450 he thought she owed. Two weeks ago Jenny was served with a copy of that complaint as she was walking into her office building in San Francisco.

Jenny calls you for legal advice. What will you tell her? What are the legal issues presented by this hypothetical?

TheMobileSolution

Date 12-10-02 Location S.M. Dealer Code CA2876 Salesperson John B.

Customer Information

Name (First, Last) Jimmy Hendricks			Street Address 628 Chalker St. Apt. #"D"	
City 0186	State CA	Zip Code 93446	Social Security Number 504-99-8064	Date of Birth 1-10-82
Home Number (805-644-8191)	Work Number		Drivers License Number B9694683	Exp. Date 7-10-06

Customer Invoice

Promotion	$ 0
Employee discount	$ 0
15 day	$ 0
Promotion E	$ 0
Not Many 15 day Buy REMORSE *	
	Tax $
Method of payment (Circle One) Cash Check Credit Card	Total $

Wireless Service Information

Application Number 66837	Credit Score	Deposit Amount 0	Payment Method Customer Int. JH
Carrier Att	Activation Fee 10.–		Service Commitment 2 year
Rate Plan 120	Monthly Service Fee		Included Minutes 1400 unlimited night
Promotional Offer linked	Free		long w/ slak 5

Mobile Number:	Phone Type:	ESN:	Rate Plan:
1 805 766-2484	Panasonic	1930 66684	2 aa9
2 805 766-2486	"	1930 55841	
3 805 766-2488	"	199316487	

Wireless Service Agreement

Customer (int.) JH **and Guarantor (int.)** ________ understand, accept and agree to the following:

a.) Each "Mobile Number" with AT&T Wireless named as "Carrier", shall remain active a minimum of 181 consecutive days beginning on the date of this agreement. Customer is the service user and shall not cancel or suspend service during this period. Guarantor shall pay on behalf of customer all obligations created by this agreement and shall not cancel or suspend service during this period.

b.) Customer and guarantor warrant that the customer(s) listed above has/have not cancelled or suspended any service with "Carrier" within the 181 days prior to the date of this agreement. I/We personally guarantee that the customer(s) listed above shall not cancel or suspend any existing service with "Carrier" for 181 days from the date of this agreement. **Customer (int.)** JH **Guarantor (int.)** ________

c.) The Mobile Solution receives a promotional payment from "Carrier", which has been used to give a $400.00 discount toward the purchase and/or activation of the above Electronic Serial Number(s) "ESN". Should either of the conditions (a) or (b) be broken, which will cause The Mobile Solution to lose it's promotional payment, or if the "Carrier" charges back The Mobile Solution for any reason, I/We will immediately pay The Mobile Solution $400.00 per infraction as compensation for it's loss.

Guarantor's Security Deposit

I choose the following method of payment of securing this contract:

Customer (int.) JH **Guarantor (int.)** ________ **I. Credit Card/Debit Card Deposit.** I authorize The Mobile Solution Corporation to charge my credit card/debit card account any amounts that become due under this contract. This agreement will act as my signed receipt in the amount of $400.00 per mobile number activated to be utilized in the event that amounts become due pursuant to conditions above

Customer (int.) ________ **Guarantor (int.)** ________ **II. Cash/Money Order Deposit.** I am leaving $150.00 cash/money order deposit per mobile number subject to the condition above. If any amounts become due under this contract, my deposit will be applied toward the balance. If at the end of the above-mentioned minimum period in section (a) no amounts become due the deposit shall be returned.

Jimmy Hendricks — Jimmy Hendricks — 12-10-02
Customer print name — Customer signature — Date

Guarantor print name — Guarantor signature — Date

John B — John Benedetto — 12-10-02
Employee print name — Employee signature — Date

This is the entire agreement between all parties and is not subject to oral or written modification

Refund Policy: No refunds after 15 days. Phones may be exchanged within 15 days from the date of purchase. Returns and exchanges must be in new condition and include all original packaging and paperwork. Returns/ exchanges without phone, battery, home charger, handsfree kit, owners manual, and original receipts will not be accepted. JH (Cust. Int.) ________ **(Guar. Int.)**

IMPRINT CREDIT CARD/DEBIT CARD HERE

Check List:

Copy of I.D. for customer and guarantor? ______
Initials in item b.) and above? ______
Print, sign and date for customer and guarantor? ______
Method of payment circled? ______
All items purchased listed, even if given away? ______
Initial refund policy statement? ______
Credit Card authorization for $1.00 if necessary? ______

White copy (customer) Yellow copy (office)

HYPOTHETICAL – THE CASE OF THE FREELOADING RELATIVE

Following your successful graduation at Cal Poly, your family holds a party to celebrate. One of the people attending is a relative, whom you haven't seen for years. Near the end of the party, when people are beginning to clean up, your relative sidles up to you and asks if you ever studied contracts in the business law course you took. You tell her that regrettably, yes, you were required to take that class and that you did, in fact, study the subject of contracts. She pulls out of her handbag a crumpled piece of paper with handwriting on it, and thrusts it at you. [See attached Exhibit A on the next page] She tells you that you could do her a really big favor if you would just review the document and tell her what you think. She says she and another friend of hers are really interested in buying the property, and they had just received the letter from the owner, but they wanted to know if they write back and accept the owner's offer, whether it will result in a legally binding contract. She says that neither she nor her friend has enough money to hire a lawyer, and besides, they don't think the property will last long, and they want to get something back to the owner tomorrow.

What advice would you give to your relative? Are there enough terms there and are they definite enough and enforceable enough to be an offer? Also, is this a contract that is required to be in writing and signed by the offeror under the Statute of Frauds to be enforceable (see textbook chapter posted on Blackboard)?

EXHIBIT A

Rent or Lease To Purchase 3-7-06

ALL Propty At Wt Mt. Cafe

① Cafe
② 1 Bedroom House
③ MoteL

$1,000.00 Per Mounth Less Rental

$350.00 Per Mounth To Apply To Purchase Price Downpayment or Reduction of Principle

– Purchas Price – $100,000.00 –

– Propty As Is – Includs 1 Acer In Front of Park

* ALL Improvments To Be in Writting – Aproved *

John Smith

General info No complaints AND Binding

Course Reader Materials for the Fourth Exam

Business Entities and Organizations

Sole Proprietorships,

Ordinary Partnerships,

Limited Partnerships (LPs),

Limited Liability Partnerships (LLPs),

Limited Liability Companies (LLCs),

and Corporations

142 Introduction To Business Entities—Forms Of Business

Study Outline

*****Note that in this textbook at pages 447–455 I have inserted several newspaper articles ("Small Business, Big Decisions" and "Earthly Assets: Besieged Church Tries to Protect Vast Real Estate") that relate to and do an excellent job of setting up/introducing this material. These articles are required reading, and, are also fair game for the exam.**

*****Make *<u>sure</u>* that you also do the various sample practice problems posted on Blackboard re: business entities – forms of business as they will help you master this material, test you to see if you "really" know and understand it, etc. You can expect similar problems to be on the exam.**

I. Choosing a Form of Business -- it is one of the most important decisions made by a person beginning a business

A. **Why?** Because it has important liability and control ramifications, tax consequences, etc.

1. Important factors that drive business entity/form of business selection:
   a) Ownership and control (there are positives and negatives in sharing ownership and control with others vs. being your own boss)
   b) Continuity of life (what happens when one of the owners dies, leaves the business, retires etc.?)
   c) Transferability of interest (e.g., can one of the owners transfer his/her ownership interest in the entity to a creditor?)
   d) Tax implications (which entity minimizes the amount of tax owed to the government?)
   e) Liability (who is responsible for the legal liabilities of the business?)
   f) Cost (which one is cheap to form? which one is expensive?)
   g) Ability to attract funding/financing from investors (e.g. venture capitalists)

B. Options:

1. **Sole Proprietorship** -- has only ***one owner*** and it is merely an extension of that owner. He/she makes all management decisions, all profits are his/hers, he/she assumes greater liability (e.g.,

he/she is *personally* liable for all obligations of the business). Hence, it is both rewarding and risky!

a) Other Attributes:
   (1) A sole proprietorship is not considered to be a legal entity. Thus, it cannot sue or be sued (i.e., since the owner *is* the business, creditors must sue the owner and he/she must sue in his/her own name those who harm the business)
   (2) It automatically terminates on the death of the owner
   (3) Taxes: Is not a tax paying entity for federal income tax purposes (i.e., the owner pays all of the taxes himself as an individual; the sole proprietorship is not taxed). The same is true with respect to deducting business losses.

b) Why do/chose?
   (1) Because it's easily formed, inexpensive to form, and as a practical matter, few people consider their business form decision and it may therefore occur by default!

c) Note that part of starting an sole proprietorship involves filling out and submitting a fictitious business name statement form and posting the relevant notice in your local paper
   (1) See, for example, the form and example I have placed in this textbook at page 457–458

d) Sample practice problems:
   (1) Of the following statements concerning sole proprietorships, which is accurate?
      (a) A sole proprietorship has no existence apart from the owner of the business [Correct]
      (b) A sole proprietor's liability for business-related debts is limited to the value of the assets of the business [Incorrect]
      (c) If a sole proprietor begins operating her business entity under a trade name, the business becomes a separate entity for income tax purposes [Incorrect]
      (d) If a sole proprietor hires one or more employees, the business becomes a joint venture rather than a sole proprietorship [Incorrect]
   (2) Sal Monella is the sole proprietor of a restaurant. One of his customers was injured when she slipped on a pool of spilled gravy that Monella's waiter had negligently failed to remove from the floor of the restaurant. The customer has sued Monella, who claims that he has no personal liability and that the customer may recover damages only out of the business assets of the restaurant. Is Monella correct?
      (a) Answer: Monella is wrong. His business is a sole proprietorship, which is not its own separate legal entity. Monella faces unlimited personal liability for debts connected with his restaurant business

2. **Partnership (Ordinary Partnerships)** -- has ***two or more owners***, called ***partners***
   a) Attributes:
      (1) Partners have the equal right to make all management decisions. They also share in all profits of the business

(2) Personal liability: Partners assume ***personal liability*** for all the obligations of the business. All debts of the business are debts of the partnership

(a) If assets of the business are insufficient to pay the claims of its creditors, the creditors may require one or more of the partners to pay the claims using their individual/personal assets

(3) Partners are also liable for the torts committed in the course of the partnership business by their partners or by employees of the partnership

(4) Taxes: Is ***not*** a tax paying entity for federal income tax purposes. Instead, all income of the partnership is income to its partners and they must report on their individual tax returns. Also, losses are treated the same way

(5) Has no life apart from its owners. Thus when one partner dies or leaves, the partnership is dissolved

(6) A partner's interest in a partnership is ***not*** freely transferable. That means that a purchaser of a partner's interest in the partnership is not a partner of the partnership unless the other partners agree to admit the purchaser as a partner

b) Why do?

(1) Requires no formalities: while it is normally formed by agreement, it may be formed by default (e.g., under the Uniform Partnership Act (UPA) it may be automatically created when two or more persons own a business together without selecting another form)

(2) Each partner's right to manage the business and the deductibility of the partnership losses on one's individual tax returns are also attractive

****Note that partnerships are discussed later and in greater detail in the "Ordinary Partnerships" Study Outline and related materials (see pages 467–490 of this textbook)

3. **Limited Partnership (LP)** -- has at least one general partner and at least one limited partner

a) Attributes:

(1) General Partner(s):

(a) General partner rights and liabilities are similar to partners in a regular ordinary partnership (see above). Most importantly, the liability of a general partner is usually unlimited

(i) However, typically, and as a practical matter, the general partner is often a *corporation*, thereby protecting the human managers that make up the general partner from unlimited personal liability

(b) Tax rules that apply to general partners are the same as with partners in a regular partnership (see above)

(c) When a general partner dies or withdraws, the limited partnership is dissolved in the absence of an agreement to the contrary

(d) A general partner's rights may not be transferred to another person unless the other partners agree to admit the new person as a partner

(2) Limited Partner(s):
   (a) Limited partners usually have no personal liability once they have paid their capital contribution to the limited partnership (i.e., their liability is normally limited to what capital they paid into/contributed to the LP)
   (b) Limited partners essentially have the same rights as general partners, including the right of access to partnership books and the right to other information regarding partnership business
      (i) However, they have no right to manage the business and if they do, they may lose their personal liability protection
   (c) Tax rules for limited partners:
      (i) Must pay federal income tax on their share of the profits of the business. They may deduct their share of losses only to the extent of their investment in the business
(3) Other:
   (a) A limited partnership may have a life span apart from its owners. For example when a limited partner dies or otherwise leaves, the limited partnership is ***not*** dissolved
   (b) A limited partnership is dissolved in much the same way as an ordinary partnership
(4) Creation of an LP:
   (a) Unlike a sole proprietorship or partnership, a limited partnership may only be created by complying with a state statute permitting limited partnerships (e.g., the parties must sign a ***certificate of limited partnership*** and file it with the Secretary of State and this certificate is usually open to public inspection). Thus, it cannot be created by default

b) Why do?
   (1) By using a corporate general partner, no individual will have unlimited liability for the debts of the business
   (2) Losses of the business are deductible on the owners' individual federal income tax returns
   (3) Investors may contribute capital to the business yet avoid unlimited liability and the obligation to manage the business. Thus, the LP has the ability to attract large amounts of capital. For a business needing millions of dollars of capital and expecting to lose money in its early years, an LP is a good way to go

4. **Limited Liability Partnership (LLP)** -- a reaction to the large personal liability sometimes imposed on ***professionals*** (usually attorneys, accountants, and architects) for the professional malpractice of their partners

a) Primary Attributes:
   (1) A partner's liability for his partners' professional malpractice (i.e., negligence) is limited to the partnership's assets

(2) BUT a partner retains unlimited personal liability for his OWN malpractice (i.e., negligence) and for all NON-professional obligations of the partnership
   (a) Examples of non-professional obligations would be things like rent the LLP owes to its landlord for its office space, fees owed on a repair bill for the copy machine the LLP uses in the course of its business, etc.

b) Other attributes:
   (1) Essentially the same as a regular partnership
      (a) Note: to create, there must be an agreement by the owners and they must comply with the limited liability partnership statute (e.g. -- many states have enacted LLP statutes that you have to comply with -- you generally need to file the appropriate form with the Secretary of State, pay the annual fee, maintain a certain amount of professional liability insurance, add "L.L.P." to the name of the firm, etc.)

c) Why do?
   (1) Allows professionals, such as lawyers and accountants, the flexibility of management, while insulating them in part from personal liability
   (2) Relatively easy to establish

d) **See related "Arthur Andersen LLP" articles in this textbook at page 459–464. This material is fair game for the exam**

5. **Corporation (Regular C Corps)** -- owned by shareholders who elect a Board of Directors to manage the business. The Board then often selects officers to run the day-to-day affairs of the business. Consequently, ownership and management of the corporation may be completely separate

   a) Attributes:
      (1) No shareholder has the right to manage the corporation
      (2) Shareholders have limited liability for the obligations of the corporation (i.e., their liability is normally limited to the amount they paid for their shares/the amount the bought into the corporation)
      (3) Directors and officers have no personal liability for the contracts they or the corporation's employees negotiate in the name of the corporation
      (4) While managers have personal liability for their own misconduct, they generally have no personal liability for corporate torts committed by other corporate managers or employees
      (5) Taxes: A corporation is usually a tax paying entity for federal income tax purposes
         (a) Shareholders do not report their share of the corporation's profits on their individual tax returns. They only report when the corporation distributes profits to the shareholders in the form of dividends, or, the shareholders sell their stock at a profit. Note how this creates a double tax liability as profits

are taxed at the corporation level and again at the shareholder level when dividends are paid

(b) Also, shareholders do not deduct corporate losses on their individual tax returns. They may, however, deduct their investment loses after they have sold their shares of the corporation

(c) Federal Corporate Tax Rates (see below chart). I won't test you on the below rates, but I provide them to you so you can get a feel for what they are, how the change/increase depending on the corporation's income. Note how these tax rates go up with/as the corporation's income goes up. This level of income can help you determine whether you form a corporation, or, stay a sole proprietorship (for example) where the tax rates can be different and so as to take advantage of the lowest possible tax rate!

Federal Corporate Tax Rates (as an example – this is a recent schedule but will, of course, change as presidents come and go)

Corporate Taxable Income	Corporate Tax
$0-$50,000	15% of taxable income
$50,001-$75,000	$7,500 + 25% of income over $50,000
$75,001-$100,000	$13,750 + 34% of taxable income over $75,000
$100,001-$335,000	$22,250 + 39% of taxable income over $100,000
$335,001-$10,000,000	$113,900 + 34% of taxable income over $335,000
$10,000,001-$15,000,000	$3,400,000 + 35% of taxable income over $10,000,000
$15,000,001-$18,333,333	$5,150,000 + 38% of taxable income over $15,000,000
Over $18,333,333	$6,416,667 + 35% of taxable income over $18,333,333

(6) A corporation has a life separate from its owners and mangers. For example, when a shareholder or manager leaves/dies, the corporation is *not* dissolved.

(7) A shareholder may sell his shares of the corporation to other persons without limitation, unless there is a contract or agreement to the contrary. The purchaser then becomes a shareholder with all the rights of the selling shareholder

b) Why do?

(1) No human has unlimited liability for the debts of the business. Thus, risky businesses incorporate (e.g., a manufacturer)

(2) Corporations can attract a large amount of capital because investors can avoid unlimited liability, escape the responsibility of managing the business, and easily liquidate their investments by selling their shares

(3) With respect to S Corporations (see below), losses of the business are deductible on individual federal income tax returns. However, because S Corporations are also limited to 100 shareholders, the ability to raise capital is severely limited as it may be difficult to find investors willing to buy their shares, or they may be restricted from selling their shares pursuant to a previous agreement

c) **NOTE: THE "S" CORPORATION**

(1) Shareholders can elect to have the corporation and its shareholders taxed under Subchapter S of the Internal Revenue Code. Here, the corporation and its shareholders are taxed nearly entirely like a partnership

(a) Requirements: See textbook and class lecture for details. Among other things, a corporation electing S Corporation status can have no more than 100 shareholders

6. **Limited Liability Company (LLC)** – a relatively new business form intended to combine the non-tax advantages of corporations with the favorable tax treatment of partnerships. It is essentially a hybrid between a partnership and a corporation!

a) Attributes:

(1) LLC is owned by "members" (they are not called shareholders), who may mange the LLC themselves, or elect the manager(s) who will operate the business

(a) These members are fiduciaries of the LLC

(b) These members also have limited liability for the obligations of the LLC (i.e., their liability is limited to their capital contribution; they are not subject to personal liability for the debts/liabilities of the LLC)

(c) An LLC does not have the S-Corp's limits on the numbers or types of owners/members

(2) To create an LLC, you must have "LLC" in the name (e.g., "Jones & Co., LLC" works; "Jones & Co." does not)

(3) Like partnerships, there is no federal income taxation at the firm level. Instead, LLC owners pay taxes on their share of the firm's profits (i.e., the IRS recognizes and treats LLCs as partnerships for federal income tax purposes)

(4) However, the transfer of membership is prohibited without the consent of all the members

(5) Death, retirement, or bankruptcy of any member dissolves and forces the liquidation of the LLC, unless all the remaining members vote to continue the business (note: this factor is one of the major disadvantages of the LLC)

b) Why do?
   (1) The LLC has the limited liability advantage and the management advantage of the corporation. The LLC and its members receive the same federal tax treatment as the S Corporation and its shareholders, yet the LLC has no limit on the number or type of owners, as does an S Corporation

c) **See/read the related "LLC Offers Entrepreneurs Tax Breaks" article at page 465 of this textbook. This article is fair game for the exam**

II. On a side note, see also the "Business Entity Comparison Table – Legal Characteristics" document that is also included in this textbook at pages 537–540 for an excellent summary in table form of the legal characteristics of the entities discussed above.

*****Again, folks, I encourage you to do the various practice problems on business entities – forms of organization that I have posted on Blackboard. You may feel that you know/understand the above material, and, you may. But you also may not. So, be safe and do these practice problems. Many of them involve the <u>application</u> of the above concepts and that is a great way to learn (the only way, really) to see if you really do know and understand this material. – Prof. Carr**

143 Small Business, Big Decisions[1]

Near the Top of Entrepreneurs' List of Things to Do: What to Do About Taxes

The Wall Street Journal

ENTREPRENEURS ARE STRUGGLING through trying times. Yet thousands of Americans are being inspired or forced by circumstances to set up shop on their own for the first time.

If you're among the risk-takers who want to organize a business or a professional-service firm, one of the first things you must consider is how you want to handle federal taxes. That in turn may well determine how you frame the legal structure of your venture.

To begin with, you have two choices: either to accept the double taxation of a regular corporation in order to claim its nontax benefits, or to grab the alluring tax advantage of a so-called flow-through or pass-through entity. This is regardless of your venture's size and of whether you start out alone or with others.

'The profit of a regular corporation is reported first on its own tax return and taxed at corporate rates. Next, individual stockholders are taxed at personal rates on any dividends they get out of the after-tax profit.

However, the earnings of a flow-through concern are taxed at just one level. The business doesn't pay taxes. Instead, all of its profit (including income retained in the business) or loss generally "flows through" to the owners. Then individuals report their personal returns to be taxed at their personal rates.

There are four main types of flow-through to choose from (remember them for the midterm exam). They are the sole proprietorship for one owner, which is the simplest form; the partnership; the S corporation, which is taxed much like a partnership and is named for the Internal Revenue Code subchapter that covers it; and the limited-liability company, or LLC.

Each of these entities has its pros and cons, tax and nontax. However, according to tax advisers, the relatively new LLC has rapidly become the preferred structure for flow-through enterprises, thanks to federal-tax and other enhancement gained in the 1990s.

"Generally, people start by using some form of flow-though entity," says David A. Lifson, managing partner of the New York City accounting firm Hays & Co. For one thing, the business losses that tend to come during the early days pass through to the owners to offset taxes on their other income. Moreover, he says, "there's no tax cost associated with turning a flow-through into a regular corporation later on, but transforming a corporation into a flow-through is a taxable transaction."

---

1 **Note from Professor Carr: This article sets up nicely the business organization/entity formation material and some of the things we will be looking at/studying.**

Flow-throughs have two principal tax negatives, notes Mr. Lifson, who is a director of the American Institute of Certified Public Accountants and a former chairman of its tax executive committee. First, the top personal income-tax rate is higher currently than the corporate rate.

That drawback may be offset by the fact that the sale of a corporation can lead to taxes on both the company's and the owners' gains, while only the owners of a flow-through may be taxed on its sale, he says.

Under the 2001 tax act, the highest individual tax rate is scheduled to drop from 39.1% in 2001 to 35% in 2006, equaling the top corporate rate. In the long term that should make flow-throughs more attractive, provided that Congress doesn't reshuffle rates during the next five years.

An often more troublesome disadvantage relates to the sale of a flow-through. Mr. Lifson continues: "A regular corporation can be sold or merged into another corporation with a tax-free exchange of stock, but a flow-through can't.

Whichever form you choose, make sure that you have "a firm understanding" of all of its obligations regarding taxes, business liabilities and other matters, cautions Robert Hunt, of the Internal Revenue Service. He is deputy director of Taxpayer Education and Communication for the IRS's Small Business/Self-Employed division. His unit's tax workshops offer what he describes as "preventive information" to people who have small businesses or are planning to start them.

You certainly must consider many factors besides taxes in choosing a form for your business. They include personal protection against business liabilities, the number of owners and investors, a need to raise capital, and long-term goals. Any of them may be far more decisive than taxes in your choice and may well channel you into a regular corporation despite its double taxation.

Remember that state laws, not federal, govern the formation and operation of all business structures. Those statutes vary from state to state so you should consult an adviser about the tax pros and cons of each form in your state and how they weigh on the other considerations.

You may also take advantage of instruction from the IRS, the Small Business Administration, and other sources.

Now, let's take a closer look at these business structure.

SOLE PROPRIETORSHIP

As a single owner, you face no formalities or posts to start and run this entity, unless your state or county requires a business or professional license. It's almost ideal for an operator who has no employees or only a handful, or who has become a consultant temporarily while looking for a job, or who has a part time sideline.

The federal tax treatment is simple. Your business doesn't even file a return. You report everything on Schedule C, Profit or Loss From Business, attached to your personal Form 1040 return. About 17.4 million taxpayers filed Schedule Cs for 1998, the IRS says; more than 250,000 of them reported receipts exceeding $500,000. Consider an electrician with three employees who is a client of Nancy E. Goedecke, of Hudson, Mass., an enrolled agent (a tax specialist recognized by the IRS). The electrician has reported receipts and all expenses on Schedule C for more than 15 years. Attachments cover self-employment taxes (Social Security and Medicare), a home office and depreciation of business assets. A retailer would have to add an inventory form, Mrs. Goedecke notes. The electrician also pays quarterly estimated taxes and uses a payroll service to deal with employee-payroll taxes.

The big disadvantage of both sole proprietorships and partnerships is that the owners are liable personally for all obligations and risks arising from the business. Liability protections is the main reasons entrepreneurs form corporations or LLCs. That way, they limit their potential loss generally to their investments in the business.

But sole proprietors and partners can protect their homes and other personal assets with insurance against a variety of business risks, Mrs. Goedecke says. For example, as a sole proprietor herself, she includes errors-and-omissions insurance among her policies.

PARTNERSHIP

For two or more owners, a partnership is also relatively easy to set up. There are some formalities though and there is the cost of hiring a lawyer to draw up a comprehensive partnership agreement.
Although the partnership itself doesn't pay tax, it must file a federal informational return, Form 1065, and send a Schedule K-1 statement to each partner. The K-1 provides the information needed for partners to prepare Part II of Schedule E, Supplemental Income and Loss, for attachment to their personal 1040s.

Nearly 1.9 million partnerships with nearly 15.7 million partners filled 1065s for 1998, the IRS says.

REGULAR, OR C, CORPORATION

Liability protection isn't the only compelling reason to adopt the "C" form, so called for its chapter in the tax code. You can sell stock to raise capital and stock is easy to transfer from one owner to another. And then there's the matter of image: Some investors, lenders, customers and suppliers may prefer to deal with a corporation because it seems better organized and more substantial.

Furthermore, says Mr. Lifson, the New York CPA, "I've had clients who started, say, biotech companies with the goal of going public or selling out to a big corporation in a tax-free, stock-for-stock exchange. They formed corporations." Certain professionals, such as doctors, lawyers and accountants, may form professional corporations, which have special requirements.

Setting up a corporation can be relatively costly and complicated. States require a number of annual document fillings and fees, plus actions such as formal directors' meetings. Preparing the tax return, Form 1120, can be expensive. Dissolving a corporation raises significant tax issues that you should consider before you form one.

S CORPORATION

This structure was developed as a means of combining limited liability and the other main benefits of a corporation with the flow-through tax break of a partnership. Starting in the late 1980s, the number of S corporations grew rapidly. The IRS received nearly 2.6 million Form 1120S informational returns from them for 1998.

But this entity is subject to several restrictions, including one limiting personal deductions of its losses, and to a maximum of 100 stockholders.

The formalities and cost of setting up an S corporation are about the same as those for a regular corporation. As for taxes, the company sends K-1 statements to stockholders; and they report pro-rata results on Schedule E, Part II, attached to their 1040s.

LIMITED-LIABILITY COMPANY

These days, "substantially all" new pass-through businesses are formed as LLCs rather than partnership or S corporations, says Joe Huddleston, of Nashville, Tenn., a former Tennessee revenue commissioner who is national managing partner for state and local taxes at the CPA firm Grant Thornton.

Although Wyoming adopted the first LLC statute in 1977 to create a hybrid entity with both partnership attributes and limited liability, the form languished because the IRS long considered many LLCs to be corporations in sheep's clothing. That position gradually softened, and liberal regulations that took effect in 1997 started the boom.

Under these "check-the-box regs," the IRS treats single-owner LLCs automatically as sole proprietorships and multiple-owner companies as partnerships, unless they elect treatment as corporations. LLC owners who operate as sole proprietors or partners follow the federal tax rules for those forms. The states' tax treatment of LLCs varies; ask about taxes in your state.

All states and the District of Columbia now provide LLCs with flexible financial and management rules. While the recently adopted or rewritten state statutes aren't uniform, they generally are far more accommodating to owners and less restrictive than the laws governing other pass-throughs. As a result, "the viability of the S corporation and the partnership has declined dramatically," Mr. Huddleston says. (However, current data about the number of new formations isn't available yet.)

A related form available in most states is the limited-liability partnership, designed especially for professionals such as accountants, lawyers and doctors.

Forming and maintaining an LLC or LLP may require more state administrative filings and expense than for other pass-throughs.

LLCs are so new that one concern about them is the lack of a broad judicial history, notes Mark Luscombe, CPA, lawyer and principal analyst for federal and state taxes at publisher CCH Inc., Riverwoods, Ill. That is, the state statues haven't been tested thoroughly in litigation, in order to settle possible major issues regarding liability protection and other matters. However, that hasn't seemed to put a hold on new LLCs.

It's also important to learn all the ramifications of operating an LLC across state borders, because of statute variations, Mr. Luscombe says. But, listen to this: Tax advisers say more and more LLCs are being formed in Delaware by out-of-state operators, because that state's laws for LLCs—like its laws for corporations—are said to be the most flexible.

Finding Help Online

www.irs.gov

The Internal Revenue Service "does a great job of providing information on setting up a new business," says Stephen P. Valenti, a small-business specialist who has a CPA firm in Plainview, N.Y. "Look for the market-segment guides on the Web site; they go into tax issues for various businesses." Start exploring at "Tax Info for Business" or go directly to the small-business pages at www.irs.gov/smallbiz/index.htm and select "New Business." You may also phone the IRS at 800-829-1040.

www.sba.gov

The Small Business Administration's site has pages on "Starting Your Business" with links to many major resources. Look for Small Business Development Centers, which offer training and counseling; Score, the Service Corps of Retired Executives, who volunteer to counsel businesses; and the states' own sites. On the IRS and SBA sites, you may order a free computer CD-ROM, "Small Business Resource Guide," produced by the agencies. For general information, phone the SBA at 800-827-5722.

cch.com

CCH Inc., a Riverwoods, Ill., tax-information publisher, offers an excellent free introduction to starting a business. Select "CCH Business Owner's Toolkit."

144 Besieged Church Tries to Protect Vast Real Estate[1]

Fearing Sex-Abuse Awards, Dioceses Restructure; Incorporating the Parish

The Wall Street Journal

WITH ITS GILDED ballroom and sweeping views of Rhode Island's Narragansett Bay, the 70-room Aldrich Mansion glows with old-money opulence. It rents for $1,000 an hour for wedding receptions, $750 for baby showers. The proprietor: a corporate arm of the Roman Catholic Church.

The beachfront estate, sold for a token amount to the Providence diocese in 1939 by the heirs of Rhode Island financier Nelson W. Aldrich, is at the center of a brewing dispute confronting Catholic dioceses across the country. The church is trying to use the intricacies of corporate law to shelter the mansion and countless other assets from plaintiffs alleging sexual abuse by priests. Attorneys filing waves of lawsuits are seeking to reach behind what they consider legal facades to grab church assets that can be transformed into cash.

Some dioceses are invoking decades old corporate structures to try to keep real estate beyond plaintiffs' reach. In other cases, church lawyers have recently created new corporate boundaries they hope will protect properties.

One of the Gems

Both strategies are in play in Rhode Island, where 38 sex-abuse suits are pending in state court. The 85-acre Aldrich Mansion is one of the gems of a real-estate portfolio valued at $44.6 million that is affiliated with the Providence-based diocese, according to local tax records.

But the mansion and the other properties are legally owned by a nonprofit corporation created more than 100 years ago, which, diocesan lawyers contend, has no involvement with priests or church affairs. "The corporation is not automatically responsible for the misconduct of a cleric," says William T. Murphy, the diocese's lead attorney. Even if plaintiffs in one or more of the pending suits

1 **Note from Professor Carr: This article also nicely sets up the business organization/entity formation material we will be looking at/studying.**

After reading it, you should have a deeper understanding of how critical and important entity formation and choice of entity selection can be for a firm/business. Who would have ever thought that the Catholic Church would have had such a need for this type of legal advice?

Further, you should be able to see (or start seeing) how creditors can and will attack/try to make an end run around some of the legal protections that certain types of business entities traditionally offer/afford certain businesses.

prevail, he adds, they shouldn't be allowed to get at any of the real estate.

Phyllis Hutnak, 51 years old, who has accused a Rhode Island priest of abusing her when she was a teenager, has helped her lawyers piece together the ownership of church assets by combing through local property and tax records. Church officials "say people who pursue suits are gold diggers," she says. "They've said the money is going to come out of buildings budgets, out of schools, out of buildings. Our point was to let people know that the church was a wealthy place."

As the sex-abuse scandal shakes the Catholic church across the country, threatening to drain at least some diocesan bank accounts, the status of church-affiliated real estate has become a critical question in many communities.

In Stockton, Calif., the church limited its legal damages in one recent priest-molestation case by having earlier set up a separate Roman Catholic Welfare Corp. that owned a variety of properties. In Dallas, the church, in a controversial move, amended certain real-estate documents to protect assets in the wake of a $119 million jury award in 1997.

In Santa Fe, N.M., all of the roughly 200 sexual-abuse suits that have been filed against the diocese since the early 1990s have been settled for a total of about $30 million. The diocese there responded four years ago by creating a separate corporation to shield annual fund-raising proceeds of about $2 million. "We wanted to protect against judgments and be able to tell donors that their donations were safe," says Charles Reynolds, an attorney for the diocese. The device hasn't been tested in court yet, and there aren't any suits pending against the Santa Fe diocese.

In Denver, the diocese has experimented by separately incorporating three of its 113 parishes. One goal of separate incorporation is to wall off those parishes from any liability of the diocese, says a spokesman. The approach hasn't been tested yet in the Colorado courts. It has had mixed results elsewhere. The Denver diocese has been named in two sex-abuse suits, one of which has been dismissed because the six-year Colorado statute of limitations had expired.

At the Epicenter

At the epicenter of the sex-abuse scandal, the Boston diocese earlier this month backed out of a multimillion-dollar settlement with 86 alleged victims.

The diocesan chancellor, David Smith, say that a Massachusetts "charitable immunity" statute that caps individual jury awards against charitable organizations at $20,000 should protect the church in any future litigation. But that law is under attack in a separate federal-court case. "If the charitable immunity in the commonwealth of Massachusetts goes away, then we would have to look at [new] corporate structures, because then assets might be put at risk."

Corporations, introduced in colonial times and widely employed by the late 19th century, are a legal device designed to shield individuals from personal liability arising from the conduct of businesses they own. Corporations themselves may separately incorporate subsidiaries and other affiliates to shield one part of the organization from the liabilities of other parts.

In commercial and product-liability cases, it is common for the combatants to fight over whether various arms of a business are truly separate corporations. One key test is whether each entity has distinct management, or whether all control really traces back to a single source. If control can be traced back to a parent company, a plaintiff can potentially get at the parent's assets. A defendant that fraudulently conceals assets in the face of a suit can be held liable for the deception. But Catholic dioceses haven't been accused of that in the sex-abuse cases.

American religious organizations tend to be organized as nonprofit corporations. "Most churches that we deal with have thought of themselves as corporate entities and have taken steps to protect their assets," says attorney Wendell Bird whose Atlanta law firm specializes in this field. Churches "feel they have responsibility to donors and parishioners not to expose assets to a runaway verdict," he adds. "That's not a newfound concern. What's new is the extent of the liability" in the sex-abuse cases. Hundreds of those cases are now pending, many of them filed in the past year.

How to shield the assets of the Catholic church's 194 U.S. dioceses from priest molestation suits has been a mounting concern for church officials and lawyers since the 1980s, when abuse victims first began winning sizeable verdicts and settlements. At least as far back as 1988, attendees at the annual meeting of the National Association of Diocesan Attorneys in Washington discussed corporate organizations that would better protect diocesan assets while allowing bishops to retain as much control as possible over their parishes, recalls Charles Thomas, an attorney for the Diocese of Rockford, Ill.

"There was a weakness in the dioceses in litigation situations," Mr. Thomas explains. Many dioceses kept most of their assets under the direct legal control of their bishop. If plaintiffs "could get to the bishop," the lawyer says, "they had an advantage." In recent years many dioceses, including Rockford's, have incorporated each parish separately, as well as each new school as it is built.

Separate incorporation probably does insulate a parish from most localized cases of alleged wrongdoing, such as negligent maintenance of a playground at a parish school. But it's less clear whether separate incorporation protects church assets when the alleged wrongdoing involves negligence by a bishop who governs all of the parishes in his diocese and is accused of failing to address sexual misconduct among his priests.

Dallas Award

In 1997, the Diocese of Dallas was hit with a Texas state-court-jury award of $119 million in a suit filed by 11 abuse victims. It remains the largest verdict in a priest sex-abuse case.

But it wasn't clear where the plaintiffs would find church assets worth anything close to their award. Most of the diocese's real estate was separately incorporated and arguably off limits.

The diocese had failed, however, to separately incorporate property valued at $20 million, including two high schools, several parcels of undeveloped land, its administrative headquarters and the bishop's residence. The diocese's 66 parishes also were potentially exposed because they, too, hadn't been separately incorporated. Immediately after the verdict, the diocese scrambled to file amended real estate records in its nine-county domain to indicate the unincorporated assets were owned by the bishop, Charles V. Grahmann, "for the benefit" of the parishes.

Church lawyers say the change makes it clear that a parish had to give its consent before any of its property could be sold.

Plaintiffs' lawyers saw it differently. "They started going through their assets and shoving them back to local parishes that were not defendants in the case, with a contingent that these were assets that belonged to parishes all along but never put in their name," says Windle Turley, one of the plaintiffs' lawyers.

The diocese denies that. "We did it for clarification," says Dennis Sullivan, one of the diocese's lawyers.

The property dispute was headed for a showdown in court in 1998, when the case was settled for $23.4 million. The diocese mortgaged its unincorporated assets to secure an $11.3 million loan that it contributed to the settlement. Its insurers paid the rest.

The Dallas litigation had a side effect: Church donors, worried their money could end up in the hands of future plaintiffs, hesitated to make major contributions, says James Hodges, past board president of Bishop Lynch High School in Dallas. The school was raising money in the late 1990s for a new performing arts center and gym. In response, the school has created separate trust funds to protect donations, he says. That kept money coming in steadily, at least until Sept. 11, when there was a fall off.

The Stockton, Calif., case, which went to trial in 1998, involved two brothers molested by a family priest over 13 years, ending in 1991. The Stockton diocese became aware of other similar complaints during this period and continued to allow the priest unsupervised contact with children, according to the suit filed on behalf of the brothers. The plaintiffs' attorneys thought they had covered the diocese's main assets when they named as their sole corporate defendant a nonprofit organization named for the bishop of Stockton and all successors. That corporation owned most of the diocese's property and buildings, valued at $120 million for insurance coverage.

But halfway through presenting their case, the plaintiffs' lawyers, Laurence Drivon and Jeffrey Anderson, say they learned from testimony of a church official that another legal creation, the Roman Catholic Welfare Corp., owned two parishes, two high schools and 12 elementary schools. It was too late to add this corporation as a defendant. Mr. Anderson says the church "hid" the existence of the Catholic Welfare Corp.—an allegation flatly denied by the diocese.

The additional assets would have made a difference, says Mr. Drivon. Plaintiffs' lawyers often urge jurors to consider a defendant's total assets when weighing punitive damages. In California, total assets are vital for a different reason: State law caps punitive damages at 10% of total assets.

In the Stockton case, the jury ruled for the two plaintiffs, awarding each of them punitive damages of 10% of the $120 million figure, or $12 million. The total award of $30 million, including $6 million in compensatory damages, was reduced by the judge to $12 million. The case ultimately settled in 1998 for $7.7 million.

In Providence, plaintiffs' lawyers face a more difficult task in trying to sort out the diocese's assets. The corporation named for the Roman Catholic bishop there is only one of more than 250 separate corporations within the diocese. One hundred and fifty of those are parishes.

Just figuring out which assets go with which corporations is tricky, plaintiffs' lawyers say. Out of concern for the First Amendment's separation of church and state, religious organizations, unlike other nonprofits, aren't required to report their assets when they seek tax exemptions from the Internal Revenue Service. State reporting requirements in Rhode Island are minimal.

Since the first abuse case was filed in 1992 in Rhode Island state court, the diocese has incorporated another six entities, including an investment trust for its charitable organizations, a trust for a capital campaign begun in the mid 1990s and, two years ago, a fund to provide administrative and financial services throughout the diocese.

The 38 suits in Rhode Island have been bogged down for years in pretrial maneuvering, and the plaintiffs' side hasn't had an opportunity to use depositions and demands for documents to sort out the other side's corporate labyrinth. "What it amounts to is you've got a very sophisticated scheme to play shell games," says Timothy Conlon, one of the plaintiffs' lawyers.

The diocese calls that assertion "scurrilous." It says through its lawyer, Mr. Murphy, that the most recently created corporations serve several purposes, including insulation from liability. That does not. imply "any illegal or improper use of corporate structures," he says.

Ownership of the Aldrich Mansion and certain other valuable properties was traced to the corporation created in the name of the bishop and all successors after Ms. Hutnak and other plaintiffs launched their own investigation, Mr. Conlon says. They visited town halls throughout out the state to examine records.

"It is a way of dealing with the situation, especially when they tend to blame the victim before they do anything else," says Ms. Hutnak, who lives in Carolina, R.I., and filed suit in 1995.

Having traced the mansion and other properties to the bishop's corporation, Mr. Conlon still faces an uphill fight in arguing that the corporation should be on the hook for damages if the plaintiffs eventually win. The corporation was created in 1900 to hold and manage diocesan property.

The corporation's purpose is limited to business functions according to the diocese. It can't be liable for clergy misconduct because it has involvement in ecclesiastical affairs, such as the appointment and supervision of priests. "There is no relationship whatsoever between the alleged perpetrator priests' misconduct and the defendant corporations, the diocese contended in court pleadings in 1998.

The plaintiffs counter that the corporation has in fact become involved with a range of ecclesiastical matters, such as supervising churches, transforming it into an "alter ego" of the bishop. If plaintiffs establish the bishop's liability and the judge presiding over the suits agrees with their view of the church's corporate anatomy, that could expose the assets to being sold off to pay a jury award.

Prior attempts to get at the corporation's assets have failed however. Two years ago, the Rhode Island Supreme Court upheld dismissal of a separate suit against the bishop's corporation asserting it was liable for physical and sexual abuse of children at a Catholic orphanage near Providence in the mid-1980s.

The court found the corporation blameless because, it said, the plaintiffs had produced no evidence it "ever was involved in any hiring, retaining or supervising of [the orphanage's] staff and its operations."

145 Example of Fictitious Business Name Statement Form

NAME ____________________

ADDRESS ____________________

CITY ____________________

SEE REVERSE SIDE FOR INSTRUCTIONS

COUNTY CLERK'S FILING STAMP

FICTITIOUS BUSINESS NAME STATEMENT

THE FOLLOWING PERSON(S) IS (ARE) DOING BUSINESS AS:

1. Fictitious Business Name(s)

2. Street Address, City & State of Principal place of Business in California — Zip Code

3. Full name of Registrant — (if corporation - show state of incorporation)

Residence Address — City — State — Zip Code

Full name of Registrant — (if corporation - show state of incorporation)

Residence Address — City — State — Zip Code

Full name of Registrant — (if corporation - show state of incorporation)

Residence Address — City — State — Zip Code

Full name of Registrant — (if corporation - show state of incorporation)

Residence Address — City — State — Zip Code

4. This business is conducted by [ ] an individual [ ] a general partnership [ ] a limited partnership [ ] an unincorporated association other than a partnership [ ] a corporation [ ] a business trust (CHECK ONE ONLY)

5. Signed ____________________

Typed or Printed ____________________

If Registrant a corporation sign below:

Corporation Name ____________________

Signature & Title ____________________

This statement was filed with the County Clerk of ____________________ County on date indicated by file stamp above.

6. New Fictitious Business Name Statement ☐

7. Refile - Statement expires December 31. ☐

File No. ____________________

I HEREBY CERTIFY THAT THIS COPY IS A CORRECT COPY OF THE ORIGINAL STATEMENT ON FILE IN MY OFFICE.

____
COUNTY CLERK

BY ____________________ DEPUTY

File No. ____________________

FICTITIOUS BUSINESS NAME STATEMENT: The followings person(s) is/are doing business as Kelly Sims Photography at 312 E. Figueroa St., Unit A, Santa Barbara, CA 93101: Dyke Kelly Sims, 312 E Figueroa St., Unit A,. Santa Barbara, CA 93101. This statement was filed with the County Clerk of Santa Barbara County on June 10, 2002. This statement expires five years from the date it was filed in the Office of the County clerk I hereby certify that this is a correct copy of the original statement on file in my office. Kenneth A. Pettit, County Clerk (SEAL) by Millie van Eerde. FBN No. 2002-0001888. Published June 21, 28, July 5, 12, 2002.

FICTITIOUS BUSINESS NAME STATEMENT: The followings person(s) is/are doing business as JMTAX, The Tax Fairy at 610 Anacapa St., C7, Santa Barbara, CA 93101: Jennifer MacMillan. 5660 Pembroke Ct. Santa Barbara, CA 93111. This statement was filed with the County Clerk of Santa Barbara County on June 7, 2002. This statement expires years five years from the date it was filed in the Office of the County Clerk. I hereby certify that this is a correct copy of the original statement on file in my office. Kenneth A. Pettit, County Clerk (SEAL) by Kathy Miller. FBN No. 2002-0001884. Published June 14, 21, 28, July 5, 2002.

Note: The above are two examples of Fictitious Business Name Statements that appeared in a local business newspaper.

146 Partners Forever? Within Andersen, Personal Liability May Bring Ruin[1]

The Wall Street Journal

[LLPs]

AMONG THE LIFE-THREATENING issues facing **Arthur Andersen** LLP, one looming especially large for its partners is how effectively those three letters, LLP, shield them from potentially ruinous personal liability.

Concerns are growing among Andersen's roughly 1,750 U.S. partners that even those who had nothing to do with the firm's work for Enron Corp. could eventually face personal liability stemming from the botched audit. Worried about what protection the limited liability partnership provides them, many are now consulting lawyers for advice, with some pooling their resources to retain prominent bankruptcy attorneys to lay out options for protecting personal assets.

In Houston, for example, one group of partners is close to hiring a law firm to help about 100 partners. "There's no reason for each of us to lay out $1,000 an hour apiece," explained one Houston partner. "Whether or not we ultimately choose bankruptcy that's the type of attorney we're hiring, because they are the ones who would handle the types of issues we have."

The partners' quest for legal advice comes as options for Arthur Andersen are rapidly dwindling. Its trial date is nearing on a federal criminal charge tied to the admitted destruction of Enron-related documents. Already, the firm faces claims exceeding $1 billion from Enron investors, and the collapse last week of a $217 million settlement of a separate Arizona fraud case raised questions about the extent of Andersen's insurance coverage. Yesterday, at least two more audit clients defected and three others announced plans to explore alternatives to Andersen. Meanwhile, there is a job vacancy at the firm's global coordinating body, Andersen Worldwide. Andersen Worldwide's board of partners today in London will discuss, among other things, what to do about the vacancy, created when the global firm's chief executive quit last week.

Every day, the interests of the firm as a whole diverge more from those of the partners, the Houston partner said. "Even though it's a limited liability partnership, we want to make sure we're looking out for our interests."

The limited liability partnership is a comparatively new corporate structure, untested by the kind of stress now besetting Andersen. But that testing appears to be just around the corner as Enron creditors, shareholders and employees seek to recover the billions of dollars they have lost from someone.

1 **Note from Professor Carr: This article does an excellent job highlighting what type of a firm might form an LLP, why, how it is done, and how creditors might try to attack/make an end-run around the traditional advantages/perks that such business entities were "thought" to offer firms/businesses. See also the next article. (Same thing.)**

Because it is unclear how much protection the LLP structure will provide Andersen partners, partnership and bankruptcy lawyers are expected to be following the matter closely. "As far as I know, there has never been a litigation test of the extent of the LLP shield, and there have been very few LLP cases about liability at all," said Larry Ribstein, a law professor at George Mason University.

If I were these boys, I'd be doing some serious estate planning right now on the theory that the limited liability protection will be pierced, and I'd be held jointly and severably liable," said William Brandt Jr., president and chief executive of Development Specialists, Inc., a Chicago restructuring firm. Mr. Brandt presided over the 1997 bankruptcy-court liquidation of law firm Keck, Mahin & Cate, which wasn't a limited liability partnership. At that firm, partners and former partners each had to personally kick in between $5,000 and more than $600,000 to settle malpractice and other claims, even if they had nothing to do with the alleged malpractice.

During the past 10 years, several large general partnerships have plunged into bankruptcy, including the accounting firm of Laventhol & Horwath. In that and other cases, partners and former partners had to dig into their own pockets to satisfy creditors, prompting some to file for personal bankruptcy protection.

The limited-liability partnership was invented about a decade ago in the wake of the savings and loan debacle to protect members of partnerships from being wiped out by claims against their firms. Under the structure, capital invested by partners into the firm is fair game for creditors. In theory, no partner is supposed to lose more than what he or she has invested in the firm.

"There is a strong legal tradition that you don't pierce the corporate veil and go after individual partners except under extraordinary circumstances," said Lynn LoPucki, a professor at the University of California Los Angeles law school. "But the law is very vague and lets the court do what they feel appropriate. It is very case specific and fact intensive."

An exception arises when a partner is guilty of professional wrongdoing or negligence, partnership experts said. In those cases, that partner becomes personally liable. The courts haven't yet set clear precedent on the stickier question of who else might be personally liable. The firm's managers? The supervisors of the guilty parties? Every partner in the firm that put its imprint on a corporate audit?

Some restructuring experts question whether it will be possible for Andersen to contain potential personal liability to the circle of people involved in the Enron audit. Laws differ from state to state on the circumstances under which a claimant can pierce the corporate veil and go after individual partners. The law in Illinois, where Andersen is incorporated, isn't considered as favorable to partners as in many other states.

In 1990, prior to the advent of limited liability partnership, the accounting firm of Laventhol & Horwath filed for Chapter 11 bankruptcy-court protection, in part due to lawsuits over questionable accounting. The firm's assets were insufficient to cover the claims of creditors and litigants.

Under a plan negotiated with the firm's creditors, the 360 partners and former partners who had spent time at the firm since 1984 were required to dig into their own pockets to share a $46 million liability. Under a formula hammered out by partner Jacob Brandzel, now an executive at American Express Co. in Chicago, they were obligated to contribute between about $5,000 and $450,000 depending on factors including seniority. Managers were levied a 5% to 10% surcharge on top. Everyone was given 10 years to pay.

One fact Mr. Brandzel didn't work into the equation was which partners were involved in the audits that led to the malpractice claims. "If we tried to assess liability, we'd have been fighting every one of these things," he said.

In the panicky early days of the firm's dissolution, he recalled, "everyone thought they were going to wind up filing for bankruptcy. That, in fact, didn't happen." In the end, about 15 partners filed for personal bankruptcy protection, most of them junior partners.

147 Andersen Partners Are Enron Targets

The Wall Street Journal

[LLPs continued]

ARTHUR ANDERSEN LLP's 1,700 partners could be held personally liable for major chunks of the firm's debts, Enron Corp. creditors asserted in a bankruptcy-court filing Friday.

Enron's official committee of unsecured creditors accused Andersen of trying to protect its partners by paying off the firm's ordinary business debts, for which partners are liable, it said. That practice will leave less money to pay malpractice claims, for which most partners cannot be held personally liable, the committee claimed.

Enron's creditors have indicated they intend to press claims against Andersen stemming from its botched audit of Enron. Concern has been rampant among partners about whether they will ultimately face personal liability in connection with Enron. Andersen is incorporated in Illinois as a limited-liability partnership, a structure designed to shield partners from firmwide liabilities. But the protection such structures offer has never been tested in a case as large as Andersen's. Settlement talks between Andersen and Enron's creditors and shareholders collapsed earlier this year, leaving Enron claimants unsure how much money they will be able to extract from the rapidly shrinking accounting firm. Andersen has said that it intends to restructure as a much smaller firm and has been selling practice groups to competitors. As Andersen strikes deals with rivals, little has been disclosed about how much cash the firm is receiving or where it is going.

On May 9, the Enron creditors committee moved in federal bankruptcy court in New York to compel Andersen to make extensive disclosures about the firm's restructuring, to determine where the money is going. On May 24, Andersen opposed the requests.

In Friday's filing, the Enron creditors pointed to what they called an "uncommon feature" in Illinois limited-liability partnership law. The applicable law, the committee said, shields partners from malpractice liabilities, except for partners involved in wrongdoing. But because Andersen is incorporated in Illinois, the partners are personally liable for ordinary commercial debts like trade debt and lease obligations, the committee said. In most other states, such a partnership wouldn't be liable for such debt, according to the filing. It is unclear how much Andersen's ordinary business debt amounts to.

In the filing, Enron creditors said they may sue Andersen for "fraudulent conveyance," a tenet of bankruptcy law that bars insolvent companies from shifting assets to the detriment of creditors. The committee contended that Andersen "may now be insolvent," and that "the current payment by Andersen of its 'ordinary commercial debt,' as well as current distributions being made by Andersen to its partners, may constitute fraudulent conveyances."

If Andersen had sought bankruptcy court protection, it would be up to the court to decide how the firm's assets are divided among various classes of creditors, and malpractice claimants would be on an equal footing with other unsecured creditors. Andersen has said that it isn't currently planning to seek bankruptcy protection. A spokesman for Andersen said yesterday: "This motion has absolutely no merit. We plan to oppose it in court."

148 LLCs Offer Entrepreneurs Tax Breaks[1]

[LLCs]

FORMING AN LLC has numerous benefits as opposed to full incorporation, said Brad Lundgren, an associate attorney at Santa Barbara's Hatch & Parent. "They're a nice entity because they combine the benefits of a corporation and a partnership," he said. "The revenues aren't taxed at the entity level, so there's no double taxation, as with corporations," and LLCs aren't taxed at the federal level.

A bill signed into law last year may help entrepreneurs who start limited liability corporations decrease their tax burden and simplify their accounting.

AB 898 set permanent tax rates for California LLCs and eliminated the double taxation that once applied to multi-level LLCs.

When the California Legislature established LLCs in 1994, they also, established the gross receipts fee in place of corporate taxes. The fee ranged from $500 to $4,500, based on the LLCs' total revenues, and was adjusted every year by the state Franchise Tax Board. By 2000 the fees had crept up to between $1,042 and $9,377. AB 898 permanently sets the rates at a range of $900 to $11,790. Eliminating the uncertainty of the changing fee makes it easier for entrepreneurs to establish their businesses as LLCs. "When I can't tell them the fee will be an absolute number, it discourages them from becoming a corporate entity," said Chris Kitisaki, an attorney with Nordman, Cormany, Hair & Compton in Oxnard.

Ken Pontifex, a partner at Price, Postel & Parma in Santa Barbara, agreed. "For a business owner, predictability is second only to profitability," he said.

Though the bill actually raises the LLC fees at some revenue levels, it prevents them from continuing to increase and lowers them slightly at most levels. Even if this doesn't result in huge savings, it's a boon to small-business owners. "A couple hundred dollars is a lot of money when you are starting new company," Kitisaki said.

Prior to AB 898 one drawback of an LLC structure was that revenues from a subsidiary LLC were subject to state fees at both the subsidiary and parent levels. AB 898 does not allow LLC revenues to be taxed more than once. "You eliminate that disincentive not to use the parent/subsidiary structure," Lundgren said.

Entrepreneurs should still be careful when forming a multi-tiered structure, Lundgren said. "The thing you want to be careful about is not to put yourself in a parent/subsidiary structure where you have creditors at the parent levels," he said. "Then you lose the benefits of diversifying your liability, which is the main reason for using a multi-tiered structure."

1 **Note from Professor Carr: This article does a nice job touching on what an LLC is, how it works, some of the advantages (and disadvantages) it offers, etc.**

149 Ordinary Partnerships

Study Outline

Earlier, in connection with the "Introduction to Business Entities – Business Organizations" Study Outline, we briefly looked at ordinary partnerships. Now … let's look at them in greater detail

*****Note that in this textbook at pages 481–490 I have inserted several newspaper articles, supplementary materials, misc. documents, etc. that relate to this material. These materials are required reading, and, are also fair game for the exam.**

*****Make *<u>sure</u>* that you also do the sample practice problems posted on Blackboard ("Practice Problems re: Ordinary Partnerships") as they will help you master this material, test you to see if you "really" know and understand it, etc. You can expect similar problems to be on the exam.**

I. Partnerships

A. Today, the American common law of partnerships has been replaced for the most part by statutory law. Every state has a statute on partnership law. The Uniform Partnership Act (UPA) has been adopted in all states except Louisiana

B. The Creation of a Partnership (how do you create one??)

1. No formalities are necessary. Two or more persons may become partners by an express oral agreement, an express written agreement, or by conduct (i.e., implied)

a) Note: Although not required, it is a good idea to hire a lawyer to prepare a written partnership agreement. As an example in this textbook at pages 481–488 I have included a sample written partnership agreement. Peruse that document to see the types of things it addresses, touches upon, etc.

2. Where no written or oral agreement defining the partnership exists, courts use the definition of partnership in the UPA to determine whether one exists (i.e., under the UPA test, you may, in fact, have unwittingly formed a partnership with another even though you did not think you did, did not want or intend to, etc.!)

a) The UPA's Definition of a Partnership:

(1) Required elements (again ...note that under the UPA, a relationship may meet the legal definition of a partnership even when a person does not believe he is a partner or the parties do not think that they are "partners"!):

(a) **Association of two or more persons** -- here, the association must be a ***voluntary and consensual*** relationship, which can be express or implied

(b) **Carrying on a business** -- can be any trade, occupation or profession. Also, "carrying on a business" requires/implies a series of transactions (versus a single transaction)

(c) **Co-Ownership** -- partners must co-own the business in which they associate. There is no requirement that the capital contributions or the assets of the business be co-owned

(i) Here, the most important factors to consider are the sharing of profits (vs. gross revenue) and the sharing of management of the business

(d) **For profit** -- the owners of an enterprise must ***intend to make a profit*** to create a partnership

(i) If the enterprise suffers losses, yet the owners intended to make a profit, a partnership may still result

(e) **Intent** -- the parties must intend to create a relationship that the *law* (note that this is different than the parties) recognizes as a partnership

(i) Thus, even if the parties create a writing which states that they do not intend to form a partnership, that is not conclusive if their actions meet the UPA test!

None of the above factors is in and of itself conclusive. This is a flexible-sliding scale test that is designed/intended to do justice and equity.

Also, to help this UPA test come to life for you, be sure to see/read the article in this textbook at page 489. This is a great example of how a party (a bank) unwittingly became a "partner" of another via the UPA, and hence, had to accept all of the good and bad that came with that fact!

3. The Doctrine of Partnership By Estoppel

a) Situation -- two persons may not be partners, yet in the eyes of a third person, they may appear to be partners (i.e., it is an issue of "apparent partners")

(1) General Rule under the UPA: persons who are not partners as to each other are not partners as to third parties/persons

(2) Exception: Partnership by Estoppel

(a) Elements (all three elements must be present):

(i) A person who holds himself out or consents to being held out as a partner of another person;

(ii) A third party justifiably relies on the holding out; ***<u>AND</u>***

(iii) The third person is injured as a result of the reliance

b) The Effect of Partnership by Estoppel

(1) The person who held himself out as a partner or who consented to being held out is liable to the third party who was injured as though he were a partner

(2) Example/Practice Problem: Art, Ben and Diedre are partners of Alphabet builders, a partnership in the construction business. They meet at a restaurant with a prospective new partner, Don, who says he will decide whether to enter the partnership after discussing the matter with his wife. During the meeting, they are approached by John, with whom the partnership has been attempting to do business. Art introduced Don to John stating, "We're celebrating Don's joining Alphabet Builders." Don and John shake hands, and John says, "Congratulations!" Alphabet Builders has a very good reputation. In fact, I'm about to become one of your new clients. I signed the contract this morning." Don says nothing in response to John's statement. Subsequently, however, Don decides not to join Alphabet Builders. Nonetheless, when Alphabet Builders breaches its contract with John, John sues Don on the contract (along with the other partners). Is Don liable to John?

(a) Answer: A strong argument can be made that Don *is* liable to John via/under the doctrine of partnership by estoppel. Don said nothing (see above) when he easily could have and should have done so.

(b) As you can see by this example, the partnership by estoppel doctrine is simply a doctrine (of equity) used by courts to come in/apply and do justice to help out an innocent third party (here, John) and allow him to recover against the other parties in question by in effect treating them as a partnership, an even though those individuals never sat down and orally, impliedly or expressly (including in writing) agreed that they were a partnership!

(3) For other/additional practice problems on the partnership by estoppel doctrine, see the practice problems posted on Blackboard ("Practice Problems re: Ordinary Partnerships")!!

II. Rights Among Partners

A. The rights (and duties, authority, etc.) of partners are governed largely by the specific terms of their partnership agreement. In the absence of provisions to the contrary in the partnership agreement, the law imposes the rights (and duties, and authority) discussed below

1. Interest in the Partnership

a) A partner's interest in the partnership is a personal asset. What does this "personal asset" consist of? The following is a partial list:

(1) Compensation:

(a) General rule: a partner's compensation is his/her share of the profits of the business and he/she is ordinarily ***NOT*** entitled to a salary or wages

(b) Exception: an agreement between the partners to the contrary

(2) Sharing of Profits and Losses:

(a) Profits:
(i) General rule: partners share equally, according to the number of partners and not according to their capital contribution or the amount of time that each devotes to the partnership
(ii) Exception: partners agree otherwise
(b) Losses: same general rule and exception as with profits above
(c) **Special Note**: And if the parties expressly agreed to, say, split profits one way but did not address/were silent on how to split the losses, then they would split losses based on the number of partners (and vice versa if the agreement was/were how to split losses but they were silent on the profits)

(3) Assignment of a Partner's Partnership Interest
(a) As a co-owner, a partner has an ownership interest in the partnership. This is called a ***partnership interest*** and it is part of his personal property. Although a partner may not give his personal creditor any interest in separate items of partnership property, he may sell or assign ***his*** partnership interest to a creditor (e.g., where a partner assigned his/her share of the partnership profits over to his/her ex-spouse as part of a divorce settlment)
(i) Such an assignment entitles the buyer or assignee to the right to receive the assigning partner's share of his partnership's profits ***only***. If does ***not*** make the buyer or assignee a partner of the partnership, give the assignee the right to inspect the partnership's books, manage the partnership, make him become liable to partnership creditors, etc. (unless the other partners agree to do so)
(a) The assigning partner remains a partner and can continue to help the others manage the business
(b) The assignment by itself does not dissolve the partnership. The non-assigning partners may not exclude the assigning partner from the partnership, but they can vote to dissolve the partnership
(ii) An **example** of an assignment-of-a-partnership-interest would be a partner in a partnership assigning his/her right/cut to any profits to his/her ex-spouse as part of a divorce settlement between them. The assignment of such proceeds do NOT make the ex-spouse a partner or give him/her the right to participate in the management of the partnership – it only gives him/her the right to receive that share/cut of the profits.

(4) Creditor's Lien on a Partner's Partnership Interest
(a) A partner's interest is also subject to a judgment creditor's lien, meaning a judgment creditor who is chasing a partner for money owed can forcibly and unilaterally (via a court order) attach that partner's interest in the partnership by petitioning the court that entered the judgment to grant the creditor a ***charging order***. This order entitles the creditor to the

profits of the partner and to any asset available to the partner on the firm's dissolution. It does NOT make the creditor a partner in the partnership

(b) A charging order is different than the assignment-of-a-partnership-interest (discussed above). A charging order is where a creditor of a partner goes to court and gets a court order that allows it to attach the profit proceeds in a partnership that the partner has coming to him/her by virtue of their membership in the partnership. So, for example, if a partner busy a boat for his own use, does not make payments on it, the creditor who is owed money on that boat can go to court and get a charging order to attach that partner's profit income from the partnership to help in turn pay off the boat debt.

2. Management Rights

a) Under the UPA, all partners have equal rights in managing the partnership. Each partner has one vote in management matters regardless of the proportional size of his or her interest in the firm

(1) In ordinary partnership matters, *majority rule* controls

(2) In other matters the vote must be *unanimous* to bind the partnership (see the text for details)

(a) Rationale: such actions are so important that the unanimous agreement of the partners is required

(3) Note: Remember that the above rules can be modified by the partnership agreement!

3. Inspection of Books

a) Partnership books and records must be kept accessible to all partners

4. Accounting of Assets

a) An accounting of partnership assets or profits is required to determine the value of each partner's share in the partnership. An accounting can be performed voluntarily, or it can be compelled by a court order. Under the UPA, a partner has the right to a formal accounting in certain circumstances

5. Property Rights

a) A partner also has ownership rights in any real or personal property owned by the partnership

b) The UPA provides that: (1) all property originally brought into the partnership or subsequently acquired by purchase or otherwise, on account of the partnership, is partnership property; and (2) unless the contrary intention appears, property acquired with partnership funds is partnership property

III. Duties Of Partners -- basically derived from agency law; the following rules are therefore similar to agency law (which we studied earlier in the quarter!)

A. Fiduciary Duties

1. Partners stand in a fiduciary relationship to one another, just as principals and agents. This means that partners must:

a) **Not Secretly Profit While Transacting Business for the Partnership**

(1) A partner may not secretly profit from the transactions of partnership business. The breach of this duty requires the partner to return such profits to the partnership

b) **Not Compete Against the Partnership**

(1) A partner may not compete against the partnership in the same/closely related type or line of work/business. The remedy for the breach of this duty is the recovery of the profits made by the partner's competing venture

(a) Of course, he/she could compete against the partnership in a totally unrelated type of business/line of work (but only so long as it does not interfere with his/her duties and responsibilities owed to the partnership)

c) **Serve The Partnership and Help Run the Day-to-Day Operations of the Partnership Business**

(1) The remedies for the breach of this duty include assessing the partner for the cost of hiring a person to do his work and paying the other partners additional compensation

d) **Exercise the Skill and Care of the Ordinarily Prudent Business Manager**

(1) In conducting partnership business, each partner owes a duty to use *reasonable skill and care*, make a *reasonable investigation* before making a decision, and the decision he makes must be that of an *ordinary prudent business manager* in his position. A partner is liable to the partnership for losses incurred if this duty is breached

e) **Act Within the Actual (Express and/or Implied) Authority Possessed by the Partner**

(1) A partner obviously has a duty not to exceed his or her authority

f) **Account For the Proper Use and Disposal of Partnership Funds and Property**

(1) Partners have a duty to account for their use or disposal of partnership property, as well as their receipt of any benefit or profit from such property; any purchases they make for the partnership; the sale of any partnership property; any funds received by them as agents of the partnership, etc.

(2) This also includes the duty to keep reasonable records of business conducted, to make those records available for inspection, a right to a formal *accounting* of the partnership affairs, etc.

g) **Other:**

(1) ***Indemnify*** other partners for expenditures they made from their personal funds and for liabilities they reasonably and in good faith incurred on behalf of the partnership; maintain the ***confidentiality*** of partnership information; ***disclose*** to the other partners information material to the partnership business; and inform partners of ***notices*** he or she has received

Note: be sure to see/do the "Practice Problems re: Ordinary Partnerships" on Blackboard – in particular the ones dealing with fiduciary duties (there are some good and fun ones); that way you can practice spotting and applying the above rules re: fiduciary duties

IV. Authority of Partners

A. Each partner is a general manager which can bind the partnership and his other individual partners for acts within the ***ordinary affairs of the partnership business***, and thereby bind the partnership to a third party creditor

1. Note: The concepts and principles of actual (express or implied) authority and apparent authority that we studied earlier in the quarter under agency law apply here!! (I.e., you need to remember what actual authority is, what apparent authority is, etc., as you will see some questions on this topic on the exam! If you don't remember that material, you should flip back and review it to refresh your memory – see pages 281 and 289–292 of this textbook)

a) Again, remember that actual authority can be express or implied!! Also, remember that apparent authority is something that someone else/an entity does (or does not) do to give a third party the impression that another has the authority to act on his/her/its behalf

b) Example/Practice Problem:

(1) Art is a partner of Alphabet Builders, a trading partnership in the construction business. The three partners of Alphabet Builders have agreed that the partnership may not borrow money unless all the partners approve the borrowing. In the name of the partnership but without the consent of his partners, Art borrows money from a bank. Art tells the bank that the partnership will use the money for general purposes. Art indorses the loan check in the name of the partnership but deposits the money in his personal account. Art uses the money to go to Vegas, party and gamble. Art loses the money at the craps tables in Vegas. The bank sues Alphabet Builders and its partners on the loan. Are Alphabet Builders and its partners liable to the bank on the loan?

(a) Answer: Yes, under/via the doctrine of apparent authority. Also, the fact that Art and his partners had an agreement to not borrow money unless all of them approve is NOT binding on the bank as the bank was not a party to that agreement, had no knowledge of it, etc.

(2) For other examples on this topic see the practice problems posted on Blackboard ("Practice Problems re: Ordinary Partnerships")

2. Also, the doctrine of ratification applies in that a partnership may *ratify*, after the fact, the unauthorized acts of any partner

B. If the act in question is not within the "ordinary affairs of the partnership business," such an act is generally not binding on the partnership unless ratified by/with the unanimous consent of all of the other partners

V. Liability of Partners For Torts And Crimes Committed by Other Partners

A. Torts

1. The standards and principles of agency law's ***respondeat superior*** are applied in determining the liability for the partnership and of the other partners for the torts of partners and other partnership employees (note that we studied *respondeat superior* earlier in the quarter in connection with Agency Law – so if you don't remember that concept/material, go back to that material and refresh your memory – see pages 281–283, 293–302 of this textbook)

a) What about intentional torts (e.g., assault, battery, fraud, sexual harassment, etc.)?

(1) General Rule: Neither a partnership or any of its partners are liable for the intentional tort of a partner

(a) Rationale: intentional torts are not normally within the course and scope of partnership business or within the ordinary authority of a partner

(2) Exception: a partner who authorizes a partner to commit an intentional tort is liable for such a tort

(3) Exception: where a partner has a history of committing intentional torts (e.g., sexual harassment) and the partnership allows him to engage in activities where such torts may forseeably recur, the partners and the partnership are liable

B. Crimes

1. General Rule: Partners are not criminally liable for a crime committed by another partner in the course and scope of transacting partnership business

2. Exceptions: A partner participates in the act or authorizes its commission; he knows of the other partner's criminal tendencies and still places him in a position in which he may commit a crime; ***or*** the crime of a partner is foreseeable because of the past conduct of that partner

C. Miscellaneous

1. Joint and Several Liability

a) In most states, partners who are both jointly liable and *severally*, or individually, liable for partnership debts and contracts. *Joint and several liability* means that a third party may sue (and collect against) any one or more of the partners without suing all of them or the partnership itself

VI. The Dissolution, Winding Up, And Termination Of Partnerships

A. **Dissolution**

1. It is characterized by a partner's ceasing to take part in the carrying on of the partnership business. It involves a change in the partners' relations/relationship

2. In the absence of an agreement on the issue, a partner may have the ***power*** to dissolve at any time, but not the ***legal right*** to do so

   a) Non-Wrongful Dissolution
      (1) Where the partner has both the power ***and*** the legal right to dissolve (i.e., to do so does not violate the partnership agreement)
         (a) Actions that constitute a non-wrongful dissolution
            (i) End of the term stated in the partnership agreement
            (ii) The partnership's accomplishment of it's objective
            (iii) Withdrawal of a partner at any time from a partnership at will
            (iv) Withdrawal of a partner in accordance with the partnership agreement
            (v) Expulsion of a partner in accordance with the partnership agreement
            (vi) Unanimous agreement of the partners
            (vii) Illegality of the partnership business
            (viii) Death of a partner
            (ix) Insolvency (e.g., bankruptcy) of a partner
            (x) Judicial dissolution due to the adjudicated insanity of a partner
            (xi) Judicial dissolution due to the inability of a partner to perform the partnership contract
            (xii) Judicial dissolution due to the inability of the partnership to conduct business except at a loss
         (b) Amplification: A partner has the POWER to disassociate fro the partnership at any time, such as by withdrawing from the partnership. A partner does not, however, always have the legal RIGHT to disassociate. When a partner's disassociation does not violate the partnership agreement and is otherwise non-wrongful, the partner has the legal right to disassociate from the partnership. Such disassociation is non-wrongful. When a partner's disassociation violates the partnership agreement or is otherwise wrongful (see below), the partner has the power – but not the right – to disassociate from the partnership. Such a disassociation is wrongful, and the consequences that follow from a wrongful disassociation are different than those for a non-wrongful disassociation (see below)
      (2) Consequences of a non-wrongful dissolution
         (a) Each partner may demand that the partnership be "wound up"

   b) Wrongful Dissolution
      (1) Where the partner dissolves the partnership in violation of the partnership agreement

(a) E.g. – Retiring before the partnership accomplishes its stated objective of completing a subdivision in SLO County

(2) Actions which constitute a wrongful dissolution

(a) Any dissolution that violates the partnership agreement

(b) Judicial dissolution due to a partner's conduct the prejudicially affects the business

(c) Judicial dissolution due to a partner's willful and persistent breach of the partnership agreement or his/her fiduciary duties

(3) Consequences of a wrongful dissolution

(a) The "bad guy" partner cannot demand that the business be wound up; he/she cannot participate in the winding up of the partnership; the goodwill cannot be taken into account when valuing his/her interest; also, the value of his share in the partnership is reduced by any damage he cause to the partnership through his/her wrongful act

c) Acts That Do ***Not*** Normally Cause a Dissolution

(1) A partner's assignment of a partnership interest (e.g., to a creditor)

(2) A creditor's obtaining a charging order against a partnership interest

(3) Addition of a new partner to a partnership

(4) Disagreement among the partners that does not threaten partnership assets or profitability

(5) Death or withdrawal of a partner, when the partnership agreement states that death or withdrawal shall not cause a dissolution

B. **Winding Up the Partnership Business**

1. This is the next step after dissolution. It essentially involves the orderly liquidation of the assets of the business

a) This can be accomplished by selling each asset separately, selling the business as a whole, possibly making *distributions-in-kind* to the partners, etc.

2. Partner Authority During Winding Up

a) During the wind up, a partner has the ***express authority*** to do anything that the partners agree a partner may perform, and he also has the ***implied authority*** to do those acts ***reasonably necessary*** to winding up (e.g., preserve and enhance assets (for example, by borrowing money), sell assets, complete executory contracts, enter into new contracts if they aid in the liquidation process, etc.)

b) With respect to ***apparent authority***, that normally will continue unless appropriate ***notice*** is given to the appropriate parties, creditors, etc. Thus, a partner may have not express or implied authority to act in a certain way, but he may (will) have apparent authority to do so!!

(1) The lesson here to the other partners is that to protect themselves, they need to provide some type of adequate and effective notice to the public that the "bad guy" partner does NOT have the authority to do certain things/anything on behalf of the partnership!

(2) For an example, be sure to see the practice problems ("Practice Problems re: Ordinary Partnerships") posted on Blackboard

3. Disputes Among Winding Up Partners

a) When more than one partner has the right to wind up the partnership, the partners may disagree concerning which steps should be taken during winding up.

(1) Rule: For decisions in the ordinary course of winding up, the decision of the majority of the partners controls

(2) Rule: When the decision is an extraordinary one (e.g., continuing the business for an extended period of time), unanimous partner approval is required

C. **When The Business Is Continued**

1. When the business is not wound up, and is instead continued, the claims of creditors against the partnership and the partners may be affected. Thus, what are the rules?

a) The Successor Partnership's Liability for the Predecessor Partnership's Obligations

(1) Creditors of the old partnership are creditors of the new partnership continuing the business.

(2) Also, the original partners remain liable for obligations incurred prior to the dissolution of the partnership unless there is an agreement with creditors to the contrary. Thus, partners may not usually escape liability by forming a new partnership (or corporation) to carry on the old business of the partnership

b) The Outgoing Partner's Liability for Obligations Incurred by the Partnership While He Was a Partner

(1) General Rule: such partners remain liable for partnership liabilities incurred while they were partners

(2) Exception: if a novation occurs they are not liable

(a) A novation is essentially an agreement between the partnership, creditor and outgoing partner (*note that there are three parties to this agreement -- the partnership, creditor, and outgoing partner*) to release the outgoing partner from the debt or liability at issue

(i) A novation can be express or implied.

(ii) Note: do not get hung up on the details and technicalities of what it takes to create a novation. Just know the big picture of what it is and how it works

c) An Outgoing Partner's Liability for Obligations Incurred by the Partnership After He Leaves the Partnership

(1) General Rule: an outgoing partner has no liability for such debts or claims

(2) Exception: if the doctrine of partnership by estoppel applies (see above), he will be liable for such debts or claims

(a) Thus, how should the outgoing partner protect himself?

(i) He/she should provide some type of notice that he/she is no longer with the partnership to the appropriate persons and parties

d) The Liability of Incoming Partners

(1) Such a person obviously has unlimited personal liability for all partnership obligations incurred ***after*** he becomes a partner

(2) For obligations incurred ***before*** he became a partner, he is as liable as if he had been a partner when the obligations was incurred! However, his liability is limited to the partnership's assets only, and the creditor cannot come after him individually/for personal liability once (and if) the partnership's assets have been exhausted (unless, of course, he expressly or impliedly agreed to undertake unlimited liability for any such prior obligations -- which is sometimes done, for example, when an incoming partner agrees to assume the outgoing partner's partnership obligations)

Practice Problem re: the above rules and scenarios under b), c) and d):

Art retires from Alphabet Builders, a partnership with Ben and Diedre. Zack agrees to replace Art in the partnership. Zack signs an agreement with Art assuming Art's liability for all partnership obligations. After Art leaves the partnership, Alphabet Builders falls behind in the payments to its creditors including the following:

a) The bank from which Art obtained the loan in the name of the partnership prior to his leaving the partnership.

b) The partnership owed money on several multi-million dollar contracts with several sub-contractors which were entered into after Art left and Zack entered the partnership.

What is Art's liability on these obligations? What about Zack?

Answer re: Art:

Re: the bank loan, Art probably remains liable. He was an outgoing partner and this debt was incurred while he was a partner. Further, based on these facts, it does not appear that any type of novation occurred (i.e., the novation exception does not apply).

Re: the sub-contractor contracts, this one is tricky for Art. For example, he was an outgoing partner, and this obligation was incurred after he left the partnership. Thus, the general rule says he is not liable (see above). However, it may very well be that these creditors could argue that the exception the doctrine of partnership by estoppel (also see above) applies, as nothing in the facts indicate that Art cut off this doctrine by, for example, giving notice to all creditors and customers of the partnership that he had retired and was no longer with the partnership.

Further, the fact that Art signed an agreement with Zack whereby Zack assumed all of Art's liabilities for partnership obligations is irrelevant as none of the creditors involved (the bank or the subcontractors) signed that agreement, were a party to it, had notice of it, etc.

Answer re: Zack:

Re: the bank loan, he is an incoming partner and this is a debt that was incurred by the partnership before he became a partner. Under the above generally rule, he would be liable only to the extent of his capital contribution to buy into the partnership. However, the exception also states that if he expressly or impliedly agrees (which he did) to undertake responsibility for such obligations, then he is on the hook for unlimited personal liability!!

Re: the subcontractor contracts, these were contracts that were entered into after he became a partner. Thus, under partnership law, Zack is fully liable for these obligations – i.e., he stands to lose not just his capital contribution to buy into the partnership, but, he also remains personally liable for these contracts as well!!

For additional practice on these rules and concepts, see the practice problems posted on my web site ("Practice Problems re: Ordinary Partnerships")

e) Rights of Outgoing Partners
   (1) They are entitled to receive the value of their partnership interest and they become a creditor of the new partnership for the value of their partnership interest. However, their claims are subordinate to the claims of other creditors of the partnership
      (a) Valuation of an outgoing partner's interest
         (i) <u>Determined at the time of dissolution</u>
         (ii) Includes goodwill
            (a) Note: In valuing the interest of a *wrongfully discharged* partner, goodwill is excluded (see above), and the valuation of that interest is further reduced by the damages that he has caused his partners due to his causing a wrongful dissolution!

D. Distribution Of Assets

1. After the partnership is wound up, how are its assets distributed?

   a) Under the UPA they are distributed as follows (and these rules cannot be changer per an agreement to the partners to the contrary):
      (1) Those owing to creditors, other than partners
         (a) E.g. -- a debt owed to the landlord who rented the office space to the partnership; wages owed to partnership employees, etc.
      (2) Those owing to partners other than for capital contributions and profits

(a) E.g. -- maybe one of the partners was entitled to a salary (in addition to his/her share of the profits – see below)

(3) Those owing to partners for capital contributions

(a) E.g. -- what the partners paid or contributed to get the partnership started (e.g., money, a truck, a building, etc.) or to buy into and become a member of the partnership

(4) Those owing to partners in respect to their share of profits

E. **Termination**

1. After the assets of a partnership have been distributed, termination of the partnership automatically occurs

***Again, folks, I encourage you to do the various practice problems ("Practice Problems re: Partnerships") that I have posted on Blackboard. You may feel that you know/understand the above material, and, you may. But you also may not. So, be safe and do these practice problems. Many of them involve the <u>application</u> of the above concepts and that is a great way to learn (the only way, really) to see if you really do know and understand this material. – Prof. Carr**

150 Example of a Written Partnership Agreement

Note that a partnership agreement can be oral; but, of course it makes sense/is wise to put it into writing.

PARTNERSHIP AGREEMENT

This Partnership Agreement is entered into this _______ day of _______________, _________, by and between the following partners: ______________________________

____

____who agree as follows:

1. **Name of Partnership.** The name of the partnership shall be: _______________

____.

The name under which the partnership shall conduct business shall be:

____.

2. **Principal Place of Business.** The partnership's principal place of business shall be:

____.

3. **Purpose of Partnership.** The purposes of the partnership are: _______________

____.

In addition to the specific purposes set forth above, the purpose of the partnership is also to conduct any lawful business in which the partners, from time to time, may agree to become engaged.

4. **Term of Partnership.** The partnership shall become effective as of the date of this agreement, and shall continue until it is dissolved by all of the partners, or until a partner leaves for any reason including incapacity or death, or until otherwise dissolved by law.

5. **Contributions of Partners.** The partners shall make the following initial contributions to the partnership:

Partner	Type of Contribution	Value
____________	____________	______
____________	____________	______
____________	____________	______
____________	____________	______

6. **Loans of Cash.** The following partners agree to loan the partnership the amount listed below, for the period of time and at the annual interest rate stated:

Partner	Amount	Period	Interest Rate

7. **Loans of Property.** The following partners agree to loan the partnership the property listed below, which shall remain the property of such partner and shall be returned to that partner upon termination of the partnership unless another time for return is specified:

Partner	Description of Property

8. **Additional Contributions.** No additional funds shall be required of any partner, unless the partners unanimously vote to contribute additional funds. In the event additional funds are needed, and a unanimous vote is not achieved, those partners desiring to continue the business may purchase the interest of any partner not desiring to make further contributions; or may make contributions with the ownership and voting rights of the partners being adjusted according to each partner's total contributions; otherwise the partnership shall be terminated and wound-up.

9. **Profits and Losses.** The partners shall share in the profits and losses of the partnership according to the following percentages:

Partner	% of Profits	% of Losses

A. **Distribution of Profits.** Any profits to which a partner shall be entitled, shall be determined and paid on a monthly basis.

B. **Limitation on Distribution of Profits.** Upon the majority vote of the partners, some or all of the total partnership profits shall be retained by the partnership for reinvestment in the partnership business, with the balance, if any, being distributed among the partners.

10. Ownership Interests. Each partner's share of ownership in the partnership, with voting rights equal to each partner's percentage, shall be as follows:

Partner	% of Ownership
______________________	__________
______________________	__________
______________________	__________

11. Voting Rights. All partnership decisions shall be made by a majority vote of the partners. Each partner shall have a certain number of votes, which shall be equal to his or her percentage of ownership in the partnership as set forth in this agreement. In the event any proposal does not receive a majority vote, that proposal shall be deemed defeated.

12. Participation in Partnership Business. Each partner shall participate in the partnership business in the following capacity:

Partner	Capacity
__________________	____________________________________
__________________	____________________________________
__________________	____________________________________

Each partner shall work a minimum of ________ hours per week in the partnership business, provided that each partner shall be entitled to the following vacation, sick, and holiday leaves:

Vacation: ____

Sick Leave: ____

Holidays: ____

13. Salaries to Partners. Partners may be paid a reasonable salary or wages for work performed in the partnership business, but only as determined in writing by a majority vote of the partners.

14. Partnership Accounting Records. The partnership shall maintain proper and complete accounting records, in accordance with generally accepted accounting principals. Such records shall be kept at the partnership's principal place of business, and shall be available and open to all partners, or their representatives, for inspection at any time during regular business hours.

15. Accounting to Partners. An accounting of the partnership business, including profits and losses, shall be made to all partners at the close of each quarter. In addition, an accounting shall be made at any time upon the written request of any partner.

16. Partnership Bank Accounts. The partnership shall maintain at least one bank checking account, which shall bear the partnership name. Other bank accounts may be maintained as determined necessary by the partners, however, all such accounts shall bear the partnership name. All partnership funds shall only be deposited in accounts bearing the partnership name. All checks drawn on partnership checking accounts must be signed by at least ________ partners. All withdrawals of funds from other partnership accounts must be on the signature of at least ______ partners.

17. Expense Accounts. The partners listed below shall receive a monthly expense account in the amount indicated for actual, necessary and reasonable expenses incurred in the regular course of partnership business. Each such partner shall keep a record of his or her expenses, and shall submit such record monthly for payment.

Partner	Amount	Partner	Amount

18. Insurance.

A. **Insurance of Business.** The partnership shall maintain policies of insurance to cover liability and business assets. Business asset insurance shall be sufficient to replace such assets. Liability insurance shall be in an amount determined by a majority vote of partners.

B. **Life Insurance on Partners.** The partnership shall maintain a life insurance policy on each partner in the face value of $____________. Said policy shall be an asset of the partnership.

C. **Disability Insurance on Partners.** The partnership shall maintain a disability insurance policy on each partner in the face value of $____________. Said policy shall be an asset of the partnership.

19. **Partnership Meetings.** In order to discuss partnership business, the partners shall meet ____, or at such other times as determined by a majority vote of the partners.

20. **Transfer of Partner's Interest in Partnership.**

A. **Option of Partnership to Purchase / Right of First Refusal.** In the event any partner leaves the partnership; for whatever reason including voluntary withdrawal or retirement, expulsion, incapacity, or death; the remaining partner(s) shall have the option to purchase said partner's interest from said partner or his or her estate. In the event any partner receives, and is willing to accept, an offer from a person who is not a partner to purchase all of his or her interest in the partnership, he or she shall notify the other partners of the identity of the proposed buyer, the amount and terms of the offer, and of his or her willingness to accept the offer. The other partner(s) shall then have the option, within 30 days after notice is given, to purchase that partner's interest in the partnership on the same terms as those of the offer of the person who is not a partner.

B. **Option of Partnership to Sell or Dissolve Partnership.** In the event a partner leaves or receives an offer to purchase his or her interest as provided for in Paragraph 20. A., above, and the remaining partner(s) do not exercise the option to purchase, the remaining partners have the option to put the entire business up for sale, or to dissolve the partnership.

C. **Valuation of Partnership.** In the event the remaining partners exercise their right to purchase another partner's interest as provided above, the value of the partnership shall be determined by an independent appraisal. The cost of the appraisal shall be shared equally by the departing partner and the partnership.

D. **Payment Upon Buy-Out.** In the event the remaining partners exercise their right to purchase another partner's interest as provided above, they shall pay the departing partner for his or her interest by way of a promissory note of the partnership, dated as of the date of purchase, which shall mature in not more than ______ years, and shall bear interest at the rate of ______% per annum. The first payment shall be made ______ days after the date of the promissory note.

21. **Expulsion of a Partner.** A partner shall be expelled from the partnership for any of the following reasons:

a. Upon a unanimous vote of the other partners to expel a partner.
b. When the partner files a petition for relief under the Bankruptcy Code.
c. When the partner files for, or becomes subject to an order or decree of, insolvency under any state law.
d. When the partner files for, consents to, or becomes subject to, the appointment of a receiver or trustee over any of his or her assets which is not vacated within _____ days.
e. When the partner consents to, or becomes subject to, an attachment or execution of his or her assets which is not released within _____ days.
f. When the partner makes an assignment for the benefit of creditors.

Upon the occurrence of any of the above events, the expelled partner shall cease to be a partner and shall have no interest in the partnership or partnership property. Said partner's rights, powers and authorities, including the right to share in partnership profits, shall also cease. The expelled partner shall be considered a seller of his or her interest in the partnership as set forth in this agreement. In the event of any such expulsion, the partnership shall not be dissolved, but shall continue its business without interruption. The expulsion of any partner as provided above shall not be subject to mediation, arbitration, or review by any court.

22. **Partnership Business Name.** The business name of the partnership, ______________ ____, is owned by the partnership. No partner may use said name after leaving the partnership.

23. **Ownership of Trade Secrets.** All trade secrets used or developed by the partnership, including customer lists, supply sources, and computer programs, shall be owned and controlled by the partnership.

24. Dispute Resolution.

A. Mediation of Disputes. In the event of any dispute arising under this agreement, all partners agree that a resolution shall first be sought through mediation. As mediation is voluntary, all partners agree to cooperate with the mediator in attempting to resolve the dispute. It is agreed that ______________________________ shall serve as mediator, and that if such person is unable or unwilling to serve as mediator another mediator shall be chosen by mutual agreement of the partners to the dispute. Mediation shall be initiated by a written request for mediation, which shall be delivered to the other partners and the mediator. Mediation shall commence within _____ days after the request for mediation is delivered. Any agreement reached at through mediation shall be reduced to writing, shall be signed by all of the partners, and shall be binding upon all of the partners. Any costs of mediation shall be shared equally by all partners to the dispute.

B. Arbitration. In the event of any dispute arising under this agreement which could not be resolved through mediation, all partners agree that a resolution shall be sought through arbitration. Arbitration shall be initiated by a written request for arbitration, which shall state the nature of the dispute, the requesting party's position, and shall name one person to serve as an arbitrator. Such request shall be delivered to the other partners. Arbitration shall proceed as follows:

1. Within 3 days after receiving the request for arbitration, the other partners shall have the right to deliver a response, which shall name a person to serve as the second arbitrator, and may state the responding partners' position. This response shall be delivered to the other party to the dispute.
2. Within 3 days after receiving a copy of the request and the response, the two designated arbitrators shall select a third arbitrator.
3. Within 7 days after selection of the third arbitrator, the arbitrators shall hold a hearing, at which time either party may present oral or written evidence. No partner may be represented by an attorney or any other third party.
4. The arbitrators shall issue a written decision within 7 days of the hearing date, which shall be delivered to both parties, and shall be binding upon them.
5. Any costs of arbitration shall be shared equally by all partners to the dispute.

25. **Continuity of Partnership.** In the event of a partner's voluntary withdrawal, expulsion, death, or incapacity, the partnership shall not terminate or dissolve, but shall continue its business without any break in continuity.

26. **Governing Law.** This agreement shall be governed by the laws of ____.

27. **Severability.** If any part of this agreement is adjudged invalid, illegal, or unenforceable, the remaining parts shall not be affected and shall remain in full force and effect.

28. **Binding Agreement / No Other Beneficiary.** This agreement shall be binding upon the parties, and upon their heirs, executors, personal representatives, administrators, and assigns. No person shall have a right or cause of action arising or resulting from this agreement except those who are parties to it and their successors in interest.

29. **Entire Agreement.** This instrument, including any attached exhibits, constitutes the entire agreement of the parties. No representations or promises have been made except those that are set out in this agreement. This agreement may not be modified except in writing signed by all the parties.

30. **Paragraph Headings.** The headings of the paragraphs contained in this agreement are for convenience only, and are not to be considered a part of this agreement or used in determining its content or context.

______________________ Signature	______________________ Signature
______________________ Signature	______________________ Signature
______________________ Signature	______________________ Signature

151 Lender Liable for $6.6 Million[1]

The National Law Journal

[Article relating to the Uniform Partnership Act test for determining the existence of a partnership]

NEWARK, N.J.—A CONSTRUCTION lender that exercises authority over management of a job site can be held liable for defects in a building, a New Jersey court has found.

Superior Court Judge John Himmelberger, in Atlantic City, on Nov. 2 let stand a $6.6 million punitive damages verdict against the Bank of America, which financed a condominium complex rife with defects.

Lawyers in consolidated cases—*Gardner v. Bank of America,* No. ATL-L-184-99, and *Ocean Club Condominium Association v. Bank of America,* No. ATL-L-256-99—said it may be the first time in New Jersey a bank has been held liable for building defects absent a loan default by the developer.

Paul Sandars, a partner at Lum, Danzis, Drasco, Positan & Kleinberg in Roseland, N.J., the lawyer for Ocean Club Condominium Association of Atlantic City, argued that flaws in the complex, such as crumbling balconies, could be pinned to Bank of America's heavy-handed supervision of the project.

Plaintiff Albert Gardner, half of a partnership that developed the two-building, 32-story project, wanted a contractor experienced in high-rise construction on oceanfront sites, which present special problems of soil condition, wind and salt air. But Bank of America insisted on a New York contractor, with which it had a business relationship.

On Sept. 17, after a three-month trial on liability, the industry found that Bank of America had deviated from accepted standards of banking practice and had improperly exercised effective control over the construction. Himmelberger, who planned to have all damages tried separately, was about to excuse the jurors when Gardner's lawyer, Arthur Shanker, of counsel to the Law Offices of Richard Weiner of Montvale, N.J., said that *Herman v. Sunshine Chemical Specialties,* 133 N.J. 329 (1993), requires the jury that found liability to decide punitive damages. The judge agreed, despite protests from bank lawyer Paul Giordano of Philadelphia's Monteverde, McAlee & Hurd.

The jury returned its $6.6 million punitive damages verdict on Sept. 25; on Nov. 2 Himmelberger denied Giordano's motion for a judgment

1 **Note from Professor Carr: This is a good example of how a partnership can unexpectedly arise/be deemed to be formed in the eyes of a jury/court. Note that here, there was no express or implied oral or written partnership between this bank and its customer. However, under the Uniform Partnership Act (UPA), the jury/court said that there WAS a partnership, so the bank therefore has to take/accept all of the benefits and disadvantages that come with it ... See this textbook at pages 467–468 for the factors that courts apply under the UPA to determine whether a partnership (from a LEGAL standpoint) has been formed between two or more parties).**

notwithstanding the verdict. A separate trial on compensatory damages with a new jury is set for next summer.

152 Limited Partnerships: LPs, LLPs and LLCs

Study Outline

Earlier, in connection with the "Introduction to Business Entities – Business Organizations" outline, we briefly looked at LPs, LLPs and LLCs. Now ... let's look at them in greater detail

*****Note that in this textbook at pages 459–465 I have inserted several newspaper articles, supplementary materials, misc. documents, etc. that relate to this material. These materials are required reading, and, are also fair game for the exam.**

*****Make *<u>sure</u>* that you also do the sample practice problems posted on Blackboard ("Practice Problems re: Limited Partnerships (LPs), Limited Liability Partnerships (LLPs) and Limited Liability Companies (LLCs)") as they will help you master this material, test you to see if you "really" know and understand it, etc. You can expect similar problems to be on the exam.**

I. Limited Partnerships (LPs)

A. Benefits
1. Allows an infusion of capital from investors, yet does not surrender managerial control to such investors; investors are also relieved of management responsibilities and they can limit their liability to the amount of their investment

B. Features
1. General partners
    a) Contribute capital to the business, manage it, share in its profits, and possess unlimited liability for its obligations
2. Limited partners
    a) Contribute capital and share profits, but possess no management powers and have liability which is limited to their capital investment in the business
3. Other
    a) See textbook and class lecture

C. Use of Limited Partnerships

1. Used primarily in tax shelter ventures (e.g., real estate investment, oil and gas drilling, mining, professional sports, etc.). For other tax details and ramifications, see textbook and class lecture

II. Creation of Limited Partnerships (LPs)

A. In order to form a limited partnership you must comply with the applicable state statute called the Revised Uniform Limited Partnership Act (RULPA). Under the RULP requirements are fairly minimal:
   1. Certificate of Limited Partnership
      a) This certificate must be signed and filed with the secretary of state, and it must be signed by all of the general partners
         (1) The certificate ***must*** contain
            (a) The name of the limited partnership, which must contain the words "limited partnership"
            (b) The name and address of each general partner. (Each general partner must also sign the certificate.)
            (c) The latest date the limited partnership will dissolve
            (d) The name and address of an agent for service of legal process on behalf of the LP
   2. Any "person" may be a general or limited partner. A "person" includes a natural person, partnership, limited partnership, trust, estate, association, or corporation
      a) Note: Again, a corporation is normally the sole general partner of a limited partnership. As a result, ordinarily no natural person will have unlimited liability!
   3. The RULPA permits partners to make capital contributions of cash, property, services rendered, a promissory note, or a binding promise to contribute cash, property, or services

III. Rights and Liabilities of Partners in Limited Partnerships

A. Rights and liabilities shared by general and limited partners

   1. Each partner is obligated to make capital contributions
      a) This obligation may be enforced by the limited partnership itself, or by any of its creditors

   2. Profits and losses
      a) General Rule: under the RULPA, profits and losses are shared on the basis (or %) of the value of each partner's capital contribution to the LP

      b) Exception: a written agreement to the contrary

   3. Voting rights
      a) The partnership agreement may provide that certain transactions be approved by general partners, limited partners, both, etc. The RULPA states that limited partners have no

inherent right to vote as a class and they may receive such right only by an agreement of the partners

4. Admission of new partners
   a) No new partner may be admitted unless each partner has consented to the admission (or in accordance with the limited partnership agreement)

5. Partnership interest
   a) Each partner in an LP owns a partnership interest, which is his personal property that he may sell or assign to others

6. Right to withdraw
   a) Partners in an LP can obviously withdraw and when they do so, they are entitled to receive the fair value of their partnership interest so long as it does not impair the limited partnership's ability to pay its creditors

B. Other rights of general partners
   1. Basically, they are the same as in an ordinary partnership (e.g., same agency powers, no right to compensation beyond his share of the profits absent an agreement to the contrary, etc.)

C. Other liabilities of general partners
   1. Generals have unlimited personal liability to the creditors of the LP, they also owe certain fiduciary duties to the LP and to the limited partners (e.g., to not misuse partnership property or secretly profit from limited partnership transactions, etc.)

D. Other rights of limited partners
   1. Limiteds have the right to be kept informed about partnership affairs by the generals; they can sue to enforce an LP right of action against a person who has harmed the LP (this is called a *derivative suit*); when the LP is sued and the generals fail to defend it, the limiteds can appear on behalf of the LP and assert a defense

E. Other liabilities of limited partners
   1. **General rule**: once the limited partners have contributed their capital contribution, they normally no longer have any further liability for partnership losses or obligations

   2. **Exception**: when the limiteds engage in "too much" management activity, they lose their limited liability
      a) ***Limited partner engaged in "too much" management activity***
         (1) Under the RULPA, a limited who participates in control is liable only to those persons who transact business with the limited partnership reasonably believing, based on the limited partner's conduct, that the limited partner is/was a general partner. Three elements need to be satisfied:

(a) The limited partner must participate in the "control" of the limited partnership;
   (i) Note: "Control" generally means participation in the firm's **day-to-day management decisions**, as opposed to isolated involvement with major decisions
(b) That participation leads a person to reasonably believe that the limited is a general partner; **AND**
(c) That person must transact business with the limited partner while holding that belief

(2) Note: the following activities under the RULPA which may be performed by a limited without becoming personally liable for partnership debts (i.e., they are okay for a limited partner to do/engage in)
   (a) Being an agent, an employee or a contractor for the LP or a general partner; or being an officer, director, or shareholder of a general partner that is a corporation
   (b) Being a consultant or adviser to a general partner
   (c) Acting as a surety for the limited partnership or guaranteeing or assuming specific obligations of the limited partnership
      (i) Note that if a limited partner assumes personal liability on a specific partnership obligation, he/she does NOT thereby forfeit his/her limited liability concerning *other* partnership obligations
   (d) Pursuing or attending a meeting of partners
   (e) Proposing or voting on such partnership matters as dissolution, sale of substantially al the assets, changes in the nature of the business, admissions and removals of general or limited partners, and amendments to the partnership agreement
   (f) Winding up the limited partnership as permitted by the RULPA
   (g) Suing to enforce the fiduciary duties that other partners owe to the LP

(3) Note: for some good examples of and practice applying the above "limited partner engaged in management" rules and concepts, see and do the practice problems posted on Blackboard ("Practice Problems re: LPs, LLPs and LLCs")

IV. Dissolution And Winding Up Of A Limited Partnership

A. Dissolution

1. There are 5 causes of dissolution of an LP, and they are: expiration of the term specified in the certificate of limited partnership; upon the happening of events specified in writing in the partnership agreement; by the consent of all partners; upon the withdrawal of a *general* partner; and, by court order
   a) Events NOT causing a dissolution of an LP:

(1) Death, bankruptcy, insanity, or withdrawal of a ***limited partner*** does not result in dissolution unless the Certificate of Limited Partnership compels a dissolution in such circumstances

(2) The addition of a partner -- general or limited – also does not cause a dissolution

B. Winding up

1. Basic Rules:
   a) Generals who have not wrongfully dissolved an LP may perform the winding up
   b) Limiteds may wind up if there are no surviving generals
   c) Any partner may ***ask a court*** to perform a winding up
   d) Beyond the above, the other winding up principles/rules are pretty much the same as for ordinary partnerships

2. Distribution of assets
   a) The RULPA rules for the distribution of limited partnership assets. From highest priority to lowest, they are:
      (1) To firm creditors, including partners who are creditors, except for unpaid distributions to partners
      (2) To partners for unpaid distributions, including the return of capital to previously withdrawn partners
      (3) To partners to the extent of their capital contributions
      (4) To partners in proportion in which they share distributions. Hence the partners share the proceeds that remain after all other claimants have been paid
   b) Note that these priority distribution rules are *different* than the distribution rules for ordinary partnerships discussed earlier in this textbook!

3. Continuation of the business
   a) Usually the assets are sold. However, all the assets of the business of an LP could be sold to someone who desired to continue the business

V. **Limited Liability Partnerships (LLPs)** – see pages 442–443 of this textbook

VI. **Limited Liability Companies (LLCs)** – see pages 445–446 of this textbook

*****Again, folks, I encourage you to do the practice problems ("Practice Problems re: Limited Partnerships (LPs), Limited Liability Partnerships (LLPs) and Limited Liability Companies (LLCs)") that I have posted on Blackboard. You may feel that you know/understand the above material, and, you may. But you also may not. So, be safe and do these practice problems. Many of them involve the application of the above concepts and that is a great way to learn (the only way, really) to see if you really do know and understand this material. – Prof. Carr**

153 Corporations

Study Outline

Earlier, in connection with the "Introduction to Business Entities – Business Organizations" outline, we briefly looked at corporations. Now … let's look at them in greater detail

*****Note that in this textbook at pages 507–536 I have inserted several newspaper articles, supplementary materials, misc. documents, etc. that relate to this material. These materials are required reading, and, are also fair game for the exam.**

*****Make *sure* that you also do the various sample practice problems posted on Blackboard ("Practice Problems re: Corporations") as they will help you master this material, test you to see if you "really" know and understand it, etc. You can expect similar problems to be on the exam.**

I. The Nature of the Corporation

A. Introduction

1. See the "Business Entity Comparison Table – Legal Characteristics" document that is also included in this textbook at pages 537–540 for an excellent summary of the characteristics of corporations.

B. Corporate Personnel

1. The shareholders own the corporation. They elect a board of directors to govern the corporation. The board of directors hires corporate officers and other employees to run the daily business of the corporation

C. Taxation

1. Remember, the corporation pays income tax on its net profits; shareholders pay income tax on declared and disbursed dividends that they receive from the corporation (hence, double taxation occurs and Uncle Sam/the government can get two bites at the tax revenue apple!!).

a) Note: Be sure to go back and see/take a look at page 444 of this textbook ("Federal Corporate Tax Rates") for how tax rates change with the level of corporate income.

II. The Classification of Corporations

A. For-Profit Corporations

1. They issue stock to their shareholders, who hope to earn and be paid profits (which are usually in the form of *dividends*)

2. They can be "publicly-held," which means that its shares are generally available to public investors

3. They can also be a "***close corporation***," where the controlling shareholders are the only managers of the business. Most family based/held corporations are close corporations
   a) Note: Close corporations are allowed greater latitude than publicly-held corporations in the operation of their internal affairs and in complying with/being excused from the relevant corporation rules and requirements (*e.g.*, most state corporation statutes permit close corporations to dispense with many management formalities and the shareholders are able to get away with much more than the shareholders in an ordinary corporation with respect to such things as exercising management and control, dispensing with the adherence to corporate formalities, *etc.* As a practical mater, close corporations are essentially "incorporated partnerships"!)

4. They can also be an "S corporation"
   a) Remember that S corporations ***cannot have more than 100 shareholders***
   b) S corporations also eliminate the double-taxation penalty of ordinary corporations (see earlier discussion on S-Corps in the "Introduction to Business Entities" Study Outline found earlier in this text.

B. Non-Profit Corporations

1. They do not issue stock and do not expect to make a profit. Instead, they provide services to their members under a plan that eliminates any profit motive. These corporations also have ***members*** rather than shareholders, and none of the surplus revenue from their operation is distributed to the members; rather profits are put back into the business
2. They also generally pay no income tax, so they can reinvest a larger share of their income in the business than can for-profit corporations
3. Typical examples -- churches, cooperative grocery stores, charities, fraternal organizations

III. The Organizational and Financial Structure of Corporations

A. The Promotional Activities of Corporate Promoters

1. Promoters (are also sometimes called/referred to as "incorporators")
   - a) Definition:
     - (1) Someone who incorporates a business, organizes its initial management, and/or raises its initial capital; *i.e.*, he or she helps turn an idea into a corporate reality
   - b) The relation of a promoter/incorporator and prospective corporation
     - (1) A promoter/incorporator of a nonexistent corporation is not an agent of the prospective corporation
       - (a) Rationale: the corporation did not and could not have appointed him as an agent because it does not exist!
     - (2) However, the promoter/incorporator nonetheless *does* owe fiduciary duties to the corporation
       - (a) What are those duties?
         - (i) Ones such as full disclosure, honesty, not to divert a business opportunity from the corporation to himself, not purchase shares at a lower price than that paid by the public shareholders, not to secretly transact business with the corporation, etc.
     - (3) Make sure you know/understand/can recognize what a promoter/incorporator is! See practice problems posted on Blackboard for lots of good examples in this regard

2. A **promoter's/incorporator's** liability on pre-incorporation contracts
   - (a) To begin, an example of a **pre**-incorporation debt or contract would be a promoter/incorporator signing a lease for commercial office space before the corporate entity has been formed/legally come into existence. An example of a **post**-incorporation debt or contract would be first forming the corporate entity and then going out and buying a company car to be used by the corporation and its members (further, the contract to buy the car would be signed by one of the corporate officers). See also the practice problems posted on Blackboard re pre vs. post incorporation debts and contacts
   - **(b)** **General Rule**: the promoter/incorporator is personally liable for any contract they make, even though made on behalf of a corporation to be formed at a later date
   - **(c)** **Exception**: the promoter/incorporator is NOT liable <u>IF</u> the contracting party knows the corporation is not yet in existence but nevertheless agrees (express or implied) to look <u>solely</u> to the corporation and not to the promoter/incorporator for payment (i.e., the contracting party expressly or implicitly agrees to release the promoter from liability)

3. A **corporation's** liability on pre-incorporation contracts entered into by the promoter/incorporator
   a) **General rule**: the corporation is not liable on such a contract
      (1) Rationale: the corporation cannot be held liable if it does not yet exist!
   b) **Exception**: after the corporation is formed, its Board of Directors adopts the contract
      (1) Note: The corporation must do so with full knowledge; also, the adoption can be express or implied

4. The **liability of the corporation to the promoter/incorporator** for services rendered and/or expenses incurred on behalf of the soon to be formed corporation
   a) **General rule**: a corporation is generally not required to pay or compensate the promoter for his or her promotional services or even his or her expenses
      (1) Rationale: the promoter/incorporator is self-appointed, and acts for a corporation that is not yet in existence. Thus, of the promoter chooses to go forward, he or she does so at their own risk!
   b) **Exception**: the corporation expressly agrees to compensate the promoter/incorporator after the promoter/incorporator performed the work (or incurred the expense)

B. Incorporation Procedures

1. To become a corporation, a business must ***incorporate*** by complying with the state incorporation statute

2. First issue is usually, ***where to do it (i.e., incorporate)?***
   a) If the corporation's business will primarily be ***intrastate***, it is usually cheaper to incorporate in that state. If the corporation's business will primarily be ***interstate,*** the corporation may benefit by incorporation in a different state than where the corporation has its business (e.g., Delaware is the most common state you hear about)

3. **Steps in incorporation**:
   a) Preparation and signing of the Articles of Incorporation (note that in this textbook at pages 507–510 I have included a sample Articles of Incorporation for you to take a look at to see what they look like, how they read, etc.). **The reason you need to know and appreciate the steps in incorporation is because in some states, those who make wholly defective and ineffective attempts to incorporate a business may be treated as partners with unlimited personal liability for the obligations of the business!!**
      (1) The Articles of Incorporation ***must*** contain:
         (a) The name of the corporation
         (b) The number of shares that the corporation has the authority to issue
         (c) The address of the initial registered office of the corporation and the name of its registered agent for service of process
         (d) Than name and address of each incorporator

(2) The following ***may*** be included in the articles:
   (a) The names and addresses of the individuals who are to serve as the initial directors
   (b) The purpose of the corporation
   (c) The duration of the corporation
   (d) The par value of shares of the corporation
   (e) Additional provisions not inconsistent with law for managing the corporation, regulating the internal affairs of the corporation, and establishing the powers of the corporation and its directors and shareholders

b) Signing the articles by one or more of the promoters/incorporators
c) Filing the Articles of Incorporation with the Secretary of State, accompanied by the payment of specified fees
d) Holding organizational meeting for the purpose of adopting ***bylaws***, electing officers and the transaction of other business
   (1) The bylaws
      (a) The bylaws essentially supplement the articles of incorporation by more precisely defining the rights and responsibilities of the parties involved in the corporate structure
      (b) The bylaws ***must*** contain the following (note that in this textbook at pages 511–512, I also include a sample set of bylaws for you to take a look at so you can see what they look like, how they read, etc.):
         (i) The authority of the officers and the directors, specifying what they may or may not do
         (ii) The time and place at which the annual shareholders meetings will be held
         (iii) The procedure for calling special meetings of shareholders
         (iv) The procedures for shareholder's and directors' meetings, including whether more than a majority required for approval of specified actions
         (v) Provisions for special committees of the board, defining their membership and the scope of their activities
         (vi) The procedures for the maintenance of share records
         (vii) The machinery for the transfer of shares
         (viii) The procedures an standards for the declaration and payment of dividends

C. Financing The Corporation

1. Equity securities
   a) Equity securities are commonly called ***shares***. Subject to minimum guarantees contained in the state corporation law, the shareholders' rights are a matter of contract and appear in the articles of incorporation, in the bylaws, in a shareholder agreement, and/or on the share certificates

(1) Common shares/stock

(a) Shareholders of common stock often occupy an inferior position to that of other investors, notably creditors and preferred shareholders. The claims of these shareholders are subordinate to the claims of creditors and other classes of shareholders when liabilities and dividends are paid and when assets are distributed upon liquidation. In return for subordination, however, these shareholders have an exclusive claim to the corporate earnings and assets that exceed the claims of creditors and other shareholders. Thus, these shareholders bear the major risks of the corporate venture, yet stand to profit the most if it is successful

(b) Note that common shareholders have the exclusive right to elect the directors, who in turn manage the corporation.

(2) Preferred shares/stock

(a) These are shares that have preferences with regard to assets or dividends over other classes of shares. They are customarily given liquidation and dividend preferences over common stock shareholders. Also, a corp. may have different classes of preferred stock

D. Consideration For Shares

1. Introduction

a) The board of directors has the power to issue shares on behalf of the corp., and it must decide at what price and for what type of consideration it will issue the shares. Corporation statutes restrict the discretion of the board in accepting certain kinds of consideration and in determining the value of the shares it issues

2. Quality of consideration for shares

a) Not all kinds of consideration in contract law are acceptable as legal consideration for shares in corporation law. To protect creditors and other shareholders, most state statutes require legal consideration to have ***real value***

3. Quantity of consideration for shares

a) The board is required to issue shares for an adequate dollar amount of consideration. Whether shares have been issued for an adequate amount of consideration depends in part on the ***par value*** of the shares. The more important concern, however, is whether the shares have been issued for ***fair value***

(1) Par Value

(a) An arbitrary dollar amount that may be assigned to the shares by the articles of incorporation. It does ***not*** reflect the fair market value of the shares, but is the minimum amount of consideration for which the shares may be issued

(i) Par value attempts to protect creditors by ensuring that the corp. has a minimum equity cushion

(2) Fair Value

(a) The Model Business Corporation Act (MBCA) purports to eliminate the concept of par value as it affects the issuance of shares. In such cases, the board must exercise care to ensure that the corp. received the fair value of the shares it issues. The boards' judgment as to the amount of consideration that is received for the shares is ***conclusive*** when/if the board acts in good faith, exercises the care of ordinarily prudent directors, and acts in the best interests of the corp.

(i) I.e. -- If the Business Judgment Rule is satisfied (see below for details)

(3) Miscellaneous

(a) Watered shares: when the board of directors impermissibly overvalues the consideration given for the shares; both the board and the shareholder are liable to the corp. for the difference

IV. Defective Attempts to Achieve and/or Maintain Corporate Status

A. **Piercing the Corporate Veil**

1. Background: See blackboard readings, this textbook and class lecture for details

2. Effect if the Corporate Veil is Pierced:

a) It may cause one or more of a corporation's shareholders to lose his/her limited liability!

3. Two requirements that must apply in order for the corporate veil to be pierced:

a) **Domination of the corporation by its shareholders**

(1) Examples: the shareholders directing a corporation to pay a shareholder's personal expenses; shareholders causing the corporation to not/fail to observe corporate formalities such as failing to hold shareholder and director meetings; running personal expenses through the corporation, etc.

(a) Note: domination usually occurs most often, and is usually easiest to prove, in and for close corporations

b) **Using that domination for an improper purpose**

(1) Examples: defrauding creditors (e.g., through thin or inadequate capitalization; looting (such as when the corporation's assets are transferred to shareholders for less than fair market value); shareholders pay themselves excessive salaries or dividends, etc.); circumventing a statute; or evading an existing obligation

(a) Note that the temptation for looting often comes up when a parent corporation owns at least a majority of the shares of the subsidiary; it can also occur when two corporations have the same shareholders and one corporation loots the other or they both loot each other

c) **For some excellent examples of how the corporate veil can be pierced, see pages 451-455 and 513–516 of this textbook ("Besieged Church Tries to Protect Vast Real Estate"**

and "Examples of Piercing the Corporate Veil" handout and the "Dos and Don'ts" handout); see also the practice problems posted on Blackboard!!

V. Directors' And Officers' Duties To The Corporation

A. Background

1. Directors and officers are in a position of trust, and as such, they owe fiduciary duties to the corp., such as:
   a) The duty to act within the authority conferred on them by the articles of incorporation, the bylaws, and the board of directors
   b) The duty to exercise due care
      (1) What is the standard of care that officers and directors are held to?
         (a) Answer: the "ordinarily prudent person in the same circumstances"
            (i) Note that this is NOT an ordinarily prudent *business* person
            (ii) Also note that this standard also requires officers and directors to make a reasonable investigation and honestly believe that their decision is in the bests interests of the corporation
            (iii) Also, mangers will not be judged based on 20-20 hindsight. A manager need merely consider the information available at the time the decision was made
               (a) I.e., it is an objective test!
      (2) **The Business Judgment Rule – what is it?**
         (a) The directors' and officers' duty of care is sometimes expressed as this rule. It comes often comes up when/after one or more of the shareholders have sued the directors/officers because they unhappy with a decision made by them which they felt damaged the corporation (and most likely the price/value of their shares as well!)
         (b) The Business Judgement Rule (BJR) states that absent bad faith, fraud, or breach of fiduciary duty, the judgment of the board or directors is *conclusive*, and as a consequence, a court will not substitute its judgment for the judgment of management
         (c) Requirements for the BJR to apply/be satisfied to in turn protect the Board from liability:
            (i) The managers must make an informed decision;
            (ii) The managers must not have any conflicts of interest; **AND**
            (iii) The managers must have a rational basis for believing that the decision is in the best interests of the corporation
               (a) The rational basis element requires only that the managers' decision have a ***logical connection to the facts*** revealed by a reasonable investigation or that the decision not be ***manifestly unreasonable***

(b) Also, some courts have held that the managers' wrongdoing must amount to ***gross negligence*** for the directors to lose the protection of the BJR

(3) Board opposition to the acquisition of control of a corporation

(a) Many outsiders (typically called ***raiders***) make a ***tender offer*** for the shares of a corporation (typically called the ***target corporation***), by making an offer to the shareholders to buy their shares at a price above the current market price. The raider hopes to acquire a majority of the shares, which will give it control of the target corporation. A board's tactics to defend against hostile tender offers has created special problems for courts' deciding whether to apply the BJR

(i) **General Rule:** directors are not liable for opposing a tender offer because the BJR applies to a board's decision to oppose a tender offer

(ii) **Exception:** the BJR will not apply when the directors make a decision to oppose the tender offer before they have carefully studied it and/or they oppose the tender offer in order to save their jobs. In such cases, the directors will be liable to the corporation and its shareholders

(4) **Be sure to read/see the articles relating to the Business Judgment Rule that I have inserted in this textbook at pages 517–528. These are fair game for the exam. Also, see the practice problems on the BJR that I have posted on Blackboard ("Practice Problems re: Corporations")**

c) The duty of loyalty

(1) This means that directors and officers cannot self-deal, usurp a corporate opportunity, oppress minority shareholders, trade on inside information, etc.

VI. Liability for Torts and Criminal Acts

A. The liability of the corporation for the torts and crimes of its agents, officers and directors

1. Torts

a) General rule: the corporation is liable for the torts committed by its agents, officers or directors within the course and scope of their employment (i.e., the doctrine of *respondeat superior* applies)

b) Exception: the tort was not committed by such a person in the course and scope of their employment (i.e., the doctrine of *respondeat superior* is <u>not</u> satisfied)

2. Crimes

a) The traditional view was that an "entity" such as a corporation or a partnership could not be held liable for crimes because it, as an entity, could not form the requisite *criminal intent* and/or a corporation was not a "person" for purposes of criminal liability

b) Today, most courts have little difficulty finding an entity such a corporation or partnership liable for a crime (and be fined) for the criminal acts of its agents, employees, partners, etc. In certain situations, corporate officers and employees, partners, etc. may also be held personally liable for corporate/partnership crimes

(1) **For some excellent examples of this fact, see the Arthur Andersen articles I have inserted in this textbook at pages 529–536**

B. The liability of directors and officers for torts and crimes

1. Torts
    a) Liability of directors and officers for their own torts
        (1) A person is always liable for his <u>own</u> torts, even when committed on behalf of his principal. Thus, officers and directors are personally liable when they commit torts or crimes during the performance of their corporate duties
    b) Liability of directors and officers for the torts of others
        (1) A director or officer is usually ***not*** liable for the torts of the other employees of the corp. unless he ***authorized the tort or participated in its commission***

2. Crimes (where people can go to jail!)
    a) Liability of directors and officers for their own crimes
        (1) A director or officer is always responsible for his/her <u>own</u> crimes, even when committed on behalf of his/her principal
    b) Liability of directors and officers for the crimes of others
        (1) A director or officer normally has criminal liability only if he/she ***requests, authorizes, conspires, or aides and abets*** the commission of a crime by another employee

*****Again, folks, I encourage you to do the practice problems on "Practice Problems re: Corporations" that I have posted on Blackboard. You may feel that you know/understand the above material, and, you may. But you also may not. So, be safe and do these practice problems. Many of them involve the <u>application</u> of the above concepts and that is a great way to learn (the only way, really) to see if you really do know and understand this material. – Prof. Carr**

State of California
OFFICE OF THE SECRETARY OF STATE

CORPORATION DIVISION

I, *MARCH FONG EU*, Secretary of State of the State of California, hereby certify:

That the annexed transcript has been compared with the corporate record on file in this office, of which it purports to be a copy, and that same is full, true and correct.

IN WITNESS WHEREOF, I execute this certificate and affix the Great Seal of the State of California this

OCT 4 1989

March Fong Eu
Secretary of State

Articles of Incorporation

of

World Suits.Com, Inc.

ENDORSED
FILED
In the office of the Secretary of State
of the State of California

SEP 21 1989

MARCH FONG EU, Secretary of State

1. Name. The name of the corporation is World Suits.Com, Inc.

2. Purpose. The purpose of the corporation is to engage in any lawful act or activity for which a corporation may be organized under the General Corporation Law of California other than the banking business, the trust company business or the practice of a profession permitted to be incorporated by the California Corporations Code.

3. Directors. There shall be no fewer than 3 and no more than 4 Directors of the corporation. The number of directors shall be fixed by vote of the shareholders from time to time. The names and addresses of the persons appointed as initial Directors of the Corporation are:

Billbo Baggins
555 Higuera Street, Apt. A
San Luis Obispo, CA 93401

Dion Sanders
777 Pismo Beach Drive
Pismo Beach, CA 93444

Chris Carr
Cal Poly
College of Business
Accounting and Law Department
Room 436
San Luis Obispo, CA 93407

4. Agent for Service of Process. The name and address of the corporation's agent for service of process are:

Chris Carr
Cal Poly
College of Business
Accounting and Law Department
Room 436
San Luis Obispo, CA 93407

5. Stock. The total number of authorized shares is 100,000 shares of Common Stock.

World Suits.Com, Inc. -- Articles of Incorporation

Execution

The undersigned, who are the incorporators and initial directors of this corporation, have executed these Articles of Incorporation on September 13, 1989.

Billbo Baggins

Billbo Baggins
Incorporator & Director

Dion Sanders (aka "Prime Time")

Dion Sanders
Incorporator & Director

Chris Carr

Chris Carr
Incorporator & Director

Acknowledgment

State of California
County of San Luis Obispo

On this September 13, 1989, before me, a notary public for the State of California, appeared Julia Roberts, proved to me on the basis of satisfactory evidence to be the person whose name is subscribed to this instrument, and acknowledged that he executed it.

IN WITNESS WHEREOF, I hereunto set my hand and official seal.

OFFICIAL SEAL
NOTARY PUBLIC - CALIFORNIA
SAN LUIS OBISPO COUNTY
My Comm. Expires March 16, 1990

Julia Roberts

State of California

March Fong Eu
Secretary of State

P.O. Box 944230
Sacramento, CA 94244-0230
Phone: (916) 445-2020

STATEMENT BY DOMESTIC STOCK CORPORATION

THIS STATEMENT MUST BE FILED WITH CALIFORNIA SECRETARY OF STATE (SEC. 1502, CORPORATIONS CODE)

A $5 FILING FEE MUST ACCOMPANY THIS STATEMENT

WHEN COMPLETING FORM, PLEASE USE BLACK TYPEWRITER RIBBON OR BLACK INK

IMPORTANT—Please Read Instructions On Back Of Form

World Suits.Com, Inc.
P.O. Box 40776
San Luis Obispo, CA 93403

DO NOT ALTER PREPRINTED NAME. IF ITEM NO. 1 IS BLANK, PLEASE ENTER CORPORATE NAME — DO NOT WRITE IN THIS SPACE

THE CALIFORNIA CORPORATION NAMED HEREIN, MAKES THE FOLLOWING STATEMENT

	ROOM NO.	CITY AND STATE	ZIP CODE
2. STREET ADDRESS OF PRINCIPAL EXECUTIVE OFFICE: 3555-D South Higuera		2A. San Luis Obispo, CA	2B. 93401
3. STREET ADDRESS OF PRINCIPAL BUSINESS OFFICE IN CALIFORNIA (IF ANY): Same		3A. San Luis Obispo, CA	3B. 93401
4. MAILING ADDRESS: Same		4A.	4B.

THE NAMES OF THE FOLLOWING OFFICERS ARE: (Sec. 312, Corporations Code requires 3 officers.)

NAME	STREET ADDRESS (SEE REVERSE SIDE)	CITY AND STATE	ZIP CODE
5. CHIEF EXECUTIVE OFFICER: Billbo Boggins	5A. 555 Higuera Street	5B. San Luis Obispo, CA	5C. 93401
6. SECRETARY: Dion Sanders	6A. 777 Pismo Street	6B. Pismo Beach, CA	6C. 93449
7. CHIEF FINANCIAL OFFICER: Chris Carr	7A. Cal Poly College of Business	7B. San Luis Obispo, CA	7C. 93407

INCUMBENT DIRECTORS, INCLUDING DIRECTORS WHO ARE ALSO OFFICERS (Attach supplemental list if necessary)

NAME	STREET ADDRESS (SEE REVERSE SIDE)	CITY AND STATE	ZIP CODE
8. Billbo Boggins	8A. 555 Higuera Street	8B. San Luis Obispo, CA	8C. 934[illegible]
9. Dion Sanders	9A. 777 Pismo Beach Drive	9B. Pismo Beach, CA	9C. 934[illegible]
10. Chris Carr	10A. Cal Poly College of Business	10B. San Luis Obispo, CA	10C. 93407

11. THE NUMBER OF VACANCIES ON THE BOARD OF DIRECTORS, IF ANY:

DESIGNATED AGENT FOR SERVICE OF PROCESS (Only one agent may be named)

12. NAME: Chris Carr

13. CALIFORNIA STREET ADDRESS IF AGENT IS AN INDIVIDUAL (DO NOT USE P.O. BOX—DO NOT INCLUDE ADDRESS IF AGENT IS A CORPORATION): Cal Poly-College of Business (A Grande Avenue) San Luis Obispo, CA 93407

14. DESCRIBE TYPE OF BUSINESS OF THE CORPORATION NAMED IN ITEM 1: Suit sales business

15. I DECLARE THAT I HAVE EXAMINED THIS STATEMENT AND TO THE BEST OF MY KNOWLEDGE AND BELIEF, IT IS TRUE, CORRECT AND COMPLETE.

Chris Carr — TYPE OR PRINT NAME OF SIGNING OFFICER OR AGENT
Chris Carr — SIGNATURE — CFO
8-12-91 — DATE

16. I DECLARE THERE HAS BEEN NO CHANGE IN THE INFORMATION CONTAINED IN THE LAST STATEMENT OF THE CORPORATION WHICH IS ON FILE IN THE SECRETARY OF STATE'S OFFICE. DOES NOT APPLY ON INITIAL FILING.

(READ INSTRUCTIONS BEFORE COMPLETING THIS ITEM)

☐ (CHECK HERE) — TYPE OR PRINT NAME OF SIGNING OFFICER OR AGENT — SIGNATURE — TITLE — DATE

155 Sample/Example of a Set of Bylaws

BY-LAWS OF
COLLEGE BETTERMENT
CORPORATION

ARTICLE I

SHAREHOLDERS' MEETINGS

Section 1. Place of Meetings.

All meetings of the shareholders shall be held at the office of the corporation in the State of California which may be designed for that purpose from time to time by the Board of Directors.

Section 2. Annual Meetings.

The annual meeting of the shareholders shall be held on the __ day of ____ each year, at the hour of ___ o'clock ___m., at which time the shareholders shall elect by plurality vote a Board of Directors, consider reports of the affairs of the corporation, and transact such other business as may properly be brought before the meetings.

Section 3. Special Meetings.

Special meetings of the shareholders, for any purpose or purposes whatsoever, may be called at any time by the President or by the Board of Directors, or by any two or more members thereof, or by one or more shareholders holding not less than one-fifth (1/5) of the voting power of the corporation.

Section 4. Notice of Meetings.

Notice of meetings, annual or special, shall be given in writing to shareholders entitled to vote by the Secretary or the Assistant Secretary, or if there be no such officer, or in case of his neglect or refusal, by any director or shareholder.

Such notices shall be sent to the shareholders' address appearing on the books of the corporation, or supplied by him to the corporation for the purpose of providing notice, not less than seven days before such meeting.
Notice of any meeting or shareholders shall specify the place, the day and the hour of the meeting, and in case of special meetings as provided by the Corporations Code of California, the general nature of the business to be transacted.

When a meeting is adjourned for thirty days or more, notice of the adjourned meting shall be given as in case of an original meeting. In all other cases, it shall not be necessary to give any notice of the adjournment of the meeting or of the business to be transacted at an adjourned meeting other than by announcement at the meeting at which such adjournment is taken.

Section 5. Consent to Shareholders' Meetings.

The transactions of any meeting of shareholders, however called and noticed, shall be valid as though had at a meeting duly held after regular call and notice, if a quorum be present either in person or by proxy, and if, either before or after the meeting, each of the shareholders entitled to vote, not present in person or by proxy, sign a written waiver of notice, or a consent to the holding of such meeting, or an approval of the minutes of the shareholders' meeting. All such waivers, consents or approvals shall be filed with the corporate records or made a part of the minutes of the meeting.

An action which may be taken at a meting of the shareholders may be taken without a meeting if authorized by a writing signed by all of the holders of shares who would be entitled to vote at a meting for such purpose, and filed with the Secretary of the corporation.

Section 6. Quorum.

The holders of a majority of voting shares, whether present in person, or represented by proxy, shall be requisite and shall constitute a quorum at all meetings of the shareholders for the transaction of business. If, however, such majority shall not be present or represented at any meeting of the shareholders, the shareholders entitled to vote, whether present in person, or by proxy, shall have the power to adjourn the meeting from time to time, until the requisite amount of voting shares shall be present. At such adjourned meeting at which the requisite amount of voting shares shall be represented, any business may be transacted which might have been transacted at the meeting as originally notified.

Section 7. Voting Rights; Cumulative Voting.

Only persons in whose name shares entitled to vote stand on the stock records of the corporation on the day of any meeting of shareholders, unless some other day be fixed by the Board of Directors for the determination of shareholders of record, then on such other day, shall be entitled to vote at such meeting.

Every shareholder entitled to vote at any election for directors of any corporation for profit may cumulate his votes a give one candidate a number of votes equal to the number of directors to be elected, multiplied by the number of votes to which his shares are entitled, or distribute his votes on the same principle among as many candidates as he thinks fit.

The candidates receiving the highest number of votes up to the number of directors to be elected are elected.

Section 8. Proxies.

Every shareholder entitled to vote, or to execute consents, may do so, either in person or by written proxy, executed by the shareholder or his duly authorized agent, and filed with the Secretary of the corporation.

156 Examples of Piercing the Corporate Veil

EVENT	PROOF OF DOMINATION	PROOF OF IMPROPER PURPOSE	RESULT
Sole shareholder/director causes corporation to pay shareholder's personal debt.	Only shareholder/director controls corporation's use of assets.	Creditors defrauded when corporate assets used to pay shareholder's debt, not corporation's debt.	Shareholder liable to creditors of corporation.
Shareholders/directors fail to hold annual shareholders' and directors' meetings.	Shareholders and directors control corporation's decision to hold meetings.	Circumvention of incorporation statute requiring annual meetings.	Shareholders liable to creditors of corporation.
To avoid union contract, shareholders vote to transfer business of corporation to new corporation owned by the same shareholders.	Shareholders' vote controlled corporation's decision to transfer business to new corporation.	Obligation to employees evaded by the business.	New corporation liable to employees under union contract.
Parent of wholly owned subsidiary causes subsidiary to buy asset from parent at price higher than fair market value.	Parent owns 100% of subsidiary, elects its directors, and thereby controls subsidiary.	Creditors of subsidiary defrauded when parent gives fewer assets to subsidiary than subsidiary gives to parent.	Parent liable to creditors of subsidiary.
Shareholders organize corporation by contributing \$1,000 of capital and by loaning \$99,000 to corporation. The loan is secured by all the corporation's assets.	Shareholders control organization of corporation.	Nonshareholder creditors defrauded by thin capitalization.	Part or all of loans treated as capital, thereby subordinating shareholder's loans to claims of nonshareholders.

157 "DOs and DON'Ts" Re: Piercing the Corporate Veil

The following list of "dos" and "do nots" is intended to serve as a checklist to help you maintain the limited liability of your shareholders, and to establish other good practices for doing business in the corporate form.

I. DO

A. Hold Meetings
   1. Your annual shareholders' meeting is set in your bylaws.
   2. Your bylaws call for an annual board of directors' meeting to be held immediately afterwards.
   3. Additional special meetings of the board should be held when matters of importance come up such as:
      a) Entering into a lease of new premises;
      b) Entering into a substantial funding commitment;
      c) Entering into a substantial leasing commitment;
      d) Entering into any other significant contractual agreement or new venture;
      e) Changing an officer's salary;
      f) Filing a vacancy in the board or officer complement;
      g) Considering the sale, in whole or in part, of the assets or the dissolution of the business.

B. Develop a Planning Mechanism
   1. Review each year's activities during the final month of the fiscal year.
   2. Budget ahead for the longest period reasonably possible and review and analyze results at least semi-annually.
   3. Review the results of 1. and 2. with your CPA to ensure tax planning is properly emphasized.
   4. Begin to develop formal long range planning capacities beyond budgeting if not already in place.

C. Sign all contracts in the name of the corporation in substantially the following form:

—[NAME OF CORPORATION]—
By: ________________________________
—[Title]—

D. Issue all orders in the name of the corporation.

E. Maintain corporate funds in a corporate account or accounts separate and apart from any other account.

II. **DO NOT**

Do not fail to hold meetings.

Do not commingle corporate accounts and personal funds and/or loans.

Do not negotiate loans, leases, *etc.* between the corporation and a principal other than on an arm's length basis.

Do not use corporate assets continually for personal use.

Do not fail to carry reasonable insurance on the corporation having due regard to the risks inherent in the corporation's business.

Do not fail, in addition, to have a reasonable initial capital base in the corporation.

Do not fail to set up a review mechanism as to decisions, so that all aspects of a proposed course of action will be considered.

158 TRW Rebuffs Northrop, Offers Own Plan[1]

The Wall Street Journal

[Business judgement rule]

TRW INC. FOR a second time rejected Northrop Grumman Corp.'s hostile take-over bid of $5.9 billion, and instead urged its shareholders to support an ambitious restructuring plan that it says would unlock greater shareholder value.

That plan, as approved by TRW's board Tuesday, calls for the company to be split into separate automotive-parts and defense concerns and for the cash sale of its aeronautical-systems business in order to pare debt. The restructuring, which TRW hopes will be completed by year end, puts pressure on Northrop to increase its offer.

TRW's board argues its plan would be better for shareholders than the bid by Northrop, which it again categorized as "an opportunistic attempt" to buy the $16 billion in revenue company on the cheap.[2] Defense concern Northrop has offered to pay $47 in stock for each TRW share, plus assume $5.5 billion in debt. The bid represents a 4% increase over what TRW's stock was trading at prior to its chief executive's sudden departure for another top post on Feb. 19.

Northrop's offer, made two days after, "has been on the table for weeks, and now we're moving ahead with our own plan," said TRW's acting chairman, Philip Odeen, in an interview.

By their own estimates, TRW executives say their company, after being broken in two, is worth between $55 and $60 a share, significantly higher than Northrop's offer. "These businesses are in a better strategic position [separated] than they are in the company as a whole," said Robert Swan, TRW's chief financial officer.

Such a valuation, though, is significantly higher than TRW's stock has traded recently. For most of the past two years, the company's shares have traded below $50. They closed Wednesday at $51.17, up 89 cents, in New York Stock Exchange 4 p.m. composite trading.

Los Angeles–based Northrop proposed a similar breakup when it made its surprise acquisition offer in late February, saying it would either sell or spin off TRW's auto parts business and combine the

1 **Note from Professor Carr: This article nicely highlights the application of the Business Judgment Rule. For example, by rejecting Northrop's bid, in your view, if TRW's Board of Directors was sued by TRW shareholders for that decision, should they (TRW's Board) be able to seek/claim the protection of the Business Judgment Rule and thereby avoid personal liability?**

Also, obviously, if you were on TRW's Board of Directors you might have an incentive to reject Northrop's bid as you would likely find yourself out of a Board of Director's job when Northrop took over your company/TRW, right? ☺

2 **Question from Professor Carr: Do you agree or disagree? I.e. is this a true or contrived reason?**

company's military and aerospace assets with its own.

But for now, Northrop officials say they will pursue their proxy fight instead. "We believe our offer and the ability to get with Northrop gives shareholders more certainty than the potential of several future transactions" by TRW, said Northrop Chairman Kent Kresa. "If TRW believes they have more value [than $47 a share], then we need to do due diligence and look at that."

TRW has called a special shareholder meeting, set for April 22, to put both proposals up for a vote. If Northrop decides to hold its position until then, shareholders will have to decide whether to accept $47 in Northrop stock now or give TRW management time to carry out its plan, something that has been studied for several years but never acted on.

"People had hoped they'd do this all along;" says Jim O'Mealia, managing director of Fox Asset Management in Little Silver, N.J., which owns about one million shares of TRW. "The important thing is that a restructuring is at hand and the game is afoot."

For much of its 101-year history, TRW has been in both the automotive and aerospace businesses. The auto-parts side, which makes air bags, steering columns and braking systems, is by far the larger of the two, with $10.1 billion in annual revenue.

But it is TRW's military operations that increasingly have been seen as attractive. The company's space and electronics businesses, as well as its systems units, play major roles in building the missile-defense systems the Bush administration has made a top priority. These two units had combined revenue in 2001 of $5.17 billion, and TRW officials said they expect both businesses to grow quickly along with increased Pentagon spending.

Under terms of TRW'S plan, the company will sell its aeronautical-systems unit, which had $1.1 billion in revenue last year and makes engine controls and flight controls, among other things. The most likely bidders for this operation are **United Technologies** Corp., **Honeywell International** Inc. or possibly a European company, say people familiar with the sale. Honeywell's top executive, David Cote, knows the business best, since he just left TRW three weeks ago for his current job.

TRW insists a sale of this business could happen soon. "We've had a larger number of inquiries," said Mr. Odeen, "but we are in negotiations with one company now." He declined to identify it. Honeywell and United Technologies declined to comment. TRW executives said the key to the company's restructuring is paring its hefty debt load, using operational earnings and the proceeds from the sale of the aeronautics division. The goal is to shave as much as $1.7 billion in debt by the end of the year, bringing the total to about $3.8 billion. Then that would be split between the two new organizations, with about $2.7 billion in debt being applied to the auto business and $1.1 billion to the systems and space units.

Investors say they still believe another company could bid for TRW. For their part, TRW executives

No Thanks

TRW rejects Northrop Grumman's $47 per-share offer calling it an "opportunistic attempt to acquire TRW's premier franchise." The company's objections to the offer include:

- **It grossly undervalues** TRW's businesses and opportunities.
- **Opinion of TRW's** independent financial advisors that the offer is inadequate from a financial point of view.
- **Offer remains** below the current market price of TRW's common stock, which is at $51.16.
- **Proposal is highly** conditional resulting in significant uncertainty that deal will be consummated.
- **Offer is subject** to a collar which could result in a price of less than $47 per share.

Source: TRW

say they have received unsolicited bids from a number of third parties "for each of [TRW's] operating businesses as well as a private equity investment in the entire company." They declined to say who had contacted them, but industry executives say a stand-alone TRW defense business wouldn't stay that way for long. Military contractors, angling for a bigger piece of Pentagon spending, have been consolidating for more than a decade, and that pace has stepped up again recently.

At the same time, TRW said it is proceeding with its search for a new CEO. Mr. Odeen had been pulled out of semiretirement when Mr. Cote left for Honeywell.

159 Enron Board's Actions Raise Liability Questions[1]

The Wall Street Journal

[Business judgement rule]

IT IS A QUEASY time to be an Enron Corp., director.

This week's disclosure that the board of the collapsed Houston energy company twice waived the corporate ethics code to allow creation of controversial partnerships raises significant red flags about directors' potential liability. According to a report that Houston law firm Vinson & Elkins prepared for Enron, the full board twice suspended the company's ethics code during 1999 in order to allow two outside partnerships to be headed by a top Enron executive who stood to financially benefit from them.

The subsequent widespread disclosure of those partnerships last fall fueled Enron's downward spiral toward a bankruptcy-court filing.

The law-firm report could increase Enron directors' legal exposure and represents another example of "a culture of sloppiness on conflict-of-interest issues," says Nell Minow," a veteran shareholder activist and editor of the Corporate Library, an online database of corporate-governance information. Enron board members seem to have "a real sense of unreality about conflicts of interest," she adds.

An Enron spokeswoman didn't comment yesterday. In the past, the company has defended its actions regarding the partnerships. Also, individual Enron directors didn't return phone calls or couldn't be reached to comment.

Things could soon get even messier for its 15-member board. Several insurance carriers that underwrite liability coverage for Enron directors and officers are exploring ways they might suspend their policies, says an individual close to the situation. One possibility: declare that Enron misled insurers by renewing D&O policies based on earnings that it subsequently restated. In November, weeks before its bankruptcy-court filing, Enron reduced its previously reported net income dating back to 1997 by $586 million, or 20%, mostly due to improperly accounting for its dealings with partnerships run by some company officers.

It is increasingly common for insurance companies to seek rescission of D&O policies "based on fraudulent applications" for new or renewed coverage, says Stephen Weiss, a partner with Holland & Knight, a Washington law firm and an expert on D&O insurance. "A restatement in earnings can

1 **Note from Professor Carr: Yet another application and example of the Business Judgment Rule. For example, wouldn't you say/think that Enron Board of Directors blew it "big-time" here and if they are sued by their shareholders (and I can assure you they will be!!), will they be able to/should they be able to argue that their decisions and activities as described in this article are protected by the Business Judgment Rule and that they should therefore not have any personal liability to their shareholder??**

certainly raise the specter of insurers seeking to rescind their policies on the basis of apparent fraud." A spokesman for Minnesota-based St. Paul Cos., one of Enron's providers of D&O insurance, declined to comment on whether it intends to maintain the coverage.

Canceling such coverage following earnings restatements doesn't always get insurers off the hook, however. Consider Sunbeam Corp.

A unit of New York–based American International Group Inc. dropped liability insurance for Sunbeam directors and officers shortly after the Boca Raton, Fla., consumer-products concern restated financial results for the six quarters ended March 1998. The restatement covered essentially the entire tenure of Albert J. Dun [...], who was ousted as chairman and chief executive in mid-1998 amid massive accounting irregularities.

Sunbeam subsequently sued the AIG unit in federal district court in Miami, [...] king restoration of its halted coverage. Under a settlement reached early last year, the AIG unit agreed to pay Sunbeam [...] million—but refused to reinstate the canceled policy, informed individuals say. The extent of Enron directors' potential [...]oility for waiving the ethics code may depend on whether a court decides this is intentional misconduct. "Any time [directors] abrogate a company's code of conduct, you raise serious questions," said Charles Elson, a board member at three publicly traded concerns who runs the University of Delaware business school's Center for Corporate Governance. "Are their actions reckless or negligent?"

On the other hand Mr. Weiss noted that corporate codes of ethics sometimes permit waivers under appropriate circumstances. You can't automatically assume that suspending an ethics code is wrong, he added.

At Enron, the first waiver occurred in June, 1999, when finance chief Andrew Fastow was looking to set up and run a private partnership to be known as LJM Cayman LP. Because the partnership would do business with Enron, Mr. Fastow needed a special ruling from the board that his activities wouldn't violate company rules regarding outside business interests by Enron officials.

According to minutes of the company's June 28, 1999, board meeting, there was a "discussion" of Mr. Fastow's involvement in the LJM partnership. The minutes don't go into details about what was discussed. However, the board adopted a resolution that ratified a recommendation from top management that Mr. Fastow's partnership participation "will not adversely affect the interests of the Company," according to the minutes.

At that special board meeting directors' approval of the partnership also included the board's "waiver of Enron's code of ethics to permit Mr. Fastow to act as the general partner" of the partnership, the Vinson & Elkins report stated.

The waiver involved a suspension of corporate policies intended to protect against executives being involved in activities that might pose a conflict of interest or be detrimental to Enron. Later that year, Mr. Fastow was looking to set up and run the much larger and more ambitious LJM2 Co-Investment LP. (LJM Cayman had about $16 million from outside investors; LJM2 had nearly $400 million.)

An excerpt from an Oct. 11, 1999, meeting of the finance committee of Enron's board recounts Mr. Fastow telling the committee that Enron's "Conduct of Business Affairs Policies" would "prohibit him from participating in LJM2 as managing partner ... absent appropriate reviews and waivers from the Board." The excerpt shows that on the motion of director Jerome Meyer and seconded by director Norman Blake, the finance panel voted to recommend such a waiver to the full board.

The next day, Oct. 12, the full board approved that waiver for Mr. Fastow on LJM2, according to an excerpt of that meeting's minutes. The resolution used essentially the same language as in the case of LJM Cayman. Enron estimates that Mr. Fastow eventually made over $30 million from the two partnerships. Enron probably has between $250 million and $350 million in current D&O coverage, according to one person close to the situation. But even if the concern retains all of its insurance for directors and officers, no one knows whether that will be enough to cope with the massive amount of pending litigation. The full board is named in nearly all of the 50 pending shareholder derivative suits.

Meanwhile, Enron directors are conducting their own internal investigation of the mess. A three-member special investigative committee consists of Herbert S. Winokur Jr., chairman and chief executive of Capricorn Holdings Inc. and a board member since 1985, and Enron's two newest directors. The pair are William C. Powers, dean of the University of Texas School of Law, and Raymond Troubh, a 75-year-old retired New York financial consultant.

Apparently, Securities and Exchange Commission investigators aren't going full tilt on the federal probe of Enron until they see the board committee's report, which could come by early next month.

160 After Enron, Companies Confront Dearth of Willing Board Members[1]

The Wall Street Journal

[Business judgment rule and directors and officers' liability insurance]

NEW YORK—AS IF new companies didn't already have their hands full trying to raise money, now they're facing a new struggle.

It seems no one wants to sit on boards of directors anymore.

As the job of running a start-up at the board level gets harder, with cash tight and the market uncertain, and new corporate-governance scrutiny brought on after Enron Corp.'s collapse, many independent board candidates are staying away.

In many cases, filling a boardroom has been just as difficult for new companies as attracting financing.

"You're fighting over human capital instead of investment capital," said Whitney Bower, a principal at Bain Capital in Boston.

The nature of board responsibilities has changed profoundly since the Internet boom years of the late 1990s. Boards back then had a certain star power. The idea was to pack a board with well-known names as a sort of window-dressing prior to an initial public offering. The more big names on a company's board, the thinking went, the better shot the offering had of attracting investors.

An extreme example, perhaps not surprisingly, was from an Internet incubator, divine interVentures Inc., which went public in July 2000 with a 43-member board of directors, which included people such as basketball great Michael Jordan and chewing-gum magnate William Wrigley Jr. At the time, one IPO analyst quipped that the board was "bigger than some state legislatures."

The company, which has since become a software firm and changed its name to divine Inc., cut its directors to 11 in February of last year, though many of the former board members joined a separate advisory board.

Nowadays, start-ups in particular would be lucky to find three outside board members, let alone 43. One big problem is the workload. Companies could pack boards because there were few demands placed

1 **Note from Professor Carr: This article does a nice job of highlighting how even WITH the traditional protection that the Business Judgment Rule has and is supposed to offer the Board of Directors of a company, they still can and often do face the risk of liability and litigation. Some folks, and as this article points out, are no longer willing or are hesitant to accept that risk and are opting out of serving on such boards.**

One way, of course, to minimize this type of liability risk is for Board members to purchase what is called "directors and officers" insurance.

But, and as the next page and article points out, such insurance in becoming more difficult to get and/or may be becoming prohibitively expensive.

on the directors. They would attend a few meetings a year, carve out some hours for conference calls, and often rubber-stamp most of the moves made by company executives and other board members affiliated with the venture capitalists who funded the companies.

As the IPO markets closed, valuations slipped, mergers became impractical and cash dried up, the job of a director became more intense. Directors often found themselves needing to roll up their sleeves and get more involved in the day-to-day operations of companies.

"It went from an easy, almost social activity to being some pretty difficult work," Bain's Mr. Bower said. Many executives, some of whom have been trying to keep their own companies afloat, simply lack the time needed now to help steer another company to viability as a board member.

Some don't want the liability that comes along with the job. Board meetings rarely get scrutiny at public companies, let alone at small start-ups, but that changed when the lights shined on the actions—or inaction—at Enron's board as that company was coming undone. Investors wondered where the board was when many of Enron's off-balance-sheet partnerships were being created.

If the collapse of Enron hadn't been so traumatic, some moves by the board might seem almost comical. Former chief executive Jeffrey Skilling, for instance, told Congress earlier this year that he couldn't recall details of a board conversation about the partnerships because the lights had gone out in the room where the meeting took place.

"The pool of interested people is fewer," said Mike Brooks, general partner with private-equity firm Venrock Associates in New York. "They don't want the risk. There's no insurance for them."

It gets even worse trying to get independent directors to serve on board audit committees. The audit committees, which supervise the external audits and monitor companies' accounting processes, need to be made up of outside, independent directors. But, again, with Enron's accounting under such scrutiny and the hobbling of Arthur Andersen, it's a job most people don't want to take.

"When I talk to some people in the corporate world, they say, 'I'll be director, but I'm not taking an audit committee role,'" Mr. Brooks said.

Venture capitalists are trying to fix the problem by recruiting outside directors earlier in the life of the company, hoping that that approach will somehow make it easier to attract talent to the boardroom.

But getting directors early in the process has its own set of problems. The younger the company, the more acute the funding needs, so start-ups now are missing even the venture capitalists who typically come on board once they fund a company, said Joseph Bartlett, an attorney with law firm Morrison & Foerster in New York.

"It's a function of the market," Mr. Bartlett said. "It's not just getting the directors, the bigger problem is getting the money."

A Smart Investment

161

Publicly Traded Companies Are Looking to Directors and Officers Insurance to Protect Them from Investor Lawsuits, Which Are on the Rise.

Best's Review Property/Casualty Insurance Edition

[The business judgment rule and directors and officers' liability insurance]

As companies like Conseco Inc., Aetna and Reliance Group Holdings Inc. face an ever-growing rash of investor lawsuits, the need for directors and officers insurance is increasing as well, according to insurance professionals.

Robert Hartwig, vice president and chief economist for the Insurance Information Institute, said he wasn't surprised financially troubled companies like Reliance and Conseco, whose stock prices have plummeted in the past couple years, are defendants in investor-generated lawsuits. That can happen to any publicly traded company facing financial turmoil, he said.

In other words, investor lawsuits are simple reality in the rollercoaster world of publicly traded companies.

"I would be surprised if there weren't lawsuits," Hartwig said. "In general, when a company suffers a severe decline in share price, like both of these companies have, you often see a directors and officers law- suit. There are attorneys specializing in this, claiming to look out for the rights of shareholders. He said the directors and officers line of insurance is now approaching $3 billion in gross premiums written. "Because of the general interest of the public in investing, and the trial bar in suing, you have a potent combination driving D&O insurance," Hartwig said.

A Profitable Line

D&O insurance is "one of the most profitable insurance lines an insurer can write" said Eric Simpson, senior vice president and head of A.M. Best Co.'s property/casualty division. It wasn't uncommon for insurance carriers to generate combined ratios in the 70s and 80s a decade or two ago. It has "drifted" into the 90s and recently closed in on 100 in some cases, Simpson said, but that's still good compared to standard commercial lines, for example, where combined ratios are commonly in the 110 to 115 range. A combined ratio below 100 represents a profit; above 100 represents a loss.

Looking ahead, Simpson said capacity is stable and at an all-time high. Rates began flattening more than a year ago, he said, and multiyear deals are declining, which would allow D&O writers a chance to make premium increases at renewals, if warranted.

Some of the biggest writers of D&O include Chubb and Executive Risk, which was bought by Chubb in 1999; American International Group

Inc.; and Reliance, although its future as a D&O writer is uncertain. These are companies with the longest histories of writing D&O.

Most companies and their boards have some basic D&O coverage, Simpson said, but the question is whether it's sufficient as liabilities increase.

The average size of a shareholder D&O liability claim award rose to $8.67 million in 1999, the highest ever, according to the "1999 Directors and Officers Liability Survey," an annual study by Tillinghast-Towers Perrin, a management and human resources consulting firm in Chicago.

Though claim awards have risen, prices for D&O coverage declined for the fourth consecutive year in 1999, according to the study's author, Mark Bob Card, director of risk management for Risk International Services, Houston, a professional services firm with specialty practices in risk management, claim management & recovery, risk science, strife victims and insurance archaeology.

Typically, most, if not all, the actual defense costs and settlement value of these suits are covered by insurance, he said. Although this relieves the defendant company in the short run, insurance premiums over the subsequent years may increase as a result of one or more shareholder suits.

These lawsuits are labor intensive, especially because management credibility is at stake, Card said. Senior managers face pressure not only to succeed in the suit, but to assure that the company's long-term reputation with shareholders and customers is not compromised. The attention spent on the lawsuit reduces the amount of concentration on managing the company.

162 Andersen Ex-Party Pleads Guilty, In a Significant Blow to the Firm[1]

The Wall Street Journal

THE ARTHUR ANDERSEN LLP partner in charge of the Enron Corp. account pleaded guilty in federal court in Houston to obstruction of justice, turning the tables on his former employer and handing prosecutors a potent weapon in their criminal case against the firm.

David Duncan's move could have a profound impact on the case, which has roiled the world-wide accounting industry and spurred congressional calls for greater oversight of corporate governance. It raises the chances that Andersen, struggling for its survival, will have to accept the government's terms if it wants to settle the pending obstruction indictment against the firm. His testimony could also prove valuable in the broader investigation of Enron and the executives who presided over its efforts to inflate profit and hide debt before its bankruptcy filing late last year.

Mr. Duncan's cooperation has give prosecutors new information and could bring more indictments of former Andersen colleagues, according to investigators and lawyers close to the case. Nancy Temple, who was a lawyer in the firm's Chicago office, and Michael Odom, a manager in Houston who was also alleged to have been involved in shredding of Enron-related documents last fall, could face federal prosecution, the lawyers close to the case said.

Prosecutors said in federal court Tuesday that Mr. Duncan "knowingly, intentionally and corruptly" directed efforts in Andersen's Houston office last fall to alter, withhold and destroy documents and records, just as a Securities and Exchange Commission investigation was getting under way.

"On Oct. 23, I instructed local people at Arthur Andersen to begin destroying documents, with the knowledge and intent that those documents would be unavailable to the SEC and others," Mr. Duncan declared. I also personally destroyed such documents and knew they would be unavailable to the SEC," he said. "I accept that my conduct violated federal criminal law and am fully responsible."

Mr. Duncan appeared before the packed courtroom in a charcoal suit and burgundy tie, and during the brief afternoon hearing uneasily read his statement to U.S. District Judge Melinda Harmon. He answered her questions in a quiet, deep voice

1 **Note from Professor Carr: This article should take you back to our discussion and study of agency law. As you will recall, under certain circumstances, a company/principal is liable (civilly) for certain torts committed by its agent/employee. But here, we have a different situation. The company is being charged with a crime (criminal law—not civil law) for an act of one of its agents/employees. And, as this article (and pages 505–506 of this textbook) points out the rules of the game are a little different—i.e., it is in many ways easier for a company to be held criminally (not civilly) liable for a crime committed by one of its employees.**

See also the related articles on the following pages for related information and issues.

and swayed noticeably on his feet when she told him that the charge could carry as much as a 10-year prison term.

Among the evidence that prosecutors have obtained against Andersen are e-mail directories showing widespread deletions, and a videotape in which a senior manager advises employees on shredding documents, investigators and lawyers close to the case said. In the video, Mr. Odom tells employees that if the firm's document policy is followed, and "litigation is filed the next day, that's great ... whatever there was that might have been of interest to somebody is gone and is irretrievable."

Ms. Temple's attorney has said his client didn't break the law; Mr. Odom's lawyer declined to comment Tuesday.

Rusty Hardin, an Andersen attorney in Houston, said after Mr. Duncan's court appearance Tuesday, "We are surprised and disappointed by Mr. Duncan's statement in court, as it completely contradicts what he has stated up until this point. For months, Mr. Duncan has contended that he had no intent to violate the law.

But others at the besieged accounting firm said they now believe the decision to [...] Duncan on Jan. 15 and publicly blame him for the shredding was a major blunder expected to provide evidence to back up the government's charge that the effort [...] documents took place not just in Houston, but also in Portland, Ore., London an[...]

Mr. Duncan is expected to meet again shortly with Federal Bureau of Investigation and appear before the grand jury. Because of his former position, he has direct knowledge of many of the transactions that are now under criminal scrutiny in the Enron investigation. He was intimately familiar with the creation of the so-called Chevron and Raptor partnerships which are alleged to have been used to inflate Enron pr[...] hide debt, those close to the case said.

Mr. Duncan's plea could quicken the pace of settlement efforts, which began last week. The government and Andersen lawyers have already discussed a settlement app[...] could include some sort of deferred prosecution agreement, with an admission of wrongdoing by Andersen.

Mr. Duncan's plea weakens Andersen's hand in any talks. "The mere fact that ar[...] of Andersen has committed a crime is devastating for Andersen itself, because that may be attributed to Andersen if he was acting within the scope of his employment it looks like he was," says Ted Fiflis, a law professor at the University of Colorado, Boulder. "The DOJ might be able to win right now after this plea, at least on leg[...]

"They [Andersen] are back to Plan A," said Peter Romatowski, a defense lawyer [...] Day in Washington, who is a former federal prosecutor. "The original strategy [was] to throw Duncan overboard, and say he is the wrongdoer, and that we should not responsible for what he did." Later, the Andersen trial team embraced Mr. Duncan, arguing that he hadn't committed a crime. "That was Plan B," said Mr. Romatowski [...] isn't involved in the Andersen or Enron cases. "Now, it is back to Plan A."

"As a technical legal matter, his guilty plea is sufficient to bind the company," Mr. Romatowski said. Lynn Turner, a former chief accountant for the SEC, is more [...] calling the cooperation deal "a grand-slam hit" for the Justice Department.

Now, Andersen lawyers will have to regroup again, and will likely have to argue [...] Duncan is agreeing to the plea only to avoid prison, and that he never really [intended to] commit a crime. While the government and Mr. Duncan haven't come to terms [...] sentence, a court filing by the government that described Mr. Duncan's cooperat[...] it clear that the defendant's substantial assistance to prosecutors would ease his [...] which is scheduled for Aug. 26.

163 Arthur Andersen Breaks Off Talks to Settle Criminal Case[1]

The Wall Street Journal

ARTHUR ANDERSEN LLP broke off settlement talks with the Justice Department aimed at resolving its criminal indictment, a decision that places the firm's future in doubt and complicates the government's broader investigation of Enron Corp.[1]

The abrupt move by the embattled accounting firm came amid signs of an unraveling of its contemporaneous discussions to settle civil litigation in a class-action suit by Enron shareholders and creditors.

Andersen's about-face underscores the riskiness of its legal strategy. Since federal prosecutors unsealed the obstruction-of-justice indictment March 14, Andersen has resisted entering a settlement with prosecutors unless it could also resolve the class action and a Securities and Exchange Commission civil investigation. Andersen reckoned that if it couldn't settle all its litigation, there wouldn't be much of a firm worth saving.

Now, Andersen faces a federal trial on the obstruction charge scheduled to begin May 6 in Houston.

By breaking off talks, Andersen walked away from a federal offer of "deferred prosecution" that would have lifted the felony indictment and in effect put the firm on probation. Some legal specialists said that, given the strength of the Justice Department's case, turning such an offer down was almost an act of self-destruction. "If you walk away from this attractive a [deal] and the company ultimately fails, its death should be attributed not to murder by the Justice Department but to suicide," said John Coffee, a law professor at Columbia University.

Settlement discussions could always be resumed. That didn't appear to be in the cards yesterday. "We are no longer in talks with DOJ, and nothing is planned in the immediate future," said Rusty Hardin, Andersen's Houston-based trial lawyer."

Andersen's decision seemed to doom any hope of creating a new audit-only model for the accounting industry, said Paul A. Volcker, the former Federal Reserve chairman Andersen appointed this year to design an overhaul of the firm. Mr. Volcker's plans have rested on, among other things, the government dropping its indictment. Asked about the chance of success of his proposal now, Mr. Volcker said, "Let's say it's a lame horse." Andersen management has been giving Mr. Volcker little insight into the settlement discussions.

This month, the government scored a major victory by securing a guilty plea on a felony obstruction-of-justice charge from Andersen partner David Duncan. Mr. Duncan, Andersen's lead auditor on

1 **Note from Professor Carr: In your view, after reading these articles, was the government unfairly picking on Anderson, or, did they/it in effect put a gun to its own head and elect to commit business suicide by not settling the case and electing to go to trial??**

the Enron account, agreed to cooperate with prosecutors. The upshot is that about all Justice has to do to win a conviction against Andersen is prove Mr. Duncan acted within the scope of his job when he ordered the destruction of tons of Enron-related documents.

The decision to end settlement talks has broad implications for both Andersen and the government. For Andersen it heightens the chances that the firm will quickly implode. Even before the indictment, the nation's fifth-largest accounting firm was bleeding. It has lost about 225 of its 2,300 U.S. publicly owned clients this year. Partners are fleeing and the firm has been scrambling to sell off chunks of its operations in the U.S. and overseas to other accounting firms.

As for the Justice Department, it had been counting, as part of a settlement, on winning total cooperation from the accounting firm and its partners and employees in the Enron case. This would give prosecutors unfettered access to all the accounting firm's records. Perhaps more significant: Andersen's personnel could be used to identify which Enron executives took part in key meetings at which the energy company's aggressive accounting moves were devised.

A lack of cooperation from Andersen hardly will paralyze the Enron investigation. Prosecutors still have the cooperation of Mr. Duncan, who was Andersen's lead partner on the Enron audits. And they still can exert huge pressure on other Andersen partners and employees to turn state's evidence or risk prosecution themselves.

During settlement talks, Andersen had tentatively agreed to provide information on any improper activities by Andersen employees, further bolstering the government's leverage. Now, the government may find itself impugning the testimony of Andersen employees at one trial—that of Andersen in May—and then defending those same employees if they provide information about activities at Enron.

As recently as a week ago, a criminal settlement agreement seemed all but certain. Under a proposed deal, the government would have lifted the obstruction indictment, and Andersen would have admitted that some of its partners and other employees committed criminal wrongdoing for destroying documents in its botched audits of Enron. Andersen would have publicly stated that it was responsible for those actions as a firm.

The firm would have been placed under a probation period of at least two years. If it violated the firms of its probation, the indictment would have been reinstated.

As it pursued the discussions, Andersen had begun to pursue a package of reforms designed by Mr. Volcker under which the firm is divesting itself of all operation except auditing, to eliminate potential conflicts of interest.

Andersen's precise strategic reasons for refusing to reach a criminal settlement unless it could also settle the civil litigation remain fuzzy. Even if Andersen had settled with Justice weeks ago, it's unlikely that attorneys for Enron's share-holders and creditors, or the SEC, could have demanded more money from the firm as compensation for their clients' Enron-related losses.

Tentatively, Andersen and opposing attorneys in the class action agreed on a $300 million settlement pact. Given that Andersen's liabilities potentially run into the billions of dollars, the figure was based almost solely on how much Andersen could afford to pay. The SEC was seeking relatively nominal amounts in fines from Andersen.

Settlement discussions in the class-action case took a turn for the worse this week. A long-running dispute erupted between William Lerach, attorney for the lead shareholder in the case, and several commercial banks and securities firms that are both creditors of Enron and defendants in the class action. Mr. Lerach, of Milberg Weiss Bershad Hynes & Lerach, had demanded that the banks, including J.P. Morgan Chase & Co. and Citigroup Inc., sign waivers relinquishing their right to have any future trial judgments reduced to reflect Andersen's proportionate liability for Enron's collapse. The banks have consistently refused to do so.

What's more, an attorney for J.P. Morgan on Wednesday night publicly criticized Mr. Lerach for continuing to insist on the waivers, accusing him of costing his clients "hundreds of millions of dollars." The court-appointed mediator in the class-action case, Eric Green, yesterday blasted the J.P. Morgan attorney for criticizing Mr. Lerach publicly and said his comment had significantly disrupted the settlement talks.

Mr. Lerach declined to comment, other than to say the negotiations are "continuing." J.P. Morgan said it stands by its attorney's comments.

Some lawyers involved in the civil talks privately doubt there will be an agreement. Other issues left to resolve include how to divy up the $300 million between shareholders, creditors and other parties. Mr. Green, the mediator, said settlement discussions in the class-action case are continuing. "Until I report to the court that we have terminated our negotiations, they are ongoing," he said.

164 Corporations Aren't Criminals[1]

The Wall Street Journal

[Criminal liability of a business entity]

NOW THAT SETTLEMENT talks have collapsed, the Justice Department is proceeding to trial with its criminal case against Arthur Andersen. Auditor David Duncan has pleaded guilty to charges of obstruction of justice and agreed to testify for the government. But do his actions really indict an organization with 85,000 employees?

The Justice Department can cite precedents and statutes that justify criminal prosecutions of business entities. Indeed, federal prosecutors have been indicting corporations for decades, usually under the auspices of the 1970 Racketeer Influenced and Corrupt Organizations Act. Two justifications are most often carted out. First, the complexity of modern corporations is said to justify criminal liability due to the difficulty of proving the responsibility of a particular individual. Second, it is argued, corporations ought not to benefit from the criminal acts of their agents.

What prosecutors seem to have forgotten, however, is that individuals—not organizations—commit crimes. Criminal indictments of groups or other entities conflict with, and cloud, the whole purpose of criminal law, which is to make judgments about individual moral responsibility. From what is known about the Andersen and Enron cases, numerous individual criminal actions probably occurred. But Justice seems to be operating on the premise that widespread wrongdoing by individuals in a company justifies a criminal indictment of the company itself.

This reflects a larger trend within the legal profession in favor of viewing criminal law and tort law as basically indistinguishable, except for the remedies available: jail vs. fines. More importantly, it ignores the moral basis on which substantive criminal law rests—the requirement that a defendant be personally responsible for his actions. Under the common law, a corporation could not be guilty of a crime because it could not possess mens rea, a guilty mind. Generally speaking, the moral basis of criminal law, the requirement of personal moral fault, remained fairly firm in the U.S. until recent decades. In large part, this was due to the fact that most crimes are matters of state law, which has adhered relatively closely to the common law.

1 **Note from Professor Carr: Now, as to whether it is right or fair to hold an entity criminally liable for a crime committed by one of its agents/employees, I leave it up to you to read this article and decide for yourself. Reasonable minds can and will certainly disagree on such a topic/debate. But one thing to consider after read this article; If the government/our society were to adopt the position taken by the author of this Wall Street Journal op-ed piece, could we/how would we effectively ever be able to deter/discourage/punish such behavior and thereby be able to prevent another Enron type situation/meltdown from occurring?**

The indictment of Arthur Andersen undermines the idea of individual responsibility.

Since about 1970, however, the federal government has greatly expanded the reach of federal crimes to cover areas previously reserved for the states. Addressing this overreach, the Supreme Court has handed down two important decisions since 1995 forcefully reaffirming that the federal government does not possess a general police power. Nevertheless, the Justice Department continues to indict corporations for violations of ethical standards and government regulations that do not necessarily constitute crimes.

Justice is often more interested in going after entire corporations than the individuals responsible for wrongdoing. Some of the better known examples of corporate indictments are Hughes Aircraft, for conspiring to defraud and make false statements to the federal government, and the Bank of New England, for violations of the Currency Transaction Reporting Act.

This trend reached an extreme in 1985 when the Justice Department indicted E.F. Hutton on mail- and wire-fraud charges without indicting a single individual. Justice explained that it was forced to indict Hutton because it could not prove the guilt of any individuals involved. Logically, this problem should have led one to question the proof of the corporation's guilt. Nevertheless, the federal government and the corporation entered into a plea bargain whereby Hutton pleaded guilty (and subsequently went bankrupt) without any individuals being charged.

If corporations can be convicted without proof of personal guilt, it should not be surprising if individuals are also convicted without sufficient concern for personal guilt. The Justice Department has taken the right approach by charging Mr. Duncan with the crime of obstruction of justice, but using his plea to go after the firm instead of other individuals involved in criminal activity would do a disservice to the notion of personal responsibility under the law. Thus, the reason for rejecting corporate criminal liability is not a bias in favor of corporations, but rather a concern for the dignity of individual rights reflected in the rejection of collective guilt.

The indictment of Andersen is a dangerous precedent that will be cited, along with the E.F. Hutton case and others, to justify more indictments of public companies. Executives have come to fear tort lawyers as a threat to corporate capitalism. But against suits, even class actions, corporations at least have the possibility of negotiating a settlement short of bankruptcy; after all, all the plaintiffs' lawyers want is money. As the indictment of Arthur Andersen should make clear, the business community has as much, if not more, to fear from well-meaning, but misguided, federal prosecutors.

Mr. Baker, a law professor at Louisiana State University, is a former state prosecutor and consultant to the Reagan Justice Department.

165 Business Entity Comparison Tables

Legal Characteristics

[Summary chart/table of business entity/business organization attributes and characteristic]

I put this table at the end of the business organizations/entities material for the simple reason that now that we have completed/you are at the end of this material, the below information should be a lot clearer and make a lot more sense!!

	Sole Proprietorship	General Partnership	Limited Partnership	C Corporation	S Corporation	LLC
How business profits are taxed	individual tax rates of sole proprietor	individual tax rates of general partners	individual tax rates of general and limited partners	split up and taxed at corporate rates and individual tax rates of shareholders	individual tax rates of shareholders	individual tax rates of members, unless LLC files IRS Form 8832 and elects corporate taxation
Tax-deductible fringe benefits available to owners who work in business	Sole proprietor may set up IRA or Keogh retirement plan; may deduct a portion of medical insurance premiums.	general partners and other employees may set up IRA or Keogh plans; may deduct a portion of medical insurance premiums	same as general partnership	full tax-deductible fringe benefits for employee-shareholders; may fully deduct medical insurance premiums and reimburse employees' medical expenses	same as general partnership, but employee-shareholders owning 2% or more of stock are restricted from corporate fringe benefits under partnership rules	can get benefits associated with sole proprietorship, partnership or corporation, depending on tax treatment of LLC
Automatic tax status	yes	yes	yes, upon filing certificate of limited partnership with state filing office	yes, upon filing Articles of Incorporation with state corporate filing office	no; must meet requirements and file tax election form with IRS (and sometimes state); revoked or terminated tax status cannot be re-elected for five years.	yes unless LLC wishes to elect corporate tax treatment (by filing IRS Form 8832)
Deductibility of business losses	Owner may use losses to deduct other income on individual tax returns (subject to active-passive investment loss rules that apply to all businesses)	partners may use losses to deduct other income on individual tax returns if "at risk" for loss or debt	Same as general partnership, but limited partners may only deduct "nonrecourse debts" (for which general partners are not specifically liable)	corporation may deduct business losses (shareholders may not deduct losses)	shareholders may deduct share of corporate losses on individual tax returns, but must comply with special limitations	follows sole proprietorship, partnership or corporate loss rules depending on tax status of LLC
Tax level when business is sold	personal tax level of owner	Personal tax level of individual general partners	Personal tax level of individual general and limited partners	two levels: shareholders and corporation are subject to tax on liquidation	normally taxed at personal tax levels of individual shareholders, but corporate level tax sometimes due if S corporation was formerly a C corporation	follows sole proprietorship, partnership or corporate tax rules depending on tax status of LLC

	Sole Proprietorship	General Partnership	Limited Partnership	C Corporation	S Corporation	LLC
Source of start-up funds	sole proprietor	general partners	general and limited partners	initial shareholders (in California, cannot invest with promise to perform services or to pay later (unless note is adequately secured)	same as C corporation —but cannot issue different classes of stock with different financial provisions	In California, members can invest by promising to perform services or contribute cash later
How business usually obtains capital, if needed	sole proprietor's contributions; working capital loans backed by personal assets of sole proprietor	capital contributions from general partners; business loans from banks backed by partnership and personal assets	investment capital from limited partners; bank loans backed by general partners' personal assets	flexible; outside investors (may offer various classes of shares); bank loans backed by shareholders' personal assets (if corporation has insufficient credit history); may go public if need substantial infusion of cash	generally same as C corporation—but can't have foreign partnership or corporate shareholders; must limit number of shareholders to 100; can't offer different classes of stock to investors except for shares with different or no voting rights	capital contributions from members; bank loans backed by members' personal assets (if LLC has insufficient credit history)
Ease of conversion to another business form	may change form at will; legal paperwork involved	may change to limited partnership, corporation or LLC; legal paperwork involved	may change to corporation or LLC; legal paperwork involved	may change to S corporation by filing simple tax election; change to LLC can involve tax cost and legal complexity	generally same as C corporation—may terminate S tax status to become C corporation but cannot reelect S status for five years after	may change to general or limited partnership or corporation; legal paperwork involved
Is establishment or sale of ownership interests subject to federal and state securities laws?	generally not	generally not	issuance or transfer of limited partnership interests is subject to state and federal laws	issuance or transfer of stock subject to state and federal securities laws	same as C corporation	no, if all members are active in the business
Who generally finds this the best way to do business?	owner who wants legal and managerial autonomy	joint owners who are not concerned with personal liability for business debts	joint owners who want partnership tax treatment and some nonmanaging investors; general partners must be willing to assume personal liability for business debts	owners who want the built-in formality and structure of the corporate form and the ability to split business income (plus limited liability)	owners who want the built-in formality and structure of the corporate form with the pass-through of corporate profits to individual owners (plus limited liability)	owners who want a less formal legal structure and automatic pass-through of profits (plus limited liability); LLC can elect corporate tax treatment when it wishes to split business income

	Sole Proprietorship	General Partnership	Limited Partnership	C Corporation	S Corporation	LLC
Who owns business?	sole proprietor	general partners	general and limited partners	shareholders	same as C corporation	members
Personal liability for business debts	sole proprietor personally liable	general partners personally liable	only general partner(s) personally liable	no personal liability of shareholders	same as C corporation	no personal liability of members
Restrictions on kind of business	may engage in any lawful business	may engage in any lawful business	same as general partnership	some states prohibit formation of banking, insurance and other special businesses	same as C corporation —but excessive passive income (such as from rents, royalties, interest) can jeopardize tax status	same as C corporation in California, licensed professionals cannot form LLC (lawyers & accountants can form RLLP instead)
Restrictions on number of owners	only one sole proprietor	minimum two general partners	minimum one general partner and one limited partner	One-person corpora- tions allowed	same as C corporation, but no more than 100 shareholders permitted who must be US citizens or residents	Before 2000, California required two members. After 2000, one-member LLCs allowed
Who makes management decisions?	sole proprietor	general partners	general partner(s) only (not limited partners)	board of directors number of board members, if less than 3, must at least be equal to number of shareholders	same as C corporation	ordinarily members; or managers if manager managed LLC
Who may legally obligate business?	sole proprietor	any general partner	any general partner (not limited partners)	directors and officers	same as C corporation	ordinarily any member; or any manager if manager- managed LLC
Effect on busi- ness if on owner dies or departs	dissolves automatically	dissolves automatically unless otherwise stated in partnership agreement	same as general partnership	no effect	same as C corporation	most LLC agreements say that LLC dissolves unless members vote to continue business
Limits on trans- fer of ownership interests	free transferability	consent of all general partners usually required under partnership agreement	same as general partnership	transfer of stock may be limited under securities laws or restrictions in Articles of Incorporation or Bylaws	same as C corporation —but transfers limited to persons and entities that qualify as S corporation shareholders	most LLC agreements require membership consent to admit new member
Amount of organizational paperwork and ongoing legal formalities	minimal	minimal; partner- ship agreement recommended	start-up filing required; partner- ship agreement recommended	start-up filing required; Bylaws recom- mended; annual meetings of share- holders required	same as C corporation	start-up filing required; operating agreement recommended; meetings not normally required

CPSIA information can be obtained
at www.ICGtesting.com
Printed in the USA
FSOW03n0905180917
38825FS

9 781935 551997